THE IMPACT OF BEHAVIORAL SCIENCES ON CRIMINAL LAW

THE IMPACT OF BEHAVIORAL

SCIENCES ON CRIMINAL LAW

EDITED BY NITA A. FARAHANY

OXFORD
UNIVERSITY PRESS

OXFORD
UNIVERSITY PRESS

Oxford University Press, Inc., publishes works that further Oxford University's objective of excellence in research, scholarship, and education.

Oxford   New York
Auckland   Cape Town   Dar es Salaam   Hong Kong   Karachi   Kuala Lumpur   Madrid   Melbourne
Mexico City   Nairobi   New Delhi   Shanghai   Taipei   Toronto

With offices in
Argentina   Austria   Brazil   Chile   Czech Republic   France   Greece   Guatemala   Hungary   Italy
Japan   Poland   Portugal   Singapore   South Korea   Switzerland   Thailand   Turkey   Ukraine
Vietnam

Published by Oxford University Press, Inc.
198 Madison Avenue, New York, New York 10016

Oxford is a registered trademark of Oxford University Press
Oxford University Press is a registered trademark of Oxford University Press, Inc.

Library of Congress Cataloging-in-Publication Data

The impact of behavioral sciences on criminal law / edited by Nita A. Farahany.
   p. cm.
  Includes bibliographical references and index
  ISBN 978-0-19-534052-5 ((hardback) : alk. paper)
1. Criminal behavior–Genetic aspects. 2. Criminal psychology.
3. Criminal behavior. 4. Behavior genetics. I. Farahany, Nita A.
  K5028.5.I47 2009
  345'.04–dc22   2008050363

1 2 3 4 5 6 7 8 9
Printed in the United States of America on acid-free paper

Note to Readers
This publication is designed to provide accurate and authoritative information in regard to the subject matter covered. It is based upon sources believed to be accurate and reliable and is intended to be current as of the time it was written. It is sold with the understanding that the publisher is not engaged in rendering legal, accounting, or other professional services. If legal advice or other expert assistance is required, the services of a competent professional person should be sought. Also, to confirm that the information has not been affected or changed by recent developments, traditional legal research techniques should be used, including checking primary sources where appropriate.

(Based on the Declaration of Principles jointly adopted by a Committee of the American Bar Association and a Committee of Publishers and Associations.)

You may order this or any other Oxford University Press publication by visiting the Oxford University Press website at www.oup.com

THE IMPACT OF BEHAVIORAL

SCIENCES ON CRIMINAL LAW

EDITED BY NITA A. FARAHANY

OXFORD
UNIVERSITY PRESS

OXFORD
UNIVERSITY PRESS

Oxford University Press, Inc., publishes works that further Oxford University's objective
of excellence in research, scholarship, and education.

Oxford   New York
Auckland   Cape Town   Dar es Salaam   Hong Kong   Karachi   Kuala Lumpur   Madrid   Melbourne
Mexico City   Nairobi   New Delhi   Shanghai   Taipei   Toronto

With offices in
Argentina   Austria   Brazil   Chile   Czech Republic   France   Greece   Guatemala   Hungary   Italy
Japan   Poland   Portugal   Singapore   South Korea   Switzerland   Thailand   Turkey   Ukraine
Vietnam

Library of Congress Cataloging-in-Publication Data

The impact of behavioral sciences on criminal law / edited by Nita A. Farahany.
      p. cm.
   Includes bibliographical references and index
   ISBN 978-0-19-534052-5 ((hardback) : alk. paper)
   1. Criminal behavior–Genetic aspects. 2. Criminal psychology.
3. Criminal behavior. 4. Behavior genetics. I. Farahany, Nita A.
   K5028.5.I47 2009
   345'.04–dc22   2008050363

1 2 3 4 5 6 7 8 9

Printed in the United States of America on acid-free paper

Note to Readers
This publication is designed to provide accurate and authoritative information in regard to the subject
matter covered. It is based upon sources believed to be accurate and reliable and is intended to be current
as of the time it was written. It is sold with the understanding that the publisher is not engaged in rendering
legal, accounting, or other professional services. If legal advice or other expert assistance is required, the
services of a competent professional person should be sought. Also, to confirm that the information has
not been affected or changed by recent developments, traditional legal research techniques should be used,
including checking primary sources where appropriate.

(Based on the Declaration of Principles jointly adopted by a Committee of the
American Bar Association and a Committee of Publishers and Associations.)

CONTENTS

ACKNOWLEDGMENTS

CHAPTER 1
The authors thank the twins and their families for their participation in the USC Twin Study and the twin project staff for assistance in data collection and scoring. The authors and the USC Twin Study were supported by grants to Laura A. Baker from NIMH (R01 MH58354), to Serena Bezdjian from NIMH (Predoctoral Fellowship Award F31 MH068953) and to Adrian Raine from NIMH (Independent Scientist Award K02 MH01114-01).

CHAPTER 6
The author thanks his indefatigable research assistant, Sean Rodriguez, for his hard work, and Nita Farahany for her patience and for a useful conversation.

CHAPTER 7
The authors thank Doriane L. Coleman, Joseph C. Davis, Amanda A. Farahany, John C.P. Goldberg, Nancy J. King, Noah A. Messing, Robert K. Rasmussen, Nicholas Quinn Rosenkranz, William W. Van Alstyne, and Christopher S. Yoo for their comments and insights. Nita A. Farahany also extends a special thanks to her parents, Amir H. Farahany and Afsaneh Farahany for their support and encouragement.

CHAPTER 8
The author thanks Ed Greenlee for invaluable help. As always, my personal attorney, Jean Avnet Morse, provided sound, sober counsel and moral support.

CHAPTER 9
The authors thank Ronald Salomon, M.D., and Cindy L. Vnencak-Jones, Ph.D., who reviewed the manuscript and made helpful suggestions. We thank Stephen A. Montgomery, M.D., and James S. Walker, Ph.D., for providing some of the case material used in this chapter.

CHAPTER 10
The author is most grateful to Marianna Gebhardt for her superb insights and research support on all aspects of this Chapter. The author would also like to thank William Bernet, Daniel Rinaldi, and Julie Salwen for helpful commentary, Eileen McNerney for excellent legal research assistance, and Christina Newhard for creating Charts 1–3 in Appendix A. Fordham University School of Law provided generous funding for this project.

CHAPTER 11

The author is grateful to Ira Ellman, Jeffrey Murphy, James Nickels, and James Weinstein for discussions of several of the issues considered in this article, and to Paul Appelbaum, Irving Gottesman, and Mark Rothstein for comments on a draft of this chapter.

Chapters 1, 2, 4–5, 7–8, and 10–13 were adapted from 69 LAW & CONTEMP. PROBS. 259 (2006).

CONTRIBUTORS

Anas Alkhatib, M.D., Child and Adolescent Psychiatrist, Riverbend Center, Florence, Alabama.

Abigail A. Baird, Ph.D., Assistant Professor of Pyschology, Department of Psychology, Vassar College.

Laura A. Baker, Ph.D., Associate Professor of Psychology, Department of Psychology, University of Southern California.

Erica Beecher-Monas, M.S., J.D., LL.M., J.S.D., Professor of Law, Wayne State University Law School.

William Bernet, M.D., Director, Vanderbilt Forensic Services, and Professor, Department of Psychiatry, Vanderbilt University School of Medicine.

Serena Bezdjian, Ph.D., Post-Doctoral Research Scholar, Department of Psychiatry, Washington University School of Medicine.

James E. Coleman, Jr., J.D., Professor of the Practice of Law, Duke University School of Law.

Deborah W. Denno, M.A., J.D., Ph.D., Arthur A. McGivney Professor of Law, Fordham University School of Law.

Nita A. Farahany, M.A., A.L.M., J.D., Ph.D., Assistant Professor of Law, Assistant Professor of Philosophy, Vanderbilt University.

Mark S. Frankel, Ph.D., Director of the Scientific Freedom, Responsibility and Law Program of the American Association for the Advancement of Science (AAAS).

Edgar Garcia-Rill, Ph.D., Director for the Center for Translational Neuroscience, research arm of the Jackson T. Stephens Spine & Neuroscience Institute, and Professor in the Department of Neurobiology and Developmental Sciences and the Department of Psychiatry at the University of Arkansas for Medical Sciences.

Brent Garland, M.S., J.D., currently in private practice, formerly a Senior Program Associate with the Scientific Freedom, Responsibility and Law Program of the American Association for the Advancement of Science (AAAS).

Henry T. Greely, J.D., Deane F. and Kate Edelman Johnson Professor of Law and Professor (by courtesy) of Genetics, Stanford University.

Owen D. Jones, J.D., Professor of Law and Professor of Biological Sciences, Vanderbilt University.

Jonathan Kaplan, Ph.D., Associate Professor of Philosophy, Oregon State University.

D.H. Kaye, M.A., J.D., Regents' Professor, Sandra Day O'Connor College of Law, School of Life Sciences, and Fellow, Center for the Study of Law, Science and Technology, Arizona State University.

Stephen J. Morse, J.D., Ph.D., Ferdinand Wakeman Hubbell Professor of Law and Professor of Psychology and Law in Psychiatry, University of Pennsylvania.

Adrian Raine, D.Phil., Robert G. Wright Professor of Psychology, Department of Psychology, University of Southern California.

Karen Rothenberg, M.P.A., J.D., Dean and Marjorie Cook Professor of Law, University of Maryland School of Law.

Alice Wang, J.D., Staff Attorney, Appellate Division, Public Defender Service for the District of Columbia.

INTRODUCTION

NITA A. FARAHANY, EDITOR

Recent scientific progress has dramatically advanced our understanding of the biological, neurological, and environmental contributions to human behavior. The scientific study of behavior has already moved beyond descriptive accounts to predictive ones by linking gene variants and neurological variations to behavioral variation in violence, aggression, and antisocial personality disorder. The growing interest and demand for scientific explanations about human behavior has become increasingly more evident. On any given day of the week, one can simply open any major newspaper or tune into any popular press outlet, where there will be some report about a newly discovered link between our genes, our brains, and our behavior or preferences.

Nowhere is the demand for understanding human behavior more evident than in the U.S. criminal justice system. The groundswell for biological and neurological explanations for criminal conduct helped motivate the John D. and Catherine T. MacArthur Foundation to fund a three-year, $10 million project on Law and Neuroscience, to consider how courts should deal with breakthroughs in neuroscience as they relate to matters of criminal law. Whether to excuse, to blame, to treat, or to simply understand, scientists and society appear closer now than ever to answers about the causes of and contributing factors to criminal conduct. But far outstripping the enormous promise of eventual discoveries concerning human behavior has been the introduction of behavioral genetics and neuroscience into the U.S. criminal justice system. The frequency and application of this evidence in the criminal justice system is increasing, although its use continues to be haphazard, ad hoc, and often ill conceived. Defense attorneys have introduced biological and neurological predisposition evidence to exculpate defendants, to bolster preexisting legal defenses, and to mitigate a defendant's culpability and punishment. Prosecutors have seized upon the double-edged potential of this evidence, using it to denigrate the defendant's character and to demonstrate a defendant's likely future dangerousness. And as the science continues to develop, its potential use in criminal investigations, interrogations, and predictions of dangerousness has been widely speculated. The discovery of more specific biological and neurological contributions to violence, aggressiveness, impulsivity, substance abuse, and so forth foreshadows the inevitable reexamination of the U.S. criminal justice system. The United States Supreme Court has already become involved in evaluating the relevance of biological predispositions to criminal culpability: in September of 2006, it granted certiorari to address, in part, whether a defendant's genetic predisposition to violence should inform whether he should be sentenced to death for first-degree murder.

To enlighten these rapidly developing changes, this book brings together the leading scientists, legal academics, physicians, public policymakers, and philosophers to provide essential reading for anyone interested in this ongoing genomics and neuroscience revolution and its implications for criminal law. Building in part on a recent multidisciplinary conference hosted at Duke University School of Law, and drawing in a number of leaders in the MacArthur Law and Neuroscience Initiative, this collection offers a comprehensive discussion of the ramifications of behavioral genetics and neuroscience in criminal cases. Unlike any other related publication, this book offers a thorough interdisciplinary perspective to the multifaceted concerns at issue. Together, the authors in this volume discuss the scientific progress and limitations in behavioral science research relating to criminal conduct, as well as the ethical concerns and the practical implications of introducing behavioral science evidence into criminal cases. Included is a detailed discussion of criminal cases in which biological and neurological predisposition testimony has been introduced, the implications for criminal responsibility and punishment, the consequences for DNA databank research, new directions in predictions of future dangerousness, and the concerns for ethnic and racial minorities arising from this research.

PART I

Part I of the volume provides a scientific primer by experts in the fields of behavioral genetics and neuroscience research. Together, they introduce recent scientific strides in the fields of behavioral genetics and neuroscience and their limitations in explaining the causes of human behavior. In the first chapter, *Behavioral Genetics: The Science of Antisocial Behavior*, renown behavioral geneticists, Laura A. Baker, Serena Bezdjian, and Adrian Raine discuss the methodologies and results of behavioral genetics studies focusing on such traits as antisocial behavior, aggression, and behaviors associated with criminal conduct. Their chapter describes in detail the classic methods as well as more recent research designs of behavioral genetics studies, along with the various assumptions, strengths, and weaknesses of each approach. They survey the leading scientific research in antisocial personality disorder, including their own, and explain the known biological and environmental contributions. They proceed through an integrated discussion of environmental and other related factors, underscoring that genetic predispositions do not mean genetic determinism. Baker et al. also provide a compelling description of why behavioral genetics explains population-wide, rather than individual, differences in behavior. This has tremendous import in criminal law where individual defendants seek to use such data for exculpatory or mitigating purposes.

Jonathan Kaplan's, *Misinformation, Misrepresentation, and Misuse of Human Behavioral Genetics Research*, focuses a more skeptical lens on scientific studies purporting to decipher the relationships among genes, behavior, and development. Bringing his expertise in philosophy of science to bear, he discusses the limitations of human behavioral genetics studies, highlighting the research limitations inherent in studying humans and the narrow policy and legal applicability of results arising from studying variation in human behavior. His chapter provides an important cautionary message regarding mis- or over-interpretation of research results from behavioral genetics studies. He concludes that, from a scientific perspective, behavioral genetics provides little relevant information regarding defendants in the criminal justice system.

In *The Developmental Neuroscience of Criminal Behavior*, Abigail A. Baird defines a relationship between cognition and emotion that together produce predictable behavior. Baird provides a sophisticated and yet accessible view into the neurological developmental process underlying human emotion and ultimately ethical behavior in adults. Her account explains not only the neurological processes involved but also the environmental influences on emotional development. Baird's work has been critical in a number of landmark cases in the U.S. criminal justice system, in part because of the stage-based developmental model of the human brain underlying emotional and cognitive development that she describes. The integrity of this developmental process, Baird explains, determines whether individuals can conform to social mandates and social norms.

PART II

The next three chapters, in Part II, by Owen D. Jones, Brent Garland and Mark S. Frankel, and by Henry T. Greely place the research in behavioral genetics and neuroscience into a broader scientific, legal, and policy context. Jones's chapter, *Behavioral Genetics and Crime, in Context*, situates the discussion of behavioral genetics by grounding it within broader areas of the law and other fields of behavioral biology. His framework provides a taxonomy for discussing behavioral genetics and neuroscience as part of behavioral biology and behavioral sciences more generally, highlighting how the discussions and conclusions in this volume fit within a much broader debate. As one of the most widely noted scholars in law and behavioral biology, Jones is well justified in his prediction that the criminal law is but one of many legal fields potentially impacted by the emerging behavioral sciences.

In *Considering Convergence: A Policy Dialogue About Behavioral Genetics, Neuroscience, and Law*, Brent Garland and Mark S. Frankel emphasize the timeliness of this volume by calling on scientists, lawyers, courts, and lawmakers to begin a critical dialogue about the implications of scientific discoveries and technological advances on criminal law. They stress the need to discuss the behavioral sciences now, before their use in the criminal justice system becomes unchecked. Garland and Frankel contribute the perspective of the American Association for the Advancement of Science (AAAS), a world-class organization steeped in the tradition of bringing scientific issues to the public policy forefront, and powerfully contextualize this volume within the broader public dialogues about behavioral genetics and the neurosciences. Their article demonstrates the natural parallels between neuroscience and behavioral genetics and explains their predictions for the broad ways in which such evidence may be used in criminal law: in mitigation of criminal responsibility for defendants addicted to drugs and alcohol, and in "preformal" situations, that is, those occurring before criminal charges are filed. Through their discussion of the shared history of neuroscience and behavioral genetics, the actual and potential use of these disciplines, and the differences between the two fields, Garland and Frankel provide a compelling case for the urgency of addressing the implications of behavioral sciences in criminal law.

Finally, Henry T. Greely, one of the most frequently quoted and relied upon bioethicists in the U.S., provides a much needed and authoritative voice on the overlap and differences between behavioral genetics and neuroscience, and their likely implications for criminal law. He deftly contextualizes the scientific fields as overlapping and yet distinct, and explains the claims that emerge from each. Based on this important discussion, Greely then offers four ways in which neuroscience is likely to have different implications for criminal law than will behavioral genomics: the association with criminal behavior, the reproducibility of the science, the likelihood to promote eugenic interventions, and the call for treatment alternatives. Finally, in a manner that helpfully contextualizes the focused chapters that follow, Greely broadly canvases and provides unique insights into the distinct and yet related ways that behavioral genomics and neuroscience may impact criminal law, particularly as it relates to questions including who committed the criminal act in question and how to best punish or otherwise respond to that criminal transgression.

PART III

Building upon the scientific and contextual foundation of Parts I and II, the chapters that follow offer in-depth study of particular issues at the intersection of neuroscience, behavioral genetics, and criminal law. The chapter by Nita A. Farahany and James E. Coleman, Jr. and the one by Stephen J. Morse opine that, scientific models of human behavior such as those described by behavioral genetics and neuroscience are unlikely to fundamentally change the legal concept of criminal responsibility. In *Genetics, Neuroscience, and Criminal Responsibility*, Coleman and I discuss the attempted use of behavioral genetics and neuroscience evidence in criminal cases and explain why, as a matter of criminal responsibility theory, such evidence has and should have limited impact. Our discussion details claims by defendants using behavioral genetics and neuroscience evidence, including attempts to negate the voluntary act requirement or mens rea, to satisfy the requirement of mental disease or defect for insanity defenses, or to offer mitigation evidence during sentencing. We then explain that in spite of their potential scientific utility and potential use for disease models, these behavioral sciences do not inform criminal responsibility as a matter of criminal law theory. In so doing, we explain the meaning and characteristics of the concepts underlying criminal responsibility, with a detailed consideration of the components of criminal liability and the operation of the reasonable person standard in justifications and excuses to negate criminal liability.

Stephen J. Morse's article, *Addiction, Science, and Criminal Responsibility*, offers an unparalleled and detailed analysis of the relevance of scientific evidence about drug and alcohol addiction to criminal responsibility. Morse, a leading expert on criminal responsibility and mental health, offers an in-depth background on phenomenology of addiction, including the concepts of craving, seeking, and using. His analysis, like that of the preceding chapter, contrasts the legal versus scientific concepts of human behavior, but here with the powerful and specific lens of addiction to elucidate the distinction. Morse then offers a robust and positive account of our present system of criminal responsibility, explaining how addiction fits within that model while dispelling confusion and myths about criminal responsibility. His chapter provides a careful and step-by-step analysis of moral versus legal accountable for addiction, the role of genetics and neural systems in addiction, and the role of individual and social responsibility in addiction related conduct. He concludes that the disease model cannot fully inform the social or legal policy of addiction, because intentional or volitional human action is inevitably involved.

PART IV

In *Genomics, Behavior, and Testimony at Criminal Trials*, William Bernet and Anas Alkhatib provide a unique insider's perspective on expert testimony introduced in behavioral genetics and neuroscience cases. Bernet, a forensic psychiatrist and frequent expert in criminal cases, details some of the scientific evidence that he relies upon when he serves as an expert witness in criminal cases about the relevance of behavioral genetics and neuroscience to criminal conduct. Together, Bernet and Alkhatib survey the scientific evidence and studies regarding the relevance of genotype in medical or psychiatric diagnosis and in explaining a person's violent or criminal behavior. Their article provides insight on both the general claims being made in criminal cases—where genetic and environmental evidence is used to support a diagnosis of a particular condition—to the more revolutionary claims—where a gene-environment interaction is not used as the basis of a diagnosis, but to explain the criminal conduct in question.

Deborah W. Denno's chapter, *Behavioral Genetics Evidence in Criminal Cases: 1994–2007*, provides an essential follow-up to Bernet and Alkhatib's discussion. Denno provides an invaluable update to her earlier work detailing the potential implications arising from the high-profile case of Stephen Mobley, who sought to introduce a then-cutting-edge theory that violence could be based on a genetic or neurochemical abnormality as mitigating evidence during capital sentencing. Denno, the first scholar to publish on and follow the controversy, discusses the original use of genetic evidence at the time of Mobley's trial, including such concerns as the potential for its abuse, the relationship between behavioral genetics and free will, the impact such evidence information has on jurors, and the potential stigma associated with genetic predispositions. Now a leading expert on the use of behavioral genetics in criminal law, she reevaluates her earlier concerns in light of the significant scientific progress that has been made in the field since *Mobley*. The review of cases in her chapter affords a complementary perspective to the cases that Coleman and I discuss by looking at the procedural posture of the cases when such information was introduced and the procedural hurdles leading to rejection of such evidence by the courts. Based on her review, she explains that in spite of her earlier predictions, the role of behavioral genetics in the criminal law still remains largely theoretical and has yet to gain widespread acceptance. Denno's chapter, together with her comprehensive appendix of cases from 1994 to 2007 at the end of the volume, offers the most detailed account, to date, of the use of behavioral genetics in criminal cases, particularly within the context of mitigation and sentencing.

David H. Kaye, one of the most cited scholars in the U.S. on the use and implications DNA databanks, addresses the politically important issue of the potential use of potential use and development of DNA databanks from behavioral genetics research. The increased frequency by which law enforcement officials rely upon DNA screens for crime investigation highlights the pressing political import of this issue. In his chapter, *Behavioral Genetics Research and Criminal DNA Databases: Law and Policies*, Kaye addresses the concern that DNA databanks serve as a limitless repository for future research and that the samples used in the databanks could be used for research into a "crime gene." Kaye explains why, given the nature of the samples used in DNA databanks and the difficulties and limitations of behavioral genetics studies, the search for a "crime gene" is unlikely by scientists. Nonetheless, he agrees that the concerns about the limitless use of these samples cannot be so easily dismissed. He provides a thorough review of state and federal DNA databank legislation and explains that although such legislation likely prohibits "crime gene" investigations, greater protections for privacy are needed to ensure that future amendments do not override such protections. Finally, he addresses some of the bioethical and social arguments against "crime gene" research using samples stored in DNA repositories, particularly given the involuntary contribution of many such samples and the ethics of retaining these samples at all. He significantly advances the policy debate on this issue by proposing mechanisms for guarding against unauthorized use of DNA repositories.

Bringing an interdisciplinary perspective to predictions of future dangerousness, Erica Beecher-Monas and Edgar Garcia-Rill consider the unfortunate probability that behavioral genetics evidence will be misused as substantiation in their chapter, *Genetic Predictions of Future Dangerousness: Is There a Blueprint for Violence?* Beecher-Monas, an expert in law and science, and Garcia-Rill, a scientist who is at the forefront of studying schizophrenia and anxiety, together discuss the problems with using actuarial instruments to refine the accuracy of future dangerousness predictions. These actuarial instruments are employed in contexts including death penalty proceedings, sex offender registrations, and post-sentence commitments. They offer significant detail regarding the scientific reality of behavioral genetics evidence, by offering a step-by-step account of the complex interaction between genes, proteins, nerve cells, biochemical and neurochemical pathways, and the environment, which combine to give rise to human behavior. Their account underscores the volume and complexity of information necessary before behavioral genetics can offer meaningful insight into predictions of future dangerousness. Their chapter provides significant support excluding behavioral genetics research for predictions of future dangerousness without significant further scientific progress.

In the closing chapter, *The Scarlet Gene: Behavioral Genetics, Criminal Law, and Racial and Ethnic Stigma*, Karen Rothenberg and Alice Wang grapple with the broader social implications of researching traits of interest to criminal law. The PBS television program *Genes on Trial: Genetics, Behavior, and the Law* provides a chilling frame, where participants discuss the situation of the fictitious Tracy Islanders, an ethnic group with a higher incidence of alcoholism attributable in part to the increased incidence of a particular gene variant in the population. Their collaboration brings a new perspective to the issue—Rothenberg is an expert in law and health issues and participated in the PBS trial, whereas Wang practices as a federal public defender and faces the very issues raised by the special in her practice. The chapter delivers their unique perspective as they consider the social impact for participants in behavioral genetics studies, particularly when such research focuses on behaviors associated with criminal behavior, like drug or alcohol addiction. Rothenberg and Wang explain that such studies often target discrete and insular ethnic groups because of their relatively homogeneous gene pools. Such groups may suffer stigmatization if particular genetic variations are discovered that contribute to behavioral variations in that population. Finally, Wang and Rothenberg discuss the potential for genetic reductionism and determinism that arises from behavioral genetics research, which would shift the focus away from other contributions to violence (including environmental and societal ones) and instead narrowly address the genetic contributions of behavioral differences. The ethical concerns raised lead them to deliberate whether certain types of research should be conducted at all, or introduced into criminal cases.

In sum, this book affords an in-depth introduction to and analysis of critical issues arising from behavioral genetics and neuroscience research and their use in the criminal justice system. Together, the authors address many of the inevitable complexities that have and will continue to arise from the introduction of behavioral genetics, neuroscience, and behavioral science into criminal law. Now is the time for scholars, practitioners, and the public to discuss these issues, before the unchecked use of behavioral sciences eclipses any meaningful debate.

PART ONE

THE SCIENCE OF CRIMINAL CONDUCT

1. BEHAVIORAL GENETICS: THE SCIENCE OF ANTISOCIAL BEHAVIOR

LAURA A. BAKER, SERENA BEZDJIAN,
AND ADRIAN RAINE

I. INTRODUCTION

Social scientists generally agree that a paradigm shift has occurred over the course of the last three decades of research in human behavior: the zeitgeist has moved away from a culturally centered, social learning model toward a more balanced perspective in which both genetic and environmental factors are understood to explain the wide variations observed in human behavior. This perspective now applies in the areas of mental health and illness, as well as across several domains of normal, varying psychological constructs, such as intelligence, personality, interests, and attitudes. The study of antisocial behavior is no exception to this paradigm shift. There is now abundant evidence that both genetic and environmental influences—and probably their interaction—are of major importance in explaining individual differences in antisocial behavior, including differences in criminal behavior.

Evidence for a genetic basis of antisocial behavior stems from several different lines of research. First, behavioral genetic studies of twins and adoptees have demonstrated that heredity plays a role in antisocial behavior, including various forms of aggression and criminality, by finding greater concordance for such behavior in genetically related individuals compared to nonrelatives living in the same environment. Second, various correlates of antisocial behavior, including personality factors such as impulsivity, sensation-seeking, risk-taking, and callous-unemotional traits, are known to be at least partly genetically influenced. Third, psychiatric outcomes related to antisocial behavior, including antisocial personality disorder, gambling, and substance use and abuse, have also been investigated in genetically informative designs, and each of these has demonstrated significant genetic influence.

This paper summarizes the heritability of each of these aspects or correlates of antisocial behavior and discusses research attempting to unpack the genetic and environmental "black boxes" involved in antisocial behavior, including studies investigating the influence of both biological and social risk factors and how they might be mediated by genetic and environmental factors. Examples of biological risk factors could be neurotransmitters, physiological arousal, frontal lobe function, and hormones, while social risk factors would include socioeconomic status, peer characteristics, and parental monitoring and discipline.

Biological risk factors may not necessarily be entirely genetically based, and social risk factors may not be purely environmental in origin; this high-lights the complexity of the relationships between risk factors and antisocial behavior.

This paper also reports studies that have identified specific genetic associa-tions with antisocial behavior. Yet genetic predispositions, though important, are more deleterious in the presence of adverse environments. This view dove-tails with other biosocial theories of antisocial behavior in which the effects of biological risk factors have been found to be moderated by social circumstances. An overarching biosocial model of antisocial behavior is presented here, along with a discussion of a few key findings that demonstrate interactions of social and biological factors in the development of antisocial behavior.

Finally, this paper considers the implications of behavioral genetic research on antisocial behavior for understanding individual responsibility. No individ-ual's behavior can ever be explained entirely, either in terms of genetic predispo-sitions or in terms of cumulative experiences, and an explanation of an individual's behavior, even if it were complete, would not necessarily excuse that behavior. Even with increasing understanding of the genetic bases of human behavior, a cautious approach is warranted both in making inferences about a given individual and in considering changes to the legal system that might now take a defendant's experiences and disposition into account.

II. RESEARCH DESIGNS IN BEHAVIORAL GENETICS

Before delving into the evidence for genetic and environmental influences on antisocial behavior, it may be helpful to review the basic research designs in behavioral genetics: (1) classical genetic designs, which infer global genetic and environmental influences through analyzing resemblance among family mem-bers of varying degrees of genetic and environmental relatedness, including twins, nuclear families, and adoptive families; and (2) quantitative trait loci (QTL) designs, in which specific DNA sequences are identified and tested for functional significance or associations with such complex traits as antisocial behavior. Although classical approaches are considered more "global" in that they broadly determine whether genes are important and estimate the magni-tude of genetic influences, the QTL designs provide a more "molecular approach" because they attempt to specify more precisely what underlying genetic and bio-logical mechanisms might increase an individual's risk of engaging in antisocial behavior.

A. Classical Genetic Designs
The traditional approach to studying genetic and environmental influences on human behavior does not involve any direct examination of DNA, but infers

observed individual differences (phenotypic variance) in a given trait, such as antisocial behavior through examination of patterns of resemblance among individuals who are related genetically, environmentally, or both.[1] The general approach partitions the phenotypic variance (V_P) into genetic (V_G) and environmental (V_E) factors. Environmental influences are typically divided further into those shared by family members (V_{Es}) and those not shared but unique to each individual in the family (V_{Ens}). Different types of genetic influences can also be distinguished; some are due to additive effects of genes at various loci (V_A), while others are the result of nonadditive genetic effects due to dominance (interactions between different forms of a gene at one locus) (V_D) and epistasis (interactions between genes at various loci) (V_I). The distinction between shared and nonshared environments is almost always made in classical genetic designs, although additive and nonadditive genetic effects are not always separated. Studies rarely attempt to estimate epistatic genetic effects, since their total contribution to observable variance is widely thought to be small even when such effects are present. These components of variance add to the total variance in a linear fashion:

$$V_P = V_G + V_E = V_A + V_D + V_I + V_{Es} + V_{Ens} \tag{1}$$

Dividing both sides of the equation by V_P yields proportional effects of each class of influence, indicating the relative amount of phenotypic variance explained by various types of genetic and environmental factors:

$$1 = h^2 + e^2 = a^2 + d^2 + i^2 + e_s^2 + e_{ns}^2 \tag{2}$$

The relative effect of genetic factors on phenotypic differences among individuals (h^2) is the heritability of the trait, while environmental influences (e^2) are the environmentality of the trait. When distinguishing among different types of genetic influence, it is possible to calculate broad-sense heritability (h^2_B), which encompasses all genetic influences ($a^2 + d^2 + i^2$), or narrow-sense heritability (h^2_N), which reflects only additive effects (a^2).[2]

This distinction between additive and nonadditive genetic influences warrants further elaboration, since their differences are often not well understood upon first encounter. The extent to which different genes "add up" in their

---

1. *See generally* ROBERT PLOMIN et al., BEHAVIORAL GENETICS 72–92 (4th ed. 2001) (reviewing basic structure of adoption and twin designs); Laura A. Baker, *Methods for Understanding Genetic and Environmental Influences in Normal and Abnormal Personality, in* DIFFERENTIATING NORMAL AND ABNORMAL PERSONALITY (S. Strack ed., 2006) (reviewing the major classical genetic designs as well as their assumptions, strengths, and weaknesses).

2. Genes do not always act in a dominant or recessive fashion (such that one gene masks the effects of another gene). Instead, each gene at a given locus may contribute additively to the phenotype. Even when dominant genes are involved, however, additive effects can appear.

contributions to a given phenotype reflect the additive effects, whereby each different allele at every locus may add incrementally to one individual's observed trait value (e.g., his or her height, intelligence, or probability of engaging in criminal behavior). That is, those individuals with a greater number of relevant genes portray a higher trait value. In contrast, nonadditive genetic effects result when it is not the *number* of genes but instead different *combinations* of various genes that determine phenotypic expression. In the simple case of two gene forms (alleles) at a single locus (A and a), an additive genetic model is implied if the heterozygous individuals (Aa) display an intermediate phenotype between the two groups of homozygotes (aa and AA). If one allele is dominant, however, the heterozygote and AA homozygote are phenotypically indistinguishable, indicating nonadditive genetic effects (i.e., having two copies of the A allele is no different from having only one copy). The same principles of additive and nonadditive effects extendto more complex traits in which many genes at different loci contribute to the phenotype. Gene expression at one locus may be modified by genes at other loci (i.e., gene × gene interaction, or epistasis), contributing further to nonadditive genetic effects.

In general, additive genetic effects lead to similarity among relatives roughly in accordance with the overall genetic relatedness between pairs of individuals (e.g., equal similarity would be expected among parents and offspring, who share exactly 50 percent of their genetic material, and among siblings, who share 50 percent of their genes on average). When genetic nonadditivity occurs, such as dominant or recessive gene action or interactions among genes at two or more loci, the similarity between relatives is affected in a more complex manner—for example, parent-offspring resemblance is not affected by nonadditive genetic effects, since these two classes of individuals do not share the same combinations of genes, while sibling and twin resemblance increase because such individuals can inherit the same combinations of genes. Moreover, genetic nonadditivity increases MZ twin resemblance much more than DZ twin or sibling resemblance, since MZ pairs always share the exact combinations of genes while this occurs for only a subset of DZ twins and siblings.

An illustration of these relative effects as portions of the total phenotypic variance for a given trait is provided in Figure 1.1, which also shows that the effects of measurement error may be taken into account as a separate component of variance.

These effects might be estimated algebraically or through complex model-fitting algorithms on the basis of observed correlations (or covariances) among various pairs of relatives. A path diagram representing one given pair of relatives in a classical genetic design is shown in Figure 1.2.

In twin studies, for example, monozygotic (MZ) twins share 100 percent of their genetic material, while dizygotic (DZ) twins on average share only 50 percent of their genes. The expected correlations between co-twins (the two

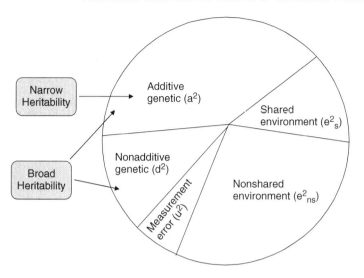

FIGURE 1.1 COMPONENTS OF GENETIC AND ENVIRONMENTAL VARIANCE

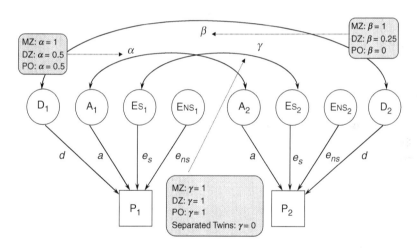

FIGURE 1.2 PATH MODEL OF COVARIANCE BETWEEN TWO RELATIVES (P₁ AND P₂)

individuals in a given twin pair) may be derived from the model shown in Figure 1.2 as follows:

$$r_{MZ} = a^2 + e^2_s \qquad (3)$$

$$r_{DZ} = \tfrac{1}{2} a^2 + e^2_s \qquad (4)$$

Assuming that both types of twins share environments to the same degree—a reasonable assumption, given their contemporaneous age and development—any increased similarity in MZ compared to DZ twins is taken to imply the importance of genetic factors on the trait under study. In particular, narrow-sense heritability (a^2) may be calculated from the correlations between MZ co-twins (r_{MZ}) and DZ co-twins (r_{DZ}) as

$$a^2 = 2(r_{MZ} - r_{DZ}) \tag{5}$$

The shared and nonshared environmental effects may also be calculated as

$$e^2_s = r_{MZ} - a^2 \tag{6}$$

$$e^2_{ns} = 1 - r_{MZ} \tag{7}$$

Other comparisons among family members may also be used to estimate effects of heredity and environment on a given trait. For example, the similarity of full siblings raised in the same home compared with the similarity of siblings separated at birth and raised in different homes may be used to infer the importance of shared family environment. Alternatively, resemblance between biological parents and their offspring given up for adoption may be used to estimate narrow-sense heritability. The resemblance between MZ twins separated at birth and raised apart also provides a direct estimate of broad-sense heritability, while unrelated (adoptive) siblings provide a direct estimate of the influence of a shared family environment. This general variance-partitioning approach in behavioral genetic designs is considered more "global," since it broadly classifies genetic and environmental effects and does not specifically identify either the genetic or environmental mechanisms involved in a phenotype.

Although equations such as those above may be used to estimate global genetic and environmental effects in traits or behaviors such as antisocial behavior, complex model-fitting routines are more typically used to compute these effects. Model-fitting routines often involve structural equation modeling to represent path models such as that in Figure 1.2 and employ iterative computational methods to find the best-fitting estimates of parameters (a^2, d^2, e^2_s, e^2_{ns}) from a set of observed correlations among various types of relatives. Such routines have the advantages of providing (1) parameter estimates that are constrained to be mathematically reasonable values by, for example, requiring each variance component to be between zero and one; (2) significance tests of each parameter; and (3) goodness-of-fit indices to evaluate the adequacy of the genetic model.

B. Molecular Genetic Designs

A variety of other genetic designs attempting to identify specific genes with associations or to identify genes of functional importance in behavior have become increasingly popular in recent years. One design includes studies of QTLs, genes which exert small but significant associations with complex (quantitative) traits.[3] Whereas the classical designs are useful in identifying broad classes of genetic and environmental influences on complex traits, QTL designs are considered to be a "molecular" approach in that they narrowly specify DNA sequences that increase risk for antisocial behavior.

Two primary approaches taken in QTL designs are (1) a between-family, or population, approach, in which unrelated individuals with varying DNA sequences are compared on some aspect of antisocial behavior, and (2) a within-family approach, in which two or more genetically varying relatives are compared.[4] Although both approaches can be informative, most researchers agree that within-family designs provide more powerful tests of association between specific genes and traits or behaviors of interest.[5]

Within-family QTL designs are similar to the classical genetic designs, with the important exception that specific alleles or genotypes are measured for each relative, instead of being inferred from the overall genetic relationship of two individuals.[6] For example, a pair of siblings (including DZ twins) could be specified as sharing zero, one, or two alleles at a particular locus. Sibling pairs can be grouped according to their allele-sharing and their phenotypic similarity computed within each group in a manner similar to that of a classical twin study with groups of genetically identical (MZ) and nonidentical (DZ) pairs. A path diagram similar to that in Figure 1.2, but depicting a sibling design with measured genotypes at a single locus, is provided in Figure 1.3.

Most evidence for a genetic basis of antisocial behavior stems from classical studies estimating the global effects of genes and environment, yet several molecular studies are beginning to emerge identifying specific genetic associations.[7] Replications of the more recent molecular genetic studies will be critical for wide acceptance of these results.

III. EVIDENCE FOR A GENETIC BASIS OF ANTISOCIAL BEHAVIOR

A large number of twin, family, and adoption studies using the classical approach have provided abundant evidence for both genetic and environmental influences

---

3. Quantitative traits are those that exist on a continuum, such as height, weight, extraversion, or general intelligence; qualitative traits are usually all-or-nothing phenomena such as disease status, eye color, or criminal convictions. The term "complex" is often used synonymously with "quantitative."

4. *See generally* Pak Sham, *Recent Developments in Quantitative Trait Loci Analysis, in* BEHAVIORAL GENETICS IN THE POSTGENOMIC ERA 41 (Robert Plomin et al. eds., 2003).

5. *Id.*

6. An "allele" is a variation of a particular gene at a given locus. "Genotype" refers to the combination of alleles at a given locus, or more generally to a combination of alleles at two or more loci.

7. *See infra* Part IV.B.

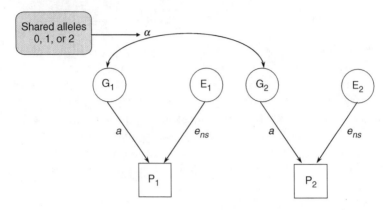

FIGURE 1.3 PATH MODEL FOR TWO SIBLINGS (P₁ AND P₂) WITH MEASURED GENOTYPE

on antisocial behavior. These studies vary widely in both their definitions of anti-social behavior and the ways in which it is measured, and results concerning the relative importance of genes and environment vary across both definitions and measures. Before turning to the evidence for genetic and environmental factors in antisocial behavior, it may be helpful to consider how measures and defini-tions actually vary.

Behavioral genetic studies of antisocial behavior have included studies of juvenile delinquency and adult criminal behavior, of *DSM-IV* psychiatric disor-ders related to antisocial behavior, and of trait aggression in both children and adults.[8] Definitions of antisocial behavior vary widely across these studies, from violations of rules and social norms to various forms of aggression, including self-defense or other reactive forms and proactive behaviors such as bullying.[9] Definitions of antisocial behavior have also included serious patterns of disrup-tive and aggressive behavior, such as those observed in conduct disorder or anti-social personality disorder.[10] Methods of measuring antisocial behavior also vary across studies; some studies are based on official records such as police arrests, court convictions, or school records,[11] while others rely on behavioral ratings pro-vided by parents or teachers or on self-reporting.[12] Each assessment method has advantages and disadvantages, with no one definition or method of assessment

---

8. *See* Soo Hyun Rhee & Irwin D. Waldman, *Genetic and Environmental Influences on Antisocial Behavior: A Meta-Analysis of Twin and Adoption Studies*, 128 Psychol. Bull. 490, 491–92 (2002) (referencing example studies).

9. *Id.*

10. *Id.*

11. *Id.*

12. *Id.*

being clearly superior.[13] In surveying these studies, it is apparent that males have been more extensively studied, although several investigations of females have also been made.[14] Antisocial behavior has also been studied across a large portion of the lifespan, from childhood to adolescence to adulthood.[15]

Several reviews of these studies are available, including the most recent meta-analysis by Soo Hyun Rhee and Irwin Waldman.[16] Rhee and Waldman initially considered nearly 12 dozen published studies of antisocial behavior; their review was narrowed to a group of 51 distinct studies that focused primarily on some dimension of antisocial behavior and for which sufficient information on familial correlations was available.[17] Results were quantitatively aggregated to estimate the relative effect of genetic and environmental influences. When results were combined across studies, the effects were found not to differ across males and females, with significant effects of additive genetic influence ($a^2 = 0.32$), nonadditive genetic influence ($d^2 = 0.09$), and shared ($e^2_s = 0.19$) and nonshared environment ($e^2_{ns} = 0.43$).[18] These effects are summarized in graphs in Figure 1.4. The effects of both heredity and environment on antisocial behavior are clearly apparent.

These genetic and environmental effects differ, however, according to the definition and method of assessing antisocial behavior as well as the age of the subjects when such behavior was studied.[19] The nonadditive genetic effects appear most strongly for studies of criminal convictions compared to all other definitions of antisocial behavior.[20] Shared environmental effects were stronger for parental reports of antisocial behavior compared to self-reports and official records, and these shared environmental effects also appeared to diminish from

---

13. For example, official criminal records represent clear violations of legal norms, but they may be incomplete to the extent that undetected crimes may exist. Self-reported antisocial behavior may be used to assess a broader range of behaviors, including both detected and undetected criminal activity as well as less serious, noncriminal antisocial behavior, but such self-reports will be influenced by the respondent's dishonesty. Parental ratings of antisocial behavior in young children reflect perhaps the most intimate knowledge of the children's behavior (apart from that of the children themselves); however, parents may be unable to judge the child's motivations (such as whether aggressive behavior may be proactive or the result of provocation), and parents have limited observations of the child's behavior outside of the home. Teacher reports provide useful information about school-related behaviors, but these may also lack information about the child's motivations and may not adequately distinguish between victims and perpetrators during conflicts among children.

14. *See* Rhee & Waldman, *supra* note 8, at 515.

15. *Id.* at 514.

16. *Id.*

17. *Id.*

18. *Id.*

19. *Id.* at 512–14.

20. *Id.* at 512–13.

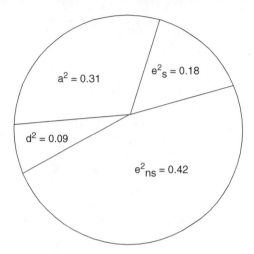

FIGURE 1.4 RELATIVE EFFECTS OF ADDITIVE GENETIC (a^2), NONADDITIVE GENETIC (d^2), SHARED ENVIRONMENT (e^2_s), AND NONSHARED ENVIRONMENT (e^2_{ns}) FACTORS IN ANTISOCIAL BHAVIOR
source: adapted from Rhee & Waldman, *supra* note 10

childhood to adulthood.[21] Nevertheless, it is also noteworthy that age and method of assessment are confounded across studies: studies of younger children tend to rely on parent or teacher reports, while studies of older populations are more apt to use official records or self-report measures of antisocial behavior.[22] Thus, the larger effect of shared environment during childhood may be due to greater reliance on parental ratings.

One recent study of antisocial behavior in nine- to ten-year-old twins attempted to evaluate the effects of raters' identity on estimates of genetic and environmental influences during childhood.[23] The study was based on a socioeconomically and ethnically diverse sample of 605 pairs of twins (MZ, DZ same-sex, and DZ opposite-sex) and their caregivers who participated in a comprehensive assessment of the twins' antisocial behavior and related risk factors.[24] Both the child and his or her caregiver provided reports of the child's antisocial behavior, in addition to teacher ratings of each child.[25] Composite measures of antisocial behavior were computed for each rater—parent, teacher, and child—based on several standardized instruments measuring rule-breaking behaviors, including

21. *Id.* at 512–14.

22. *Id.* at 495.

23. Laura A. Baker et al., Genetic and Environmental Bases of Antisocial Behavior in Children (unpublished manuscript, on file with *Law and Contemporary Problems*).

24. *Id.*

25. *Id.*

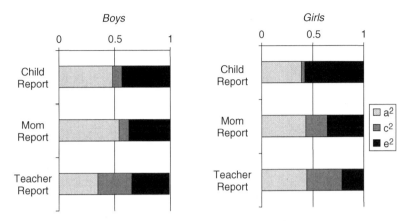

FIGURE 1.5 RELATIVE EFFECTS OF ADDITIVE GENETIC (a^2), SHARED ENVIRONMENT (c^2), AND NONSHARED ENVIRONMENT (e^2) INFLUENCES IN A COMPOSITE MEASURE OF ANTISOCIAL BEHAVIOR IN THE USC TWIN STUDY

theft and violence, as well as reactive and proactive aggression and conduct disorder symptoms, as rated by each informant.[26] The pattern of genetic and environmental influences in the composite antisocial behavior measures for these pre-adolescent children, as summarized in Figure 1.5, was similar to that found in Rhee and Waldman's meta-analytic review, in that (1) genetic effects were significant for antisocial behavior as assessed by each of the three informants; (2) shared environmental effects were larger for parent and especially for teacher ratings of antisocial behavior as compared to the children's self-report; and (3) the respective magnitudes of genetic and environmental effects were comparable for males and females.[27] A larger effect of shared environment for childhood antisocial behavior was exhibited, as rated by parents and teachers, although genetic influences are still significant at this early age. The larger shared environmental effect estimated in twin studies relying on parent or teacher ratings of antisocial behavior may thus be due in part to a form of rater bias, rather than to a true shared environmental effect.

Genetic influences in antisocial behavior are present in childhood well before the major risk period for criminality (at age 15 to 25). These effects do not appear to vary by sex, suggesting that some root biological influences may explain individual differences in antisocial behavior for both males and females. The variability in effect sizes across informants, however, suggests that observing heritability of antisocial behavior may depend on the way in which antisocial behavior is measured. It is therefore important to consider results from a

---

26. *Id.*
27. *Id. Compare* Rhee & Waldman, *supra* note 8, at 516–17, 522.

wide range of studies rather than to rely on estimates of heritability from one single study. Meta-analytic reviews are particularly helpful in drawing conclusions across behavior genetic studies.[28]

A. Developmental Changes in Genetic Influences

Genetic and environmental influences on antisocial behavior also appear to change across a lifespan. Although the Rhee and Waldman's review emphasized the decreasing importance of shared family environment (e^2_s) from childhood to adulthood,[29] other reviews have suggested that heritability may vary in importance at different ages. The direction of difference, however, varies across studies and reviews. Some studies show larger genetic effects during adulthood compared to childhood and adolescence,[30] while others suggest greater heritability of antisocial behavior during childhood compared to adolescence and adulthood.[31]

To a large extent this discrepancy of results may be due to confounding methods of measurement of antisocial behavior with age of subjects; studies of children tend to rely on parent and teacher reports, while studies of adults utilize official records, such as convictions and self-reported antisocial behavior more often.[32] Thus, the patterns of genetic and environmental influences across a lifespan are not yet clearly established. In addition, there may be different genetic and environmental influences for various subtypes of individuals with different life-course patterns of offending. It has been suggested that life-course, persistent offenders may be at greater genetic risk compared to adolescence-limited offenders, who may in turn be more influenced by social factors like peer influences.[33] The longitudinal twin or adoption studies required to establish the different genetic influences in developmental subtypes of antisocial individuals have yet to be done.

B. Genetics of Criminal Behavior

The major reviews of genetic influences in antisocial behavior typically combine a wide range of definitions for what may be considered antisocial. In a legal setting, it may be worth considering studies involving illegal behaviors specifically. Several large-scale twin and adoption studies of criminality have been conducted

---

28. *See, e.g.*, Rhee & Waldman, *supra* note 8.

29. *Id.*

30. *See, e.g.*, Donna R. Miles & Gregory Carey, *Genetic and Environmental Architecture of Human Aggression*, 72 J. PERSONALITY & SOC. PSYCHOL. 207, 207 (1997).

31. *See, e.g.*, Lisabeth Fisher Dilalla & Irving I. Gottesman, *Heterogeneity of Causes for Delinquency and Criminality: Lifespan Perspectives*, 1 DEV. & PSYCHOPATHOLOGY 339 (1990).

32. Rhee & Waldman, *supra* note 8, at 494.

33. Terrie E. Moffitt, *Adolescence-Limited and Life-Course-Persistent Antisocial Behavior: A Developmental Taxonomy*, 100 PSYCHOL. REV. 674 (1993).

in various countries, including the United States,[34] Sweden,[35] Denmark,[36] and Norway.[37] Concordance between twins for property crimes such as theft and vandalism has been generally greater for MZ twin pairs (who are genetically identical) compared to DZ twin pairs (who on average share only 50 percent of their genes).[38] Property crime convictions among adopted individuals significantly increased when a biological parent was convicted.[39] In comparison, conviction rates showed little or no increase in adopted children raised by parents with property crime convictions.[40] Thus, environmental influences on nonviolent criminality have appeared largely nonfamilial and specific to the individual rather than being shared by relatives living together.

Although large sex differences in property crime offenses are evident—males are arrested far more often than females[41]—the genetic effects on most criminal behavior are of the same magnitude across the two sexes.[42] For example, greater MZ than DZ concordance for nonviolent criminal convictions has been found in both male and female same-sex pairs. Opposite-sex DZ twins are often less similar than same-sex DZ pairs, however, suggesting that *different* genes or environments or both may be important within each sex.[43] These patterns of genetic influence for nonviolent criminality are consistent with findings for other measures of antisocial behavior, including aggression.[44] Thus, while there is little or no sex difference in the magnitude of genetic effect on antisocial behavior, some

---

34. *See, e.g.,* Remi J. Cadoret et al., *Genetic-Environmental Interaction in the Genesis of Aggressivity and Conduct Disorders,* 52 ARCHIVES OF GEN. PSYCHIATRY 916 (1995).

35. *See, e.g.,* Sören Sigvardsson et al., *Predisposition to Petty Criminality in Swedish Adoptees: III. Sex Differences in Validation of the Male Typology,* 39 ARCHIVES GEN. PSYCHIATRY 1248 (1982).

36. *See, e.g.,* Barry Hutchins & Sarnoff A. Mednick, *Registered Criminality in the Adoptive and Biological Parents of Registered Male Criminal Adoptees, in* GENETIC RESEARCH IN PSYCHIATRY 105 (Ronald R. Fieve et al. eds., 1975).

37. *See, e.g.,* S. Torgersen et al., *The Psychometric-Genetic Structure of* DSM-III-R *Personality Disorder Criteria,* 7 J. PERSONALITY DISORDERS 196 (1993).

38. *See* C. R. Cloninger & I. I. Gottesman, *Genetic and Environmental Factors in Antisocial Behavior Disorders, in* THE CAUSES OF CRIME: NEW BIOLOGICAL APPROACHES 92, 96–100 (S. A. Mednick et al. eds., 1987).

39. Hutchins & Mednick, *supra* note 36, at 110; Laura A. Baker et al., *Sex Differences in Property Crime in a Danish Adoption Cohort* 19 BEHAV. GENETICS 355, 360 (1989).

40. Hutchins & Mednick, *supra* note 36.

41. JAMES Q. WILSON & RICHARD J. HERRNSTEIN, CRIME AND HUMAN NATURE 104–12 (1985); *cf.* Janet S. Hyde, *How Large Are Gender Differences in Aggression? A Developmental Analysis,* 20 DEVELOPMENTAL PSYCHOL. 722 (1984) (discussing gender variation in aggression).

42. *See* Rhee & Waldman, *supra* note 8, at 494 (noting that genetic effects on antisocial behavior are equal between the sexes, but that genetic effects on aggression are not equal).

43. *See* Cloninger & Gottesman, *supra* note 38.

44. Rhee & Waldman, *supra* note 8.

sex-limitation (different genetic effects in males and females) may be evident whereby different genes or environmental factors or both are important within each sex.

Interestingly, the consistent finding of genetic influences on property crimes did not hold true for violent crimes. None of the major adoption studies reported any increased risk for violent conviction as a function of either biological or adoptive parent criminal background, although one twin study did find greater MZ than DZ concordance for violent convictions.[45] The findings of twin, but not of parent-offspring, similarity for violent criminal behavior suggest the possibility of nonadditive genetic effects, which would result in increased resemblance for siblings, but not for parents and offspring.

Studies of younger subjects have typically not distinguished between violent and nonviolent offending. Nor have self-report methods of assessment been frequently used in studies of delinquent behavior in children. One exception is the University of Southern California (USC) twin study of antisocial behavior.[46] These nine- to ten-year-old twins completed a self-report Delinquency Interview,[47] which provided separate scales for recording nonviolent delinquent behavior. These scales included minor rule breaking, such as watching TV without permission, theft, damaging property, and truancy.[48] The interview also contained three scales of violent behaviors, which involve hitting, shoving, or biting (1) one's twin, (2) another sibling, or (3) a child outside of one's family.[49] In contrast to the large genetic influence on criminality in adults, these childhood behaviors appeared to be explained primarily by environmental (both e^2_S and e^2_{NS}) factors.[50] There were, however, small genetic influences in minor rule breaking ($a^2 = 0.20$) and theft ($a^2 = 0.12$),[51] suggesting that these effects may begin to emerge as a propensity to engage in nonviolent delinquent behavior prior to adolescence. Consistent with research on adult offending, as well as the Rhee and Waldman meta-analysis of antisocial behavior,[52] the magnitude of genetic and environmental influences in the USC twin study were not significantly different in boys and girls.[53] It may be expected that genetic influences on

---

45. Cloninger & Gottesman, *supra* note 38.

46. Baker et al., *supra* note 23.

47. Laura A. Baker & Adrian Raine, The Delinquency Interview for Children (DI-C): A Self-report Measure of Antisocial Behavior (2005) (unpublished manuscript, on file with *Law and Contemporary Problems*).

48. *Id.*

49. *Id.*

50. Adrian Raine et al., *Biological Risk Factors for Antisocial and Criminal Behavior, in* CRIME AND SCHIZOPHRENIA: CAUSES AND CURES (Adrian Raine ed., 2006).

51. Baker & Raine, *supra* note 47.

52. Rhee & Waldman, *supra* note 8.

53. Baker & Raine, *supra* note 47.

nonviolent behaviors will increase in these children as they move into the high-risk period of adolescence.

Developmental factors may indeed play an important role in genetic influences for early rule-breaking and eventual law-breaking behaviors. Other moderating factors besides age must also be considered in understanding how genetic factors may operate in antisocial behavior. In particular, genetic influences in criminality appear to be moderated by environmental factors, as discussed below.[54]

C. Genetic Studies of Psychiatric Outcomes Related to Antisocial Behavior

Antisocial behavior and aggression play key roles in the diagnoses of three mental disorders. As discussed in this section, antisocial personality disorder in adults may involve aggressive, impulsive, reckless, and irresponsible behavior. It may also be very difficult for individuals with antisocial personality disorder to maintain jobs and personal relationships or to otherwise conform to social or cultural norms. In children, conduct disorder is thought to be indicated by the externalization of problems in the form of aggression toward people and animals, destruction of property, dishonesty, theft, and other serious violations of age-appropriate rules such as truancy. In addition, a persistent pattern of negative, hostile, overly aggressive, and defiant behavior in children is characteristic of oppositional defiant disorder (ODD). These disorders are typically diagnosed through interviews and questionnaires.

The effects of genes and environment on these psychiatric disorders have been investigated in both twin and adoption studies. Significant genetic influences have been consistently reported for antisocial personality disorder symptoms in twin samples, while shared environmental influences have been reported to be less important.[55] Furthermore, adoption studies have also found significant genetic effects for antisocial personality disorder symptom counts.[56] In addition, significant genetic influences on conduct disorder have been reported in twin[57]

---

54. *See infra* Part V.A.

55. William M. Grove et al., *Heritability of Substance Abuse and Antisocial Behavior: A Study of Monozygotic Twins Reared Apart*, 27 BIOLOGICAL PSYCHIATRY 1293 (1990); G. Carey, *Multivariate Genetic Relationship Among Drug Abuse, Alcohol Abuse and Antisocial Personality*, 3 PSYCHIATRIC GENETICS 141 (Paper Presented at the Third World Congress on Psychiatric Genetics, 1993); Michael J. Lyons et al., *Differential Heritability of Adult and Juvenile Antisocial Traits*, 3 PSYCHIATRIC GENETICS 117 (Paper Presented at the Third World Congress on Psychiatric Genetics, 1993); Michael J. Lyons, *A Twin Study of Self-Reported Criminal Behaviour, in* GENETICS OF CRIMINAL AND ANTISOCIAL BEHAVIOR 61 (Gregory R. Bock & Jamie A. Goode eds., 1996).

56. Cadoret et al., *supra* note 34; Remi J. Cadoret et al., *An Adoption Study of Genetic and Environmental Factors in Drug Abuse*, 43 ARCHIVES GEN. PSYCHIATRY 1131 (1986).

57. Lindon J. Eaves et al., *Genetics and Developmental Psychopathology: 2. The Main Effects of Genes and Environment on Behavioral Problems in the Virginia Twin Study of Adolescent Behavioral Development*, 38 J. CHILD PSYCHOL. & PSYCHIATRY 965 (1997).

and adoption studies.[58] In contrast to adult antisocial personality disorder, for conduct disorder, shared family environmental influences have been found to be of greater importance during childhood.[59]

1. Antisocial Personality Disorder Antisocial personality disorder is one of the most extensively studied personality disorders. Individuals with this disorder are impulsive, aggressive, and aloof, and are thought to have diminished capabilities for work, love, guilt, and cooperation with others.[60] Antisocial personality disorder begins in childhood with substantial behavior problems either at school or at home.[61] The disorder is typified by antisocial behavior in a broad range of social and personal contexts. Impulsive-aggressive behavior is most prominent during childhood.[62] These behaviors include fighting, setting fires, running away from home, treating animals cruelly, and engaging in conflicts with authority figures.[63] In adulthood, the impulsive-aggressive behaviors persist and are associated with impairments in work and social situations.[64] Individuals with antisocial personality disorder tend to change jobs repeatedly, both by getting fired and by quitting.[65] They also frequently use and abuse alcohol and drugs.[66]

Antisocial personality disorder is more prevalent in males than females, regardless of age or ethnicity.[67] Furthermore, rates of this disorder are higher in people who are related to someone with it when compared to the normal population.[68]

---

58. Remi J. Cadoret et al., *Evidence for Gene-Environment Interaction in the Development of Adolescent Antisocial Behavior*, 13 BEHAV. GENETICS 301 (1983); Cadoret et al., *supra* note 34.

59. Laura Baker, *The Nature-Nurture Problem in Violence, in* INTERNATIONAL HANDBOOK OF VIOLENCE RESEARCH 589 (Wilhelm Heitmeyer & John Hagan eds., 2003); Michael J. Lyons et al., *Differential Heritability of Adult and Juvenile Antisocial Traits*, 52 ARCHIVE GEN. PSYCHIATRY 906 (1995).

60. C. Robert Cloninger et al., *Epidemiology and Axis I Comorbidity of Antisocial Personality, in* HANDBOOK OF ANTISOCIAL BEHAVIOR 12 (David M. Stoff et al. eds., 1997).

61. LEE N. ROBINS, DEVIANT CHILDREN GROWN UP: A SOCIOLOGICAL AND PSYCHIATRIC STUDY OF SOCIOPATHIC PERSONALITY (1966).

62. *See* Lee N. Robins et al., *Antisocial Personality, in* PSYCHIATRIC DISORDERS IN AMERICA: THE EPIDEMILOGIC CATCHMENT AREA STUDY 258, 264 (Lee N. Robins & Darrel A Regier eds., 1991) (describing the common remission of the disorder as the individual advances into adulthood).

63. *Id.* at 259–60.

64. *Id.* at 260.

65. *Id.*

66. Marian B. M. van den Bree et al., *Antisocial Personality and Drug Use Disorders—Are They Genetically Related?, in* THE SCIENCE, TREATMENT, AND PREVENTION OF ANTISOCIAL BEHAVIORS: APPLICATION TO THE CRIMINAL JUSTICE SYSTEM 8-1, 8-1 to 8-2 (Diane H. Fishbein ed., 2000).

67. Robins et al, *supra* note 62, at 271.

68. Cloninger & Gottesman, *supra* note 38.

In addition, even though the rates of antisocial personality disorder are lower in females, affected female probands normally have more affected relatives than do male probands.[69] Thus, females may require stronger cultural and biological influences than males to become antisocial.[70]

2. Conduct Disorder Conduct disorder is a childhood onset disorder that is emerging as one of the most common child psychiatric disorders.[71] The disorder manifests as a repetitive and persistent pattern of adolescent antisocial behavior in which the basic rights of others or societal norms and rules are violated.[72] In general, conduct disorder is considered to be a relatively severe and clinical form of antisocial behavior.[73] It is associated with a plethora of negative outcomes such as depression and anxiety, drug use and abuse, and, in adults, antisocial personality disorder.[74]

Conduct disorder in childhood and adolescence is a strong predictor of antisocial behavior in adulthood. Studies using official court records have shown that 50 to 70 percent of children (youth) who meet criteria for conduct disorder, or who were arrested for delinquent acts during childhood or adolescence, are arrested in adulthood.[75] Similarly, children with high instances of antisocial behaviors have been found to have a 43 percent chance of meeting criteria for antisocial personality disorder during adulthood,[76] and 40 percent of institutionally reared boys and 35 percent of institutionally reared girls who met a relaxed *DSM-III* criteria for conduct disorder in childhood later met criteria for

---

69. Van den Bree et al., *supra* note 66, at 8-6.

70. *Id.*

71. Jane Scourfield et al., *Conduct Problems in Children and Adolescents: A Twin Study*, 61 ARCHIVES GEN. PSYCHIATRY 489 (2004). *See also* Jessie C. Anderson et al., DSM-III *Disorders in Preadolescent Children*, 44 ARCHIVES OF GEN. PSYCHIATRY 69 (1987); Patricia Cohen et al., *An Epidemiological Study of Disorders in Late Childhood and Adolescence— I. Age- and Gender-Specific Prevalence*, 34 J. CHILD PSYCHOL. & PSYCHIATRY 851 (1993) (detailing studies of common childhood disorders which include conduct disorder).

72. AMERICAN PSYCHOLOGICAL ASS'N, DIAGNOSTIC AND STATISTICAL MANUAL OF MENTAL DISORDERS 85 (4th ed. 1994).

73. Heather L. Gelhorn et al., *Genetic and Environmental Influences on Conduct Disorder: Symptom, Domain, and Full-Scale Analyses*, 46 J. CHILD PSYCHOL. & PSYCHIATRY 580, 580 (2005).

74. *Id.*

75. Rolf Loeber, *Antisocial Behavior: More Enduring than Changeable?*, 30 J. AM. ACAD. CHILD & ADOLESCENT PSYCHIATRY 393, 393 (1991). *See also* Rolf Loeber, *Development and Risk Factors of Juvenile Antisocial Behavior and Delinquency*, 10 CLINICAL PSYCHOL. REV. 1 (1990); Rolf Loeber, *The Stability of Antisocial and Delinquent Child Behavior: A Review*, 53 CHILD DEV. 1431 (1982) (detailing studies involving the development and stability of juvenile delinquency into adulthood).

76. ROBINS, *supra* note 61, at 141–42.

antisocial personality disorder in adulthood.[77] Furthermore, a study following a sample of boys and girls who had attended a large psychiatric clinic in London into their adulthood found that 43 percent of the youth who had conduct disorder during childhood also met criteria for antisocial personality disorder during adulthood, compared to only 13 percent of youth who had not had conduct disorder in childhood.[78]

Not all youth with conduct disorder engage in antisocial acts in adulthood, raising the question of what factors might set them apart and predict whether a child with conduct disorder will become antisocial as an adult. Children who meet criteria for conduct disorder and who have a biological parent with antisocial personality disorder are more likely to meet criteria for antisocial personality disorder themselves.[79] A history of antisocial personality disorder in a parent is the strongest predictor of persistence of conduct disorder from childhood into adolescence.[80]

Researchers have begun to recognize that genetic factors contribute critically to the development of conduct problems in children.[81] Recent studies have indicated that conduct disorder is significantly heritable, with estimates ranging from 27 to 78 percent.[82] Some twin studies have demonstrated the significance of shared family environmental influences in conduct disorder,[83] while several other studies have found no such significant shared factors.[84] Predominantly, significant genetic factors do appear to be influencing antisocial-behavior-related

---

77. Mark Zoccolillo et al., *The Outcome of Childhood Conduct Disorder: Implications for Defining Adult Personality Disorder and Conduct Disorder*, 22 PSYCHOL. MED. 971, 976 (1992). *See generally* Benjamin B. Lahey & Rolf Loeber, *Attention-Deficit/Hyperactivity Disorder, Oppositional Defiant Disorder, Conduct Disorder, and Adult Antisocial Behavior: A Life Span Perspective, in* HANDBOOK OF ANTISOCIAL BEHAVIOR, *supra* note 60, at 51 (describing the developmental relationship between behavior disorders in childhood and the appearance of antisocial disorders in adulthood).

78. Lahey & Loeber, *supra* note 77, at 57 (citing Richard Harrington et al., *Adult Outcomes of Childhood and Adolescent Depression: II. Links with Antisocial Disorders*, 30 J. AM. CHILD & ADOLESCENT PSYCHIATRY 434 (1991)).

79. *See* ROBINS, *supra* note 61, at 163–66.

80. *See, e.g.*, Lahey & Loeber, *supra* note 77.

81. Scourfield et al., *supra* note 71, at 489.

82. *See* Gelhorn et al., *supra* note 73; Scourfield et al., *supra* note 71; Anita Thapar et al., *Examining the Comorbidity of ADHD-Related Behaviours and Conduct Problems Using a Twin Study Design*, 179 BRIT. J. PSYCHIATRY 224 (2001); Frederick L. Coolidge et al., *Heritability and the Comorbidity of Attention Deficit Hyperactivity Disorder with Behavioral Disorders and Executive Function Deficits: A Preliminary Investigation*, 17 DEVELOPMENTAL NEUROPSYCHOLOGY 273 (2000); Eaves et al., *supra* note 57.

83. Gelhorn et al., *supra* note 73, at 588; Thapar et al., *supra* note 82, at 226. Cadoret et al., *supra* note 34.

84. Scourfield et al., *supra* note 71, at 494; Eaves et al., *supra* note 57, at 973.

psychiatric disorders such as conduct disorder and antisocial personality disorder.

3. Oppositional Defiant Disorder Similar to conduct disorder, oppositional defiant disorder is a behavioral disturbance characterized by aggressive and antisocial acts.[85] Oppositional defiant disorder encompasses primarily verbal aggression, such as losing one's temper, and inharmonious interpersonal behavior, such as blaming others and seeking revenge, whereas conduct disorder "includes physically aggressive behaviors ranging in severity from bullying to forced sexual activity and antisocial acts, including theft, destruction of property, and violation of age-normative rules, such as truancy."[86] When combined, oppositional defiant disorder and conduct disorder are among the most common psychiatric disorders in childhood and adolescence. Recent studies estimate the prevalence rates for oppositional defiant disorder at 1.8 to 3.9 percent, and conduct disorder at 3.3 to 6.6 percent.[87]

As with antisocial personality disorder and conduct disorder, twin studies have also been utilized to investigate the heritability of oppositional defiant disorder. Several twin studies have found significant genetic influences in oppositional defiant disorder symptoms with heritability estimates ranging from 14 to 65 percent.[88]

D. Genetic Influences on Correlates of Antisocial Behavior

Although studies reviewed so far provide direct evidence for genetic influences on antisocial behavior, numerous other investigations also provide indirect evidence by examining the genetic underpinnings of traits and behavior that predict or correlate with antisocial behavior. These traits include personality traits, such as impulsivity, and cognitive factors, such as attention and other executive function deficits. These correlates of antisocial behavior are manifested in another psychiatric disorder, attention deficit hyperactivity disorder (ADHD), which also shows comorbidity with conduct disorder and aggressive behavior in children. Reviewing evidence for genetic influences in these correlated traits can help shed light on the nature of the genetic mechanisms that may underlie antisocial behavior.

85. Emily Simonoff, *Gene-Environment Interplay in Oppositional Defiant and Conduct Disorder*, 10 CHILD & ADOLESCENT PSYCHIATRIC CLINICS N. AM. 351, 351 (2001).

86. *Id.*

87. *Id.*, at 352.

88. Coolidge et al., *supra* note 82, at 282 tbl.4 (finding a heritability estimate of 0.61); Eaves et al., *supra* note 57, at 974 tbl.3 (finding heritability of 14 percent for girls as measured by their fathers' responses to questionnaires and heritability of 65 percent for boys as measured from interviews with their fathers).

1. **Impulsivity** Individuals are differentially susceptible to antisocial behavior, due perhaps in part to variations in personality characteristics such as impulsivity.[89] These personality correlates of antisocial behavior are also heritable. Data from large twin and adoption studies have suggested that traits related to repetitive, aggressive behavior, such as impulsivity, drug abuse, and neurological deficits, are significantly heritable. In a review of 11 behavioral genetic studies on impulsive behavior and aggressive behavior, at least 5 demonstrated significant heritability for these traits.[90] In addition, three out of three studies conducted on adolescents demonstrated negative results, but three out of four studies on adults found significant heritabilities for impulsivity and aggression.[91] In the latter studies, the heritabilities found were 0.72,[92] 0.44,[93] and 0.41,[94] indicating that impulsivity and aggression are significantly heritable.[95] Furthermore, the heritability of self-reported personality traits related to impulsiveness and irritability in twins reared together and apart showed heritability rates that ranged from 20 to 62 percent.[96] Other twin studies have also indicated a strong genetic heritability for impulsivity.[97] Genes may therefore modulate behaviors that involve impulse control, which can lead to manifestations such as conduct disorder, antisocial personality disorder, ADHD, and alcoholism.[98]

2. **Attention Deficit Hyperactivity Disorder** ADHD is a highly disabling condition that normally begins during early childhood.[99] It is characterized bypervasive inattention, overactivity, and impulsiveness. Children with ADHD not only experience educational failures in school, but they also experience problems with

---

89. David Goldman & Diana H. Fishbein, *Genetic Bases for Impulsive and Antisocial Behaviors—Can Their Course Be Altered?, in* THE SCIENCE, TREATMENT, AND PREVENTION OF ANTISOCIAL BEHAVIORS: APPLICATION TO THE CRIMINAL JUSTICE SYSTEM, *supra* note 70, at 9-1, 9-2.

90. Emil F. Coccaro et al., *Heritability of Irritable Impulsiveness: A Study of Twins Reared Together and Apart*, 48 PSYCHIATRY RES. 229, 237 (1993).

91. Goldman & Fishbein, *supra* note 89, at 9-6.

92. J. Phillipe Rushton et al., *Altruism and Aggression: The Heritability of Individual Differences*, 50 J. PERSONALITY & SOC. PSYCHOL. 1192, 1194 (1986).

93. Auke Tellegen et al., *Personality Similarity in Twins Reared Apart and Together*, 54 J. PERSONALITY & SOC. PSYCHOL. 1031, 1036 (1988).

94. Coccaro et al., *supra* note 90, at 234–35.

95. Goldman & Fishbein, *supra* note 89, at 9-6.

96. Coccaro et al., *supra* note 90, at 234–35.

97. *See, e.g.,* Yoon-Mi Hur & Thomas J. Bouchard, Jr., *The Genetic Correlation Between Impulsivity and Sensation Seeking Traits*, 27 BEHAV. GENETICS 455 (1997).

98. Goldman & Fishbein, *supra* note 89, at 9-2.

99. Russell A. Barkley, *Genetics of Childhood Disorders: XVII. ADHD, Part 1: The Executive Functions and ADHD*, 39 AM. CHILD & ADOLESCENT PSYCHIATRY 1064, 1064 (2000); Anita Thapar et al., *Genetic Basis of Attention Deficit and Hyperactivity*, 174 BRIT. J. PSYCHIATRY 105, 105 (1999).

relationships and poor self-esteem.[100] In addition, they are at risk for developing behavioral, psychiatric, and social difficulties in adulthood, including antisocial behavior.

Childhood ADHD has been linked to antisocial behavior in two ways. First, research has shown that children with ADHD are more likely than children without ADHD to exhibit antisocial behavior during adolescence and adulthood.[101] Second, it appears that the persistence of conduct disorder over time is worse for youth who also display symptoms of ADHD.[102] Several studies have suggested that youth who exhibit both antisocial behavior and ADHD manifest more severe forms of antisocial behavior, particularly greater physical aggression.[103] Although some youth classified as ADHD exhibit high levels of either inattention or hyperactivity-impulsivity, most exhibit high levels of both types of symptoms. Developmentally, ADHD symptoms tend to persist. Studies have reported strong continuity in overactivity and attention problems from ages 6–7 to ages 16–18.[104]

Many classical genetic studies have examined genetic influences on ADHD,[105] as have adoption studies, which provide strong evidence suggesting a genetic basis for both inattention and hyperactivity.[106]

Early research showed higher prevalence rates of hyperactivity among biological parents and second-degree relatives of children with hyperactivity, compared with controls. Furthermore, family studies have found that full siblings of affected children show higher rates of hyperactivity than half-siblings. . . . In a [more] recent series of family studies, where standardised interviews . . . were used, relatives of affected male and female probands were found to be at increased risk for the disorder. . . . Early adoption studies found significantly higher rates of hyperactivity among biological parents of children with hyperactivity (7.5%) compared with adoptive parents (2.1%). . . . Adoption research

---

100. Thapar et al., *supra* note 99, at 105.

101. L. Hechtman, G. Weiss, & T. Perlman. *Hyperactives as Young Adults: Past and Current Substance Abuse and Antisocial Behavior*, 54 AM. J. ORTHOPSYCHIATRY 415, 415–25 (1984); or R. Satterfield, M. Rutter, & A. M. Schell, *A Prospective Study of Delinquency in 110 Adolescent Boys with Attention Deficit Disorder and 88 Normal Adolescent Boys*, 139 AM. J. PSYCHIATRY, 795, 795–98 (1982).

102. See Benjamin Lahey & Rolf Loeber, *Attention-Deficit/Hyperactivity Disorder, Oppositional Defiant Disorder, Conduct Disorder, and Adult Antisocial Behavior: A Life Span Perspective, in* HANDBOOK OF ANTISOCIAL BEHAVIOR, *supra* note 60, at 51.

103. See Lahey & Loeber, *supra* note 102; Offord et al., *Delinquency and hyperactivity*, J. NERVOUS & MENTAL DISEASE, 167, 734–41 (1979).

104. Jonna Kuntsi et al., *Genetic Influences on the Stability of Attention-Deficit/ Hyperactivity Disorder Symptoms from Early to Middle Childhood*, 57 BIOLOGICAL PSYCHIATRY 647, 647 (2005).

105. Thapar et al., *supra* note 99, at 109; BARKLEY, *supra* note 99.

106. RUSSELL A. BARKLEY, ADHD AND THE NATURE OF SELF-CONTROL 37–41 (1997).

has also found that biological parents of hyperactive children demonstrate significantly poorer performance on cognitive measures of attention, compared with adoptive parents.[107]

Another adoption study using both biologically related and unrelated international adoptees identified a strong genetic component ($h^2 = 0.47$) for attention problems, which are highly related to diagnoses of ADHD.[108]

Correlations for symptoms of hyperactivity and inattention are greater for MZ twins than for DZ twins,[109] with heritability estimates ranging from 39 to 91 percent.[110] Several large-scale twin studies have also separately examined the trait of hyperactivity-impulsivity and attribute a large portion of variance to genetic factors (with an average heritability of approximately 80 percent).[111] Furthermore, such a genetic contribution may increase as the scores along this trait become more extreme, although this issue is under debate.[112]

---

107. Thapar et al., *supra* note 99, at 106–9. Indeed, first-degree relatives of male probands were five times more likely to be diagnosed with ADHD than were relatives of the normal controls.

108. Edwin J. C. G. van den Oord et al., *A Study of Problem Behaviors in 10- to 15-Year-Old Biologically Related and Unrelated International Adoptees*, 24 BEHAV. GENETICS 193, 201 (1994).

109. Robert Goodman & Jim Stevenson, *A Twin Study of Hyperactivity—II. The Aetiological Role of Genes, Family Relationships and Perinatal Adversity*, 30 J. CHILD PSYCHOL. & PSYCHIATRY 691 (1989); Jim Stevenson, *Evidence for a Genetic Etiology in Hyperactivity in Children*, 22 BEHAV. GENETICS 337, 342 (1992); Jacquelyn J. Gillis et al., *Attention Deficit Disorder in Reading-Disabled Twins: Evidence for a Genetic Etiology*, 20 J. ABNORMAL CHILD PSYCHOL. 303, 304 (1992); Craig Edelbrock et al., *A Twin Study of Competence and Problem Behavior in Childhood and Early Adolescence*, 36 J. CHILD PSYCHOL. & PSYCHIATRY 775, 779 (1995); Anita Thapar et al., *Childhood Hyperactivity Scores Are Highly Heritable and Show Sibling Competition Effects: Twin Study Evidence*, 25 BEHAV. GENETICS 537, 539 (1995); Eaves et al., *supra* note 57; Florence Levy et al., *Attention-Deficit Hyperactivity Disorder: A Category or a Continuum? Genetic Analysis of a Large-Scale Twin Study*, 36 J. AM. ACAD. CHILD & ADOLESCENT PSYCHIATRY 737, 738 (1997); Dianne K. Sherman et al., *Attention-Deficit Hyperactivity Disorder Dimensions: A Twin Study of Inattention and Impulsivity-Hyperactivity*, 36 J. AM. ACAD. CHILD & ADOLESCENT PSYCHIATRY 745, 746 (1997).

110. Thapar et al., *supra* note 99, at 107.

111. Stephen V. Faraone, *Discussion of "Genetic Influence on Parent-Reported Attention-Related Problems in a Norwegian General Population Twin Sample,"* 35 J. AM. ACAD. CHILD & ADOLESCENT PSYCHIATRY 596 (1996); Helene Gjone et al., *Changes in Heritability Across Increasing Levels of Behavior Problems in Young Twins*, 26 BEHAV. GENETICS 419 (1996); Levy et al., *supra* note 109; Rhee & Waldman, *supra* note 8; Sherman et al., *supra* note 109; Judy Silberg et al., *Genetic and Environmental Influences on the Covariation Between Hyperactivity and Conduct Disturbance in Juvenile Twins*, 37 J. CHILD PSYCHOL. & PSYCHIATRY 803 (1996); Edwin J. C. G. van den Oord et al., *A Genetic Study of Maternal and Paternal Ratings of Problem Behaviors in 3-Year-Old Twins*, 105 J. ABNORMAL PSYCHOL. 349 (1996).

112. Neilson Martin et al., *Observer Effects and Heritability of Childhood Attention-Deficit Hyperactivity Disorder Symptoms*, 180 BRIT. J. PSYCHIATRY 260 (2002); Thapar et al., *supra*

How important are environmental factors in ADHD symptoms? Shared environmental factors contribute little, if anything, to the underlying symptoms of ADHD, typically accounting for only about 5 percent or less of the variance among individuals.[113] There has been some suggestion, however, that shared environmental influences might contribute to the *persistence* of behavior problems across development.[114]

Twin studies also indicate the importance of nonshared environmental factors, which may include unique individual experiences as well as biological factors that might not be genetic in origin.[115] Such nonshared environmental factors might be events that affected one twin but not the other, such as neurological injuries, or differences in manner or character that received different treatment from the parents of the children. Nearly 15 to 20 percent of the variance in ADHD symptoms is due to nonshared environmental factors.[116]

In summary, twin, family, and adoption studies have consistently shown a strong genetic contribution to ADHD. Influential environmental factors appear to be largely of the nonshared variety, although shared family environment could possibly influence the persistence of symptoms over time.

3. Executive Function Executive function has been defined in the literature as a unique domain of cognitive abilities that involves organization in space and time, selective inhibition, response preparation, goal attainment, planning, and cognitive flexibility.[117] This set of functions is thought to be relatively independent from other cognitive functions, such as sensations, perception, language, and memory, yet it is also thought to overlap with attention, reasoning, and problem solving.[118] The neural mechanisms underlying executive function have not been clearly defined, but it is thought that they are mediated by the prefrontal

---

note 82; Farone, *supra* note 111; Gjone et al., *supra* note 111; Levy et al., *supra* note 109; Soo Hyun Rhee et al., *Sex Differences in Genetic and Environmental Influences on* DSM-III-R *Attention Deficit Hyperactive Disorder (ADHD)*, 108 J. ABNORMAL PSYCHOL. 24, 37–38 (1999); Sherman et al., *supra* note 109; Thapar et al., *supra* note 109; Edwin J. C. G. van den Oord et al., *supra* note 111.

113. *See, e.g.,* Levy et al., *supra* note 109; Sherman et al., *supra* note 109; Silberg et al., *supra* note 111.

114. Edwin J. G. C. van den Oord & David C. Rowe, *Continuity and Change in Children's Social Maladjustment: A Developmental Behavior Genetic Study,* 33 DEVELOPMENTAL PSYCHOL. 319, 329 (1997).

115. BARKLEY, *supra* note 99, at 40–41.

116. Silberg et al., *supra* note 111, at 809; Alison Pike & Robert Plomin, *Importance of Non-shared Environmental Factors for Childhood and Adolescent Psychopathology,* 35 J. AM. ACAD. CHILD & ADOLESCENT PSYCHIATRY 560 (1996).

117. *See, e.g.,* Frederick L. Coolidge et al., *Are Personality Disorders Psychological Manifestations of Executive Function Deficits? Bivariate Heritability Evidence from a Twin Study,* 34 BEHAV. GENETICS 75, 75–78 (2004).

118. Coolidge et al., *supra* note 82.

cortices of the brain.[119] Significant differences in one or more measures of executive function have been found between children who have ADHD and control children.[120] Furthermore, deficits in executive function can arise as a consequence of many different factors, including genetic as well as traumatic brain injuries.[121]

The most typical head injuries include damage to the frontal lobes, which are responsible for planning and for the inhibition of impulsive behavior.[122] Therefore, damage to the frontal lobes will often result in increased impulsive and aggressive behavior in response to external provocation.[123] There is also a link between executive dysfunctions and antisocial behavior, whereby antisocial offenders have been found to demonstrate greater neuropsychological deficits.[124]

In contrast to the numerous studies showing high heritability of disorders such as ADHD and conduct disorder, genetic studies of executive function deficits are much scarcer. One reason might be that, unlike ADHD, conduct disorder, or even oppositional defiant disorder, the *Diagnostic and Statistical Manual of Mental Disorders* includes no established criteria for executive function deficits, so "a standard syndromal description and consensus of criteria are lacking."[125] However, heritability studies of ADHD and evidence that ADHD is comorbid with executive function deficits indirectly suggest a substantial and even primary genetic link.[126] Two recent studies that explored the etiology of executive function deficits in children demonstrated that executive function deficits are in fact highly heritable ($h^2 = 0.77$).[127]

4. Substance Use and Abuse The relationship between alcohol use and violence has been well documented[128] but is not fully understood. Illicit drug use has been connected to violence and antisocial behavior, but whether drug or

---

119. Bruce F. Pennington & Sally Ozonoff, *Executive Functions and Developmental Psychopathology*, 37 J. CHILD PSYCHOL. & PSYCHIATRY 51, 51 (1996).

120. *See id.* at 58–65.

121. Adrian Raine et al., *Neurocognitive Impairments in Boys on the Life-Course Persistent Social Path*, 114 J. ABNORMAL PSYCHOL. 38 (2005).

122. Coolidge et al., *supra* note 117.

123. *Id.*

124. *See* ADRIAN RAINE, THE PSYCHOPATHOLOGY OF CRIME: CRIMINAL BEHAVIOR AS CLINICAL DISORDER 215–16 (1993).

125. Coolidge et al., *supra* note 82, at 275; *See generally* AMERICAN PSYCHOLOGICAL ASS'N, *supra* note 72.

126. Coolidge et al., *supra* note 82, at 275.

127. *Id.*

128. Alcohol use is presumed to contribute to violence because of the pharmacological properties of the drug, as well as expectancies and societal norms surrounding these aspects. *See generally* Helene Raskin White, *Alcohol, Illicit Drugs, and Violence, in* HANDBOOK OF ANTISOCIAL BEHAVIOR, *supra* note 60, at 511.

alcohol use has a direct effect on violence has been debated.[129] In general, the nature of the association between substance use and violence may stem from several possible sources: it might be due to shared common causes, such as genetic or temperamental traits, to antisocial personality disorder, or to parental modeling of heavy substance use and violence.[130]

Recent literature has focused on family and twin studies to shed more light on the relationship between antisocial behavior and substance use.[131] Like antisocial behavior, substance dependence also tends to run in families, with most family resemblance being explained by genetic factors and not by shared family environment.[132] In addition, the relative influence of genetic and environmental factors on substance dependence tends to be the same in both men and women, although women may require greater familial loading—that is, greater genetic propensity or liability—to express these disorders.[133] Establishing that both antisocial behavior and substance dependence are heritable, however, does not necessarily mean that the same genetic or environmental factors influence both disorders. Studies that simultaneously investigate both disorders are required to understand their genetic and environmental overlap.

Several twin studies show significant genetic overlap among disinhibitory syndromes, such as conduct disorder and alcohol dependence, child and antisocial behavior, and alcohol and drug dependence.[134] Men and woman both exhibit a similar pattern of genetic and environmental effects.[135] Although there is significant genetic overlap among these disorders, genetic and environmental risk factors can be specific to each disorder.[136] Large epidemiologic samples have identified a broad dimension of risk underlying antisocial personality disorder, conduct disorder, alcohol dependence, and drug dependence.[137] This general

---

129. White, *supra* note 128.

130. *Id.* at 512.

131. Brian M. Hicks et al., *Family Transmission and Heritability of Externalizing Disorders: A Twin-Family Study*, 61 ARCHIVES OF GEN. PSYCHIATRY 922, 922–23 (2004).

132. *Id.*

133. Kathleen R. Merikangas et al., *Familial Transmission of Substance Use Disorders*, 55 ARCHIVES GEN. PSYCHIATRY 973 (1998).

134. Hicks et al., *supra* note 131, at 923; Kenneth S. Kendler et al., *The Structure of Genetic and Environmental Risk Factors for Common Psychiatric and Substance Use Disorders in Men and Women*, 60 ARCHIVES GEN. PSYCHIATRY 929 (2003); Robert F. Krueger et al., *Etiologic Connections Among Substance Dependence, Antisocial Behavior, and Personality: Modeling the Externalizing Spectrum*, 111 J. ABNORMAL PSYCHOL. 411 (2002); Kristen C. Jacobson et al., *Sex Differences in the Genetic and Environmental Influences on the Development of Antisocial Behavior*, 14 DEV. & PSYCHOPATHOLOGY 395 (2002).

135. Hicks et al., *supra* note 131, at 923; Kendler et al., *supra* note 134; Krueger et al., *supra* note 134; Jacobson et al., *supra* note 134.

136. *See, e.g.*, Hicks et al., *supra* note 131, at 923; Kendler et al., *supra* note 134, at 929–30; Krueger et al., *supra* note 134, at 411–13; Jacobson et al., *supra* note 134.

137. *See, e.g.*, Hicks et al., *supra* note 131, at 923.

vulnerability factor is typically referred to as "externalizing behavior problems," and recent twin studies have indicated that the source of the comorbidity in these disorders can be largely attributed to common genetic factors ($h^2 = 0.60\text{–}0.80$, a broad-sense estimate).[138]

IV. UNPACKING THE GENETIC AND ENVIRONMENTAL BLACK BOXES

Although the classical genetic studies of antisocial behavior have clearly demonstrated the importance of genetic predispositions as well as environmental influences, this research does not specify the precise biological or social mechanisms that underlie these global effects. Thus, both genetic and environmental influences represent "black boxes" in our understanding of antisocial behavior based on these classical studies. Unpacking these boxes is now a primary aim of much current research in this area. Several different approaches are being used to understand the biological and social mechanisms that underlie the genetic and environmental factors for antisocial behavior. These include (1) a "measured risk factor" approach, in which multivariate genetic models are used to elucidate genetic mechanisms by studying various risk factors also known to be at least partially heritable and that are known to correlate with antisocial behavior, and (2) the "QTL approach," in which specific genes are identified and investigated for their associations and possible functional significance to antisocial behavior.

A. Multivariate Genetic Models: The Measured Risk Factor Approach

The "measured risk factor" approach investigates various traits and behaviors that are known to correlate with the risk of antisocial behavior in genetically informative designs, such as classical twin or adoption studies. Multivariate genetic models are thus used to explain sources of genetic covariance and environmental covariance that underlie these associations between risk factors and antisocial behavior.[139] This is similar to the "endophenotype approach," in which researchers identify highly heritable traits that show associations with antisocial behavior.[140] In addition to estimating the components of genetic variance important to both antisocial behavior and the risk factor, multivariate models also compute the correlation between genes influencing antisocial behavior and genes influencing the risk factor or endophenotype. To the extent that a gene or set of genes may have manifold effects on both the risk factor and antisocial behavior (called pleiotropy), a large genetic correlation should result. A simple multivariate

---

138. *Id.* at 924–27.

139. David M. Evans et al., *Biometrical Genetics*, 61 BIOLOGICAL PSYCHOL. 33, 45 (2002).

140. *See generally* Irving I. Gottesman & Todd D. Gould, *The Endophenotype Concept in Psychiatry: Etymology and Strategic Intentions*, 160 AM. J. PSYCHIATRY 636 (2003).

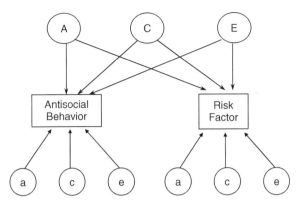

FIGURE 1.6 MULTIVARIATE GENETIC MODEL FOR ANTISOCIAL BEHAVIOR AND A MEASURED RISK FACTOR (RF)

genetic model involving antisocial behavior and a single risk factor is presented in Figure 1.6, in which common genetic and environmental effects (A, C, and E) are shown to influence both the risk factor and antisocial behavior.

To the extent that genes have pleiotropic effects—that is, to the extent that they influence more than one phenotype—common genetic influences on the risk factor and antisocial behavior should result. Close proximity—"genetic linkage"—of the genes influencing antisocial behavior to the risk factor, or certain patterns of assortative mating, such as antisocial individuals paired systematically to mates with extreme values of the risk factor, or both, can also contribute to the common genetic factors in Figure 1.6.[141] Additional genetic influences that are specific to either antisocial behavior or the risk factor are also indicated in this model (a, c, e effects for each phenotype). Thus, the total heritability for a given trait such as antisocial behavior may be parsed into components that are shared and not shared with the risk factor, in order to specify more exactly the nature of the global genetic influences in antisocial behavior.

Many of the various correlates of antisocial behavior reviewed earlier[142] may be considered as possible endophenotypes, most notably personality traits such as impulsivity and attention deficits. A wide range of other characteristics showing associations with antisocial behavior has also been identified and includes both biological and social risk factors.[143] Key biological risk factors include hormones, physiological (autonomic) underarousal, frontal lobe function

---

141. D. S. Falconer & Trudy F. C. Mackay, Introduction to Quantitative Genetics, 312–13 (4th ed., 1996).

142. See supra Part III.D.

143. See, e.g., Randy Borum, Assessing Violence Risk Among Youth, 56 J. Clinical Psychol. 1263, 1267–72 (2000).

(and dysfunction), and neurotransmitters.[144] Any of these traits may be examined for common genetic relationships with antisocial behavior, although little work has been done using this approach to date.

One example of a biological risk factor for antisocial behavior is autonomic underarousal in antisocial—including violent—individuals. Antisocial individuals have shown a lower resting heart rate and lower electrodermal (that is, skin conductance) response, as well as sma ller changes in these factors in response to novel stimuli such as auditory presentation of tones.[145] The connections of these findings to antisocial behavior have been interpreted in several ways. For example, low heart rate may reflect fearlessness, or reduced anxiety,[146] lack of socialization, poor learning abilities due to cognitive deficits or emotional withdrawal or both,[147] or reduced brain functioning in areas involved in mediating psychophysiological responding.[148] Another explanation is that low arousal may lead to stimulation-seeking behaviors, including violence, in an attempt to raise autonomic arousal to optimal levels.[149]

Although autonomic arousal in terms of heart rate and skin conductance has been shown to be at least partially heritable,[150] it is unclear to what extent underarousal may be related to antisocial behavior due to a common genetic link. This question may be addressed using multivariate genetic analyses as indicated in Figure 1.6. In the USC twin study of nine- to ten-year-old children, multivariate analyses showed that a significant genetic correlation did in fact exist between

---

144. *See* RAINE, *supra* note 124, at 40–46; Klaus A. Miczek et al., *An Overview of Biological Influences on Violent Behavior, in* 2 UNDERSTANDING AND PREVENTING VIOLENCE: BIOBEHAVIORAL INFLUENCES 1 (Albert J. Reis et al. eds., 1994); DEBRA NIEHOFF, THE BIOLOGY OF VIOLENCE 106–11, 115–49, 153–87 (1999) (describing brain imaging studies of violent offenders and explaining the "circular" relationship between hormones and behavior and between neurotransmitters and behavior); Laura A. Baker, *Theories of Violence: Biology, in* 3 VIOLENCE IN AMERICA 307, 307 (Ronald Gottesman & Richard M. Brown eds., 1999).

145. *See* RAINE, *supra* note 124, at 160–65 (referring to findings of lower skin conductance in those who have committed crimes of evasion, and pointing to two of eight studies that found antisocial individuals to have lower skin-conductance responsivity to aversive tones); *id.* at 166 (referring to findings of lower resting heart rates for "younger noninstitutionalized" antisocial individuals, but not for "institutionalized, criminal psychopaths"); *id.* at 173 (referring to the "virtually no anticipatory [heart rate] response" found in nonpsychopathic criminals); *id.* at 185 (referring to findings of low heart rate, skin conductance, and response to novel stimuli in disinhibited children).

146. *See* David P. Farrington, *The Relationship Between Low Resting Heart Rate and Violence, in* BIOSOCIAL BASES OF VIOLENCE 89 (Adrian Raine et al. eds., 1997).

147. H.J. EYSENCK, CRIME AND PERSONALITY 80–104 (1977).

148. Raine et al., *supra* note 146, at 107–24.

149. EYSENCK, *supra* note 147, at 80–104.

150. Andrew Crider et al., *Stability, Consistency, and Heritability of Electrodermal Response Lability in Middle-Aged Male Twins,* 41 PSYCHOPHYSIOLOGY 501, 502 (2004).

heart rate and antisocial behavior.[151] The heritable arousal factor, however, explained very little of the overall genetic variance in antisocial behavior in these children.[152] Thus, the heritable component in antisocial behavior remains linked but largely independent of physiological underarousal.

Environmental mechanisms may also be investigated using the same "measured risk factor" approach in multivariate genetic models. As shown in Figure 1.6, the common and specific environmental influences for the risk factor and antisocial behavior may also be estimated. This approach may be used to help elucidate the nature of environmental influences important to antisocial behavior by determining, for example, the extent to which certain measured social risk factors and antisocial behavior may have correlated etiologies. Individual social risk factors that have been identified as being important to antisocial behavior include various aspects of parenting, such as harsh discipline and monitoring or awareness of children's activities and behaviors.[153] These and other environmental factors, such as lead poisoning,[154] need to be investigated in genetically informative designs to determine the extent to which their effects may be moderated by individual genetic predispositions.

B. Identifying Specific Genes for Antisocial Behavior: The Quantitative Trait Loci Approach

A second approach for unpacking the genetic black box involves QTL designs, in which specific genes are identified as having either associations with or functional significance in antisocial behavior. These studies also help inform us about environmental influences, in that measured environmental factors can be used to understand the circumstances under which genes for antisocial behavior become expressed. The QTL methods may be considered a measured gene approach.

Although family and twin studies have shed light on the critical role of genetics in antisocial behavior, certain negative outcomes can be most effectively treated and prevented by understanding the precise mechanisms involved in the pathways from genes to behavior. This understanding can be greatly enhanced by identifying which genes are involved in antisocial behavior. Despite popular belief, genetic traits are not immutable. Although individual genes themselves cannot be easily altered, knowing which genes are involved in behavioral

---

151. *See* K. C. Jacobson et al., Abstract, *Genetic Mediation of the Relationship between Arousal and Antisocial Behavior in Pre-Adolescent Twins*, 35 BEHAV. GENETICS 832a, 832a (2005).

152. *Id.*

153. *See* Borum, *supra* note 143, at 1271.

154. *See* Kim N. Dietrich et al., *Early Exposure to Lead and Juvenile Delinquency*, 23 NEUROTOXICOLOGY & TERATOLOGY 511 (2001); Herbert L. Needleman et al., *Bone Lead Levels and Delinquent Behavior*, 275 JAMA 363 (1996).

disorders such as antisocial behavior, ADHD, oppositional defiant disorder, and conduct disorder leads to a better understanding of the underlying mechanisms and biological underpinnings of a gene.

For instance, identifying particular genes that might be associated with certain disorders and that regulate neurotransmitter activity might enable adjustment of neurotransmitter levels and functions accordingly by pharmacological or environmental methods. "Neurotransmitters are brain chemicals that transmit messages from cell to cell, enabling neural [communication]. Neurotransmitter metabolism and receptor function are crucial for most of the brain's functions, including mood, behavior, [and] emotion. . . ."[155] In the case of antisocial behavior, several neurotransmitters associated with genes have been identified, including serotonin and dopamine. These neurotransmitters or neurochemicals are highly sensitive to environmental manipulations.[156]

Of the neurochemicals examined over the past three decades for their relationship to antisocial behavior, none has been scrutinized so intensely as serotonin (5-hydroxytryptamine, or 5-HT).[157] Although the psychological mechanism underlying this relationship remains unclear, some research models speculate that low levels of serotonin increase impulsivity and inhibit sensible behavior, therefore increasing the likelihood of risky and antisocial behavior.[158] Thus, deficiencies in serotonin have been linked with several types of impulsive behavior, including drug abuse, antisocial personality disorder, and gambling.[159] In particular, the "[l]evel of brain serotonergic activity appears to have a profound influence on the production of impulsive-aggressive behavior. In [laboratory studies conducted on] rats, lesions of the septal area and other structures dense with serotonergic connections produce rage and attack [behaviors]." Moreover, "one of the most widely reproduced findings in neuropsychiatry is that indicators of serotonin activity are lower in humans characterized as impulsive and violent towards themselves and others."[160] Therefore, "deficits in brain serotonergic

155. Goldman & Fishbein, *supra* note 89, at 9-4.

156. David E. Comings, *The Role of Genetics in ADHD and Conduct Disorder—Relevance to the Treatment of Recidivist Antisocial Behavior*, in THE SCIENCE, TREATMENT, AND PREVENTION OF ANTISOCIAL BEHAVIORS: APPLICATION TO THE CRIMINAL JUSTICE SYSTEM, *supra* note 70, at 16-1.

157. Todd M. Moore et al., *A Meta-Analysis of Serotonin Metabolite 5-HIAA and Antisocial Behavior*, 28 AGGRESSIVE BEHAV. 299 (2002).

158. *Id.* at 300.

159. Scott D. Lane & Don R Cherek, *Biological and Behavioral Investigation of Aggression and Impulsivity*, in THE SCIENCE, TREATMENT, AND PREVENTION OF ANTISOCIAL BEHAVIORS: APPLICATION TO THE CRIMINAL JUSTICE SYSTEM, *supra* note 70, at 5-1.

160. Marie Åsberg et al., *Psychobiology of Suicide, Impulsivity, and Related Phenomena*, in PSYCHOPHARMACOLOGY: THE THIRD GENERATION OF PROGRESS 655, 657–58 (Herbert Y. Meltzer ed., 1987); Alex Roy et al., *Serotonin in Suicide, Violence, and Alcoholism*, in SEROTONIN IN MAJOR PSYCHIATRIC DISORDERS 185, 187–89 (Emil F. Coccaro & Dennis L. Murphy eds., 1990);

activity produce behavioral disinhibition, resulting in an increased likelihood of impulsive aggressiveness or other excessive and inappropriate behavior."[161]

In addition, specific 5-HT genes have also been identified in association with aggressive and violent behavior; these genes are particularly good candidates for conduct disorder and aggressive behavior.[162] For example, very aggressive behavior has been observed in mice in which the HTR_{1B} gene has been functionally removed.[163] Similarly, in humans the "5-HT_{1B} gene has been localized to chromosome 6."[164] In subjects with antisocial personality disorder, a decrease in the frequency of a polymorphism (a variant form) of the 5-HT_{1B} gene has been found as compared to normal controls.[165]

A second serotonergic gene showing relationships to antisocial behavior is the HTR_{2A} gene. A variant polymorphism of this gene, the serotonin$_{2A}$ receptor gene, was examined in a sample of Caucasian substance abusers and age- and ethnically matched controls.[166] The results demonstrated that this gene was associated with the amount of money spent on drugs, histories of shoplifting, vandalism, or rape, and elevated scores on assault and hostility scales.[167]

A third serotonergic gene associated with antisocial behavior is the HTR_{1DA} gene, which is purported to play a role in 5-HT metabolism.[168] The C variant of this gene was found to be significantly more common in adult offenders with antisocial personality disorder and in childhood conduct disorder than in normal controls.[169]

Matti Virkkunen et al., *Relationship of Psychobiological Variables to Recidivism in Violent Offenders and Impulsive Fire Setters*, 46 ARCHIVES GEN. PSYCHIATRY 600, 600–1 (1989).

161. Goldman & Fishbein, *supra* note 89, at 9-9. *See also* Oliver Cases et al., *Aggressive Behavior and Altered Amounts of Brain Serotonin and Norepinephrine in Mice Lacking MAOA*, 268 SCIENCE 1763 (1995).

162. HTR_{1B}, HTR_{2A}, and HTR_{1DA} denote serotonin receptor genes, which influence the function of serotonin. Some or most of these genes may have variants. Each gene receptor may be localized to a specific chromosome and may perform a different and/or particular function.

163. Frederic Saudou et al., *Enhanced Aggressive Behavior in Mice Lacking 5-HT_{1B} Receptor*, 265 SCIENCE 1875 (1994).

164. Comings, *supra* note 156, at 16-9. *See also* Matti Virkkunen et al., *Serotonin in Alcoholic Violent Offenders, in* GENETICS OF CRIMINAL AND ANTISOCIAL BEHAVIOR, *supra* note 55, at 168.

165. *Id.*

166. *Id.*

167. *Id.* at 16-9 to 16-10.

168. Richard A Glennon & Malgorzata Dukat, *Serotonin Receptor Subtypes, in* PSYCHOPHARMACOLOGY: THE FOURTH GENERATION OF PROGRESS 415, 421 (Floyd E. Bloom & David J. Kupfer eds., 1995).

169. Comings, *supra* note 156, at 16-10.

The last 5-HT gene associated with antisocial behavior is the TDO2 (trypto-phan 2,3-dioxydase) gene. Tryptophan is a known precursor of 5-HT.[170] Increased activity of TDO2 is associated with low levels of 5-HT and, in turn, is associated with aggressive behaviors.[171] Several identified genetic polymorphisms of this gene were found to be associated with alcoholism, drug abuse, ADHD, and Tourette's syndrome.[172]

Additionally, sociocultural factors such as socioeconomic status, stress, and nutrition may play a role in the relationship between neurotransmitters and behavior.[173] For example, diets low in or otherwise blocking the uptake of trypto-phan (a dietary precursor of serotonin) have been found to lower levels of sero-tonin in the brain such that previous levels are never fully recovered, even after the individual returns to a normal diet.[174]

Dopamine is another major neurotransmitter considered to play a role in behavioral activation, reward mechanisms, and goal-directed behaviors. Results from animal studies indicate that increased dopamine functioning is usually associated with increases in defensive aggression.[175] It has also been suggested that dopamine activity may be positively associated with aggressive or impulsive behavior in humans.[176] Results of central neurochemical studies of humans, however, parallel those of serotonin studies, indicating that dopamine activity is inversely correlated with aggressive behavior.[177] For example, cerebrospinal fluid homovanillac acid, a dopamine metabolite, has been found to be negatively correlated with a life history of aggression.[178] In addition, low levels of cerebro-spinal fluid homovanillac acid appear to discriminate recidivist violent criminal offenders from nonrecidivists and incarcerated offenders with antisocial

---

170. *Id.; see also* P. S. Timiras et al., *Lifetime Brain Serotonin: Regional Effects of Age and Precursor Availability*, 5 NEUROBIOLOGY OF AGING 235, 236–37 (1984) (studying the effects of reducing serotonin by reducing the amount of its precursors, including tryptophan).

171. Comings, *supra* note 156, at 16-10.

172. *Id.*; David E. Comings et al., *Polygenic Inheritance of Tourette Syndrome, Stuttering, Attention Deficit Hyperactivity, Conduct, and Oppositional Defiant Disorder: The Additive and Subtractive Effect of the Three Dopaminergic Genes—DRD2, D H, and DAT1*, 67 AM. J. MED. GENETICS 264 (1996).

173. Moore et al., *supra* note 157, at 313.

174. *Id.*

175. *See, e.g.*, Petra Netter & Thomas Rammsayer, *Reactivity to Dopaminergic Drugs and Aggression Related Personality Traits*, 12 PERSONALITY & INDIVIDUAL DIFFERENCES 1009 (1991); Michael R. Spoont, *Modulatory Role of Serotonin in Neural Information Processing: Implications for Human Psychopathology*, 112 PSYCHOL. BULL. 330 (1992).

176. Graham Rogeness et al., *Neurochemistry and Child and Adolescent Psychiatry*, 31 J. AM. ACAD. CHILD & ADOLESCENT PSYCHIATRY 765, 775–77 (1992).

177. Mitchell E. Berman et al., *Neurotransmitter Correlates of Human Aggression*, in HANDBOOK OF ANTISOCIAL BEHAVIOR, *supra* note 60, at 305, 310.

178. *See, e.g.*, Rhona Limson et al., *Personality and Cerebrospinal Fluid Monoamine Metabolites in Alcoholics and Controls*, 48 ARCHIVES GEN. PSYCHIATRY 437, 439 (1991).

personality disorder from those with paranoid or passive-aggressive personality disorders.[179]

The DRD2 gene, a specific dopamine receptor gene, has been positively linked not only to ADHD but also to a range of impulsive, compulsive, and addictive behaviors.[180] The prevalence of a particular gene variant of DRD2 (the Taq A1 allele) has been studied in a range of disorders.[181] In addition to its link with disorders such as ADHD, the A1 allele has also been shown to be significantly elevated in conduct disorder, posttraumatic stress disorder, alcoholism, and drug abuse.[182] This gene was also examined for being potentially related to violent behavior.[183] The results indicated that those who carried the A1 allele were significantly more likely to have engaged in fighting behavior in school and to have been incarcerated for violent crimes as adults.[184] Thus these findings indicate that the DRD2 gene may be one of the genes involved in aggressive behavioral disorders.[185]

Monoamine oxidase (MAO) A and B are two enzymes that metabolize dopamine, norephinephrine, and serotonin.[186] MAO activity has been utilized as an index of central presynaptic serotonergic functioning in impulsive and aggressive individuals.[187] When MAO levels are low, these neurotransmitters become imbalanced. Abnormally low levels in MAO have been linked with a wide range of disorders, including ADHD, alcoholism, drug abuse, and impulsive and risk-taking behaviors.[188]

Significant associations have been found between longer base-pair alleles of the MAOA gene, an X-chromosome gene, and various behavior disorders, including ADHD, conduct disorder, major depressive disorder, drug abuse,

---

179. *See* Berman et al., *supra* note 177, at 305.

180. Comings, *supra* note 156, at 16-6.

181. *Id.; see also* Comings et al., *supra* note 172 (examining the relationship between the gene variant to such disorders as Tourette's syndrome, stuttering, and ADHD).

182. Comings, *supra* note 156, at 16-6.

183. *Id.* at 16-6 to 16-7.

184. *Id.*

185. *Id.* at 16-11 to 16-12.

186. *Id.*

187. Berman et al., *supra* note 179, at 307.

188. Eric J. Devor et al., *Association of Monoamine Oxidase (MAO) Activity with Alcoholism and Alcoholic Subtypes*, 48 AM. J. MED. GENETICS 209 (1993); Anne-Liis Von Knorring et al., *Platelet Monoamine Oxidase Activity in Type 1and Type 2 Alcoholism*, 26 ALCOHOL & ALCOHOLISM 409 (1991); Walid O. Shekim et al., *Platelet MAO Activity and Personality Variations in Normals*, 27 PSYCHIATRY RES. 81 (1989); Monte S. Buchsbaum et al., *The Biochemical High-Risk Paradigm: Behavioral and Familial Correlates of Low Platelet Monoamine Oxidase Activity*, 194 SCIENCE 339 (1976); C. G. Gottfries et al., *Lowered Monoamine Oxidase Activity in Brains from Alcoholic Suicides*, 25 J. NEUROCHEMISTRY 667 (1975).

alcoholism, and learning disabilities.[189] Furthermore, genetic deficiencies in MAOA have been linked with aggression in mice and in humans.[190] In the Brunner study of MAOA deficiencies in a Dutch family sample, a null allele at the MAOA locus was associated with antisocial behavior in males.[191]

V. MODELS OF COMPLEX INTERACTIONS IN ANTISOCIAL BEHAVIOR

Genetic influences on antisocial behavior—even if specified at the level of DNA—are by no means simple. As in many other phenotypes, gene expression for antisocial behavior may well depend on a variety of other factors, including the effects of other genes as well as numerous environmental circumstances. Several classical genetic studies have provided strong evidence for interactions between genes and environment, and these effects have also begun to emerge in QTL studies examining specific genes and more narrowly specified environments. Outside of genetically informative studies, there is also a growing acceptance of more comprehensive models that encompass both biological and social risk factors for antisocial behavior, as well as their interactions.

A. Gene X Environment Interactions

The extent to which genetic effects vary as a function of environmental factors is referred to as a gene × environment (G×E) interaction.[192] A statistical G×E interaction has been consistently found in all major adoption studies of criminal convictions, such that the genetic predispositions, indicated by biological-parent antisocial behavior, present the greatest risk to the adopted offspring in the presence of adverse environmental conditions, indicated by adoptive-parent antisocial behavior. Figure 1.7 provides an illustrative example of a G×E interaction in criminality identified in a Danish adoption study.[193]

As shown here, the property-crime conviction rate in adopted sons is significantly higher for those with a biological father previously convicted of a property offense, both in families with and without a convicted adoptive father.[194] This increase in the conviction rate is greatest, however, when the adoptive father has

---

189. *See* Comings, *supra* note 156, at 16-11 to 16-12.

190. J. C. Shih et al., *Monoamine Oxidase: From Genes to Behavior*, 22 ANN. REV. NEUROSCIENCE 197, 210 (1999).

191. H. G. Brunner et al., *Abnormal Behavior Associated with a Point Mutation in the Structural Gene for Monoamine Oxidase A*, 262 SCIENCE 578 (1993).

192. This is a statistical interaction, which is distinct from the general notion that both genes and environment may combine together to produce phenotypic outcomes.

193. Sarnoff A. Mednick et al., *Genetic Influences in Criminal Convictions: Evidence from an Adoption Cohort*, 224 SCIENCE 891 (1984).

194. *Id.*

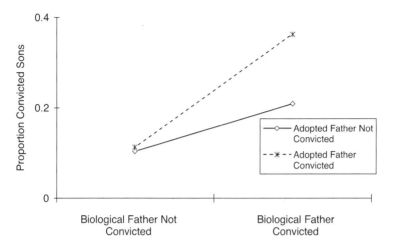

FIGURE 1.7 PROPERTY CRIME CONVICTIONS IN DANISH ADOPTED SONS AND THEIR FATHERS
source: adapted from Hutchings & Mednick, *supra* note 38

also been convicted.[195] In other words, negative environmental factors stemming from being raised by antisocial parents may exert their greatest effects on individuals who are genetically predisposed toward antisocial behavior.[196] A remarkably similar pattern of results has been found in adoption studies in both Scandinavia[197] and the United States.[198]

More recently, this global G×E interaction has begun to be seen at the specific gene level. In particular, a deleterious MAOA gene, which has been linked to aggression in both humans[199] and mice,[200] has been demonstrated to have the greatest influence on violence and other antisocial outcomes in individuals who have experienced severe maltreatment (including physical abuse) during childhood.[201] As other specific genes are more clearly identified and replicated, specific environmental factors may be shown to moderate their effects.

These results also have profound implications for our understanding of the role of parents and of other environmental aspects in producing aggressive and other antisocial outcomes in children. At the very least, the findings of

195. *Id.*

196. *Id.*

197. *See* Cloninger & Gottesman, *supra* note 38.

198. *See* Cadoret et al., *supra* note 58.

199. *See* Brunner et al., *supra* note 191.

200. Shih et al., *supra* note 190.

201. *See* Caspi et al., *Role of Genotype in the Cycle of Violence in Maltreated Children*, 297 SCIENCE 851 (2002).

GxE interactions in antisocial behavior highlight the complexity of gene-behavior relationships. Even when strong genetic effects are found, these may be enhanced or reduced by a variety of factors.

B. Biosocial Model of Antisocial Behavior

Over the past fifty years, important progress has been made in delineating replicable psychosocial risk factors for antisocial and violent behavior.[202] Within the past fifteen years, important progress has also been made in uncovering biological risk factors that predispose individuals to antisocial behavior.[203] Despite this progress, until recently we have learned surprisingly little about how these different sets of risk factors *interact* in predisposing individuals to antisocial behavior. Furthermore, even though heuristic and theoretical references are frequently, if incidentally, made to such interactive influences, remarkably few investigators have conducted serious empirical research on this interface in humans.[204]

Very recently, however, there has been renewed interest in biosocial interaction effects. In this context, Figure 1.8 depicts a heuristic biosocial model that emphasizes the importance of risk and protective factors, the interaction of social and biological variables, and different forms of antisocial behavior. A key conceptual issue is the assumption that joint assessment of both social and biological factors is a critical interdisciplinary approach that will yield innovative insights into the development of antisocial behavior. In the following section, broad processes are outlined to accommodate the many constructs that biosocial researchers use and to allow some degree of specificity and testability.

---

202. *See, e.g.*, MICHAEL RUTTER et al., ANTISOCIAL BEHAVIOR BY YOUNG PEOPLE (1998); David P. Farrington, *Psychosocial Predictors of Adult Antisocial Personality and Adult Convictions*, 18 BEHAV. SCI. & L. 605 (2000); Stephen P. Hinshaw & Carolyn A. Anderson, *Conduct and Oppositional Defiant Disorders*, in CHILD PSYCHOPATHOLOGY 113 (Eric J. Marsh & Russell A. Barkley eds., 1996); Rolf Loeber & David P. Farrington, *Never Too Early, Never Too Late: Risk Factors and Successful Interventions for Serious and Violent Juvenile Offenders*, 7 STUD. ON CRIME & CRIME PREVENTION 7 (1998); Joan McCord, *Psychosocial Contributions to Psychopathy and Violence*, in VIOLENCE AND PSYCHOPATHY 141 (Adrian Raine & José Sanmartín eds., 2001).

203. *See, e.g.*, Rutter et al., *supra* note 202; Benjamin B. Lahey et al., *Psychobiology*, in CONDUCT DISORDERS IN CHILDREN AND ADOLESCENTS 27 (G. Pirooz Sholevar ed., 1995); Terrie E. Moffitt, *The Neuropsychology of Juvenile Delinquency: A Critical Review*, 12 CRIME & JUST. 99 (1990); Elizabeth J. Susman & Jordan W. Finkelstein, *Biology, Development, and Dangerousness*, in CLINICAL ASSESSMENT OF DANGEROUSNESS 23 (Georges-Frank Pinard & Linda Pagani eds., 2001).

204. *See* Raine et al., *Biosocial Bases of Violence: Conceptual and Theoretical Issues*, in BIOSOCIAL BASES OF VIOLENCE 1 (Adrian Raine, Patricia A. Brennan, David P. Farrington, & Sarnoff A. Mednick, eds. 1997).

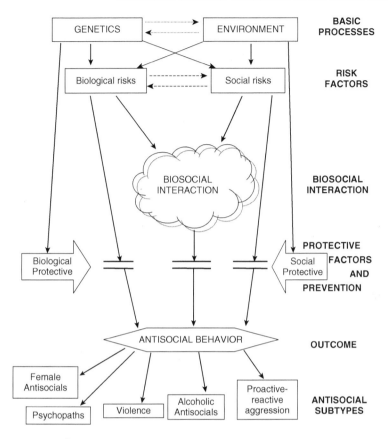

FIGURE 1.8 BIOSOCIAL MODEL OF ANTISOCIAL BEHAVIOR

1. **The Biosocial Model** The right side of the figure outlines the key processes in the model. From top to bottom, they are as follows:

(1) *Genes and environment as determinants of risk and protective factors*: Both forces are assumed to be the building blocks for later processes, and each may directly influence both sets of risk factors (solid straight and crossed arrows from "genetics" and "environment" to "biological risks" and "social risks"), as well as protective factors. The model also suggests, however, that these forces may interact (dotted arrows connecting "genetics" and "environment"); environmental forces can give rise to the expression of a latent genetic trait and vice-versa.

(2) *Reciprocal relationships between biological and social risk factors*: Biological and social risk factors may have reciprocal relationships, as indicated by broken lines connecting "biological risks" and "social risks." For example,

the social risk factors of early life stress or negative parenting may mitigate the biological risk factor of autonomic activity.

(3) *Biological and social risk factors—direct pathways*: Biological risk factors
may directly result in antisocial behavior independently of social risk factors and vice-versa (solid lines from "biological risks" and "social risks" to
"antisocial behavior"). The vast majority of research to date assumes these
direct-effect pathways.

(4) *Biosocial interactions*: The much-less-tested proposition is that biological
and social risk factors interact to produce antisocial behavior (solid lines
from "biological risks" and "social risks" to "biosocial interaction"). This
is the crux of the model and is elaborated further below.

(5) *Protective factors and prevention*: Importantly, biological and social protective factors (and preventive programs) can break all three pathways
(biological, social, and biosocial) to antisocial behavior (interruption of
lines from "biosocial interaction" to "antisocial behavior" by protective
factors).

(6) *Antisocial subtypes*: Risk factors give rise to both a general predisposition
to antisocial behavior and to several different antisocial subtypes with
potentially different etiological bases, such as psychopathy or violence.

2. Examples of Biosocial Interactions If genetic factors interact with the environment in predisposing individuals to antisocial behavior, then it is incumbent
on researchers to identify the specific biological factors that interact with the
specific environmental processes in giving rise to such behavior. A recent review
of this literature identified 39 empirical examples of biosocial interaction effects
for antisocial behavior from the areas of genetics, psychophysiology, obstetrics,
brain imaging, neuropsychology, neurology, hormones, neurotransmitters, and
environmental toxins.[205] Two main themes emerged. First, when biological and
social factors are grouping variables and when antisocial behavior is the outcome, then the presence of both risk factors exponentially increases the rates of
antisocial and violent behavior.[206] Second, when social and antisocial variables
are grouping variables and biological functioning is the outcome, then invariably
the social variable moderates the antisocial-biology relationship such that these
relationships are strongest in those from benign home backgrounds.[207]

With respect to the first theme, several studies have shown that babies who
suffer birth complications are more likely to develop conduct disorder and delinquency, to commit impulsive crime, and to behave violently in adulthood when
other psychosocial risk factors are present. Specifically, obstetric factors interact

---

205. *See* Adrian Raine, *Biosocial Studies of Antisocial and Violent Behavior in Children
and Adults: A Review*, 30 J. ABNORMAL CHILD PSYCHOL. 311 (2002).
206. *Id.* at 323.
207. *Id.*

with psychosocial risk factors in relation to adult violence. Birth complications have been found to interact with a disruptive family environment, characterized by maternal separation, illegitimacy, marital discord, parental mental health problems, or paternal absence in predisposing individuals to delinquency.[208] In 4269 live male births in Denmark, similar results were obtained in a prospective assessment of birth complications and maternal rejection at the age of one.[209] Birth complications significantly interacted with maternal rejection of the child in predicting violent offending at the age of 18.[210] Four percent of the sample had both birth complications and maternal rejection, but this small group accounted for 18 percent of all the violent crimes committed by the entire sample.[211] This finding from Denmark has recently been replicated in four other countries in the context of a variety of psychosocial risk factors, and it consequently appears robust.[212]

With respect to the second theme, previous research has indicated that violent offenders have reduced functioning of the prefrontal cortex.[213] One positron emission topography (PET) study addressed how psychosocial deficits moderate

---

208. Emmy E. Werner, *Vulnerability and Resiliency in Children at Risk for Delinquency: A Longitudinal Study from Birth to Young Adulthood, in* 10 PREVENTION OF DELINQUENT BEHAVIOR 16, 22–28 (John D. Burchard & Sara N. Burchard eds., 1987, vol. 10 of PRIMARY PREVENTION OF PSYCHOPATHOLOGY).

209. Adrian Raine et al., *Birth Complications Combined with Early Maternal Rejection at Age 1 Year Predispose to Violent Crime at Age 18 Years,* 51 ARCHIVES GEN. PSYCHIATRY 984, 984 (1994).

210. *Id.*

211. *Id.*

212. Sheilagh Hodgins et al., *Obstetric Complications, Parenting, and Risk of Criminal Behavior,* 58 ARCHIVES GEN. PSYCHIATRY 746 (2001) (finding pregnancy complications interacted with poor parenting in predicting adult violence in a large Swedish sample); Liisa Kemppainen et al., *The One-Child Family and Violent Criminality: A 31-Year Follow-Up Study of the Northern Finland 1966 Birth Cohort,* 158 AM. J. PSYCHIATRY 960 (2001) (finding that perinatal risk interacted with being an only child in raising the odds of adult violent offending by a factor of 4.4 in a sample of 5587 Finnish males); Louise Arseneault et al., *Obstetrical Complications and Violent Delinquency: Testing Two Developmental Pathways,* 73 CHILD DEV. 496 (2002) (finding in Canada that serious birth complica tions interacted with an adverse family environment in predisposing to violence at ages 6 and 17 and that this effect accounted for the continuity in violence between these ages); Alex Piquero & Stephen Tibbetts, *The Impact of Pre/Perinatal Disturbances and Disadvantaged Familial Environment in Predicting Criminal Offending,* 8 STUD. ON CRIME & CRIME PREVENTION 52 (1999) (finding in a prospective longitudinal study of 867 males and females from the Philadelphia Collaborative Perinatal Project that those with both pre- or perinatal disturbances and a disadvantaged familial environment were much more likely to become adult violent offenders).

213. Nora D. Volkow et al., *Brain Glucose Metabolism in Violent Psychiatric Patients: A Preliminary Study,* 61 PSYCHIATRY RES.: NEUROIMAGING 243 (1995).

the relationship between prefrontal dysfunction and violence.[214] A sample of murderers was divided into those who came from relatively good home backgrounds and those who came from relatively bad ones, as defined in the study. Ratings of psychosocial deprivation took into account early physical and sexual abuse, neglect, extreme poverty, foster home placement, having a criminal parent, severe family conflict, and a broken home. Compared to normal controls, deprived murderers showed relatively good prefrontal functioning, while nondeprived murderers showed significantly reduced prefrontal functioning.[215] In particular, murderers from good homes had a 14.2 percent reduction in the functioning of the right orbitofrontal cortex; damage to this brain area results in reduced fear conditioning as well as personality and emotional deficits that parallel criminal psychopathic behavior,[216] or what some have termed "acquired sociopathy."[217] These results extend findings from several psychophysiological studies showing especially reduced autonomic functions in those from benign home backgrounds and again suggest that biology-violence relationships are potentiated in those lacking psychosocial risk factors for violence.

VI. CONCLUSION

Genetic influences are clearly important in antisocial behavior, including criminality. Numerous classical twin and adoption studies, as well as more recent studies of specific genes, support this conclusion. Heritability estimates suggest as much as one-half of the variation in propensity toward antisocial behavior can be explained by genetic differences among individuals. Moreover, various traits correlated with antisocial behavior appear heritable, including impulsivity, autonomic arousal, and attention and other cognitive deficits. Although some specific genes for antisocial behavior have been suggested by QTL studies, the global genetic influence indicated by the moderate heritability estimate remains largely unspecified. Several biological risk factors have also been identified, although the extent to which their relationships to antisocial behavior may be genetically mediated remains unknown.

Genetic research, however, also makes a strong case for the importance of environment in influencing antisocial behavior. In fact, the more we know about genetics of behavior, the more important the environment appears to be.

---

214. Adrian Raine et al., *Prefrontal Glucose Deficits in Murderers Lacking Psychosocial Deprivation*, 11 NEUROPSYCHIATRY, NEUROPSYCHOLOGY & BEHAV. DISORDERS 1 (1998).
215. *Id.*
216. *Id.* at 5–6.
217. Jeffrey L. Saver & Antonio R. Damasio, *Preserved Access and Processing of Social Knowledge in a Patient with Acquired Sociopathy Due to Ventromedial Frontal Damage*, 29 NEUROPSYCHOLOGIA 1241 (1991).

Heritability estimates are far from being in agreement, leaving much room for environmental variations to influence antisocial outcomes. Most importantly, the environment itself appears to play a critical role in the expression and magnitude of genetic influences in antisocial behavior, as evidenced by the well-replicated findings of G×E interactions in several adoption studies, as well as by more recent studies of specific genes such as MAO.[218]

What does heritability of antisocial behavior imply for individuals? Very little. Heritability estimates provide information about individual differences in behavior within a group of individuals, and these estimates are specific to historical time, age cohort, and the given culture from which the sample is drawn. Even within the population, heritability is merely a statistical description of variance within that particular group, and it has little or no predictive value for any one individual. That is, when risk rates for criminality might be computed for groups of individuals, such as the relatives of a convicted felon, errors in prediction for a given individual would be quite large. Heritability estimates do not provide any information about one individual's DNA or genetic risk and thus cannot be used to understand one person's behavior or risk for future behavior.

Unlike heritability estimates from classical genetic designs, however, QTL studies do provide more detailed information at an individual level. As more specific genes are shown to play a role in the risk for antisocial behavior, predictions of individual behavior could become increasingly accurate. Still, genes rarely, if ever, operate deterministically such that a given behavior can be predicted with any reasonable degree of certainty. Although individual genes can be more highly predictive of individual behavior, there will always be large errors in prediction. Moreover, the effects of specific genes can often be modified through environmental interventions. Such interventions have already proven to be feasible even for highly heritable traits, such as phenylketonuria (PKU), a single-gene disorder resulting in mental retardation, which can be ameliorated by omitting phenylanine from the diet. This point is underscored by the G×E interactions for antisocial behavior as well as by the biosocial model, both of which emphasize the moderating effects of social factors on biological risks for antisocial behavior.

In spite of our increasing ability to identify specific genes important to antisocial behavior—and to identify individuals who inherit high-risk genes—our ability to understand and predict any one individual's behavior is still far from perfect and will probably remain so indefinitely. Specific genes that show associations with complex traits are likely to have small effects on risk partly because of the moderating effects of other genes, as well as that of environmental factors. Although genes may, for example, increase propensity for criminality, they do

218. *See* Caspi et al., *supra* note 210, at 851.

not determine it—the preponderance of individuals with the same gene are likely not to have engaged in serious antisocial behavior.

The wide variation in behavior observed for individuals sharing the same gene or set of genes (recall that MZ correlations for antisocial behavior or concordance for conduct disorder or antisocial personality disorder are far from being in agreement) is further evidence that genes do not operate in any deterministic way. Given this lack of genetic determinism, behavioral genetic research does not provide a sufficient basis for arguing against the notion of individual responsibility for one's behavior.

The genetic and environmental influences in antisocial behavior themselves still remain as large "black boxes." Understanding the genetic and social mechanisms underlying antisocial behavior is still in its infancy. These mechanisms are likely to be clarified over the next few decades, however, with increasing numbers of QTL studies in this area. As understanding the root causes of antisocial behavior increases, we may be optimistic that a more therapeutic approach will emerge for treating individuals who engage in or appear to be at risk for antisocial behavior.

2. MISINFORMATION, MISREPRESENTATION, AND MISUSE OF HUMAN BEHAVIORAL GENETICS RESEARCH

JONATHAN KAPLAN

I. INTRODUCTION

"Behavioral genetics" does not describe a single field with a single set of methodological tools, nor does it describe a single explanatory project. Rather, different researchers are interested in answering different questions about the relationship(s) between genes, behaviors, and development, and they use different methodologies to answer their questions. The same diversity holds for human behavioral genetics: different researchers are interested in different questions, and in attempting to answer those questions they use different approaches.

At the broadest level, one can distinguish between (1) research into the *differences* in behaviors between different individuals and (2) research into behaviors *shared* by (most) individuals. It is obvious that some traits vary between people. Different people tend to act differently—when, for example, someone is said to be shy, it follows that, in general, they act differently at parties than people who are said to be gregarious. It is equally obvious that some traits do not vary much between people—although different people may speak different languages, all normal human adults (unlike other animals) use some complex language and learn that language while growing up.

Researchers interested in the differences within a population will focus on the variation within that population. For example, within normal human populations, some people are taller than others, some people score higher on standardized intelligence tests than others, and some are more prone to violent behavior than others. Researchers interested in such differences attempt to discover how these differences are associated with the presence or absence of particular genes or environments. In other words, are particular genes associated with being more (rather than less) prone to violence? Do particular environments in which children grow up result in their being more (rather than less) likely to score highly on intelligence quotient (IQ) tests?

More generally, such research focuses on particular differences in the resources used in organismal development. Humans, for example, develop over time from a single fertilized egg to an adult capable of a variety of complex behaviors, behaviors that require a body consisting of an astonishingly complex organization of many different types of cells. The development of any complex organism requires a variety of resources. Some of these resources are genetic (the genetic material inherited from the parents), some are environmental (from the prenatal environment of the mother, to the provision of food, and so forth), and some are hard to classify (the complex subcellular systems that, in conjunction with genes, make proteins, etc.). The outcome of this development is a complex organism that differs from (and, of course, resembles) other organisms in the population in a variety of ways. The goal of research focused on differences is to find ways to associate different phenotypes with differences in how the organisms developed—whether different phenotypes had, for example, different genes or experienced different environments.[1] In these projects, the hope is that researchers will be able to explain how differences in available resources produce different outcomes.

Specifically, human behavioral genetics research that is focused on variation in human behavioral tendencies tries to associate different behavioral tendencies with genetic differences. It asks, for instance, if people who are more prone to violent behavior are also more likely to have certain genes, or if people who tend to score highly on standardized intelligence tests also share particular genetic traits.

On the other hand, researchers interested in behaviors that do not vary significantly within a population have other goals. In the study of behaviors shared by (most) humans, the purpose is to figure out how particular traits are produced

---

1. It is traditional in genetics research to distinguish between an organism's *genotype* and its *phenotype*. The genotype of an organism is the complete complement of genetic material—all of its DNA. DNA consists of a deoxyribose sugar and phosphate "backbone" linked to nitrogen-based bases. These bases, adenine (A), guanine (G), cytosine (C), and thymine (T) are the *nucleotides*, and each location on a DNA molecule where one of these bases can occur is a nucleotide site. Particular stretches of DNA are called nucleotide *regions*, which are simply a "mapping" convenience and which can be entirely arbitrary. *Genes*, on the other hand, are generally thought to be *functional* nucleotide regions (*but see* Box 1, *infra*, at 51). The most obvious functional regions are those that code for proteins; nucleotide *triplets* (three base-pairs) or *codons* can specify which of 20 amino acids gets used in forming a protein. It is these proteins, consisting of many amino acids, that are used in the cellular processes resulting in growth, reproduction, development, and the like. Famously, DNA forms a *double-helix;* these helixes themselves are wrapped tightly, and form *chromosomes*, each of which is a linear arrangement of the DNA.

An organism's *phenotype* consists of all the measurable traits of the organism *except* its DNA sequence. So while, for example, the height of a plant is an aspect of its phenotype, so would be the concentration of a particular protein in a particular leaf of that plant. As with most distinctions in biology, there are fuzzy areas—for example, the way a particular chromosome is folded can influence which genes are expressed, what proteins get made, and so forth; is this folding pattern an aspect of the organism's genotype or phenotype? Most researchers would consider them phenotypic, though they are not obviously so.

in normal development. For instance, all normally developing humans acquire the ability to use language, despite growing up in different environments and having a different complement of genes. What makes this possible? How is our ability to use language produced in the process of normal human development? The goal of these studies is to discover the particular developmental pathways— the biological systems that direct development—that transform developmental resources (genes, environments, etc.) into (nearly) universal outcomes, even though only some resources are shared universally.

Researchers interested in understanding either the causes of variation in human behaviors or how human behaviors develop are at a disadvantage compared to researchers interested in answering similar questions associated with nonhuman organisms. First, ethical restrictions on human experimentation make many kinds of experiments that are standard in other model organisms impossible to perform on humans. Second, compared to traditional model organisms used in the study of behavior (nematode worms, fruit-flies, mice, etc.), human development is a very slow process. The average human lifespan is very much longer, the behavioral repertoire of humans is larger, and the individual behaviors of interest are often more complex than those of other model organisms. Despite these disadvantages, there have been active research programs in human behavioral genetics for the past century, and although progress in human behavioral genetics has been uneven, the field has advanced remarkably, given the difficulties inherent in such research. Indeed, human behavioral genetics research programs have generally been quick to take advantage of the advances in molecular biology and human genetics.

This piece will explore some of the limits of human behavioral genetics research, focusing especially on how these limits affect the reasonableness of the interpretations and uses of the research results. Despite enormous improvements in the techniques used by human behavioral genetics research, especially over the past decade, it is still too easy to mis- or overinterpret the results of particular research projects. As the power and reliability of the tools used by researchers increases, it is especially important to keep in mind the conceptual limitations of the methodologies employed in human behavioral genetics research. Even when the technical results themselves are impeccable (itself a rarely achieved feat, given the methodological difficulties in carrying out human genetics research of any sort), one must be very careful when interpreting—and especially when using—those results. This is particularly true in areas where the results might be (mis)interpreted as having public policy or other social implications. Studies of the relationship between human behavioral genetics and the criminal law provide ample room for such dangerous mis- and overinterpretations. Given the focus of this current volume, then, there are good reasons to be particularly alert to the possibility of such misleading (and mistaken) interpretations.

II. DEVELOPMENTAL BIOLOGY AND THE INTERACTIONIST CONSENSUS

To fully understand the conceptual strengths and weaknesses of the various research techniques and the particular difficulties with adapting these techniques to studies of human behavioral genetics, one must first be familiar with what has become known as the interactionist consensus.[2] According to the interactionist consensus, organisms and all their traits are the products of development processes that involve the interaction of genetic and environmental resources at every stage. Hence, every trait of an organism is the result of the interaction of various genes and environments during the developmental process. In order to be successful, organismal development always requires the presence and coordinated actions of various kinds of resources (genetic, epigenetic, and environmental, to name a few), so it makes no sense to ask if a particular trait is genetic or environmental in origin. Understanding how a trait develops is not a matter of finding out whether a particular gene or environment causes the trait; rather, it is a matter of understanding how the various resources available in the production of the trait interact over time.

However, too many references to the interactionist consensus fail to address, or even to suggest, the complexity of those interactions between genes and environments. The very possibility of the development of any given trait requires the coordinated actions of many genes and many aspects of the developmental environment. For example, the production of a working human hand is contingent on the development of a more or less normal human body, which itself requires a vast array of genes and many environmental resources (proper food, shelter, and such).

Indeed, when it comes to the interaction of genes and environments, it is often not even particularly clear what a gene is. The same stretch of DNA (the same nucleotide region) can be involved in the production of many different proteins (through various forms of alternative splicing), and this can occur at different times and in different amounts (via regulatory genes).[3] Furthermore, proteins coded by different genes can interact to form different proteins (physical epistasis) or can merely complement or impede the action of one another (statistical epistasis).[4]

Similarly, references to the developmental environment tend to downplay the complexities and ambiguities inherent in this concept. Developmental environments include not only external environmental factors (such as food, shelter, and parental care), but also the cellular structures and organization that make coordinated protein synthesis possible. For example, the formation of new

---

2. *See generally* Susan Oyama, Paul E. Griffiths & Russell D. Gray, *Introduction: What Is Developmental Systems Theory?*, in CYCLES OF CONTINGENCY 1 (Susan Oyama, Paul E. Griffiths, & Russell D. Gray eds., 2001) (providing a brief history and discussion of the concept).

3. For a very brief review of DNA and "genes," *see supra* note 1.

4. *See* Box 2.1.

membranes (a necessary step for cellular reproduction, and hence for life as we know it) is impossible without preexisting template membranes; changes in the membranes used as templates have been implicated in important speciation events.[5] Hence, the entire environment makes possible the development of all the traits that make up the organism's phenotype, and variations in either external environmental factors or cellular structures can influence development in any number of complex ways.

Essentially, many factors contribute to developmental environments; they can be inherited from the organisms' ancestors, found in the world, or constructed by the organisms themselves.[6] Development is emphatically not merely a matter of genes providing the heritable instructions and the environment providing the raw materials. Although such an image remains popular, it is deeply misleading and empirically inadequate. Even though, in a sense, the interactionist consensus itself perpetuates this image by artificially dichotomizing the resources involved in development into genes and everything else, it is better to keep clearly in mind that genes (or, more precisely, nucleotide regions) are simply one developmental resource among many.

Box 2.1. Genes and Gene Expression

In the classic gene concept, a gene codes for one protein. Structurally, each gene is a string of nucleotides identifiable by starting with a triplet of bases that form a start codon and ending with another triplet of bases that form a stop codon However, contemporary genomic research has painted a very different picture of the relationship between the physical triplets of base-pairs and the proteins that are produced; the one gene–one protein picture is no longer even remotely viable. Some ways in which the current picture is more complex are the following roles for various genes:[7]

(1) Regulatory Genes. Regulatory genes include sequences of nucleotides that, by binding particular proteins, result in other

Continued

---

5. Eva Jablonka & Marion J. Lamb, Evolution in Four Dimensions: Genetic, Epigenetic, Behavioral, and Symbolic Variation in the History of Life 121 (2005).

6. *See generally* Lenny Moss, What Genes Can't Do 75–117 (2003); F. John Odling-Smee, Kevin N. Laland & Marcus W. Feldman, Niche Construction: The Neglected Process in Evolution (2003); Susan Oyama, The Ontogeny of Information: Developmental Systems and Evolution (2d ed. 2000).

7. *See id.* at 6–9; Karola Stotz, Paul E. Griffiths & Rob D. Knight, *How Biologists Conceptualize Genes: An Empirical Study*, 35 Stud. Hist. Phil. Biol. & Biomed. Sci. 647, 649–54 (2004).

Box 2.1.—Cont'd

genes being made more or less active. So-called promoter regions enhance the protein production associated with other genes, whereas so-called silencer regions act to suppress the production of proteins associated with other genes.

(2) Frame Shifting. In frame shifting, one continuous stretch of DNA is involved in the production of two (or more) different proteins as the two different messenger-RNA (mRNA) strands are produced from overlapping parts of that stretch of DNA.

(3) Overlapping Genes. In the case of so-called overlapping genes, one continuous stretch of DNA is involved in the production of two (or more[8]) different proteins as the different mRNA strands are produced, each from parts of the DNA stretch.

(4) Trans-splicing. In trans-splicing, two (or more) discontinuous stretches of DNA are involved in the production of two (or more) separate pre-mRNA strands that then combine to form a single mature RNA strand. The stretches involved in trans-splicing may also be involved in the production of other mRNA strands, and hence other proteins.

(5) Physical Epistasis. In the case of physical epistasis, two (or more) discontinuous stretches of DNA are involved in the production of two (or more) separate mRNA strands and two (or more) different proteins that then interact to form a third protein, which has a developmental function different from that of either of the two proteins that interact to form it.

Gene action can also be influenced by such heritable epigenetic mechanisms as the following:

(6) DNA-methylization. Methyl groups are attached to the DNA strand, influencing the activation of gene transcription. These attachments can be reliably inherited through nongenetic pathways, primarily via physical imprinting.

(7) Chromatin condensation. The shapes into which chromosomes fold influence which genes will be most easily accessed and transcribed. Variation in chromatin condensation patterns is heritable by nongenetic pathways—again, primarily by physical imprinting.

---

8. Documented cases of nineteen—and more—exist!

A sense of the complexity of the interactionist element of the interactionist consensus is apparent in a brief summary of behavioral genetics research on the nematode worm *C. elegans* by Kenneth F. Schaffner; the summary lists eight rules governing the relationship between the worm's genes and behaviors.[9] These rules include the expectation that

(1) any given gene will affect many different behaviors, in part by affecting many different neurons (pleiotropy—one gene affects many traits);

(2) any given neuron will be affected by many different genes (statistical epistatis—each trait is affected by many genes);

(3) different genes will interact in complex ways to affect the development of particular neuron(s) (physical epistatsis—gene products interact to form new proteins);

(4) any given behavior will involve many different neurons;

(5) any particular neuron will be involved in multiple behaviors;

(6) different developmental environments will result in different behaviors in genetically identical organisms (phenotypic plasticity);

(7) development is stochastic—genetically identical organisms raised in seemingly identical environments will express different behaviors via different neuron formation (caused by developmental noise and unique environmental influences); and, finally,

(8) gene expression depends on (often heritable) epigenetic factors, such that the local developmental environment of the gene(s) in question can be expected to influence behavior.

Given the relative simplicity of the *C. elegans* nervous system and of the behaviors studied, Schaffner argues that these rules should be regarded as the default assumptions for the study of the behavioral genetics of any multicellular organism.[10] There might be cases in which the particular organism is simpler than these assumptions imply, but these will likely be very rare. Usually, the developmental pathways between genes, developmental environments, and behaviors will demonstrate at least the level of complexity these rules suggest.

---

9. Kenneth F. Schaffner, *Genetic Explanations of Behavior: Of Worms, Flies, and Men,* *in* GENETICS AND CRIMINAL BEHAVIOR: METHODS, MEANINGS, AND MORALS 88–90 (David Wasserman & Robert Wachbroit eds., 2001). Schaffner is a researcher involved in the conceptual bases of behavioral genetics.

10. *See* Box 2. Shaffner, *supra* note 10, at 89–91.

Box 2.2. *C. Elegans*—the Reductionist's Delight

The nematode *C. elegans* has been a staple of developmental biology research since the 1960s, in large part because of its relative simplicity and its straightforward developmental progress (in addition to the advantage of its being mostly transparent, a boon for researchers wishing to keep track of which cells end up where).[11] Indeed, studying its development in a step-wise fashion seems so straightforward that Robert Cook-Deegan has referred to it as "the reductionist's delight."[12]

C. elegans has two forms—a hermaphrodite and a male form. The adult hermaphrodite has 959 somatic cells; of these, 302 are neurons, making its nervous system by far its largest organ.[13] The male is far less common in the wild, and it has slightly more somatic cells (1031); of these, 381 are neurons.[14]

In many ways, the development of *C. elegans* is very well understood. For example, it is known how each cell in *C. elegans* arrives at its final location in the organism, including which cells suffer programmed cell death as *C. elegans* grows. It is even possible to produce a wiring diagram that shows how the synapses connect the neurons to each other and to the somatic cells.

C. elegans has a relatively small genome (about 97 million base-pairs), and a number of *C. elegans* genomes have been sequenced.[15] Although researchers have begun to understand how different genes and different environments influence the behavioral repertoire of *C. elegans*, they have not yet, despite extensive effort, determined all the genes and developmental pathways involved in, for example, the mating behavior of *C. elegans*.[16] Even though that mating behavior (involving four separate steps) is considered quite complex, it is of course vastly simpler than most human behaviors of interest to researchers involved in human behavioral genetics.

Such complexities highlight the difference between research that attempts to understand the development of traits that are widely shared

---

11. Shaffner, *supra* note 9, at 85–86.

12. ROBERT COOK-DEEGAN, GENE WARS 53 (1994).

13. *C. elegans* has 95 muscle cells, the second largest system.

14. *See, e.g.,* THE NEMATODE CAENORHABDITIS ELEGANS (William B. Wood ed., 1988).

15. A variety of *C. elegans* genomes are available for download from http://www.wormbase.org.

16. *See* Caenorhabditis Elegans, http://elegans.swmed.edu/ (last visited Sept. 25, 2005) (providing recent *C. elegans* papers, research, and the like).

within a population of organisms and research that attempts to find associations among differences in such traits. *C. elegans* researchers focus on how worms develop shared traits. For instance, in studying the worms' ability to exhibit mating behavior, they seek to identify the genes used in producing certain physical traits and to investigate the role of different aspects of the environment. This kind of work permits them to explain, in some detail, how a particular behavior is produced—what physically causes that behavior and how the structures necessary for that kind of behavior come to exist in a particular worm. This kind of research requires techniques different from those used in research focused on differences between individuals. Research focused on differences can, for the most part, ignore any environmental or genetic resources that are shared by all members of a population. If there is no variation in a resource, then there can be no variation in traits associated with differences in that resource.[17]

For behavioral genetics research that attempts to understand the causes of individual variation in particular *human* behaviors, it is appropriate to focus on differences, in particular developmental resources (genes and environments, for example) that are causally associated with the behavioral variation. For instance, when studying why some people are more prone to violence than others, it may be appropriate to study variation in their home lives—for example, whether they were abused as children. However, this is not the same task as determining which resources are involved in the development of the trait more generally. Again, if resources do not vary within the population, they will not be identified by research programs attempting to explain individual variation in a trait, even if those resources are of fundamental importance to the proper development of the trait. On the other hand, research that attempts to understand the development of behaviors more generally, including behaviors that are (essentially) universal in the populations in question, will tend to focus on all the different kinds of resources used in producing traits, including all the developmental pathways that produce organisms capable of those kinds of behaviors and that result in those sorts of behaviors being expressed.

---

17. *See generally* Robert Plomin, John C. DeFries, Ian W. Craig & Peter McGuffin, *Behavioral Genetics, in* BEHAVIORAL GENETICS IN THE POSTGENOMIC ERA 531–40 (Robert Plomin et al. eds., 2003) (outlining how this distinction is used in behavioral genetics more generally).

III. TECHNOLOGIES AND TECHNIQUES: RESEARCH METHODOLOGIES AND (SOME OF) THE LIMITS OF CONTEMPORARY HUMAN BEHAVIORAL GENETICS

Since its inception, human behavioral genetics has pursued research into the possible biological bases of violence and criminality.[18] Although in recent years this research has often been seen as politically and socially controversial,[19] various research programs have continued to generate results receiving extensive attention in both scientific journals and the popular press. The following discussion introduces some of these contemporary research programs into the possible biological bases of violence and criminality[20] as examples of research techniques pursued by human behavioral genetics research programs.

This discussion will highlight two fundamentally different problems: first, the empirical difficulties facing these research programs, and, second, the conceptual limitations of the techniques these programs use. The first problem is fundamentally practical in nature. Some of the research techniques currently used in behavioral genetics research are generally very difficult to adapt to human behavioral genetics. Studies that attempt to do so produce results that are often less reliable than one might wish. Though these are empirical problems, some of them are likely unsolvable, for example because ethical restrictions on human experimentation make certain kinds of information regarding human development very likely unobtainable. On the other hand, the second problem is conceptual in nature. For some techniques, critiquing the reliability of the data obtained is less important than understanding the limits of the data's legitimate uses and interpretations. In these cases, the techniques in question, even if applied perfectly, answer very specific questions in very specific domains. As such, the results of these studies cannot simply be extended to other domains, nor can they be used to answer other kinds of questions.

A. Statistical Analysis of Variance: Heritability, Plasticity, and All That . . .

1. **What Is Heritability and How Is it Measured?** Heritability is perhaps the most controversial concept in human genetics research, especially in human behavioral genetics. Over at least the past three decades, various authors have criticized both the techniques used to generate estimates of heritability in human populations and the interpretations and uses of these estimates. This is especially

---

18. *See, e.g.*, Daniel J. Kevles, In the Name of Eugenics: Genetics and the Uses of Human Heredity (1985).

19. *See, e.g.*, Natalie Angier, *Disputed Meeting to Ask if Crime Has Genetic Roots*, N.Y. Times, Sept. 19, 1995, at C1; Natalie Angier, *At Conference on Links of Violence to Heredity: A Calm After the Storm*, N.Y. Times, Sept. 24, 1995, at C8.

20. *See also* Nita A. Farahany, *The Impact of Behavioral Sciences on Criminal Law*, (New York: Oxford University Press, 2009), Chapter 1.

true for behavioral traits.[21] However, since researchers in human behavioral genetics, including those working on biological associations with variation in violence and criminality, continue to cite heritability estimates relatively often,[22] it is worth briefly covering some of the traditional difficulties inherent in the concept.

Heritability is usually interpreted as a measure of the proportion of the variance in a particular trait in a particular population that is associated with genetic variation in that population.[23] Put more simply, heritability is a measure of the extent to which related individuals in a population resemble each other more than they resemble unrelated individuals. It can be thought of roughly as a measure of how much children can be expected to resemble their parents more then they resemble the average member of the population. Heritability is, then, appropriate only for research programs interested in understanding the causes of

---

21. The classic critical article is Richard Lewontin, *The Analysis of Variance and the Analysis of Causes*, 26 AM. J. HUMAN GENETICS 400 (1974). *See also* Elliot Sober, *Separating Nature from Nurture, in* GENETICS AND CRIMINAL BEHAVIOR: METHODS, MEANINGS, AND MORALS, *supra* note 9, at 47.

22. *See, e.g.*, Baker et al., *supra* note 20, at 25 (citing a broad-sense heritability estimate of 0.41 for antisocial behavior); *see also* S. H. Rhee & I. D. Waldman, *Genetic and Environmental Influences on Antisocial Behavior: A Meta-analysis of Twin and Adoption Studies*, 128 PSYCHOL. BULL. 490, 490–529 (2002) (providing a meta-analysis of over 50 studies on the heritability of criminality).

23. *See* Lewontin, *supra* note 21, at 402–9; Baker et al., *supra* note 20. This refers more particularly to broad-sense heritability. Briefly, if the total amount of phenotypic variation in a particular trait in a particular population is given by the total variance in that trait, V_P (roughly, the average deviation in that population from the mean value of that trait within the population), then that variation can be partitioned out as follows:

$$V_P = V_G + V_E + V_{GxE} + e \text{ (Equation 1)},$$

where V_G is that portion of the variation from the mean phenotypic value in the population associated with genetic variation in that population, V_E is the portion of the variation from the mean phenotypic value associated with environmental variation, V_{GxE} is the portion of the variation from the mean phenotypic value associated with gene-by-environment interactions (associated with genetic and environmental variations other than the additive effects of V_G and V_E), and e is everything else (in practice this includes unique environmental effects, developmental noise, and measurement errors). Broad-sense heritability, the portion of phenotypic variation association associated with genetic variation, is therefore expressed as

$$H^2 = V_G / V_P \text{ (Equation 2)}.$$

Broad-sense heritability includes both additive and nonadditive genetic effects, whereas narrow-sense heritability includes only additive effects. Narrow-sense heritability is important in plant and animal breeding, as it provides a measure of likely response to short-term selection; it is not, however, of any particular use in human behavioral genetics.

differences between individuals within a population. Heritability will be undefined for any trait that is shared by all organisms within a population, because all the organisms in the population resemble each other equally with respect to that trait. If there is no variation in the trait, then neither genes nor environments can be associated with that variation.

It follows that heritability cannot be properly thought of as a measure of the extent to which genes are involved in the development of a particular trait. Rather, the development of a trait can involve the actions of many genes that are all critical for that trait's formation. But if those genes are shared by all organisms in the population, the trait, if it varies at all in the population, may still have a heritability of zero, since, because those genes do not vary, none of the variation in the trait is associated with genetic variation.

Accurately determining the heritability of a trait generally requires being able to sort organisms with known genotypes from a given population into known environments and to follow them throughout their development. In nonhuman animals, this is usually done through controlled breeding experiments in which organisms with known particular genotypes are physically sorted into the particular environments in which they are raised. But this only gives an estimate of heritability in the environments actually tested and for the population actually used. Accurately finding the broad-sense heritability of a trait in natural populations, where the organisms in question are not deliberately sorted into particular environments, is quite difficult; in the case of humans, it is all but impossible. That is, generating reliable estimates of heritability in humans through the sort of controlled breeding experiments done to generate estimates of heritability in nonhuman animals is not possible; it is possible, however, to generate rather inaccurate and less reliable estimates through other methods. These methods aim to separate shared genetic variation from shared environmental variation. However, because children growing up in families usually share with each other and their parents aspects of both their environment and of their genes, teasing apart any associations these different aspects might have to variation in phenotypes is tricky.

Estimates of the heritability of traits in humans are generated from studying situations in which it is thought possible to separate the influences of shared environments from the influences of shared genes. These situations include adoption studies, monozygotic (MZ) and dizygotic (DZ) twin studies, and studies about monozygotic twins reared apart.[24]

In adoption studies, the shared variation in the phenotype of interest in siblings adopted into separate families is compared to the shared variation in siblings raised together, as well as between those groups and unrelated individuals

---

24. *See, e.g.*, ROBERT PLOMIN, JOHN C. DEFRIED, GERALD E. MCCLERN & PETER MCGUFFIN, BEHAVIORAL GENETICS (4th ed. 2001) (discussing adoption studies and providing numerous examples).

adopted into the same and different families. The assumption is that those siblings adopted into separate families will resemble each other more than they resemble the population at large, only insofar as they share similar genes; on the other hand, those siblings raised together in the same family will share both genetic and the environmental components, and unrelated individuals adopted into the same families will share only the environmental components.

The assumption in monozygotic and dizygotic twin studies is that both mono- and dizygotic twins share (roughly) the same environmental influences (as they are raised in the same home), and hence any difference in the degree to which MZ and DZ twins resemble each other more than they do the population at large can be attributed to different amounts of shared genetic resemblance.[25]

If monozygotic twins are separated at birth (or, better yet, at conception, to avoid the shared gestational environment) and reared in uncorrelated environments, the heritability of the trait in question can be determined simply by the degree to which the twins resemble each other more than they resemble the population at large. Insofar as studies of monozygotic twins reared apart thus resembling each other more than others to a greater or lesser degree, the heritability of the trait of interest can be estimated.

None of these methods of study is ideal or, in practice, even very good. There are too many confounding factors, and it is too difficult to separate shared environmental influences from shared genetic similarities in humans.[26] But the accuracy of the heritability estimates of human behaviors emerging from these studies is really not the issue.

Heritability estimates, no matter how accurate, are of very limited use. They have been published for such human psychological traits as antisocial behavior and such particular behaviors as criminality and violence. Estimates of the heritability of antisocial behaviors (construed broadly) are usually said to cluster around 0.5, with only a relatively small number of studies reporting much lower or higher estimates.[27] This means that roughly half the observed variation in antisocial behavior is associated with the genetic variation present in the tested societies, rather than, say, environmental variation or other effects. Studies of violent behaviors (construed somewhat narrowly) have been less consistent, with reported estimates ranging from no discernable heritability up to around 0.5.[28] It is not surprising that different studies generate very different heritability

---

25. Monozygotic twins share all of their DNA, whereas dizygotic twins share only half their DNA (the same amount as "ordinary" siblings).

26. *See* Sober, *supra* note 21, at 55–62.

27. *See, e.g.,* Nuffield Council on Bioethics, *Antisocial Behavior, in* GENETICS AND HUMAN BEHAVIOR: THE ETHICAL CONTEXT 72–96 (2002), available at http://www.nuffieldbioethics.org/ fileLibrary/pdf/nuffieldgeneticsrep.pdf; Baker et al., *supra* note 20.

28. *See, e.g.,* Nuffield Council on Bioethics, *supra* note 27, at 87–96; Baker et al., *supra* note 20.

estimates, even when they are supposed to be measuring the same behaviors or traits. This is because estimates of heritability can easily vary with the particular methods used (for instance, MZ/DZ versus adoption studies), the particular way that the trait in question is operationalized, and the particular population tested.

However, as has often been stressed in the literature, the problem is not the difficulty of generating accurate estimates of heritability in human populations; rather, the problem is due to the locality of the measure itself and the extent to which estimates of heritability are uninformative with respect to the causal pathways involved.[29] These two problems are briefly addressed below.

2. The Locality of Heritability A trait that is highly heritable in one environment may have a very low heritability in another environment. For example, the heritability of adult human hair color is rather high in cultures with no tradition of dyeing hair, but it is likely much lower in cultures with such a tradition. Less trivially, in populations in which individuals have radically different access to adequate food, such environmental differences may be strongly associated with adult height, so the heritability of height may be reduced; in cultures in which adequate access to food is more common, the role of that environmental difference will be reduced, and genetic differences will be more strongly associated with height variation. Heritability estimates, then, are local—the heritability of a trait can vary with variations in the environment or with the makeup of the population. One classic approach to making the locality of heritability perspicuous is to consider the genotype's norm of reaction for a particular trait, given the possible developmental environments of interest—that is, to consider what the resulting phenotype will be, given a particular genotype and a particular developmental environment.[30] Dobzhansky, one of the founders of modern genetics, claimed that although it was incorrect to think of an organism's genotype as determining its phenotype, it was correct to think of the genotype as determining the "reaction norm" of the phenotype.[31]

Of course, Dobzhansky was quick to note that the complete reaction norm of a genotype could never be completely known, since that would require knowing how the particular organism would develop in every possible combination of environments.[32] Partial norms of reaction represent how one trait varies when some aspect of the environment is varied. They are incomplete in that they fail to account for how variation in other aspects of the environment might affect the trait. Even so, partial norms of reaction remain a good way to understand phenotypic plasticity—that is, the differences in phenotype that emerge in different environments, even in organisms with the same genotypes. A phenotypic trait is

---

29. Lewontin, *supra* note 21. *See also* Sober, *supra* note 21, at 47.
30. Lewontin, *supra* note 21. *See also* Sober, *supra* note 21, at 47.
31. Theodosius Dobzhansky, Evolution, Genetics, and Man 74–75 (1955).
32. *Id.*

plastic insofar as it varies with variation in the developmental environment of the organism. For example, in humans, the number of limbs is generally non-plastic (most developmental environments result in people having the same number of limbs), whereas the specific language spoken is highly plastic (whether one speaks French or English, for example, depends almost entirely on the language heard during development).

Technically, generating even partial norms of reaction requires raising genet-ically identical organisms in a particular set of environments. In practice, when a group of organisms is thought to possess a particular, similar genotype (by virtue, say, of their having adapted to a particular local condition), the norm of reaction is often associated with organisms with that sort of genotype, rather than with being the genotype's norm of reaction per se.[33] This is exemplified in Cooper and Zubek's work on rats bred to be either particularly good (maze-bright) or bad (maze-dull) at running mazes.[34] Cooper and Zubek started with rats that were either maze-bright or maze-dull when raised under normal labora-tory conditions. However, when reared in enriched environments, such as labo-ratory cages with lots of toys, the maze-dull rats improved immensely, while the maze-bright rats did not get much better: in the enriched environment, the two lines of rats performed similarly well. On the other hand, when raised in impov-erished environments (in gray cages with no mobile objects), the maze-dull rats did not get much worse, but the performance of the maze-bright rats suffered enormously; under these conditions, the two lines of rats performed similarly poorly. Graphed, these three performances under each of the three environ-ments can be thought of as a partial, or generalized, norm of reaction.[35]

The maze-running ability of these rats show significant *plasticity* with respect to the environment in which they are raised; neither kind of rat performed equally well in all the environments. Further, the two populations display plastic-ity under different environmental conditions. The maze-dull rats show little plasticity in performance between impoverished and normal environments, whereas the maze-bright rats show significant plasticity in that range. The maze-dull rats, however, show significant plasticity in performance between the normal and the enriched environments, whereas the performance of the maze-bright rats is unaffected by that variation. In all three environments the rats' behavior displays a strong gene-by-environment interaction effect. That is, varia-tion in the performance of the rats cannot be accounted for by simply adding the overall effects of the environmental variation and the overall effects of the

---

33. These have been called "generalized" norms of reaction. *See, e.g.,* Sahotra Sarkar & Trevon Fuller, *Generalized Norms of Reaction for Ecological Developmental Biology,* 5 EVOLUTION & DEV. 106 (2003).

34. R.M. Cooper & John P. Zubek, *Effects of Enriched and Restricted Early Environments on the Learning Ability of Rats,* 12 CANADIAN J. PSYCHOL. 159 (1958).

35. *See* Figure 2.1.

FIGURE 2.1 HERITABILITY, PLASTICITY, AND COOPER AND ZUBEK'S RATS

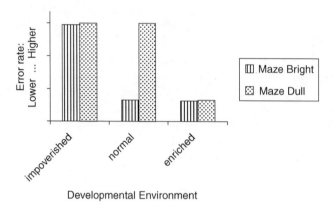

Developmental Environment

Figure 2.1: This partial norm of reaction shows the different ways in which two different kinds of genotypes respond to three different developmental environments. Rats bred under normal laboratory conditions to be either very good or very bad at running mazes show a significant difference in maze-running ability when raised in those normal conditions. However, when raised in an impoverished environment, the difference in the ability of the maze-bright rats compared to that of the maze-dull rats is not statistically significant. When raised in an enriched environment, again, there is no statistically significant difference in the maze-running abilities of the two strains. Although the maze-dull rats show marked improvement between normal and enriched environments, the maze-bright rats show no such improvement. Similarly, while maze-bright rats do show a marked improvement between the impoverished and the normal environments, the performance of maze-dull rats is unchanged.

genetic variation. Rather, different genotypes interact differently with the various available environments.

So what is the heritability of maze-running ability in these rats? The question simply cannot be answered without more information—in fact, the question does not make sense unless one knows the environments and structure of the two rat populations. If one looked only at the normal laboratory environment, the heritability of maze-running ability would be quite high; most of the variation in maze-running ability would be associated with the genetic differences between the two kinds of rats in the population. However, if one looked only at the impoverished and enriched environments, the heritability of maze-running ability would be quite low (essentially zero), since most of the variation in maze-running performance would be associated with the different environments in which the rats were reared; there would be no statistically significant difference in ability associated with the genetic differences in the two strains of rats. Given a particular population of rats, with particular numbers of maze-bright and maze-dull rats distributed in a particular way in the developmental environments, heritability could of course be calculated, but that number would hold only for that particular population. If one changed the distribution of rats in the environments, one would likely change the heritability of maze-running ability as well. It may be difficult or impossible to perform similar studies on humans, but this generalization still holds true: just because a trait (say, antisocial behavior) has a particular heritability in a particular population at a particular time, this does not necessarily mean it will have a similar heritability in other environments or in other populations.

Heritability, then, is emphatically not a measure of the degree to which a particular trait is genetically determined. A trait can have a heritability of one hundred percent in one developmental environment, but a heritability of zero percent in another. The heritability of a trait can be one hundred percent in each of two populations, but its average difference in each population can be due entirely to environmental factors.[36] And the development of a trait can critically involve any number of genes, yet the trait itself can have a heritability of zero.[37]

Box 2.3. Heritability, Locality, and Genetic Determinism

(1) A trait can have a heritability of one hundred percent in one environment, yet a heritability of zero in another environment. In the case of Cooper and Zubek's rats, the heritability of maze-running ability in the normal environment would be quite high; however, in the impoverished and enriched environments, it would be zero.

(2) The heritability of a trait can be one hundred percent in each of two populations, but the difference in the mean value of the trait between the populations can be entirely environmental in origin. Example: Two (genetically distinct) varieties of corn, type 1 and type 2, are planted in two different fields, A and B. Each field is uniform with respect to water, nutrients, and so forth, but field A is fertilized better than B. In each field, the differences in performance between type 1 and type 2 corn will be due to the genetic differences, but the difference in performance between the fields may be due entirely to the different environmental treatments the two fields received.

(3) The development of a trait can critically involve any number of genes, yet the trait itself can have a heritability of zero. Example: normal limb development in humans involves the activity of a large number of different genes, yet the heritability of the number of legs in humans is essentially zero—almost all the variation in leg numbers in humans is associated with environmental causes (usually trauma), and not with genetic variation.

---

36. *See, e.g.,* Lewontin, *supra* note 21.
37. *See* Box 2.3.

3. Heritability and Alternative Causal Pathways Given the difficulty in sorting humans with particular genotypes into particular developmental environments, estimating the heritability of traits in humans is likewise hard. Estimates of the heritability of particular human behavioral traits tend to vary widely between studies, but this is hardly surprising, given the difficulties with estimating heritability in humans and the locality of heritability as a measure. But the difficulties involved in human experimentation add an additional level of uncertainty to heritability estimates. In humans, even if the heritability of a trait is known, the causal pathways through which the trait's heritability is expressed are very difficult to disentangle.

For example, in the American population as a whole, African Americans score, on average, significantly lower on standardized IQ tests than do white Americans.[38] Combined with the heritability of performance on IQ tests,[39] these statistics have been interpreted by some to imply that genetic differences in the two populations are responsible for the difference in scores.[40] Leaving aside for the moment the different environments experienced by each population and the impossibility of using heritability estimates to support a trait's heritability when the two populations experience different environments,[41] good reasons support assuming that the causal pathway is unclear. Steele and Aronson, for example, demonstrate that African American students perform significantly worse when told they are taking an IQ test than when told they are taking a test unrelated to IQ; white American students do not perform significantly differently under these circumstances.[42] Steele and Aronson attribute the underperformance of African American students on IQ tests to "stereotype threat"—the threat that performing badly on an IQ test will reinforce a particular harmful stereotype—a worry that white students simply do not share. Given that skin color is heritable and that these stereotypes do exist in our society, the performance differences in IQ tests will be heritable, but not because of any genetic difference causally

---

38. *See generally* Ned Block, *How Heritability Misleads About Race*, 56 COGNITION 99 (1995) (arguing that authors frequently misinterpret the concept of heritability, leading to fallacious conclusions about race).

39. Nuffield Council on Bioethics, *supra* note 27, at 72 (reporting estimates ranging between 0.35 and 0.75).

40. *See, e.g.*, RICHARD J. HERRNSTEIN & CHARLES MURRAY, THE BELL CURVE: INTELLIGENCE AND CLASS STRUCTURE IN AMERICAN LIFE (1994); Arthur R. Jensen, *How Much Can We Boost IQ and Scholastic Achievement?*, 39 HARVARD EDUC. REV. 1 (1969); J. PHILIPPE RUSHTON, RACE, EVOLUTION AND BEHAVIOR (1999).

41. *See* Box 2.3, II, *supra* p.

42. Claude M. Steele & Joshua Aronson, *Stereotype Threat and the Intellectual Performance of African Americans*, 69 J. PERSONALITY & SOC. PSYCHOL. 797 (1995). Indeed, merely being asked to indicate one's race on the test form (by checking a box) lowered the average scores of black students, but had no effect on the average scores of white students.

related in any ordinary way to IQ test-taking skills. Rather, these differences will be associated with a particular social environment—associating one's race with particular stereotypes. If that environment were changed, then the heritability of test performance would also change. The lesson here is that even an accurate estimate of heritability can say little about the causal pathways involved in generating the variation in any one trait.

Some researchers interpret these limitations to imply that finding the heritability of a trait is only a first step, which, ideally, should be followed with studies into the mechanisms necessary for that trait to develop, focusing especially on those differences in the available developmental resources that make a difference in the development of the phenotype involved. Thirty years ago, when the discovery that a particular trait in model organisms was heritable was sometimes the first step into studying the complexities of the developmental process, this line of argument was more plausible. Now, however, researchers in model organisms tend to skip estimating heritability and move directly to approaches that attempt to identify nucleotide regions associated with the observed differences. If researchers attempting to estimate the heritability of various behavioral traits in humans were more cautious and circumspect about the claims they made respecting their research results, this first-step characterization of the research would seem, if not convincing, at least harmless. However, estimates of heritability get reported in ways that make interpreting them as full-blown causal accounts all too easy. These estimates are then used in legal cases and in framing public policy issues without the appropriate cautions.[43]

4. **Heritability, Causation, and Changes** Heritability, then, is a local measure—it can, and often does, change with changes in the environment or in the population more generally. It must not be interpreted as a measure of the extent to which genes are involved in the development of a trait, nor should it be thought of as revealing the causal processes by which a trait is produced. However, despite all that is known theoretically and empirically about the locality of heritability and about heritability's inability to provide causal information, strong claims continue to be made regarding what knowing the heritability of a trait entitles one to say about, for example, the possibility of changing that trait, the causal genesis of that trait, and the social policies relevant to that trait that ought to be pursued. For example, Hamer and Copeland take the high heritability of performance on standard IQ tests to mean that "no other single factor is more important than genes in determining cognitive ability."[44] They claim that the very high heritability ("70 to 90 percent") of very shy or inhibited personality types is "probably the reason such personalities do not change much

---

43. *See, e.g.*, JONATHAN M. KAPLAN, THE LIMITS AND LIES OF HUMAN GENETIC RESEARCH: DANGERS FOR SOCIAL POLICY (2000).

44. DEAN HAMER & PETER COPELAND, LIVING WITH OUR GENES—WHY THEY MATTER MORE THAN YOU THINK 219 (1998).

during a lifetime."[45] The same kind of causal language appears when Kendler argues that the frequency of "stressful life events" encountered is "genetically influenced" through the high heritability of temperament, and that it is "because of differences in genetic constitution" that people "select themselves into high versus low risk environments."[46]

Once such causal language is accepted, then applied to explain behavior, its use in support of social policy recommendations is rarely far behind. Infamously, Murray and Hernstein argue from the high heritability of IQ to conclusions regarding appropriate social policies. Starting from the kinds of claims made by human behavior genetics researchers, they argue that in a society that sorts itself according to ability, some people are going to be stuck at the bottom because of genetically mediated, inherited differences in ability. Therefore, they conclude that nothing much could, or should, be done about this; social programs aimed at helping the children of poor parents to achieve academic success are, in this view, a waste of money.[47] In a slightly more cautious vein, DiLalla and Gottesman argue from the high heritability of "anti-social behavior" (citing estimates of around 0.5) to the conclusion that understanding "intergenerational transmission" of violence and abusive behavior will require understanding the "genetic and biological factors" that "influence violent crime," and that "social policy decisions" formed without such an understanding will likely be "faulty."[48] Their conclusion implies that knowing the heritability of a trait can, and should, influence social policy.

The same kind of reasoning has also been used in legal cases. For example, Judge Parslow, deciding the famous custody battle of *Johnson v. Calvert* in California, cited the high heritability of IQ and other behavioral traits as a reason why genetic parenthood should determine custody.[49] Because of the high heritability of these traits, the genetic parents of a child will resemble that child more than other individuals and will thus be in a better position to understand the child. Interestingly, some authors have argued from the high heritability of IQ to the conclusion that a child's best interests might not lie in giving custody to his

45. *Id.* at 66–67.

46. Kenneth S. Kendler, *Major Depression and the Environment*, 31 PHARMOCOPSYCHIATRY 5, 7–8 (1998).

47. *See* HERRNSTEIN & MURRAY, *supra* note 40, at 10 ("[B]ecause IQ is substantially heritable, because economic success in life depends in part on the talents measured by IQ tests, and because social standing depends in part on economic success, it follows that social standing is bound to be based to some extend on inherited differences."); Jensen, *supra* note 40.

48. Lisabeth F. DiLalla & Irving I. Gottesman, *Biological and Genetic Contributors to Violence—Wisdom's Untold Tale*, 109 PSYCHOL. BULL. 125, 128 (1991).

49. Johnson v. Calvert, 286 Cal. Rptr. 369, 380–81 (Cal. 1993) (upholding the trial court's decision to give custody to a child's "natural" genetic mother rather than the child's surrogate birth mother).

or her genetic parents, since that child would probably fare about the same in life, whatever the environment.[50] When the developmental environment is not strongly associated with variation in those traits, the parent's identity just does not matter that much.

In cases involving liability for lead poisoning, the high heritability of IQ has been used to justify testing the intelligence of parents and other relatives.[51] The theory was, apparently, that if the parents are none too bright and if IQ is heritable, then lead probably was not at fault for the child's cognitive problems, after all.

But if one takes what is known about the locality of heritability estimates seriously, it is immediately obvious that none of these claims is supportable by heritability estimates, no matter how high or how accurate that estimate may be. Hamer just gets it wrong when he writes that the high heritability of IQ implies that "no other single factor is more important than genes in *determining* cognitive ability."[52] The only supportable claim in this regard is far more cautious— namely, that within the developmental environments experienced with reasonably high frequency by the populations tested, the high heritability of IQ implies that genetic differences are more strongly associated with differences in the scores achieved on IQ tests than are other factors. But this is not Hamer's claim. Differences in performance on IQ tests might be strongly associated with any number of environmental factors, but if these factors did not happen to vary in the populations tested, their influence would be missed by analyses of variance and hence would not appear in heritability estimates.

Replacing language of association with more causal language would be misleading—possibly in socially dangerous ways. Development of complex phenotypes (including the ability to engage in complex behaviors) is marked by systems of complex feedback between the different resources available to human development. As such, a particular gene does not do the same thing throughout development, and the environment it encounters changes as the organism develops. So, for example, the development of a complex behavior could easily be influenced by environmental differences that themselves emerged from the development of an entirely different and otherwise independent phenotype. Thus the trait would show high heritability if the independent phenotype was heritable, but the heritability of the trait would be the result of the different environments encountered. Under such circumstances, to say genes associated with the

---

50. *See, e.g.*, George J. Annas, *Crazy Marking: Embryos and Gestational Mothers*, Hastings Center Rep. Jan.–Feb. 1991, at 35, 37 (1991); Todd M. Krim, *Beyond Baby M*, 5 Annals Health L. 193 (1996); Steven Pinker, The Blank Slate (2002) (offering a more contemporary spin on this idea).

51. *See* Jennifer Wriggins, *Genetics, IQ Determination, and Torts: The Example of Discovery in Lead Exposure Litigation*, 77 B.U. L. Rev. 1025, 1059–65 (1997).

52. Hamer & Copeland, *supra* note 44, at 219 (emphasis added).

differences in the independent phenotype *caused* its differences would stretch the ordinary meaning of cause almost beyond recognition.

In controlled breeding studies, these kinds of effects can usually be disentangled, but not through estimates of heritability. Rather, what environmental factors might co-vary (that is, be systematically related to each other) and how particular environmental variations might co-vary (perhaps in complex ways) with genetic differences must be considered. The experiments can then be repeated, eliminating the kinds of co-variation concerned. In the case of Cooper and Zubek's rats, for example, some researchers claimed that maze-bright and maze-dull rats did not differ in learning ability per se, but rather in curiosity. Under normal conditions, the more curious rats performed better on maze-running tasks than the less curious rats, and hence they appeared to be better learners; but on other tests of learning ability, in which curiosity was not a factor, this effect could be eliminated.[53]

The problem is that such studies are impossible in human populations; one cannot simply breed a new population of people and systematically test the effect of changing the environment they grow up in. So one is left with the results of research done in a particular environment, and those results are of very limited generality. A high heritability for behavioral tendencies such as antisocial behaviors or violence does not reveal the developmental causes of such behaviors or personalities. Nor does it necessarily offer a window into how such behaviors might, or might not, be modified. Again, variation in a particular trait can have a heritability of 100 percent, yet a change in the developmental environment can result in the radical modification of that trait in part or all of the particular population. As Figure 1 shows, any argument that the high heritability of maze-running ability in Cooper and Zubek's rats in a normal laboratory environment signified the irrelevance of environmental interventions would be *false*.

B. Differences and QTLs: Statistical Correlations Made Physical

Improvements in gene mapping and sequencing over the last few decades have made finding genetic markers associated with phenotypic differences much easier. Though the power of such techniques is still somewhat limited, further improvements can be expected to make finding the particular genes (or at least small chromosomal regions) associated with phenotypic differences possible, even when the associations are weak. One technique is quantitative trait loci (QTL) analysis.

QTL analyses seek chromosomal regions that are statistically associated with differences in the particular phenotype of interest. In medical genetics, QTL studies have revealed that variations in certain regions of particular chromosomes are

---

53. *See* Norman D. Henderson, *Relative Effects of Early Rearing Environment and Genotype on Discrimination Learning in House Mice*, 75 J. Comp. & Physiological Psychol. 243, 247–48 (1972).

associated with different likelihoods of disease; so, for example, women with mutations in the BRCA1 and/or BRCA2 genes are more likely to develop breast cancer than women without those mutations, all else being equal.[54] Importantly, these techniques are essentially statistical in nature. A successful QTL analysis reveals only that differences in a particular chromosomal region are associated with differences in the phenotype of interest; it does not provide information about the developmental pathways (if any) with which the genes in that region are involved. Indeed, at least currently, QTL analyses do not find the gene or genes associated with any particular phenotypic variation.[55] Instead, they simply identify the chromosomal region in which the putative gene can be supposed to lie. And, of course, QTL analyses are essentially tools to be used for exploring differences in traits, such as how likely a person is to develop a disease or whether a person is more or less prone to violent behavior. The analysis cannot discover the genes involved in the development of any traits for which there is no variation in the particular population involved.[56]

It follows that a QTL analysis done in one environment might reveal an association between a particular chromosomal region and differences in a particular trait, but the same analysis done in another environment might reveal nothing. Imagine if the genotypic difference between the maze-bright and the maze-dull rats was at a single locus. In the normal environment, a QTL analysis would show an association of this locus with the difference in maze-running performance. However, QTL analyses done in either the enriched or impoverished environments would reveal no associations between chromosomal regions and differences in maze-running ability.

In fact, exactly this kind of plasticity has been reported in human behavioral genetics research focused on violence and antisocial behavior. In the early 1990s, researchers studied a family in the Netherlands in which many of the men (but none of the women) had a record of abnormal behavior (including violent and antisocial behaviors). Biochemical testing revealed these men to be severely deficient in Monoamine Oxidase A (MAOA), and genetic testing revealed a

---

54. Andrea Veronsi et al., *Familial Breast Cancer: Characteristics and Outcomes of BRCA 1-2 Positive and Negative Cases*, 5 BMC CANCER 70 (2005).

55. On the difficulties inherent in defining and identifying genes, *see* Box 1.

56. *See, e.g.*, Sober, *supra* note 21, at 48–55. To explore how genes for which there is no natural variation in the pertinent population play roles in development, one can, in model organisms, design "knock out" experiments. In such studies, the target gene is rendered nonfunctional at some point in development. Alternatively, one can trace the activity of genes with RNA transcription in particular tissues. But ethical restrictions prevent the use of knock-out studies in humans (it is also too hard to control for confounding factors in natural experiments), and they likewise prevent the results of micro-array activation studies from being aggressively pursued. For these reasons, naturally occurring genetic variation and appeals to the results of studies in model organisms remain the primary source for the generation and testing of hypotheses in the human case.

"nonsense point" mutation in the MAOA gene explaining the absence of MAOA.[57] But it rapidly became clear that complete MAOA deficiency was extremely rare, and studies attempting to link partial MAOA deficiency to aggressive antisocial behavior tended to be inconclusive.[58] A study subsequently performed on a population in Dunedin, New Zealand, considered the effects of the early developmental environment (mainly, the extent to which the developing child was exposed to physical abuse in the home) and found a strong relationship between growing up in an abusive household and the likelihood of aggressive violent behavior later in life. This association was much stronger in people with low levels of MAOA activity.

In the Dunedin study, children were categorized according to the likely level of physical abuse in their homes, abuse generally directed at the children and their mothers. Three categories of abuse were identified: "likely none," "probable/moderate abuse," and "likely severe abuse."[59] The likely MAOA level of the children was determined by the genotype of their MAOA promoter region. Children who grew up in households rated as likely nonabusive had the same low risk of becoming violent adults, regardless of their level of MAOA. However, children who grew up in abusive households had a much greater risk of becoming violent adults if they had promoter regions associated with low-MAOA activity than if they had promoter regions associated with high-MAOA activity.[60]

A QTL analysis would find an association between the MAOA promoter regions and antisocial behaviors only if the children were exposed to fairly serious abuse in their homes. In other environments, the different promoter regions were not associated with statistically significant differences in the likelihood that violent or antisocial behaviors would develop. This kind of plasticity may partly explain why it has been so difficult to replicate many of the studies that found

---

57. Han G. Brunner et al., *Abnormal Behavior Associated with a Point Mutation in the Structural Gene for Monoamine Oxidase A.*, 262 SCIENCE 578, 579 (1993). A nonsense point mutation is one that prevents the formation of a protein that is usually produced; because of the redundancy of the genetic code, some mutations will have little or no effect on the protein produced, and others will result in a different protein being produced. Nonsense mutations stop transcription and prevent the protein from being produced.

58. *See, e.g.,* Avshalom Caspi, Joseph McClay, Terrie E. Moffitt, Jonathan Mill, Judy Martin, Ian W. Craig, Alan Taylor & Richie Poulton, *Role of Genotype in the Cycle of Violence in Maltreated Children,* 297 SCIENCE 851 (2002). This study has not been replicated, and while it appears to have been very well performed, the results may not be general in the way suggested here. But these doubts are secondary to the more significant conceptual issues discussed below.

59. *Id.,* at 297. Based on previous studies, longer promoter regions were associated with greater MAOA activity.

60. *See infra* Figure 2.2.

FIGURE 2.2 THE DUNEDIN STUDY: A GENERALIZED NORM OF REACTION—THE RELATIONSHIP BETWEEN CHILDHOOD ABUSE, LIKELY MAOA LEVEL, AND THE RISK FOR ANTISOCIAL BEHAVIORS

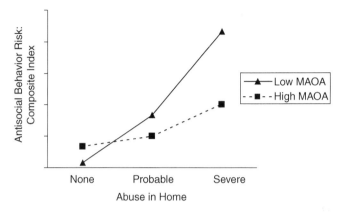

Figure 2.2: This graph demonstrates the relative risk of antisocial behavior for adults who grew up in households with no abuse, probable abuse, or severe abuse, given likely low levels of MAOA or likely high levels of MAOA. The difference between the risk of becoming a violent adult is not significantly different for children with low and high MAOA levels in houses without abuse or in houses with probable (and likely mild) abuse. Children who grow up in households with severe physical abuse have a significantly higher risk of becoming violent adults than those who grew up in houses without abuse, *whatever* their MAOA levels. But in those households, those with low MAOA levels have a significantly higher risk of this than do those with higher MAOA levels. This graph does not highlight the extensive variation in antisocial behaviors within each category.[61]

loci associated with particular behavioral traits.[62] Similarly, since in this case the heritability of antisocial behaviors will vary based on the prevalence of abuse in the society in question, studies of the heritability of antisocial behaviors will yield very different numbers in different social environments.

The same problem—that genes associated with a difference in one environment may not be so associated in another environment—holds for differences in the genetic environment, as well. Epistasis, the phenomenon in which genes affect the expression of other genes, is a central fact of development. A gene associated with a particular form of a trait in one genetic context may not be associated with that form of the trait in another genetic context.[63] Indeed, with

---

61. Redrawn from Caspi et al., *supra* note 59. On the concept of a generalized norm of reaction *see* Sarkar & Fuller *supra* note 34, at 71.

62 *See, e.g.*, D.C. Rowe, *Assessing Genotype-Environment Interactions and Correlations in the Postgenomic Era, in* Behavioral Genetics in the Postgenomic Era, *supra* note 17, at 71.

63. See the developmental rules above, especially rules 2 and 3.

several diseases associated with particular genes in humans, the different expression of the genes in individuals is likely to be associated with differences in their genetic background. For example, how much the presence of genes associated with breast cancer raise one's lifetime risk of breast cancer is currently an area of active research. It seems likely that the answer depends on the presence of other genes. For instance, in some genetic contexts the BRCA1/2 mutations may raise the lifetime risk of breast cancer to over 80 percent, whereas in the presence of other genes, the same mutations are associated with only a 20 percent lifetime risk.[64]

Like studies of heritability, QTL analyses are a good first step in research aimed to untangle the complex developmental pathways involved. Finding chromosomal regions associated with particular differences can provide an entry into research focused on understanding those developmental processes more generally. For example, further work can be done narrowing the chromosomal region and looking for particular candidate genes. Differences found in these genes can be analyzed with an eye toward understanding what functional differences they make to development. And that, of course, leads to the differences in development that matter to the production of different versions of the trait in question. But, again, in the case of associations between genetic markers and human behavioral traits, such research is just the first step; all too often it suggests a promise for the future, not a conclusion for the present. What gets reported and unwisely used in the framing of social and political debates, as well as in legal decisionmaking, is not the work that remains to be done (and the complex context that work involves), but that a "gene for" some behavioral trait or other has been discovered.[65]

Research into the relationship between variation in the MAOA promoter regions and antisocial behaviors can reasonably claim to have gone beyond generating mere statistical associations. For example, the MAOA system is known, at least in animal models, to be involved with metabolizing various neurotransmitters, and differences in neurotransmitters are implicated in behavioral differences (including aggression) in those model organisms.[66] It is therefore hardly a

64. *See, e.g.,* Colin B. Begg, *On the Use of Familial Aggregation in Population-Based Case Probands for Calculating Penetrance,* 94 J. Nat'l Cancer Inst. 1221, 1221 (2002) (reporting estimates of BRCA1/2 risks); *accord* Ulrich Wolf, *Identical Mutations and Phenotypic Variation,* 100 Hum. Genetics 305 (1997) (examining similar data for cystic fibrosis, tumors, and a number of other human disorders); Barbara R. Grubb & Richard C. Boucher, *Pathophysiology of Gene-Targeted Mouse Models for Cystic Fibrosis,* 79 Physiological Rev. 193 (1999) (examining the effect of the genetic background in mouse models).

65. Jonathan M. Kaplan & Massimo Pigliucci, *Genes 'For' Phenotypes: A Modern History View,* 16 Biology & Phil. 189 (2001) (providing examples and a general critique of speaking about a gene being "for" a phenotype).

66. *See, e.g.,* Brunner et al., *supra* note 57, (correlating a mutation in part of "the MAOA structural gene" with an increase in impulsive aggression).

stretch to suspect that the associations found involve causally salient differences at the level of the developmental pathways.

Even so, it would be unwise to assume that the results of the Dunedin study will be easily replicated in other populations since development can be sensitive to many different environmental factors; so the correlations found in Dunedin may not be found elsewhere. But even if Dunedin results do turn out to be typical, it is unclear what, if any, policy implications they might have. After all, significant variation in antisocial behavior cannot be accounted for by associations between environments or by the different promoter regions. That is, low-MAOA activity, even when coupled with growing up in a violent household, does not guarantee that a violent or antisocial adult will result; conversely, high-MAOA activity, even when coupled with growing up in a nonviolent household, does not guarantee that the result will be a nonviolent adult. And surely the most important lesson of the Dunedin study is that growing up in a violent household is associated with an increased risk of antisocial behavior, whatever version of the promoter region one has.

This suggests in part that—despite the claim of the Dunedin researchers that the link between low MAOA, childhood exposure to violence, and antisocial behavior implies that "these findings could inform the development of future pharmacological treatments"[67]—any reasonable public health approach to reducing the prevalence and impact of violent behaviors in society ought to focus on reducing violent abuse in the home rather than on MAOA levels. No pharmacological interventions are currently available; but even if they were, they would still very likely be less effective than programs aimed at reducing the prevalence of domestic violence. And given the other effects of domestic violence (including not only the direct physical and psychological harms, but also such subtler harms as the reduction of IQ scores in children exposed to domestic violence),[68] even if such programs were not wholly successful, they would still seem to be more worthwhile than pharmacological interventions.

From the standpoint of human behavioral genetics research more generally, limits in the current understanding of the developmental pathways that produce particular personality types or behavioral tendencies are to be expected; such limits do not count as a criticism of the field. Indeed, that substantial variation in the particular behaviors cannot be associated with variation in either genetic or environmental developmental resources should be expected in the study of any complex behavior, or, for that matter, that of any complex trait more generally.[69] But these limits mean that current research does not point towards any substantial

---

67. *See* Caspi, *supra* note 58, at 853.

68. *See, e.g.*, Karestan C. Koenen, Terrie E. Moffitt, Avshalom Caspi, Alan Taylor & Shaun Purcell, *Domestic Violence Is Associated with Environmental Suppression of IQ in Young Children*, 15 DEV. & PSYCHOPATHOLOGY 297 (2003).

69. See the developmental rules above, especially rule 7.

predictive abilities respecting the behavior of individuals. Any public policy implications drawn from this research are very limited, indeed, and will likely remain so for the foreseeable future.

C . Evolutionary Accounts

Some researchers interested in human behavioral genetics have appealed to evolutionary accounts of particular behavioral traits. These appeals have taken several distinct forms. For instance, evolutionary psychology aims to uncover universal developmental systems that could be adaptive responses that evolved to solve particular kinds of problems in ancestral humans.[70] So some hypotheses suggest that the development of linguistic ability in humans was a solution to the problem of social coordination, and that the preference for sweet, high-fat foods as a solution to the problem of food choice for hunter-gatherers in broadly unstable environments. Evolutionary psychiatry is a related project that attempts to account for particular kinds of psychopathologies by reference to the mismatch between an adaptive behavioral response in the ancestral environment and current environmental conditions.[71] Insofar as a taste for high-fat foods is no longer adaptive (because it is associated with obesity), an evolved preference for such foods would represent a mismatch of this sort. Researchers engaged in more traditional behavioral genetics research will sometimes appeal to evolutionary accounts in order to explain the continued presence of particular kinds of heritable variation in traits.[72]

However, evolutionary psychology has been widely criticized, and these criticisms apply in large part to evolutionary psychiatry as well.[73] The primary difficulty with accounts of the adaptive evolution of human behaviors is that studying evolutionary adaptations in humans is notoriously difficult. All the standard techniques used in evolutionary biology to gather evidence that phenotypic traits

---

70. *See, e.g.,* JEROME H. BARKOW, LEDA COSMIDES & JOHN TOOBY, THE ADAPTED MIND: EVOLUTIONARY PSYCHOLOGY AND THE GENERATION OF CULTURE 3 (1992).

71. *See* MICHAEL MCGUIRE & ALFONSO TROISI, DARWINIAN PSYCHIATRY vii–x (1998).

72. *See, e.g.,* Henry C. Harpending & Patricia Draper, *Antisocial Behavior and the Other Side of Cultural Evolution, in* BIOLOGICAL CONTRIBUTIONS TO CRIME CAUSATION 293, 293 (Terrie E. Moffitt & Sarnoff A. Mednick eds., 1988) (developing a theoretical framework "in which antisocial behavior makes evolutionary sense").

73. *See, e.g.,* DAVID J. BULLER, ADAPTING MINDS: EVOLUTIONARY PSYCHOLOGY AND THE PERSISTENT QUEST FOR HUMAN NATURE 93–106 (2005) (arguing that there are "intractable obstacles to discovering our psychological adaptations via evolutionary" analysis because (1) it is impossible to specify what adaptive problems our ancestors faced or what would solve them, and (2) even if we could determine how our ancestors adapted, "no reliable chain of inference" connects our ancestor's adaptive problems to our current problems); Jonathan M. Kaplan, *Historical Evidence and Human Adaptations,* 69 PHIL. SCIENCE 294 (2002) (arguing that it is difficult or impossible to apply information from even the closest extant relatives to humans to evolutionary psychology because (1) either the traits studied are not widely shared in the species, or (2) the difference betwwween humans and their relatives is big enough that any information about the relatives is likely too simplistic).

(including behaviors) are adaptations are either impossible to perform or of somewhat limited use in humans.[74] Moving from a plausible account of how a particular behavioral tendency might have been adaptive in some ancestral environment to being able to provide compelling evidence that the tendency is itself an adaptation is, at best, very difficult.

Box 2.4. Evolutionary accounts and human adaptations

The following table lists some standard techniques used to find evidence in support of adaptive hypotheses in evolutionary biology, the kind of evidence each technique is supposed to gather, and the difficulties with using that technique in the human case.

Technique	Evidence Gathered	The Trouble with Humans
Phenotypic manipulation (laboratory or field). In these studies, the trait in question is modified by the researcher.	Fitness consequences of the traits in question, causal mechanisms associated with traits and fitness consequences.	Ethical constraints; no controls in natural cases (trauma, genetic diseases, etc.).
Transplant studies. In these studies, organisms are physically moved from one location to another location with a different environment.	Fitness consequences, hypotheses about local selective pressures, hypotheses about local adaptations to local environmental factors.	Ethical constraints; few ways to control for confounding variables in natural cases; little known systematic (behavioral) variation between populations.
Laboratory evolution. Here, populations of organisms are kept and bred under controlled conditions.	Robustness of pathways (given the same environment, does the same trait develop?), strength of constraints.	Ethical constraints; also, humans are very poor model organisms due in part to their long lifespans.

Continued

---

74. *See* Box 2.4.

Box 2.4.—Cont'd

Optimism analyses. These investigate what the best trait would be, given some ancestral version of the trait, problems posed by the environment, and variation in developmental resources.	Qualitative assessments (for quantitative plausibility), sensitivity, path-dependence.	Little extant knowledge of relevant selective history.
Phylogenetic analyses. These studies focus on the history of the lineage of the organisms in question—what traits do they share or not share with other species that share a recent common ancestor?	History of trait; homology (shared trait derived from common ancestor) versus homoplasy (similar traits with independent evolutionary origins).	Very sparsely populated clade (few extant relations, none of them very close); little known about environment of speciation events.
Regression analyses and comparative analyses. These compare particular versions of various traits to each other and to environmental changes over time.	Relationship between trait and environmental variables, strength of relationship, relationship between trait and fitness, relationship between trait and other traits.	Very little known about environment-trait relationships; little known about current or historical trait-fitness relationship; little known systematic variation within populations.

Nevertheless, evolutionary accounts that attempt to explain the prevalence of violent behaviors in societies have been presented in the literature. These include models that link the development of particular kinds of violent tendencies to particular environments, as well as models of frequency-dependent selection that maintains genetic variation for a propensity to violence. An example of the first is an influential article in which Margo Wilson and Martin Daly argue that many behavioral features of "violent criminals" who grew up in "high-crime" neighborhoods could be explained as rational, adaptive responses to the particular developmental environments in which they found themselves.[75] Working within the framework of evolutionary psychology, Wilson and Daly hypothesize that human psychological development reveals adaptive plasticity with respect to particular kinds of developmental environments. They argue that the development of human behavioral tendencies is determined by a number of universal developmental programs that respond to local environmental variation in ways that would have been adaptive in the environments in which their ancestors evolved. All people share the same potential to develop various psychological traits; whether they actually develop any particular trait will depend on the developmental environment they experience.[76]

Since our brains evolved to solve "important" problems regarding maximizing reproductive success within complex social systems, Wilson and Daly suggest that we should expect to find that behavioral tendencies will vary based on the developmental environment encountered and that we should thus be especially sensitive to the social environment. One upshot of this is that everyone will share the same potential to become a violent adult; whether someone actually becomes a violent adult will depend on whether he or she experiences environments that, in the past, made being violent a good strategy to adopt.[77] In environments in which the average lifespan is relatively long, rates of violent death relatively low, opportunities for low-risk social advancement widely available, and reasonable levels of social success widely distributed (that is, social environments with relatively low levels of social inequality), Wilson and Daly suggest that adopting a long time-horizon would be adaptive (which is to say, such a strategy will tend to increase reproductive fitness). This would include delaying reproduction, pursuing relatively low-risk, long-term strategies, and avoiding risk-taking—behaviors that all lead to broadly nonviolent psychological features. On the other hand, in environments in which the average lifespan is relatively short and the chance of dying early through violence is relatively high, in which there are large social inequalities and low-risk strategies are unlikely to accrue reasonable amounts of social success (so-called "winner take all" societies), and in which risk-taking may have large social rewards, Wilson and Daly argue it is in fact adaptive to adopt a short time-horizon. This would include early reproduction, high-risk pursuits, and high-reward strategies, including violent ones.

Wilson and Daly claim the neighborhood patterns of life expectancy, homicide rates, and reproductive timing in the United States conform to this hypothesis.[78] Neighborhoods with relatively little violence are those with relatively long

---

75. Margo Wilson & Martin Daly, *Life Expectancy, Economic Inequality, Homicide, and Reproductive Timing in Chicago Neighbourhoods*, 314 BRIT. MED. J. 1271 (1997).

76. *See, e.g., id.* at 1271–72.

77. *See, e.g., id.* at 1273–74; *see generally* MARTIN DALY & MARGO WILSON, HOMICIDE (1988).

78. Wilson & Daly, *supra* note 75, at 1273–74.

life expectancies (and better overall health), relatively little economic inequality (and overall reasonably high incomes), and relatively numerous educational and economic opportunities. The most violent neighborhoods are those with relatively short life expectancies (and poor overall health), great economic inequality (and overall very low incomes), and relatively few educational and economic opportunities.[79]

Based on such data, some authors suggest that searching for biological differences between more and less violent people may, in general, be pointless.[80] Instead, the differences between people may not lie in different biologies per se but rather in the different developmental environments to which the people were exposed. Although different developmental environments may produce different behavioral phenotypes that are related to different brain chemistries, for example, these latter features are best thought of as caused by environmental differences.[81]

Evolutionary psychology as a field has come under serious attack,[82] but its methodological weaknesses and poorly supported assumptions are not, fundamentally, the most serious problems facing its published results. Indeed, although Wilson and Daly acknowledge the "daunting" number of complex "feedback loops" in the pathways between the developmental environment, reasonable expectations regarding life expectancies and life strategies involving violence do not, and cannot, address the developmental biology of the behaviors in question. From the standpoint of how, developmentally, particular behaviors come to be expressed in particular individuals, these kinds of evolutionary accounts are silent.

Rather, the kind of evolutionary approach favored by Wilson and Daly is supposed to reveal the ultimate causes of violent behaviors[83]—to explain why such behaviors exist, not how those behaviors develop. For this reason, such approaches count as behavioral genetics only insofar as the evolution of stable developmental pathways involves the selection and maintenance of particular genes. However, it has become increasingly clear that adaptations may not involve the selection of particular genes, but rather the selection of developmental mechanisms that result in the resources available (including genetic resources) being

---

79. *Id.*

80. Alan Gibbard, *Genetic Plans, Genetic Differences, ioand Vlence: Some Chief Possibilities, in* GENETICS AND CRIMINAL BEHAVIOR 169, 192–94 (David Wasserman & Robert Wachbroit eds., 2001).

81. *See, e.g., id.;* Vernon L. Quinsey, *Evolutionary Theory and Criminal Behaviour,* 7 LEGAL & CRIMINOLOGICAL PSYCHOL. I (2002).

82. *See* Kaplan, *supra* note 73.

83. *See, e.g.,* Quinsey, *supra* note 81, at 1–2 (explaining the concept of "ultimate" causes compared to "proximal" causes in this context).

used in different ways.[84] So, even if a particular set of evolutionary accounts is correct, it may not point toward particular genes that are uniquely involved in the production of the behaviors in question.

It may be that projects like these that attempt to uncover ultimate evolutionary accounts would be intellectually interesting if they were better supported,[85] but because they do not address the causal pathways involved, they cannot support arguments surrounding individual differences in behavior except through the statistical associations between those behaviors and particular environments. As it is already well established that growing up in a violent society with high levels of economic and social inequality and so on is statistically associated with becoming a violent adult, the additional evolutionary account does not seem to add anything to the explanation of differences within particular populations. It certainly adds nothing that would be of value to social policies directed at individual variations in behaviors.

A second approach to using evolutionary accounts to explain violent human behaviors links genetic variation associated with behavioral differences to the likelihood of antisocial or violent behavior.[86] It does so by appealing to evolutionary accounts that could generate or maintain such genetic variations, either between or within populations. In the case of between-population differences, people in different populations might face different environments due either to the structure of the societies or to other local environmental features. These differences might, in turn, lead to local populations adapting to these local features and hence having different distributions of genes.[87] In the case of within-population differences, an evolutionary equilibrium might occur in which different strategies, associated with different genetic features, might exist at stable levels. However, neither the account in terms of equilibrium strategies nor the account in terms of local adaptations does much to explain the differences in rates of violence between or within populations, and neither has been seriously investigated in recent years, so neither is particularly helpful in explaining associations between genes, behavior, and environment.

---

84. *See, e.g.,* Moss, *supra* note 6, at 75–116.

85. *But see* Richard Lewontin, *The Evolution of Cognition: Questions We Will Never Answer, in* 4 METHODS, MODELS, AND CONCEPTUAL ISSUES, AN INVITATION TO COGNITIVE SCIENCE 107, 118–30 (Don Scarborough & Saul Sternberg eds., 1998) (presenting a compelling argument that, in this case, the required evidence is not, and will never be, available).

86. *See* Ian Pitchford, *The Origins of Violence: Is Psychopathy an Adaptation?* 1 HUM. NATURE REV. 28 (2001); Harpending & Draper, *supra* note 72, at 293–307.

87. *See* Massimo Pigliucci & Jonathan Kaplan, *On the Concept of Biological Race and its Applicability to Humans, in* 70 PHIL. OF SCI. 1161 (Supp. 2003) (discussing the possibility of human ecotypes (locally adapted populations)).

IV. CONCLUSION: EVIDENCE AND THE USES OF EVIDENCE

Despite well over a quarter-century of criticism of the methodological limitations of human behavioral genetics research and the weak evidence offered for linking particular variations in human behaviors to particular biological features,[88] the standards required to publish and publicize particular claims in human behavioral genetics still remain disappointingly low. This should not come as a surprise: in nonhuman behavioral genetics and in evolutionary biology more generally, the evidence generally required to link particular behaviors to particular biological differences or to particular accounts of adaptation is also relatively weak. But there is an important difference. In the case of accounts involving, say, locally adapted populations of plants or fruit flies, the willingness to formulate and publish hypotheses on the basis of weak evidence is not deeply problematic. Nor is the acceptance or rejection of any particular adaptive account based on nonhuman studies; even if criticism of poor evidence and new hypotheses does not occur for some time, it is unlikely that any real or lasting harm will be done by the (temporary) acceptance of the original, poorly supported hypothesis about plants or fruit flies.

The situation in commercial plant and animal breeding might be considered rather different. Here, mistaken hypotheses, if not discovered quickly, could be costly. But commercial plant and animal breeders have important advantages over researchers hoping to understand the development of traits in natural populations. Studies relevant to commercial plant and animal breeding can, and do, control the environments in which the experiments are performed. This is not problematic in the least, as the goal is not to mimic some range of natural environments, but rather to recreate the artificial environments in which those plants or animals are usually raised. For this reason, studies involving commercial plant and animal breeding do not need to control for the manipulation of their subjects; the subjects of such studies are always manipulated.

Similarly, in principle it would be possible to pursue human behavioral genetics research that would be accurate, as long as one could selectively breed humans in controlled environments, and as long as all one wanted to know was the relationship between particular genes and particular behaviors in those populations and in those controlled environments. However, even if such studies were ethically feasible (not to mention practically feasible), they would still be inadequate

---

88. *See generally* PHILIP KITCHER, VAULTING AMBITION: SOCIOBIOLOGY AND THE QUEST FOR HUMAN NATURE (1985); RICHARD C. LEWONTIN, BIOLOGY AS IDEOLOGY: THE DOCTRINE OF DNA (1991); Richard C. Lewontin, *The Evolution of Cognition: Questions We Will Never Answer,* in METHODS, MODELS, AND CONCEPTUAL ISSUES, *supra* note 75, at 107. RICHARD C. LEWONTIN, STEVEN ROSE & LEON J. KAMIN, NOT IN OUR GENES: BIOLOGY, IDEOLOGY, AND HUMAN NATURE (1984); HILARY ROSE & SEVEN ROSE, ALAS POOR DARWIN (2000); MICHAEL RUSE, SOCIOBIOLOGY: SENSE OR NONSENSE? (2d ed. 1979).

for understanding the relationship between variation in human genetics and variation in human behavior. Human behavioral genetics is not—and ought not be—interested in the relationship between particular genes and particular behaviors in some particular, artificially structured population and in some artificially controlled environment. The goal of behavioral genetics is not to find associations that hold true within artificial environments or artificially created populations. Rather, the environments of interest to human behavioral genetics are those natural environments in which the populations of interest develop.

Further, insofar as human behavioral genetics is expected to generate research results with public policy implications, there are good reasons to reject any research model that fails to focus on the actual environments encountered during development and on the actual populations experiencing those environments. Public policy decisions cannot be sensibly made on the basis of what might happen to a particular population in a particular controlled environment. Rather, such decisions should take into account the ways in which the developmental environments encountered vary within populations, between populations, and especially over time.

Even if contemporary approaches to finding biological correlates to violent, antisocial, or criminal behavior are successful, the research results are unlikely to contribute meaningfully to shaping public policy, to making better legal decisions, or to improving our understanding of the causes of violence within societies. Because contemporary techniques cannot reveal the causal pathways of development in the human case, they cannot be used to predict how particular developmental resources will be used in different developmental environments. Hence, they cannot predict the results of any particular social policies. Changes in social policy are, after all, environmental changes, and changes in the developmental environment may well change the associations between particular genes and particular behaviors. As a result, any social changes made in response to research might change the associations uncovered by the research itself. The conceptual limitations of the techniques employed by these research programs simply do not permit the results of such research to be used in the kinds of explanations or predictions that could meaningful influence social policy.

A substantial literature is emerging from moral philosophy, legal studies, and the social sciences on how to deal with possible discoveries of links between biology and violent crime. Various authors have argued that some possible discoveries would force a major rethinking of basic moral intuitions or major revisions in the public policies surrounding violent crime.[89] In these hypothetical cases, one is often asked to imagine discovering biological correlates to criminal violence that predispose an individual to commit violent acts in every possible developmental environment or biological correlates that make an individual

---

89. *See especially* Part II of GENETICS AND CRIMINAL BEHAVIOR, *supra* note 9.

much more impulsive and thus more unable to control his or her temptations than the norm.[90] More dramatically, one could imagine discovering biological pathways that make it certain an individual will commit violent acts—pathways that would determine him or her to be a violent or antisocial adult.[91]

Interesting as they are, perhaps, as an intellectual exercise, these hypothetical cases should not be permitted to distract from what is already known about how to reduce the prevalence and ameliorate the impact of violent, antisocial, and criminal behaviors. And despite the over-bold claims of some human behavioral genetics researchers, it is not at all likely that more biological data would even help in reducing such behaviors. Rather, what seems to be missing from attempts to deal seriously with these problems is a willingness to act on what is already known about techniques for reducing them. It seems reasonable to suggest, therefore, that people concerned with actually reducing the prevalence and impact of violent behavior in societies or interested in finding ways to reform the legal and penal systems should focus on these broader political questions. To reduce the prevalence and ameliorate the impact of violent, antisocial, and criminal behavior within societies, such people should treat biological research as, at best, intriguing distractions from the hard work ahead.

---

90. *See* Marcia Baron, *Crime, Genes, and Responsibility, in* GENETICS AND CRIMINAL BEHAVIOR, *supra* note 10, at 204–05.

91. *See* Peter Van Inwagen, *Genes, Statistics, and Desert, in* GENETICS AND CRIMINAL BEHAVIOR, *supra* note 10, at 225 (discussing the moral culpability of individuals genetically predisposed to commit violent acts).

3. THE DEVELOPMENTAL NEUROSCIENCE OF CRIMINAL BEHAVIOR

ABIGAIL A. BAIRD

I. INTRODUCTION

In Europe, a woman was near death from cancer. One drug might save her, a form o f radium that a druggist in the same town had recently discovered. The druggist was charging $2000, ten times what the drug had cost him to make. The sick woman's husband, Heinz, went to everyone he knew to borrow the money, but he could get together only about half of what it should cost. He told the druggist that his wife was dying and asked him to sell it cheaper or to let him pay later. But the druggist said no. The husband got desperate and broke into the man's store to steal the drug for his wife.

Should the man have stolen the medicine?[1]

The way in which individuals answer this question, taken from Lawrence Kohlberg's well-known test of moral reasoning, is believed to reflect their level of moral reasoning. According to this conceptualization the answer that reflects the highest level of moral reasoning is something akin to, "Yes, Heinz was right to steal the medicine, the life of his wife is more important than property." The justification for Heinz's behavior is based on the idea that morally advanced individuals place human life above all else. This is a universally appealing strategy at the level of the individual (and their kin). Heinz is ethically correct to prioritize his wife, but in doing so he has lost sight of the fact that human beings live in large societal groups. The inclusion of society in this dilemma adds a second, far more complicated layer to the ethics of his decision. For example, what might Heinz have done if the druggist happened to be present while he was attempting to steal the medicine? It would be in Heinz's best interest to take the medicine even if in doing so he harmed the druggist. In the animal world, if dog 1 wants dog 2's meal, a fight ensues and the *fittest* dog goes home with dinner. In sharp contrast, humans have created a system of policies that ensure the health and well-being of each individual as a function of the health and well-being of society. As long as there have been societies, there have been systems of laws. These systems consistently have been based on rules to be observed by all citizens and on sanctions for individuals who violate the rules. The Heinz

---

1. LAWRENCE KOHLBERG, ESSAYS ON MORAL DEVELOPMENT, VOL. I: THE PHILOSOPHY OF MORAL DEVELOPMENT (1981).

Dilemma underscores that legal and moral dicta are not always in agreement. In response to a princess who inquired about the statutes of appropriate conduct, the philosopher Descartes has been quoted as saying, "Although each of us is a person distinct from all others . . . we must always remember that none of us could exist alone. . . . The interests of the whole, of which each of us is part, must always be preferred to those of our individual personality."[2] More recently, legal scholar Steven Shavell has described the way in which society recognizes this and seeks to control the behavior of individuals through moral statute, legal statute, and a combination of the two. Shavell underscores the need for this distinction:

> My conclusion is that for most of the acts that society has chosen to control through the law and through morality, the use of moral incentives alone would not function well because of some combination of the following factors: substantial private benefits from committing bad acts, inadequacy of internal and external moral sanctions to counter the private benefits, and/or the presence of amoral subgroups. The imperfect performance of our moral system as a regulator of conduct, together with very high social costs of failure to control conduct, warrants use of our costly legal system.[3]

Importantly, this thought underscores the need for both moral and legal influence when the personal or social stakes are high. The Heinz Dilemma serves as an excellent example of the potential conflict between individually-based morality and socially-based legal statues. While Heinz's moral stance protects his wife's life, the presence of law ensures the life and well-being of the druggist. It can be argued that Heinz made the decision to steal the medicine because his wife's life was more important to him than the druggist's property. Psychologists would posit that Heinz made the decision he did because his feelings regarding his wife exerted a more powerful influence on his decision than did his feelings about the druggist, the druggist's property, or the law. In making his decision, it is possible that Heinz thought about the possible legal consequences of his actions; however his behavior demonstrates that these thoughts did not produce a level of aversive emotion greater than that produced by the thought of his wife's death. One can also envision a scenario in which the thought of legal consequences produced a level of emotional aversion that resulted in different behavior. These scenarios all support the idea that in moments requiring decisive action, the behavioral response is largely the product of the specific stimuli (often among many) that are capable of producing the strongest emotional response, independent of legal or moral origin. It is important to note, however, that the emotional response is derived from a number of interactions

---

2. JEROME KAGAN, THE NATURE OF THE CHILD 116 (1984).
3. STEVEN SHAVELL, *Law versus Morality as Regulators of Conduct*, 4 AM. L. & ECON. REV. 227, 248–49 (2002).

with cognition. This intricate and complex interaction is discussed in detail in the pages that follow.

This chapter will explore how cognition and emotion work together synergistically to produce predictable behavior, independent of its utility. Although many scholars (correctly) draw distinctions between moral and legal behavior, this chapter argues that at their core they share a number of fundamental attributes, and as such, for present purposes, they will be referred to collectively as ethical behavior. It will also be demonstrated that in high-stakes situations emotional response (whether automatic or cognitively mediated) ultimately drives behavior. A developmental model will be presented elucidating the ways in which maturation of the human brain supports the development of a coordinated relationship between emotional and cognitive processes, a relationship whose integrity is critical to the production of behavior in accordance with personally or socially mandated standards. Conditions under which emotion and cognition are less synchronized, such as in situations of high psychological stress and in cases involving specific neuropsychological disorders, are offered as additional support for this model. Finally, implications for legal scholarship and policy will be discussed.

II. THE DEVELOPMENTAL PERSPECTIVE

Collectively, the scientific literature has described the function of human development as enabling the individual to pass his or her genetic material to the next generation. This predisposition makes development an extremely flexible process, enabling human infants to follow an infinite number of developmental trajectories. Ideally, the developmental path is constrained by environmental demands that not only complement the individual's biology, but also forge behavioral outcomes that result in the individual's eventual reproductive success.[4] Certain processes within human development build upon themselves, and this can be seen in both neural development and behavioral development.[5] Other processes develop in such a way that each period constitutes a unique time, characterized by individual environmental demands and idiosyncratic milestones.[6] The acknowledgment of both trajectories is critical to understanding how events at one stage are likely to ripple their way through later stages of development.

Because human beings come with a predisposition for pro-social behavior, *specific* social behaviors are not hardwired in humans. It is therefore up to developmental processes to produce specific pro-social behaviors. At the core of this

---

4. C. H. WADDINGTON, THE EVOLUTION OF AN EVOLUTIONIST (1975).

5. STEPHEN J. GOULD, ONTOGENY AND PHYLOGENY (1977).

6. D. F. Bjorklund, *The Role of Immaturity in Human Development*, 122 PSYCHOL. BULL. 153 (1997).

process is the developmental coordination of emotion and cognition. This inter-action changes form in response to individual social, emotional, and cognitive demands, and manifests in both continuous and discontinuous change during development. During the course of development, the relationship between cog-nition and emotion changes both quantitatively and qualitatively, reaching its apex during a sensitive period in early adolescence as the individual prepares to become part of adult society. The developmental synergy between emotion and cognition relies heavily on individual differences in visceral sense, sensitivity to that sense, as well as individual differences in cognitive ability, insight, and emo-tionality. Although complex, the presence and interaction of these factors (and likely others) make human behavior surprisingly malleable. Neuropsychological plasticity is undoubtedly one of the great accomplishments of human evolution. Developmental processes, however, work on an "honor principle," meaning that most rely on the integrity of brain structure and function as well as the utility of the feedback received from the environment. The earliest form of feedback given to human beings takes place in the context of infant/caregiver relationships and is delivered in the form of emotional exchange.

III. HUMAN EMOTION

Charles Darwin was among the first to theorize about different types of emotion in an integrated way.[7] Darwin described emotion as a group of functional behav-iors that originated and persist in human beings for the same reason that any aspect of function originated and persists in any species: because of its ability to advance survival and enhance reproductive fitness. In this way he saw emotion as an intrinsic part of the human neurobehavioral repertoire. Darwin viewed emotion as originating in our phylogenetic past, part of which we share with other animals. Many other species are critically dependent upon the synchronous exchange of emotion with one another for survival. Early life represents an impor-tant period during which input heavily influences and shapes the organism. Among the functions that emotion serves during this time is that of providing an innate language that possesses seemingly hardwired predispositions alongside mechanisms that enable extremely sensitive, rapid, perhaps even single-exposure, learning. This type of learning provides the scaffolding for split-second communication between social animals.[8]

Paul MacLean[9] has written extensively about the "triune" brain. According to MacLean's model, the human brain is best understood within a sociocognitive

---

7. CHARLES DARWIN, THE EXPRESSION OF THE EMOTIONS IN MAN AND ANIMALS (1872).

8. Joseph E. LeDoux, *Memory Versus Emotional Memory in the Brain, in* THE NATURE OF EMOTION (Paul Ekman & Richard J. Davidson, eds., 1995).

9. P. D. MACLEAN, THE TRIUNE BRAIN IN EVOLUTION (1990).

context by dividing it into three regions. The primary and phylogenetically oldest part is the brainstem, which is responsible for the most basic and primitive survival-oriented functions, such as breathing, cardiac function, and basic arousal. The second region, which emerged more recently in evolutionary terms, is the limbic system. The limbic system comprises a number of structures that together make up a nexus of social and emotional behavior. The limbic system also exerts influence on a number of cognitive processes, most notably many forms of memory. Finally, the phylogenetically newest part of the brain is the neocortex, most specifically the prefrontal cortex. This evolutionary advancement is credited with hurling the human being up the food chain by giving them the capability for symbolic representation, the cornerstone of most complex cognitive processes.[10] Greater detail about these regions and their interactions is provided (within their behavioral contexts) in the sections that follow.

The basic neurophysiology of emotion relies heavily on the interaction of the brainstem and the limbic system. The brainstem houses the centers controlling basic autonomic function and thus heavily influences the somatic expression of emotion. Via the sympathetic and parasympathetic nervous system, emotion induces considerable and varied alterations in a wide range of physiologic parameters, including cardiovascular, respiratory, gastrointestinal, reproductive, sexual, and perhaps even immunologic functions. Regions located in the dorsal brainstem such as the periacqueductal gray (PAG) and the ventral tegmental area (VTA) have substantial roles in behavior related to high-stakes emotional situations. The PAG region receives a variety of inputs from other brain regions and is responsible for orchestrating behavior associated with the fight-or-flight response. Through its connections with the spinal cord and autonomic nervous system, the PAG is able to increase heart rate and mobilize increased blood flow to major muscle groups, thereby enabling the physical manifestation of the fight-or-flight response. Whether to fight or to flee is a critical behavioral dichotomy, and one for which the PAG relies on communication with "higher" parts of the brain, namely the limbic system and the prefrontal cortex.[11]

The VTA resides in a section of the brainstem called the midbrain and subserves multiple appetitive motivational behaviors. There are two major projections of neural fibers from the VTA. The first, the mesolimbic pathway, connects the VTA to the nucleus accumbens, a brain region notable for its involvement in experiences of reward and pleasure; the second, the mesocortical pathway, connects the VTA with the frontal cortex.[12] It has been well established that this

---

10. MERLIN DONALD, ORIGINS OF THE MODERN MIND (2005).

11. Joseph L. Price, *Free Will Versus Survival: Brain Systems That Underlie Intrinsic Constraints on Behavior*, 493 J. COMP. NEUROLOGY 132 (2005).

12. Adena L. Svingos et al., *Opioid Receptors in the Ventral Tegmental Area are Targeted to Presynaptically and Directly Modulate Mesocortical Projection Neurons*, 41 SYNAPSE 221 (2001); Albert Adell & Francesc Artigas, *The Somatodendritic Release of Dopamine in the Ventral*

brain region, especially the mesolimbic pathway, is involved in reward and plea-sure processing, making the VTA a key focus of research on addictive behavior. Opiate agents such as cocaine, marijuana, nicotine, and caffeine have been shown to activate the VTA. The release and reception of endogenous opioids in the VTA is the mechanism believed to be responsible for the execution of para-doxical self-initiated stressful behaviors (e.g., mating, altruistic deeds, socially challenging behaviors). According to this idea, the reward mediating mesocorti-cal and mesolimbic pathways counteract any instinctive sensorily triggered aver-sion to a normally unpleasant behavior, properties that make the region a critical contributor to human social behavior.

The limbic system subserves a number of survival-related behaviors, possess-ing rich reciprocal connections with both the brainstem and the neocortex.[13] At its most basic, the limbic system has been described as a series of neural structures that are critical for human emotion, motivation, and some forms of emotional/social learning.[14] There is, however, some disagreement with regard to which specific structures are included in the limbic system. Given the purpose of the present discussion, description of the limbic system will be limited to structures involved in emotionally driven behavior, which includes the amygdala, the ventral striatum, and portions of the cingulate cortex.

LeDoux and colleagues[15] have stressed the importance of the amygdala in fear detection and conditioning, describing it as "a neural system that evolved to detect danger and produce rapid protective responses without conscious partici-pation." The central nucleus of the amygdala has been described as essential for the expression of autonomic and somatic fear responses elicited by both learned and unlearned threats. These responses are controlled through efferent connec-tions from the central amygdala to brainstem nuclei.[16] The amygdala has also been characterized as a higher order "convergence zone" for the social, homeo-static, and survival-related meanings of complex stimuli.[17] Taken together, these lines of evidence describe the amygdala as a structure that has evolved to help the human animal recognize and learn the emotional meaning of stimuli in their environment and produce appropriate behavioral responses.[18]

Tegmental Area and Its Regulation by Afferent Transmitter Systems, 28 NEUROSCIENCE AND BIOBEHAVIORAL REV. 415–31 (2004).

13. M. Davis, *The Role of the Amygdala in Fear and Anxiety*, 15 ANN. REV. NEUROSCIENCE 353 (1992).

14. J. E. LeDoux et al., *Different Projections of the Central Amygdaloid Nucleus Mediate Autonomic and Behavioral Correlates of Conditioned Fear*, 8 J. NEUROSCIENCE 2517 (1988).

15. J. E. LeDoux, *Emotion, Memory and the Brain*, 270 SCI. AMER. 32 (1994).

16. M. T. Rogan & J. E. LeDoux, *Emotion: Systems, Cells, Synaptic Plasticity*, 85 CELL 469 (1996).

17. A. R. DAMASIO, DESCARTES' ERROR: EMOTION, REASON, AND THE HUMAN BRAIN (1994).

18. M. Davis & P. J. Whalen, *The Amygdala: Vigilance and Emotion*, 6 MOLECUL. PSYCHIATRY 34 (2001).

The ventral striatum comprises portions of the basal ganglia that are found on the underside of the brain, along its midline. Although the ventral striatum is made up of both the nucleus accumbens (NAC) and the olfactory tubercle, the nucleus accumbens is most relevant to the present discussion. The NAC is located at the head of the caudate nucleus and has been implicated in a number of processes involving reward, pleasure, and addiction. The NAC receives inputs from a large number of limbic structures and sends projections to structures that mediate behavioral expression. As a result of its connectivity, the NAC is thought to represent a limbic-motor interface.[19] Cardinal and colleagues provide a detailed description of the primary functions of the NAC. In short, this area of the brain is required for goal-directed instrumental behavior, and it typically accomplishes this through its influence on the motivational aspects of appetitive conditioning, specifically conditioned locomotor approach. Given the role of the NAC in reward, it is also of note that it promotes response to delayed reward. Due to its connections to memory for rewards, the NAC has been shown to remain active during delays when a reward is expected in natural settings, thus increasing the likelihood that individuals are able to delay gratification, a behavior critical to social functioning.[20]

The cingulate cortex lies along the midline of the brain, in each hemisphere, just dorsal to the corpus callosum. The cingulate has been functionally and cytoarchitectonically segregated into four distinct regions.[21] The anterior cingulate bends around the anterior portion of the corpus callosum and has a primary role in emotion and in the integration of visceral and cognitive information (an idea that will be addressed in greater detail in later sections). The midcingulate cortex lies posterior to the anterior cingulate and is involved in response selection, particularly among competing stimuli. Next is the posterior cingulate, which is closely tied to personal orientation, both in terms of visual spatial information and self-relevance assessment. Finally, the retrosplenial cortex is the most posterior region. The least understood region of the cingulate cortex, the retrosplenial cortex is believed to be closely involved in memory formation and retrieval, with preference for valenced information.

The prefrontal cortex is of paramount interest in human development largely because of its well-understood function with regard to cognitive, social, and emotional processes in adulthood. Converging evidence of prolonged development

19. R. N. Cardinal et al., *Emotion and Motivation: The Role of the Amygdala, Ventral Striatum, and Prefrontal Cortex*, 26 NEUROSCIENCE BIOBEHAVIORAL REV. 321 (2002).

20. J. J. Day & R. M. Carelli, *The Nucleus Accumbens and Pavlovian Reward Learning*, 13 NEUROSCIENTIST 148 (2007).

21. Brent A. Vogt et al., *Human Cingulate Cortex: Surface Features, Flat Maps, and Cytoarchitecture*, 359 J. COMP. NEUROLOGY 490 (2004).

and organization throughout childhood and adolescence[22] underscores the important parallel between prefrontal development and cognitive development. Data from both healthy and brain-damaged individuals has provided consistent evidence underscoring the central role that the frontal lobes play in executive function. Patients with damage to the prefrontal cortex show impairment in judgment, organization, planning, and decision making,[23] as well as behavioral disinhibition and impaired intellectual abilities. Even though selective aspects of executive function may appear intact in patients with frontal lobe damage, when coordination of a number of functions is required, either in a testing or real-life situation, patients with frontal damage are often unable to perform the required task.[24] Again, this underscores the significance of the frontal cortex in the generation and coordination of multiple processes that result in appropriate, goal-driven behavior. In a clever meta-analysis Duncan and Owen[25] compared a variety of tasks posited to tap executive function and identified three areas that were reliably active across tasks. The studies examined in the meta-analysis manipulated a particular task demand: response conflict, task novelty, working memory load, memory delay, or perceptual difficulty. For each of these demands, five or more studies assessed the effects of manipulating that demand. Three main clusters were distinguished: the dorsal anterior cingulate, a mid-dorsolateral frontal region, and a mid-ventrolateral frontal region. The authors concluded that a common network, involving these three regions, is recruited by diverse cognitive demands. However, they did not rule out the possibility that there may be finer specializations within this network. The investigators suggest that it is possible that the three regions subserve different functions, but that these functions are sufficiently abstract to be involved in many different complex cognitive tasks. In developing children, the emergence of empathy and theory of mind are thought to rely heavily on early gains in executive function and frontal lobe maturation. This idea has also received support from Fuster,[26]

---

22. *See* Adele Diamond & Chaya Herzberg, *Impaired Sensitivity to Visual Contrast in Children Treated Early and Continuously for Phenylketonuria*, 119 BRAIN 523 (1996); Adele Diamond, *Abilities and Neural Mechanisms Underlying AB Performance*, 59 CHILD DEV. 523 (1988); H. T. Chugani, *Positron Emission Tomography Study of Human Brain Functional Development*, 22 ANN NEUROL 487 (1987); P. R. Huttenlocher, *Synaptic Density in Human Frontal Cortex—Developmental Changes and Effects of Aging*, 163 BRAIN RES. 195 (1979).

23. D. T. Stuss & D. F. Benson, *Neuropsychological Studies of the Frontal Lobes*, 95 PSYCHOL. BULL. 3 (1984).

24. D. T. Stuss & M. P. Alexander, *Executive Functions and the Frontal Lobes: A Conceptual View*, 63 PSYCHOL. RES. 289 (2000); R. Elliot, *Executive Functions and Their Disorders*, 65 BRIT. MED. BULL. 49 (2003).

25. J. Duncan & A. M. Owen, *Common Regions of the Human Frontal Lobes Recruited By Diverse Cognitive Demands*, 23 TRENDS NEUROSCIENCE 475 (2000).

26. JOAQUIN M. FUSTER, THE PREFRONTAL CORTEX (1997).

Pribram,[27] and Nelson.[28] These investigators have stressed the integrative function of the prefrontal cortex. Fuster and Pribram have described the prefrontal cortex as being responsible for retrospective aspects of working memory, anticipatory components of impending tasks, and inhibiting behavior that is not consistent with a desired behavioral goal. Nelson has taken a more neurophysiological perspective, arguing that the integrative aspects of dorsolateral prefrontal function stem from its abundant anatomical connections with both cortical and sub-cortical regions.

Regarding the expression of emotional behavior, it is also important to highlight the relationship between the brainstem and the hypothalamic-pituitary-adrenal (HPA) axis. The HPA axis is a group of structures within the neuroendocrine system whose primary function is to regulate various bodily responses to stress. In human beings, there are rich connections between the hypothalamus (the body's "master gland") and the amygdala, the hippocampus, and the brainstem.[29] Given this link, it is easy to understand the direct role of the HPA axis in the production of somatic expressions of emotion.

The section above has provided a brief overview of the very complex neural substrates of human emotion. As initially emphasized by Darwin, human emotion exists and has evolved because of its ability to promote survival and fitness.[30] It is important to recognize, however, that no human is born with the full compliment of emotional behaviors and skills that will assure long-term survival. One consequence of this relative immaturity is the need to learn about the social world. This occurs first within the context of attachment.

A. Attachment

As conceptualized by British psychoanalyst John Bowlby, attachment behaviors are those that have the predictable outcome of maintaining proximity/contact with the mother.[31] Bowlby proposed that the presence of these behaviors was evidence of a biologically-based behavioral system that serves to promote the viability of the infant by the formation of a bond with its mother. This bond, according to Bowlby, occurs within the first year of life and promotes the survival of the infant by ensuring the proximity of a protecting adult. In a broader sense, mammalian infant attachment, unlike imprinting in birds, is not a singular, instantaneous event. Infant attachment represents a constellation of various

---

27. K. H. Pribram, *Neurological Investigations of the Associative Structure of Memory*, 19 CLIN. NEUROSURGERY 397 (1972).

28. Charles A. Nelson, *The Ontogeny of Human Memory: A Cognitive Neuroscience Perspective*, 31 DEVELOPMENTAL PSYCHOL. 723 (1995).

29. J. P. Herman et al., *Neuronal Circuit Regulation of the Hypothalamo-Pituitary-Adrenocortical Stress Axis*, 10 CRITICAL REV. NEUROBIOLOGY 371 (1996).

30. CHARLES DARWIN, THE EXPRESSION OF THE EMOTIONS IN MAN AND ANIMALS (1872).

31. JAMES BOWLBY, ATTACHMENT, VOL. I (2d ed. 1983).

behavioral-physiological interactions that begin prenatally and continue to evolve postnatally.[32] In this view, from the first day of life, mother and infant are participating in a vital exchange of signals that will have crucial implications for neurodevelopment and, hence, for the nature and capacities of the adult that the infant will become. From the earliest encounter, the caregiver is participating in the regulation of the homeostatic state and the neurodevelopment of the infant with whom she is engaging.

Neurophysiologically, human attachment is believed to rely heavily on the hormone oxytocin and the neural structures with which it interacts. Oxytocin is produced in the hypothalamus and released into the bloodstream through axonal terminals in the pituitary gland. Research has demonstrated the importance of oxytocin in complex forms of social memory such as offspring recognition and pair bonding[33]. It is thought that social memory is highly reliant upon the expression of oxytocin receptors in the nucleus accumbens, a portion of the caudate nucleus previously noted for its role in reward and learning.

All mammals are perpetually dependent upon the synchronous exchange of emotion with others for stability. Early life, however, represents an important period during which input heavily influences and shapes the organism. Amini and colleagues[34] review a great deal of evidence supporting the hypothesis that human infants are equipped with a functional memory system at birth (well before the capacity for explicit memory of events and concepts is present) that is most adequately suited for implicit-type learning. Implicit memory, which is paramount in the function of emotion and attachment, has been described as being both functionally and structurally more archaic than other types of memory. This type of memory describes skills and "automatic" operations that are not stored with respect to time or place. The human organism is capable of demonstrating long-lasting changes in behavior in response to information and experiences that have no conscious representation. This system is able to preserve information that is not available for conscious recollection or awareness, but that is still able to create enduring and observable changes in behavior[35]. The underlying patterns and regularities in the attachment relationship are thus detected, extracted, encoded, and stored. In this manner the growing infant collects knowledge regarding what relationships are like, how they are conducted,

---

32. Thomas R. Insel, *A Neurobiological Basis of Social Attachment*, 154 AM. J. PSYCHIATRY 726 (1997).

33. Isadora F. Bielsky et al., *Profound Impairment in Social Recognition and Reduction in Anxiety-Like Behavior in Vasopressin V1a Receptor Knockout Mice*, 29 NEUROPSYCHOPHARMACOLOGY 483 (2004).

34. F. Amini, et al., *Affect, Attachment, Memory: Contributions Toward Psychobiologic Integration*, 1996 PSYCHIATRY 59 (1996).

35. B. Milner et al., *Further analysis of the Hippocampal Amnesia Syndrome: 14-year follow-up study of H.M.* 6 NEUROPSYCHOLOGIA 215 (1968).

and according to which "rules" behavior is regulated. However, because the operative memory system is implicit, knowledge is acquired in the form of generalizations and rules are extracted from experience, and it later operates to influence behavior in an unthinking, reflexive manner. In a process that may be somewhat analogous to the learning of motor skills, people proceed in later life to enact attachments in accordance with "rules" or prototypes they have extracted based on their prior experiences. The memory of the attachment relationship is an enduring neural structure that exerts a significant influence on emotional behavior related to attachment behavior.

The successful development of a human infant relies critically on his ability to create implicit memories for emotional information over time. The infant's gradual internalization of the emotionally laden interchange with his surroundings and his caretaker organizes and determines the structure and function of neurobehavioral systems, as well as the psychology of the child's mind; both features are fundamentally intertwined. The relationship between emotion and memory is a reciprocal one, in which the character and development of emotion is as much influenced by memory processes as these processes are influenced by emotion. More precisely, emotional development is the process by which children learn to recognize, identify, and communicate affective states. Extreme emotional experiences are thought to influence an individual's interpretation and reaction to affective information.[36] These well-documented effects of experience demonstrate that emotion and memory are intimately related. Furthermore, this relationship may involve neurophysiological functioning that is affected by both genetics and environmental events. Cicchetti and Tucker argue that brain function and development are governed primarily by one's active strivings for self-organization.[37] As a result, portions of brain development that involve self-organization may be particularly sensitive to environmental influences at certain life stages. The implication inherent in this argument is that neural development may be uniquely goal oriented. Depending upon one's experiences, neural development may proceed to incorporate specific pathways intended to facilitate behavior that is uniquely adaptive.

B. Infancy and Early Childhood

The primary role of emotion during infancy is to facilitate communication with attachment figures. During infancy, learning is based almost exclusively on the implicit memory system. Infants do not possess spoken language, advanced reasoning abilities, or great aptitude for explicit memory. The reason for this is

36. Christina Heim & Charles B. Nemeroff, *The Role of Childhood Trauma in the Neurobiology of Mood and Anxiety Disorders: Preclinical and Clinical Studies*, 49 BIOL PSYCHIATRY 1023 (2001).

37. Dante Cicchetti & D. Tucker, *Development and Self-Regulatory Structures of the Mind*, 6 DEV. PSYCHOPATHOL.] 533 (1994).

simple: not only do infants not need these skills, but these processes would very likely interfere with learning things that are important to learn in infancy. Imagine the inefficiency in learning how to drink from a bottle by remembering the specific bottle, what your caregiver was wearing, what time of day it was, and so on. These explicit features are rarely consistent, but the idea of where to suck from and how to hold the bottle remain constant and therefore are the important lessons (procedures) to retain.[38]

During infancy, behavioral outcomes are guided by emotionally laden implicit memory, most of which is the product of conditioning. Conditioning describes the process by which the organism learns to associate specific stimuli with specific responses. This process produces virtually all of infant behavior. In the case of desired behavior, parents are able to impart an aversive (or rewarding) sensory response to certain infant behavior that will influence the likelihood of the behavior reoccurring. For example, if an infant bites the mother's nipple while nursing, the mother is likely to respond by abruptly removing the nipple from the infant's mouth, displaying an angry face, and perhaps delivering a sharp "No!"; all three of these events are aversive to an infant. In this example, the infant is neither able to reflect on past experience or potential outcomes of biting, and therefore has no reason to not bite. Once the infant is able to associate his actions with concomitant outcomes (i.e., punishment or smiles and coos in response to desirable nursing behavior), it becomes possible to shape his behavior. Conditioning in infants has been demonstrated empirically with infants as young as four months of age.[39] This basic understanding—that others may impose an emotionally salient, sensory-based consequence in response to behavior—forms the foundation of human attachment and the scaffolding for social learning.

As a result of this early learning system, children's first behaviors are based on the avoidance of punishment and the seeking of reward (such as a smile or comforting embrace). Parents (or caretakers) exclusively supply the rules of the world, and there is no questioning of these rules. At this point in human development, a conditioned fear response looks much like it does in most animals. Upon perceiving a disapproving "No or "Stop" from the caretaker, the child's amygdala will send a signal to the PAG to freeze and await further instruction. Infants and toddlers follow their parent's instructions without conscious reasoning; they do so because they have come to associate their parents' emotional displeasure with a personally aversive outcome. This conditioning also enables the child to orient his attention toward the caretaker and await additional instruction. Again, this authority is highly functional, as the infant benefits from the caretaker's experience and care without interference from the child's potentially immature reasoning, which is not able to see the larger context of decisions or to contemplate

---

38. MERLIN DONALD, ORIGINS OF THE MODERN MIND (1991).

39. Carolyn Rovee-Collier, *Dissociations in Infant Memory: Rethinking the Development of Implicit and Explicit Memory*, 104 PSYCHOL. REV. 467 (1997).

long-term outcomes. Finally, these conditioned emotional exchanges between parent and child are remarkably enduring. For example, most adults acknowledge having strong emotional and physiological responses to warm or disparaging facial expressions from their parents well into their own adult years.[40]

The next important gain in emotional reasoning takes place following the emergence of the child's ability to reflect on the past and to integrate past and present. In the toddler years, the infant enters a new phase of development, whichsome have called the separation/individuation phase.[41] These years are marked by the full maturation of the perceptual and motor systems. The child also makes great strides in the development of cognition, memory (especially representational memory), and language. With increased perceptual and motor skills, the child becomes able to turn his attention away from the attachment relationship toward an active interest in the external environment. The child experiences various states of elation and considerable pleasure in mastery by using this increased autonomy to effectively negotiate the new world and discover new abilities. Emergence of the advances described above requires that individuals be capable of modifying their present behavior based on either past experience or environmental response (most often that of the parent or caretaker). At this point, children are able to regulate many aspects of their behavior and are increasingly aware that they may be responsible for acts that cause harm to others. Improvements in children's ability to remember and integrate experiences, as well as better modulate their own behavior, result from improvements in the neural architecture supporting executive function. The term "executive function" has been used to define complex cognitive processing requiring the flexible coordination of several subprocesses to achieve a particular goal.[42] When these systems break down or are immature, behavior is poorly controlled, disjointed, and disinhibited.[43] The structure and function of the frontal lobes are intimately tied to executive processes. There is a growing body of literature that suggests one way in which the frontal cortex may enable executive function is by flexibly coordinating with other cortical and subcortical regions. This is not surprising given the fact that the prefrontal cortex has been demonstrated to have reciprocal connections with nearly every part of the brain.[44]

---

40. Debra Umberson, *Relationships Between Adult Children and Their Parents: Psychological Consequences for Both Generations*, 54 J. MARRIAGE FAM. 664 (1992).

41. Margaret S. Mahler, *On the Current Status of the Infantile Neurosis*, 23 J. AM. PSYCHOANALYTIC ASS'N 327 (1975).

42. Shintaro Funahashi, *Neuronal Mechanisms of Executive Control By the Prefrontal Cortex*, 39 NEUROSCI RES. 147 (2001).

43. For a review, *see* ELLIOT, *supra* note 24.

44. M. Petrides & D. N. Pandya, *Comparative Cytoarchitectonic Analysis of the Human and the Macaque Ventrolateral Prefrontal Cortex and Corticocortical Connection Patterns in the Monkey*, 16 EUR. J. NEUROSCIENCE 291 (2002).

The ability to shift perspective and appreciate the experiences of others is critical to the emergence of empathy, theory of mind, and deception. Basic empathy, the ability to infer the most basic information about others states (usually as a function of the child's own experience), is known to emerge sometime around the second birthday. In a classic study, Jerome Kagan allowed children about two years old to play with a pair of ski goggles that had been modified to make the lenses opaque. As a result the children were not able to see clearly while wearing them. When a child grew bored with the goggles, the attending parent would pick up the goggles and put them on. Without any cue from the parent, the child would begin to lead the parent around, behaving in a manner consistent with the idea that the child was aware that the parent was not able to see clearly.[45] The emergence of this ability is thought to rely on the child's improvement in frontal lobe–based memory function. The child is able to remember his own experience for a short time, and keep it in mind while simultaneously observing the parent. In a miraculous feat of frontal lobe coordination, the child is able to transfer his own sensory experience to another person. The fact that not being able to see might have engendered slightly elevated levels of emotion only serves to strengthen the memory by involving limbic systems as well as frontal systems. This most basic form of empathy—of understanding the perceptual state of another—sets the stage for the emergence of theory of mind, between the second and third year of life, which similarly requires knowledge of the perceptions of others, but in addition requires an understanding of their thoughts and feelings. Importantly, theory of mind allows children to realize that their thoughts are unique and not identical to, or available to, those around them. As a result, children come to understand that others have beliefs, desires, and intentions of which they may be completely unaware. Perhaps the most readily obtainable index of theory of mind ability is deception. Prior to three years of age (on average) children will rarely attempt to deceive their caretakers, even if the caretaker was not present at the time of a transgression. At this point in development, children still believe that adults are omnipotent. That children become capable of deceiving their caretakers serves as compelling evidence of cognitive advancement[46] and again suggests improvements in executive function and concomitant frontal lobe maturation. No sooner has this ability emerged, however, than caretakers impose a new set of standards for children to learn, which take their cognitive and emotional development into account.

The toddler years are characterized by great strides in cognitive development. The child develops the capacity for genuine mental representations: flexible,

---

45. Jerome Kagan, The Nature of the Child (1984).

46. Charles V. Ford et al., *Lies and Liars: Psychiatric Aspects of Prevarication*, 145 Am. J. Psychiatry 554 (1988).

symbolic representations as opposed to more rudimentary schemas.[47] The capacity for symbolic representation sets the stage for the integration and differentiation of the representational world and the development of an organized representation for the psychological sense of self.[48] During this phase, the heretofore relatively autonomous lines of affective and representational development become integrated. From this point in development and thereafter, affective states become associated with the inner experience of self and object representations. At around five years of age, children become aware that their prior actions could have been modified, and this realization forms the foundation of the emotional experience of guilt.[49] Guilt at this stage, however, is fundamentally different from that experienced by most adults (which will be reviewed below). "Guilt" associated with transgressions at this age is a cognitive awareness, following a violation of internalized standards that triggers the previously acquired conditioned fear response.

The emergent complex constellations of affective states and cognitive representations of experiences, however, remain primarily affective in nature. During this time, affective experience undergoes a change in function. Affect now functions not only as a response to external stimulation or as communication with the caregiver, but also as a signal for the ongoing changes within the representational world. Certain constellations of internal self-representations, object representations, or both may become activated or deactivated in particular situations. The changes in affective experiences correspond to shifts in internal representations as much as to shifts in external stimulation. In this sense, affective states become partially separated from external stimulation and interactions with others with whom they were originally associated. These developmental improvements in cognition precipitate a new class of emotions called self-conscious emotions.

Self-conscious emotions are a set of complex emotions that emerge relatively late in development and require certain cognitive abilities for their elicitation.[50] Whereas the primary emotions that appear early, such as joy, sadness, fear, and anger, have received considerable attention, the later-appearing self-conscious emotions have received relatively little attention. There are likely many reasons for this. One reason may be that self-conscious emotions cannot be described solely by examining a particular set of facial movements; they necessitate the observation of bodily action more than facial cues.[51] The elicitation of self-conscious emotions

---

47. Stanley I. Greenspan & Reginald S. Lourie, *Developmental Structuralist Approach to the Classification of Adaptive and Pathologic Personality Organizations: Infancy and Early Childhood*, 138 AM. J. PSYCHIATRY 725 (1981).

48. HEINZ KOHUT, THE ANALYSIS OF THE SELF (1971).

49. *See* KAGAN, *supra* note 45.

50. MICHAEL LEWIS, HANDBOOK OF EMOTIONS (2d ed. 2004).

51. *See* DARWIN, *supra* note 30.

involves elaborate cognitive processes that have, at their heart, the notion of self. It is the way we think or what we think that becomes the elicitor of pride, shame, guilt, or embarrassment.

Darwin not only described the basic, primary—or early—emotions, but also theorized about self-conscious emotions. Darwin saw these later emotions as involving the self. For example, he believed that blushing was caused by how we appear to others, "the thinking about others, thinking of us . . . excites a blush" (p. 325). Darwin repeatedly emphasized the idea that these emotions were qualitatively unique, in that they relied exclusively on the opinion of others, regardless of the valence of that opinion. This requirement also indicates something special about the cognitive processes that contribute to the formation of self-conscious emotions, because they require a cognitive awareness of not only the existence of the thoughts of others, but also the ability to speculate regarding the contents of these thoughts. The reliance upon additional cognitive processes for the generation of self-conscious emotions also distinguishes them from primary emotions in terms of their neurophysiology. Many researchers, including Darwin, have described the primary emotions as being "hardwired" or genetically determined, but the number of these must remain relatively small. These are the universal emotions that are consistent across cultures and are believed to derive from basic human instincts or propensities.[52] In this way, primary emotions are a bit like primary colors, in that by varying the combinations and intensities the entire spectrum can be created. To have these more complex and subtle emotions cemented in our genetic code or neurophysiology would limit the capacity for learning and plasticity that make us unique as humans. That is why their appearance, both behaviorally and in terms of the brain structures that enable them, is the work of development. The emergence of self-conscious emotion closely parallels the changes in neural physiology described in the previous section. In addition to requiring extensive cognitive and emotional awareness of self, the emergence of self-conscious emotion also relies on social feedback.

When children are young, parents serve as the primary source of social and emotional feedback. Parents and caretakers create and reinforce desirable and undesirable behavior. Furthermore, they act as the authority that oversees the development of an individual's ethical reasoning. In many ways, parents can be conceptualized as "external frontal lobes" for their children, helping to interpret environmental demands and to construct and execute appropriate responses. Given the behavioral consequences of having an immature frontal cortex, parents subsume a number of frontal functions by instructing a child in the absence of his own capacity for abstract reasoning. Parents attempt to maintain control of where and with whom a child goes in order to minimize behavioral

---

52. Ralph Adolphs, *Neural Systems for Recognizing Emotion*, 12 CURR. OPIN. NEUROBIOLOGY 169 (2002).

transgressions in the absence of the child's ability to make good decisions. Importantly, parents also provide feedback that allows the child to modify his behavior. However, total memory capacity during this phase of development is unstable, so the emerging organization of representations is still vulnerable to fragmentation in response to the contingencies associated with this developmental period.[53] The next significant advance in development takes place during adolescence when abstract thought enables an individual to envision and anticipate situations that they have not directly experienced. This is also a time in which social cognition takes center stage and the role of behavioral dictator shifts from primarily parent to primarily peer.[54]

Adolescence marks the transition from concrete operational thinking to formal operational thinking.[55] The hallmark of adolescent cognition is the qualitative change that adolescent thinking undergoes. Their thought becomes more abstract, logical, and idealistic. Adolescents are more capable of examining their own thoughts, others' thoughts, and what others are thinking about them. In addition, adolescents are much more likely than their younger counterparts to interpret and monitor the world around them. These changes suggest that the primary change in adolescent cognition is a dramatic improvement in the ability to think and reason in the abstract. Piaget believed that adolescents are no longer limited to actual, concrete experiences as anchors for thought. They can cognitively generate make-believe situations, events that are entirely hypothetical possibilities, or strictly abstract propositions. The primary gain in adolescent cognition is that in addition to being able to generate abstract thought, they are able to reason about the products of their cognition. This "thinking about thinking" forms the foundation for both metacognition and introspection.

Adolescent thought emerges in phases. In the first phase, the increased ability to think hypothetically produces unconstrained thoughts with unlimited possibilities. In fact, early adolescent thought often disregards the constraints of reality.[56] During the later phases, adolescents learn to better regulate their thoughts, measuring the products of their reasoning against experience and imposing monitoring or inhibitory cognitions when appropriate. By late adolescence, many individuals are able to reason in ways that resemble adults. However, it is clear that the emergence of this ability depends in great part on experience and therefore does not appear across all situational domains simultaneously. Simply put, adult-like thought is more likely to be used in areas where adolescents

---

53. B. Bradford Brown et al., *Parenting Practices and Peer Group Affiliation in Adolescence.* 64 CHILD DEV. 467 (1993).

54. J. Lawrence & John H. Taylor, *Family Interactions and the Development of Moral Reasoning,* 62 CHILD DEV. 264 (1991).

55. JEAN PIAGET, THE CONSTRUCTION OF REALITY IN THE CHILD (1954).

56. John M. Broughton, *Criticism of the Developmental Approach to Morality,* 8 CATALOG OF SELECTED DOCUMENTS IN PSYCHOL. 82 (1975).

have the most experience and knowledge.[57] During development, adolescents acquire elaborate knowledge through extensive experience and practice in multiple settings (e.g., home, school, sports environment). The development of expertise in different domains of life bolsters high-level, developmentally mature-looking thought. Experience and the ability to generalize about it give older adolescents two important improvements in reasoning ability. Greater experience and an improved system for organizing and retrieving the memories of experience enable the adolescent to recall and apply a greater number of previous experiences to new situations. Additionally, an increased ability to abstract and generalize may allow adolescents to reason about a situation that they have not directly experienced. Improvements in cognition result largely from synergistic maturation in working memory capacity, selective attention, error detection, and inhibition, all of which have been shown to improve with maturational changes in brain structure and function.

Perhaps the most consistently reported finding associated with adolescent brain development is the decrease of gray matter and the increase of white matter throughout the cortex, most significantly within the frontal cortex.[58] The decline of gray matter in the prefrontal cortex in adolescence has been taken to be a marker of neural maturation as a result of synaptic pruning.[59] This decrease in synaptic density during adolescence coincides with the emergence of newly integrated cognitive and emotional phenomena. The secondary process that is taking place during this time is the fortification of synaptic connections that will remain into adulthood. There has been further speculation that this "use it or loose it" process may represent the behavioral and, ultimately, physiological suppression of immature behaviors that have become obsolete due to the novel demands of young adulthood.[60] One can imagine that a response to a particular event in the environment will be potentiated by repeated exposure and subsequent strengthening of the relation between the event and the generation of the appropriate response. The delayed maturation of this brain region allows neural and behavioral plasticity, which in turn enables the individual to adapt to the particular demands of their unique environment.

---

57. Susan Carey, *Are Children Fundamentally Different Kinds of Thinkers and Learners Than Adults?* in COGNITIVE DEVELOPMENT TO ADOLESCENCE (Ken Richardson & Sue Sheldon, eds., 1988).

58. Jay N. Giedd et al., 2 *Brain Development During Childhood and Adolescence: A Longitudinal MRI Study*, NAT NEUROSCI 861–863 (1999); Elizabeth R. Sowell et al., *Localizing Age-Related Changes in Brain Structure Between Childhood and Adolescence Using Statistical Parametric Mapping*, 9 NEUROIMAGE 587 (1999).

59. Jean-Pierre Bourgeois et al., *Synaptogenesis in the Prefrontal Cortex of Rhesus Monkeys*, 4 CEREB CORTEX 78 (1994); Martin P. Paulus et al., *Increased Activation in the Right Insula During Risk-Taking Decision Making Is Related to Harm Avoidance and Neuroticism*, 19 NEUROIMAGE 1439 (2003).

60. B. J. Casey et al., *Structural and Functional Brain Development and Its Relation to Cognitive Development*, 54 BIOL. PSYCHOL. 241 (2000).

The work of Casey and colleagues has revealed a functional consequence of decreasing gray matter in adolescence that consistently demonstrates an increased volume of cortical activity in younger adolescents who perform *less well* on tasks of cognitive control and attentional modulation. This pattern of greater brain activity in children relative to adults is suggestive of a gradual decrease in the brain tissue required to perform the task. Many researchers have documented that while there are age-related decreases in gray matter in the prefrontal cortex, the overall cortical volume does not change significantly. Not surprisingly, the overall cortical volume remains stable due to simultaneous increases in white matter volume that are equally important for brain development. The observed increase in frontal white matter observed during adolescence is the result of increased axonal myelination. Myelin is the fatty sheath that covers and insulates the neural wires (axons) of the brain. It has been well established that myelination has a direct impact on the speed and efficiency of neural processing. At the level of the neuron, increased myelination leads to increased action potential propagation speed and reduced signal attenuation. At a macroscopic level this type of maturation facilitates synchrony and coordination, both regionally and across the whole brain.

One specific frontal region within which increases in myelination have been observed is the anterior cingulate cortex,[61] an area known for its prominent role in the mediation and control of emotional, attentional, motivational, social, and cognitive behaviors.[62] A significant positive relationship between age and total anterior cingulate volume (which has been attributed to increases in white matter) has been well documented.[63] It is thought that this relationship may reflect improved cortical-cortical and cortical-subcortical coordination. The observed projections from both the cortical and subcortical regions to the cingulate in adult subjects are known to contribute to the coordination and regulation of cognitive and emotional processes. A critical question with regard to human development has been the exact developmental course of these projections. Activity of the dorsal portion of the anterior cingulate cortex has been shown to play a crucial role in autonomic control and the conscious interpretation of somatic state. In addition, maturation of the dorsal anterior cingulate cortex has been consistently related to self-control and behavioral inhibition.[64] The dorsal anterior cingulate may be an important center for the creation of second-order

---

61. Craig M. Bennett & Abigail A. Baird, *Anatomical Changes in the Emerging Adult Brain: A Voxel-Based Morphometry Study*, 27 HUM. BRAIN MAPP. 1031 (2006).

62. Brent A. Vogt et al., *Functional Heterogeneity in Cingulated Cortex: The Anterior Executive and Posterior Evaluative Regions*, 2 CEREB. CORTEX 435 (1992).

63. B. J. Casey et al., *The Role of the Anterior Cingulate in Automatic and Controlled Processes: A Developmental Neuroanatomical Study*, 30 DEV. PSYCHOBIOL 61 (1997).

64. Yoshikazu Isomura & Masahiko Takada, *Neural Mechanisms of Versatile Functions in Primate Anterior Cingulate Cortex*, 15 REV. NEUROSCIENCE 279 (2004).

representations of body state. Second-order representations are the product of integrating first-order sensory information from insular and somatosensory cortices with cognitive and contextual information available to the cingulate. Critchley and colleagues[65] found that the right anterior cingulate and the left posterior cingulate were key areas for the creation of second-order representations. Finally, the anterior cingulate is believed to play a specific executive role in the integration of autonomic responses with behavioral effort.[66]

The neural maturation described above sets the stage for the integration of emotion and cognition, which is fundamental not only to adult decision making, but also to the formation of adult-like social attachments. The adolescent has the capacity to discern future feelings and to make subtle distinctions regarding expressed emotion. Moreover, affective states become integrated with formal thought operations. The development that takes place in adolescence, namely the initial integration of visceral emotion with social cognition, is essential for fully developed ethical reasoning that functions preemptively, with minimal cognitive effort. This integration will undergo further development, largely as a function of social learning. During adolescence emotion is translocated from the self to self-in-relationship, a domain where the complex unfolding of emotional states in both the self and other can be mutually recognized.

IV. THE IMPORTANCE OF PEERS

Part of leaning how to respond to environmental demands relies on knowing one's self and one's position in the world. An adolescent's self-concept changes as a function of the great strides made in both emotional and cognitive development described above. Specifically, adolescents undergo a profound change in how they perceive themselves, as individuals within multiple (often contrasting) contexts. However, being an individual does not necessarily describe much about one's specific identity or how to fit into the different domains of one's life. Teens desire validation and approval from various groups of people in their lives (e.g., parents, other family members, adults, friends, and classmates). These people all contribute to an adolescent's perception of his identity, but all have different values and expectations. The juxtaposition of these different social pressures may explain why adolescents often adopt different "selves" in different social contexts.[67]

---

65. H. D. Critchley et al., *Neuroanatomical Basis for First- and Second-Order Representations of Bodily States*, 4 NAT. NEUROSCI. 207 (2001).

66. Hugo D. Critchley et al., *Neural Systems Supporting Interoceptive Awareness*, 7 NAT. NEUROSCI. 189 (2004).

67. Susan Harter et al., *The Development of Multiple Role-Related Selves During Adolescence*, 9 DEV. PSYCHOPATHOLOGY 835 (1997).

Adolescence forever changes the interaction between parents and their children. As children mature, they must learn new social skills in order to renegotiate their relationships with family members and peers. As discussed previously, the maturation of the frontal cortex produces significant improvements in behavioral and emotional control, decision making, and, perhaps most importantly, abstract reasoning. If everything has gone according to plan, the adolescent is well on his way to being proficient at independent thought and autonomous ethical reasoning. Despite the cognitive advances that take center stage during adolescence, the actual purpose of puberty (the biological changes that underlie the sociocultural phenomenon of adolescence) remains reproduction. As teenagers develop a functionally reproductive adult body, they also develop increased interest in sex. So, while the body is preparing for this, the mind is trying to line up the combination of behaviors that will gain an individual access to potential mates. Teenagers focus more of their energy on peer groups. Within peer groups, teens learn how to talk, walk, and act around each other.[68]

Research has suggested that it is not wholly accurate to refer to this time as a switch "from" parents "to" peers. It is more precise to describe this time as one in which the parent's role changes and peers are more prominently added to the lives of adolescents. Theorists such as Piaget and Kohlberg have argued that parents have a minimal and nonspecific role in their children's ethical development, primarily because of their position of unilateral authority. Both theorists have expanded on this to say that the role of the parents and family, while not unimportant, pales in comparison to the critical contributions of peers to the adolescent's ethical development. What parental influence does offer the developing adolescent, however, is an ethical perspective forged from a great deal more experience. Because parents are more frequently operating at a higher stage of ethical reasoning than their children, they offer a consistent source from which their children can learn. Despite the fact that peers most effectively dispense the knowledge necessary to navigate specific ethical dilemmas, overarching ethical concepts are best imparted by those with higher-level ethical reasoning.[69] Much like the idea of language being best taught under the conditions of shared attention, so too is the case of ethical development. In describing the ideal conditions under which to learn language, Vygotsky examined how language develops via social interactions with significant people in a child's life[70] (this effect has been more recently replicated by Kuhl and colleagues).[71] As a

---

68. Lawrence J. Walker & et al., *Parent and Peer Contexts for Children's Moral Reasoning Development*, 71 CHILD DEV. 1033 (2003).

69. Lawrence J. Walker & John H. Taylor, *Family Interactions and the Development of Moral* Reasoning, 62 CHILD DEV. 264 (1991).

70. LEV S. VYGOTSKY, THOUGHT AND LANGUAGE (MIT Press 1986) (1934).

71. Patricia K. Kuhl et al., *Foreign-Language Experience in Infancy: Effects of Short-Term Exposure and Social Interaction on Phonetic Learning*, 22 PROC. NAT'L ACAD. SCI. 9096 (2003).

result of these meaningful exchanges, children come to internalize the linguistic components of their culture including speech patterns, written language, and other symbolic knowledge. In this way, under conventional circumstances, the development of language serves as a conduit for the construction of many forms of knowledge. Vygotsky placed a great deal of importance on the social component of learning. In this view, known as the social cognition learning model, culture teaches children not only *what* but also *how* to think. This model underscores an important point regarding social learning. Voygotsky's work has provided clear and consistent evidence that children learn best within a socially meaningful context. What is often left out of this model, however, is that in order for the social connection to be effective, the child/adolescent must "care" about the person with whom he is interacting. As vague as this description may seem, "caring," in this instance, refers to being emotionally attached. By virtue of being emotionally invested in (connected to) another, the adolescent is able to engage in the kind of meaningful exchange described above (see the section on attachment). This results in an up-regulation of arousal, which (ideally) is in proportion to the importance of the imparted information and as a result optimizes learning. For example, if a parent were to say, "You know, going swimming at the quarry is not such a great idea," delivered in a quiet monotone, with little eye contact or emotional expression, the statement will be easy to ignore. Contrast this to a middle schooler who comes rushing to a friend's locker waving her arms and shouting, "Oh my God, oh my God, the coolest guys are hanging out at the quarry after school today, we SO have to go!" This type of behavioral exchange guarantees a high-charged emotional interaction and the undivided attention and cognitive focus of one's peers. Based on these kinds of interactions, it is easy to understand how emotional investment (i.e., attachment) facilitates development of ethical reasoning.

Theorists contend that friends have *coercive* power, that is, friends give reinforcement for socially approved behaviors and punishment for noncompliance with group standards.[72] This power is wielded through discrete, subtle means of approval and reward, or disapproval, teasing, and rejection.[73] Within friend groups, this type of social feedback is probably healthy and constructive because it helps adolescents develop mature social skills (e.g., empathy, perspective taking, good listening skills). If there is anything consistent among kids who are perceived as socially potent or "popular," it is that they are good at managing their coercive power. Coercive power is achieved through a number of strategies including the manipulation both of interpersonal relationships and of the portrayal of the imagined audience (e.g., "Don't wear that, *everyone* will hate you,"

---

72. Laurence Steinberg, *Friendship and Peer Relations, in* AT THE THRESHOLD: THE DEVELOPING ADOLESCENT, 277–307 (S. S. Feldman & G. R. Elliot eds., 1990).

73. Ritch C. Savin-Williams and Thomas J. Berndt, *Motivation and Achievement, in* AT THE THRESHOLD: THE DEVELOPING ADOLESCENT, 277–307 (S. S. Feldman & G. R. Elliot eds., 1990).

or, conversely, "*Everyone* thought you were awesome in yesterday's game").[74] Given the attention paid to peers, it is likely that this coercive power exerts its irresistible influence via the limbic system, making adolescents "feel" that peer-related behaviors are critical to their survival. This basic emotional influence could mean that peers inspire teammates to work harder in practice, encourage other members of the orchestra to practice their instruments, or challenge others to try out a new activity. Conversely, it could mean that they pressure their friends into sneaking out, drinking alcohol, or participating in other dangerous risk-taking behaviors.

V. THE EMERGING ADULT

In terms of acquiring an ethical sense, adolescence and early adulthood represent an extended "practice time." While adolescents share responsibility for the regulation of their behavior with their external frontal lobes (i.e., their caretakers), they are increasing able to integrate their own cognitive and emotional processes and learn from the consequences of their decisions. As they mature, adolescents' own frontal systems become increasingly autonomous and able to effectively regulate, or converse with, their limbic systems (which by this point is very well coordinated with the individual's brain stem and HPA axis). As young adults emerges from adolescence, their decision-making processes begin to approximate those observed among mature individuals.

Consistent with the cognitive demands of everyday reasoning, lesion studies implicate the dorsolateral prefrontal cortex (DLPFC) as being essential for everyday reasoning.[75] In addition, research by a number of cognitive neuroscientists examining both inductive reasoning[76] and deductive reasoning[77] have underscored the dominant role of the dorsolateral prefrontal cortex in tasks that demand high-level reasoning. More recently, Goel and Dolan[78] demonstrated

---

74. David Elkind, *Egocentrism in Adolescence*, 38 CHILD DEV. 1025 (1967).

75. Tim Shallice & Paul Burgess, *Deficits in Strategy Application Following Frontal Lobe Damage in Man*, 114 BRAIN 727 (1991); Stuss & Alexander, *supra* note 24.

76. Vinod Goel & Raymond J. Dolan, *Anatomical Segregation of Component Processes in an Inductive Inference Task*, 12 J. COGN. NEUROSCI. 110 (2000); Carol A. Seger et al., *Hemispheric Asymmetries and Individual Differences in Visual Concept Learning as Measured by Functional MRI*. 38 NEUROPSYCHOLOGIA 1316 (2000).

77. Vinod Goel et al., *Neuroanatomical Correlates of Human* Reasoning, 10 J. COGNI NEUROSCI 293 (1998.); Lawrence M. Parsons & Daniel Osherson, *New Evidence for Distinct Right and Left Brain Systems for Deductive versus Probabilistic Reasoning*, 11 CEREB CORTEX 954 (2001); Daniel Osherson et al., *Distinct Brain Loci in Deductive Versus Probabilistic Reasoning*, 36 NEUROPSYCHOLOGIA 369 (1998).

78. Vinod Goel & Raymond J. Dolan, *Differential Involvement of Left Prefrontal Cortex in Inductive and Deductive Reasoning*, 93 COGNITION 109 (2004).

preferential DLPFC activity during an inductive reasoning task (relative to a task that required deductive reasoning). Inductive reasoning is more sensitive to background knowledge rather than logical form, and it is essential for knowing which ideas generalize and which do not. The increased activity in the dorsolateral prefrontal cortex may thus be due to use of world knowledge in the generation and evaluation of hypotheses,[79] which is the basis of inductive reasoning.

Recent work has added to this idea by emphasizing the role that emotional experience plays in decision making. Once individuals are capable of higher-order abstraction of emotion, they are capable of using abstract emotional information to inform decision making and other forms of higher cognition. While other animals can anticipate an emotional response based on previous experience, only humans can abstractly combine estimates of future emotional state with rational decision-making processes. The somatic marker hypothesis[80] offers that external or internal stimuli are capable of creating a specific emotional state that is represented within both the brain and the body (soma). Further, this somatic state becomes quickly and indelibly associated with the specific stimuli that initiated the body state. These markers function to guide behavior by biasing selection toward actions that result in pleasurable somatic markers (while avoiding actions resulting in aversive somatic markers). This hypothesis additionally argues that emotional states associated with prior decision outcomes are used to guide future decisions based on the potential emotional (somatic) consequence. For example, when a choice followed by a bad outcome occurs, an emotional reaction becomes associated with that choice. Once the emotional reaction is sufficiently well established, the reaction occurs before a choice is made. In other words, anticipation of a potentially bad outcome prevents the bad choice and leads, instead, to a more beneficial choice. Thus somatic anticipation (markers) of good and bad options facilitates optimal decision making. In summary, according to the somatic marker hypothesis, optimal decision making is not simply the result of rational, cognitive calculation of gains and losses but, rather, is based on the good or bad emotional reactions to prior outcomes of choices. In essence, rational choice is guided by emotional reactions that bias decision making. Over time, somatic markers help to reduce the complexity of decision making by providing a "gut" feeling that does not require effortful cognition.[81]

Within the context of the somatic marker hypothesis, the insula has been described as critical for the initial representation as well as the reenactment of

---

79. Jordan Grafman, *The Structured Event Complex and the Human Prefrontal Cortex*, in THE FRONTAL LOBES (D. T. Stuss & R. T. Knight eds., 2002).

80. Antonio R. Damasio, *The Somatic Marker Hypothesis and the Possible Functions of the Prefrontal Cortex*, 351 PHIL. TRANSACTIONS: BIOL. SCI. 1413 (1996).

81. John M. Hinson et al., *Somatic Markers, Working Memory, and Decision Making*, 2 COGNITIVE, AFFECTIVE & BEHAV. NEUROSCIENCE (2002).

somatic markers.[82] In this view, increased activation in the insula also signals the intensity of the somatic state. The insula is of particular interest in this regard because of its well-known role in the perception of disgust. A number of studies have demonstrated a consistent relation between the human emotion disgust and the subjective body state that accompanies insular activity. It is thought that activity in the insula signals distress in the central viscera, and that the emotion of disgust has evolved to reside amid the neural circuitry used to learn food aversions (i.e., the hardware that makes you intensely avoid any food that has ever made you sick). Disgust is a universal human emotion tied to a set of nonverbal behaviors that clearly and rapidly convey a visceral, repulsive sensation. This has been most closely studied through the conditioned taste aversion paradigm in nonhuman species.[83] In humans, the sensation of disgust discourages approach and predicts poison, mutilation, sickness, or contamination. It has been established that the capacity to recognize something noxious as disgusting is a simple survival mechanism whose social transmission helps the perceiver avoid potential harm. It can be argued that the way in which shame and guilt are nonverbally communicated is nearly identical to the expression of disgust. More specifically, nonverbal behaviors are believed to communicate the undesirability of certain objects (e.g., rotten food) or behaviors (e.g., hitting a child on the playground) to an individual before the individual has performed his own cognitive appraisal of why something may be disgusting or shameful. This saves a great deal of the perceiver's time. The social signal of disgust is remarkably potent because of the fundamental necessity to avoid noxious agents. In most animals, a single exposure to a toxic substance (in a nonlethal dose) is enough to produce a strong and extremely enduring avoidance of that substance. In addition to similar behavioral signals, disgust and guilt also rely on virtually identical neural hardware, namely the amygdala and the anterior insula.[84] Evidence supporting this argument comes from literature that has relied primarily on visual presentation of disgust-invoking stimuli[85] and guilt-invoking sentences or autobiographical recall.[86] Collectively, these studies have consistently demonstrated that activity within the anterior insula is closely related to feelings of both disgust and guilt.

82. A. Bechara, *Neurobiology of Decision-Making: Risk and Reward*, 6 SEMINARS CLINICAL NEUROPSYCHIATRY 205 (2001).

83. J. Garcia & R. A. Koelling, *A Comparison of Aversions Induced By X-Rays, Toxins, and Drugs in the Rat*, 7 RADIATION RES. SUPPLEMENT 439 (1967).

84. Bruno Wicker et al., *Both of Us Disgusted in My Insula: The Common Neural Basis of Seeing and Feeling Disgust*. 40 NEURON 655 (2003).

85. Pierre Krolak-Salmon et al., *An Attention Modulated Response to Disgust in Human Ventral Anterior Insula*, 53 ANN OF NEUROL 446 (2003); P. Wright et al., *Disgust and the Insula: fMRI Responses to Pictures of Mutilation and Contamination*, 15 NEUROREPORT 2347 (2004).

86. Lisa M. Shin et al., *Activation of Anterior Paralimbic Structures During Guilt-Related Script-Driven Imagery*, 48 BIOL PSYCHIATRY 43 (2000); Daniel A. Fitzgerald et al., *Neural*

Despite the strong similarity that disgust and guilt share, there is one way in which they differ considerably. Upon close examination of the two, it becomes evident that disgust is inherent to certain sensory perceptions whereas guilt regarding one's actions is learned from active participation in social exchanges. Guilt is experienced in relation to another person's emotional state and in association with a particular event. One of the challenges in studying guilt with the tools of neuroimaging is the likelihood that experiences provoking guilt also incite other negative emotions—anxiety being one of the more likely candidates—that are associated with insular activation.[87] The experience of guilt conceptually presupposes self-awareness and counterfactual reasoning, and, on a more basic level, an awareness of another person's feelings and potential emotional reactions (empathy). Finally, guilt has been associated with a desire to compensate others and engage in self-punishment.[88] Taken together the evidence described above suggests that the relatively complex emotion of guilt has, over evolutionary time, co-opted the neural hardware that enables enduring avoidance of noxious stimuli, following just a single experience. This primary response has been elaborated on in the social realm, where the very same social signals that reduce the probability of an individual ingesting toxic substances are also able to significantly reduce the chances of an individual violating an important social norm. Finally, activity within the insula is associated with aversive somatic markers and therefore, a relatively large activation during a decision-making situation could arguably signal a potentially aversive outcome and guide the subject to avoid the selection of an undesirable alternative.[89] This perspective has also been espoused by legal scholars:

> The effectiveness of the enforcement of moral rules depends in part on the magnitude of the moral incentives, that is on how much guilt and virtue, and admonition and praise, matter to individuals. The degree to which they matter is shaped by, and determined hand in hand with the socialization and inculcation that governs the absorption of the rules themselves.[90]

Somatic feelings of "bad behavior" are learned based on functional neural structures and informative social feedback. In an ideal developmental schema, over time learned somatic markers constitute or inform rapid automatic

---

Correlates of Internally-Generated Disgust Via Autobiographical Recall: A Functional Magnetic Resonance Imaging Investigation, 370 NEUROSCI. LETT. 91 (2004).

87. M. L. Phillips et al., *A Specific Neural Substrate for Perceiving Facial Expressions of Disgust*, 389 NATURE 495 (1997).

88. S. Berthoz et al., *Affective Response to One's Own Moral Violations*, 31 NEUROIMAGE 945 (2006).

89. Martin P. Paulus et al., *Increased Activation in the Right Insula During Risk-Taking Decision Making Is Related to Harm Avoidance and Neuroticism*, 19 NEUROIMAGE 1439 (2003).

90. SHAVELL, *supra* note 3.

responses to emotionally significant dilemmas. A developmentally constrained progression exists in the maturation of emotional decision making whereby conditioned behavior precedes explicit cognition, and through the social learning that takes place in adolescence, thoughts and behaviors become associated with emotions that, in their most evolved/mature state, produce socially appropriate behavior with relatively little cognitive influence. Autonomous high-stakes decision making requires the integration of many developmental processes, and it is heavily reliant upon not only the integrity of these processes but also the extent to which lessons learned from experience can be generalized to larger social norms.

VI. ETHICAL BEHAVIOR IN ADULTS

As a result of the developmental progression described above, evidence suggests that adults are equipped with two comingled systems that enable the production of ethical behavior. The first can be thought of as a "bottom-up" system, which relies heavily on instantaneous input from somatic markers and implicit associations that together have become automatic. The second system is based on more abstract processes and is "top-down" in nature. This system is based largely on cognitive reasoning and the ability to envision outcomes and consequences. Both systems are detailed below.

A. Bottom-Up: Primal Perfection

When it comes to keeping a person alive, few systems are better than the human amygdala and the regions with which it communicates. In developing infants this system instills the basic rules and regulations of life with their caretakers. This system, where learning begins as emotionally charged conditioning, makes very clear what is "right" or "safe" and what is "wrong" or "dangerous." By virtue of coordination between the limbic system, the HPA axis, and the brainstem, these simple associations are able to regulate infant/child behavior and form a foundation for important socially grounded heuristics. These lessons, as well as the process by which they are laid down, provide the basis for more complex learning. Perhaps the most obvious example of this involves harming conspecifics. Quite simply, the vast majority of adults do not harm members of their own species. There are arguably a number of possible deterrents, but among the first, most salient, and most intense is an old, amygdala-mediated memory that makes committing such acts highly emotionally aversive. As the individual matures, this system is built upon, mainly through the addition of the somatic marker, which is primarily grounded in the connectivity of the insular cortex. As the insula becomes increasingly involved in decision making, an important shift occurs whereby the emotion of guilt shifts from being largely based on fear, to being driven by the highly aversive emotion of disgust. In doing so, the developing human preserves the fight-or-flight response for genuinely life threatening situations and comes to rely on the somatic manifestation of insular activity (i.e., disgust, repulsion, visceral distress) to inform decision making. This primitive and highly effective system remains in place throughout life and continues to inform the most primary decisions. For example, consider the behavior of gentiles who helped Jews during the World War II. On being asked why she consented to help hide Anne Frank and her family, Miep Gies answered, "My decision to help Otto [Frank, Anne's father] was because I saw no alternative." This serves as a prime example of how the more primitive emotional system is capable of overriding the "higher" system that relies on cognition to weigh the various possibilities. If Miep Geis had given greater priority to the realities of the situation, her cognitive awareness would likely have reminded her that she could be killed by the Nazis for her actions. Given that many gentiles had already met such a fate, Miep would have been wise to heed this real world warning, but her gut sense would not let her do so. The limbic system, in coordination with both the brainstem and the frontal systems, will always determine behavior in these high-stakes situations. There are many situations, however, in which the abstract abilities of the prefrontal cortex are able to mobilize the resources of the limbic system. This "top-down" approach is described below.

B. Top-Down: It's the Thought That Counts

Have you ever jumped from the second-story window of a house? No? Would you like to? Most adults would refuse this request, despite never having tried it themselves. This is a prime example of how abstract reasoning is able to generate a visceral response and in turn inform cognition about potential emotional consequence. The prefrontal cortex is able to draw on previous experiences, and by integrating them with current situational demands, generate "possible scenarios." The maturation of the prefrontal system locally, along with improvements in coordination with limbic structures, provides the hardware necessary for generating ideas about future occurrences and possible outcomes or consequences. This idea has been elegantly studied using "controlled generation" paradigms.[91]

Ochsner and Gross reviewed three basic ways in which cognitive processes can generate an emotional response. The first, and most widely studies, is the phenomenon of anticipation. In paradigms examining anticipation, participants are informed of an impending aversive event and then forced to wait for an undisclosed amount of time. In a classic report of this phenomenon,[92] participants had an electrode capable of delivering an aversive (but not painful) shock

---

91. Kevin N. Ochsner & James J. Gross, *The Cognitive Control Of Emotion*, 9 TRENDS COGNITIVE SCI. 242 (2005).

92. Elizabeth A. Phelps et al., *Activation of the Left Amygdala to a Cognitive Representation of Fear*, 4 NAT. NEUROSCI. 437 (2001).

attached to their hand while they underwent neuroimaging. Participants were told that they would be viewing a variety of shapes of different colors, but that one in particular would precede a shock being delivered to their hand. Importantly, no participant had a preexisting association with colored shapes and aversive outcomes, nor did the colored shapes possess any symbolic qualities associated with danger of any sort. Finally, and perhaps most importantly, no one was shocked, even when the warning shape was presented. Brain activity was then parsed into the time periods during which participants had viewed shapes that had no cognitive information attached to them and the periods when they had viewed the "warning" shape. Viewing warning shapes was associated with increased activity in the amygdala, the insula, and the cingulate cortex; this activity was not seen when viewing the other shapes. This study critically demonstrated that explicit, abstract, and unintuitive cognitive information can reliably produce limbic system activity that is nearly indistinguishable from that produced when participants are in actual distress. Additional investigations have examined the effect of abstract information on anticipatory reward and have shown that, in addition to the limbic regions just described, the nucleus accumbens, known to respond to rewarding, is highly active in studies of reward anticipation.[93] It has also been demonstrated that top-down influence is capable of modifying, and even overriding, previous experiences or beliefs. Two recent studies have demonstrated that stimuli not normally perceived as painful can be used to activate limbic representations of pain if the cognitive beliefs about the stimuli are modified through informational exchange.[94] Finally, Ochsner and colleagues[95] demonstrated a compelling distinction between top-down and bottom-up influence on frontal regulation of limbic activity. The investigators asked participants to either view negative/aversive images (bottom-up) or view neutral images in negative ways (top-down). The amygdala was found to be active in both conditions. Interestingly, the frontal regions (anterior cingulate, lateral prefrontal cortex, and medial prefrontal cortex) were only active in the top-down condition. The activity of these frontal regions in conjunction with the amygdala activity in response to viewing neutral images provides convincing support for the notion that cognitive processes are very capable of mobilizing limbic resources to modify behavior. What this means more practically is that humans

---

93. B. Knutson et al., *Dissociation of Reward Anticipation and Outcome with Event-Related fMRI*, 12 NEUROREPORT 3683 (2001).

94. Nobukatsu Sawamoto et al., *Expectation of Pain Enhances Responses to Nonpainful Somatosensory Stimulation in the Anterior Cingulate Cortex and Parietal Operculum/Posterior Insula: An Event-Related Functional Magnetic Resonance Imaging Study*, 20 J. NEUROSCI 7438 (2000); Alexander Ploghaus et al., *Exacerbation of Pain by Anxiety Is Associated with Activity in a Hippocampal Network*, 21 J. NEUROSCI. 9896 (2001).

95. Kevin N. Ochsner et al., *Reflecting Upon Feelings: An fMRI Study of Neural Systems Supporting the Attribution of Emotion to Self and Other*, 16 J. COGN NEUROSCI. 1746 (2004).

are able to derive emotional response, and in turn emotional information, from abstract concepts.

Together these two systems provide the means by which individuals are able to follow both obvious and abstract moral or legal ideals. In order to follow the law, you need to either *feel* that the deed you are about to commit is wrong or *think* that it is wrong. In thinking, or believing, that a particular action is wrong, frontal systems allow the individual to "feel the future," whereby frontally pro-voked and mediated amygdala, insula, and cingulate activity ensure a socially desirable outcome. What is important to highlight about the way these two sys-tems work together is that the subcortex, or emotional "gut," dictates behavioral output. The recruitment of emotional resources might come from frontal cogni-tion and may in some cases be mediated by frontal regulation, but the evolution-arily "newer" prefrontal cortex is no match biologically for the subcortically-based survival system (the limbic system and the brainstem). People follow ethical stat-utes because they fear what will happen if they do not, they feel guilty if they do not, or they feel good from following ethical statutes. Most of life's everyday deci-sions are high-stakes in nature, but in every decision that human beings make, there is a conscious (however small) avoidance of bad feeling, or motivation toward a good feeling. As a result of this highly evolved system, individuals are able to "feel the future," a process that is critical for many forms of ethical behavior. What remains is for the individual to make use of the information to enact the desired behavior. This most commonly takes the form of behavioral regulation, a pro-cess that significantly improves as the individual matures.

VII. BEHAVIORAL REGULATION

The previously described interaction between the frontal system and the limbic system clearly is critical in generating socially appropriate behavior. In predict-ing actual behavior, one more factor must be considered. Behavioral regulation is the process by which individuals come to integrate individual motivations with situational and societal constraints. Behavioral regulation improves dramatically between childhood and adolescence, and then again between adolescence and young adulthood.[96] A great deal of empirical evidence supporting these age-related improvements comes from developmental comparisons of performance on go/no-go tests, response inhibition tasks, and other batteries designed to evaluate the capacity to cognitively assess decisions before executing them as

---

96. B.J. Casey et al., *Clinical, Imaging, Lesion, and Genetic Approaches Toward a Model of Cognitive Control*, 40 DEV. PSYCHOBIOL. 237 (2001); Silvia A. Bunge & Samantha B. Wright, *Neurodevelopmental Changes in Working Memory and Cognitive Control*, 17 CURR. OPINI. NEUROBIOL. 243 (2007).

well as the efficiency of response inhibition.[97] Together, these studies have shown that humans demonstrate consistent age-related improvement in the capacity to inhibit irrelevant salient information and conform to situation-based social constraints.

Paradoxically, while adolescents closely resemble adults with regard to logical reasoning, they lag noticeably behind in terms of their relatively poor capacity to regulate impulsive decision making or to avoid involvement in high-risk activities. Adolescents have been shown to be as well *informed* as adults with regard to the consequences of their actions, suggesting that their deficits in behavioral regulation are not a result of difficulties with information processing.[98] Impulsive decision making may result in actions that carry negative long-term consequences. Impulsive actions may also be maladaptive in other ways, such as antisocial or self-destructive behaviors. Bunge and colleagues[99] revealed that children (ages 8–12) show a distinct pattern of increased neural activity in cases of successful response inhibition whereas adults do not, which implies that younger individuals need to recruit greater neural resources to accomplish adult-like behavior. Neural regions that were more active in children relative to adults included the bilateral parietal cortex, the right premotor cortex, the right globus pallidus, the bilateral middle temporal gyrus, and the bilateral occipital cortex. These data underscore the differences, in both brain and behavior, in terms of cognitive control between adults and younger individuals.

Performance on cognitive control tasks has provided a great deal of evidence highlighting the importance of ventrofrontal-striatal pathway maturation to inhibitory control.[100] The basal ganglia are also known to contribute both directly and indirectly to the regulation of cortically mediated behavior. The basal ganglia, consisting largely of inhibitory projections, are believed to have a primary role in overriding competing behaviors/cognitions during executive function tasks handled by the prefrontal cortices. Thus, Durston and colleagues place the emphasis in cognitive control not exclusively on the frontal cortex per se, but on its modulatory connectivity with the basal ganglia. Using a similar experimental paradigm, Bunge and colleagues reported that the right ventrolateral prefrontal cortex was significantly active in adults, but not among children who responded incorrectly to a go/no-go task. Children who responded correctly, however, demonstrated activity in the same ventrolateral and ventrofrontal-striatal circuitry

---

97. Sarah Durston et al., *A Neural Basis for the Development of Inhibitory Control*, 5 DEVELOPMENTAL SCI. 9 (2002).

98. Laurence Steinberg, *Risk Taking in Adolescence*, 162 CURRENT DIRECTIONS IN PSYCHOLOGICAL SCI. 55 (2007).

99. Silvia A. Bunge et al., *Immature Frontal Lobe Contributions to Cognitive Control in Children: Evidence from fMRI*, 33 NEURON 301 (2002).

100. Sarah Durston et al., *A Shift from Diffuse to Focal Cortical Activity with Development*, 9 DEVELOPMENTAL SCI. 1 (2006).

recruited by adults during the control task. Additionally, posterior activation of association cortices in children was highly correlated with adult-like responding, indicating that the prefrontal cortices are likely just one part of the maturing brain that influences response inhibition, indispensably complemented by maturational changes across the parietal cortex and the midtemporal gyrus.

Based on the extent to which the prefrontal cortex contributed to the regulation of adult behavior, the protracted myelination of the prefrontal circuits prevents most immature individuals from coordinating the projections that inhibit/regulate the nucleus accumbens (NA) in mature individuals. The NA, along with the ventral tegmental area (VTA) becomes increasingly attune to novelty and reward contingencies. The VTA sends excitatory projections to the NA that increase the individual's interest in, and response to, novel, rewarding, and therefore, motivational, stimuli. By virtue of developmental stage, this excitation takes place in the absence of the mature regulatory influence of the frontal cortices. In the course of healthy development, as adolescence wanes, activity in the VTA seems to attenuate. As a result, projections from the prefrontal cortex and the limbic region, as well as those from the more mature VTA, aid in the modulation of the NA. These projections together create a system that allows motor output (action) to be appropriately governed by the integrated influence of several regions.[101] Years of learning and experience facilitate the development of the described neural system, such that a great deal of ethical reasoning comes to rely on largely unconscious and automatic processes. These decision-making and behavioral processes that take a great deal of behavioral and neural time to mature are also vulnerable to dysfunction under a fair number of circumstances. Some of these conditions are described below.

VIII. PATHOLOGY

This chapter has devoted a great deal of space to describing how the decisions that guide everyday life are a product of the hardware (brain) and the software (experience) of human development. Given the recursive complexity of human development, missteps at different points may have very different outcomes. There are two basic categories of problems that are likely to occur early in development: those that have their origins in neurobiology (hardware) and those related to environment (software). It is important to acknowledge, of course, that by the time an individual reaches adulthood the interactions of brain and experience often make it impossible to discern the original source of pathology. In many ways a problem in childhood resembles removing a stone from a

---

101. R. Andrew Chambers, *Developmental Neurocircuitry of Motivation in Adolescence: A Critical Period of Addiction Vulnerability*, 160 AM. J. OF PSYCHIATRY 1041 (2003).

mountainside: under some conditions there is little or no consequence from this action, whereas in other scenarios this small action can set off a massive landslide.

As previously discussed, medial temporal lobe structures are functionally mature very early in life, while the human frontal cortex does not reach full functional maturity until after puberty. Therefore, it is plausible that early in development, many aspects of behavior may be regulated by medial temporal lobe structures. Furthermore, it is conceivable that during later development, frontal regions begin to exert a more powerful influence so that what were once largely survival-based "unconscious" behaviors become increasingly entwined with more "conscious" cognitive and social processes. To date, however, few studies have explored the developmental trajectory of this functional connectivity. It has been established that during adolescence there is a substantial increase in the density and myelination of projections between medial temporal regions and frontal cortices.[102] Investigations using nonhuman primates have suggested that selective aspects of normal frontal development may rely on medial temporal lobe integrity.[103] Additional studies of nonhuman primates suggests that early damage to the amygdala has a deleterious effect on later social and emotional learning and behavior, while lesions of the amygdala in adulthood do not produce the same types of behavioral impairments.[104] It is not entirely clear, though, how these findings extend to human development. It is possible that the functionality of early developing brain regions (i.e., temporal lobe structures) may serve to guide, at least in part, later developing regions (i.e., frontal cortices). Taken together, the studies above suggest a model of functional connectivity that in early life begins with medial temporal influence of the frontal cortices and later is driven by frontal regulation of medial temporal lobe structures. This is a process that takes place over many years and is the product of both preprogrammed neural development and environmental influence. Implicit in this development sequence is the assumption that the information available from the environment is not only advantageous for the individual, but also in accord with the ethical standards of that individual's society.

---

102. Francine M. et al., *Increased Interaction of Dopamine Immunoreactive Varicosities with GABA Neurons of Rat Medial Prefrontal Cortex Occurs During the Postweanling Period*, 23 SYNAPSE 237 (1996); Jeffrey L. Cummings, *Anatomic and Behavioral Aspects of Frontal-Subcortical Circuits*, 15 ANNALS NY ACAD. SCI. 769 (1995).

103. A. Bertolino et al., *Altered Development of Prefrontal Neurons in Rhesus Monkeys with Neonatal Mesial Temporo Limbic Lesions: A Proton Magnetic Resonance Spectroscopic Imaging Study*, 7 CEREB. CORTEX 740 (1997).

104. J. Bachevalier, *Memory Loss and Socio-Emotional Disturbances Following Neonatal Damage of the Limbic System in Monkeys: An Animal Model for Childhood Autism*, in ADVANCES IN PSYCHIATRY AND PSYCHOPHARMACOLOGY (C. Tamminga & S. Schulz eds., 1991).

In order for the complex transitions that take place during adolescence to go smoothly, all of the requisite building blocks must be sturdy and available for assembly. Adolescence bears some resemblance to the first group performance of an orchestra whose sections have been practicing independently for some time. If the conductor taps the music stand, raised the baton, and the horns are out of tune, or absent all together, the resultant sound will suffer. Simply put, the intense and complex transformations of adolescence rely on the integrity of the developmental processes (both behavioral and neurobiological) that have preceded it. Not surprisingly, adolescence is also a time when the chances of non-adaptive change significantly increase.

Defining pathology within a developmental context is a rather complex endeavor. Behavior that is not in accord with social norms is fairly easy to detect, but often quite difficult to explain. For the purposes of the present discussion, explanation of ethical transgressions will be divided into two general categories: "not knowing" and "knowing." Transgressions resulting from "not knowing" describe behaviors that are the result of individuals' lack of knowledge either of the expected social norm or of the full consequence of their behavior. These violations mostly likely involve problems with learning and may trace back to initial attachment issues or to general deficits regarding the coordination of emotion and cognition. It is important to note that "knowing" in this context can be either emotional or cognitive, or both. There are also instances when individuals possess sufficient knowledge of social norms as well as the potential repercussions of their actions, but are unable or unwilling to regulate their behavior. Violations of this nature are likely related to problems with behavioral regulation. Additionally, it is important to note that both types of transgressions can result from disruptions at the level of the hardware (neurobiological) or the installed software (inappropriate information from the environment), or both. Unfortunately, even when neural development and experiential learning are within normal limits, exceptional environmental circumstances can produce highly deviant behavior. As such the discussion of pathology will close with a review nonpathological conditions that produce this type of behavior, including intense psychological stress, immaturity, and different forms of intoxication.

A. Developmental Neuropathology

The first stage of ethical development requires that infants acquire the ability to pair their own actions with concomitant outcomes. These outcomes range from highly pleasurable to highly aversive, and it is through the conditioned association of the infant's behavior with sensory-based consequences that the earliest forms of learning are instantiated. Disruptions in this ability have been consistently associated with early amygdalar dysfunction and acquired psychopathy. More recently, Blair demonstrated that individuals with early amygdalar damage were not capable of learning a conditioned response based on the facial expressions of others, but showed no deficits in conditioned learning when the stimulus was a basic threat such as bared teeth.[105] Disruptions of this early stage often lead to pervasive difficulties in social and emotional processing (most prominently social attachments), where ethical transgressions appear alongside a multitude of maladaptive behaviors.[106] In the most recent revision of the Diagnostic and Statistical Manual of Mental Disorders (DSM-IV-TR), a childhood diagnosis of conduct disorder is required for an adult to be diagnosed with antisocial personality disorder. Conduct disorder in children is best described as a pattern of repetitive behavior (strikingly similar to that which is seen in adults with antisocial personality disorder) where the rights of others or the social norms are violated. Symptoms often include highly aggressive behavior, cruelty toward people and animals, as well as destructive behaviors.[107] In addition, a great number of children with conduct disorder also show evidence of hypoarousal, most commonly manifest in a relatively lower resting heart rate. In his 2002 review, Raine[108] provides evidence for a number of reasons why a low resting heart rate may be a valuable correlate/predictor of unethical behavior. In a meta-analysis of 29 independent samples, low autonomic arousal (hypoarousal) was the biological variable most consistently associated with antisocial and criminal behavior in both children and adolescents.[109] Importantly, additional studies have eliminated the possibility that a low resting heart rate is the product of a delinquent way of life. A low heart rate has also been shown to be a specific predictor of antisocial behavior, meaning that not only is hypoarousal not observed in other psychiatric conditions, but *hyper*arousal is more frequently associated with psychiatric conditions such as depression, anxiety, alcoholism, and schizophrenia. Finally, it has been reported that a low heart rate interacts with poor familial relationships during development and that this combination is more likely to produce violent adult offenders.[110] It has been consistently suggested that hypoarousal results from the interaction of a hypoactive amygdala and the brainstem. Given the amygdala's primary role in the fight-or-flight response, it is not surprising that hypoaroused individuals are often described as "fearless."

105. R. J. R. Blair, *Applying a Cognitive Neuroscience Perspective to the Disorder of Psychopathy*, 17 DEVEL. PSYCHOPATHOLOGY 865 (2005).

106. Abigail A. Baird et al., *Developmental Precipitants of Borderline Personality Disorder*, 17 DEVEL. PSYCHOPATHOLOGY 1031 (2005).

107. AMERICAN PSYCHOLOGICAL ASSOCIATION DIAGNOSTIC AND STATISTICAL MANUAL OF MENTAL DISORDERS DSM-IV-TR (4th ed. 2000).

108. Adriane Raine, *Biosocial Studies of Antisocial and Violent Behavior in Children and Adults: A Review*, 30 J. ABNORMAL CHILD PSYCHOL. 311 (2002).

109. Adriane Raine, *Autonomic Nervous System Factors Underlying Disinhibited, Antisocial, and Violent Behavior, Biosocial Perspectives and Treatment Implications*, 20 ANNALS NY ACAD. SCI. 46–59 (1996).

110. D. P. Farrington, *The Relationship Between Low Resting Heart Rate and Violence*, *in* BIOSOCIAL BASES OF VIOLENCE 89–106 (A. Raine, P.A. Brennan, D.P. Farrington, & S. A. Mednick eds., 1997).

In addition to having difficulties with fear conditioning, these individuals may lack the motivation to learn from social and emotional Eisenberg has drawn a connection between fearlessness and an inability to develop guilt within the attachment relationship.

> A mutual interpersonal orientation between parent and child enhances the socialization process. However, a positive cooperative interactive set, as reflected in a secure attachment between parent and child and maternal responsiveness, seems to be especially important for the development of guilt in relatively fearless children, a finding consistent with the notion that children's temperament moderates the association between parental socialization-related behaviors and the development of conscience.[111]

It is not uncommon for deficits of this nature in children to remain undetected, or largely overlooked, mainly because children are not held to the same ethical standards as adults. Perhaps most striking about this type of primal deficit is that among individuals with average or above average cognitive functioning, their inability to extract meaning from social and emotional cues in childhood often garners little attention; it is not until the multifaceted pressures of adolescence "force the hand" of the individual that maladaptive behavior becomes apparent. Due to the nature of human development, specifically its tendency to build on itself, it is possible for a seemingly uneventful developmental process to unmask a previously hidden diathesis. To use another analogy, not being able to steer a car is not a problem prior to the age at which one is expected to be able to drive. If one is not able to learn to steer, however, the entire process of learning to drive a car is likely to collapse. As a result of trying to learn to drive, one now has knowledge of a previously silent "steering disorder." Quite simply, adolescent development requires the acquisition of increasing complex cognitive, social, and emotional process that rely heavily on those that precede them, and it is conceivable that the expectations associated with adolescent development may in and of themselves serve to uncover and perhaps even exacerbate previously unseen diatheses.

Dysfunction of areas within the frontal cortex, specifically the orbital, ventromedial prefrontal, and cingulate cortices, has been consistently associated with criminal behavior.[112] There is consistent and compelling evidence that some, but not all, of the characteristics associated with criminal behavior may also be acquired following damage to the ventromedial as well as orbitofrontal regions

---

111. Nancy Eisenberg, *Emotion, Regulation, and Moral Development*, 51 ANN. REV. PSYCHOL. 665 (2000).

112. ANTONIO R. DAMASIO, DESCARTES' ERROR: EMOTION, REASON, AND THE HUMAN BRAIN (1994); Adriane Raine et al., *Selective Reductions in Prefrontal Glucose Metabolism in Murderers*, 15 BIOL. PSYCHIATRY 365 (1994); Kent A. Kiehl, *A Cognitive Neuroscience Perspective on Psychopathy: Evidence for Paralimbic System Dysfunction*, 142 PSYCHIATRY RES. 107 (2006).

of the prefrontal cortex.[113] Specifically, pathological lying, irresponsibility, promiscuous sexual behavior, labile emotion, and impenitence are just a few of the behaviors that are seen in individuals following damage to the ventromedial cortex or the orbitofrontal cortex. Though damage to these regions does not inevitably result in the development of criminal behavior, individuals with this type of damage are likely to demonstrate behaviors associated with conventional descriptions of psychopathy (i.e., impulsivity, remorselessness, problems with emotional processing).

Although there is little doubt that disruption of frontal cortical systems contributes significantly to the symptomatology of criminality, it is equally plausible that the neural systems underlying this personality disorder have both local and distributed components. Blair has argued that dysfunction of the amygdala may be primarily responsible for behavior associated with psychopathy and, in turn, criminality. As previously detailed, damage to the amygdala often results in impairments in emotion recognition and fear conditioning. It is also noteworthy that the amygdala is critical for producing functional levels of social anxiety. In this context "functional" social anxiety refers to the amygdala's ability to discern and attach social and emotional significance to people and events, which over time helps individuals to follow social norms. For example, a mild anxiety in response to meeting new people is highly functional as it ensures that one's arousal will increase slightly and in turn so too will short-term memory and attention to self-regulation.

It is conceivable that the severe dysfunction in the amygdala *or* one of the frontal regions detailed above could lead to the manifestation of socially anomalous, but not criminal, behavior. That is, individuals with a hyporesponsive amygdala might demonstrate some of the behavioral problems associated with fearlessness, but not the personality style differences (i.e., manipulative behavior, Machiavellian traits, callousness, etc). In contrast, individuals with specific prefrontal dysfunctions may manifest personality problems or impulsivity problems, but not the fearlessness associated with damage to the amygdala. It is compelling, based on the current literature, to consider the possibility that the profound behavioral differences seen in criminal and clinical populations require dysfunction of both the frontal and subcortical regions.

B. Intact Hardware, Corrupt Software

Human beings are fundamentally social animals that rely on the fluid exchange of social, emotional, and cognitive knowledge for survival. This fluidity enables

---

113. John M. Harlow, *Passage of an Iron Rod Through the Head*, 34 Bos. Med. and Surgical J., 389–93 (1848); Adam K. Anderson & Elizabeth A. Phelps, *Lesions of the Human Amygdala Impair Enhanced Perception of Emotionally Salient Events*, 411 Nature 305 (2001); Joseph Barrash et al., *Acquired Personality Disturbances Associated With Bilateral Damage to the Ventromedial Prefrontal Region*, 18 Develop. Neuropsychology 355 (2000).

highly dynamic and adaptive behavioral output. Improvements in abstract thinking during adolescence enable significant advances in understanding other individuals' experience. Knowledge of the thoughts, beliefs, and feelings of others is the well from which springs the capacity for both great compassion and great harm. A visceral aversion to violating ethical standards is not hardwired. Given this, the emotional importance of following moral and legal statutes must be taught. Individuals who reach maturity without these associations very likely suffer from one of two pathogenic mechanisms. First, as discussed above, individuals may lack the necessary neural hardware to learn what is needed to understand or act in accordance with appropriate ethical standards. The second pathogenic scenario involves an environment where ethical standards are not taught, or standards that differ significantly from those of society are imparted. If the neural hardware is intact and capable of emotional learning, both of these scenarios create conditions under which an individual learns dysfunctional sociocultural norms and is more likely to violate ethical standards. Raine[114] has described this second type of criminal in great detail. In a rather ingenious study, Raine and colleagues examined the prefrontal function, as measured by resting glucose metabolism, in two groups of convicted murderers. One group came from relatively deprived psychosocial backgrounds, whereas the other group came from nondeprived psychosocial backgrounds. Ratings of psychosocial deprivation were based on the presence of physical abuse, sexual abuse, neglect, extreme poverty, foster home placement, a criminal parent, severe family conflict, and a broken home. It was discovered that murderers from deprived backgrounds not only showed higher frontal metabolism than murderers from nondeprived backgrounds but also that the frontal functioning in deprived-background murderers was greater than that seen in the control participants. These data suggest that individuals from deprived backgrounds lack obvious neurological impairments and are in fact more frontally active than most non-murderers. These findings very clearly demonstrate that there are some criminals who have very functional brains, but as a result of deprived backgrounds either have learned dysfunctional ways of interacting with othersor did not receive the experience necessary to associate aversive emotional states with ethical violations.

IX. LEGAL IMPLICATIONS

Individuals who spend long periods of time in prison also learn ethical principles that cannot be generalized to the larger society. Prison is a place where the

---

114. Adriane Raine et al., *Prefrontal Glucose Deficits in Murderers Lacking Psychosocial Deprivation*, 11 NEUROPSYCHIATRY, NEUROPSYCHOL, & BEHAV. NEUROLOGY 1 (1998).

majority of social and ethical lessons learned are a matter of life or death. Because of this, in order to survive in prison, you must learn the lessons fast and they must be enduring. Perhaps this accounts for some of the statistics on recidivism. In recent years a number of states have moved the adjudication of certain juvenile offenses from juvenile court to adult criminal court. Sentences for youths adjudicated in adult court are served in adult prisons. Many states have espoused the belief that this change would provide greater deterrence to youthful offenders by raising the stakes of their punishment. Criminologists and psychologists are showing that they could not have been more wrong. First, for reasons previously discussed, adolescents have trouble generating abstract thoughts about the future; they are about as able to envision adult prison as they are able to imagine their day-to-day life as parents. That is, they simply cannot. Not surprisingly, moving juvenile offenses to adult court has had no effect on deterring these violations[115]. Second, as a result of the offender's age, adolescents are at increased risk for indelibly learning the culture of prison. For an individual whose brain is at its peak for social and emotional peer learning, placement in a prison ensures that they will learn that culture and function best within it for the rest of their lives. Research has shown that this is precisely the case. Four different studies in four different states have demonstrated significantly higher rates of recidivism among juveniles incarcerated in adult prisons relative to those placed in juvenile detention facilities.[116] These studies, considered in the context of what is known about human development, suggest that if the goal of incarceration is to prevent future violations, there may be ways to capitalize on the critical time of adolescence. Instead of surrounding a juvenile offender with experienced "mentor" criminals, a better outcome might be achieved by sentencing them to the football team or the drama club. This is not meant to sound glib, but instead meant to underscore the tremendous neurobiological plasticity of development and how its interaction with environmental influences can be used to enable desired outcomes.

A. Do "Normal" People Ever Commit Criminal Acts?

The simple answer to this question is "Yes." "Crimes of passion" or "temporary insanity" are ideas that have been incorporated into the social and legal comprehension of why an individual with no prior pattern of criminal behavior could "snap" and commit a criminal act. More recent legal philosophy has described

---

115. Donna M. Bishop, *The Transfer of Juveniles to Criminal Court: Does It Make a Difference?*, 42 CRIME & DELINQ. 171 (1996).

116. Jeffrey Fagan, *The Comparative Advantage of Juvenile versus Criminal Court Sanctions on Recidivism among Adolescent Felony Offenders*, 18 L. & POL'Y 77 (1996); Lawrence Winner et al., *The Transfer of Juveniles to Criminal Court: Reexamining Recidivism Over the Long Term*, 43 CRIME & DELINQ. 548 (1997); Donna Bishop, *Juvenile Offenders in the Adult Criminal System*, 27 CRIME AND JUST. 81 (2000).

"temporary insanity" as an irresistible impulse, which is defined as an act that a person may have known was illegal but because of a mental impairment was unable to control. Crimes committed in a "fit of passion" are considered acts of insanity and are not seen as guilty in the eyes of the court. In most human beings a "fit of passion" is more commonly known as a version of the fight-or-flight response, an intense response of the amygdala and the HPA axis that prepares the body and mind for life-threatening situations. In animal models, life-threatening situations are fairly straightforward; unfortunately this is not the case with humans. Because of the complex cognitive processes humans posses, rather abstract situations (e.g., sexual jealousy) can trigger the intense fight-or-flight response. Via its influence on the HPA axis and the brainstem, the amygdala is able to instantaneously increase arousal in preparation for fighting or fleeing. As previously noted, a small to medium amount of stress produces improvements in cognitive functions[117]; in the case of the fight-or-flight response, however, the concomitant arousal response is large enough to produce significant impairments in attention, memory, and problem-solving ability. Since all of these functions rely heavily on the prefrontal cortex, it is reasonable to think that intense stress inhibits prefrontal functioning, which inhibits both rational decision making and behavioral regulation.[118] Reducing neural resources devoted to "higher cognition" makes a great deal of sense, if in fact the individual is in a life-or-death situation. Simply put, the laborious, more thoughtful processes of the prefrontal cortex are not going to keep an individual alive if he is in immediate danger, they are simply too slow. Survival in cases of intense arousal depends on implicit, more primitive, behavioral responses. This response system is marvelously effective if one needs to get away from an angry bear, but much less so when one is overcome by sexual jealousy. In the case of sexual jealousy, one's life is not in jeopardy, but the combination of personal disposition and environmental cues has been known to trigger the sort of "blind rage" described by the fight-or-flight response in the absence of cognitive regulation, resulting in the harming (or even killing) of other individuals. The law has taken such momentary "lapses in judgment" into consideration. For example, as a precondition to punishment, criminal law requires conduct to be voluntary. If something interferes with the capacity of the individual to choose to break the law, this should be reflected by an excuse or exculpation. The law is challenged with balancing the need to be fair to the individual wrongdoer with providing protection to society from a person who may not have complete control over his behavior. This reasoning makes a great deal of common sense, particularly when one considers situations like that of Heinz in the dilemma presented at the beginning of this chapter. The stress of

117. Robert M. Yerkes & John D. Dodson, *The Relation of Strength of Stimulus to Rapidity of Habit Formation*, 18 J. COMP. NEUROLOGY AND PSYCHOL. 459 (1908).

118. S. J. Lupien & B. S. McEwen, *The Acute Effects of Corticosteroids on Cognition: Integration of Animal and Human Model Studies*, 24 BRAIN RES. REV. 1 (1997).

his wife's life-threatening illness provoked an uncontrollable urge to steal the medicine from the pharmacist. It is easy to imagine a judge or jury being lenient in this situation, realizing that due to extreme emotional stress, his behavior may not have been under his direct control. Understanding that Heinz's behavior was based on an actual, tangible neurobiological process sheds a different light on how we might come to interpret any number of human behaviors in regard to how "excusable" they are in the eyes of the law.

As compelling as these accounts of brain behavior are, there are several critical caveats that must be mentioned. Based on our current understanding, the human brain does not correspond with human behavior in a direct fashion. As a result, the complex relationships between brain structure, brain function, human behavior, and psychopathology require cautious speculation. Implicit in this discussion is also the idea that the brain and behavior have a reciprocal relationship, meaning that experience is fully capable of rendering pathological anomalies in brain structure or function.[119] While human neuroscience has a great deal to offer with regard to the likely causes of human behavior, it is not yet capable of predicting—or for that matter, explaining—any individual's specific intentions or behaviors. It is tempting to draw great truth from brightly colored pictures of brain activity (which are actually statistical maps of the probability of activity in those regions, not the actual activity),[120] but it would be wrong to do so with regard to the actions of an individual. Through the close study of groups of individuals, psychology and neuroscience have come a long way in helping us understand the conditions under which unethical behavior is likely to happen. However, baring gross neurological pathology, these scientific advances have little or nothing to offer about the individual offender. It is for this and other obvious reasons that science and law need to continue their discussion in hopes of eventually creating a system that is as informed as possible and able to make the best decisions both for society and for its individual members.

---

119. John C. Mazziotta, *Imaging: Window on the Brain*, 57 ARCHIVES NEUROLOGY 1413 (2000).

120. S. M. Kosslyn, *If Neuroimaging Is the Answer, What Is the Question?*, 354 PHILOS. TRANSACTIONS ROYAL SOC'Y LONDON 1283 (1999).

PART TWO

CONSIDERING THE BROADER CONTEXT

4. BEHAVIORAL GENETICS AND CRIME, IN CONTEXT

OWEN D. JONES

I. INTRODUCTION

Two experiences clarified for me precisely how worried people can get about the legal implications of behavioral genetics. First, I attended the 1994 conference on genes and crime,[1] at which interrupting protestors famously chanted, "Maryland conference, you can't hide; we know you're pushing genocide." Two signs illustrated their concerns. One read: "Jobs, Not Prozac." The other read: "This Conference Predisposes Me to Disruptive Behavior Disorder."

The second experience was in 1997, when I was a panelist on the subject "Biological Aspects of Human Action" at a conference of social scientists. When my turn came, I had barely begun the opening sentences, which would start in the most general terms to lay a foundation for why law should care about biological influences on behavior, when a woman in the front row began to shake her head—then her entire body—with obvious passion. I paused, and asked what I had said that had so offended her. Her reply, which was just as much a non sequitur in the original as it will come across here, was, "I just don't believe we should put people in jail before they've done anything wrong."

In each of these instances, the yawning gulf between what I or anyone else was actually saying (or about to say) and the preemptive assumption about what we must mean, intend, and advocate was breathtaking. The leaps of logic necessary to cross this divide typically reflect misunderstandings about the relationships between biology and behavior, the relationships between genes and environments, the implications of those relationships, the ways in which those implications will be considered, the goals a speaker is pursuing, and the way those goals might be translated—if at all—into social, legal, or political action. Some of these subjects I will touch on here, in an effort to provide some context for considering the relationships between behavioral genetics and crime.

One thing seems clear: misunderstandings or no, issues at the intersection of behavioral genetics and crime will be with us for some time. Behavioral genetics is developing at a quickening pace, and developments within that field continue

---

1. The conference—"Research on Genetics and Criminal Behavior: Scientific Issues, Social and Political Implications"—was held September 22–24, 1995, at the Aspen Institute's Wye Center in Queenstown, Maryland.

to inspire efforts to use them, principally in postarrest contexts. The *Landrigan* death penalty litigation illustrates this point.[2]

The defendant in *State v. Landrigan*[3] (later *Landrigan v. Stewart*[4] and *Schriro v. Landrigan*[5]) was born Billy Hill. Billy's biological father—the son of a man who was killed in a shootout with police—allegedly raped Billy's mother the first time they met. The two later became step-siblings and subsequently married. Billy's mother apparently abused alcohol and drugs while pregnant with Billy. After Billy was born, his father went to prison and his mother relinquished parental rights and ties.

When six months old, Billy was adopted by the Landrigan family and renamed Jeffrey Landrigan. After a markedly troubled childhood, Landrigan was sentenced to prison in Oklahoma for killing his best friend. While there, a fellow inmate commented that Landrigan looked just like a man on death row in Arkansas who—it later turned out—was Landrigan's biological father. Landrigan subsequently escaped from prison and traveled to Arizona, where he committed and was convicted of another murder. The trial court sentenced Landrigan to death, noting that Landrigan appeared to be an exceptionally amoral person, utterly lacking remorse.[6]

On direct appeal, the Arizona Supreme Court affirmed the death sentence.[7] Subsequently, the federal public defender replaced prior counsel and sought habeas corpus relief on the grounds that, among other things, Landrigan's first counsel was ineffective for failing to investigate, develop, and introduce genetic and other biological evidence.[8] Upon preliminary exploration of various biological angles, Landrigan's attorneys argued that Landrigan was entitled to present evidence of mitigating factors at a resentencing hearing. Specifically, they sought to introduce evidence of genetic predisposition for disordered behavior, in utero

---

2. Landrigan's various circumstances as related here are drawn from several sources, including: State v. Landrigan (*Landrigan*), 859 P.2d 111 (Ariz. 1993); Landrigan v. Stewart (*Landrigan II*), 272 F.3d 1221 (9th Cir. 2001); Brief of Petitioner-Appellant, *Landrigan II*, 272 F.3d 1221 (No. 00-99011); Brief of Respondents-Appellees, *Landrigan II*, 272 F.3d 1221 (No. 00-99011); Landrigan v. Stewart (*Landrigan III*), 397 F.3d 1235 (9th Cir. 2005); *60 Minutes: Murder Gene; Man on Death Row Bases Appeal on the Belief That His Criminal Tendencies are Inherited* (CBS television broadcast February 27, 2001) [hereinafter *60 Minutes: Murder Gene*].

For more detail on the Landrigan litigation, *see* Chapter 10 in this volume, Deborah W. Denno, *Behavioral Genetics Evidence in Criminal Cases: 1994–2007, in* THE IMPACT OF BEHAVIORAL SCIENCES ON CRIMINAL LAW (Nita A. Farahany, ed., 2009).

3. 859 P.2d 111 (Ariz. 1993).

4. 272 F.3d 1221 (9th Cir. 2001).

5. 127 S.Ct. 1933 (2007).

6. *Landrigan, supra* note 2, at 117 (quoting the trial judge).

7. *Landrigan, supra* note 2.

8. Brief of Petitioner-Appellant, *supra* note 2, at 45–51.

poisoning due to maternal drug and alcohol abuse during pregnancy, early maternal rejection, and severe drug and alcohol addictions.[9] They claimed that "Landrigan's behavior and activities from infancy into childhood, and through adulthood, were not the products of 'free will' as society defines this term because Landrigan lacked the ability to make non-impulsive, considered choices about his life's path."[10] In other words, Landrigan's actions had been caused principally by his various genetic and other circumstances.

The United States District Court denied habeas corpus relief. The Court of Appeals for the Ninth Circuit affirmed, indicating that the genetic argument was "exotic" and that "assuring the court that genetics made him the way he is could not have been very helpful."[11] Highlighting the double-edged nature of genetic evidence, the court also concluded, "Although Landrigan's new evidence can be called mitigating in some slight sense, it would also have shown the court that it could anticipate that he would continue to be violent."[12] Landrigan successfully petitioned for a rehearing en banc, arguing among other things that the panel had neglected other independent biological arguments, including both organic brain damage and the interaction of genetic and in utero environmental influences. En banc, the Ninth Circuit affirmed in part, reversed in part, and remanded for an evidentiary hearing,[13] in an opinion thought to reflect "openness and receptivity [to] Landrigan's efforts to introduce mitigating genetic and family evidence history."[14] The Supreme Court subsequently reversed and remanded, concluding that the District Court had not abused its discretion in refusing to provide Landrigan with a new evidentiary hearing, and agreeing with the Ninth Circuit's initial panel view that the genetic and other mitigating information was weak, and would not have helped Landrigan.[15]

It remains unclear what genetic evidence Landrigan would have introduced. And it remains unclear whether a defendant less distasteful, less singularly remorseless, and less flauntingly menacing might in the future succeed in introducing more rigorous and relevant behavioral genetics evidence. In the meantime, the Landrigan case illustrates the criminal justice purposes for which some defense attorneys hope to use behavioral genetics. And it seems likely that cases like Landrigan's will arise with increasing frequency. This is due not only to advances in behavioral genetics (which, rightly or wrongly, are perceived to offer hope to defendants) but also to every defense attorney's obligation to mount a

---

9. *Id.* at 6.

10. *Id.* at 6–7.

11. *Landrigan II, supra* note 2, at 1228–29.

12. *Id.*

13. Petition for Panel Rehearing and Rehearing En Banc, *Landrigan III*, 397 F.3d 1235 (No. 00-99011); Landrigan v. Schriro, 441 F.3d 638 (9th Cir. 2006) (en banc).

14. Denno (this volume) at Part IV.B.1.

15. 127 S.Ct. 1933 (2007).

rigorous defense. One way or another, the criminal justice system will need to continue grappling with how to assess specific findings within behavioral genetics, whether to admit genetic evidence, and how to do so (for example, with what limitations and implications). One researcher explains the situation this way:

> Although it has been previously argued that genetics play no part in shaping antisocial and criminal behavior, a growing literature base has served to substantiate that genetic factors are as important to the development of some forms of criminal activity as are environmental factors.
>
> This attitudinal shift has occurred for several reasons. First, there are simply too many studies, in too many countries, using different methodologies that converge on the same conclusion: genes do play a role. Second, other, potentially less controversial fields of behavioral trait research have not only identified heritability in psychiatric disorders such as autism, schizophrenia and reading disability, but also in personality traits such as political conservatism. Thus, it would be surprising if criminal behavior—particularly recidivistic crime—was not in some way influenced by genetic factors.[16]

Such views and developments have already sparked a number of scholars to consider what behavioral genetics might mean for the criminal justice system. For example, Friedland considers and critiques ways in which a "genetically oriented criminal justice system" might differ from current approaches in contexts of pretrial release, character evidence at trial, posttrial release, sentencing, and parole.[17] Greely has asked the important question: how accurate would a genetic test have to be (at predicting future dangerousness, for instance) before it should be given significant weight?[18]

Others in this symposium will provide more detailed updates on the latest findings from behavioral genetics and the latest cases in law to confront issues raised by behavioral genetics.[19] My task here is more general. Part II attempts to

---

16. Sharon S. Ishikawa & Adrian Raine, *Behavioral Genetics and Crime*, in THE NEUROBIOLOGY OF CRIMINAL BEHAVIOR 81, 81–82 (Joseph Glicksohn ed., 2002) (internal citations omitted).

17. Steven I. Friedland, *The Criminal Law Implications of the Human Genome Project: Reimagining a Genetically Oriented Criminal Justice System*, 86 KY. L.J. 303 (1997–98).

18. Henry T. Greely, *Prediction, Litigation, Privacy, and Property*, in NEUROSCIENCE AND THE LAW: BRAIN, MIND, AND THE SCALES OF JUSTICE: A REPORT ON AN INVITATIONAL MEETING CONVENED BY THE AMERICAN ASSOCIATION FOR THE ADVANCEMENT OF SCIENCE AND THE DANA FOUNDATION 114, 120–23 (Brent Garland ed., 2004) [hereinafter NEUROSCIENCE AND THE LAW].

19. Some relatively recent overviews appear in Ishikawa & Raine, *supra* note 11; L. F. Lowenstein, *The Genetic Aspects of Criminality*, 8 J. HUM. BEHAV. SOC. ENV'T 63 (2003); Richard P. Epstein & Robert H. Belmaker, *Genetics of Sensation or Novelty Seeking and Criminal Behavior*, in THE NEUROBIOLOGY OF CRIMINAL BEHAVIOR, *supra* note 11, at 5l. The Human Genome Project's introduction to Behavioral Genetics appears at http://www.ornl.gov/sci/techresources/Human_Genome/elsi/behavior.shtml. A recent

situate behavioral genetics, criminal law, and their overlap within larger contexts of law and biology. Part III attempts to situate the inquiries of this symposium issue within the context of work to date on behavioral genetics and crime. To help avoid needless duplication of efforts, it also provides a brief summary of views, gleaned from a variety of different sources, on which it appears the majority of relevant scientists and commentators have reached at least tacit agreement. Part IV then outlines some of the complications and implications of discussing behavioral genetics and crime, including definitional and methodological challenges, as well as implications for free will and responsibility. Finally, Part V raises two issues worth exploring. The first concerns how the respective contributions of behavioral genetics and behavioral ecology will compare over time, and how those efforts might best be joined. The second issue concerns what it would mean to put environmental considerations and genetic considerations on equal footing in the criminal justice system—and whether such a thing would be desirable.

II. CONTEXTUALIZING BEHAVIORAL GENETICS AND CRIME

On the one hand, taking behavioral biology into account in criminal law is not, in itself, new. For example, we implicitly take developmental biology into account when defining different levels of civil or criminal responsibility on the basis of age—as when state contract law allows minors to void contracts or the Supreme Court holds that a state cannot constitutionally execute an adult for a crime he committed when under the age of eighteen.[20] Numerous states allow that various mental diseases (such as schizophrenia) and various brain injuries (such as those damaging the prefrontal cortex) can reduce moral blameworthiness.[21] And epilepsy can, in some circumstances, preclude blameworthiness entirely.[22] On the other hand, there is a general perception that steadily quickening developments in biology will enable greater and greater biological insight into the causal processes underlying human behavior, with consequences both important and disturbing for criminal law.

---

overview prepared in association with the American Association for the Advancement of Science (AAAS) and The Hastings Center is CATHERINE BAKER, BEHAVIORAL GENETICS: AN INTRODUCTION TO HOW GENES AND ENVIRONMENTS INTERACT THROUGH DEVELOPMENT TO SHAPE DIFFERENCES IN MOOD, PERSONALITY AND INTELLIGENCE (2004). A more thorough introduction appears in ROBERT PLOMIN ET AL., BEHAVIORAL GENETICS (Robert Plomin ed., 4th ed. 2001).

20. Roper v. Simmons, 125 S. Ct. 1183, 1200 (2005).

21. See C. T. Drechsler, Annotation, *Mental or Emotional Condition as Diminishing Responsibility for Crime*, 22 A.L.R. 3d 1228, §§ 1–2, 5–9 (1968; 2005).

22. Eunice A. Eichelberger, Annotation, *Automatism or Unconsciousness as Defense to Criminal Charge*, 27 A.L.R. 4th 1067, § 6(a) (1984).

To situate the specific topic of behavioral genetics and crime, two points need noting at the outset. First, behavioral genetics is but one of many fields within behavioral biology that are potentially relevant to crime. Second, crime is but one area of law to which behavioral genetics is potentially relevant.

A. Behavioral Genetics within Behavioral Biology

For those interdisciplinary legal thinkers who draw principally on the social sciences and humanities, the corpus of biology relevant to behaviors that are in turn relevant to law is generally undifferentiated—if indeed biological influences on behavior are contemplated at all. Unfortunately, lumping all of behavioral biology together prevents meaningful consideration of where biology is most and least likely to be useful in law.

In fact, scientists study the biology of behavior in a wide variety of biological subdisciplines in addition to behavioral genetics. These include, for example, evolutionary biology, evolutionary ecology, animal behavior, developmental biology, cognitive neuroscience, and behavioral ecology, as well as neuroanatomy, brain chemistry, evolutionary psychology, Darwinian medicine, Darwinian psychiatry, psychopharmacology, neurophysiology, brain imaging, and, most recently, neuroeconomics. Although the boundaries between these fields blur at the edges, as one might expect, the fields yield different insights, from different perspectives, from scientists trained differently.

Put another way, behavioral geneticists are not the only biologists to study the effects of genes on behavior, nor do all biologists studying behavior study genes. For example, neurological damage (particularly brain damage)—whether prenatal or postnatal—can affect behavior regardless of a person's genetic complement.[23] Fetal maldevelopment, cortisol, testosterone, hypoglycemia, lead ingestion, and various birth complications, as well as nicotine or cocaine exposure during pregnancy, are among the many other biological phenomena that can have powerful effects on behavior relevant to law.[24]

B. Crime within Behavioral Genetics

Just as behavioral genetics is but one of many fields within behavioral biology that are potentially relevant to crime, crime is but one area of law to which behavioral genetics is potentially relevant. One could imagine that if behavioral

---

23. *See* Hanna Damsio, et al., *The Return of Phineas Gage: Clues about the Brain from the Skull of a Famous Patient*, 264 Sci. 1102 (1994) (providing discussion of a classic case of behavioral changes consequent to brain damage).

24. Useful discussion appears in Adrian Raine, The Psychopathology of Crime: Criminal Behavior as a Clinical Disorder 191–213 (1993). *See also* Diana H. Fishbein, *How Can Neurobiological Research Inform Prevention Strategies?*, *in* The Science, Treatment, And Prevention Of Antisocial Behaviors: Application To The Criminal Justice System 25–1 (Diana H. Fishbein ed., 2000).

genetics were to usefully illuminate predispositions relevant to crime, it might also help illuminate predispositions relevant to many other areas of law. For example, scholars continue to debate the proper effects on health law (insurance coverage, for example) of discernible genetic effects on susceptibility to disease. Possible genetic effects on sexual preferences could affect family law, genetic effects on risk perceptions could affect various regulatory policies, and genetic effects on acquisitive behavior could affect corporate law, and the like.

III. POINTS OF (NEAR) CONSENSUS

There are many ways to approach the intersection of behavioral genetics and crime. Some of the many relevant questions include: (a) What do we think we know? (b) How might that knowledge aid various legal goals? (c) Would the likely benefits of incorporating such knowledge—given the potential for error, misunderstanding, or misuse—exceed the likely costs? (d) What kinds of knowledge are and are not likely to emanate from behavioral genetics in the future? The existing literature on behavioral genetics and crime suggests that there are a number of points on which everyone, or nearly everyone, seems to agree:[25]

(1) Behavior is a complex phenomenon, neither attributable to single causes nor easily parsed among multiple causes.

(2) All behavior results from the interaction of genes, environments, developmental history, and the evolutionary processes that built the brain to function in the ways it does.

(3) Genes and learning are not mutually exclusive explanations for behavior, because genes affect learning and contribute to cultural patterns that are common to the species.

(4) The human organism is neither genetically determined nor environmentally determined, but rather possesses multiple potentials that arise through the successive interactions of genes and environments.

(5) To say something is genetically influenced is not to say that environmental influences are irrelevant.

---

25. These are distilled from a wide range of sources, including RAINE, *supra* note 19; Ishikawa & Raine, *supra* note 11; David Wasserman & Robert Wachbroit, *Introduction: Methods, Meanings, and Morals, in* GENETICS AND CRIMINAL BEHAVIOR 1 (David Wasserman & Robert Wachbroit eds., 2001); Elliot Sober, *Separating Nature and Nurture, in* GENETICS AND CRIMINAL BEHAVIOR, *supra*, at 47. *See also* Gregory Carey & Irving I. Gottesman, *Genes and Antisocial Behavior: Perceived versus Real Threats to Jurisprudence,* 34 J.L. MED. & ETHICS 342 (2006).

(6) To say a behavior is genetically influenced—even with high heritability—is not to say it is inevitable, unalterable, or "determined" in any inflexible sense. A predisposition is not a predestination.[26]

(7) A high statistical correlation between the presence of a particular allele[27] and a behavior does not necessarily indicate any particular causal connection between that allele and the behavior.

(8) There is no gene or set of genes (or allele or set of alleles) that are for—or directly responsible for—criminal behavior.

(9) Criminal behavior is influenced by both environmental and genetic forces, as well as by their interaction.

(10) To say that genes influence behaviors relevant to crime does not mean that genetics can explain why certain individuals commit crime.

(11) To say a behavior is natural, biological, or genetically influenced is never to say it is for that reason good or excusable, or automatically entitled to any legal deference or relevance whatsoever. Explanation is not exculpation.

(12) A person's behavior can be genetically influenced and still be subject to legitimate moral condemnation.

(13) The extent to which different alleles of genes influence behaviors relevant to crime provides no justification for human eugenics.

(14) The extent to which different alleles of genes influence behaviors relevant to crime provides no justification for discrimination.

These points of consensus or near-consensus highlight the extent to which all human behavior—the criminal necessarily included—is a complex phenomenon. It is difficult to know what one can say with reasonable confidence about the probability that biology generally or behavioral genetics specifically will be useful to the criminal law.

For example, one commentator argues that "our judicial system ultimately must address[] the criminal responsibility one will bear for committing a crime when the actions are determined by the actor's genetic makeup. . . . which rendered him unable to exercise free and independent will to restrain from

---

26. Arguably, there are some very limited exceptions. So far as we know, for example, everyone with the allele for Huntington's Disease eventually will display behavioral manifestations of the disease, if they live long enough. Yet even here there can be significant variation in age of onset and rapidity of the course of the disease.

27. Alleles are different variants (forms) of two or more genes that reside at a specifically named genetic locus. Discussions of genetic differences among individuals ordinarily refer not to individuals having different genes per se, but rather to individuals having different alleles of genes.

committing the offense. . . ."[28] On the one hand, the commentator seems right to raise a question about how behavioral genetics will affect the legal system's approach to criminal behavior. On the other hand, the commentator seems distinctly outside the biology mainstream to frame the question in terms positing that actions may be "determined by the actor's genetic makeup." As has often been noted, imagining that an individual's behavior is determined by genes in any hard sense, irrespective of environment, is a bit like imagining that the area of a rectangle is the product only of its length, irrespective of its width.[29] So it seems likely that questions framed in this way have more rhetorical than actual use.

IV. COMPLICATIONS AND IMPLICATIONS

David Wasserman—a scholar who has long been thinking about genes and crime—captures the present situation this way: "No serious researcher believes that there are genes for crime; no responsible critic believes that genetic differences have no effect on personality and behavioral disposition."[30] If the statement is true (I believe it is), and if most commentators would agree the statement is true (I believe they would), then why do commentators so frequently talk past one another? The principle reasons can be divided into three general categories: definitions, methods, and implications.

---

28. Marcia Johnson, *Genetic Technology and Its Impact on Culpability for Criminal Actions*, 46 CLEV. ST. L. REV. 443, 444, 466 (1998). In a similar vein, the commentator states:

Once genes for behavior are identified, many geneticists believe a person's genetic predisposition to violent behavior can be shown. When that predisposition is so compelling that a person cannot overcome the compulsion to act in accordance with noncriminal behavior, then he or she is not responsible for his or her actions. A criminal defendant suffering such a genetic predisposition could be found not guilty by reason of genetic predisposition. . . .

Id. at 470.

29. The key point is that genetic determinism is incoherent. Nonetheless, the rectangle analogy requires additional explanation, highlighting the initially counterintuitive result that although it is impossible to ascertain separate contributions of genes and environment to an individual's behavior, it is simultaneously possible (at least in theory) to closely estimate the separate contributions of genes or environment to the *variance* in behavior across a population. Plomin usefully illustrates this in his discussion of the often misunderstood concept of "heritability." He notes length and width contribute equally and indivisibly to the area of a single rectangle. At the same time, given a population of rectangles having (for instance) a constant width, one could state with confidence that one hundred percent of any variance among the rectangles in area can be attributed to differences among the rectangles in their lengths. *See* PLOMIN ET AL., *supra* note 14, at 85–91.

30. David Wasserman, *Research into Genetics and Crime: Consensus and Controversy*, 15 POL. & LIFE SCI. 107, 107 (1996).

A. Definitions

There are at least two kinds of definitional problems. The first concerns the different meanings attributed to words used in discussion of behavioral genetics and crime. For example, one person might be using the term "behavioral genetics" loosely—perhaps intending to refer broadly to biological influences on behavior—while another uses or understands the term according to its more precise meaning.[31] Similarly, discussants may part ways when using the words "heritable" or "heritability." One might intend to refer generally to the capacity of a trait to be inherited genetically; the other may use or understand heritability in its more technical sense as "the proportion of phenotypic variance that is attributable to genotypic variance."[32] Some might be using "gene" (knowingly or unknowingly) as a shorthand for "allele of a gene," "a combination of genes," or "a combination of alleles," while a listener interprets the usage more literally.

The second definitional problem concerns the link between an allele and a given criminal behavior. That link in fact spans a great distance. Consider that genes code for amino acid sequences, which string together in long chains to make proteins, which in turn are used to build neural architecture, which is in turn influenced by environmental conditions, which conditions may also affect what genes are active when, which may in turn affect information processing in ways that in turn lead to increases or decreases in the probability of defined behaviors.

But what behaviors, really, are we talking about? Labeling a behavior as "criminal" is not meaningfully similar, in this respect, to labeling a behavior as chewing, drinking, or swallowing. The latter words code for very specific behavior on which all but the most philosophical would agree. What is criminal, on the other hand, varies by culture, time, and context—it is socially rather than biologically defined. And as Rutter put it, "Genes do not, and cannot, code for socially defined behaviors."[33] In addition, things socially defined as crimes are often quite different from one another and, within their own categories, are not meaningfully homogenous.[34] As Epstein and Belmaker note, "Criminality is a

---

31. For more on that meaning, *see infra* Part V.

32. PLOMIN ET AL., *supra* note 14, at 349.

33. Michael Rutter, *Concluding Remarks, in* GENETICS OF CRIMINAL AND ANTISOCIAL BEHAVIOR 266 (Gregory R. Bock & Jamie A. Goode eds., 1996).

34. Pamela J. Taylor, *Forward, in* THE NEUROBIOLOGY OF CRIMINAL BEHAVIOR, *supra* note 11, at xiiv, xiv–xvi; Troy Duster, The Implications of Behavioral Genetics Inquiry for Explanations of the Link between Crime, Violence, and Race 6–7 (Dec. 15, 2003) (unpublished manuscript, on file with author, cited by permission of Troy Duster); Troy Duster, *Selective Arrests, An Ever-Expanding DNA Forensic Database, and the Specter of an Early-Twenty-First-Century Equivalent of Phrenology, in* DNA AND THE CRIMINAL JUSTICE SYSTEM: THE TECHNOLOGY OF JUSTICE 315 (David Lazer, ed., 2004) [hereinafter Duster, *Selective Arrests*]. *See also* Tabitha M. Powledge, *Genetics and the Control of Crime*, 46 BIOSCIENCE 7, 7

complex phenotype and is characterized by a wide spectrum of acts, from non-violent white collar crimes to serial killings."[35]

Perhaps as a partial reaction to definitional ambiguities, there is a marked tendency in discussions of behavioral genetics and crime to focus on violent behaviors, notwithstanding the fact that a great deal of crime is theft. But this offers little analytic comfort, for even if we were to explicitly limit a discussion to a subset of criminal acts—such as violence—even this does not represent a single behavioral category.[36] Premeditated murders are meaningfully different from bar-room brawls—as are beatings, rapes, and torture. And even these phenomena are not uniform. Moreover, we know that the motives for committing even a single criminal act can vary dramatically, with implications for the principal goals of criminal law: deterrence, retribution, isolation, and rehabilitation. For instance, a person might commit arson because she is a pyromaniac, because she wants to cover up evidence of a separate property crime, because she wants the insurance money, because she seeks revenge, or for a variety of other reasons.

B. Methods

Much of the inherent difficulty in figuring out the relationship between genes, crime, and the criminal justice system flows from the same difficulties encountered in other areas linking science and potential legal implications. What have studies actually shown? How confident are we that the findings may be generalized? What are the possible implications of what we believe to be true? What are the projected costs and benefits of those implications? How should variations in the kinds of implications affect how confident we should be in scientific findings before acting in reliance upon them? In what legal contexts, and how, should science make a difference?

In addition to carrying these typical law–science difficulties, human behavioral biology carries at least four more, each of which compounds problems significantly. First, with only rare exceptions, each organism in a sexually reproducing species is genetically unique. Second, each human organism is environmentally unique, encountering its own combinations of experiences from womb to tomb. Third, obvious ethical constraints accompanying differences between humans and other animals mean that only a tiny fraction of the potential experiments that might control for various confounds can be administered.

(1996) ("[T]hat motley mass of disparate actions—ranging from stock fraud to serial homicide—we lump under the catchall rubric *crime*.").

35. Epstein & Belmaker, *supra* note 14, at 51.

36. *See* Stephen C. Maxson, *Issues In The Search For Candidate Genes In Mice As Potential Animal Models Of Human Aggression, in* GENETICS OF CRIMINAL AND ANTISOCIAL BEHAVIOR, *supra* note 28, at 21, 24.

Fourth, the proximate mechanisms linking genes and behavior are incredibly complex, as Schaffner, among others, has vividly described. Schaffner notes that behaviors are generated by groups of neurons acting together, a single genetic change can affect multiple neurons, a single neuron can affect multiple behaviors, and multiple neurons can affect the same behavior.[37] In addition, many genes can affect one neuron, development can affect neuronal connections, differences in environment can yield different behaviors through short-term environmental influence (such as learning), environments can create long-term environmental influence (by affecting the expression of genes that affect behavior), and one gene can affect another gene that can in turn affect behavior.

Each of these four difficulties poses important problems for what can be learned from dissimilar human subjects, what can be predicted about subjects not yet studied, and with what confidence we should hold our tentative conclusions about the relationships between behavioral genetics and crime. Chastened but uncowed by these problems, scientists simply endeavor to do the best they can with what they have. For example, studying identical and fraternal twins reared apart, and comparing those groups, provides useful controls for genetic variation.[38] Comparing findings from genetic studies of prison populations with findings of such studies in unincarcerated populations may also yield important clues, if allele frequencies at a particular genetic locus were to differ significantly between the two populations.

Such studies are nevertheless imperfect, as a number of critics have argued.[39] For example, adoption placements are not random, and selective placement factors can confound efforts to extract useful and reliable information from adoption studies.[40] Moreover, such studies occasionally lead us down a path that later proves incorrect—as was the case with early studies suggesting that the unusual XYY chromosomal complement meaningfully predisposed its bearer to violent

---

37. Kenneth F. Schaffner, *Complexity and Research Strategies in Behavioral Genetics, in* BEHAVIORAL GENETICS: THE CLASH OF CULTURE AND BIOLOGY 61 (Ronald A. Carson & Mark Rothstein eds., 1999). The balance of this paragraph is drawn from *id.* at 74, 76.

38. For discussions of methods generally, *see* Ishikawa & Raine, *supra* note 11; RAINE, *supra* note 19, at 54–78. For further information, *see* NANCY L. SEGAL, INDIVISIBLE BY TWO: LIVES OF EXTRAORDINARY TWINS 2–3 (2005); Stephanie L. Sherman & Irwin D. Waldman, *Identifying the Molecular Genetic Basis of Behavioral Traits, in* BEHAVIORAL GENETICS: THE CLASH OF CULTURE AND BIOLOGY, *supra* note 32, at 35; Dorret Boomsma et al., *Classical Twin Studies and Beyond,* 3 NAT. REV. GENET. 872 (2002).

39. *See, e.g.,* Sober, *supra* note 20; Lowenstein, *supra* note 14. Useful discussions of some limitations to methods appear in David Wasserman, *Is There Value in Identifying Individual Genetic Predispositions to Violence?,* 32 J.L. MED. & ETHICS 24 (2004); and Duster, *Selective Arrests, supra* note 29.

40. Lowenstein, *supra* note 14, at 67.

criminal activity.[41] In addition, important questions also surround the validities of measurements, as well as complications arising from the search not just for genes, but also for relevant interactions of genes and environments.

C. Implications

It is, of course, in the realm of implications that the future for behavioral genetics and crime is most hotly contested. Many others (including many contributing to this symposium) have mapped and continue to map this territory in detail. What follows here provides several introductory but key concepts about the implications of behavioral genetics for criminal law that are also useful when navigating the terrain.

1. **Free Will and Responsibility** As is well known, the criminal law is one of the few areas of law in which motive matters. In general, the criminal law cares whether a person has requisite mental intent, choosing freely to perform an act, and choosing with an awareness of distinctions between right and wrong. It is therefore in criminal law that issues of free will are often raised—and it is in the context of free will that the influence of biology on behavior generates concerns.

A key question, of course, is whether free will exists in the first place. On the one hand, all but the most physically or mentally constrained humans perceive life as an endless series of choices. Economic, social, political, and religious conditions, among others, may present constraints within which choice will be exercised. But at some meaningful level individuals still choose what to do, when to do it, and, indeed, whether to abide by many of the social constraints encountered. So human will seems "free," even if it does not result in limitless possibilities.

---

41. Wasserman and Wachbroit summarize the episode succinctly:

In 1965, researchers found an apparently high prevalence of [the XYY chromosomal combination] among prison inmates in Britain. That is to say, the percentage of prison inmates with XYY was higher than the percentage of XYY males in the general population. Unfortunately, many people quickly took this finding to be evidence of a direct link between an extra Y chromosome and a tendency to hyperaggressivity and violence. That assumption was eventually rejected by genetic researchers, but it held sway in the popular imagination long enough to stigmatize a generation of XYY males and (reportedly) lead to the abortion of a significant number of [XYY] fetuses. . . . It is now widely believed that if an extra Y chromosome leads to incarceration, it is by a indirect route. XYY individuals are no more aggressive than average, but they may be taller and less intelligent, hyperactive, and generally more impulsive. Their increased risk of arrest or conviction may stem from an increased likelihood of getting caught, or of committing crimes more likely to be detected, rather than from heightened aggressiveness or greater disregard for social norms.

Wasserman & Wachbroit, *supra* note 20, at 9 (citations omitted).

On the other hand, all choices emerge from the human nervous system. And each state of the nervous system is, in part, a function of the prior state of that nervous system. The system is composed of molecules, in turn composed of atoms, and it is driven by chemical reactions and electrical circuits. The nervous system and its brain are therefore part of a material world in which present events are caused by prior events, extending back to the beginning of time and matter. If genes we inherit affect our nervous systems in ways that affect our behavior, in what sense is our will free?

This question opens the door to a series of pressing and yet seemingly intractable problems, many of which have challenged commentators for ages.[42] How free must will be in order to justify the law's punishment of actors who behave criminally? Is free will binary, such that you have it or you don't? If not binary, is there any reliable way to measure the proportion in which a person's action was free? If there were such a way to measure free will, how much, in a given context, will be necessary for purposes of exculpation at trial, or mitigation at sentencing?[43]

Most commentators subscribe to beliefs within a grey zone of compatibilism. The central idea of compatibilism is that—in all but the rarest cases—adult humans should be deemed to have free will in sufficient quantities (whatever that may mean) to justify holding them legally accountable for their behaviors. As always, however, the precise location of the threshold is unclear. And here behavioral genetics presents complications that are new in detail, but in fact old in kind. Behavioral genetics may afford us tools for more clearly understanding the multiple causes that lead to behavior, but whether that behavior reflects the operation of a normal brain is a question the legal system has already been asking in the mental health context for a long time.[44]

---

42. *See generally* Michael S. Gazzaniga & Megan S. Steven, *Free Will in the Twenty-First Century: A Discussion of Neuroscience and the Law, in* NEUROSCIENCE AND THE LAW, *supra* note 13, at 51; Stephen J. Morse, *New Neuroscience, Old Problems, in* NEUROSCIENCE AND THE LAW, *supra* note 13, at 157; Wasserman & Wachbroit, *supra* note 20, at 201–327; Richard Lowell Nygaard, *Freewill, Determinism, Penology, and the Human Genome: Where's A New Leibniz When We Really Need Him?*, 3 U. CHI. L. SCH. ROUNDTABLE 417, 423 (1996); Matthew Jones, Note, *Overcoming the Myth of Free Will in Criminal Law: The True Impact of the Genetic Revolution*, 52 DUKE L.J. 1031 (2003).

43. A number of these issues are explored in Gazanniga & Steven, *supra* note 37; Morse, *supra* note 37; Steven Goldberg, *Evolutionary Biology Meets Determinism: Learning from Philosophy, Freud, and Spinoza*, 53 FLA. L. REV. 893 (2001); Owen D. Jones & Timothy H. Goldsmith, *Law and Behavioral Biology*, 105 COLUM. L. REV. 405, 485–88 (2005).

44. *See, e.g.,* Christopher Slobogin, *Is Atkins the Antithesis or Apotheosis of Anti-Discrimination Principles?: Sorting Out the Groupwide Effects of Exempting People with Mental Retardation from the Death Penalty*, 55 ALA. L. REV. 1101 (2004); Christopher Slobogin, *Rethinking Legally Relevant Mental Disorder*, 29 OHIO N.U. L. REV. 497 (2003).

2. The Separate Realms of "Is" and "Ought" Even if we were able to identify, with reasonable specificity, some combination of alleles and environment that significantly increased the likelihood of certain behaviors labeled criminal, it is a separate question whether that information ought to play any role in criminal justice. We could not, for example, legitimately conclude that simply because a convicted individual has certain alleles relevant to the behavior at issue, he is entitled to greater leniency.

The reason is simple: the realms of fact and meaning are logically distinct. That is, the realm of what "is" and the realm of what "ought-to-be" are as necessarily separate as description and prescription. Explanation is not justification. And one simply cannot move from facts to normative conclusions without passing through a prism of human values. Arguments to the contrary—which seek to draw causal arrows directly from fact to normative conclusion—have long been recognized as committing the grave logical error labeled the "naturalistic fallacy."[45]

Moreover, even if we were able to identify, with reasonable specificity, some combination of alleles and environment that significantly increased the likelihood of certain behaviors labeled criminal, and even if we were inclined to find normative meaning in biological fact, it would often be unclear what that normative meaning would be. Genetic information can cut in different directions simultaneously. For instance, we could conclude it mitigates (if responsibility seems materially lessened), we could conclude it exacerbates (if greater deterrence seems advisable to offset greater proclivities), or we could conclude it has no or some other implication.

In any case, there are no convenient shortcuts from "is" to "ought." We cannot avoid the hard work of netting out our often competing values by imagining that increasing advances in behavioral genetics will make our legal responsibilities easier.

3. The "Isms" Over time, people have found cause—often good cause—to be concerned about ways that biology can be invoked in the service of sexism, racism, genetic determinism, eugenics, and Social Darwinism (more properly though less commonly known as Social Spencerism[46]). These collected subjects, each significant in its own right, serve as an important backdrop against which all discussions of behavioral genetics and crime take place. Consequently, no effort to put behavioral genetics and crime in context could be complete without acknowledging that history gives ample reason to be skeptical about the uses to which biological information will be put. Missteps are not uncommon, as is

---

45. The term apparently was coined by G. E. Moore in *Principia Ethica*. *See* G. E. Moore, Principia Ethica 90 (Thomas Baldwin ed., rev. ed. 1993). The concept traces back, however, to David Hume's *A Treatise of Human Nature*. *See* David Hume, A Treatise of Human Nature 469–70 (L. A. Selby-Bigge & P. H. Nidditch eds., Oxford, 2d ed. 1978) (1739–40).

46. Jones & Goldsmith, *supra* note 38, at 492–93.

illustrated by reexamining the history of phrenology, craniometry, and the XYY controversy.[47]

Although it is important to be alert to the possibility that people will either misunderstand the biology in a way that leads to misuse, or count on other people misunderstanding the biology in a way that opens the door to intentional misuse, two things bear noting. First, it is important to recognize that there is nothing inherent *in the underlying biological reality* that justifies any of these uses.[48] The uses are always a function of the injection of various human values, many of which have nothing to do with the biology itself. Second, it is rarely clear *ex ante* that we are better off without information that could be misused, since the lack of information also imposes its own costs.[49]

4. The Wide Variety of Criminal Justice Contexts to Consider When discussing possible interactions of behavioral genetics and the criminal law, it is important to keep in mind the wide variety of potential interactions, spanning the preventive, the corrective, and the therapeutic. Each creates its own fork in the analytic road. Are we interested in pre-offense identifications? If so, what kind of screenings— if any—could legitimately be implemented? Are we interested in pre-offense interventions? If so, of what kind? Are we interested in post-offense treatment? If so, are social, chemical, or genetic treatments worth pursuing? Each choice risks a misstep, warranting more than customary caution and deliberation.

V. TWO ISSUES WORTH EXPLORING

The preceding survey of some of the many themes bearing on this conference is necessarily short. There are many possible launching points for further discussion. Here are two worth exploring.

A. Relative Contributions of Behavioral Genetics and Behavioral Ecology

It is often noted that people tend to misunderstand behavioral biology.[50] One of the key misunderstandings concerns the distinction between behavioral

---

47. Duster, *Selective Arrests*, *supra* note 29, at 8–10. Useful discussions of the XYY controversy appear in Raine, *supra* note 19, at 47–53; Deborah Denno, *Legal Implications of Genetic and Crime Research*, in Genetics of Criminal and AntiSocial Behaviour, *supra* note 28, at 248; Deborah Denno, *Human Biology and Criminal Responsibility: Free Will or Free Ride?*, 137 U. Penn L. Rev. 615 (1988).

48. This is explored in much greater detail in Jones & Goldsmith, *supra* note 38, at 484–99.

49. *See* Jones & Goldsmith, *supra* note 38, at 499. Nygaard phrases this idea somewhat differently—"[I]gnorance can also be used for illegitimate purposes"—and suggests the results can be at least as or even more culturally destructive. Nygaard, *supra* note 37, at 430.

50. For example, some commentators note the importance of distinguishing the study of behavior generally from the study of behavioral differences attributable to differences

genetics and an area of study that goes by various names, including behavioral ecology.

The distinction, essentially, is this. Behavioral genetics often focuses on how different behaviors from different individuals can arise from genetic differences among the individuals. Behavioral ecology generally focuses on how different behaviors from different individuals can arise when evolved and algorithmic predispositions that are widely shared among brains encounter different environmental circumstances.[51] The important distinction between behavioral genetics and behavioral ecology is not whether environments affect behavior; in both fields environmental conditions are vitally important. The important difference in disciplinary focus is that behavioral genetics often looks for differences in behaviors that can be attributed largely to genetic differences, while behavioral ecology generally looks for differences in environments that lead organisms with evolved neural architectures that are fundamentally similar to behave differently from one another.

These two related subfields provide complementary rather than competing perspectives—two sides of a coin. The question is not which one is right. Instead, the questions are: (1) how might each perspective aid legal efforts to achieve social goals; and (2) how do the perspectives differ on dimensions relevant to their ultimate utility in law?

One initially tempting approach to answering these questions is to think that behavioral ecology is more useful at the broad policy level, while behavioral genetics may be more useful in litigation contexts. That is, some might be tempted to conclude that behavioral ecology is the more useful of the two perspectives when legal thinkers and lawmakers are attempting to change, through law, environmental conditions a large population encounters—to reduce violent aggression in society, for example. And some might be tempted to conclude that behavioral genetics is the more useful of the two perspectives when an individual's behavior is at issue.

Yet the utilities of behavioral ecology and behavioral genetics are probably not so neatly divisible. For one thing, both behavioral ecology and behavioral genetics can be important tools for identifying the kinds of environmental conditions that are likely to increase the probability of criminal acts, either through the

---

in genetics. *See* Wasserman & Wachbroit, *supra* note 20, at 5; Martin Daly, *Evolutionary Adaptationism: Another Biological Approach to Criminal and Antisocial Behavior, in* GENETICS OF CRIMINAL AND ANTISOCIAL BEHAVIOR, *supra* note 28, at 183. Others have argued for the importance of incorporating evolutionary perspectives on crime. *See* MARTIN DALY & MARGO WILSON, HOMICIDE (1988); RAINE, *supra* note 19, at 27–46; Alan Gibbard, *Genetic Plans, Genetic Differences, and Violence: Some Chief Possibilities, in* GENETICS AND CRIMINAL BEHAVIOR, *supra* note 20, at 169; and Jones & Goldsmith, *supra* note 38, at 484–98.

51. Efforts to represent this distinction graphically appear in Owen D. Jones, *Proprioception, Non-Law, and Biolegal History*, 53 FLORIDA L. REV. 831, 840 (2001) and in Jones & Goldsmith, *supra* note 38, at 501.

conditional and algorithmic processes behavioral ecology studies or through the context-sensitive, gene-environment interactions that behavioral geneticists study.[52] For another, both fields are inherently probabilistic, rather than deterministic. Application to given individuals is therefore, under any circumstances, complicated and indeterminate, at best. For instance, even if an individual convicted of a crime bears a genetic sequence positively correlated in a population with behavioral predispositions relevant to the crime he committed, behavioral genetics still does not answer a question often important at the sentencing phase: why did this individual commit this criminal act?

If one of our main interests is in reducing crime, rather than in simply increasing the number of contexts in which behavioral genetics is used, then the advantages and disadvantages of behavioral genetics and behavioral ecology should be explored. More particularly, we should consider ways in which those perspectives—each of which identifies biological processes that can be simultaneously operating in every person—can be usefully integrated in furtherance of a synthetic, and hopefully improved, approach.

For example, one weakness of the way behavioral genetics information tends to be understood by nonscientists is that it inclines people to think that crime is somehow principally the result of criminals having genes (or, more precisely particular alleles of genes) that noncriminals do not have. This can mislead us into thinking that crime comes far more from "criminal minds" than from what we might call "criminal moments"—opportunities to gain personal advantage through means society defines as criminal that the species-typical brain will notice and find tempting. The behavioral ecology perspective suggests that even if we were to magically and instantaneously sequester all those who had ever committed a crime, the positive effect on subsequent crime rates would be dampened by the probability that otherwise law-abiding citizens would move opportunistically into the vacuums created.

Conversely, one weakness of the way insights from behavioral ecology can be internalized is that the foregoing could be misunderstood to suggest that all people are materially the same, and that therefore genetic differences are irrelevant to criminal behaviors. This could distract attention from those probably rare but significant contexts in which a person who behaved criminally bears some

---

52. *See, e.g.*, Fishbein, *supra* note 19 (proposing structuring the environment to minimize risk factors). Fishbein notes that neurobiological research can be used to help identify individual vulnerabilities as a function of genetic, biological, and environmental conditions; assist in identifying environmental conditions that trigger antisocial behavior and drug-taking behaviors, among other vulnerabilities; signal which prevention programs under which specific conditions will likely be most effective (including methods for early detection, interventions, treatments, and primary prevention strategies); and decrease reliance on incarceration by emphasizing the superiority of public health and medical approaches. *Id.* at 25-3.

highly influential genetic trait that, while not determining his behavior, could have played a sufficient role such that a just society would want to consider whether that role might be mitigating at a sentencing phase. The behavioral genetic perspective suggests that, even when encountering environmental conditions that most people find irrelevant or only trivially relevant to the probability that they would commit a criminal act, some people will find such an environment disinhibiting.

This suggests we should neither categorically nor cavalierly exclude evidence of the sort Landrigan sought to introduce in his case. At the same time, it is not going to be easy, given the inherent complications explored above, for legal thinkers and behavioral biologists to settle on a sensible, fair, and administratively workable approach that balances the inherent uncertainties of science with the aspiration to do immediate individual justice in the courts.

B. The Parity Principle, Bias, and Varying Standards

Another aspect of using behavioral genetics in criminal contexts concerns the comparative uses of the social sciences and the life sciences in criminal trial contexts. Except in the rarest circumstances, information attempting to explain extenuating causes of a defendant's behavior should not be wholly exculpatory in criminal contexts. Nevertheless, one can readily imagine that information from advances in behavioral genetics will from time to time be admitted in criminal trials, during liability phases, sentencing phases, or both. Whether in the end admitting this evidence is good or bad depends on a variety of factors. These include the precise purpose for which the information is offered, the soundness of the underlying science, and the like. But four points bear noting.

First, genes do not "determine" behavior to any extent greater than environments do. It is true that, in any given case, the behavioral variation between two groups of people can be explained to a greater or lesser degree by genes or environment.[53] But that fact alone provides no support for the idea that, when genetic effects are identifiable and present, they should necessarily have an effect on criminal justice outcomes.

Second, and at least in the context of assessing moral blameworthiness, our concerns about the extent to which genes "determine" criminal behavior should not be thought categorically different from our concerns about the extent to which environments "determine" behavior. If we were somehow trying to apportion among various causal elements the extent of influence over a defendant's behavior, it would initially appear to makes no sense to be more concerned about an x percent environmental influence than about an x percent genetic influence. Causes are causes, and what we often attempt to evaluate—the degree to which a person's behavior was "free"—should be sensitive to the extent that a cause

---

53. *See* discussion *supra* note 24.

imposes on freedom, not to the kind of cause it is. That is, one could legitimately say that although genetics evidence should not receive any special admissibility privileges, nor should it receive any lesser privileges than those afforded environmental evidence.[54] We might refer to this view as *the parity principle.*

Third, this parity principle is problematic when one considers its application rather than its theoretical justification. Because even when genetic information about causes and environmental information about causes may share similar promise and limitations, these types of information may be—and probably are— dissimilarly incorporated into the minds of judges and jurors. That alone may provide sufficient justification for treating these two kinds of evidence differently at trial. This asymmetry in the application of the two kinds of evidence in the minds of decision makers undoubtedly traces, in part, to common misunderstandings about how biology affects behavior generally, how behavioral genetics affects behavior specifically, and what statistical and probabilistic language does and does not mean.[55] It may trace, in part, to the ease with which, and the length of time during which, environmental conditions—physical abuse, injuries, sociocultural milieu—are observable at the macroscopic level, compared to the relative difficulty of detecting genes, the relative novelty of our ability to do so, and the manifest difficulty in understanding what genes do and how. It likely also has something to do with apparently widespread public interest in, and frequent over-ascription of sufficiency to, explanations from the natural sciences, when such explanations can be offered. But the bottom line is this: if jurors were likely to endow a quantum of information from behavioral genetics with more significance than an equivalent quantum of information from the social sciences, treating genetics and environment identically for analytic purposes may result in systematic bias in favor of genetic explanations. Education may be an antidote to this bias. But the potential for bias nonetheless warrants caution and concern.

Finally, there is a potential for bias that cuts precisely the other way. It results in potential over-favoring of social science insights over behavioral genetic ones. The problem is this: if social and natural sciences are often (perhaps improperly) deemed competitive in legal arenas, they should be held to similar standards for purposes of admissibility.[56] For example, holding information from behavioral genetics to a higher standard than information from psychology would inevitably favor the latter. Why, for example, should an inherently uncertain prediction

54. Among those who have argued similarly, *see* Joseph S. Alper, *Genes, Free Will and Criminal Responsibility*, 46 Soc. Sci. Med. 1599 (1998).

55. As an example of the latter, a probability can be dramatically higher in one set of people when compared with another set, at the same time that the absolute incidence of the behavior on a per capita basis is still quite low.

56. Owen D. Jones, *Brains, Evolution, and Law: Applications and Open Questions*, 359 Phil. Trans. R. Soc. Lond. B 1697 (2004).

of future dangerousness, based on either individual or statistical analysis by a psychologist, be admitted any more easily than an equally uncertain prediction of future dangerousness based on either individual or statistical analysis by a behavioral geneticist? The likelihood of the information being held to different standards in law is exacerbated by each discipline's having its own standards of what it takes to establish some proffered piece of information as more probably true than not. Some might say the natural sciences are more reserved on this score. And the problem of varying standards between social and life sciences is further compounded by the unavoidable fact that our legal system already (and quite properly) deploys different standards in different contexts (such as trials versus legislative action).

VI. CONCLUSION

We are learning a great deal from the bio-behavioral sciences about how and why humans behave as they do. We now recognize that animals of each species—including humans—come evolutionarily equipped not only with behavioral pre-dispositions, but also with proclivities to learn some behaviors far more easily than others. Evolutionary theory, together with animal studies in both natural and experimental conditions, helps clarify the patterns in which social systems can evolve. Technological advances have enabled neurobiologists to investigate the operations of single nerve cells in neural circuits of active animals, to clarify how neurons operate on known principles of physics and chemistry, and to local-ize cognitive activities in human brains by using noninvasive techniques, such as functional magnetic resonance imaging. And researchers in evolutionary anthropology and evolutionary psychology are helping to illuminate features of human behavior shared widely around the world.

We have come increasingly to understand how even the tiniest brains—such as those of ants—have sufficient complexity to enable highly sophisticated social behavior, as well as flexible and successful navigation of environmental chal-lenges. We can see how synaptic connections in the human brain ebb and flow—not only over long periods, but also across a single day. And we can not only see how different parts of the brain perform different functions, but we can also observe in real time how different parts of a brain operate when it is thinking, analyzing, deciding, or experiencing emotions.

Amidst the swirl of all this activity, the discovery of DNA's structure in 1953 opened the door to a host of related discoveries about the operations of genes and development. Developmental biology examines the processes by which genes and environments interact and guide a brain's construction and function, with consequences for developmental psychology, learning, and the evolution of behavior. And behavioral genetics has helped us to understand some of the important ways that genes influence behavioral predispositions—some of which in turn contribute to behaviors that law classifies as criminal. The task now is to keep the constraints as well as the insights of behavioral genetics in perspective as it continues to develop as a field and as it continues to intersect with criminal law. In this brief overview, I have attempted to situate some of the many issues addressed by other authors in this symposium issue within the larger biological context. I have also summarized some points of widespread agreement, highlighted a few complications and implications, and raised a variety of issues at the intersection of genes and crime that seem worth exploring.

5. CONSIDERING CONVERGENCE: A POLICY DIALOGUE ABOUT BEHAVIORAL GENETICS, NEUROSCIENCE, AND LAW

BRENT GARLAND AND MARK S. FRANKEL

I. INTRODUCTION

As the poet Mark Strand said, "The future is always beginning now."[1] When considering the social impact that neuroscience and behavioral genetics will have on the criminal justice system, scientists, lawyers, courts, and policymakers might do well to keep Strand's words in mind. Too often it is assumed that for developments in science and technology, there is time to start the policy dialogue in "the future." Those who would address the issues later typically assert that the science in question is too immature, that it is too early, that the discussion is too speculative. While such objections sometimes have merit, it seems society is more often too slow in promoting a public dialogue.

Open public dialogue is an important tool in considering and weighing public reaction, in informing the public and policymakers, and in building public consensus about appropriate and responsible uses of science and technology. Scientific advancements can result in strong, negative public reactions, as with nuclear power in the United States, genetically modified food crops in the European Union, and human research cloning in a variety of nations. This negative backlash can in turn influence scientists and science policy and slow the progress of socially valuable research. When the social risks are great, it may be prudent to slow the pace of research. However, when the risks are minimal, and the negative reaction is based on incomplete or inaccurate information about the science, then restraints on research serve little purpose.

Now is the time to call on scientists, lawyers, courts, and lawmakers to begin a sustained dialogue focused on the impact that scientific discoveries and technological advances might have on the criminal law. The dialogue should focus on developing appropriate policies to address the legal and social issues raised by such advances. Such a dialogue is necessary, in particular, concerning the focus of this chapter: the impact of neuroscience and behavioral genetics on criminal law.

This chapter first briefly considers some of the commonalities and differences between behavioral genetics and neuroscience as they relate to the criminal law,

---

1. Mark Strand, *The Babies, in* REASONS FOR MOVING, DARKER & THE SARGENTVILLE NOTEBOOK 19, 20 (1992).

including topics addressed by both fields, as well as how each field might be applied in criminal proceedings. The article then focuses on a common concern raised by both fields in this context—the possible misuse of science in the criminal law. It concludes with a proposal to address the need for a continuing policy dialogue about the law and scientific developments in neuroscience and behavioral genetics.

II. A POLICY PERSPECTIVE

The American Association for the Advancement of Science (AAAS)[2] has sought to advance the public and policy dialogues in both behavioral genetics and neuroscience in the past few years.[3] It is reasonable to ask why anyone would consider the effect on the criminal law of *two* broad scientific fields, rather than deal with each separately. It seems increasingly clear, though, that when describing, predicting, and understanding human behavior, numerous scientific discussions may be considered part of one larger discussion; various scientific fields converge in their exploration and explanation of human actions. It makes some scientific sense to talk about neuroscience and behavioral genetics together; indeed, the disciplines overlap and interact—for example, a person's genes affect how his brain develops.[4] It similarly makes legal sense to consider a larger behavioral biology, and it makes sense to consider the two fields together from a policy perspective. Moreover, public dialogues at AAAS and elsewhere on behavioral genetics and neuroscience suggest that both disciplines are ripe for further discussion about their nexus with criminal law and policy.

---

2. AAAS is a nonprofit, nongovernmental organization located in Washington, DC. It is the largest general scientific organization in the world and publisher of the journal SCIENCE. According to its Web site, "AAAS serves some 262 affiliated societies and academies of science, serving 10 million individuals." About AAAS, http://www.aaas.org/aboutaaas. AAAS is "open to all and fulfills its mission to 'advance science and serve society' through initiatives in science policy; international programs; science education; and more." *Id.*

3. For more information, please see the Web site for the Scientific Freedom, Responsibility & Law Program, http://www.aaas.org/spp/sfrl/about/mission.shtml. Of particular relevance are the Behavioral Genetics Project site, http://www.aaas.org/spp/bgenes, and the Neuroscience and the Law Web site, http://www.aaas.org/spp/sfrl/projects/neuroscience. Project publications are available for free download at both Web sites.

4. Another example of this overlap can be found in the emergence of a new, complex behavioral biology—one that will ultimately be not only descriptive but predictive. *See* Owen D. Jones & Timothy H. Goldsmith, *Law and Behavioral Biology*, 105 COLUM. L. REV. 405 (2005). Many scientific disciplines will contribute to the knowledge base that will underlie such a biology.

III. COMMON ISSUES OF INTEREST

Behavioral genetics and neuroscience converge on a number of scientific, legal, social, and ethical issues—in particular, on two areas of interest to the criminal justice system: the prediction of behavior and the use of behavioral information in the preliminary stages of criminal processes.

A. Prediction of Behavior: Mitigation

Both neuroscience and behavioral genetics have focused considerably on explaining and predicting behavior.[5] Much discussion has focused on "ultimate" issues such as free will, determinism (genetic or mechanistic), and their effect on whether the concept of criminal culpability will be undone by new scientific discoveries. This seems unlikely, at least in the near future.[6] A more intriguing and immediate concern is how scientific findings will affect the criminal law regarding the mitigation of criminal responsibility. For example, neuroscience and behavioral genetics seem particularly likely to play a role in addressing drug addiction, as findings in both fields may be relevant to how society chooses to

---

5. Courts and prosecutors currently use prediction constantly—in plea bargaining, sentencing, decisions about levels of probation, and case diversion, among other proceedings. As the parties involved seek to weigh future risks, including the likelihood of recidivism, they do so knowing that our predictive models and abilities are really very poor. To the extent that neuroscience and behavioral genetics can better inform such predictions, the courts and criminal justice system could stand to benefit significantly.

The risk, of course, is that predictive decisions will be based on poor or incomplete science. Additionally, neuroscience- or genetics-based predictions may be given undue weight as "scientific predictions" while still being prone to the problems inherent in current risk prediction models, including construction bias in the normative or sample groups and the inability of predictive measures to provide information about any specific individual beyond probabilistic information about a group to which the subject belongs.

The pressing need for courts to make decisions about sentencing and risk management increases the risk for early adoption of immature "predictive models." The courts are in a difficult place with prediction—they cannot wait for the next round of peer-reviewed research results. *See generally* Erica Beecher-Monas & Edgar Garcia-Rill, *Danger at the Edge of Chaos: Predicting Violent Behavior in a Post-Daubert World*, 24 CARDOZO L. REV. 1845 (2003) (discussing this challenge, particularly that juries should get both predictive information as well as details as to the limitations of such information).

6. Nor, indeed, will it be undone in the long term. As Stephen Morse has argued in the context of neuroscience, the idea of criminal responsibility is not an artifact of science, but, like law itself, a human construct that is mind-dependent; since we are constrained by our view of ourselves as rational agents, our constructs will reflect these views. This is admittedly a gross simplification of Morse's argument. *See* Steven J. Morse, *New Neuroscience, Old Problems, in* NEUROSCIENCE AND THE LAW: BRAIN, MIND AND THE SCALES OF JUSTICE 157 (Brent Garland ed., 2004).

handle criminal behavior that accompanies addiction, such as drug possession.[7] Neuroscience has shown that the brains of addicts are different from those of nonaddicts,[8] and there appears to be a genetic predisposition toward addiction.[9] As with criminal behavior generally, the question arises whether such information (neuroscientific or genetic) should mitigate criminal responsibility, at least when there is evidence of neurological or genetic differences in the accused.

Neuroscience adds a gloss to this question by providing highly effective pharmaceutical treatments for opiate addiction that are currently available and yet not widely in use.[10] One drug, naltrexone, serves to block the pleasurable or rewarding effect of the opiates by blocking the receptors to which the opiates bind, preventing their euphoric effects.[11] As long as the individual is compliant in taking naltrexone, relapse, in the sense of experiencing the pleasurable aspects of opiate use, is impossible. Successful drug treatment not only reduces the health risks associated with drug use, but it also eliminates the legal risk of incarceration for possession of drugs or drug paraphernalia. Drug addicts could, in theory, be diverted to a mandatory treatment program at a much lower cost than incarceration. Thus, by changing the way that society views and understands addiction, drug use, and treatment, neuroscience has the potential to reshape our policies on criminalization and incarceration as they pertain to drug-related offenses.

Indeed, mitigation is the most obvious issue that the scientific, legal, and policy communities must face with some immediacy. This need was highlighted most recently by the Supreme Court decision in *Roper v. Simmons*, which barred capital punishment for juvenile offenders under the age of eighteen.[12] The opinion

---

7. The potential upside for better understanding addiction is important since treating addiction is viewed by many as a long-term, if not lifelong, process. The relapse rate is high, and the legal penalties for illegal drug use are substantial.

8. *See, e.g.*, Alan I. Leshner, *Addiction Is a Brain Disease, and It Matters*, 278 SCIENCE 45 (1997); Nora D. Volkow, *Beyond the Brain: The Medical Consequences of Abuse and Addiction*, NIDA NOTES, Feb. 2004, at 3.

9. For a brief review article, see Eric J. Nestler, *Genes and Addiction*, 26 NAT. GENET. 277 (2000).

10. Neuroscience can offer a brain-based treatment in a way that behavioral genetics cannot—that is, behavioral genetics is unlikely to offer a form of gene therapy for addiction anytime soon. *See, e.g.*, Charles P. O'Brien, *A Range of Research-Based Pharmacotherapies for Addiction*, 278 SCIENCE 66 (1997); *see also* Charles P. O'Brien, *Mandating Naltrexone among Court-Referred Patients: Is It Ethical?* 31 JSAT 107 (2006).

11. For a brief overview of these treatments, see Christian A. Heidbreder & Jim J. Hagan, *Novel Pharmacotherapeutic Approaches for the Treatment of Drug Addiction and Craving*, 5 CURR. OPIN. PHARMACOL. 107 (2005). Opiates are not the only drugs for which new treatments are being developed. For example, one vaccine, TA-CD, reduces the euphoric effects of cocaine. *Cocaine Vaccine Trials Progress*, BBC NEWS, Apr. 2, 2002, http://news.bbc.co.uk/1/hi/health/1906823.stm.

12. 125 S. Ct. 1183 (2005).

referred to "the scientific and sociological studies"[13] cited by the respondent and amici as confirming a "lack of maturity and an underdeveloped sense of responsibility" found in the young.[14] Several amici briefs[15] cite brain studies as offering evidence of immaturity and lack of judgment sufficient to mitigate a juvenile's culpability, even when the juvenile engages in the worst behavior—behavior for which society reserves the death penalty.[16]

In comparison, the well-known Brunner study of a Dutch family in the 1990s[17] helped raise a similar question regarding whether behavioral genetics should be considered in mitigation. The study discovered a very rare defect in the gene encoding for monoamine oxidase A (MAOA), an enzyme that helps break down certain neurotransmitters.[18] The defect appeared to correlate with antisocial behavior,[19] which raised the obvious question of how such a finding might be used in arguing for mitigation in criminal cases.

Shortly after the research was published, defense counsel in a death penalty case filed a motion seeking funds to determine whether their client suffered from a deficiency of enzymatic activity for MAOA, with a request for follow-up genetic testing as well.[20] The trial court denied the defense request, "finding that the theory behind the request for funds will not have reached a scientific stage of verifiable certainty in the near future and that [the defendant] could not show that such a stage will ever be reached."[21]

Although the court was correct in rejecting the science as premature, research continues on the correlation between MAOA and antisocial behavior. Subsequent research published in 2002 suggests that children with low MAOA expression

---

13. *Id.* at 1195.

14. *Id.* (quoting Johnson v. Texas, 509 U.S. 350, 367 (1993)).

15. *See* Juvenile Death Penalty Amicus Briefs, http://www.abanet.org/crimjust/juvjus/simmons/ simmonsamicus.html (last visited May 24, 2005).

16. Although the Court did not directly cite any specific amicus brief, several amici supporting the respondent cited neuroscientific support for their position. Although none could conclude that neuroscience was controlling the Court's decision in *Roper*, it is reasonable to expect that lawyers will be citing neuroscience developments in the future. For example, the amicus brief filed by the American Psychological Association and the Missouri Psychological Association argued that neuropsychological research suggests that the adolescent brain is not as developed as the mature adult's brain; similarly, the brief filed by the American Medical Association made a similar "immature brain" argument. *See id.*

17. H. G. Brunner et al., *Abnormal Behavior Associated with a Point Mutation in the Structural Gene for Monoamine Oxidase A*, 262 SCIENCE 578 (1993).

18. *Id.* at 579.

19. *Id.*

20. Mobley v. State, 455 S.E.2d 61, 65 (Ga. 1995). *See also* Deborah W. Denno, *Legal Implications of Genetics and Crime Research, in* GENETICS OF CRIMINAL AND ANTISOCIAL BEHAVIOR 248, 251–53 (Gregory R. Bock & Jamie A. Goode eds., 1996).

21. *Mobley*, 455 S.E.2d at 66.

who are maltreated may be at a greater risk for antisocial behavior,[22] though a more recent study failed to replicate those findings.[23] Similar MAOA challenges are likely in the future as the literature evolves.

Even if MAOA challenges or other arguments based on behavioral genetics are accepted by courts in the future, it is not always clear which way scientific knowledge will cut when introduced at trial. For example, while a defendant could argue for mitigation due to some genetic propensity or neurological defect ("bad genes" or a "bad brain" led him astray), the prosecution could make a counterargument for aggravation, saying that the defendant is even more dangerous because he is *biologically predisposed* to commit crime, and thus he should be incarcerated rather than given probation. This mirror side to mitigation arguments should also be included in the policy dialogue.

B. Preformal Uses

Neuroscience and behavioral genetics converge on issues other than mitigation related to how and when to use possibly relevant findings from these sciences:

> [A significant fear], both in the behavioral genetics area and with [neuroscience], is that there are no [rules of evidence] that control the use of these kinds of technologies in the preformal stages of criminal processes. When it gets to the formality of sentencing, the cry will come up, but the ability of judges and prosecutors to make decisions about whether they're going to initiate charges, [whether] they're going to accept diversion [from criminal prosecution] for people, et cetera—using [neuroscience tests] that haven't been validated—is a serious risk that the technology poses.[24]

Such concerns offer a good example of a policy question that also needs to be addressed in the near future: how neuroscience and behavioral genetics findings might be used by the legal system in preformal settings—that is, prior to bringing criminal charges. For example, defense counsel could bring test results to prosecutors as part of a precharging dialogue, seeking dismissal, reduction of charges, or some other outcome.[25] Such usages would essentially be unreviewable and possibly nonpublic. In addition, such information could be considered

---

22. Avshalom Caspi et al., *Role of Genotype in the Cycle of Violence in Maltreated Children*, 297 SCIENCE 851 (2002).

23. Brett C. Haberstick et al., *Monoamine Oxidase A (MAOA) and Antisocial Behaviors in the Presence of Childhood and Adolescent Maltreatment*, 135 AM. J. MED. GENETICS (PART B: NEUROPSYCHIATRIC GENETICS) 59 (2005).

24. NEUROSCIENCE AND THE LAW, *supra* note 6, at 38 (quoting neuroscientist participant).

25. To give the prosecution their fair share of concern, district attorneys could seek genetic or neuroscientific information in deciding to bring charges, or use it in arguments to a grand jury to secure an indictment.

without even the minimal protections offered by the *Daubert*[26] or *Frye*[27] tests regarding admissibility in formal proceedings.[28] Although the exact nature of these preformal usages is unclear, it seems prudent for policymakers, lawyers, and scientists to consider how such uses might be addressed in ways that are socially, legally, and scientifically appropriate.

IV. INSTRUCTIVE DIFFERENCES

Both genetics and neuroscience raise many of the same policy questions when it comes to issues such as prediction of behavior, but there are obviously areas in which the fields differ. Nevertheless, even when there are differences, the policy dialogue can be enriched by considering the two fields together. The dialogue that has already begun about genetics may serve to inform and shape the way society thinks about neuroscience, and neuroscience may have some lessons for behavioral genetics as well. For example, genetics in general garnered a fair amount of early attention from the public and policymakers. As the human genome project advanced, lawmakers in several states enacted laws to protect genetic information and to guard against potentially discriminatory uses.[29]

---

26. *See* Daubert v. Merrell Dow Pharmaceuticals, Inc., 509 U.S. 579 (1993), *superseded by statute*, FED. R. EVID. 702.

27. *See* Frye v. United States, 293 F. 1013 (D.C. Cir. 1923).

28. The admissibility of scientific information into evidence at trial is generally governed by two approaches:

(1) The *Frye* standard allows for the admission of scientific evidence when the scientific technique, data, or method is generally accepted by the scientific community in the relevant field. 293 F. at 1014. The courts relied on the members of the relevant scientific discipline for the standard, with "general acceptance" usually being proven through additional expert testimony, the citing of standard reference materials in the discipline, and various other methods. *Id.*

(2) The newer approach, and the one now codified in the Federal Rules of Evidence, is the *Daubert* standard, which offers four criteria for courts to use in their evaluations: (a) falsifiability, which asks if the theory or technique can be (and has been) tested; (b) subjection of the theory or technique to peer review; (c) the known or potential error rate of the methodology or technique; and (d) a *Frye*-like general acceptance criteria. 509 U.S. at 592–95. The four elements form a flexible rule, one whose focus should be on determining scientific validity, meaning the evidentiary relevance and reliability. *Id.* at 594–95.

29. After years of debate, the U.S. Congress passed and President Bush signed the Genetic Information Nondiscrimination Act of 2008, Pub. L. 110–233, 122 Stat. 881, which prohibits the improper use of genetic information in health insurance and employment. Under the Act, health insurers cannot deny coverage or charge higher premiums based solely on a person's genetic predisposition to develop a disease, nor can employers use individuals' genetic information when making hiring, firing, or promotion decisions.

This was an unusual and entirely proactive approach to policy making, as there had generally been no litigation about genetic discrimination at that point. The mere specter of risk of misusing genetic information had caused lawmakers to act.

Yet no such actions have been spurred on by recent developments in neuroscience. The link between brain and behavior is much closer than the link between genes and behavior, but the attention to genetics research and its broad social implications has far outweighed that given to neuroscience and technology.[30] Neuroscience could likely benefit from the same public consideration and policy dialogue.

A. Essentialism and Exceptionalism

The potential impact of genetic "exceptionalism"[31] and genetic "essentialism"[32] is an area in which the policy dialogue in genetics has outpaced the dialogue in neuroscience and in which the thinking on genetics has been especially instructive. Both exceptionalism and essentialism deal with the idea that the public may perceive scientific information about a person as being more powerfully determinative than it in fact is.

For genetics, these constructs seem to have worked well in guiding discussion and in thinking about appropriate policy. However, the essentialism argument may not be as obvious in neuroscience as it is in genetic science.[33] People may see their brains as being much more "who they are" than their genes, and they may accordingly offer less resistance to using neuroscientific information in criminal and other court proceedings. This aspect of brain science may not

---

See also, Sonia M. Suter, *The Allure and Peril of Genetics Exceptionalism: Do We Need Special Genetics Legislation?,* 79 WASH. U. L.Q. 669 (2001) (providing a brief overview and analysis of some state genetic information laws).

30. *See Open Your Mind,* THE ECONOMIST, May 23, 2002, at 79 (discussing the legal implications of neuroscientific research).

31. In genetics, a concern has arisen that passing laws and special rules for genetic discrimination (rather than treating such matters under current antidiscrimination schemes, like the Americans with Disabilities Act, 42 U.S.C. §§ 12101–213 (2000)), will result in a perception by the public that genetic factors are more important and determinative of our well-being and behavior than they actually are. This singling out of genetic information for special protection seems to indicate an exceptionally powerful amount or type of knowledge—hence, genetic exceptionalism. A similar concern would arise regarding neuroscientific information.

32. Essentialism is the idea that the person is reducible to some limited element of their biology, that is, "I am my genes" or "I am my brain."

33. As Stanford law professor Henry Greely observed in the AAAS neuroscience and law meeting, "It seems to be quite possible that I am my mind or I am my brain in a way that I'm quite clear I am not my genes. My genes are not me. My mind, my brain, well, maybe that is me." NEUROSCIENCE AND THE LAW, *supra* note 6, at 34 (quoting Greely).

have even been considered as potentially problematic, had it not been for the genetics policy debates.

B. Truth telling

Neuroscience may have something instructive to offer behavioral genetics in the field of truth telling,[34] since it is more likely than behavioral genetics to develop techniques to tell when someone is lying. The development of accurate and reliable neuroscience-based lie detection is already being vigorously explored by researchers, and this has obvious value to the law.[35] If such technology were to be successfully developed, lie detection could be used to evaluate the testimony of witnesses and defendants, to challenge jurors' responses in voir dire, or to poll the jury following a verdict. Courts would have to determine whether witnesses or defendants could be compelled to be tested for truthfulness and whether the judge or jury should be allowed to consider the refusal of a witness to take such a test. All of these would be just the tip of the iceberg.

Issues surrounding the acceptability and legality of compelled neuroscience-based testing, including court decisions regarding when and how to use lie detection technology, would likely be instructive for any behavioral genetics tests

---

34. Lie-detection tests have frequently been held to be inadmissible, in part due to concerns about the accuracy and reliability of techniques such as the polygraph. *E.g.*, United States v. Scheffer, 523 U.S. 303, 309–12 (1998). For the types of questions discussed in the body of this paper, it is assumed that neuroscience is likely to eventually produce substantially more accurate and reliable testing for it to be admissible and relevant.

For a more in-depth discussion of some legal implications of neuroscience-based lie detection, *see* Henry T. Greely, *Prediction, Litigation, Privacy, and Property: Some Possible Legal and Social Implications of Advances in Neuroscience, in* NEUROSCIENCE AND THE LAW, *supra* note 6, at 114. Greely notes several bases for excluding lie-detection tests from court proceedings, including accuracy concerns and invasion of the purview of the jury in its role as finder of fact. *Id. See also* Laurence R. Tancredi, *Neuroscience Developments and the Law, in* NEUROSCIENCE AND THE LAW, *supra* note 6, at 71.

35. This is an area of strong research interest and is becoming increasingly sophisticated. For example, one of the most significant hurdles facing accurate lie detection is what could be termed "the problem of unintentional deceit." Although techniques might be developed to detect when someone is intentionally lying, there might be real difficulty in detecting when someone is merely mistaken—that is, when they are engaging in *unintentional deceit*, subjectively telling the truth but being factually in the wrong. *See* Paul Root Wolpe, et al., *Emerging Neurotechnologies for Lie Detection: Promises and Perils*, 5(2) AM. J. BIOETHICS 1 (2005) (detailing some of the overall problems associated with lie detector technology). Yet, even this difficult problem seems to be gradually yielding to researchers. *See* Scott D. Slotnick & Daniel L. Schacter, *A Sensory Signature That Distinguishes True from False Memories*, 7 NAT. NEUROSCI. 664 (2004); Daniel L. Schacter & Scott D. Slotnick, *The Cognitive Neuroscience of Memory Distortion*, 44 NEURON 149 (2004), available for reading online at http://www2.bc.edu/~slotnics/articles/schacter_slotnick04_neuron.pdf.

that are developed (such as one to determine a propensity for impulsive violence for use in either mitigation or evaluations of future risk).

V. A SHARED HISTORY

Just as both fields share common areas of interest and application, they share a common problem—the problem of history. The history of criminal law and science is one that makes people cautious. Prior uses of science to underpin law by politicians and policymakers include examples in which developing science was misused, and sometimes exploited, occasionally to brutal ends.[36] Because of this history, any attempt to understand criminality from the basis of biology will suffer from suspicion and doubt, and many will have concerns that any such research findings or technologies will be used in oppressive and reactionary ways. These public concerns about the possible abuse of science push just as strongly for a broad policy dialogue as do the hopes for valuable uses.[37] One might call this "the curse of Lombroso"[38]—the haunting risk that immature science could be adopted and used for political and social purposes that feed into the worst of human behavior.

History provides several examples of misguided efforts to apply science to the study of criminality and to use such findings to make policy and law. By now the examples are familiar—from Lombroso's work in the 1800s to identify criminals by anthropomorphic measurements, to the hereditarian theories of some phrenologists, to the development of degeneration theory in the early twentieth century.[39] Perhaps the most horrible American example of science being misused

---

36. *See, e.g.,* NICOLE HAHN RAFTER, CREATING BORN CRIMINALS (1997) (offering an overview of biological theories of criminality from the nineteenth and twentieth centuries); Paul A. Lombardo, *Genes and Disability: Defining Health and the Goals of Medicine: Taking Eugenics Seriously: Three Generations of ??? Are Enough?*, 30 FLA. ST. U.L. REV. 191 (2003) (considering contemporary genetic science in the context of the history of eugenics in America).

37. The potential for discriminatory or eugenic uses of modern genetics research is a good example of a modern public concern. *See* Garland E. Allen, *Is a New Eugenics Afoot?*, 294 SCIENCE 59 (2001) (providing a historical overview of the development of the eugenics movement). *See also* Paul A. Lombardo, *Medicine, Eugenics, and the Supreme Court: From Coercive Sterilization to Reproductive Freedom*, 13 J. CONTEMP. HEALTH L. & POL'Y 1 (1996) (discussing how the eugenics laws continue to play a role in our modern legal thinking).

38. Cesare Lombroso was a nineteenth-century Italian physician who developed the idea that criminals could be detected scientifically through anthropomorphic measurements. Lombroso put forth the idea of the "born" criminal; while his theories were disproven, other concepts of the "born" criminal (or of innate criminality) would continue to play a dangerous role well into the twentieth century, including through the American eugenics movement.

39. *See generally* RAFTER, *supra* note 36, (detailing a history of these examples).

in policy and the law was the development of eugenic sterilization laws in the 1920s and 1930s—laws that sought to forcibly sterilize the "feeble-minded," spurred at least in part by the intent to eliminate "inherited criminality." Anyone with any interest in this topic remembers the chilling words of Justice Holmes in *Buck v. Bell*, "Three generations of imbeciles are enough."[40] Perhaps the coldest chill, however, comes from the sentences preceding that famous line:

> It is better for all the world, if instead of waiting to execute degenerate offspring for crime, or to let them starve for their imbecility, society can prevent those who are manifestly unfit from continuing their kind. The principle that sustains compulsory vaccination is broad enough to cover cutting the Fallopian tubes.[41]

The Supreme Court upheld the compulsory eugenic sterilization laws of Virginia, other states took them as a model, and many people were forcibly sterilized under these laws.

Although the history of American eugenics may be one of the most inflammatory examples of science being misused to make bad law and bad policy, not every time science and criminal law meet means a disaster in the offing. The law is not always easily swayed by attempts to use bad or immature science. For example, during the 1960s a theory emerged regarding males who possessed an additional Y-chromosome.[42] These so-called XYY males were thought to be particularly aggressive and inclined to violence and criminality.[43] In general, courts rejected attempts to admit such information.[44] The impact on the law, such as it was, was rather mild, and eventually, the concept of the XYY male as someone who posed a high risk for criminal behavior was discredited.[45]

What the eugenics experiment and the XYY theory have in common is the extent to which developing science was seized upon and used by nonscientists—policymakers, politicians, judges, and lawyers—who sought to dress their agendas in the trappings of legitimate scientific debate. In part, the ability to misuse science (and for lawyers to ineffectively combat such misuse) comes from the different approaches of the two cultures. Science has a narrowing, problem-focused method, and its discoveries are seen as part of a continuing dialogue, open to change in light of new information. The timeline is long, the knowledge slowly built up, but the entire system is open to complete upheaval—hypotheses, after all, prompt disproof as well as proof. Science values consensus and replicability.

---

40. 274 U.S. 200, 207 (1927).

41. *Id.*

42. Deborah W. Denno, Comment, *Human Biology and Criminal Responsibility: Free Will or Free Ride?*, 137 U. PA. L. REV. 615, 619–20 (1988).

43. *Id.*

44. *Id.* at 620.

45. *See id.* at 622.

Lawyers and judges, on the other hand, often operate with little knowledge of science and the scientific method, and they work on a more pressing timeline to solve the problems immediately before them. Law moves forward on advocacy— using the tools available at the time the conflict must be addressed.

Policymakers add a third approach to the mix—one driven by political concerns and marginally limited by what issues can be considered in formulating positions. Lawyers and scientists are somewhat constrained by the rules of law and peer review, respectively. Policymakers, on the other hand, have broad, wide-sweeping powers, and they can seize on and implement policies with far-reaching impacts that, once in place, can be quite difficult to revise.

VI. CONCLUSION

The potential impact of neuroscience and behavioral genetics on the criminal law, the extent to which the fields converge on common areas, the history of science and the criminal law, and the potential for policymakers to seize on early findings for political goals all lead to this conclusion: the time for a deep, broad, science-driven policy discussion is now. Both neuroscience and behavioral genetics sit at the courtroom door.[46] The issues at the forefront are not the more academic and philosophical ones of causation, free will, determinism, and responsibility, but rather those posed by technologies that are poised to come into courtroom and preformal use soon. These technologies will lay the legal foundations for how courts think about and utilize these developing sciences, possibly for years to come.[47]

---

46. In fact, neuroscience has already entered the courtroom for a visit. *See* Roper v. Simmons, 125 S. Ct. 1183 (2005) (forbidding the death penalty for juvenile offenders in light of their ongoing psychological and emotional development).

47. Oftentimes, the fear is that weak or immature science will be accepted into evidence by a court, to be followed by a flood of decisions influenced by bad science. There are other possible negative effects as well, including when the introduction of science seen as weak or immature results in a ban on all such evidence. For example, in Virginia, a line of cases bars any and all testimony regarding a defendant's mental state, unless an insanity defense is being asserted:

> The state of knowledge in the fields of medicine and psychiatry is subject to constant advance and change. The classifications and gradations applied to mental illnesses, disorders, and defects are frequently revised. The courts cannot, and should not, become dependent upon these subtle and shifting gradations for the resolution of each specific case.

Stamper v. Commonwealth, 324 S.E.2d 682, 688 (Va. 1985) (citing Fisher v. United States, 328 U.S. 463 (1946), and Wahrlich v. Arizona, 479 F.2d 1137 (9th Cir. 1973)). The level of scientific proof and relevance needed to reverse the ruling in *Stamper* remains unclear. In the interim, the evidentiary bar would appear to preclude any and all testimony about mental state, be it psychiatric, psychological, medical, or neurological.

Members of the scientific, legal, and criminal justice professions should join forces to advise and inform policymakers and the public on the scientific, legal, and social issues associated with advances in neuroscience and behavioral genetics. This effort should strive to engage policymakers to make better, more fully informed decisions about science, criminal law, and policy—decisions that would hopefully reduce the risks of the following: unwarranted backlash to developments in science and technology, poorly informed legislation, and judicial decisions based on inappropriate or immature science. If this multidisciplinary effort were successful in establishing itself as a valued resource and authority, the models it develops for assisting in the policy process could be applied to other areas of science, technology, and law.

The proposal is not intended as a "thought experiment" or an academic exercise. Failure to try such an approach will leave these matters to the vagaries of the political process or to a court system that is unprepared to address complex issues of science. The very structure of the court system works against the development of coherent and unified policies—courts develop policies in response to specific legal challenges, not from a proactive, forward-looking approach. As a consequence, the results may impair scientists' ability to conduct research and society's ability to benefit from useful technology. Moreover, the adoption of controversial, poorly understood, and immature science by the courts or law enforcement could undermine public confidence in the legal system, as well as unfairly affect the rights of citizens.

The initial political challenge facing such an effort will be to convince policymakers in all branches of government that the analysis is timely and relevant to them in governing. To achieve this goal, the analysis must be capable of transcending narrow partisan and professional interests, and it should therefore reach out to a broad range of stakeholders in a genuine dialogue based on mutual respect for differences of opinion. Such a dialogue should help to confer legitimacy on various policy options. It is not enough that the dialogue be only among colleagues in a particular discipline, but it must also be conducted across fields, so that both the participants and the larger group of stakeholders may understand the wider context. Broad, integrative thinking about what the sciences

---

This bar has precluded testimony regarding the mental capacity of a defendant in a malicious wounding case in which the defendant, who had an established history of mental retardation and an estimated IQ of 65, shook and injured his infant son. Funk v. Commonwealth, No. 1821-02-4, 2003 Va. App. LEXIS 383 (2003). *See also* Peeples v. Commonwealth, 519 S.E.2d 382, 386 (Va. Ct. App. 1999) (upholding the exclusion of expert testimony from psychologist in aggravated malicious wounding case, where defense sought to admit evidence to rebut assumption of malice and to bolster self-defense claim). *Stamper* has also been interpreted to bar admission of psychiatric testimony that the defendant "lacked the capacity to form the necessary premeditation to commit the offense of capital murder as charged in the indictment." Smith v. Commonwealth, 389 S.E.2d 871, 879–80 (Va. 1990) (citing *Stamper*, 324 S.E.2d at 688).

reveal to us about how we behave will help to shape better policy—from statutes and regulations to courtrooms.

The ultimate challenge, however, is how to have a substantial and long-lasting effect on policy making. The proposed effort must connect to government, but it cannot be captured by it, or else it becomes just another partisan battleground. So the question arises: how do you create a private body to exert influence on the policy-making process without being part of the government itself? The question of how best to assist policymakers with questions that span multiple areas of expertise, such as science and law, is complicated. As the sheer volume of scientific knowledge has increased, it seems clear that governmental and quasi-governmental bodies cannot by themselves fully advise and educate policymakers on all of the scientific, legal, and social issues associated with advances in science and technology. In short, there are simply too many issues that would need to be addressed and too few governmental bodies to meet that need.

Instead, the professional communities that have the relevant knowledge and expertise to educate and inform policymakers should combine efforts to serve as a nongovernmental, nonpartisan advisory body. This ongoing neuroscience and law task force would monitor and assess future scientific developments as they occur and report on these developments to policymakers and the public. In addition to its ongoing deliberations, the task force could serve as "first responder" to emerging events that could affect neuroscience research as well as legal and policy decisions. In this latter capacity, the task force would consider requests from scientists, legal professionals, and policymakers to review and comment on issues of pressing importance and provide information and guidance on these complex matters.

The impact of neuroscience and behavioral genetics on criminal law offers an opportunity to start such an effort on a small scale, by building on the types of discussions that are included in this volume and in other relevant proceedings. Without such an effort in place, the public policy dialogue will go along in fits and starts—and our policies will be constantly playing catch up as the science surges forward.

6. "WHO KNOWS WHAT EVIL LURKS IN THE HEARTS OF MEN?": BEHAVIORAL GENOMICS, NEUROSCIENCE, CRIMINAL LAW, AND THE SEARCH FOR HIDDEN KNOWLEDGE

HENRY T. GREELY

In an old radio show, the question in this chapter's title was answered, "The Shadow knows." In the modern American criminal justice system, people increasingly want to answer "The Scientist knows." Behavioral genomics,[1] in spite of false starts of the eugenics era and the XYY fiasco in the late 1960s, continues to attract attention, but neuroscience, particularly through neuroimaging, may now be generating even more excitement for its potential to deal with crime.

These two approaches inspire hope that they will teach us something useful, and otherwise unknown, about individual defendants and criminals, their tendencies, and their crimes. Each also invokes the social authority of "Science"—objective, impartial, and definitive. These similarities lead to them sometimes being treated together, as in this book. And yet for all that they share, the two approaches also differ in important ways.

This chapter explores the differences between the implications of behavioral genomics and neuroscience for criminal justice.[2] As behavioral genomics has been discussed for several decades—and provides the subject for most of the chapters in this book—this chapter will focus on how the consequences of possible neuroscientific methods differ from those of behavioral genomics. It will

---

1. This field has more commonly been referred to as behavioral genetics. The semantic line between "genetics" and "genomics" is not entirely clear; at times it seems that genomics is being used as a trendier version of genetics. To the extent there is a meaningful distinction, though, it is that "genetics" deals with discrete and usually individual genes, while genomics deals with information drawn from throughout an individual's genome, from genes and nongenes, from one site or many. I have used the term genomics in this chapter both because genomics encompasses genetics and because, increasingly, our important discoveries will come from genomics and not from the traditional single gene approach associated with genetics.

2. I have, earlier, explored some of the differences between the ethical, legal, and social issues that arise in genetics (ELSI) and those that spring from neuroscience. Henry T. Greely, *Neuroethics and ELSI: Similarities and Differences*, 7 MINN. J. L. SCI. & TECH. 599–637 (May 2006). That discussion overlapped only partially with this chapter, but focused more on the history and development of the ethical analysis of the two fields.

first sketch the sciences involved and some of their plausible technological applications to criminal justice. It will then analyze some general ways in which neuroscience is likely to have different effects from those of behavioral genomics. Finally, it will contrast the likely power of neuroscience with that of behavioral genomics in two specific aspects of the criminal justice system: deciding who did it and then determining what to do with him.

I conclude that, in the context of criminal law, neither science is likely to provide much help in determining, based on their predispositions, *who* committed a crime. Neuroscience, however, may well answer other important questions in solving crimes. Both behavioral genomics and neuroscience will provide some information useful, at least occasionally, for determining responsibility, sentencing, or "treatment" of criminal behaviors. For the most part, however, however weak or strong behavioral genomics will be, neuroscience is likely to be stronger. Although the consequences of either science for criminal law are uncertain, neuroscience, although it will not undermine the foundations of criminal justice, has a far greater potential to shake—and to reshape—those foundations.

THE SCIENCES

Genomics and neuroscience are not exactly different things. Genomics is, in fact, one tool that neuroscience uses to examine the brain. Behavioral genomics, as behavior comes from the brain, is effectively one kind of neuroscience. But for present purposes, I will distinguish between behavioral genomics, on the one hand, and neuroscience that does not directly use genomic (or genetic) techniques, on the other.

Behavioral Genomics

Behavioral genomics depends on correlating certain behaviors with particular genomic variations. The use of human behavioral genomics in individual criminal cases will generally be to produce evidence that the suspect, defendant, or convict has a particular genomic variation and, from that, to infer some otherwise hidden or deniable characteristic, such as a strong tendency to violent criminal behavior.[3]

We most often think of those variations as involving different variations in DNA sequences, but they can also be variations in the number of copies of a particular chromosome, gene, or "non-gene" stretch of DNA. People with Down syndrome (caused by having three copies of chromosome 21) or men with an extra Y chromosome (the XYY karyotype), for instance, have too many copies of

---

3. The prosecution's ability to introduce such evidence, at least at trial (as opposed to on sentencing) may be affected by other evidence rules or by the defendants' decisions about, for example, introducing character evidence.

some of their DNA. These differences will typically be found in all of the individual's cells, all descended from the initial copy of the genome found in the early embryo. (One might try to examine the "functional genome" as opposed to this "structural genome," by looking at what genes are expressed, when and how, in the brain, but getting that information from the brains of living humans is quite difficult.)

In its purest form, behavioral genomics would be able to go from a person's genotype to a reliable statement about that person's behavior. A person with three copies of chromosome 21 (trisomy 21) will almost always exhibit the behavior of mental retardation as part of Down syndrome.[4] A boy whose X chromosome does not carry a properly functioning copy of the gene HPRT1, which directs the creation of the protein hypoxanthine-guanine phosphoribosyltransferase, will be diagnosed with Lesch-Nyhan syndrome and will develop self-mutilating lip- and finger-biting behaviors in his second year.[5] And in the one Dutch family in which the condition has been identified, males with a nonfunctional version of the gene MAO-A, which codes for the protein monoamine oxidase A, develop antisocial and violent behavior, along with mental retardation.[6] In all of these cases the connection between the genetic variation and the resulting behavior is extremely strong; the "penetrance"—the percentage of those with the genotype who will develop the behavior—is quite high, possibly 100 percent.

---

4. The National Institute of Health provides a useful summary of Down syndrome: National Institute of Child Health and Human Development, *Down syndrome*, http://www.nichd.nih.gov/health/topics/down_syndrome.cfm.

By the way, the condition is often called "Down's syndrome," named, as many diseases are, for a physician who described it, in this case J. Langdon Down, an English doctor who described the syndrome in 1866. In recent years patient advocates and others for several diseases have tried to make the point that the discoverer did not "invent" or "own" the disease and so write the disease names as Down syndrome or Alzheimer disease, without an 's.

In this case, however, Down received the credit inappropriately, as a French physician named Edouard Séguin had already described it in print twenty years earlier. Furthermore, Down viewed the syndrome in a racist context as a case of reversion of the "higher" European race to a "lower" "Mongoloid" level. Some suggest, as a result, naming the syndrome trisomy 21, indicating it solely by its cause—three copies of chromosome 21.

5. National Institute for Neurological Disorders and Stroke, Lesch-Nyhan Syndrome Information, http://www.ninds.nih.gov/disorders/lesch_nyhan/lesch_nyhan.htm. See also ONLINE MENDELIAN INHERITANCE IN MAN (hereafter "OMIM"), Lesch-Nyhan Syndrome, http://www.ncbi.nlm.nih.gov/entrez/dispomim.cgi?id=300322.

6. OMIM, Monoamine Oxidase A, http://www.ncbi.nlm.nih.gov/entrez/dispomim.cgi?id=309850; See also Brunner, H. G., et al., *X-linked borderline mental retardation with prominent behavioral disturbance: phenotype, genetic localization, and evidence for disturbed monoamine metabolism.* 52 AM. J. HUM. GENET. 1032–39 (1993) and OMIM, *Brunner Syndrome*, http://www.ncbi.nlm.nih.gov/entrez/dispomim.cgi?id=300615.

Known examples of genetic variations that are highly penetrant for behaviors are rare. Other claims have been made for less penetrant variations associated with particular behaviors. For example, many genetic variations have been claimed to be linked to schizophrenia, a mental illness characterized by a number of unusual behaviors. In all cases, the estimated effect of the genetic variation on the risk of being diagnosed with schizophrenia is fairly small. In many cases, the links between the disease and some of those genetic variations have not been strongly replicated and are not widely accepted.[7] Similarly, claims have been made for associations between particular genetic variations and high intelligence. Perhaps the most prominent such finding, based on a study of extraordinarily intelligent children, concluded that the genetic variation involved accounts for only 2 percent of the variation of the subjects' intelligence from average.[8]

It may turn out that the relative paucity of strong associations between genetic variations and human behavior is an artifact of the early stage of our genetic knowledge. Perhaps, in 10 or 20 years, when we know much more about our genomes, we will discover that links between genetic variations and behaviors are both much more numerous and, in a substantial number of cases, much stronger than we now expect.

Or perhaps not. Behaviors are often difficult to define; blue eyes are relatively easy to recognize, but what are the boundaries of a personality trait like shyness, or a condition like autism, or a behavior like "criminality"? Difficulty in defining the phenotypes for behaviors makes establishing genomic links harder. Also, it seems quite plausible that behaviors are strongly influenced by more factors than physical traits are as an individual develops from a zygote, with a fixed genome, to an adult. For example, men differ genetically from women because men, but not women, carry a Y chromosome with about 80 genes, which code for about 25 different proteins.[9] We believe that men and women, on average, differ in some of their behaviors, but jumping from the genes to the behavior is very hard because of all the other ways in which men and women have different

---

7. Patrick F. Sullivan, *The Genetics of Schizophrenia*, 2 PLoS MEDICINE e212 doi:10.1371/journal.pmed.0020212 (July 26, 2005).

8. M. J. Chorney, et al., *A Quantitative Trait Locus Associated with Cognitive Ability in Children*, 9 PSYCH. SCI. 183-189 (May 1998). See Nicholas Wade, *First Gene To Be Linked With High Intelligence Is Reported Found.*, THE NEW YORK TIMES A 16 (May 14, 1998). Interestingly, Plomin's group later were unable to replicate this finding with a similarly-sized sample. Hill L et al. *A Quantitative Trait Locus Not Asssociated with Cognitive Ability: A Failure to Replicate.* 13 PSYCH SCI,561 (2002). The second article does not appear to have been reported in THE NEW YORK TIMES.

9. See Mark A. Jobling and Chris Tyler-Smith, *The Human Y Chromosome: An Evolutionary Marker Comes of Age*, 4 NATURE REVIEWS GENETICS 598–612 (Aug. 2003), which estimates that the Y chromosome codes for 27 unique proteins. Other sources suggest there are 23 proteins. The estimate of 80 genes includes DNA that codes for small RNAs and other nonprotein products.

experiences and environments that could, and in many cases certainly do, influence behavior. And even if all the differences were to be "explained" by genomics, we would still face the reality that some men will display some behaviors more commonly found in women and vice versa. This intermixing of genomes and environments (and chance) seems particularly likely to be important in the development of the immensely complex and, to a large extent, self-organized human brain and the behaviors it produces.

Neuroscience

Neuroscience is a much larger field than behavioral genomics or, indeed, than genetics and genomics in general. For present purposes, though, we are interested in those applications of human neuroscience that may be relevant to the criminal justice system. Most of those will involve neuroimaging, looking at the structure or the function of the human brain. Structural MRI is a complex technology but the result is straightforward: a computer-generated image that can reveal the shape and size of the living brain in exquisite detail. Functional MRI (fMRI) is less direct. Instead of looking for structure, it looks for the ratio of oxygenated hemoglobin to deoxygenated hemoglobin in thousands of little cubes (voxels) in the brain. A higher level of oxygenated hemoglobin is thought, under the BOLD hypothesis (Blood Oxygenation Level Dependent), to be the result of the "firing" of neurons in that region about two seconds earlier. A subject in an MRI machine will be shown an image, asked to think about something, made to listen to a sound, or have his mind engaged in some other way. The MRI will then detect which parts of his brain have more or less oxygenated hemoglobin two seconds later, leading to an inference that the regions with higher levels (regions that "are activated" or, more familiarly, that "light up") are involved in the mental processes of that task.

This neuroimaging research will often be relevant to criminal law in the same way as behavioral genomics. A suspect, defendant, or convict will be shown to have a certain brain structure or pattern of brain function. An inference will be drawn from the neuroimaging results to certain hidden or deniable characteristics or mental states. In some cases it will be the same as the example given for behavioral genomics—that the subject has a strong tendency to violent criminal behavior.

While determining a genomic sequence or set of copy number variations is becoming increasingly routine and cheap, neuroimaging remains very complicated, particularly functional neuroimaging. The machines are finicky and the subject's cooperation is essential—a few head movements can ruin a neuroimaging session. Functional MRI is particularly tricky. The results are often acutely sensitive to how the MRI data is treated—the setting of various cut-off levels for counting a particular voxel as "activated," for example, can make enormous changes in the conclusions. And the statistical analysis of the patterns of activation can be even more difficult to interpret than genomic associations.

There are further complications. Functional MRI studies are experiments, where the human subject, in the scanner, is being exposed to or doing something. The precise design of that experiment can be crucial. For example, for a study of lie detection, one would not want to have the subject press the "yes" button every time he told the truth and the "no" button only when lying because the pattern of brain activation might be the difference between "yes" and "no," not the difference between "truth" and "lie." The cost of doing fMRI studies is roughly comparable to the cost of doing a whole genome scan on one individual (roughly $500 to $1000 per subject), but fMRI studies typically are done with far fewer subjects than genomic research but are done by many more individual researchers. As a result, the published literature on fMRI studies comprises thousands of studies, all with small numbers of subjects, almost all with different experimental designs, and almost never subject to precise attempted replication. All of this makes functional neuroimaging research trickier, in some respects, than behavioral genomics research.

Neuroimaging research is currently the most discussed new neuroscience method, with reports of imaging studies, particularly fMRI studies, appearing regularly in major newspapers and magazines. It is by no means, however, the only one relevant to criminal law. Neuroimaging is observational; various interventional methods may also prove important. These include everything from neurosurgical removal of some brain regions to the implantation of deep brain stimulating electrodes to the use of external and transient electrical or magnetic fields to stimulate or repress brain neurons. Each of these methods has the potential to teach us something about the roots of criminal behavior or even its "cure." These methods also have their own sets of limitations.[10]

BEHAVIORAL GENOMICS, NEUROSCIENCE, AND CRIMINAL LAW: GENERAL DIFFERENCES

The consequences of neuroscience for criminal law seem likely to differ from those of behavioral genomics in four general ways. First, neuroscience findings are likely to be strongly associated with criminal behavior more often and more strongly than will genomic findings. Second, it is likely that any genomic findings ultimately could be reproduced, often more powerfully, as neuroscience findings. Third, neuroscience findings will be less likely to promote eugenic interventions, but, fourth, both behavioral genomics and neuroscience are likely to suggest plausible near-term "treatments" for criminal behavior. These differences will neither

---

10. See Henry T. Greely, *Neuroscience and Criminal Justice: Not Responsibility but Treatment,* 56 KAN. L. REV. 1103-38 (2008).

be universal nor always be differences of kind rather than degree, but they are worth noting.

Association Strength

Whether structural or functional, neuroimaging studies will deal with the criminal's (or potential criminal's) brain *now*, when the behaviors are relevant. The exact shape and size of the subject's amygdala or the interactions between his anterior cingulate cortex and his limbic system, which might influence criminal behavior, are visible and having their influence, if any, today. The amygdala or the pattern of interactions between two brain regions were almost certainly different 20 years earlier and were completely nonexistent until some point well into the person's prenatal development. The subject's genome, however, was set shortly after fertilization took place, when the sperm's genome merged with the egg's genome (barring postconception mutations, which are unlikely to be important for any given individual).

As a result, the connection between criminal behavior and brain structure and function is immediate. A criminal's brain acts in particular ways immediately before and during the crime to cause the crime to occur. The consequences of genomic differences for criminal behavior are likely to be much less direct. If there is any connection, it will usually be because the genomic variations found in the zygote will have influenced the developing individual in ways that ultimately correlate with the criminal behavior. But a near-infinite number of other things—from parenting, to experiences, to nutrition, to drugs, to chance—will have joined the initial genome in shaping that growing brain and its behavior. As a result, compared with links between existing brain structures or function and crime, identifying genomic variations that correlate with criminal behavior is likely to be much more difficult and, more importantly, the strength of such variations (the "penetrance" of the genome) seems likely to be much lower.

Ascertainment Overlap

Even when the genomic influences are strong, as in, for example, Down syndrome, ultimately neuroscience, because it studies the current brain, should be stronger still. The genes can *only* affect behavior through changes they make in the brain, changes that neuroscience, in one of its forms, should ultimately be able to detect.[11] Thus, any strong genomic associations with behavior should be trumped by stronger neuroscience associations.

---

11. It also seems likely that genomic differences will be linked to criminal behavior in a causal way—they will be at least one of the "causes" of the behavior. That's not necessarily true of neuroimaging findings. If a particular region "lights up" during criminal behavior, that activation may be the cause of the behavior or one of its consequences. This difference may not be very important. For detecting a propensity to criminal behavior, a strong correlation may be quite useful even if the correlation is not causal. If every time

Thus, while Down syndrome can be diagnosed through genomics, at some point it should be diagnosable through neuroimaging and other neuroscience methods. (Of course, in some cases, like this one, simpler methods of diagnosis, like physical and behavioral examinations, may well be cheaper, easier, and as definitive.) Neuroscience has the further advantage of being likely to say more about severity than behavioral genomics. People with Down syndrome exhibit a wide range of severity of mental retardation, from severe to mild. Genomic analysis, at this point, can tell us little if anything about the severity of mental retardation in Down syndrome. Presumably, as the severity of the mental retardation must be a product of the structure and function of the brain, neuroscience will be better able to provide information about severity than genomics.

Now, as a practical matter, this may not always be true. Go back to that Dutch family with the nonfunctional MAO-A gene. The affected men in that family do not make any working copies of the MAO-A protein. That might have had long-term effects on their brain development (and, in fact, seems likely to have done so, at least with regard to their mental retardation), but it may also have a continuing effect through the continuing absence of that protein. Neuroscientists could, in theory, detect the absence of normal copies of that protein directly, but getting samples of tissue or fluid from the brains of living humans is neither safe nor easy. The structure of the gene could be used powerfully to infer the contemporary lack of protein function as reliably and more easily than that current function, as a matter of current biochemistry, could be directly tested. Such a case, though, seems likely to be the exception, not the rule, in part because many aspects of brain function may be relatively easily ascertained by neuroimaging. Genomic variations are likely to work through influencing brain development, not by changing immediate brain function.

As a result, in terms of telling us something about behaviors or behavioral propensities, particularly those that are not immediately detectable, it is likely that anything behavioral genomics will be able to do, neuroscience will be able to do, and better. Behavioral genomics may remain important as a way of understanding the biochemical causes of various behaviors or behavioral tendencies, but, in the criminal justice system, it is not clear that it will have any significant role (even *if* strong, and not rare, genomic associations with criminal behavior are discovered, which remains to be seen). For the criminal justice system, behavioral genomics may well have become obsolete during its infancy.

Eugenics

The next point seems straightforward. If behavioral genomics were to produce evidence for genomic variations powerfully associated with criminal behavior,

---

A happens, we see B, B is a good signal for A whether it is a cause or not. For some purposes, though, such as potential treatments, causation will matter. And for scientists seeking to understand how the brain works, causation will also be important.

one way to intervene might be through eugenics. One method would be to ban genetic reproduction by people at risk for having children with those variations. ("Non-genetic" reproduction through use, for example, of donor eggs or sperm that did not carry the relevant genomic sequence should be permissible.) Alternatively, people at risk for having a child with this genetic trait could be required to use preimplantation genetic diagnosis to select for implantation only unaffected embryos or to use prenatal genetic testing followed by the abortion of any affected fetuses.

The nature of the genomic risk would be relevant here. In a traditional single gene trait, the chances that a couple at risk would have a child who carried the dangerous variation would be 25 percent, 50 percent, or 100 percent, depending on the method of inheritance (autosomal dominant, autosomal recessive or X-linked, or mitochondrial) and how many risky alleles each of the parents carried (zero, one, or two). If the risk depended on a particular combination of several different alleles (or copy number variations, translocations, or other changes), the child's probabilities would be lower.

With a neuroscience connection to criminal behavior, without any genomic connection, eugenic solutions would be meaningless. Parents with the trait would not be any more, or less, likely, to pass this nongenetic trait on to their genetic children. Note, however, that if it were believed that the parents were likely, through their parenting, to cause their children to have that behavior, the state might still want to limit their ability to be parents—not, so much, to be genetic parents but to *raise* children. And this constraint would apply not only to their genetic children, but any adopted children, step-children, or children from donor eggs, donor sperm. This could turn out to be more intrusive—and crueler—than limiting genetic reproduction.

"Treatments"

Finally, both behavioral genomic and neuroscience findings are likely to suggest interventions to "treat" the "disorder" of some particular criminal behavior, though in different ways.

For genetic conditions, treatments that might come to mind involve molecules, introduced either as drugs or as genes. If we discover connections between particular sets of genetic variations and certain criminal behaviors, the connections are likely to suggest interventions. The genomic variations will operate through molecules, usually proteins but sometimes small RNAs. The variations will change the sequence of these molecules or when and in what quantities they appear. These kinds of associations will offer possibilities for similarly molecular interventions, changing the nature, timing, or quantities of these molecules in the offender's brain.

These treatments may well be pharmacological, aimed at changing the proportions of different molecules or different versions (isoforms) of the same molecules in the brain. Or they could use genomic clues to try to block or stimulate certain cell receptors in order to change behavior. Each method could function directly through administering drugs, either the proteins or RNAs themselves or small molecules designed to block or assist their functions.

But pills, shots, or infusions are not the only ways of delivering molecules inside human brains. Another method is cell therapy. In this approach people who suffer from DNA that makes the wrong molecules (or the right molecules at the wrong time, in the wrong place, or in the wrong quantity) will receive transplants of cells that make the molecules properly. These cells will then deliver the molecules in ways that fix the problem. One biotech company, StemCells Inc., is currently conducting a clinical trial of such a therapy, using brain stem cells (derived from aborted fetuses, not from embryonic stem cells) to try to treat Batten's Disease, a fatal neurodegenerative disorder.[12]

At the extreme, the treatment could involve "gene therapy," more properly called, at this point, gene transfer research. This approach transfers "good" copies of the relevant genes into a living person's cells where they will make, *in situ*, the "right" molecules. This approach does have the substantial problem that, in spite of over 25 years of trying, it has not yet been proven safe and effective—and has, in fact, almost never been shown to be effective at all. The strongest evidence of success came in a French trial for disease called Severe Combined Immunodeficiency—X-linked. Eleven children were cured of this condition but three of them developed leukemia as a result of the treatment. At least one of those children died.[13]

It is, of course, a long way from the discovery of an association between genomic variations and a behavior to the creation of a safe and effective treatment for it, but it is certainly conceivable. Of course, even the development of therapies that succeed in getting the right molecules to the right places at the right times might not provide a very useful intervention for criminal behavior. If the behavior is the result of the influences of genomic variations during development, gene therapy later in life, such as at the time of criminal conviction, may be futile. (If the genomic variation has continuing effects, such as, for example, the possibly continuing effect of MAO-A deficiency on criminal behavior, successful gene therapy might be useful.)

Neuroscience associations to crime will appear in the person's existing brain. The brain structures or patterns of brain activity linked with the behavior will suggest immediate interventions. In some cases those may be through removal of a brain structure. Thus, both Chinese and Russian hospitals removed or destroyed brain regions of heroin addicts in the early 2000s in order to "cure"

---

12. Carl T. Hall, *Trials for Stem-Cell Treatment for Brain Disease*, SAN FRANCISCO CHRONICLE, A18 (Oct. 21, 2005). The company's discussion of the trial can be found at http://www.stemcellsinc.com/rdprograms/nervoussystem.html#batten.

13. Jocelyn Kaiser, *Panel Urges Limits on X-SCID Trials*, 307 SCI 1544–45 (Mar. 11, 2005).

them of their addiction.[14] Other connections might suggest not removing but stimulating or repressing neuronal activity in some regions. Deep brain stimulation, approved by the FDA for various motion disorders, including Parkinson's disease, is now being used experimentally on a variety of mental illnesses, such as depression, and other behaviors, including overeating and aggressiveness.

Of course, this dichotomy between genomics and neuroscience is too stark. In behavioral genomics, even if the underlying genomic flaw cannot be corrected, other interventions may prevent or mitigate the symptoms in some cases. For example, phenylketonuria (PKU) is an autosomal recessive disease where the affected person's body does not produce a protein necessary to help transform the amino acid, phenylalanine, into another amino acid, tyrosine. Phenylalanine is essential to life, but an excessive amount is deadly to neurons in developing brains, leading to severe mental retardation. The nonfunctional genes in phenylketonuria cannot be replaced or "corrected" and we cannot deliver the protein to the right place in the right quantities at the right time. By limiting affected children to diets very low in phenylalanine, however, their brains can be saved.

None of these four general differences between behavioral genomic and neuroscientific approaches to criminal behavior will always apply. Nonetheless, in general, neuroscience is likely to produce stronger connections to criminal behavior, avoid the temptation to eugenic interventions, and suggest more treatments, especially during adolescence or adulthood, than behavioral genomics.

BEHAVIORAL GENOMICS VERSUS NEUROSCIENCE: TWO TYPES OF APPLICATION

Let's now get more specific and look at how behavioral genomics and neuroscience are likely to vary in their effects on two different aspects of the criminal justice system. The first involves "Who did it?"—evidence, or, in some cases, "facts" generated during the investigation of a crime whether or not they are ever actually introduced in evidence at a trial. The second concerns "What to do with him?"—issues of criminal responsibility, such as insanity or mitigation; of sentencing; and of "treatment."

Who Did It?

Genomics (or genetics) is already very useful in determining who committed a crime (or, in some cases, whether an offense has been committed at all[15]);

---

14. Wayne Hall, *Stereotactic Neurosurgical Treatment of Addiction: Minimizing the Chances for Another "Great and Desperate Cure,"* 101 ADDICTION, 1–3 (2006).

15. Consider the use of DNA technologies to determine whether particular artifacts came from a protected species or not.

neuroscience is likely to be increasingly important. Neither *behavior* genomics nor the *behavioral* uses of neuroscience are likely to be very helpful for these purposes, although, in the event they are, neuroscience is likely to be more useful.

The use of genomic information has been a major breakthrough in forensic science over the last twenty years. DNA from a crime scene can be compared with DNA from suspects, providing powerful evidence of guilt or innocence. It can be matched with DNA profiles stored in massive databases, implicating those in the database in further crimes. Partial matches between crime scene DNA and the DNA of a second person can even be used to cast suspicion on relatives of the second person.[16] It can be used for identification of nonhuman DNA in other criminal contexts, from identifying materials from endangered species to associating DNA from a suspect's pet with a crime scene.[17] All of these uses can take place during the investigation of a crime and can be crucial whether or not the information is ever introduced as evidence at trial. (And, in fact, that information may be so powerful as to prevent a trial by leading defendants to plead guilty.)

It is hard to imagine much use of *behavioral* genomics information in the investigation of a crime. Presumably if a witness testified that the perpetrator behaved in a distinctive way, associated with some genomics variations, one could test suspects for that genetic variation.[18] On the other hand, one could usually determine more directly whether the suspect exhibited that particular behavior by observing the suspect's behavior. Thus, if a witness said the defendant appeared to be mentally retarded, one could presumably do genetic tests to determine if a suspect had a form of mental retardation known to be associated with particular genomic patterns—but there are easier ways to determine mental retardation. (And in most cases mental retardation is not associated with any known genomic variations, or anything else—most cases of mental retardation have unknown causes.)

If the behavior cannot necessarily be observed in a suspect because it is only a propensity—an increased likelihood of acting in a particular way—rather than an invariant behavior, genomic analysis might indeed show whether a particular

---

16. See Henry T. Greely, Daniel P. Riordan, Nanibaa' A. Garrison, Joanna L. Mountain, *Family Ties: The Use of DNA Offender Databases to Catch Offenders' Kin*, 34 J. L. MED. & ETHICS 248–262 (Summer 2006); Frederick R. Bieber, Charles H. Brenner, David Lazer, *Finding Criminals Through DNA of Their Relatives*, 312 SCI. 1315–16 (June 2, 2006).

17. See George Sensabaugh and D. H. Kaye, *Non-human DNA Evidence*, 38 JURIMETRICS J. 1–16 (1998).

18. Arguably crimes committed entirely or almost entirely by men, such as forcible rape, could be considered an exception, as maleness has extremely strong, though not quite perfect, genomic associations (though whether the DNA is the cause of the behavior or not remains unclear). Of course, a test that leaves half the human species in the suspect pool is not that helpful, even apart from the fact that genomic analysis will almost never be needed to determine whether a person is male.

person had that higher likelihood. But the fact that the behavior is not invariant is, in itself, evidence that that person might not have exhibited it at the relevant time. And, of course, it cannot show that the suspect was *the* person who exhibited that behavior in the course of the crime. This is particularly true if, as I assume, there are fundamentally no criminal behaviors that are restricted only to people with behavioral genomic predispositions to them.

Consider the strongest known behavioral genomic association with crime: the Dutch family without a functional MAO-A gene. Males with the nonfunctional gene seem to have a very high likelihood of committing arson at some time (though not, of course, at every possible time). How useful would even that extreme example be in determining whether an apparent arson in the Netherlands had been committed by such a person? Or as a defense to the arson charge from a person with a normal MAO-A gene? That information is just not very useful—people with the genomic variation will not be the only people to exhibit such a behavior. It may not be entirely useless, at least in the investigation stage. It might help the Dutch police to know which men have nonfunctional MAO-A genes and to include them as suspects in arson cases, just as they would include people previously convicted of arson. If the propensity is strong enough, of course, most of those with the genetic predisposition will eventually be suspects as a result of earlier convictions.

And on top of all these logical problems with the weakness of the link between the genes and punishable behavior are actual legal issues. It is not clear that genomic evidence of a propensity to commit crimes would be admissible at trial. American evidence law restricts the use of "character," "predisposition," or "similar crimes or acts" evidence at trial.[19] I will not discuss these restrictions in any detail, but, in general, such evidence is viewed with suspicion and admitted, at most, grudgingly. (Evidence of similar past crimes or acts by the defendant in a criminal or civil case for sexual assault or child molestation is an exception; the rules make it generally admissible but establish a process to help assure that it is used fairly.)

Neuroscience evidence of propensity to particular behaviors will face all the same barriers and then some. For one thing, neuroscience tests to be used as evidence about who committed the crime will *never* be done at the time of the crime (except in the very unlikely situation of a crime committed from inside an

---

19. Federal Rules of Evidence 404 and 405 deal with character evidence. Rules 412 through 416 deal with sex. Rule 412 concerns evidence of an alleged victim's past sexual behavior or alleged sexual predispositions. Rules 413 and 414 deal with evidence of similar past crimes in sexual assault and child molestation cases, respectively. Rule 415 deals with evidence of similar acts in civil sexual assault or child molestation cases. In addition, Rule 406 concerns evidence of habit or routine practice, which possibly could be stretched to cover some predisposition evidence.

MRI machine). And, like behavioral genomics tests, they will reveal only propensities, not certainties.

For the reasons discussed earlier, however, neuroscience tests are likely to reveal such propensities more strongly than genomic tests would. Consider, for example, a male defendant in the forcible rape of a woman who argues that he did not commit the crime because, among other things, he is gay. It is plausible that various neuroscience-based tests (or even more traditional psychological tests) would reveal a suspect's sexual preference much more powerfully than any "straight" or "gay" genes. But even such evidence would not necessarily mean that the suspect had not raped a victim of the "wrong" sex for his usual preference. Similarly, neuroscience evidence of a strong aversion to violence would not necessarily mean that, at one moment, the suspect had not acted violently. Neuroscience evidence of relevant predispositions is likely to be stronger than behavioral genomics evidence but neither will be very strong or very useful—certainly at trial and probably in investigations.

So, at least with respect to the revelation of propensities for some behaviors, neuroscience, like behavioral genomics, is unlikely to provide very useful information about particular crimes. But neuroscience has its own equivalent of the use of genomics, through forensic DNA, in criminal cases; other uses of neuroscience may well be quite important in criminal law. These include areas such as lie detection,[20] determination that a person "recognizes" something,[21] possible testing of the quality of memories, assessing bias, and others. It is these applications, not the detection of behavioral propensities, that may well make neuroscience even more useful than the use of DNA for identification in investigating crimes.

What Should We Do With Him?

A defendant's mental state can have a wide range of effects in criminal law. At trial, it may lead to a verdict of not guilty by reason of insanity or an acquittal for lack of intent or of relevant knowledge (perhaps through the lack of the capacity to form that intent or have that knowledge). It could lead to lesser charges, such as manslaughter rather than premeditated murder, or lesser punishment, as a result of having been provoked or having acted from better rather than worse motives. It can also affect what happens after trial by affecting the defendant's criminal sentence, civil commitment, or other intervention.

---

20. See Henry T. Greely and Judy Illes, *Neuroscience-Based Lie Detection: The Urgent Need for Regulation*, 33 Am. J. Law & Med. 377–431 (2007); Paul R. Wolpe, Kenneth R. Foster, David D. Langleben, *Emerging Neurotechnologies for Lie-Detection: Promises and Perils*, 5 Am. J. Bioethics 38 (2005).

21. See Daniel V. Meegan, *Neuroimaging Techniques for Memory Detection: Scientific, Ethical, and Legal Issues*, 8 Am. J. Bioethics 9 (2008).

Behavioral genomics is unlikely to say much about the first of these issues, the degree of responsibility the defendant will bear for his actions. Even in those few cases where the mental state could be strongly associated with particular genomic variations—where, for example, a lack of relevant knowledge might be inferred from mental retardation caused by Down syndrome or Fragile X syndrome—the mental retardation will typically not need to be proven by genomic information. The behavior can usually be observed directly. Even in a jurisdiction that still recognizes an "irresistible impulse" as grounds for a successful insanity defense, genomic evidence seems very unlikely to provide evidence for such a strong, effectively uncontrollable, predisposition. The penetrance of the genomic variations just will not be that strong. One exception might arise when a defendant is suspected of feigning mental retardation as the basis of a defense. In those cases, the presence of a powerful genomic association with mental retardation (such as Down syndrome, Fragile X syndrome, and a wide variety of other, rarer, genetic conditions) could be good evidence that the defendant really was mentally retarded.

Neuroscience may provide information relevant to criminal responsibility in far more situations. Mental illness, psychopathy, or a variety of other mental conditions of potential relevance to criminal responsibility may have nongenetic causes. In those cases, behavioral genomics adds nothing; neuroscience may add much.

To take an extreme example, in a case described in the medical literature, a 40–year-old married man suddenly developed an interest in child pornography and was eventually arrested for improper behavior with his prepubescent stepdaughter.[22] He was charged and convicted of child molestation and, after being unable to control his sexual urges during an inpatient rehabilitation program, was scheduled to be sentenced to prison. The day before sentencing, he came to a hospital emergency room, complaining of a severe headache, but also exhibiting other neurological signs. He turned out to have an egg-sized brain tumor. After it was removed, he retook and passed the rehabilitation program and was released. Ten months later he began collecting pornography again; an MRI showed that his tumor had grown back. It was removed again and his inappropriate sexual urges again faded. Exactly how the criminal justice system should deal with such a case is debatable, but the neuroscience information seems at least relevant. Behavioral genomics would offer no information in a case like this.

Similarly, in a criminal case where an insanity defense is pleaded, the prosecution may suspect that the patient is lying about having visual or verbal hallucinations in an effort to bolster a claimed diagnosis of schizophrenia. If the

---

22. Jeffrey M. Burns and Russell H. Swerdlow, *Right Orbitofrontal Tumor with Pedophilia Symptom and Construction Apraxia Sign*, 60 ARCH. NEUROLOGY 437–40 (2003). For a less scientific discussion, see, *Doctors Say Pedophile Lost Urge After Brain Tumor Removed*, USA TODAY, July 28, 2003.

person was subject to an fMRI scan while having such hallucinations, he should show activity in his brain in the visual or auditory cortex. Behavioral genomics, at most, might be able to say that a person with his genome had a higher than average chance of being schizophrenic; neuroscience can provide more direct evidence of that person's mental state.

The ultimate importance of neuroscience information for criminal responsibility is being debated vigorously.[23] Without taking a position on that question here, I will only say that however important it is (or is not), because the brain's current structure and function will always be more closely associated with behavior than a person's inherited genome will be, it should be *more* important than behavioral genomics.

Issues of the disposition of the defendant—to probation, to prison, to civil commitment, or to other outcomes—generally follow the same pattern, but at a different level. Evidence standards are lower on sentencing than on trial; future behavior is often explicitly considered. This will make information about behavioral propensity more relevant than at trial, but neuroscience evidence will remain always, or almost always, more powerful than genomic evidence.

Consider an example from capital punishment. The U.S. Supreme Court has held that the death penalty may not constitutionally be imposed on the mentally retarded.[24] At least for those defendants with genomically-determined mental retardation, such as Downs or Fragile X syndromes, behavioral genomics would seem useful. The U.S. Supreme Court, however, left open the definition of mental retardation to the states. The mildly mentally retarded may not qualify, which could mean that, while the presence of an extra chromosome 21 or a long repeat in the fragile X gene would be some evidence of mental retardation, it may not be determinative evidence that the retardation was sufficiently severe for purposes of the state's capital punishment law. Psychological testing would be required for that determination, perhaps bolstered, in cases where feigning was suspected, with neuroscience evidence.

And, of course, with mental retardation, the *absence* of genomic variations associated with mental retardation is not strong evidence of the absence of mental retardation; most mentally retarded people do not have any known genomic cause of their condition. Indeed, for most cases of mental retardation,

---

23. See, e.g., Dean Mobbs, Hakwan C. Lau, Owen D. Jones, Christopher D. Frith, *Law, Responsibility, and the Brain*, 5 PLoS Biology 4, e103 doi:10.1371/journal.pbio.0050103 April 17, 2007) and Stephen J. Morse, Moral and Legal Responsibility and the New Neuroscience in Neuroethics: Defining the Issues in Theory, Practice, and Policy (ed. Judy Illes Oxford Univ. Press 2005); Joshua Greene and Jonathan Cohen, *For the Law, Neuroscience Changes Nothing and Everything, in* Law and the Brain 207 (eds. Semir Zeki and Oliver Goodenough, 2006); Robert Sapolsky, *The Frontal Cortex and the Criminal Justice System, in* Law and the Brain (eds. Semir Zeki and Oliver Goodenough, 2006).

24. *Atkins v. Virginia*, 536 U.S. 304 (2002).

particularly moderate or mild retardation, the cause is entirely unknown. As mental retardation is a pathological condition of the brain (or, perhaps more accurately, a description of the outward consequences of several different brain pathologies), neuroscience evidence should eventually be able to help decide whether anyone is mentally retarded. Both the presence and the absence of neuroscientific signs could be useful, and possibly determinative, in making that decision. (It would be interesting to see what the courts would do if a rigorous neuroscience-based definition of mental retardation were developed that differed, in some ways, from the lay understanding of the term.)

It is only in "treatments" for criminal behaviors that behavior genomics might rival neuroscience. As discussed above, behavioral genomics may give us clues that could lead to treatments, through drugs, gene therapy, or otherwise, that could reduce or eliminate propensities for some antisocial behaviors. We do not (yet) typically "sentence" criminals to long term drug treatment, but some states do, for some criminals.

"Chemical castration" is a possible sentence for certain sex offenders in seven American states and several European countries.[25] The procedure involves administration of drugs to suppress testosterone and hence behaviors associated with testosterone. (In the United States, Depo-provera, a drug invented for female contraception and approved by the FDA, is used.) The drug has some direct physiological effects with consequences for behavior; it reduces the convict's ability to have erections or ejaculations. It does not, however, seem to reduce those abilities to zero. Its stronger function is to change the convict's behavior, reducing his previously compulsive interest in sex from a scream to a whisper.

Although this is not exactly behavioral genomics—we knew the association between testosterone and various male behaviors before we knew in detail the genomic pathways involved in testosterone production—it may be an example of possible future treatments for criminal behavior that may be discovered as a result of behavioral genomics. If so, it should be a cautionary one. Men are being given doses of Depo-provera more than ten times higher than the doses tested and approved for use in women with basically no studies of its long-term safety, even though Depo-provera for contraception now bears a "black box" warning because of an association with osteoporosis. In the name of changing their behavior, we may be condemning these sex offenders to a later life of crippling bone disease.[26] We will need to ensure that any use by the criminal justice system of drug or gene therapy treatments derived from behavioral genomics has been proven safe and effective.

---

25. See the very useful discussion in John F. Stinneford, *Issues Surrounding Punishment of Sex Offenders: Incapacitation Through Maiming: Chemical Castration, the Eighth Amendment, and the Denial of Human Dignity*, 3 U. St. Thomas L.J. 559, 560 (2006). See also Greely, *supra* at n. 10.

26. See Greely, *supra* at n. 10.

Even here, more purely neuroscience methods might prove more powerful than behavioral genomics methods. Criminal behavior might be treated not just through drugs but also through neurosurgery or deep brain stimulation. Both have been tried for intractable aggression. In the 1960s researchers tried removing the amygdala, an important brain region, to reduce aggression in seriously impaired subjects,[27] while others removed another important region, the hypothalamus.[28] More recently, other researchers have tried to reach the same results by implanting an electrode in a different area of the brain and using it for deep brain stimulation.[29] Both kinds of research are a far cry from use of "regular" violent criminals, but either could expand in that direction.

The cautions about the safety of drugs derived from behavioral genomics apply at least equally powerfully to these more direct brain "treatments" for criminal behavior. Chinese and Russian hospitals, mentioned above, "cured" heroin addiction with neurosurgery. Both reported success in eliminating heroin addiction, though it is not clear what else was eliminated.[30] More distantly, the prefrontal lobotomy was performed on over 30,000 Americans for a wide range of mental illnesses or behavioral traits. Its inventor, Egas Moniz, won the 1949 Nobel Prize in Medicine or Physiology for its development.[31] Within 20 years the procedure was abandoned as barbaric. Our next efforts may be better informed but will not necessarily be more successful.

Beyond safety, of course, such "treatments" for criminal behavior raise a host of other issues that are beyond the scope of this chapter. It is not clear that we will, or should, use direct methods to "treat" the brains of criminals in order to "cure" them of criminal behaviors. It does seem clear, though, that both behavioral genomics and neuroscience will hold out the prospect of this kind of intervention.

CONCLUSION

We are in the middle of revolutions in both human genomics and human neuroscience. Both hold out the promise of being able to reveal things otherwise

---

27. See Kostas N. Fountas and Joseph R. Smith, *Historical Evolution of Stereotactic Amygdalotomy for the Management of Severe Aggression*, 106 J. NEUROSURG 710–13 (2007).

28. K. Sano, M. Yoshioka, M. Ogashiwa, B. Ishijima, and C. Ohye, *Postero-Medial Hypothalamotomy in the Treatment of Aggressive Behaviors*, 27 CONFIN. NEUROL. 164–67 (1966).

29. Angelo Franzinia, Carlo Marrasa, Paolo Ferrolia, Orso Bugiania, and Giovanni Broggia, *Stimulation of the Posterior Hypothalamus for Medically Intractable Impulsive and Violent Behavior*, 83 STEREOTACT. FUNCT. NEUROSURG. 63–66 (2005).

30. See Hall, *supra*, at n. 12.

31. Victor W. Swayze, *Frontal Leukotomy and Related Psychosurgical Procedures in the Era Before Antipsychotics (1935–1954): A Historical Overview*, 134 AM. J. PSYCHIATRY 505–15 (1995).

unknowable about our pasts, our futures, and our thoughts. We, as a culture, are both drawn to and repelled by this promise of revealing hidden knowledge. Our criminal justice system is no exception.

Behavioral genomics and neuroscience both are likely to provide some information that will be useful for the criminal justice system, but neither will provide the kind of information that most attracts, and most frightens, us—information that clearly, definitely, and inalterably tells us something important about someone's future behavior. Instead, they will offer us information that is usually weak—less weak with neuroscience than with behavioral genomics, but never, in itself, determinative. And in other ways, ways to which we have not paid enough attention, such as lie detection, sentencing, or, "treatment" neuroscience, and to a lesser extent behavioral genomics, may well change the criminal justice system. We need to focus on those technologies and the challenges they will present and be less concerned about methods to see the inner realities of defendants, to learn "what evil lurks in the hearts of men." No technology is ever likely to answer that question for us fully; in spite of the best geneticists and neuroscientists—and writers of radio fiction—it is likely to remain seen only in shadows.

PART THREE

REVISITING CRIMINAL RESPONSIBILITY

7. GENETICS, NEUROSCIENCE, AND CRIMINAL RESPONSIBILITY

NITA A. FARAHANY AND JAMES E. COLEMAN, JR.

I understand by responsibility nothing more than actual liability to legal punishment.
It is common to discuss this subject as if the law itself depended upon the result of
discussions as to the freedom of the will, the origin of moral distinctions, and the nature
of conscience. Such discussions cannot be altogether avoided, but in legal inquiries
they ought be noticed principally in order to show that the law does not really depend
upon them.[1]

I. INTRODUCTION

Human behavioral genetics and neuroscience may enhance our understanding
of human behavior and yet have little relevance to assigning responsibility in the
criminal law. Both disciplines seek to understand the contribution of genetics,
neurobiology, and the environment to observed variations in human behavior.
Although the science is in early stages of discovery, and scientists quarrel over
basic methodology and the definitions and metrics for measuring behavior,
criminal law has already seized upon behavioral genetics and neuroscience evidence for a variety of purposes: as exculpatory evidence, to bolster preexisting
legal defenses, and as mitigating evidence during sentencing. As these fields
progress and gain credibility, scientific results demonstrating a genetic or neurological contribution to behavioral differences in violence, aggression, hyperactivity, impulsivity, drug and alcohol abuse, antisocial personality disorder, and
other related traits will continue to be introduced into the criminal law. This
chapter discusses practitioners' attempts to use behavioral genetics and neuroscience in U.S. criminal law cases, and explores the relationship between behavioral genetics, neuroscience, and criminal responsibility as it operates in the
U.S. criminal justice system. It argues that irrespective of understanding
the underlying contributions to human behavior, as a matter of criminal law
theory, such evidence is unlikely to unhinge current assessments of criminal
responsibility.

Several observations about the science underlying these disciplines inform
the arguments presented herein. First, neither behavioral genetics nor neuroscience supports the perspective that human actions are fixed or caused by genes or

---

1. James F. Stephen, A History of The Criminal Law of England 96 (MacMillan 1883).

our brain. In other words, neither science supports behavioral determinism. To the contrary, the science supports a complex interaction of biology and the environment that gives rise to behavioral differences between individuals.

Second, behavioral genetics studies in particular are designed to generate a population statistic about the correlation between behavioral and genetic variation in a population, termed an estimate of "heritability."[2] Heritability provides a statistical approximation of the relative contribution of genetic differences versus environmental differences to observed behavioral differences among individuals in a population.[3] In contrast, it does not explain the relationship between the genetic profile of an individual and his or her behavior, nor does it explain the causes of any particular act by an individual.[4] As a population statistic, heritability may vary by the age, culture, and environment of the population under study.[5] Moreover, the old adage in statistics rings true here as well: correlation does not imply causation. A statistical correlation between genetic or neurological differences and behavioral variation in a population does not translate into a causal explanation about the behavior of interest.[6] In short, heritability does not explain the *causes* of an individual's behavior, or the causes of any specific act by an individual.[7] And while neuroscience has focused more closely on changes in individuals based on specific brain abnormalities, these differences again have meaning only by understanding the differences from a population norm. A brain abnormality can only have meaning if there is some concept of a population norm for brain activity, structure, and corresponding function.

Third, studies in both fields reveal that even if biological or neurological differences provide insight into why individuals behave as they do, biology contributes only one part to the overall story.[8] In studies of antisocial or criminal

---

2. This is explained in considerable detail in Chapter 1, Laura A. Baker, Serena Bezdjian & Adrian Raine, *Behavioral Genetics: The Science of Antisocial Behavior, in* THE IMPACT OF BEHAVIORAL SCIENCES ON CRIMINAL LAW (Nita A. Farahany, ed., 2009), and separately in Chapter 2 by Jonathan Kaplan, *Misinformation, Misrepresentation, and Misuse of Human Behavioral Genetics, in* THE IMPACT OF BEHAVIORAL SCIENCES ON CRIMINAL LAW (Nita A. Farahany, ed., 2009).

3. Kaplan, *supra* note 2, at 55–58.

4. *Id.*

5. *Id.*

6. Thus, if a study of aggression in a population generated a heritability estimate of 0.2, one could not say that twenty percent of the behavior is explained by genetics, only that the differences in observed aggression between the individuals in that population were twenty percent correlated with genetic differences in that population.

7. *See* Baker, Bezdjian & Raine, *supra* note 2.

8. A criminal defense claiming a 1:1 correlation between genetic differences and behavior would be unsupportable. *See supra* note 7. However, if new scientific discoveries emerged demonstrating that humans in fact operate as automatons, acting solely in reaction to their biological programming, the foundations of criminal law doctrine discussed in this chapter would naturally be challenged. Setting aside such an extreme

behavior, for example, behavioral geneticists report heritability estimates between 0.12 and a high of 0.62, meaning the genetic differences in the study population correlated with 12 to 62 percent of the differences in observed ntisocial or criminal behavior in that population. Thus, biological differences failed to account for 38 to 88 percent of the observed behavioral variation in the population.

These observations—that behavior is not deterministic, that heritability estimates refer to population rather than individual differences, and that biological or neurological differences alone do not explain behavioral differences between individuals—would alone support limiting the introduction of genetic or neurological predisposition evidence into criminal cases. Nonetheless, practitioners continue to introduce behavioral genetics and neuroscience evidence in criminal cases. Thus, rather than focusing on ever-changing scientific limitations, this chapter instead demonstrates why, as a matter of criminal law theory, such evidence should not inform the assessment of criminal responsibility in a any meaningful way.

Part II reviews the introduction by practitioners of behavioral genetics and neuroscience in recent U.S. criminal cases and the corresponding response by courts. This review illustrates that the present use of behavioral genetics and neuroscience evidence in criminal cases remains limited, and judges have by and large rejected its use. The rationales stated in both majority and dissenting opinions, however, leave the door open for future use of such evidence in the criminal law.

Parts III and IV discuss the relevance of these behavioral sciences to assigning criminal responsibility. "Criminal responsibility," as that term is used in this chapter, encompasses two distinct processes in the criminal law: the determination of liability and the evasion or diminution of responsibility.

Criminal liability, discussed in Part III, follows from the determination that an actor engaged in criminal conduct by inquiring (1) whether the defendant voluntarily engaged in proscribed conduct (voluntary act), and (2) if he did, whether he was aware of the circumstances that made his conduct criminal (mens rea).[9] We conclude that behavioral genetics and neuroscience should have limited

---

improbability, this chapter assumes behavioral genetics will not support strong genetic determinism.

9. GEORGE P. FLETCHER, RETHINKING CRIMINAL LAW 454–58 (1978). Fletcher describes the distinction as wrongdoing and attribution. He explains that there is a distinction between objective wrongdoing and the subjective attribution of wrongdoing. We adopt similar reasoning, such that liability, as de scribed in this chapter, is analogous to Fletcher's concept of wrongdoing, while the discussion of justification and excuse parallels Fletcher's discussion of attribution of wrongdoing. Unlike Fletcher, this chapter presents the attribution of wrongdoing as an objective determination, governed by the juror's assessment of whether the defendant's conduct deviated from social norms. Nonetheless, Fletcher points out two individualized characteristics relevant to criminal responsibility that this chapter does not discuss: infancy and insanity. These two characteristics may exempt an individual from

bearing on the determination of whether an act is voluntary or whether the defendant acted with the requisite mens rea.

Part IV analyzes justifications and excuses to criminal responsibility, by which a criminal defendant may evade or mitigate criminal liability. This part explains how justifications and excuses serve as a societal check on liability by comparing the defendant's conduct with that expected of a reasonable person—the embodiment of societal norms of conduct.[10] As a result, a defendant's behavioral predispositions—while potentially relevant to the motivations underlying his conduct—lack probative value. Because behavioral science does not inform either liability or justifications and excuses, behavioral genetics and neuroscience should have little use in determining criminal responsibility.

Criminal responsibility, as discussed herein, is distinct from criminal punishment, although they are naturally interrelated. A defendant's criminal responsibility corresponds with whether and to what extent he will be punished. And punishment depends upon a defendant's personal culpability, which turns in part on criminal responsibility and potentially according to the individual characteristics of the defendant. The rigidity of the present sentencing schemes, however, may limit the extent to which both the criminal and the crime receive consideration. In spite of these limitations, this chapter proposes that the present system of U.S. criminal law limits the relevance of individual characteristics (such as behavioral predispositions) to questions of culpability, rather than responsibility.

II. CURRENT USE OF BEHAVIORAL GENETICS AND NEUROSCIENCE IN CRIMINAL CASES

Courts have so far been skeptical of practitioners' attempts to introduce evidence of biological predispositions as grounds for obviating criminal responsibility or mitigating punishment. The decisions in these cases have sometimes provoked dissents, however, and even the majority opinions (perhaps reflecting a healthy instinct for incrementalism) have not closed the door on such arguments in future cases. This chapter illustrates that at least as to criminal responsibility, the door should be kept closed.

---

wrongdoing, but do so as narrowly circumscribed anomalies. Neither exemption should afford inroads for behavioral genetics in defenses to criminal responsibility.

10. *Id.* at 459. Fletcher describes this inquiry slightly differently: he explains that justifications and excuses may negate liability for a defendant, but those justifications do so by negating the wrongfulness of the act, while excuses suggest an absence of personal accountability on the part of the actor. This chapter proposes that the reason an actor lacks personal culpability in the case of excuses is because social norms suggest the circumstances negate the extent of wrongdoing by an actor—that actor.

A. Behavioral Genetics, Neuroscience and Involuntariness

A handful of criminal defendants claimed to have committed a criminal act because of a genetic or neurological predisposition to addiction, violence, impulsivity, or other behavioral traits, as if they were moved by reflex or convulsion, rather than by free will.[11] Most courts considering the claim that a defendant's biologically based "overpowering compulsion" excuses him from criminal liability have rejected it.[12] Because the defense of involuntariness itself is quite rare and limited by statute, the use of genetic or neurological evidence to bolster a defendant's claim of involuntariness is likewise quite infrequent. Yet practitioners continue to introduce these claims, and scholars persist in supporting their attempts.

The defense of "involuntariness" based on a genetic or neurological predisposition to compulsion has been most prevalent in the context of drug or alcohol addiction.[13] As a general rule, voluntary intoxication is not an excuse to criminal liability. But in these cases, the defendant disavows responsibility by claiming to have acted under the influence of a drug or alcohol addiction for which he had a genetic predisposition. He claims that because he labored involuntarily under the influence of drugs or alcohol, the criminal act was involuntary. The U.S. Court of Appeals for the District of Columbia Circuit summarized this defense in *United States v. Moore:*

> Appellant's position seems to be that if a defendant is compelled to use narcotics due to a serious physical craving (addiction) . . . the court can find no free will on the part of the defendant, since he acts as a result of compulsion, not from choice. Indeed, so the argument goes . . . there is really no guilt involved, merely disease.[14]

---

11. Some commentators argue an individual with a genetic defect may be "so emotionally distressed and out of touch with his surroundings that he is unable to refrain from the act that results in a crime, and therefore, may not satisfy the voluntary act requirement. If so, the man would be entitled to acquittal on that ground." Susan Horan, Comment, *The XYY Supermale and the Criminal Justice System: A Square Peg in a Round Hole*, 25 Loy. L.A. L. Rev. 1343, 1372 (1992).

12. *See, e.g.*, United States v. Moore, 486 F.2d 1139 (D.C. Cir. 1973).

13. *See, e.g., id.*; State v. Boushack, No. 94-1389-CR, 1995 Wisc. App. LEXIS 378, at *4–*8 (Wis. Ct. App. Mar. 21, 1995) (rejecting defendant's argument that his genetic defect limited his self control generally and made his intoxication involuntary); *see also* Chapter 8, Stephen J. Morse, *Addiction, Genetics, and Criminal Responsibility, in* The Impact of Behavioral Sciences on Criminal Law (Nita A. Farahany, ed., 2009).

14. 486 F.2d at 1150. Although this case did not specifically address addiction from the perspective of behavioral genetics, an expert on drug addiction testified the defendant "was an addict of long-standing, that appellant's addiction had the characteristics of a disease, and that as a consequence appellant was helpless to control his compulsion to obtain and use heroin." *Id.* at 1143.

In response to this defense, the court posited that an individual's self-control is guided by two factors with respect to drug addiction:[15] the physical craving for the drug and the moral standards of the defendant.[16] Against this backdrop, "[i]n any case where the addict's moral standards are overcome by his physical craving for the drug, he may be said to lose 'self-control,' and it is at this point, and not until this point, that an addict will commit acts that violate his moral standards."[17] From this perspective of the defense, every criminal defendant who could demonstrate a predisposition to drug or alcohol addiction could claim that his will succumbed to his addiction. Consequently, every criminal defendant with a biological predisposition to drug or alcohol addiction could claim to have acted involuntarily and so evade criminal liability. The court found it unwise to recognize such an expansive defense.[18]

The defendant in *Ex Parte John Wayne Rice*[19] raised a similar claim, arguing that his frontal lobe damage rendered his act of homicide involuntary. The defendant appealed his conviction of voluntary manslaughter, arguing that psychiatric testimony at trial demonstrated he suffered from frontal lobe damage, and "a person with physical damage to the frontal brain lobes might respond with greater emotion than a normal person to any particular situation . . . [S]uch an emotional response is not voluntary if it results from frontal lobe brain damage."[20] The court rejected Morris's claim, because "there was no evidence that [the defendant] involuntarily pulled his gun and shot [the victim]. The forensic psychiatrist who testified stated that a person with frontal lobe brain damage could have an impaired ability to control his emotional reaction to stimuli.

In essence, defendants who raise a genetic or neurological predisposition to drug or alcohol addiction challenge the temporal principle articulated in *People v. Decina*,[21] that the defendant who causes harm while unconscious may be considered to have acted voluntarily by reason of his earlier conduct. In *Decina*, the defendant suffered an epileptic seizure while driving his car and killed four children.[22] The court, viewing the timeframe of the culpable conduct broadly, held the defendant responsible for the homicide because he was aware of the likelihood that he could suffer an epileptic seizure and he still chose (voluntarily) to drive.[23] By contrast, the defendant with a genetic or neurological predisposition to addiction claims that he at no point made a voluntary choice. A defendant who raises

---

15. *Id.* at 1145.
16. *Id.*
17. *Id.*
18. *Id.* at 1146–48.
19. 415 S.E.2d 819 (S.C.Ct. App. 1991).
20. *Id.* at 821.
21. 138 N.E.2d 799 (N.Y. 1956).
22. *Id.* at 801, 803.
23. *Id.* at 803–04; *see* JOSHUA DRESSLER, UNDERSTANDING CRIMINAL LAW 91 (3d ed. 2001).

the defense of a genetic or neurological predisposition to drug or alcohol addiction must overcome the rationale of the *Decina* line of cases; that is, if he is aware of his genetic or neurological predisposition, then the choice to take drugs or alcohol could itself be treated as the relevant voluntary act in committing the separate criminal offense.

In contexts other than addiction, courts' receptiveness to claims that a defendant's predisposition negates the actus reus required for criminal liability has been mixed. For example, the Supreme Court of South Carolina was persuaded by the argument that the defendant's mental disease—severe depression arising from a genetic predisposition—rendered the homicide a product of disease, disassociated from the will, rather than a voluntary criminal act by the defendant. In *Von Dohlen v. State*,[24] the defendant was initially convicted and sentenced to death for the armed robbery and murder of a shop employee he shot in the back of the head.[25] His conviction and sentence were affirmed on direct appeal, and his subsequent application for post-conviction relief was denied.[26] In support of Von Dohlen's application for post-conviction relief, a psychologist testified on his behalf that as a result of "his altered mental state '[the murder] was not a volitional thing but out of his conscious awareness or control.'"[27] On appeal, the court reversed the denial of post-conviction relief, finding the psychological testimony created a "reasonable probability the outcome of the trial might have been different had the jury heard the available information about [the defendant's] mental condition."[28] This suggests the court's receptivity to the view that a mental condition arising from a biological or neurological predisposition may render the act of homicide the product of disease, rather than a voluntary act attributable to the defendant.

Earlier, however, the same court cited with approval the rejection of a closely analogous claim in a case in which the defendant argued that a predisposition to overly emotional responses arising from frontal lobe brain damage rendered his act of homicide involuntary.[29] In *State v. Morris*,[30] the defendant appealed his conviction of voluntary manslaughter, arguing that psychiatric testimony at trial demonstrated that he suffered from frontal lobe damage and "a person with physical damage to the frontal brain lobes might respond with greater emotion

---

24. Von Dohlen v. State, 602 S.E.2d 738, 743 (S.C. 2004), *cert. denied*, 125 S. Ct. 1645 (2005).

25. *Id.* at 740.

26. *Id.*

27. *Id.* at 742.

28. *Id.* at 743.

29. State v. Pickens, 466 S.E.2d 364, 366 (S.C. 1995) (noting that in *State v. Morris*, 415 S.E.2d 819 (S.C. Ct. App. 1991), the defendant had intentionally shot his gun and therefore could not claim involuntary manslaughter).

30. 415 S.E.2d 819 (S.C. Ct. App. 1991).

than a normal person to any particular situation. . . . [S]uch an emotional response is not voluntary if it results from frontal lobe brain damage."[31] The South Carolina Court of Appeals rejected Morris's claim:

> [T]here was no evidence that Morris involuntarily pulled his gun and shot [the victim]. The forensic psychiatrist who testified stated a person with frontal lobe brain damage could have an impaired ability to control his *emotional* reaction to stimulus. He stated . . . that he had not evaluated Morris with regard to the specific *act* involved in the [the victim's] shooting.[32]

The Court's rationale in *Morris* underscores a concern courts repeatedly express regarding the implications of behavioral predispositions for criminal responsibility: the lack of an explicit causal link between behavioral predispositions in the abstract and the specific criminal act in question. In other words, courts have recognized that genetic or neurological conditions alone do not explain the causal relationship between a defendant's physiology and his behavior, nor do they provide a complete explanation of the defendant's criminal act. For Morris, the causal disconnect between the frontal lobe damage and his specific criminal conduct bolstered the trial court's conclusion that Morris voluntarily and intentionally engaged in criminal conduct.[33]

A recent concurring opinion by Ninth Circuit Judge Berzon[34] suggests that additional jurists are open to a claim that a defendant's behavioral predisposition vitiated his volitional control. In *Dennis ex rel. Butko v. Budge*, the defendant Terry Dennis, at the time a Nevada state prisoner, pled guilty to first-degree murder and was sentenced to death.[35] During the penalty phase of his trial, a psychiatrist testified that Dennis suffered from mental illness and had a long history of suicide attempts.[36] The Nevada Supreme Court affirmed the conviction and sentence on direct appeal,[37] and the state district court dismissed his subsequent petition for writ of habeas corpus.[38] Before his appeal reached the Nevada Supreme Court, Dennis notified the relevant authorities that he wished to withdraw his appeal and to submit to execution.[39] Dennis's trial attorney then filed a next-friend petition for habeas corpus in the federal district court, arguing that Dennis could not competently waive his rights or make rational choices

31. *Id.* at 821.
32. *Id.* at 821–22.
33. *Id.* at 822.
34. Dennis ex rel. Butko v. Budge, 378 F.3d 880, 895 (9th Cir. 2004) (Berzon, J., concurring).
35. *Id.* at 882.
36. *Id.*
37. Dennis v. State, 13 P.3d 434 (Nev. 2000).
38. Budge, 378 F.3d at 882.
39. *Id.* at 882–83.

regarding his defense because of his mental illness.[40] The district court rejected that claim, and the Ninth Circuit affirmed, holding that no clear or persuasive evidence demonstrated that Dennis irrationally chose to forego his appeal or that his suicidal tendencies or mental disorder fixed his choice.[41]

Although Circuit Judge Berzon agreed with the Ninth Circuit majority on the ultimate outcome, she rejected the rationale of their decision:

> [The majority assumes] a vision of mental processes which precludes the possibility that an individual with intact cognitive capacity may, nonetheless, be unable to make a rational choice, not so much because the choice is not rational in an objective sense, or because the individual in general lacks the capacity to make rational choices, but because, for the person making the *particular* decision it is not a *choice*. Instead, the individual's mental disorder dictates the outcome.[42]

In contrast to the majority view, Judge Berzon believes an individual may be competent and yet lack the capacity to make voluntary decisions:

> In effect, such a prisoner, though otherwise lucid, rational and capable of making reasonable choices is, in a Manchurian Candidate-like fashion, volitionally incapable of making a choice other than death when faced with the specific question here at issue—namely, whether to pursue legal proceedings that could vacate the death penalty or to abandon them. . . . To make a "choice" means to exercise *some* measure of autonomy or free will among the available options, at least to the degree that an individual who does not suffer from a mental disorder is able to do so.[43]

Although *Budge* concerns the voluntariness of a decision to forego further appeals, rather than the voluntary-act requirement for criminal liability, Judge Berzon's concurring opinion signals receptiveness to a claim of involuntariness based on behavioral biology.[44] Employing reasoning such as this, some jurists

---

40. *Id.* at 886–87.

41. *Id.* at 889–95.

42. *Id.* at 895.

43. *Id.* at 899 (explaining that, although Judge Berzon was persuaded that Dennis's biological predisposition kept him from exercising a rational choice, the finder of fact was entitled to find otherwise).

44. Dennis's argument was not that he had a genetic predisposition to mental infirmity, nor does Judge Berzon's opinion rely solely on a genetic predisposition to mental infirmity. One could read the following line as recognizing a distinction between genetic predispositions and the mental disorders at issue in this case: "Indeed, how can a mental infirmity or disorder be distinguished from the myriad . . . memories, experiences and genetic predispositions that go to make up each individual's unique personality?" *Id.* Although the opinion does not squarely address genetic predispositions, it demonstrates

may find it persuasive that an individual may lack the capability to exercise "free will" based on a biological predisposition.[45]

B. Behavioral Genetics, Neuroscience, and Negation of Mens Rea

Defendants are increasingly introducing behavioral genetics and neuroscience to negate or diminish their mental state during the commission of the crime.[46] This approach has not won significant success, in part likely because of the conceptual difficulty of explaining why a behavioral predisposition would negate scienter as that notion is understood in the criminal law.[47] Nevertheless, some defendants have successfully mitigated murder to manslaughter or first-degree premeditated murder to second-degree murder without premeditation using genetic or neurological claims. More frequently, though, defendants offered such evidence to bolster an insanity defense.[48]

In *People v. Ledesma*,[49] for example, the defendant claimed his murder conviction should be reversed because the evidence was insufficient to prove he had the intent to murder—specifically that he lacked malice and did not premeditate the

---

receptiveness to the idea that an act may be viewed as involuntary based on the subjective mental state of the actor, rather than by an objective determination of wrongdoing.

45. *See generally id.* at 902–07 (Berzon, J., concurring).

46. We discovered no case in which the defendant relied solely and specifically on a genetic predisposition to negate mens rea. Nonetheless, several defendants have made the closely analogous claim that they could not form the requisite intent for the crime because of low serotonin levels, which predispose the defendant to violence or impulsiveness. *E.g.*, People v. Uncapher, No. 246222, 2004 Mich. App. LEXIS 923 (Mich. Ct. App. Apr. 13, 2004) (arguing defendant's biological problem of low serotonin diminished his ability to reason and control his impulses); Hall v. State, No. W2003-00669-CCA-R3-PD, 2005 Tenn. Crim. App. LEXIS 3 (Tenn. Crim. App. Jan. 5, 2005), *appeal denied*, No. W2003-00669-SC-R11-PD, 2005 Tenn. LEXIS 590 (Tenn. June 20, 2005) (presenting expert testimony that defendant's low serotonin levels were correlated with violent acts, and as a result, the defendant was "unable . . . to achieve the mental state . . . [of] the absence of passion and excitement" necessary for a finding of criminal liability); State v. Payne, No. W2001-00532-CCA-R3-CD, 2002 Tenn. Crim. App. LEXIS 998 (Tenn. Crim. App. Nov. 20, 2002) (arguing that defendant's low serotonin level rendered the defendant unable to form the requisite mental state required for second-degree murder); State v. Godsey, No. E2000-01944-CCA-R3-CD, 2001 Tenn. Crim. App. LEXIS 926 (Tenn. Crim. App. Dec. 4, 2001) (introducing evidence that because of defendant's low serotonin levels and resultant aggressive impulses, he could not form the requisite mental state required for second-degree murder). Moreover, although we do not address separately the defense of diminished capacity, a more detailed discussion of the issue is available in Nita Farahany, Rediscovering Criminal Responsibility Through Behavioral Genetics (2006) (unpublished Ph.D. dissertation, Duke University) (on file with author).

47. *See* WAYNE R. LAFAVE, CRIMINAL LAW § 5.1 (4th ed. 2003).

48. *See infra* Part II.C.

49. People v. Ledesma, 140 P.3d 657, 722 (Cal. 2006).

killing. In support of his claim, the defense introduced a diminished capacity defense, arguing the defendant was "incapable of premeditating or forming the intent to kill at the time the crimes occurred, because of his extensive use of . . . PCP . . . combined with . . . the effects of brain damage."[50] A clinical psychologist and psychiatrist testified that the defendant's history of brain damage as a result of head traumas could have rendered him more susceptible to drugs or that it could have produced lapses in his judgment.[51] The court sustained his conviction on appeal because a reasonable juror could have rejected the expert testimony as inconsistent with the objective indications of the defendant's subjective intent.

In *State v. Idellfonso-Diaz*,[52] the State directly appealed a trial court ruling that the defendant, who was charged with two counts of first-degree-premeditated murder and one count of first-degree-felony murder, could present expert testimony at trial about his diminished mental capacity at the time of the crimes. At the suppression hearing, a defense expert witness testified that he examined defendant with MRI, PET, and EEG brain scans that revealed very minor brain abnormality. The expert testified that these factors, when taken together with his history of abuse, likely had an impact on the defendant's capacity when he shot a pregnant woman after a traffic accident. On cross-examination, the expert could not conclude that the defendant lacked complete capacity to premeditate but only that his capacity was somewhat impaired. The appellate court held that expert testimony regarding diminished capacity is relevant only when it can show that a defendant lacked the capacity to form the culpable mental state due to mental disease or defect. Because the expert in this case believed the defendant's capacity was only somewhat impaired, his testimony was irrelevant and inadmissible.

Relying on the link between genetics and depression, the defendant in *State v. Davis*[53] claimed that a mental defect, arising from his genetic predisposition to depression and mental illness, impaired his ability to form the requisite intent for his alleged criminal conduct. Davis, charged with shooting a classmate, argued at trial that his mental condition prevented him from forming the requisite intent to commit first-degree murder, reckless endangerment, or possession of a weapon on school property.[54] He presented psychiatric testimony that, at the time he committed the alleged crimes, he suffered from a depressive disorder that severely impaired his capacity to deliberately commit homicide.[55]

---

50. *Id.* at 659.

51. *Id.* at 660.

52. 2006 WL 3093207 (Tenn.Crim.App. 2006).

53. No. M1999-02496-CCA-R3-CD, 2001 Tenn. Crim. App. LEXIS 341 (Tenn. Crim. App. May 8, 2001).

54. *Id.* at *18.

55. *Id.*

The psychiatrist testified that Davis had a "genetic predisposition" for depression and mental illness, as shown by the history of severe depression in his family.[56] The jury rejected his claim,[57] and the court affirmed on appeal, noting the perceived manifestations of Davis's intent prior to and during the commission of the alleged crime had properly informed the jury's determination of his mental state.[58]

Oftentimes, the motivation for the act, rather than the legal intent, is challenged by behavioral science. But motivation is not the legal standard for determining criminal liability. Hence, in *People v. Bobo*,[59] the California Court of Appeal rejected an insanity defense that turned into a mens rea challenge by drawing a distinction between the defendant's motive for killing her children and the determination of whether she acted with the requisite legal intent required for first-degree murder. Diane Rochelle Bobo methodically stabbed and then drowned her three children.[60] The jury convicted her of three counts of first-degree murder.[61] During the guilt phase of her trial, a psychiatric expert testified that Bobo suffered from delusions,[62] and a court-appointed psychologist testified that he believed Bobo suffered from paranoid schizophrenia, triggered by genetic factors, biochemical elements, and developmental experiences.[63] These delusions and psychological conditions were introduced to inform her motive for killing her children. The jury nevertheless found Bobo to have been legally sane when she committed the crimes.[64] On appeal, Bobo challenged the sufficiency of the evidence to prove that she harbored malice or deliberately killed her children.[65] The California Court of Appeals rejected her claim,[66] noting, with regard to defendant's alleged lack of malice, the distinction between an intention and the motivation to kill. Because the evidence sufficiently demonstrated that Bobo had planned and deliberately killed her children, her reasons for doing so were irrelevant to whether she acted with mens rea.[67]

Finally, the XYY cases of the late 1960s and early 1970s represent the mixed use of biological predisposition both to negate mens rea and, alternatively, to support an insanity defense. This parallels the use of mental illness to support a claim of insanity and to prove the lack of capacity to form a requisite mental state.

---

56. *Id.* at *12.
57. *Id.* at *19.
58. *Id.* at *19–*26.
59. 3 Cal. Rptr. 2d 747 (Cal. Ct. App. 1990).
60. *Id.* at 749–50.
61. *Id.* at 748.
62. *Id.* at 751–52.
63. *Id.* at 752–53.
64. *Id.* at 748.
65. *Id.* at 755.
66. *Id.* at 755–56.
67. *Id.* at 762.

In the 1969 case of *People v. Farley*,[68] for example, a defendant with XYY chromosome and a history of antisocial behavior asserted as a defense to the vicious rape and murder of a young woman that his deviant chromosome structure, coupled with a past history of psychiatric difficulties, rendered him incapable of formulating the necessary intent to commit murder. Farley's attorney argued that "the killing was unplanned, impulsive, the product of a sick, psychotic and warped mind, while he was in a psychotic state, out of touch with reality."[69] Farley's defense failed, resulting in his conviction for murder.[70] The record leaves unclear the significance of the claim of incapacity for mens rea. His courtroom efforts understandably focused on a garden-variety defense of not guilty by reason of insanity.[71] A successful claim that a defendant lacks the capacity to form mens rea is hard to imagine, whatever the alleged basis claimed for incapacity.

C. Behavioral Genetics, Neuroscience and the Insanity Defense[72]

In most jurisdictions, insanity may be asserted as an affirmative defense to criminal liability,[73] requiring proof that the defendant suffered a disease of the mind, lacked awareness of his actions, could not appreciate the nature and quality of his actions, or lacked the ability to distinguish right from wrong.[74] Due in large

---

68. The case is unpublished, but its facts and outcome are described in *People v. Yukl*, 372 N.Y.S.2d 313, 320 (N.Y. Sup. Ct. 1975); *see also* David B. Saxe, *Psychiatry, Sociopathy, and the XYY Chromosome Syndrome*, 6 TULSA L.J. 243, 243 (1970).

69. *See* Edith Evans Asbury, *"Chromosome Slaying Trial" Begins in Queens*, N.Y. TIMES, April 16, 1969, at 54 (quoting the opening statement by Farley's defense attorney Marvyn Kornberg).

70. Saxe, *supra* note 62, at 244.

71. Edward C. Burks, *Genetic Defense Sought in Slayings*, N.Y. TIMES, Feb. 15, 1969, at 12; Telephone Interview with Marvyn Kornberg, Defense Attorney for Farley (Sept. 9, 2005). Nevertheless, previous articles have mistakenly characterized the defense as negating mens rea rather than a presentation of the insanity defense. *E.g.*, Saxe, *supra* note 62, at 243–44 ("For the first time in the United States, the defense attempted at the trial stage to prove that this deviant chromosome structure coupled with a past history of psychiatric difficulties made the defendant incapable of formulating the necessary *mens rea* to commit murder.").

72. We introduce the empirical use of behavioral genetics in cases of insanity but do not explore the theoretical role of insanity in the criminal law. Farahany's dissertation, *supra* note 44, explores the complicated relationship between insanity, criminal liability, and criminal responsibility in further depth.

73. LAFAVE, *supra* note 45, § 7.1, at 369.

74. *Id.* § 7.2, at 377–85. More recently, juries also have had the option of finding a defendant guilty but mentally ill, which further obscures the determination being made. *E.g.*, MICH. COMP. LAWS SERV. § 768.36 (2005). A successful insanity defense results in indefinite commitment to a mental institution, incarceration, or both, depending on the law of the governing jurisdiction. LAFAVE, *supra* note 45, § 7.1, at 369.

part to the mental illness or defect element of the insanity defense, the majority of defendants who have asserted a genetic theory of insanity have failed to reach a jury with their claim. Courts have almost summarily rejected theories of mental illness based solely on a behavioral predisposition by differentiating between a biological predisposition and the traditional diagnoses of mental disease, such as mental illnesses, including schizophrenia or bipolar disorder, that form the foundation of the insanity defense. In *State v. Johnson*,[75] for example, the trial court rejected the defendant's attempt to introduce evidence that he could not form the mental state required for the crime because a genetic predisposition, coupled with bad nutrition, caused him to react to stress in a compulsive, abnormal fashion.[76] The appellate court concluded that although such a defense might have relevance to the unrecognized partial defense of diminished capacity, the alleged genetic predisposition did not constitute a mental defect, a threshold requirement for the insanity defense.[77]

The rejection of an insanity defense based on the defendant's chromosomal or behavioral predispositions has historic roots. In the XYY claims previously mentioned, several defendants argued that their XYY chromosomal abnormality established the mental defect element of the insanity defense. Aside from *People v. Farley*,[78] in no reported case[79] did these claims reach a jury. In *People v. Tanner*,[80] the trial court denied the defendant's motion to change his guilty plea to not guilty by reason of insanity, which he had based on the theory that his aggressive behavior was a result of his XYY chromosomal abnormality.[81] The Court of Appeals for the Second District of California affirmed, explaining that "experts [do] not suggest that all XYY individuals are by nature involuntarily aggressive. Some identified XYY individuals have not exhibited such behavior."[82] The court noted two additional deficiencies: (1) the expert testimony did not link Tanner's specific act of aggression to his chromosomal abnormality, and (2) his experts did not testify that an extra Y chromosome satisfied the mental defect component of California's variation on the *M'Naghten* rule.[83] The appellate court in

---

75. 549 N.E.2d 565 (Ohio Ct. App. 1989).

76. *Id.* at 566.

77. *Id.*

78. *See supra* Part II.B.

79. Based on a review of cases available in Westlaw and Lexis databases.

80. 91 Cal. Rptr. 656 (Cal. Ct. App. 1970).

81. *Id.* at 659.

82. *Id.*

83. *Id.* The California variation of the *M'Naghten* rule reads as follows: "Insanity . . . means a disease or deranged condition of the mind which renders a person incapable of knowing or understanding the nature or quality of his act, or unable to distinguish right from wrong in relation to that act." *Id.* at 658 n.4. *See generally* M'Naghten's Case, 8 Eng.Rep. 718 (1843).

Millard v. State[84] similarly observed that the "mere fact" that the defendant had an extra Y chromosome would not satisfy the test for legal insanity because, even if individuals with XYY are more "prone to aggression, are antisocial, and continually run afoul of the criminal laws, it is hardly sufficient to rebut the presumption of sanity."[85]

Two decades later, in *State v. Thompson,* the Court of Criminal Appeals of Tennessee expanded upon the rationale used by earlier courts to reject claims of insanity in the XYY cases, recognizing a distinction between evidence that an individual with a particular behavioral predisposition will likely act in a certain manner and evidence that the particular criminal defendant committed the act in question *because* of his behavioral predisposition.[86] Essentially, the court recognized the correlation-or-causation problem inherent in behavioral sciences.[87] Thompson offered expert testimony at trial that he suffered from "mild to moderate" impairment in the frontal lobe of his brain, which he claimed "could affect 'impulse control, delay, the ability to think ahead and plan and suppress what would be an immediate reaction.'"[88] Expert psychiatric testimony also suggested that frontal lobe impairment "would have affected [Thompson's] ability to appreciate right from wrong . . . [and] could have prevented him from conforming his acts."[89] Although the appellate court opined that the psychiatric evidence rebutted the initial presumption of Thompson's sanity, it nevertheless held that a reasonable juror could ultimately conclude, based on Thompson's behavior leading up to and during the crime, that his frontal lobe deficiency did not affect him in the relevant ways that such an impairment *could* affect an individual.[90] Consequently, the court affirmed the jury's finding that Thompson was sane when he committed the crimes and reinstated the verdicts for first-degree murder.[91]

These cases highlight the incongruity between behavioral predispositions and the mental conditions traditionally required for legal insanity. In case after case, courts have concluded that a defendant can appreciate the wrongfulness of his conduct and conform to the law notwithstanding any behavioral predisposition to aggression.[92] On the other hand, criminal defendants have

---

84. 261 A.2d 227 (Md. Ct. Spec. App. 1970).
85. *Id.* at 231.
86. No. E2002-02631-CCA-R3-CD, 2003 Tenn. Crim. App. LEXIS 736 (Tenn. Crim. App. Aug. 27, 2003).
87. *Id.* at *42–*43. *See generally* Kaplan, *supra* note 2.
88. *Thompson,* 2003 Tenn. Crim. App. LEXIS 736, at *13–*14.
89. *Id.* at *17.
90. *Id.* at *42–*43.
91. *Id.* at *43.
92. Kenley v. State, 759 S.W.2d 340, 344–48 (Mo. Ct. App. 1988) (rejecting defendant's ineffective assistance of counsel claim because it was reasonable trial strategy for the attorney to exclude psychiatric testimony regarding defendant's genetic background

had some success using evidence of a biological predisposition to bolster expert diagnosis of a mental condition.[93] In *People v. Urdiales*,[94] for example, the defendant was charged and convicted of first-degree murder and sentenced to death. At trial, the defendant entered a plea of guilty but mentally ill, but the judge rejected his insanity defense. To satisfy the statutory requirements of a legal insanity plea, the defense presented expert testimony and evidence, including MRI and SPECT scan data, to demonstrate that the defendant's sufferance from shrinkage of the brain could be linked to his criminal conduct. The court instead credited the States' expert who rebutted the diagnosis of organic brain disease and testified that the defendant's actions at the time of the murder did not bespeak someone who suffered significant impairments of the central nervous system.

In light of current standards for admission of scientific evidence, using behavioral genetics and neuroscience to bolster an insanity defense will likely be of more benefit to the criminal defendant than a theory of insanity grounded solely in a predisposition to violent, aggressive, or antisocial behavior.[95]

D. Behavioral Genetics, Neuroscience and Punishment

1. Predisposition as Mitigating Evidence Criminal defendants most often offer behavioral predispositions as evidence to mitigate punishment after a finding of guilt, rather than as a defense to criminal liability.[96] The claim that a behavioral predisposition mitigates the defendant's degree of criminal responsibility for purposes of punishment often resembles claims already discussed here: the defendant's biology dictated his choices and he therefore acted involuntarily, or his behavioral predisposition prevented him from forming the requisite intent.

---

and childhood history of violence because it did not satisfy the legal requirements for insanity)

93. For example, in *Robison v. Johnson*, 151 F.3d 256 (5th Cir. 1998), an expert abstained from testifying at trial because he believed Robison's behavior to be drug-induced. On appeal, the expert filed an affidavit that he now believed Robison's behavior to be caused by schizophrenia rather than drugs, because of new evidence that Robison's sister and other family members had been diagnosed as manic depressives and schizophrenics, demonstrating Robison's genetic predisposition to the disease.

94. 871 N.E.2d 669 (Ill. 2007).

95. *E.g.*, People v. Weinstein, 591 N.Y.S.2d 715, 722, 724–25 (N.Y. App. Div. 1992) (holding that a theory of violence based on biological factors could not be introduced into evidence because a theory of behavior must have reached general acceptance to be introduced, although each factor considered in diagnosing a medical condition need not satisfy the relevant scientific admissibility standard).

96. *See, e.g.*, People v. Sapp, 73 P.3d 433, 469–73 (Cal. 2003) (introducing the defendant's psychological and neurological factors contributing to the homicide as mitigating evidence).

Simplistically put, defendants claim that behavioral genetics mitigates their culpability by arguing "it's not my bad character; it's my bad genes."

Biological predispositions, in its many variations—whether as a genetic or neurological predisposition, a family history of violence, or a cycle of violence—appears frequently as one of many mitigating factors during sentencing in criminal cases. The typical case involves introduction of expert testimony regarding the defendant's socioeconomic upbringing; childhood trauma; family history suggesting a genetic or neurological predisposition to impulsive, antisocial, or violent behavior;[97] or evidence of a genetic or neurological predisposition to drug or alcohol abuse.[98] More recently, criminal defendants have introduced biological predisposition as the principal theory of mitigation during sentencing in capital cases, rather than one of several mitigating factors.

In *Hill v. Ozmint*, defense counsel sought to demonstrate in the sentencing phase of the defendant's capital trial that the defendant suffered from serotonin deficiency, "attributable to genetics," from which his aggressive impulses arose.[99] After his arrest and incarceration, Hill had begun prescription medication that, according to the treating physician, successfully curbed his aggressive impulses.[100] The theory of mitigation was that "the death penalty was not warranted because Hill's aggressive behavior was genetic (thus, beyond his control) and treatable,"[101] and that Hill in fact had been treated successfully and now behaved appropriately. Three experts proffered testimony in support of Hill's claim: one who discussed serotonin deficiency generally, one who had diagnosed Hill's serotonin deficiency, and one who would have testified about Hill's successful treatment

---

97. *E.g.*, Corcoran v. State, 774 N.E.2d 495, 502 (Ind. 2002) (opining that the defendant's genetic predisposition to being a "loner" or a "hermit" based on diagnosis of schizotypal personality disorder was outweighed by quadruple killing in imposing the death penalty); Cauthern v. State, 145 S.Wd.3d 571, 588 (Tenn. Crim. App. 2004) (noting that genetic predisposition to impulsive behavior could have been developed and introduced as mitigating evidence at the time of trial).

98. *E.g.*, State v. Mata, 916 P.2d 1035, 1049 (Ariz. 1996); State v. Hartman, 476 S.E.2d 328, 342 (N.C. 1996) (rejecting defendant's argument that instruction to jury prevented jury from considering alcoholism as arising from genetic predisposition and "[w]ithout this focus, the fact of [defendant's] alcoholism was more likely to be viewed simply as weakness or unmitigated choice"); State v. Scott, 800 N.E.2d 1133, 1148-49, 1151 (Ohio 2004) (weighing genetic predisposition to drug and alcohol addiction, based on family history of drug abuse, as mitigating evidence during capital sentencing), *cert denied*, 542 U.S. 907 (2004), *application for reopening denied*, 811 N.E.2d 1148 (Ohio 2004).

99. 339 F.3d 187, 201–2 (4th Cir. 2003).

100. *Hill*, 339 F.3d at 202; Brief of Appellant at 19, Hill v. Ozmint, No. 03-1 (4th Cir. 2003).

101. *Hill*, 339 F.3d at 202.

with Prozac.[102] The jury nevertheless sentenced Hill to death.[103] The U.S. Court of Appeals for the Fourth Circuit affirmed the death sentence on appeal[104] without addressing the merits of Hill's genetic mitigation theory.[105] This case, however, illustrates the typical attempt by defense counsel to use behavioral genetics to distinguish between defendant's choices that arise from his bad character (presumptively within his control) and choices that are the product of his genetic predisposition (presumptively outside of his control).[106]

The defendant in *Crook v. State*[107] fared better with a similar mitigation claim based on brain damage. He claimed that his organic brain damage[108] predisposed him to fits of violence. During his initial sentencing hearing, expert witnesses testified that Crook suffered from frontal lobe brain damage and impulse control disorder arising from "his organic brain dysfunction rather than any character disorder."[109] The trial court sentenced Crook to death without considering the expert's testimony.[110] The Supreme Court of Florida vacated Crook's death sentence and remanded the case to the trial court: "[C]learly, the existence of brain damage is a significant mitigating factor that trial courts should consider in deciding whether a death sentence is appropriate in a particular case."[111] On remand, the trial court again imposed the death penalty,[112] and Crook appealed the proportionality of his sentence in light of the substantial evidence

---

102. *Id.* Instead of testifying about Hill's favorable response to the medication, the third expert had a nervous breakdown on the stand and could not respond to questions on direct- or cross-examination; all the while the jury laughed at this fiasco. *Id.;* Brief of Appellant, *supra note 93*, at 19.

103. *Hill*, 339 F.3d at 189.

104. Hill appealed to the Fourth Circuit after the denial of federal writ of habeas corpus in the district court. *Id.* at 190.

105. *Id.* at 202–03.

106. *E.g.*, Mobley v. State, 455 S.E.2d 61, 65–66 (Ga. 1995). That case is discussed in this volume. *See* Chapter 10, Deborah W. Denno, *Behavioral Genetics Evidence in Criminal Cases: 1994–2007*, *in* THE IMPACT OF BEHAVIORAL SCIENCES ON CRIMINAL LAW (Nita A. Farahany, ed., 2009).

107. 813 So.2d 68 (Fla. 2002) [hereinafter *Crook* I] (vacating death sentence for failure to consider Crook's brain damage and mental retardation as mitigating factors); *see also* Crook v. State, 908 So.2d 350 (Fla. 2005) [hereinafter *Crook* II] (vacating death sentence after resentencing by finding the death sentence was disproportionate in light of evidence of extreme mitigation).

108. Experts testified that Crook's brain damage arose from his genetic background, socioeconomic deprivation, head trauma, substance abuse, and birth trauma. *Crook* I, 813 So.2d at 72.

109. *Id.* at 70–71.

110. *Crook* II, 908 So.2d at 354.

111. *Crook* I, 813 So.2d at 74–76.

112. *Crook* II, 908 So.2d at 355.

of the neurological and genetic basis for his behavior.[113] The Supreme Court of Florida again reversed the decision, finding Crook's mental deficiencies were highly relevant to his degree of culpability for purposes of punishment and focusing on "the unrefuted testimony of the mental health experts that relate the rage and brutal conduct in this crime to the defendant's brain damage and mental deficiencies."[114]

With scientific progress, particularly in the relationship between specific genetic factors, brain abnormalities, and specific behaviors, mitigation theories such as Hill's and Crook's likely will become more prevalent. But whether biological predisposition testimony serves as the principal theory of mitigation or as only one of several proffered mitigating factors, courts currently have little guidance for interpreting or weighing this evidence, particularly in light of the complexity of showing a causal connection between a behavioral predisposition and a specific criminal act. Courts have relied on experts who have linked the defendant's general behavioral propensity and his specific criminal act in only a few cases;[115] the majority of defendants have failed to show such a causal link. In *Roberts v. State*,[116] the Arkansas Supreme Court focused on the absence of such a link in affirming the death sentence of Karl Douglas Roberts. Roberts, convicted of the capital murder of a twelve-year-old girl, had introduced psychological and neurological evidence during his pretrial competency hearing, during his trial to negate criminal liability and responsibility, and during the sentencing phase to mitigate his punishment.[117] The court held that Roberts had failed to connect evidence of his brain damage to his ability to control his emotions and actions, or to his ability to function socially.[118] Other courts express similar concern about "how this [evidence] relates to the murder"[119] and what weight to assign it.[120]

---

113. *Id.* at 356.

114. *Id.* at 358.

115. *E.g., id.* (finding that an expert's testimony explained how the defendant's fit of rage exhibited in the homicide was causally related to his behavioral predisposition to rage and impulse control).

116. 102 S.W.3d 482 (Ark. 2003).

117. *Id.* at 486–88.

118. *Id.* at 496–97.

119. Morris v. State, 811 So.2d 661, 668 (Fla. 2002). This is similar to remarks made by courts in the XYY cases. In *State v. Roberts*, 544 P.2d 754, 758 (Wash. Ct. App. 1976), for example, the court explained that the behavioral impact of the XYY defect had not been precisely determined nor had the causal connection between the XYY defect and criminal conduct been established.

120. *See, e.g., Morris*, 811 So.2d 661. An expert testified that "people with [frontal lobe damage] typically make choices against the odds, that when they commit crimes, they are unplanned and disorganized crimes." *Id.* at 668. The court was "left with the overall impression that impulsiveness is the dominant feature. The defendant is not powerless to control his behavior, but his ability to do so may be substantially impaired." *Id.* Consequently, the court gave this evidence some weight as a mitigating factor to the death

2. Predisposition as a Double-Edged Sword Not only have criminal defendants experienced little success by introducing predisposition testimony during sentencing, but in some cases, it has cut against the defendant. Courts have regarded the biological predisposition of defendants as a potential aggravating sentencing factor or circumstance. The Ninth Circuit's opinion in *Landrigan v. Stewart*[121] provides a stark example of how this double-edged sword might cut against a criminal defendant. Jeffrey Landrigan filed a petition for federal habeas corpus relief, claiming ineffective assistance of counsel during the penalty phase of his capital case because his attorneys, following the defendant's explicit instruction, failed to present mitigating evidence during the penalty phase of Landrigan's trial.[122] Four years after sentencing, however, Landrigan argued that notwithstanding his instructions at trial, he would have cooperated had his attorneys attempted to offer mitigating evidence demonstrating that his "biological background made him what he is."[123] The original Ninth Circuit panel was not persuaded that such evidence would have helped with Landrigan's sentence:

> [We find it] highly doubtful that the sentencing court would have been moved by information that Landrigan was a remorseless, violent killer because he was genetically programmed to be violent, as shown by the fact that he comes from a family of violent people, who are killers also. . . . [A]lthough Landrigan's new evidence can be called mitigating in some slight sense, it would also have shown the court that it could anticipate that he would continue to be violent. . . . As the Arizona Supreme Court so aptly put it when dealing with one of Landrigan's other claims, "[i]n his comments, defendant not only failed to show remorse or offer mitigating evidence, but he flaunted his menacing behavior." On this record, assuring the court that genetics made him the way he is could not have been very helpful.[124]

The Ninth Circuit recently reheard this case en banc, and partially reversed the district court's decision. The United States Supreme Court then granted certiorari, in part, on the question of whether a genetic predisposition to violence was

---

penalty but still concluded that the death penalty was proportional to the crime. *Id.* at 669

121. 272 F.3d 1221 (9th Cir. 2001), *reh'g en banc granted, vacated,* 397 F.3d 1235 (9th Cir. 2005). The Ninth Circuit reheard this case en banc. *See* Landrigan v. Schriro, 441 F.3d 638 (9th Cir. 2006) (en banc) (affirming in part and reversing in part district court's denial of a capital habeas petition because Petitioner demonstrated colorable claim of ineffective assistance of counsel during penalty phase based on counsel's failure to investigate and present mitigating evidence including Petitioner's family history and mental illness, which could have resulted in sentence other than death).

122. *Id.* at 1224.

123. *Id.* at 1228.

124. *Id.* at 1228–29 (internal citations omitted).

mitigating evidence.[125] Although it decided the case on other grounds, the majority went on to conclude that evidence of a genetic predisposition to violence was weak mitigating evidence, and quoted the initial Court of Appeals, when it stated that ". . . On this record, assuring the court that genetics made him the way he is could not have been very helpful."[126]

The case of *Schriro v. Landrigan* may give some courts and defense counsel future pause about the double-edged nature of this evidence. But, in past cases, it seems evident that the double impact of this evidence has escaped attention. In *State v. Creech*, the appellate court affirmed the trial court's finding of the statutory aggravating circumstance "propensity to commit murder,"[127] defined as "that person who is a willing, predisposed killer, a killer who tends toward destroying the life of another, one who kills with less than the normal amount of provocation."[128] The state had established this aggravating factor based on evidence of Creech's past history of violence—including his guilty plea for the first-degree murder of a fellow inmate while serving a life sentence in the Idaho State Correctional Institute[129]—supported by evidence of a genetic predisposition to violence that the defendant offered in mitigation.[130]

Apparently unaware of the two-sided effect of his evidence, Creech claimed the trial court had not given appropriate mitigating weight to his biological predisposition to violence.[131] A psychologist had testified on Creech's behalf during sentencing about a probable "biological component to Creech's violent personality."[132] The appellate court concluded the trial court had accorded Creech's biological predisposition due weight by accepting for sentencing purposes "that the defendant may be biologically predisposed to violence."[133]

---

125. 550 U.S. __ (2007).

126. Id. at *14.

127. 966 P.2d 1, 11 (Idaho 1999); *see also* Gregg v. Georgia, 428 U.S. 153 (1976) (allowing aggravating factor of propensity to commit murder).

128. *Creech*, 966 P.2d at 11.

129. *Id.* at 5–6.

130. *Id.*

131. *Id.* at 15.

132. *Id.* at 16.

133. *Id.* At the 1995 sentencing hearing, a psychologist testified Creech had a "biological component" to his problems. At the same time, the psychologist agreed that "[e]verything we do has a biological component" but noted that this was the only instance in which he had testified about a "genetic contribution." He explained:

[Such evidence] is relevant in capital sentencing. It does not mean Tom Creech is not competent to stand trial. It does not—I don't think it has any bearing on whether or not he is criminally responsible. And in normal sentencing, I don't think it is relevant. But I do think in a capital sentencing, the fact that he has a biological contribution is relevant. . . . [H]e had no choice over his genes. And that probably helped contribute to his messed-up nervous system.

Neither defense counsel's brief[134] nor the appellate court's opinion acknowledged that Creech's predisposition and history of violence were treated as mitigating at the same time they were deemed sufficiently aggravating to justify the death sentence.[135]

Baker v. State Bar of California[136] demonstrates the double-edged nature of behavioral predisposition evidence in noncapital cases. The State Bar of California found attorney John David Baker had misappropriated client funds, failed to perform services for clients, and abandoned clients without notice.[137] As mitigating evidence, Baker introduced his drug and alcohol abuse.[138] The court posited that such evidence might be mitigating if it suggested the conduct would not recur.[139] Generally, drug use, itself illegal, and alcoholism, which adversely affects an attorney's ability to practice, could be grounds for attorney disbarment.[140] By contrast, however, the court considered newly discovered evidence of Baker's "genetic predisposition" to alcoholism and drug abuse to be potentially mitigating because it gave credence to his claim that having now learned about his genetic predisposition, he would abstain from future drug and alcohol abuse.[141] Consistent with the bad character versus bad genes distinction of other cases, the court distinguished between misconduct that "was the product of a physical or mental disorder, or substance abuse," and misconduct that arose from a voluntary choice.[142] Without his genetic predisposition to drug and alcohol abuse, Baker likely would have been disbarred, but his discipline instead included only protracted probation with strict conditions, in part because of Baker's "concession that he has a genetic predisposition to addiction."[143]

In a less direct way, prosecutors may use predisposition evidence to stigmatize or denigrate the character of the criminal defendant. For example, the prosecutor

---

Brief of Respondent, State v. Creech, 966 P.2d 1 (Idaho 1998) (No. 22006), 1997 WL 33769519, at 54.

134. Appellant's Brief, State v. Creech, 966 P.2d 1 (Idaho 1998) (No. 22006), 1997 WL 33769521.

135. Although there is no discussion about the reason this evidence could be both aggravating and mitigating, it is possible this is another case of "bad character" versus "bad genes," in which the aggravating factor addressed Creech's bad character, while the mitigating factor addressed his bad genes. But this possibility would simply underscore the point: depending on how the evidence is perceived, behavioral genetics could be used as an aggravating or mitigating factor in sentencing.

136. 781 P.2d 1344 (Cal. 1989).

137. *Id.* at 1349, 1353.

138. *Id.* at 1352–53.

139. *Id.* at 1351 n.6.

140. *Id.*

141. *Id.*

142. *See id.* at 1354.

143. *Id.* at 1345.

in *Johnston v. Love*[144] referred to the defendant's family history of crime during his closing statement to the jury by accusing Johnston as coming from a "family of crime."[145] Although the court acknowledged that in some contexts, "this statement might be inappropriate, as it might indicate (for instance) a genetic predisposition to crime," in this case the court was unconcerned because it considered the statement merely hyperbolic, not grossly denigrating.[146] Because of cases such as these, some defense counsel will refuse to offer evidence of defendant's predisposition to violence, aggression, and related behavioral traits in fear that the evidence will backfire against the defendant.[147] Unless such evidence can be used in a way that avoids the double edge, refusing to use it may be a prudent choice: a judge and jury are much more likely to be influenced in sentencing decisions by the defendant's antisocial conduct and the suggestion of his continued dangerousness than by a possible biological explanation for it.

At this stage of knowledge about behavioral genetics and neuroscience, defense lawyers must carefully consider whether evidence of an alleged genetic defect will help or hurt the defendant. As one commentator noted, to focus on the genetic defects of the individual defendant creates the danger that "he will be punished, or treated, for what he is or is believed to be, rather than for what he has done. If his offense is minor but the possibility of his reformation is thought to be slight, the other side of the coin of mercy can be cruelty."[148] This point seems unassailable.

III. CRIMINAL LIABILITY AND BEHAVIORAL PREDISPOSITIONS

The above cases illustrate the varied attempts by defendants to advance claims based on behavioral genetics and neuroscience to negate or mitigate criminal liability. These defendants have encountered problems in showing a causal connection linking the biological claim and the specific act in question, between the motivation to act and the intent to act, and in satisfying the mental illness or defect element of the insanity defense. Such obstacles, however, relate to the validity of the science and the crafting of the claim, rather than the legal relevance of behavioral genetics evidence. Parts III and IV explain instead why

---

144. 940 F. Supp. 738 (E.D. Pa. 1996).

145. *Id.* at 753 n.17.

146. *Id.*

147. *E.g.*, State v. Ramsey, 864 S.W.2d 320, 340 (Mo. 1993) (noting that it was not ineffective assistance of counsel to choose not to introduce psychiatric testimony regarding defendant's potential predisposition to crime based on history of criminality in his family and past criminal acts).

148. Henry M. Hart, *The Aims of the Criminal Law*, LAW & CONTEMP. PROBS. 401, 407 (Summer 1958).

behavioral genetics and neuroscience evidence clashes with criminal responsibility theory. Although the following discussion comports with the majority of case outcomes discussed above, it challenges the rationale employed in those opinions and provides a more robust reason to reject the claims presented. Moreover, the analysis in Parts III and IV goes against the scholarly grain[149] by explaining why, even if one could fairly draw inferences between a genetic or neurological endowment and propensity toward criminal misconduct, that evidence has little relevance to determining a defendant's criminal liability or his justifications or excuses to such liability.

A finding of criminal liability requires the government to prove that the actor voluntarily engaged in a harmful or threatening act proscribed by criminal law and did so with the requisite mental awareness of the circumstances of fact that made the conduct criminal.[150] These concepts are often referred to as actus reus and mens rea; both are prerequisites to a finding of criminal liability.[151] Circumscribing both of these concepts is the presumption in the criminal law that individuals are responsible agents capable of making choices and intend the natural consequence of their actions. Several commentators have opined that behavioral science requires a retooling of this system of liability because scientific advances challenge its validity.[152] Such arguments ignore the fact that the criminal law does not depend on individual capabilities: "Acts are judged by their tendency under known circumstances, not by the actual intent which accompanies them."[153] Free will, actus reus, and mens rea are tools to aid in the narrow determination of a defendant's liability for a crime.

---

149. *See* Brock & Buchanan, *supra* note 153, at 68 (noting that an increase in genetic knowledge might increase our propensity to believe in determinism and affect human belief in free agency; alternately, it may not affect such beliefs if individuals neither act nor feel they are unfree); Deborah W. Denno, *A Mind to Blame: New Views on Involuntary Acts*, 21 BEHAV. SCI. & L. 601, 603 (2003); Bernadette McSherry, *Voluntariness, Intention and the Defense of Mental Disorders: Toward a Rational Approach*, 21 BEHAV. SCI. & L. 581, 593 (2003).

150. *See* LaFAVE, *supra* note 45, §§ 5.1, 6.1(c).

151. Although some criminal offenses do not require proof of mens rea, those offenses are beyond the scope of this chapter.

152. *E.g.*, Marcia Johnson, *Genetic Technology and Its Impact on Culpability for Criminal Actions*, 46 CLEV. ST. L. REV. 443 (1998) (equating a genetic predisposition with genetic determinism and claiming that a defense based on a genetic predisposition negates free will and the elements of criminal responsibility); John L. Hill, Note, *Freedom, Determinism, and The Externalization of Responsibility in the Law: A Philosophical Analysis*, 76 GEO. L.J. 2045 (1998) (claiming that if determinism reflects reality, then the criminal law lacks coherence when it holds individuals criminally responsible); Note, *The XYY Syndrome: A Challenge to Our System of Criminal Responsibility*, 16 N.Y.L. SCH. L. REV. 232 (1970) (using the XYY syndrome to argue that the concept of criminal responsibility rests on flawed notions of free will).

153. OLIVER WENDELL HOLMES JR., THE COMMON LAW 66 (Dover Publ'ns, Inc. 1991) (1981).

A. Legal versus Theoretical Free Will

When discussing behavioral genetics and criminal law, some scholars apparently feel obliged[154] to reconcile the broad concept of free will (hereinafter referred to as theoretical free will) with new scientific discoveries about human behavior. These arguments miss the point. Theoretical free will, which encompasses the philosophical, metaphysical, psychiatric, and biological perspectives on this topic, does not inform the understanding and use of free will in the criminal law (hereinafter referred to as legal free will).[155] Our hope is that by articulating the limited purpose of legal free will, we may quiet claims that behavioral genetics and neuroscience undermine the assumption of free will underlying criminal liability.

---

154. Of course, many scholars also recognize that behavioral genetics does not change our conception of human agents in criminal law. The participants in this symposium agreed that behavioral genetics does not support a deterministic view of human behavior, and little, if any, discussion of free will took place during the conference held at Duke University School of Law on April 8–9, 2004. *But see, e.g.,* WILLIAM R. CLARK & MICHAEL GRUNSTEIN, ARE WE HARDWIRED: THE ROLE OF GENES IN HUMAN BEHAVIOR 265 (2000) (asking whether free will actually exists and inquiring into the biological basis of free will); Note, *The XYY Chromosome Defense,* 57 GEO. L.J. 892, 912 (1968–69) ("If it is shown that the XYY individual finds it more difficult to control his behavior than does a 'normal' individual, he obviously would not have 'free will' and thus could not be accommodated by an objective theory of penal law."). Still others believe that an increased understanding of a genetic contribution to behavior could expand notions of personal responsibility. *E.g.,* Robert F. Schopp, *Natural-Born Defense Attorneys, in* GENETICS AND CRIMINALITY: THE POTENTIAL MISUSE OF SCIENTIFIC INFORMATION IN COURT 82, 88–90 (Jeffrey R. Botkin, William M. McMahon & Leslie Pickering Francis eds., 1999).

155. Scientifically speaking, one could causally describe every human action by examining the biological and environmental chain of events involved. For example, to explain the cause of raising one's hand to ask a question, one would describe the environmental and cultural influences that compel an individual to raise his hand, the neurological and physiological pathways involved in formulating the question, the neurological and physiological pathways involved in deciding to raise one's hand after formulating the question, and finally, the physiological description of the actual movement of the hand. Depending on the scientific instruments available, every physiological, neurological, and biochemical change in the body could be described with varying degrees of specificity in the complex pathway between deciding to raise one's hand and the final movement of the hand. But this does not suggest that the act of hand-raising is predetermined or outside the conscious control of the individual. Similarly, even if genes or gene variants involved in the causal pathway of behavior were discovered, no behavioral geneticists could with any credibility claim that those genes predetermine or fix the expression of any complex behavior, just as no credible claim can be made that one's environmental upbringing fixes or predetermines one's future behavior. Because behavioral sciences do not support a deterministic view of human behavior, they should have little impact on the debate over the existence of theoretical free will.

Whatever the interrelationship may be among the psychological, neurological, biological, and environmental factors that give rise to human conduct, the criminal law presumes that individuals actively and consciously choose to engage in criminal conduct.[156] The criminal law views human beings as autonomous actors, not because of a preference for arguments in support of theoretical free will, compatibilism, or determinism,[157] or "because it is empirically verifiable."[158] Instead, the criminal law recognizes the autonomy of human choice as fundamental to the operation of a modern system of laws[159] and a necessary presumption to foster "better social arrangements" and "greater individual liberty."[160] The presumption derives, in part, from the belief that "[s]ocial systems are strengthened by holding people responsible for their conduct,"[161] and undermined by shifting responsibility to the many factors affecting human behavior such as environmental influences or family upbringing. The criminal law proceeds, then, by assuming that humans are responsible agents, capable of exercising control over their impulses, desires, and actions.[162] And it influences responsible conduct with both a carrot and a stick: the system obligates members of society to abstain from prohibited conduct by threatening punitive sanctions and moral stigmatization, while reflecting and reifying societal norms to encourage more law-abiding behavior.[163] Such an approach may strengthen the

---

156. HERBERT FINGARETTE, THE MEANING OF CRIMINAL INSANITY 72–73 (1972).

157. Determinism embodies the idea that all human behavior is the "product of the broad array of causal factors that govern the choices we make," and is thus determined by the causal factors leading to our choices. Jeffrey A. Kovnik, *Juvenile Culpability and Genetics, in* GENETICS AND CRIMINALITY, *supra* note 145, at 213.

158. Robert Batey, *Law and Popular Culture: Literature in a Criminal Law Course: Aeschylus, Burgess, Oates, Camus, Poe, and Melville,* 22 LEGAL STUD. FORUM 45, 60 (1998) (citing HERBERT PACKER, THE LIMITS OF THE CRIMINAL SANCTION 74–75 (1968)).

159. *Cf.* United States v. Moore, 486 F.2d 1139, 1241 (D.C. Cir. 1973) (Wright, J., dissenting) ("[I]n determining responsibility for crime, the law assumes 'free will' and then recognizes known deviations 'where there is broad consensus that free will does not exist' with respect to the particular condition at issue.").

160. Batey, *supra* note 149, at 60 (citing PACKER, *supra* note 149, at 74–75 (1968)).

161. Seymour L. Halleck, M.D., *Responsibility and Excuse in Medicine and Law: A Utilitarian Perspective,* 49 LAW & CONTEMP. PROBS. 127, 127 (Summer 1986).

162. *See* Gregg Cartage & Storage Co. v. United States, 316 U.S. 74, 79–80 (1942); Dan W. Brock & Allen Buchanan, *The Genetics of Behavior and Concepts of Free Will and Determinism, in* GENETICS AND CRIMINALITY, *supra* note 145, at 69–75.

163. *See* Brock & Buchanan, *supra* note 153, at 69–75; *see* John C.P. Goldberg & Benjamin C. Zipursky, *Accidents of the Great Society,* 64 MD. L. REV. 364, 392 (2005) (making the analogous argument in tort law, by explaining that tort law is "not limited to functioning as a carrot or stick, although it can so function," meaning that it functions not only through pricing and prohibition, but also by being connected in "an organic way to obligations already recognized in familiar forms of social interaction," and by so doing may enjoy greater efficacy).

concept of criminal responsibility by preventing actors from viewing themselves as responsible actors in the "impoverished sense" that they are "'responsible when [the] government concludes that it is in the public interest that I be held responsible.'"[164]

Nonetheless, some persist in arguing that the tenets of criminal law must evolve to comport with a more scientifically robust understanding of human behavior.[165] So the claims go, as science discovers new contributions to human behavior, the criminal law must accordingly redefine its system of criminal responsibility. [166] Such claims subjugate the field of criminal law to metaphysics or science and presume that the foundation and objectives of the criminal justice system are and must be rooted in metaphysical or scientific explanations of human behavior.[167] Practitioners subscribing to the appeal of such claims attempt to defend criminal defendants by arguing that the defendant's "overwhelming compulsion" to engage in the criminal act negates the "free will" necessary to hold him criminally responsible for his action.[168] The erroneous association between theoretical free will and legal free will is encouraged when judges (thus far, usually in dissent) express a sympathetic view of the merits of such arguments.[169]

---

164. Goldberg & Zipursky, *supra* note 154, at 394.

165. *See supra* note 140.

166. Some commentators share the view that the "failure of the Anglo-American criminal justice system to consider differences in individual capacities in determining blame and punishment can be viewed as a conceptual and structural flaw, which renders it fundamentally unjust and inefficient." Halleck, *supra* note 152, at 141.

167. FINGARETTE, *supra* note 147, at 76 ("[T]here is a set of legal concepts and a different set of metaphysical concepts. . . . [T]hat the determinist or free-willist uses the word 'free' or 'compelled' should not mislead us into thinking that he is talking about the issues that are relevant in law.").

168. Gorham v. United States, 339 A.2d 401, 410 (D.C. Ct. App. 1975); *see* United States v. Moore, 486 F.2d 1139, 1146 (D.C. Cir. 1973) ("[I]f it is the absence of free will which excuses the mere possessor-acquirer [for possessing narcotics], the more desperate bank robber . . . has an even more demonstrable lack of free will from precisely the same factors as appellant argues should excuse the mere possessor.") (emphasis omitted).

169. *See Gorham*, 339 A.2d at 444–47 (Fickling, J., dissenting). The genesis of mens rea is discussed at length:

Since Congress and medical experts agree that drug dependence is characterized by "a strong compulsion" which reaches the level of loss of "the power of self-control" with reference to the individual's drug dependence, the question for us is whether this compulsion is strong enough to negate *mens rea* as to possession and PIC for the addict's own use.

. . .

[W]ithout a free exercise of will, there can be no guilty mind. . . . Over the centuries the law has come to recognize a number of situations where an individual lacks "free will"

In fact, criminal law adopts an entirely different concept from psychology of human behavior by assuming that

> [t]here is a faculty called reason which is separate and apart from instinct, emotion, and impulse, that enables an individual to distinguish between right and wrong and endows him with moral responsibility for his acts. This ordinary sense of justice still operates in terms of punishment. To punish a man who lacks the power to reason is as undignified and unworthy as punishing an inanimate object or an animal. A man who cannot reason cannot be subject to blame. Our collective conscience does not allow punishment where it cannot impose blame.

> Psychology [on the other hand] is concerned with diagnosis and therapeutics and not with moral judgments. It proceeds on an entirely different set of assumptions. It does not conceive that there is a separate little man in the top of one's head called reason whose functions it is to guide another unruly little man called instinct, emotion, or impulse in the way he should go. The tendency of psychiatry is to regard what ordinary men call reasoning as a rationalization of behavior rather than the real cause of behaviour.[170]

Each discipline and field operates from assumptions that best serve the needs of the field. The criminal justice system assumes human actors can choose to engage or refrain from criminal conduct and creates societal standards of conduct and responsibility by "assigning blame and imposing punishment."[171] The medical or scientific models employ a deterministic view of human behavior because human conduct, human disease, and all natural phenomena must be

---

> and is therefore not to be held criminally liable for knowingly engaging in prohibited conduct.
>
> . . .
>
> Although some addicts may retain the ability to choose methadone maintenance rather than continued use of heroine, they should not be precluded from raising a defense of drug dependence. Sick persons, whether mentally ill, alcohol dependent, epileptic, etc., are not precluded from asserting a defense because they failed to take advantage of available treatment. The relevant inquiry is into the defendant's mental and physical condition at the time of the alleged offense, *i.e.*, the addict's "power of self-control with reference to his addiction."

Id.; see also State v. Johnson, 399 A.2d 469, 471 (R.I. 1979) (explaining that the law proceeds from the postulate that individuals are autonomous actors and "seeks to fashion a standard by which criminal offenders whose free will has been sufficiently impaired can be identified and treated" in a humane manner)

170. Holloway v. United States, 148 F.2d 665, 666–67 (D.C. 1945).

171. Richard C. Boldt, *Construction of Responsibility in the Criminal Law*, 140 U. PA. L. REV. 2245, 2304–5 (1992).

causally determined to allow for diagnosis and treatment.[172] To abandon the legal perspective of human behavior and shift now from a presumption of conscious control to the assumption of determinism would enable defendants to introduce an endless string of diversionary defenses claiming weakness of the human spirit in order to avoid criminal responsibility.[173] Such defenses stand opposed to the historical rejection of theoretical free will in favor of an intentional suspension of disbelief in humans as free agents.[174] In short, the legal system did not rely upon a theoretical understanding of free will to begin with,[175] and need not do so now.

B. The Voluntary Act[176]

Just as legal free will imputes agency to individuals, the criminal law assumes that when an individual acts, he reveals his choice to have acted. Notwithstanding the claims in *Moore*,[177] *Von Dohlen*,[178] and *Budge*,[179] or others, and scholars claiming otherwise, behavioral genetics and neuroscience cannot answer whether an individual acted "voluntarily," as defined by the criminal law.

As a legal term of art,[180] actus reus embodies a deeply entrenched principle of the criminal law: liability may not be imposed in the absence of a criminal act[181]

---

172. *Id.* at 2304.

173. *See* United States v. Moore, 486 F.2d 1139, 1147 (D.C. Cir. 1973) (opining that to allow the defense of addiction to justify certain types of criminal conduct in furtherance of one's addiction would enable the same defense to bank robberies, street muggings, burglaries, and any other crime "which can be shown to be the product of . . . compulsion.").

174. *See* Brock & Buchanan, *supra* note 153, at 69; *see also* HOLMES JR., *supra* note 144, at 50–51 (explaining that the common law assumes "that every man is as able as every other to behave as they command," with only a few exceptions when the "weakness is so marked as to fall into well-known exceptions, such as infancy or madness").

175. FINGARETTE, *supra* note 147, at 67–69. Fingarette rejects the idea that the legal construct of human will must make sense from the perspective of a psychiatrist because it is not designed to make psychiatric sense but to serve the purposes of criminal law.

176. A comprehensive and principled theory is beyond the purview of this chapter, which instead, focuses on demonstrating why behavioral genetics does not inform the objective system of criminal responsibility. We seek here to demonstrate only that whether one adopts Austin's, Hart's, the MPC's, or the "control" theory of voluntary conduct, the behavioral predispositions of an individual do not negate the presumption of voluntary conduct.

177. 486 F.2d 1139 (D.C. Cir. 1973).

178. 602 S.E.2d 738 (S.C. 2004).

179. 378 F.3d 880 (9th Cir. 2004).

180. LaFave, *supra* note 45, at 302–3; MODEL PENAL CODE § 1.13(10) (Official Draft and Revised Commentaries 1985).

181. DOUGLAS N. HUSAK, PHILOSOPHY OF CRIMINAL LAW 78 (1987).

attributable to the defendant.[182] Absent evidence to the contrary, however, the criminal law presumes the defendant intended the specific act in question.[183] Because the criminal law presumes that an act implies a choice to have acted, actus reus focuses on the act rather than on the actor (or the crime rather than the criminal).

The criminal law does, however, enable a defendant to challenge the presumption of agency, by deeming "involuntary" bodily movements that arise from natural phenomena or external forces.[184] In the language of the criminal law, only a voluntary act satisfies the actus reus requirement; an involuntary act caused by natural or other phenomena will not suffice.[185] Part III.A demonstrates practitioners' attempts to capitalize on these exceptions with biological and neurological evidence.

Although definitions of *voluntary* vary, none is undercut by claims of genetic and neurological predispositions. In *Lectures on Jurisprudence*, John Austin opined that a voluntary act means an external manifestation of the will.[186] Commentators have criticized his approach because it presumes active deliberation prior to bodily movement, a fact his opponents argue rarely occurs.[187] H.L.A. Hart refuted Austin's approach by arguing that *voluntary* pertains to behavior that would have been a different one had the individual willed or chosen so.[188] Hart introduced this alternative primarily to account for unconsciousness or epilepsy, instances in which he posited that an actor could not have chosen to act otherwise. Another approach is to disclaim a positive definition of a voluntary act, defining it instead by reference to the conditions rendering an act involuntary.

---

182. FINBARR MCAULEY & J. PAUL MCCUTCHEON, CRIMINAL LIABILITY: A GRAMMAR 121 (2000).

183. In other words, a "voluntary act" in criminal law names a different concept than a "voluntary act" in other disciplines. *See* Kevin Jon Heller, *Beyond the Reasonable Man? A Sympathetic but Critical Assessment of the Use of Subjective Standards of Reasonableness in Self-Defense and Provocation Cases*, 26 AM. J. CRIM. L. 1, 14 (1998); Jeffrie G. Murphy, *Involuntary Acts and Criminal Liability*, 81 ETHICS 332, 333 n.3 (1971). Criminal law provides that a criminal act may be attributed to the accused (and therefore "voluntary") by making two presuppositions: first, individuals have control over their behavior (legal free will), and second, a human agent causes the actions he performs by the exercise of his capacities and control. Thus, one can infer a defendant chose to act from proof that he engaged in the prohibited act. Because criminal law allows this inference, the question whether the defendant engaged voluntarily in an act does not usually arise.

184. *See supra* Part III.A (providing examples of practitioners attempting to capitalize on these exceptions with the use of behavioral genetics).

185. *Id.*

186. JOHN AUSTIN, LECTURES ON JURISPRUDENCE OR THE PHILOSOPHY OF POSITIVE LAW 411 (Robert Campbell ed., 5th ed. 1885) (1861).

187. MCAULEY & MCCUTCHEON, *supra* note 173, at 124–25.

188. H.L.A. HART, PUNISHMENT AND RESPONSIBILITY: ESSAYS IN THE PHILOSOPHY OF LAW 105 (1968).

The Model Penal Code (MPC) adopted this view[189] by enumerating involuntary acts without offering a positivist account of voluntary conduct.[190]

One could deduce that by defining instances of involuntary conduct, the MPC incorporates the assumptions of legal free will, such that, except when otherwise enumerated, criminal law allows the inference that the operative will governed the act in question. Conceptually, the MPC creates a rebuttable presumption to legal free will by putting beyond the purview of criminal law bodily movements arising during unconsciousness (for example, sleep, coma, or reflex) and presumed unconsciousness (hypnosis). Carving out these exceptions effectively limits criminal law to punishing deliberate acts rather than all bodily movements or gratuitous thoughts. The commentary to the MPC supports this interpretation of its approach:

> The term "voluntary" as used in this section does not inject into the criminal law questions about [theoretical] determinism and free will. . . . There is sufficient difference between ordinary human activity and a reflex or a convulsion to make it desirable that they be distinguished for purposes of criminal responsibility by a term like "voluntary."[191]

---

189. *See* MODEL PENAL CODE § 2.01 (Official Draft and Revised Commentaries 1985). The relevant sections read:

Requirements of a Voluntary Act; Omission as Basis of Liability; Possession as an Act:

(1) A person is not guilty of an offense unless his liability is based on conduct that includes a voluntary act or the omission to perform an act of which he is physically capable.

(2) The following are not voluntary acts within the meaning of this Section:
  (a) a reflex of convulsion;
  (b) a bodily movement during unconsciousness or sleep;
  (c) conduct during hypnosis or resulting from hypnotic suggestion;
  (d) a bodily movement that otherwise is not a product of the effort or determination of the actor, either conscious or habitual.

(3) Liability for the commission of an offense may not be based on an omission unaccompanied by action unless:
  (a) the omission is expressly made sufficient by the law defining the offense; or
  (b) a duty to perform the omitted act is otherwise imposed by law.

(4) Possession is an act, within the meaning of this Section, if the possessor knowingly procured or received the thing possessed or was aware of his control thereof for a sufficient period to have been able to terminate his possession.

Id.

190. *See* L.A. Zaibert, *Intentionality, Voluntariness, and Culpability: A Historical-Philosophical Analysis*, 1 BUFF. CRIM. L. REV. 459, 479 (1998) (describing the confusion surrounding the definition of a voluntary act).

191. MODEL PENAL CODE § 2.01 cmt. at 216.

That a defendant should be assumed to have acted voluntarily except for a few enumerated exceptions also comports with Herbert Packer's explanation of the voluntary/involuntary act divide:

> The term [voluntary] is one that will immediately raise the hackles of the determinist, of whatever persuasion. But, once again, the law's language should not be read as plunging into the deep waters of free will vs. determinism, Cartesian duality, or any of a half-dozen other philosophic controversies that might appear to be invoked by the use of the term "voluntary" in relation to conduct. The law is not affirming that some conduct is the product of the free exercise of conscious volition; it is excluding, in a crude kind of way, conduct that in any view is not.[192]

Using the MPC's approach, behavioral genetics must literally or conceptually explain one of the enumerated exceptions to be relevant to the voluntary act requirement.

Several commentators[193] have adopted the "control" theory of human agency, which posits that voluntary acts arise by exercise of "an element of control on the part of the actor."[194] Its proponents claim that this theory affords the simplest and most plausible explanation of what makes an act voluntary.[195] This concept of voluntariness appears in the *Von Dohlen* case,[196] in which Von Dohlen offered expert testimony that the murder "was not a volitional thing, but out of [the defendant's] conscious awareness or control."[197] According to Finbarr McAuley and J. Paul McCutcheon, an individual need not have complete control or control of each event in the causal pathway of an action, so long as some part of the sequence lay within his control.[198] Much like Hart's concept of a voluntary act, the control theory presumes some choice on the part of the actor, and "if the actor refrained from doing that which he did, a different outcome would have resulted."[199] Deborah Denno takes a similar approach with a different solution. She proposes that voluntary acts "constitute conduct subject to an individual's control."[200] She supports this approach as the one that best comports with new scientific discoveries of human behavior, able to "accommodate new [scientific]

---

192. PACKER, *supra* note 149, at 76.

193. *E.g.*, McAULEY & McCUTCHEON, *supra* note 173, at 127; Deborah W. Denno, *Crime and Consciousness: Science and Involuntary Acts*, 87 MINN. L. REV. 269 (2002).

194. McAULEY & McCUTCHEON, *supra* note 173, at 27.

195. *See id.*

196. *See supra* Part II.A.

197. 602 S.E.2d 738, 740 (S.C. 2004).

198. McAULEY & McCUTCHEON, *supra* note 173, at 127.

199. *Id.*

200. Denno, *supra* note 184, at 363.

research on voluntariness, as well as keep the main statement of criminal liability [scientifically] accurate, even if it is incomplete."[201]

Whether voluntariness is defined according to Austin's view,[202] Hart's view, the MPC approach, or the control theory of human behavior, each positivist approach delineates certain acts as being beyond the purview of criminal law. Each of these approaches either implicitly or explicitly labels certain acts as involuntary: bodily movements during coma or when arising by another's physical force, automatic reflexes in response to external stimuli, and bodily movements while unconscious, asleep, or while sleepwalking. To hold individuals accountable for "conduct that in any view is not"[203] voluntary would render the limit of criminal sanctions to acts meaningless.[204]

As for what is not voluntary, Jeffrie Murphy offers this description, which unifies these various approaches:

> An act . . . is involuntary if and only if the behavior . . . is explainable by factors which causally prevent the exercise of normal capacities of control or eliminate such capacities entirely. By "causally prevent" here I mean simply the following: that the factors and the incapacity can be related by subsumption under a scientific law.[205]

If Murphy's definition incorporates the assumption of human agency, then normal human capacities include the capacity to suppress impulses or emotions arising from the many subconscious influences on human choice, including behavioral genetics. Given this unifying definition, the average person should be able to suppress behavioral predispositions arising in part from her genes.

Each theory or definition of involuntariness explicitly or implicitly includes simple reflexes and convulsions as involuntary acts, arising not from human autonomy but from the body's reaction to forces external to the individual. Like the reflexive knee jerk, such involuntary acts cannot be viewed as arising from human agency because the capacity to abstain from acting cannot precede and thus cannot prevent the relevant act. Whether the knee jerks does not call into question the infirmities of an individual. The same analysis applies to bodily

---

201. *Id.* at 358.

202. In accordance with Austin's view that acts arising from the will are voluntary, Herbert Fingarette and Ann Fingarette Hasse provide a simple answer that one could apply to determine that behavioral genetics would not render an act involuntary: "[W]hy should behavior that *is* willed, even though the will be 'diseased,' be called *involuntary?* This seems to be a corruption of language in order to achieve a desired conclusion, since it is natural and usual to hold that behavior, if *willed,* is voluntary." HERBERT FINGARETTE & ANN FINGARETTE HASSE, MENTAL DISABILITIES AND CRIMINAL RESPONSIBILITY 60 (1979).

203. PACKER, *supra* note 149, at 76.

204. Murphy, *supra* note 174, at 340–41.

205. *Id.* at 340.

movements during a convulsive fit.[206] An individual's convulsive movement during a seizure cannot realistically be imputed to an operative and deliberate will. Without adopting the deterministic perspective that humans act reflexively as a result of their genetic predispositions, the narrow exclusion of reflexes and convulsions as voluntary acts would not enable a criminal defendant to assert a parallelism between his reflexes, convulsions, and behavioral predispositions.

Another example: Person B overwhelms Person A by the use of external force, physically moving Person A's arm or physically forcing him to pull the trigger of a gun.[207] Under any of the voluntary act definitions described above, the criminal law would attribute the voluntary act to Person B, who compels Person A's movements, rather than to Person A. The law need not question Person A's subjective infirmities, but merely distinguish acts (in a legal sense, involving voluntariness) versus bodily movement arising by external physical force. Under any view, Person A acted involuntarily or not at all.

Although behavioral genetics and neuroscience seem irrelevant to this exception, the *Moore* and *Von Dohlen* cases underscore how practitioners may seek to use this evidence to blur this seemingly clear example of involuntary conduct. Moore claimed that because of his addiction he acted "as a result of compulsion, not from choice,"[208] while Von Dohlen's defense expert testified that the murder "was not a volitional thing, but [one] out of [the defendant's] conscious awareness or control."[209] To disclaim responsibility for the act, each defendant attributed his act to his disease as a force distinct from himself as a responsible agent. But even though each defendant conceivably established a causal factor in his decision to act (as those involved in raising one's hand to ask a question), neither proved he acted programmatically in a predetermined manner. A theory of action referencing the many subconscious factors influencing the choice to act differs in kind, then, rather than degree, from moving by the physical force of another. To accept Moore's and Von Dohlen's claims would require parsing the subjective thought processes of defendants to determine whether the act should be attributed to conscious choice or to subconscious influences, as if these were distinct entities. To accept otherwise—namely that a subconscious influence on behavior negates individual choice—would render all acts involuntary and therefore beyond the purview of criminal liability. The *Moore* court appropriately rejected this approach as antithetical to the system of criminal liability.[210]

---

206. However, under the *Decina* temporal rule discussed in Part II.A, one could still face liability if he had previous knowledge of his predisposition to convulsions by engaging in an earlier voluntary act.
207. United States v. Moore, 486 F.2d 1139, 1179 (D.C. Cir. 1973).
208. *Id.* at 1150.
209. Von Dohlen v. State, 602 S.E.2d 738, 740 (S.C. 2004).
210. 486 F.2d at 1139.

The defense of unconsciousness[211] blurs the boundaries of the voluntary-act presumption, that is, presuming that every act is the result of conscious choice (albeit one affected by subconscious influences). The defense of unconsciousness was recognized in the late 1800s by the Court of Appeals of Kentucky, which stated that because an unconscious individual lacks awareness of his outward actions, his circumstances, and his surroundings, "none of his acts during the paroxysms can rightfully be imputed to him as crimes."[212] Many courts have adopted or expanded this reasoning,[213] such that now criminal law generally recognizes that during sleep, coma, or blackout, bodily movements occur in a state of the actor's unawareness, rather than by choice. But in certain states of physical activity, such as epileptic fugue, amnesia, extreme confusion, and equivalent conditions, individuals may not be unconscious so much as they might suffer gross impairment of self-awareness.[214] These conditions create a gray area between consciousness and unconsciousness, promoting some to question the degree of unconsciousness sufficient to overcome a presumption of individual agency.[215] *Unconsciousness* in this sense is evocative of the notion that one is compelled to act, without conscious choice, by her genes. In actuality, the narrowness of the exception of unconsciousness in the criminal context suggests otherwise.

Unconsciousness[216] refers to conditions including sleep, coma, blackout, and stroke, or more generally to a defendant's lack of self-awareness or awareness of his surroundings. When an individual lacks self-awareness, his bodily movements cannot be explained by an operative will. By contrast, the individual who is grossly impaired or extremely confused has self-awareness and some understanding of his circumstances and surroundings. The presumption of voluntariness

---

211. Courts generally interpret unconsciousness to mean that the bodily movements of the individual are directed by an agency other than his own. *See* McAuley & McCutcheon, *supra* note 173, at 133.

212. Fain v. Commonwealth, 78 Ky. 183 (1879) (quoting Ray's Med. Jur. § 508).

213. Denno, *supra* note 184, at 339.

214. Model Penal Code § 2.01 cmt. at 219 (Official Draft and Revised Commentaries 1985).

215. McAuley & McCutcheon, *supra* note 173, at 133–34.

216. We discuss unconsciousness but not automatism because of the implausibility of a court's allowing the introduction of behavioral genetics to argue a defendant acted as an automaton as a result of his biological predispositions. Behavioral genetics has little relevance to automatism, a relatively rare defense, particularly as a failure-of-proof defense to the voluntary act requirement. Automatism describes the imprecisely defined condition of an individual who argues that his mental state prevented his mind from directing his bodily movement. *Id.* at 142. Usually, the individual is capable of action but not conscious of what he is doing. Michael Corrado, *The Theory of Action*, 39 Emory L.J. 1191, 1191–92 (1990). Courts vary widely on its meaning and content, and its applicability to the voluntary act requirement instead of as an affirmative defense. McAuley & McCutcheon, *supra* note 173, at 142–46.

should therefore apply to his conduct.[217] With consciousness thus understood, rarely could a defendant credibly claim that his behavioral predisposition rendered him unaware of his circumstances and surroundings.[218] Moreover, to argue one's behavioral predisposition influenced or overwhelmed a defendant's choice to act could suggest that the individual acted consciously in response to his many subconscious stimuli. The Supreme Court of New Jersey has articulated this distinction:

> Criminal responsibility must be judged at the level of the conscious. If a person thinks, plans and executes the plan at that level, the criminality of his act cannot be denied, wholly or partially, because although he didn't realize it, his conscious was influenced to think, to plan and to execute the plan by unconscious influences which were the product of his genes and his lifelong environment. So . . . criminal guilt cannot be denied or confined . . . because [the defendant] was unaware that his decisions and conduct were mechanistically directed by unconscious influences. [219]

In short, the genetically or neurologically predisposed criminal defendant acts consciously, albeit conceivably in part as a result of his genetic endowment. The logic seems inescapable that a behavioral predisposition could not satisfy this final exception to the voluntary act requirement. In practice, then, only when "under any view"[220] a bodily movement does not arise from choice and cannot causally be explained by the operative will can the resulting conduct be said to be involuntary in criminal law.

C. Mens Rea or Mental Culpability

In addition to the requirement of a voluntary act or omission, criminal liability also requires proof of a mental state that coincides with the act or

---

217. *See infra* Part IV. The defendant still has available to him the full array of justifications and excuses, and determining that the defendant engaged in a voluntary act has partially satisfied one element of criminal liability.

218. Judge Berzon's concurrence in *Dennis v. Budge*, which states that a "prisoner, though otherwise lucid, rational and capable of making choices is, in a Manchurian Candidate-like fashion, volitionally incapable of making a choice," would suggest otherwise, but no behavioral geneticist supports the view that a behavioral predisposition would render an individual programmed like a Manchurian candidate. 378 F.3d 880, 889 (9th Cir. 2004).

219. State v. Sikora, 210 A.2d 193, 202-03 (N.J. 1965).

220. The "any view" analysis from Packer could serve a potential limiting function in the criminal law, such that in the unlikely scenario that behavioral genetics reveals a 1:1 correlation between a particular behavior and a particular genetic endowment, bypassing any capacity for choice or reason, one could use behavioral genetics as a defense for involuntary conduct. The emergence of such scientific evidence, particularly from the field of behavioral genetics, is highly improbable.

omission.[221] This mental element is referred to as mens rea or the guilty mind.[222] Commentators have lamented the absence in American criminal law and in common law generally of an orderly approach to this element, "a highly complex cluster of problems for which the tag of mens rea stands as a convenient but elliptical symbol."[223] Nevertheless, it is into this complex cluster of problems that some are tempted to introduce behavioral genetics and neurological evidence. But such evidence does not contribute to the determination of whether a particular defendant had the mental state required for criminal offenses.

Mens rea derives from the early notion in criminal law that an offender should be punished only if he acted with a "vicious will."[224] To satisfy this requirement necessitated proof that either malice or an intention to engage in the legal wrong-doing actually motivated the defendant's conduct.[225] As criminal law developed, however, the requisite mental element for criminal liability (mens rea) came to mean something quite different, and the focus shifted from assessing the individual character of the defendant to the more utilitarian goal of deterring illegal conduct through the threat of moral condemnation and physical punishment.[226] Acts thus became criminal when commissioned under circumstances that likely

---

221. LaFave, *supra* note 45, § 6.3, at 322. There are some criminal offenses—not discussed here—that do not require mens rea: strict liability offenses. To the extent that behavioral genetics is relevant to strict liability offenses, the concerns, at least as they might relate to mens rea, are not distinguishable from the general concerns about making conduct that is not blameworthy criminal.

222. The MPC identifies the levels of mental culpability by the concepts of "purpose," "knowledge," "recklessness," and "negligence." *See* Model Penal Code § 2.02(2) (Official Draft and Revised Commentaries 1985). The higher levels of purpose and knowledge are defined such that the criminal act is the product of the actor's conscious mind. *Id.* The common law generally referred to these levels of culpability as specific intent. The MPC identifies the lower levels of recklessness and negligence to mean that the criminal act or omission is the result of a risk or peril that was created by the actor's conduct, which the actor unreasonably ignored (recklessness) or unreasonably failed to perceive. *Id.* The common law generally referred to these levels of mental culpability as general intent.

223. Herbert L. Packer, *Mens Rea and the Supreme Court*, 1962 Sup. Ct. Rev. 107, 108 (1962).

224. United States v. Freed, 401 U.S. 601, 607 (1971).

225. *See* Richard Singer, *The Resurgence of Mens Rea: I—Provocation, Emotional Disturbance, and The Model Penal Code*, 27 B.C. L. Rev. 243 (1986) (discussing the development of the mens rea requirement in criminal law). Singer notes:

Prior to the nineteenth century, the criminal law of England and this country took seriously the requirement that a defendant could not be found guilty of an offense unless he truly acted in a malicious and malevolent way—that he not only had "the" mental state for the crime, but that more generally, he manifested a full-blown mens rea: an "evil mind."

Id. at 243 (citation omitted).

226. Hart, *supra* note 139, at 409.

would cause or threaten an interest that criminal law sought to protect.[227] The test of criminality was the degree of danger shown by common experience to accompany that particular act or omission under those particular circumstances.[228] This test made it unnecessary to determine the actual wickedness of the defendant; conduct could instead be judged by its "tendency [to cause a certain result] under the known circumstances."[229] "By the early twentieth century, it was possible to argue that criminal law was no longer concerned with a general mens rea, but only with a more specific, constrained question of whether the defendant's conduct reflected the specific mental state required by the statute."[230] Criminal liability thus became an assessment of the defendant's conduct measured against the conduct expected of the average law-abiding citizen aware of the relevant circumstances known to the defendant. The defendant's mental state could be inferred from those circumstances alone, such that the criminal mind could be known from the crime.

The movement from focusing on the defendant's general wickedness to his conduct and the circumstances of the crime nevertheless required a moral basis for finding individual fault. Otherwise, the "the actor [would be] subjected to the stigma of a criminal conviction without being morally blameworthy."[231] This reformulated approach therefore focused on the defendant's willingness to engage in harmful conduct, rather than his general maliciousness, to inform his criminal liability. In this move from punishment for general malice or ill will to punishment for "an intention to threaten the paradigm interests protected by the criminal law," mens rea and actus reus were joined as the constituent elements of a criminal offense.[232] The defendant's awareness of, or unreasonable failure to recognize, the circumstances by which his conduct could be judged blameworthy became the primary orientation of the modern concept of mens rea.

Today, mens rea refers only to the state of mind that must accompany proof of individual elements of particular criminal offenses (such as willfulness, intention, or purposefulness); the risks created by the defendant's conduct (recklessness or negligence); the facts and circumstances surrounding the crime, or "the middle category of 'knowingly' committing an offense."[233] To determine the

---

227. HOLMES JR., *supra* note 144, at 46–47, 75.

228. *Id.*

229. *Id.* at 66.

230. *See* Singer, *supra* note 216, at 244 ("By the early twentieth century, it was possible to argue that the criminal law was no longer concerned with a general 'mens rea,' but only with a much more specific, constrained question of whether the defendant's conduct reflected the specific mental state required by the statute.").

231. *Id.*

232. McAULEY & McCUTCHEON, *supra* note 173, at 275.

233. FLETCHER, *supra* note 9, at 442.

existence of any of these mental states, the criminal law does not concern itself with the "inner posture of the actor," but focuses on the "actual risk and knowledge of risk" created by the actor's conduct and the circumstances known to the actor at the time he acts.[234] Moreover, the mental state *intent* (mens rea) differs from the *motive* for acting, as illustrated by the *Bobo* case, in which a mother intentionally killed her children, although she harbored no malice against them.[235] Thus, the trier of fact infers the relevant mental state from the circumstances under which the defendant acted, and need not inquire into the internal factors motivating the defendant's conduct.[236]

Given these very general principles about mens rea, an actor's behavioral predisposition would have little relevance to whether he acted with the requisite mental state for a criminal offense. In particular, there is an incongruity between behavioral sciences evidence and the question of whether the defendant acted with purpose, knowledge, or recklessness, as those mental states are currently

---

234. *Id.* at 447.

235. People v. Bobo, 3 Cal. Rptr. 2d 747 (Cal. Ct. App. 1990); *see supra* Part II.B.

236. If, therefore, the actor puts bullets into a gun, places the gun at his friend's temple, and pulls the trigger, the trier of fact will infer he intended to kill his friend, not because killing was his purpose, but because that assumption is the commonly understood conclusion to be drawn from the sequence of his action. The Model Penal Code makes a distinction between mental state as an objective inquiry, independent of the actor's actual awareness of the nature and circumstances of his conduct, and mental state as a subjective inquiry, but focusing upon the objective nature and circumstances of the actor's conduct and the actor's awareness of those things. MODEL PENAL CODE, *supra* note 180, at 235–36. Thus, the drafters distinguished between the Washington state code definition of "knowingly" that included the defendant's having "information which would lead a reasonable man in the same circumstances to believe that facts exist which facts are described by a statute defining an offense" and a proposed Michigan definition of "knowingly" providing, "[i]n finding that a person acted knowingly with respect to conduct or circumstances, the finder of fact may rely upon proof that under the circumstances a reasonable person would have known of such conduct or circumstances." The Washington standard is an objective one; the Michigan standard makes a subjective determination (the defendant's mental state), relying upon the objective circumstances known to the individual actor. *Id.* at 236 n.12. The drafters noted that the proposed Michigan Code only permitted the jury to "draw inferences about an actor's . . . knowledge." *Id.* They concluded,

> [e]ven without such explicit language, it will generally be true that the actual mental state of the actor in most cases will be inferred from the circumstances as they objectively appear to the jury, but the critical point is that this language [permitting the inference] should not be taken as an invitation to dispense with the need for making the inference.

Id. Another commentator noted, "it would appear that an intention to engage in certain conduct or to do so under certain attendant circumstances may likewise be said to exist on the basis of what one knows." LAFAVE, *supra* note 45, at 246.

understood, or, more broadly, with *intent*, as that term is understood to describe a culpable mental state. The Supreme Court has noted,

> [i]t is now generally accepted that a person who acts (or omits to act) intends a result of his act (or omission) under two quite different circumstances: (1) when he consciously desires that result, whatever the likelihood of that result happening from his conduct; and (2) when he knows that the result is practically certain to follow from his conduct, whatever his desire may be as to that result.[237]

The inquiry in either case is whether the defendant is "consciously behaving in a way the law prohibits" and whether "such conduct is a fitting object of criminal punishment."[238] Only the inquiry into the defendant's conscious desires are relevant for determining whether the defendant is acting intentionally, not his biological predispositions.

Behavioral genetics and neuroscience evidence likewise lacks relevance to whether a person acted recklessly or negligently, as those terms generally are used to describe culpable mental states. The drafters of the MPC noted, for example, that although its standard for negligence, as well as that for extreme emotional disturbance and duress, invites consideration of the "care that a reasonable person would observe in the actor's situation," this was not an invitation to make the inquiry turn on individual quirks: "The heredity, intelligence or temperament of the actor would not be held material in judging negligence, and could not be without depriving the criterion of its objectivity. The Code is not intended to displace discriminations of this kind, but to leave the issue to the courts."[239] The same can be said with respect to determining whether a person acted recklessly, the only difference being that in addition to determining whether the defendant created a criminal risk, the jury also would have to find that the defendant was aware of the risk.

The defendants in *Smith* and *Bobo* did not claim that they were not conscious of their conduct; rather, their real claim was that their conscious conduct was the product of mental illnesses, for which they alleged a genetic origin. That, however, amounts to nothing more than a claim that the defendant was unable to conform his conduct to law. But, as one commentator has noted, the obligations established by criminal law are ones that "normal members of the community will be able to comply with, given the necessary awareness of the circumstances

---

237. United States v. United States Gypsum Co., 438 U.S. 422, 445 (1978) (quoting W. LaFave & A. Scott, Criminal Law 196 (1972)). The MPC divides "intent" into acting "purposefully" and acting "knowingly," which corresponds to the two ways the Court identifies for acting "intentionally."

238. *Id.*

239. Model Penal Code § 2.02 at 242 (Official Draft and Revised Commentaries 1985) (internal citations omitted).

of fact calling for compliance."[240] When the actor actually lacks the ability to comply, which is what behavioral genetics evidence has been offered, as in *Bobo*,[241] to show,

> the traditional law provides materials for solution of the problem when inability negatives blameworthiness. . . . The materials include doctrines . . . providing for the exculpation of those individuals who because of mental disease or defect are to be deemed incapable of acting as responsible, participating members of society.[242]

A claim of irresponsibility is more than just a claim that the actor cannot be deterred, "or else the more hardened the criminal, the better would be his claim of irresponsibility."[243] What also is involved "is reaching for criteria which will avoid attaching moral blame where blame cannot justly be attached, while, at the same time, avoiding a denial of moral responsibility where the denial would be personally and socially debilitating."[244] Criminal law now finds that balance by determining mental states through objective analysis. There is no place for behavioral genetics and neuroscience in the analysis of the nature and circumstances of the actor's conduct as informed by ordinary human experiences.[245]

---

240. Hart, *supra* note 139, at 414 (emphasis omitted).

241. *E.g.*, People v. Bobo, 271 Cal. Rptr. 277 (Cal. Ct. App. 1990); State v. Davis, 2001 Tenn. Crim. App. LEXIS 341 (Tenn. Crim. App. 2001).

242. Hart, *supra* note 139, at 414.

243. *Id.* at 414 n.13.

244. *Id.*

245. Unrestrained and misguided efforts to introduce behavioral genetics evidence into the analysis of culpable mental states could result in preemptive legislative or judicial action to preclude such evidence altogether, making it difficult to reconsider its relevance as scientific knowledge advances. Could the state preclude the defendant from presenting an entire available category of evidence, such as behavioral genetics, to negate proof of a requisite mental state? The answer appears to be yes. In *Montana v. Egelhoff*, 518 U.S. 37 (1996), the Supreme Court considered a state statute that precluded the jury's consideration of the defendant's voluntary intoxication in determining whether he "purposefully" or "knowingly" caused the death of the victim. In a concurrence Justice Ginsburg agreed with the plurality if the statute has been "simply a rule to keep out 'relevant exculpatory evidence' . . . Montana's law offends due process." *Id.* at 57. But the statute did something more: it redefined the mental element of the offense charged, which wholly eliminated any due process concern. "[A] 'state legislature certainly has the authority to identify the elements of the offenses it wishes to punish' . . . and to exclude evidence irrelevant to the crime it has defined." *Id.* (Ginsburg, J., concurring) (quoting *id.* at 64 (O'Connor, J., dissenting)). Montana, she thought, had extracted "the entire subject of voluntary intoxication from the mens rea inquiry." *Id.* at 58 (Ginsburg, J., concurring) (quoting Mont. Code Ann. § 45-2-205 (1995)). "Defining *mens rea* to eliminate the exculpatory value of voluntary intoxication does not offend a 'fundamental principle of justice.'" *Id.* at 59.

IV. STANDARDS OF CONDUCT AND EVADING OR
DIMINISHING CRIMINAL RESPONSIBILITY

The development of criminal jurisprudence has left little room for genetic and neurological evidence in negating the actus reus or mens rea requirements for criminal liability. Likewise, such evidence has limited potential to bolster a defendant's attempts to evade[246] or diminish the attribution of criminal responsibility to him[247] by arguing that the circumstances warrant (justification) [248] or partially excuse[249] his behavior (excuse).[250]

When evaluating the merits of a justification or excuse, the trier of fact compares the defendant's acts to societal norms or standards of conduct.[251] Put otherwise, the criminal law allows a determination of whether the circumstances warrant attributing to the actor criminal responsibility for the crime.[252] Although there are exceptions to the general proposition that excuses include an invariant

---

It seems safe to assume that a statute excluding evidence of behavioral genetics as irrelevant to culpability likely would not offend the Constitution. In his dissent Justice Souter acknowledged the right of the state to "so define the mental element of an offense that evidence of a defendant's voluntary intoxication . . . does not have exculpatory relevance." *Id.* at 73.

246. Hart, *supra* note 139, at 414.

247. *See* FLETCHER, *supra* note 9, at 510; HART, *supra* note 179, at 15.

248. DRESSLER, *supra* note 21, at 202; FLETCHER, *supra* note 9, at 459 ("A justification negates the wrongfulness of the act and denies the element of wrongdoing.").

249. FLETCHER, *supra* note 9, at 798 ("The focus of the excuse is not on the act in the abstract, but on the circumstances of the act and the actor's personal capacity to avoid either an intentional wrong or the taking of an excessive risk."). But it is not the actor's personal capacity to avoid such wrongdoing or risks that matters, but the capacity of the *reasonable person* to do so.

250. George P. Fletcher, *The Right and the Reasonable*, 98 HARV. L. REV. 949, 957 (1985).

251. Dolores A. Donovan & Stephanie M. Wildman, *Is the Reasonable Man Obsolete? A Critical Perspective on Self-Defense and Provocation*, 14 LOY. L.A. L. REV. 435, 459 (1981) ("[T]he question of attribution is to be viewed in light of all relevant facts and circumstances of the individual case."). Donovan and Wildman adopt Fletcher's characterization that such facts and circumstances imply a subjective determination. Such determinations are in fact standards of general applicability, rather than inquiries into the unique infirmities of the individual defendant.

252. *Id.* Insanity is the only outlier. It is either an anomaly in jurisdictions with the defense of not guilty by reason of insanity (which is theoretically inconsistent with the structure of criminal responsibility) or it represents a carefully delineated category of those individuals who are exempt from criminal responsibility. This narrow group would nevertheless not permit the introduction of subjective mental infirmities of an individual during the determination of criminal responsibility. *See* Saxe, *supra* note 62, at 253 ("Unless a court can make a finding of insanity, the criminal law does not seek to understand the uniqueness of the mental deficiency of the criminal defendant.").

legal standard, these are narrowly circumscribed and remain consistent with society's expectations of the norms of human behavior.[253] Justifications and excuses thereby serve as a check against holding a defendant to a higher standard of conduct than the average or reasonable person in society could be expected to meet under the circumstances. Because these defenses serve as an external check on liability, they rarely implicate the defendant's unique psychological characteristics and instead rely on comparison with societal expectations for norms of conduct.[254] The criminal law enables this external check by reference to a fictitious "reasonable person," who represents the average person of society and the norms of behavior that society expects that person to meet. In the few defenses that enable the defendant to introduce his unique perspective, a separate showing of reasonableness is likewise required.[255]

As of yet, few criminal defendants have sought to introduce behavioral genetics or neuroscience to establish a justification or excuse. Recent legal scholarship, however, reveals a growing movement to transform the objective assessment of certain defenses into a more subjective one by reformulating the reasonable-person standard in criminal law.[256] Proponents of this change support augmenting

---

253. Paul H. Robinson, Criminal Law § 9.1, at 488–89 (1997) (explaining that insanity, involuntary acts, and involuntary intoxication do not seem to incorporate an objective standard, but that one would be mistaken "to assume that these defenses excuse without regard for whether the actor has met society's collective normative expectations for efforts to avoid a violation"). As discussed in Part II.C, behavioral genetics could bolster psychiatric testimony in insanity cases, but it should not stand alone to satisfy the mental defect element of insanity.

254. Id. § 9.1, at 488, § 9.4, at 532–33 (explaining that "in practice, all modern excuses hold an actor to some form of objective standard in judging his or her efforts to remain law-abiding," and that an excuse does not derive from a defendant's disability, because even if "an actor was unfairly burdened in having to resist or avoid committing an offense [this] will not excuse him or her if, with reasonable effort, he or she could have successfully avoided the violation").

255. Again, insanity serves as an outlier. Insanity is best understood as a categorical exemption from criminal responsibility when presented as "not guilty by reason of insanity." The "guilty but mentally ill" verdict has little benefit for the criminal defendant and holds him fully responsible for his criminal conduct.

256. See, e.g., Donovan & Wildman, supra note 242, at 465–68 (arguing in favor of a subjective reasonable-person standard because an objective standard ignores social reality and applies a false legal reality to defendant); Heller, supra note 174 (analyzing the problems with the juror cross-section concerns obviating the validity of the objective-person test, and proposing limited subjectivization of the reasonable-person standard); Eugene R. Milhizer, Justification and Excuse: What They Were, What They Are, and What They Ought to Be, 78 St. John's L. Rev. 725, 890-93 (2004) (distinguishing justifications from excuses and advocating a subjective standard, including the actor's subjective perception of the circumstances to evaluate excuses to determine the validity of the excuse); V.F. Nourse, Self-Defense and Subjectivity, 68 U. Chi. L. Rev. 1235 (2001) (demonstrating that the divide between an objective and subjective reasonable-person standard is an

the standard with the allegedly relevant individual infirmities of the defendant, so that the defendant's unique psychological perspective may more closely govern the assessment of reasonableness.[257] If these scholars succeed, the result would be a reasonable-person standard—if one could call it a standard at all—that would enable criminal defendants to introduce behavioral genetics to support claims of justification or excuse as relevant to criminal responsibility.[258] Properly viewed, however, these behavioral sciences have limited relevance to the reasonableness inquiry governing the evasion or diminution of criminal responsibility.

A. The Reasonable Person as a Standard of Conduct

In *The Common Law*,[259] Oliver Wendell Holmes described the standard of the "reasonable person,"[260] which embodies:

> an ideal being, represented by the jury when they are appealed to, and his conduct is an external or objective standard when applied to any given individual.

---

artificial one); Alan Reed, *Duress and Provocation as Excuses to Murder: Salutary Lessons from Recent Anglo-American Jurisprudence*, 6 FLA. ST. J. TRANSNAT'L L. & POL'Y 51 (1996) (comparing the English and U.S. system of reasonableness, and advocating a subjectivization of the reasonable-person standard to include unique mental characteristics of the defendant, such as timidity); Paul H. Robinson, *Criminal Law Scholarship: Three Illusions*, 2 THEORETICAL INQUIRIES L. 287, 308 (2001) (explaining that although there are calls for increased subjectivization of the reasonable-person standard, it is unclear which characteristics of a defendant should be incorporated); Lauren E. Goldman, Note, *Nonconfrontational Killings and the Appropriate Use of Battered Child Syndrome Testimony: The Hazards of Subjective Self-Defense and the Merits of Partial Excuse*, 45 CASE W. RES. L. REV. 185 (1994) (proposing that psychological characteristics of abused children should be included in the assessment of reasonableness for purposes of an excuse when the focus is on the circumstances of the defendant, rather than the crime); Sarah McLean, Comment, *Harassment in the Workplace: When will the Reactions of Ethnic Minorities and Women be Considered Reasonable?* [Watkins v. Bowden, 105 F.3d 1344 (11th Cir. 1997)], 40 WASHBURN L.J. 593, 609 (2001) (claiming that the reasonable-person standard reflects a whiteAnglo-Saxon male bias and should be reformulated to allow the subjective perceptions of women and ethnic minorities, particularly with respect to employment discrimination claims).

257. *See generally* sources cited *supra* note 247.

258. *See* Robinson, *supra* note 247, at 306 (noting that subjectivization of the reasonable-person standard could allow criminal defendants to introduce a genetic propensity to violence as a relevant characteristic to the reasonableness inquiry).

259. HOLMES JR., *supra* note 144.

260. For a succinct discussion of the reasonable-person standard, *see generally* Mark A. Rothstein, *The Impact of Behavioral Genetics on the Law and the Courts*, 83 JUDICATURE 116 (1999). Rothstein summarizes:

> The reasonable person standard, originally expressed as the "reasonable man" standard, was first applied to negligence law in England in the middle of the nineteenth century. The concept was soon adopted in the United States. By the beginning of the

That individual may be morally without stain, because he has less than ordinary intelligence or prudence. But he is required to have those qualities at his peril. If he has them, he will not, as a general rule, incur liability without blameworthiness.[261]

In Holmes's description, the individual attributes of the defendant relate only to the defendant's capacity to conform his conduct to the rules of the state. Thus the reasonable person embodies norms of behavior under the relevant circumstances against which the jury measures the defendant's conduct; in Holmes's view, there is no inquiry into what unique biological, neurological, or other factors influenced the defendant's behavior. But a second and equally powerful explanation of the reasonable person emerges from the criminal law's role in reifying and codifying societal norms of conduct. As a check on liability, the reasonable-person standard reflects conduct deemed justified by the state under the circumstances, while also providing a tool by which a jury may implement and codify societal norms of behavior by comparing the defendant's actions against that expected of the reasonable person under the circumstances.[262]

---

twentieth century the gender-neutral "reasonable person" came into use and is now used in every state. The reasonable person standard is often expressed as the reasonably prudent person, or some similar terminology, all of which have the identical meaning.

Id. at 118.

261. HOLMES JR., *supra* note 144, at 51.

262. Hisham M. Ramadan, *Reconstructing Reasonableness in Criminal Law: Moderate Jury Instructions Proposal*, 29 J. LEGIS. 233, 238 (2003) (noting that some argue that reasonableness represents societal standards of conduct, and "crystallizes the norms and values of the society and incorporates them into a set of rules that govern individuals' conduct and communicates its meaning to the public frankly"). In his treatise, *Criminal Law*, Paul H. Robinson also describes the criminal law's role in shaping societal norms:

The real power in shaping people's conduct lies in the networks of interpersonal relationships in which people find themselves, the social norms and prohibitions shared among those relationships and transmitted through those social networks, and the internalized representations of those norms and moral precepts. . . . Criminal law, in particular, plays a central role in creating and maintaining the social consensus on morality necessary to sustain norms. In fact, in a society as diverse as ours, the criminal law may be the only single mechanism that is society-wide, transcending cultural and ethnic differences. Thus the criminal law's most important real-world effect can be its ability to assist in building, shaping, and maintaining these norms and moral principles. A central role for the criminal law and the criminal justice system, therefore, is to contribute to and harness the compliance-producing power of interpersonal relationships and personal morality.

ROBINSON, *supra* note 244, § 1.2, at 21.

In such a way, the reasonable-person standard may help "to foster, sustain, and articulate norms" of behavior in society.[263]

Holmes did not fully humanize the reasonable person by giving him a gender, age, or any other defining characteristics. Holmes describes him as an ideal being because the reasonable person also reflects societal norms of conduct, but the reasonable-person standard more appropriately embodies an average or ordinary member of society—one who does not excel, who can err in his choices, and who makes mistakes, suffers fear and selfishness, and possesses other shortcomings to the extent such shortcomings manifest normal standards of community behavior.[264] Thus understood, the reasonable person exists in criminal law as a representation of ordinary and presumed human capacities of thought, choice, and reason, and does not don any particular physical characteristics or features.

The purposes underpinning the reasonable-person standard help to illuminate why it operates without regard to the defendant's individual mental infirmities or behavioral predispositions. Proponents of the objective reasonable-person standard generally rely on some combination of the following four rationales:

(1) It creates a community standard of general applicability that affords notice to all members of society (standard of conduct);[265]

(2) It fosters predictability of outcomes in criminal cases and more evenhanded enforcement of the criminal law (equality);[266]

(3) It affords ease of administration of the criminal law in light of the difficulty of knowing the subjective state of mind of individual defendants (administrative ease);[267] and

---

263. Goldberg & Zipursky, *supra* note 154, at 386 (explaining that law, and negligence law in torts, may help to reduce car accidents not only through pricing and prohibition—a stick—but also by helping to reify social norms of safe driving and thereby promote "internal deterrence").

264. Mayo Moran, Rethinking the Reasonable Person: An Egalitarian Reconstruction of the Objective Standard 132 (2003).

265. *See* Hart, *supra* note 179, at 229 (explaining that the objective standard creates standards of conduct that the largest proportion of society can meet and that to require a higher standard than that achievable by a large proportion of society lacks efficacy because such a standard could neither come into nor continue in existence); Holmes Jr., *supra* note 144, at 50–51 (expressing the reasonable person as an external standard of general application that requires every person to achieve the best possible conduct and to deviate from this conduct, even if by incapacity or infirmity, at his own peril). Holmes further noted that, "it is precisely to those who are most likely to err by temperament, ignorance, or folly, that the threats of the criminal law are the most dangerous." *Id.*

266. Moran, *supra* note 255, at 207.

267. Hart, *supra* note 179, at 175.

(4) It ensures that the most dangerous criminals will not be held the least criminally responsible (collapse of responsibility).[268]

These objectives—creating standards of conduct, ensuring equality, promoting administrative ease, and preventing the collapse of responsibility—comport with other characteristics of the criminal law—safeguarding the general welfare of society while fostering responsible members of society. More importantly, these objectives comport with the limited role of criminal responsibility: to determine if a crime was committed and, if so, what crime and by which responsible agent.

To conclude, however, that the objective reasonable-person standard is the necessary legal standard in fact, two propositions must first be established: (1) justifications and excuses operate objectively in practice, and (2) a "subjective" reasonable-person standard would not achieve the same stated goals. If the reasonable person operates objectively in fact, then evidence of a defendant's behavioral predispositions does not presently inform responsibility. But if a subjective or variable standard would achieve the same four goals, the criminal law lacks a principled reason for excluding subjective evidence in assessing responsibility.

B. The Reasonable Person: Objective in Fact

In *Murder and the Reasonable Man*, Cynthia Lee frames the typical subjective-versus-objective debate on the reasonable-person standard, opining that each extreme presents a legal fiction:

> A purely objective standard of reasonableness is one that excludes consideration of any of the defendant's particular characteristics. Under such a standard, the defendant is compared to the Reasonable Person devoid of gender, race, culture, religion and any particular strengths or weaknesses. Of course, no person is devoid of identifying characteristics.
>
> . . . .
>
> At the other end of the reasonableness spectrum is another legal fiction—a purely subjective standard of reasonableness. Under such a standard, the

---

268. Joshua Dressler, *Why Keep the Provocation Defense?: Some Reflections on a Difficult Subject*, 86 Minn. L. Rev. 959, 999–1000 (2002) (discussing which characteristics of a defendant may be properly incorporated in the reasonable-person defense and noting that the objective standard excludes certain characteristics such as short-temperedness, as necessary to the function of the standard). As one of the sources of resistance to subjective determination of liability, George Fletcher identified the "unresolved anxiety about sociological and psychological determinism that leads many to believe *tout comprendre, c'est tout pardonner*. If we know everything about the defendant, we will invariably excuse him." Fletcher, *supra* note 9, at 513; *see also* Abraham S. Goldstein, The Insanity Defense 191–92 (1967) (noting the concern that a subjective theory of judgment used for justifications or excuses other than insanity could result in more acquittals for the most dangerous defendants).

Reasonable Person is imbued with the defendant's race, gender, class, level of education, and other personal characteristics. If, however, the Reasonable Person has all the defendant's characteristics, the reasonableness standard simply collapses . . . . Under such a standard, if the defendant thinks his beliefs and actions are reasonable, the Reasonable Person with all the defendant's characteristics will likely feel the same.[269]

Lee's conception of an objective standard differs from that described here: the "objective" reasonable-person standard signifies reasonableness as a standard of conduct generally applicable to all members of society without regard to the defendant's individualized *beliefs* about the circumstances of the crime or unique psychological perspective.[270] Thus, the term *objective* names the specific idea that the trier of fact should evaluate the defendant's proffered justifications or excuses by a standard of conduct that reflects the collective expectations of society of how law-abiding members of society can and should behave under the circumstances that confronted the defendant. The personal beliefs, impulses, and desires of the defendant have little practical relevance to how law-abiding citizens can and should act under a given set of circumstances. To give an obvious example, irrespective of whether an individual defendant believes it moral to kill others for pleasure, society still expects that he will refrain from doing so precisely because an ordinary member of society can and should refrain from doing so. Thus, the defendant's belief will not excuse his behavior if he kills another individual.

The criminal law, however, has determined that certain physical characteristics of the defendant may inform how a reasonable person in society would be expected to act under the relevant external circumstances. For example, one could ask and answer how a reasonable person would likely act if attacked by an assailant with greater size and strength who is apparently armed with a deadly weapon, without regard to the defendant's actual perceptions. To answer this

---

269. CYNTHIA LEE, MURDER AND THE REASONABLE MAN: PASSION AND FEAR IN THE CRIMINAL COURTROOM 206–7 (2003).

270. George Fletcher offers four conceptions of the difference between objective and subjective:

(1) 'Objective standards' are 'standards of general application.' 'Subjective' standards by implication take 'account of the infinite varieties of temperament, intellect and education which make the internal character of a given act so different.

(2) 'Objective standards' are external; they apply regardless of whether the actor thinks he is doing the right thing; 'subjective' standards focus on the actor's state of mind.

(3) The question of wrongdoing is an objective standard, for it focuses on the act in abstraction from the actor; the issue of attribution is subjective in the sense that it focus[]es on the actor's personal accountability for wrongdoing.

(4) Standards are objective if they are factual; subjective if they require a value judgment.

FLETCHER, *supra* note 9, at 506.

question, one need not inquire into the individual beliefs or mental infirmities of the particular defendant. Instead, one need consider only easily ascertainable facts external to the mindset of the defendant—such as the size and strength of the defendant. By taking the relative size and strength of the defendant into account, the reasonableness inquiry has not been transformed into an inquiry about the individual beliefs of the criminal defendant.[271] The criminal law rationally distinguishes between the mental and physical characteristics of the defendant because the reasonable-person standard reflects a generalized standard of mental capacities, not a generalized standard of physical characteristics. Thus, the traditional, "objective" reasonable-person standard survives the incorporation of certain unusual physical characteristics of the defendant (for example, blindness) if relevant, but excludes any unusual mental characteristics by definition.[272] Against this backdrop, the following sections analyze the defenses of provocation and self-defense by battered women, both of which have been misperceived as anomalies to the objective reasonable-person standard.

C. The Defense of Provocation: A Failed Reformulation

Under the traditional formulation of the provocation excuse, the extent of criminal responsibility ascribable to a defendant will diminish from murder to manslaughter if the defendant proves he committed the homicide during a sudden quarrel.[273] To mitigate murder to manslaughter, he must prove he acted in the heat of passion caused by an adequate provocation.[274] At common law, mutual combat, assault, and adultery constituted legally adequate provocation.[275] As society came to view understandable human frailties more broadly, these categories were expanded.[276]

---

271. *See* State v. Van Dyke, 825 A.2d 1163, 1170–72 (N.J. Super. Ct. App. Div. 2003) (explaining that, although certain physical attributes such as age, physical strength, or health could be relevant to the reasonable-person standard, the appropriate standard is "based on a societal norm rather than the exceptional or substandard attributes of an individual"). Thus, the defendant's conduct "is measured against the standard . . . for the behavior of the entire community. A defendant's effort to avoid [attribution] of criminal liability should be measured by the same objective societal norm." *Id.*

272. MODEL PENAL CODE § 2.02 cmt. 4 at 242 (Official Draft and Revised Commentaries 1985) (noting that, although blindness may be relevant to the reasonable person standard and his "situation," the "heredity, intelligence or temperament of the actor would not be held material in judging negligence, and could not be without depriving the criterion of all its objectivity"); DRESSLER, *supra* note 21, at 132.

273. Donovan & Wildman, *supra* note 242, at 446.

274. *Id.*

275. *Id.*

276. *Id.* at 447.

Historically, a judge determined the adequacy of the provocation as a matter of law.[277] As new theories of provocation introduced murkiness into this consideration, the criminal law relegated to the jury the question of adequacy of provocation.[278] The criminal law imported the reasonable man or "ordinary person"[279] test from the law of negligence as a tool for juries to decide these marginal cases.[280] At its inception, then, the ordinary-person test served as a tool for use by the jury to assess the extent of criminal responsibility ascribable to the criminal defendant based on the circumstances of the crime.[281]

The traditional test for provocation has four elements:

(1) Adequate provocation which would have roused an ordinary person to the heat of passion;
(2) Actual provocation, requiring that the defendant actually have been provoked;
(3) An ordinary person would not have cooled off; and,
(4) The defendant in fact did not cool off.[282]

Although this test appears to invite an individualized determination of whether the defendant experienced actual provocation,[283] it does so in only a limited fashion. The requirement of actual provocation limits the availability of the defense to those who acted as a result of provocation rather than by another motive.[284] Several factors limit the relevance of behavioral genetics evidence to this inquiry. First, the defendant must have been provoked by the victim and not by some other unrelated cause.[285] Second, most jurisdictions generally recognize categories of provocation under which the victim's conduct must have fallen for the defendant to be entitled to claim adequate provocation, such as physical injury or mental assault, mutual combat or quarrel, illegal arrest, or adultery with the defendant's spouse.[286] These categories represent conduct by a victim, not some

---

277. *Id.*

278. State v. Ott, 686 P.2d 1001, 1005 (Or. 1984); Donovan & Wildman, *supra* note 242, at 447.

279. Several commentators, including Joshua Dressler, note the inconsistency of calling the standard a "reasonable person" standard in the context of provocation since the defense deals with unreasonableness. The defense instead recognizes that the ordinary person sometimes acts out of uncontrolled emotion rather than reason. DRESSLER, *supra* note 21, at 530–31.

280. Donovan & Wildman, *supra* note 242, at 447–48.

281. *Id.* at 448.

282. LEE, *supra* note 260, at 25; Donovan & Wildman, *supra* note 242, at 448.

283. FLETCHER, *supra* note 9, at 508.

284. DRESSLER, *supra* note 21, at 533.

285. People v. Strader, 663 N.E.2d 511, 515 (Ill. App. Ct. 1996); State v. Shane, 590 N.E.2d 272, 276 (Ohio 1992).

286. *Strader*, 663 N.E.2d at 516; *Shane*, 590 N.E.2d at 277.

internal mental deficiency of the defendant. Conceivably, a defendant could claim to have misunderstood the situation as a result of a behavioral predisposition, but such a claim raises the final concern. A claim of an abnormal response to an external stimuli, triggered by a defendant's behavioral predisposition, may itself cut against a finding of reasonableness in the determination of adequacy of provocation such that an ordinary person would have reacted as the defendant did. Otherwise put, for a defendant to claim he reacted because of his behavioral predisposition itself sets him at odds with the reasonable-person standard. Thus, under the traditional approach to provocation, the defense operates through consideration of provocation external to the psyche or behavioral propensities of the defendant, rendering his infirmities irrelevant to whether he was actually provoked, and at odds with the reasonableness inquiry that follows.[287]

In an effort to depart from the traditional approach to provocation,[288] the MPC adopted section 210.3(1)(b), which provides that criminal homicide constitutes manslaughter when "committed under the influence of extreme mental or emotional disturbance for which there is reasonable explanation or excuse. The reasonableness of such explanation or excuse shall be determined from the viewpoint of a person in the actor's situation under the circumstances as he believes them to be."[289] The MPC's reformulation has been interpreted by some as introducing the actor's actual state of mind into the previously rigidly applied provocation defense by allowing the trier of fact to evaluate reasonableness from the viewpoint of the actor.[290] Under the reformulation, the defendant first must offer a reasonable explanation for his alleged extreme emotional distress, and, second, must demonstrate the reasonableness of his reaction to it from the viewpoint of an ordinary person in the circumstances of the accused.[291] Regrettably, little guides courts on what factors to consider in assessing the circumstances from the viewpoint of the accused under the MPC approach.[292] Consequently, some courts have allowed defendants to introduce certain psychiatric and mental peculiarities as relevant to the defense, even while recognizing that "not all

---

287. FLETCHER, *supra* note 9, at 508; *see* State v. Bourque, 636 So.2d 254, 268 (La. Ct. App. 1994) ("The measure of adequacy of the provocation to cause a defendant to act in 'sudden heat of passion or heat of blood' is the average or ordinary person, and not the peculiar psychological characteristics of a particular defendant.").

288. *See* State v. Ott, 686 P.2d 1001, 1006–7 (Or. 1984) (detailing how the drafters of the MPC arrived at the revision, in part due to disdain for a particular case outcome).

289. MODEL PENAL CODE § 210.3(1)(b) (Official Draft and Revised Commentaries 1985).

290. *See* State v. Dumlao, 715 P.2d 822, 830 (Haw. Ct. App. 1986) (opining that the Model Penal Code reformulation of the provocation defense newly allows subjective mental abnormalities of the individual to be considered as part of the defense); LEE, *supra* note 260, at 207; *see also* State v. Magner, 732 A.2d 234, 241 (Del. Super. Ct. 1997) (interpreting a similar provision in the Delaware Code to include a subjective inquiry).

291. *Magner*, 732 A.2d at 241.

292. *Id.*

individual peculiarities are relevant."[293] By contrast, other courts recognize that the particular psychological condition of a defendant cannot inform adequacy of provocation, which should be judged by the mental capacities of the ordinary person.[294] To the extent that courts, as a matter of factual relevance, allow the incorporation of certain physical characteristics into the ordinary or reasonable-person standard, they do not deviate from the purpose of the excuse—to allow the diminution of responsibility for ordinary human fallibility.[295] To the extent those courts allow the incorporation of peculiar mental infirmities, they transform the defense of provocation into an individualized determination of the blameworthiness of the defendant, contrary to the limited purpose of excusing generalized human fallibility. By allowing the peculiar mental condition of the defendant to govern a determination of reasonableness, courts pervert the provocation as an excuse and conflate criminal responsibility with culpability and therefore punishment. They put the law on a "dangerously slippery slope" and risk "trivializing the normative anti-killing message of the criminal law."[296] After all, to ask from the unique psychological viewpoint of the defendant whether it seemed reasonable to kill, the answer would obviously be yes. He did, after all, choose to do so.

In short, criminal law can be deceptive. Occasionally, as in the MPC's reformulation of provocation, it speaks of personal guilt and uses subjective-sounding words when, in fact, the drafters of the MPC intended for the reasonableness prong of the excuse to continue to operate objectively.[297] Although some interpret the MPC's approach to allow a defendant to introduce his or her subjective, individualized infirmities, the provocation defense in fact operates by "rejecting evidence that a given defendant was more fearful than most, more moved to anger than most, more suggestible than most."[298] Courts should therefore interpret the MPC's reformulation as enabling the introduction of materially relevant physical traits in the circumstances, but not the defendant's unique mental infirmities or behavioral predispositions. If narrowly conceived, the reformulation will still enable the provocation defense to partially excuse human fallibility without collapsing the concept of criminal responsibility.

---

293. *Id.* at 243.

294. People v. Ali, No. A096034, 2004 Cal. App. Unpub. LEXIS 1001, at *16 (Cal. Ct. App. Jan. 30, 2004); State v. Bourque, 636 So.2d 254, 268 (La. Ct. App. 1994).

295. *See* MODEL PENAL CODE § 2.02 cmt. 4 at 242 (Official Draft and Revised Commentaries 1985) (explaining that physical characteristics may inform the reasonable person but that "heredity, intelligence or temperament of the actor would not be held material in judging negligence, and could not be without depriving the criterion of all its objectivity"); DRESSLER, *supra* note 21, at 532 ("The heat-of-passion defense recognizes the ordinary human frailty of loss of self-control in provocative circumstances.").

296. DRESSLER, *supra* note 21, at 532.

297. GOLDSTEIN, *supra* note 259, at 18.

298. *Id.*

D. The Battered Woman Syndrome: A Matter of Fact

Self-defense offers an easier challenge to the subjective-versus-objective reasonable-person debate than does provocation. A nonaggressor may use force upon another if "he reasonably believes that such force is necessary to protect himself from imminent use of unlawful force by the other person."[299] Like provocation, to succeed on a claim of self-defense, the defendant must prove he acted in accordance with an honest belief in the need to defend himself and that he had a reasonable ground for so doing.[300] Self-defense functions as a justification that negates the wrongfulness of the defendant's conduct; all 50 states allow it as a justification for homicide.[301] It focuses on the self-defensive act rather than on the actor,[302] through an external assessment of the reasonableness of the act in light of the circumstances. Consequently, a defendant will evade criminal responsibility only if "a reasonable person in defendant's circumstances would have perceived self-defense as necessary."[303] To assess reasonableness, the jury may consider all relevant circumstances in which the actor found himself.[304] Put simply, the justification of self-defense deems protecting oneself from an aggressor socially acceptable or tolerable.[305]

Under the theory of self-defense, defendants have introduced evidence of Battered Woman Syndrome (BWS) to bolster claims of self-defense and to assist the trier of fact in deciding the "reasonableness . . . of defendant's belief that killing was necessary."[306] BWS arises primarily in one of two contexts: (1) the battered woman killed her partner during an altercation, or (2) the battered woman killed her partner while he was sleeping or after a significant cooling-off period since the last violent attack.[307] Cases in the first category do not generally challenge the reasonable-person standard because they more closely fit the classic case of self-defense. In the latter category, defendants have sought to use BWS evidence both to demonstrate that the defendant acted in the honest belief of the need to self-defend and also to support the determination that the self-defense was reasonable under the circumstances.[308] The use of BWS in this second

---

299. DRESSLER, *supra* note 21, at 221.

300. *Id.* at 222. If the defendant acted sincerely but unreasonably, he would still be held criminally responsible for his act. A few states, however, would allow the partial excuse of imperfect self-defense, which mitigates the murder charge to manslaughter. People v. Humphrey, 921 P.2d 1, 6 (Cal. 1996); People v. Jaspar, 119 Cal. Rptr. 2d 470, 475 (Cal. Ct. App. 2002); DRESSLER, *supra* note 21, at 222–23.

301. Heller, *supra* note 174, at 11.

302. *Id.*

303. *Id.* at 3.

304. *Jaspar*, 119 Cal. Rptr. 2d at 476.

305. Heller, *supra* note 174, at 15.

306. *Jaspar*, 119 Cal. Rptr. 2d at 476.

307. DRESSLER, *supra* note 21, at 240.

308. *Id.* at 242.

category of cases has led some to argue that the reasonable-person standard has become more individualized, thereby paving the way toward introducing other mental infirmities, such as certain behavioral predispositions, into the calculation of reasonableness. This argument is flawed, however, because it assumes that the trier of fact compares the battered woman to a *lower* standard of conduct than the reasonable person and uses the past history of violence to justify killing the batterer. BWS does not serve this purpose in this (or any other) category of self-defense cases. In fact, the word *syndrome* seems only to confuse matters, given that BWS operates more like an evidentiary rule rather than a diminished-capacity offense. Indeed, the defendant does not argue that she acted out of rage from her repeated abuse, or in an altered and subjectively weaker state of mind than the reasonable person. Instead, she introduces the history of prior abuse and the special knowledge available to a battered woman (such as the credibility of the abuser's threat) to endow the reasonable person with additional "expertise,"[309] much like a specialist physician is held to a specialized standard of conduct in negligence cases in tort law.[310]

The history of prior abuse, for example, helps inform the jury's determination of whether the defendant honestly and reasonably believed she needed to defend herself *at the time* that she killed her partner.[311] For example, if the defendant endured a physical confrontation with her abuser that evening, when he told her he would kill her the next morning, and the history of her abuse proved his threat was credible and flight was futile, these circumstances would assist a trier of fact in deciding whether the defendant reasonably believed her batterer

---

309. *See, e.g.,* John Yoo, *Using Force,* 71 U. Chi. L. Rev. 729, 753 (2004) (noting the battered woman's defense need not be about whether the reasonable person standard is subjective or objective, but about redefining the imminence of the threat in self-defense). Thus understood, the battered woman's defense allows the use of past conduct for predicting the likelihood of future harm.

310. *E.g.,* Heinrich *ex rel.* Heinrich v. Sweet, 308 F.3d 48, 63 (1st Cir. 2002) (explaining the proper standard of care for evaluating medical negligence by a specialist physician is the skill and care required of those in the profession practicing that specialty); Deasy v. United States, 99 F.3d 354, 358–359 (10th Cir. 1996) (comparing psychiatrist failure to provide medical treatment for plaintiff's edema against the standard of care for psychiatrists); Myles v. Laffitte, No. 91-1821, 1993 U.S. App. LEXIS 3274, at *7–*8 (4th Cir. Feb. 16, 1993) (noting specialists are held to a higher standard of care than general practitioners and are measured against the relevant specialist's skill and care required); Pierce v. Hobart Corp., 939 F.2d 1305, 1309–10 (5th Cir. 1991) (noting the state act defined standard of care for specialists to be determined by those within the involved medical specialty); Lanier v. Sallas, 777 F.2d 321, 323 (5th Cir. 1985) (noting the Texas statute holds a specialist physician to the standard of care of a similar specialist under similar circumstances); McPhee v. Reichel, 461 F.2d 947, 950 (3d Cir. 1972) (jury instruction that ophthalmologist would be held to standard of care of a general practitioner was error; specialist owes higher standard of care).

311. Dressler, *supra* note 21, at 242.

presented an imminent threat to her when she killed him during his sleep.[312] In effect, because "the right of self-defense arises only when the necessity begins, and equally ends with the necessity,"[313] BWS evidence goes to reasonableness of the belief about the imminence of the aggressor's threat of bodily harm[314] rather than serving as a justification for an unreasonable belief in the threat.

A comparison with provocation provides another useful insight into BWS and genetic and neurological evidence. The battered woman, like the provoked defendant, must demonstrate that she reacted in response to the victim to prove that she acted under the honest belief that she needed to self-defend rather than in response to an internal weakness or abnormality. Moreover, like provocation, self-defense enables the defendant to introduce only certain categories of information in support of her defense, such as the history of prior abuse and her prior unsuccessful attempts to flee. Finally, if behavioral genetics and neuroscience evidence could be introduced with respect to her actual belief in the need to self-defend, the stronger the evidence that she reacted because of a predisposition to rage, aggression, or violence, the less likely it is that her conduct will be perceived as reasonable under the separate consideration of the reasonableness of her conduct.

Respecting the determination of reasonableness, experts testify about the special knowledge the battered woman develops from the threats of her specific batterer, which the average member of society would lack. In particular, "[a]s violence increases over time, and threats gain credibility, a battered person might become sensitized and thus able to reasonably discern when danger is real and when it is not."[315] Expert testimony then "enable[s] the jury to find that the battered [woman] . . . is particularly able to predict accurately the likely extent of violence in any attack on her."[316] In *People v. Humphrey*,[317] the court framed the defense in that manner, explaining that BWS evidence does not alter the objective nature of the reasonable-person standard in self-defense, but operates as a rule of evidence, allowing the jury to consider facts and circumstances known to the defendant about the particular batterer.[318] The jury then is able to evaluate whether a reasonable person, aware of the facts of circumstances known by the defendant—the specialized knowledge about the batterer and his pattern of abuse—would have believed she faced imminent danger and acted in self-defense.[319]

---

312. Yoo, *supra* note 300, at 753 (explaining that the battered woman's defense may redefine the concept of imminence in self-defense cases).

313. United States v. Peterson, 483 F.2d 1222, 1229 (D.C. Cir. 1973).

314. State v. Richardson, 525 N.W.2d 378, 381 (Wis. Ct. App. 1994).

315. People v. Jaspar, 119 Cal. Rptr. 2d 470, 476 (Cal. Ct. App. 2002).

316. *Id.*

317. 921 P.2d 1 (Cal. 1996).

318. *Id.* at 9.

319. *Id.*

The narrow relevance of BWS evidence to the inquiry must be emphasized—it informs only the homicide of the woman's batterer, but not that of some other seemingly threatening person. The battered woman defendant could not, for example, use BWS evidence to justify killing a person other than her batterer because, as a result of her abuse, she may now suffer greater fear than most or may react more forcefully than most at the first sign of physical aggression. Likewise, she could not use it to claim the abuse resulted in her psychological impairment such that she reasonably (or rather understandably) acted unreasonably.[320] Thus, although BWS may provide the battered woman with greater knowledge about her batterer, it does not generally enable her to introduce evidence regarding any mental infirmities she may suffer as a general defense to her conduct. Battered woman's syndrome evidence therefore simply endows the reasonable person, otherwise physically or mentally unaltered, with additional factual information about the batterer that is part of the circumstances contributing to the defendant's conduct. It does not transform the objective analysis of the justification of self-defense into a subjective one.

E. The Reasonable Person: Objective by Necessity

Proponents of the present reasonableness standard believe its success depends upon the exclusion of the unique mental infirmities of the defendant. They argue that should the reasonable-person standard adopt the fallibilities of each criminal defendant, rather than embody expected societal norms of conduct, the reasonable person would not create a standard of conduct at all. After all, the defendant would find his own conduct reasonable under the circumstances. With respect to administrative ease, they explain that an individualized reasonableness standard would require the jury to make conclusions about the peculiarities governing the defendant's state of mind—a task criminal law has almost always eschewed because of the unreliability and infeasibility of such determinations.[321] That some jurors may do so on an ad hoc basis would not justify institutionalizing this practice. Which standard would afford the greatest equality in practice presents the more challenging question. Although this brief review of the issue cannot fully resolve that question, it seems intuitive that a system that encourages a comparison between the defendant's conduct and a common standard of conduct would offer the most egalitarian outcomes in the assessment of criminal responsibility. The resolution of this issue, however, is a philosophical

---

320. It is possible, however, that such a claim could have relevance to the partial excuse of diminished capacity, recognized in a few jurisdictions in the United States. Farahany's dissertation explores this possibility in further detail. Farahany, *supra* note 44.

321. *See* HART, *supra* note 179, at 261–62 (noting the impossibility of making judgments about how a person with the defendant's mental abnormalities would have behaved under the circumstances, particularly given the limitations of medical science on the subject).

concern beyond the scope of this chapter. Moreover, a theoretically consistent system of criminal responsibility that focuses on the circumstances of the crime to determine responsibility, rather than individual blameworthiness, would reserve the inquiry of the personal circumstances of the defendant to the adjudication of punishment. Finally, an objective assessment of reasonableness seemingly poses the lowest risk of collapsing the societal checks on liability—justifications and excuses. By preserving the objectivity of these tests, society avoids the path of questioning the relevance of each individual infirmity that arises over time, and instead relies on norms of conduct, which may evolve over time, but are norms nonetheless.

In short, justifications and excuses, which serve as societal checks on the assignment of liability, operate objectively both in fact and in furtherance of preserving the reasonable-person standard within the constraints of the present system. Except in the limited circumstances discussed above, a defendant's behavioral predispositions should not inform these external checks on liability. And because behavioral genetics has limited utility in informing the determination of criminal liability,[322] behavioral genetics and neuroscience therefore lack a meaningful role in the assessment of criminal responsibility in the present system.

V. CONCLUSION

Behavioral genetics and neuroscience appear to offer new information about the causes of human behavior, even though scientific hurdles of discovery presently limit their reach. But even if scientists eventually discover the vast array of causal contributions to human behavior, these discoveries should not implicate criminal responsibility as it presently operates in the criminal law.

The criminal law allows ascription of criminal responsibility to an actor upon a finding of liability measured against the external check of justifications and excuses. The concepts underlying liability—legal free will, actus reus, and mens rea—do not invite an inquiry into the defendant's predispositions. Thus, behavioral genetics and neuroscience, which at best informs one aspect of the many influences on behavior, lacks a pivotal role in the assessment of liability. Although a defendant may still partially or entirely evade criminal responsibility by presenting a successful justification or excuse for his conduct, behavioral genetics and neuroscience will be unlikely to take a meaningful role in those determinations. If the defendant's conduct is justified by societal norms of conduct, he will evade all criminal responsibility. If, instead, the defendant's conduct is partially excused, the resulting diminution of criminal responsibility is ascribable to

---

322. *See supra* Part III.

the defendant. In either justification or excuse, the defendant's conduct is compared to societal norms of conduct, embodied by the reasonable-person standard. The defendant's unique infirmities have little role in the construction of the reasonable-person standard and therefore cannot serve to justify or excuse his conduct. Because genetic and neurological predisposition evidence is irrelevant to both liability and the defenses of justifications and excuses, it should have little role in the negation or mitigation of a defendant's criminal liability.

We emphasize that this chapter seeks only to reconcile behavioral genetics and neuroscience evidence with our *present* system of criminal law, by defining the concepts and purposes of the doctrines underlying criminal responsibility. Greater knowledge about human behavior or new mechanisms or purposes of criminal law could potentially inform a more effective or more just reimagined system of criminal justice. But those who advocate a reimagined system should reconcile the purposes and mechanisms of that new system with its present operation. Moreover, the conclusion that behavioral genetics and neuroscience evidence does not inform criminal responsibility may apply equally to other similar kinds of evidence relating to the subjective beliefs and predispositions influencing an actor's conduct. And although new theories regarding the causes of human behavior must be reconciled with the categories of involuntary conduct discussed in Part III.B, the broader conclusion—that the unique influences on an individual's decisions have little impact on the assessment of criminal responsibility—remains the same.

Finally, this chapter leaves open the question of how such evidence may affect criminal punishment. Theoretically, punishment depends upon both the crime and the blameworthiness of the individual defendant. But the current use of predisposition evidence during sentencing has resulted in a mixed bag for the criminal defendant. In some instances a defendant's genetic or neurological predispositions could mitigate his sentence by reducing his perceived moral blameworthiness. This would most likely occur if a criminal defendant could demonstrate that he sought and responded favorably to treatment based on a newfound awareness of his genetic or neurological predispositions and therefore no longer poses a threat to society. In other scenarios, the same evidence might serve—and has served—as aggravating evidence during sentencing by characterizing the defendant as a biologically programmed violent offender, an incorrigible danger to society. As the science develops, yet other possibilities may emerges, such as the possibility to detect, to prevent, or to treat biological predispositions of interest in criminal law. Irrespective of how one reconciles punishment theory with behavioral genetics and neuroscience, for now, the criminal defendant should beware of its double-edged potential.

8. ADDICTION, SCIENCE, AND CRIMINAL RESPONSIBILITY

STEPHEN J. MORSE

It is clear that genes build proteins, but God only knows what happens next. . . . If you want to know how the mind works, you should investigate the mind, not the brain, and still less the genome.[1]

I. INTRODUCTION

An immense proportion of alleged felons are under the influence of mind-altering substances when they are arrested, and many people arrested for drug offenses and other crimes are addicted.[2] Indeed, possession and use of illicit substances, which are necessary criteria of addiction,[3] are crimes in every state

---

1. Jerry Fodor, *Crossed Wires*, TIMES LITERARY SUPPLEMENT, May 16, 2003 at 3.

2. *See* ZHIWEI ZHANG, NATT OPINION RES. CENTER, DRUG AND ALCOHOL USE AND RELATED MATTERS AMONG ARRESTEES tbls. 3, 9 & 10 (2003) (showing that 73.9% of male adult arrestees in 39 cities tested positive for alcohol or at least one of nine controlled substances, that 37% had engaged in the heavy use of controlled substances and 39.1% were at risk for drug dependence, and that 47.9% had engaged in heavy drinking within the past 30 days and 28.6% were at risk for alcohol dependence). I recognize that there is no consensual, scientifically or clinically operationalized definition of "addiction" and that the diagnostic and statistical manual of the American Psychiatric Association uses the terms "Substance Dependence" and "Substance Abuse" to refer to substance-related disorders. AM. PSYCHIATRIC ASS'N, DIAGNOSTIC AND STATISTICAL MANUAL OF MENTAL DISORDERS (4th ed., text rev. 2000). Toward the extremes of drug use behavior, however, addiction could be characterized as Supreme Court Justice Potter Stewart characterized "hard core" pornography: Even if we can't define it, we know it when we see it. *Jacobellis v. Ohio*, 378 U.S. 184, 197 (1964). For ease of exposition, the term addiction will be used throughout the paper. Also for ease of exposition, addictions will be treated as limited to substance-related problems. Many believe that addictions encompass nonsubstance activities, such as gambling, and there is research evidence supporting this position. *See* Jon E. Grant et al., *Multicenter Investigation of the Opioid Antagonist Nalmefene in the Treatment of Pathological Gambling*, 163 AM. J. PSYCHIATRY 303 (2006) (finding that an opioid antagonist successfully reduces the symptoms associated with pathological gambling, suggesting that the disorder is not about gambling but about addiction in general). This position remains controversial, however, and arguing for it is unnecessary for the purposes of the present paper.

3. *See* Eric J. Nestler, *Genes and Addiction*, 26 NAT. GENET. 277, 277 (2000) ("Drug addiction . . . is defined solely in behavioural terms. For example, addiction can be considered . . . compulsive drug-seeking and taking despite horrendous consequences.") This definition is discussed further *infra*.

and under federal law. Assessing the moral and legal responsibility of agents who engage in such behavior is thus of paramount importance in our criminal justice system. But understanding the moral and legal responsibility of people for becoming addicted and for criminal conduct associated with their addictions has unfortunately been hindered by inadequate understanding of how explanatory models of addiction relate to responsibility. Even sophisticated people tend to think that the "man with the golden arm" is somehow an automaton, a puppet pulled by the narcotic strings of a biological disease, and that therefore the addict is not responsible for actions associated with his addiction. Evidence linking a genetic predisposition or neurological abnormality for this condition contributes powerfully, often confusingly, to this type of thinking.[4] Conversely, many people think that addiction is purely a result of moral weakness. The various characterizations of addiction may be striking and contain a grain of truth, and many models have great heuristic power. For the law's purposes, however, the metaphors and models often obscure rather than clarify issues of criminal responsibility and of social policy generally in response to the deviant behavior many addicts exhibit.

This chapter has two simple underlying theses. The first is that it is impossible to understand the relation of any variable to criminal responsibility without having in place an account of criminal responsibility. The second is that discovery of genetic, neuroscientific, or any other physical or psychosocial cause of action raises no new issues concerning responsibility, and discovery of such causes does not per se create an excusing or mitigating condition for criminal conduct or any other type of behavior.

The chapter begins in Part II with a brief description of the phenomenology of addiction, describing generally what is known about the behavioral aspects of addiction in addition to the basic criteria of craving, seeking, and using. Thinking sensibly about the relation of addiction to criminal responsibility is impossible unless it is first understood that this condition is "defined solely in behavioural terms."[5] Part III addresses the contrast between the legal and scientific images of behavior, using the disease concept of addiction, now fueled by discoveries of genetic predisposition and altered neural systems of reward, as prime examples of the contrast.

Part IV offers a general model of criminal responsibility to guide the analysis of responsibility for addiction-related criminal behavior, offering the best positive account of the present system. The model's essential criteria are behavioral, broadly understood to refer to actions and mental states. Part V deals with

---

4. *See generally* Johannes Keller, *In Genes We Trust: The Biological Component of Psychological Essentialism and Its Relationship to Mechanisms of Motivated Social Cognition*, 88 J. PERSONALITY & SOC. PSYCHOL. 686 (2005) (validating a scale to measure the belief in genetic determinism and demonstrating that such a belief affects social cognition).

5. Nestler, *supra* note 3, at 277.

persistent confusions about responsibility. Part VI describes those aspects of addiction, if any, for which persons might be held morally or legally responsible, concluding that only actions related to addiction are appropriate objects for ascribing criminal responsibility. Part VII addresses the causal role genetics and neural systems of reward play in explaining addiction. This discussion is deferred until this point because, as earlier parts explain, no particular causal explanation of any behavior, including a biological explanation, entails necessary legal consequences. In particular, the existence of a genetic or neural explanation for addiction does not demonstrate that addicts are not acting when they seek and use substances or engage in other activities related to their addiction, and a genetic or neuronal explanation produces no necessary legal conclusion concerning responsibility for such addiction-related actions.

Finally, Part VIII considers individual and social responsibility for the addiction-related actions. It begins by discussing whether addicts are responsible for becoming addicted and potentially for the foreseeable further consequences of their addiction.[6] As everyone concedes, becoming addicted virtually always involves intentional action. The addict must have intentionally used the substance, usually for prolonged periods. If the addict is responsible for substance use, then, arguably, he is also responsible for setting in motion those mechanistic, biophysical processes that partially cause addiction and that are activated or potentiated by using substances. The relation of genetic or other biological causation to responsibility for the further consequences of addiction then becomes much less important and interesting.

Part VIII then turns in detail to the meaning of those features of addiction—subjective craving and compulsion—that seem the most likely predicates for excuse or mitigation. It argues that understanding the biological roots of craving does not yet yield valid information concerning the strength of craving and seemingly compulsive behavior. This part next addresses the two leading theoretical and legal candidates for an excusing condition: internal coercion and lack of the capacity for rationality. To raise the issues most starkly and most sympathetically to the view that biological causation may play an excusing role, it is assumed that addicts are not responsible for becoming addicted. This assumption is relaxed when the part discusses whether addicts should be excused because addiction compromises their rational capacities. It concludes that most addicts should be responsible for most criminal behavior motivated by addiction, but that addiction can in some cases affect the agent's ability "to grasp and be guided

---

6. *See, e.g.*, Montana v. Egelhoff, 518 U.S. 37 (1996) (upholding the constitutionality of a state statute excluding evidence of intoxication relevant to whether the defendant in fact had the subjective mens rea required by the definition of the crime). I firmly reject such partial or complete strict liability, but it is a common feature of the criminal law. See Stephen J. Morse, *Fear of Danger, Flight from Culpability*, 4 PSYCHOL. PUB. POL'Y & L. 250, 250,254 (1998).

by reason."[7] The last section of this part considers whether society is responsible for addiction-related actions. It concludes that even if most addicts should be held responsible for addiction-related behavior, sensible social policy can do much to reduce both the prevalence of addiction and concomitant criminal behavior. The final part of the chapter discusses three legal proposals for reducing the costs associated with addictions and for treating addicts fairly.

II. THE PHENOMENOLOGY OF ADDICTION

Here, in commonsense terms, is what we know about the phenomenology of addiction.[8] A later section considers in detail attempts to define more precisely some of the key terms, such as "craving" and "compulsive."

Some people use substances for which they develop an extremely intense, insistent level of subjective desire that is apparently satisfied only temporarily by use. After the addict satisfies the craving by use, the desire to use substances quickly reasserts itself and the agent again desires to use very intensely. Addicts typically engage in repetitive seeking and using behavior, even though the drug-related actions threaten and often cause adverse, frequent, and horrendous social, health, and legal consequences. Addicts have very good long-term reasons not to engage in drug seeking and use, but they tend to be steep time discounters when they evaluate drug seeking and using. For some, use may be rational in the short term. Addicts do not seem to learn from experience, however. Thus, many continue to use and to imperil their lives. Most are ambivalent about their addictions. For some, the craving is so strong that seeking and using the substance becomes a central life activity and even central to the addict's identity. Many, and perhaps most, who quit will relapse, especially if the "drug life" has compromised functional social networks and skills. It is often inferred from the addict's report about his own thoughts and feelings and from the negative consequences of addiction-related actions that the addict is driven by an overwhelming or overpowering desire termed "craving" and that drug seeking and using are "compulsive." On the other hand, there is often reason to doubt the accuracy of

---

7. This felicitous phrase is borrowed from Jay Wallace's superb book on responsibility. R. JAY WALLACE, RESPONSIBILITY AND THE MORAL SENTIMENTS (1994). Wallace treats the phrase as encompassing both rationality and control defects. I prefer to limit it to the former, however, and will suggest that most control defects can be assimilated to rationality defects.

8. What follows in this part is boilerplate among addiction researchers. Support can be found in the many scientific studies of addiction cited in this chapter and in many first-person accounts of addiction. Part VIII.B., *infra*, addresses attempts by scientists to define craving and compulsion more precisely.

an addict's self-report and the life of addiction seems to satisfy some addicts' deepest needs.[9]

The environment and expectations play a weighty role in the addict's experience of craving and use. Addiction is a condition that is eliminated by large numbers of craving sufferers simply by intentionally ceasing to seek and use, and many cease craving after they quit. In many cases, the addict is able to quit because he finally has sufficient reason to do so, and many addicts "age out" of addiction. Even if addiction is properly and most usefully characterized as a disease, at the extreme its necessary behavioral signs are virtually all reward-sensitive or reason-responsive. An addict threatened with instant death for seeking and using will not seek and use unless he already wishes to die at that moment or does not care if he does.[10]

III. IMAGES OF ADDICTION

The concepts of illness and disease have powerful associations in our culture, most of which are inconsistent with the sufferer's responsibility for the features of the illness. People can, of course, be responsible for initially contracting or risking contracting diseases. A person who is overweight, does not exercise, and smokes surely is responsible for risking hypertension; the person who in inappropriate circumstances engages in unprotected sexual activity surely risks contracting sexually transmitted diseases. And a person who suffers from many diseases can ameliorate the consequences by intentionally adhering to a prescribed medical regimen. But hypertension and infections are themselves mechanisms. The sufferer cannot terminate all the signs and symptoms of the disease simply by intentionally choosing to cease being hypertensive or infected.

Despite the potential contribution of human agency to the cause and maintenance of some diseases, no one denies that these are fundamentally diseases.

---

9. First-person accounts of addiction often treat addiction as a psychological and emotional journey in which biological and environmental factors are considered less important than moral and spiritual affliction. Brian Hurwitz, Caroline Tapping & Neil Vickers, *Life Histories and Narratives of Addiction, in* DRUGS AND THE FUTURE: BRAIN SCIENCE, ADDICTION AND SOCIETY 485, 502 (David Nutt et al. eds., 2007). Addicts may be less ambivalent and loathe to report their true feelings because they have internalized the negative social attitudes towards addiction and drug use. See, Julian Savulescu & Bennett Foddy, *A Liberal Account of Addiction* (in press PHILOSOPHY, PSYCHIATRY AND PSYCHOLOGY, 2009).

10. The ability of many addicts to decide to quit and to be responsive to contingencies generally is an inconvenient fact for those who wish to conceptualize addiction as purely a brain disease. People do not stop being diabetics, for example, simply by deciding that their pancreases should produce more natural insulin nor does cancer abate because people have good reason to be free of this terrible disease. *See infra* Parts III & VI.

Moreover, with many and perhaps most diseases, the sufferer is not responsible for contracting the disease, and for many diseases there is little or nothing the sufferer can do to help, other than to seek and cooperate with professional help and to wait for the disease to run its course. Although people sometimes can be complicit in their own diseases, the disease model is so powerful that people who are ill are not in general considered responsible for the signs, symptoms, and consequences. The dominant image of people with diseases is that they are the victims of pathological mechanisms who deserve sympathy and help and do not deserve condemnation.

The brain disease model of addiction borrows heavily from the powerful moral and social associations of the general concepts of illness and disease. It claims that addiction is a chronic and relapsing brain disease.[11] Supported by highly technical anatomical, physiological, and genetic research demonstrating that addictions appear to have a biological basis, the brain disease model inevitably suggests that the addict is sick. The signs and symptoms of the disease—primarily compulsive drug seeking and use—are seemingly the mechanistic consequence of genetically-driven pathological brain anatomy and physiology over which the addict has no control once prolonged use has caused the pathology. The following are recent excellent examples of this mode of thought that appeared in prestigious journals. The first is by an eminent neuroscientist:

> Dramatic advances over the past two decades in both the neurosciences and the behavioral sciences have revolutionized our understanding of drug abuse and addiction. Scientists have identified neural circuits that subsume the actions of every known drug of abuse, and they have specified common pathways that are affected by almost all such drugs. Researchers have also identified and cloned the major receptors for virtually every abusable drug, as well as the natural ligands for most of those receptors. In addition, they have elaborated many of the biochemical cascades within the cell that follow receptor activation by drugs. Research has also begun to reveal major differences between the brains of addicted and nonaddicted individuals and to indicate some common elements of addiction, regardless of the substance.[12]

The second is by an addiction researcher:

> Addiction is a disorder of the brain's reward system. Functional imaging shows the vulnerable circuitry for addiction originating in the paleocortex. Paradoxically, humankind's greatest adaptive advantage, the neocortex, responsible for the phenomenon of consciousness, is at best only minimally protective from addictive disease and may pose a hurdle for recovery. Unlike most

---

11. Alan I. Leshner, *Addiction Is a Brain Disease, and It Matters*, 1 Focus 190 (2003).

12. Alan I. Leshner, *Addiction Is a Brain Disease, and It Matters*, 278 SCIENCE 45, 45 (1997).

medical disorders, in addiction a net effect of supraphysiologic reward, impaired inhibition, or both paradoxically leads the limbic drive system to reinforce exposure to the disease vector. This is in direct violation of the principle of survival of the species. In individuals with underlying vulnerabilities, limbic drive progressively recruits neocortical function to protect continued access to abused substances, the polar opposite of self-preservation.[13]

The first example, despite the concession to the behavioral sciences in its first sentence, describes solely biological advances, and the remainder of the article fails to note one "dramatic advance" in the behavioral understanding of addiction.[14] The second example treats the intentional conduct of the addict solely as the product of brain mechanisms. There is no person present, no agent acting when the "organism" seeks and uses.

For those whose thinking is driven by the brain disease model, this image is applauded and promoted. For example, an editorial in the *American Journal of Psychiatry* opens as follows:

American psychiatry has made remarkable progress in recategorizing the addictive disorders from moral failures to brain diseases, but the need for community education continues. The concept of moral failure is by no means gone from the discussion of addictive disorders, as evidenced by our country's investment in criminal justice rather than treatment.[15]

Such thinking can reflect in part battles over turf, funding, and the like, but it is doubtlessly sincerely motivated.

Virtually all mechanistic models of problems that bedevil society, including the medical model, are alluring because they imply that there are technical, "clean" solutions. Fix the "pathological mechanism," fix the social problem it produces; do not worry about refractory human behavior and messy moral accountability. The medical model is used here for rhetorical purposes because it is much in the news, and because there is heartening progress in the biological understanding of addiction. But any black-box mechanical model of the phenomenon of addiction would have done as well.

Criminal law's concept of the person, including the addict, is the antithesis of the medical model's mechanistic concept. Although all honest people will admit that biological and environmental variables beyond the person's rational control can cause an agent to be the type of person who is predisposed to commit crimes or can put the agent in the kind of environment that predisposes people to

---

13. David R. Gastfriend, *Physician Substance Abuse and Recovery: What Does It Mean for Physicians—and Everyone Else*, 293 JAMA 1513,1514 (2005).

14. Leshner, *supra* note 12.

15. Thomas R. Kosten, *Addiction as a Brain Disease*, 155 AM. J. PSYCHIATRY 711, 711 (1998); accord Alan I. Leshner, *Science Is Revolutionizing Our View of Addiction and What to Do About It*, 156 AM. J. PSYCHIATRY 1 (1999).

criminal activity, the law ultimately views the criminal wrongdoer as an agent and not simply as a passive victim who manifests pathological mechanisms.[16] Unless either the person does not act or an excusing condition is present, agency entails moral and legal responsibility that warrants blame and punishment. Suffering from a disease simpliciter, such as schizophrenia, does not itself mean that the defendant did not act or that an excusing condition obtained, although diseases and other causes may negate action or produce an excusing condition, such as gross irrationality. Action can always be evaluated morally, even if it is symptomatic of a disease state.[17] Most mental and physical diseases—even severe disorders—suffered by people who violate the criminal law do not have these exculpating effects because they do not sufficiently affect rational agency.[18] Even if addiction is properly characterized as an illness, most addicts are nonetheless capable of being guided by good reasons, including the incentives law can provide.[19] Sick people who behave immorally or who violate the criminal law are almost always responsible agents.

Why does it matter if we conceptualize drug-related problems medically as a brain disease, as the product of genetic predisposition and usurped or "hijacked" neural mechanisms of reward? After all, drugs undoubtedly cause vast and often catastrophic personal and social misery, and perhaps the program of research and intervention the biological disease model implies can ameliorate the misery. Why should internecine disputes among philosophers of biology and medicine about the boundaries of the disease concept, or the law's model of the person, or the pure moralizing of many stand in the way? They should not, of course; nothing should stand in the way of useful research and interventions. Unfortunately, however, otherwise useful images or models can have negative consequences if

---

16. In Powell v. Texas, 392 U.S. 514 (1968), a case involving a chronic alcoholic convicted of being drunk in public, the Supreme Court held that a defense of "compulsion symptomatic of a disease" was not constitutionally required. The Court wrote that public drunkenness was behavior, and thus unlike the simple status of being addicted, and it refused to hold that criminal blame and punishment were constitutionally impermissible under the circumstances. Indeed, Justice Marshall's plurality opinion observed that it was not irrational to respond to public drunkenness with the criminal sanction. Id. at 527–31. The plurality also pointed out that Powell's own cross-examination at trial suggested that he was not powerless to stop drinking after he had taken his first drink. Id. at 519–21.

17. Stephen J. Morse, Voluntary Control of Behavior and Responsibility, 7 AM. J. BIOETHICS 12 (2007).

18. Mental disorders, even severe mental disorders, seldom negate the act requirement for criminal culpability and equally rarely negate either the mens rea required by the definition of crimes or the intentionality of unlawful conduct. See Stephen J. Morse, Crazy Reasons, 10 J. CONTEMP. LEGAL ISSUES 189, 210 (1999) (considering the act requirement); Stephen J. Morse, Craziness and Criminal Responsibility, 17 BEHAV. SCI. & L., 147, 161–64 (1999) (concerning mens rea).

19. See SALLY L. SATEL & FREDERICK K. GOODWIN, ETHICS & PUB. POLICY CTR., IS DRUG ADDICTION A BRAIN DISEASE? 20–21 (1998).

they exceed their rightful boundaries. Wrong or misleading images in an inapt domain can produce misguided policies.

Whether the law should treat addiction as a disease and what that would mean are open conceptual and practical questions. Let us begin by examining the law's model of responsibility ascription.

IV. THE MODEL OF CRIMINAL RESPONSIBILITY

The criteria for criminal responsibility, like the criteria for addiction, are entirely behavioral. An agent is criminally responsible if his intentional action, accompanied by an appropriate mental state, satisfies the definition of a criminal offense. If the agent does not act at all because his bodily movement is not intentional— for example, a reflex or spasmodic movement—then there is no violation of the prohibition. There is also no violation in cases in which the agent's intentional action satisfies the offense's act definition, but the mental state required by the definition is lacking. In Anglo-American criminal law, an agent unjustifiably violating a criminal prohibition will be held not responsible and legally excused if he was incapable of rationality or was metaphorically compelled to act by being placed in a "do-it-or-else," hard-choice situation.[20] Note that in cases of metaphorical compulsion, unlike cases of no action, the agent does act intentionally. Infancy and legal insanity are doctrinal examples of rationality excuses; duress is an example of a hard-choice excuse. The criteria for the excusing conditions— lack of rational capacity and sufficiently hard choice (compulsion)—are normative. The degree of rational capacity required for responsibility and how hard choices must be to excuse can differ in response to changing moral conceptions and material circumstances.

This account of criminal responsibility is most tightly linked to retributive justifications of punishment, which hold that punishment is not justified unless the offender morally deserves punishment because the offender was at fault and responsible, and that the offender never should be punished more than he deserves. It is generally conceded that desert is at least a necessary precondition for punishment in Anglo-American law.[21] The account is also consistent with consequential justifications for punishment, such as general deterrence. No offender, however,

---

20. A justification exists if action that would otherwise be criminal is right or permissible under the circumstances. Self-defense is an example. An excuse exists if the agent acts wrongfully, but the agent is not responsible for his conduct. Legal insanity is an example. *See* Kent Greenawalt, *The Perplexing Borders of Justification and Excuse*, 84 COLUM. L. REV. 1897 (1984) (distinguishing justification and excuse and examining the often hazy boundaries between them).

21. Exceptions, such as strict liability, are few and highly controversial precisely because they permit punishment in the absence of fault.

including an addict, should be punished unless he at least deserves such punishment. Even if good consequences might be achieved by punishing nonresponsible addicts or by punishing responsible addicts more than they deserve, such punishment would require very weighty justification in a system that takes desert seriously.

This brief description is arguably the most accurate positive account of the current, dominant Anglo-American conception of responsibility. One might quibble about details,[22] but the basic thesis that responsibility is based on ordinary, commonsense behavioral criteria such as action, mental states, and rationality, and that responsibility is tied to desert is accurate. In short, responsibility depends on the folk psychological model of mind and action. Now, many people become confused about these criteria when they consider newly discovered scientific evidence concerning the causation of behavior or if they have more fundamental metaphysical doubts about the legitimacy of criminal responsibility and consequent deserved punishment. As the next part argues, such concerns are dangerous distractions that either confuse analysis or prove too much by threatening all conceptions of responsibility.

V. DANGEROUS DISTRACTIONS CONCERNING RESPONSIBILITY

A persistent but confused (and confusing) thought is that discovery of genetic, neural, or other biological causes implicates the free will versus determinism debate, and, relatedly, that causation is per se an excusing condition.[23] That determinism threatens responsibility is a truism. Although no one can know if determinism or something close to it is true, let us assume that it is. After all, the universe is massively regular above the subatomic level, and it would be strange indeed if the phenomena of the universe were mostly or entirely random or indeterministic.[24]

---

22. For example, there is a debate about whether justified conduct violates a moral or criminal prohibition. Some argue that justifiable conduct violates no prima facie obligation. See MICHAEL MOORE, PLACING BLAME: A GENERAL THEORY OF THE CRIMINAL LAW 31–33, 64–67 (1997) (arguing that justification should be treated as part of the "special part" of the criminal law). A more formalistic criminal law analysis holds that justified conduct does violate a prima facie criminal prohibition, but ultimately the conduct is judged right or at least permissible. In either case, illicit drug activity is almost never justified under current legal doctrine.

23. See, e.g., Common Addictions of the Group for the Advancement of Psychiatry, Responsibility and Choice in Addiction, 53 PSYCH. SERV. 707, 708 (2002) (pointing to genetic and biological factors responsible for addiction and suggesting that partial determinism or causation provides a partial excuse).

24. Galen Strawson calls this assumption the "realism constraint." Galen Strawson, Consciousness, Free Will and the Unimportance of Determinism, 32 INQUIRY 3, 12 (1989).

The alleged incompatibility of determinism and responsibility is founda-tional. Determinism is not a continuum concept that applies to various individu-als in various degrees. There is no partial or selective determinism. Responsibility is possible or it is not, *tout court*, if the universe is deterministic. If human beings are fully subject to the causal laws of the universe, as a thoroughly physicalist, naturalist worldview holds, then many philosophers claim that "ultimate" responsibility is impossible from the start.[25] On the other hand, plausible "com-patibilist" theories suggest that responsibility is possible in a deterministic uni-verse.[26] There seems no resolution to this debate in sight, but our moral and legal practices do not treat everyone or no one as responsible. Determinism cannot be guiding our practices. If one wants to excuse addicts because they are genetically and neurally determined or determined for any other reason to be addicts, one is committed to negating the possibility of responsibility for anything.

Our criminal responsibility criteria and practices have nothing to do with determinism or with the necessity of having so-called "free will."[27] Criminal responsibility involves evaluation of intentional, conscious, and potentially ratio-nal human action. And almost no one in the debate about determinism and free will or responsibility argues that we are not conscious, intentional, potentially rational creatures when we act.[28] We may be deterministically caused to be the type of creature that acts intentionally, but determinism is not inconsistent con-ceptually or logically with the possibility of mind-brain causation of behavior. The truth of determinism does not entail that actions and nonactions are indis-tinguishable and that there is no distinction between rational and nonrational actions or compelled and uncompelled actions. Children are less rational than adults; most people most of the time do not act under severe threats. Our current responsibility concepts and practices use criteria consistent with and indepen-dent of the truth of determinism.

A related confusion is that once a nonintentional causal explanation has been identified for action, the person must be excused. In other words, the claim is that causation and responsibility are inconsistent and that causation per se is an excusing condition. This is sometimes called the "causal theory of excuse."

If the universe were indeterministic or random, it would hardly provide a secure founda-tion for responsibility.

25. *See, e.g.*, DERK PEREBOOM, LIVING WITHOUT FREE WILL (2001).

26. *See* Wallace, *supra* note 7; Stephen J. Morse, *Reason, Results, and Criminal Responsibility*, 2004 U. ILL. L. REV. 363, 437–44 (2004).

27. Stephen J. Morse, *The Non-Problem of Free Will in Forensic Psychiatry and Psychology*, 25 BEHAV. SCI. & L. 303 (2007).

28. Some neuroscientists and other scientists claim that "conscious will" is an illusion, but these arguments are at present conceptually and empirically unpersuasive and they certainly have gained no acceptance in the law. *See* Stephen J. Morse, *Criminal Responsibility and the Disappearing Person*, 28 CARDOZO L. REV. 2545, 2566–74 (2007).

Thus, if one identifies genetic, neurophysiological, or other causes for behavior, then allegedly the person is not responsible. In a thoroughly physical world, however, this claim is either identical to the incompatibilist critique of responsibility and furnishes a foundational critique of all responsibility, or it is simply an error. I term this the "fundamental psycholegal error" because it is erroneous and, indeed, incoherent as a description of our practices.[29] Noncausation of behavior is not and could not be a criterion for responsibility because all behaviors, like all other phenomena, are caused. Causation, even by abnormal physical variables, is not per se an excusing condition. Abnormal physical variables, such as neurotransmitter deficiencies, may cause a genuine excusing condition, such as the lack of rational capacity, but then the lack of rational capacity, not causation, is doing the excusing work. If causation were an excuse, no one would be responsible for any action. Unless proponents of the causal theory of excuse can furnish a convincing reason why causation per se excuses, we have no reason to jettison responsibility practices that use other criteria for responsibility and excuse.

In short, the burden of persuasion is on critics of the positive account of responsibility that has been offered to guide our thinking about responsibility and addiction. They must show either that it is an inaccurate account or that our entire system of blame and punishment is normatively indefensible. Until they accomplish this, they must work within the model. There can be disagreement about how much lack of rational capacity excuses or how hard choices must be to excuse, but determinism and causation are simply dangerous distractions. Until the law is persuaded to abandon the folk psychological model of the person, all responsibility analysis must employ some version of that model.

VI. ASPECTS OF ADDICTION; OBJECTS OF RESPONSIBILITY

Roughly speaking, addiction has four associated aspects or phenomena that might be objects of responsibility ascription: anatomical states, physiological states, psychological states, and actions.[30] Among these, only action is a potentially appropriate object of moral and legal responsibility ascription and a

---

29. Stephen J. Morse, *Culpability and Control*, 142 U. Pa. L. Rev. 1587 (1994). Critics complain that this argument is repeated in many of my writings. I plead guilty to the charge and will continue to recidivate as long as people continue to manifest the confusion, as they routinely do. See Comm. on Addictions, *supra* note 23, Anders Kaye, *Resurrecting the Causal Theory of the Excuses*, 83 Neb. L. Rev. 1116 (2005), and John Seabrook, *Suffering Souls: the search for the roots of psychopathy*, The New Yorker, November 10, 2008, 64, 73 (quoting Jean Decety of the University of Chicago), for recent examples.

30. *See* Herbert Fingarette & Ann Fingarette Hasse, Mental Disabilities and Criminal Responsibility 148 (1979).

justification for criminal punishment; status is neither an object of ascription nor a justification for blame and punishment.[31] For the most part, people are held morally and legally responsible only for actions that are capable of being guided by reason. Although anatomical and physiological states, including one's genetic makeup, may be evaluated as desirable or undesirable, they are entirely or largely the product of mechanistic processes that are not under the agent's rational control. Those anatomical and physiological states that are signs of addiction are simply statuses of the agent's physical body, whether or not they are directly controllable through the person's rational agency. Similarly, a psychological state that is symptomatic of addiction, such as craving (or, according to many, ambivalence), is likewise just a status that is mechanistically produced by the underlying anatomical or physiological states associated with addiction and, in many cases, by environmental cues. Anatomical, physiological, and psychological states are not intentional human actions.[32] People may be responsible for the anatomical, physiological, and psychological states associated with addiction if they are responsible for becoming addicted, but the criminal law still would not punish those states because they are solely statuses.

The primary behavioral signs of addiction—seeking and using substances[33]—are intentional human actions, even if they are also signs of a disease that has genetic, anatomical, and physiological causes. Indeed, all intentional action has genetic, anatomical, and physiological causes, whether or not the action is the sign of a disease.[34] The addict has an exceptionally powerful desire—a craving to consume the addictive substance—believes that consuming it will satisfy that craving by avoiding pain, causing pleasure, or some combination of the two, and therefore forms and acts on the intention to seek and to use the substance. Such explanatory practical syllogisms are the mark of all intentional actions.

Intentional action is the primary object of responsibility ascriptions. Seeking and using and other associated actions may therefore be morally and legally assessed. To assume that the addict is not responsible for addiction-related behavior just because it has biological causes or because the action is the sign of a disease generally commits the fundamental psycholegal error and therefore

---

31. *E.g.*, Robinson v. California, 370 U.S. 660 (1962) (holding that criminal punishment solely for the status of being addicted is cruel and unusual and thus constitutionally impermissible under the Eighth and Fourteenth Amendments).

32. Intentional mental acts do exist, of course. For example, intentionally adding two and two to find the sum is an intentional act. But a subjective feeling of craving or compulsion is not per se a mental act.

33. Jordi Cami & Magi Farré, *Mechanisms of Disease: Drug Addiction*, 349 NEW ENG. J. MED. 975 (2003); Leshner, *supra* note 12, at 46 (defining the "essence" of addiction as, "compulsive drug seeking and use, even in the face of negative health and social consequences"); Nestler, *supra* note 3.

34. To claim otherwise is to deny the fundamental insight of biological physical naturalism that Darwin so profoundly explained.

begs the question of responsibility. It is natural to think people are not responsible for signs and symptoms because mostly they are statuses mechanistically
caused. But human action is distinguishable. It is not simply a status.

Before finally turning to the question of the responsibility of addicts, the role
that genetics and neural states play in causing the actions associated with addiction and how that role relates to responsibility first must be understood. The next
part undertakes that task.

VII. THE MECHANISTIC CAUSES OF ADDICTION—RELATED ACTIONS

Although environmental variables play an undeniably important role and sometimes explain a majority of the variance in the addict's behavior, the variance in
agents' initial responses to a substance, the development of craving, and the
apparently compulsive aspect of addictive behavior appear to have a genetic and
neural biological substrate. The scientific explanation of behavior is covered in
other chapters in great detail, so I shall be brief and conclusory.

Virtually all addiction experts agree that addiction is a complex, heterogeneous phenotype, that many genes contribute only small effects, that the expression of those genes may be strongly influenced by the environment, that the
heritability of most addictions probably does not exceed 50 percent, and that the
causal mechanisms are not yet well understood.[35] Indeed, it is difficult to disentangle preexisting neural vulnerabilities from the effects of chronic use.[36] Despite
the limitations in our present understanding, experts believe that there is no

---

35. *E.g.*, ROBERT PLOMIN, JOHN C. DEFRIES, GERALD E. MCCLEARN, & PETER MCGUFFIN, BEHAV.
GENETICS 265–72 (4th ed. 2001); John C. Crabbe, *Genetic Contributions to Addiction*, 53
ANN. REV. PSYCHOL. 435, 437, 451–52 (2002); Mary Jeanne Kreek, David A. Nielson &
K. Steven LaForge, *Genes Associated with Addiction Alcohol Opiate, and Cocaine Addiction*,
5 NEUROMOLECULAR MED. 85, 86 (2004); Nestler, *supra* note 3. Alcoholism is the most
intensely studied addiction. Future research will surely confirm a genetic contribution to
addiction and provide increased understanding of the causal mechanisms. *See generally*
Anne M. Glazier, Joseph H. Nadeau & Timothy J. Altman, *Finding Genes that Underlie
Complex Traits*, 298 SCIENCE 2345, 2345–46 (2002) (proposing standards for proof of discovery of genes for complex traits); Kenneth S. Kendler, *Psychiatric Genetics: A
Methodological Critique*, 162 AM. J. PSYCHIATRY 3 (2005) (reviewing the four major research
paradigms and proposing that they be better integrated with recognition of the strengths
and weaknesses of each).

36. Monique Ernst, Alane S. Kimes, & Sandra Jazbec, *Neuroimaging and Mechanisms
of Drug Abuse: Interface of Molecular Imaging and Molecular Genetics*, 13 NEUROIMAGING
CLINICS N. AM. 833, 839 (2003); *see also* Véronique Deroche-Gamonet, David Belin & Pier
Vicenzo Piazza, *Evidence for Addiction-like Behavior in the Rat*, 305 SCIENCE 1014, 1016–17
(2004) (stating the interaction of phenotypical vulnerability and length of exposure
explains the onset of addiction).

single gene or interacting set of genes that inevitably or even directly produce intentional seeking and using of drugs.[37]

Addiction may be a disease with a genetic basis, but it is not like Huntington's disease or other single-gene diseases that involve the inevitable and purely mechanistic expression of that gene. The genetic contributions to addiction instead affect "intervening" variables that can predispose the person to become addicted. For example, genetic factors may influence the following: the agent's initial response to the substance; brain adaptations, including reward circuitry and the degree to which the substance is rewarding; disinhibitory mechanisms; physical dependence; and other variables that affect whether an agent who uses substances, especially for a prolonged period, compulsively seeks and uses because he is motivated by intense craving.[38] None of these explanatory variables denies or is inconsistent, however, with the truth that seeking and using drugs and other drug-related behaviors are intentional actions. A genetic cause is just a cause. It will have no responsibility-affecting effect unless it in part produces a genuine excusing or mitigating condition. It is precisely for this reason that the neuroscience of addiction may be of importance.

The most plausible, current neural explanatory mechanism for addiction involves abnormal usurpation by drugs, especially after prolonged use in vulnerable people, of the potent dopamine system that regulates reward.[39] Such mechanisms are usually used in the service of adaptive behavior, but drug usurpation makes drugs highly salient to the addict at the expense of other, more adaptive goals, creates craving if use is delayed, and thus undermines the addict's ability to avoid seeking and using. This combination of effects explains the compulsive aspect of the addict's behavior. In short, and colloquially, the typically shorter-term "go" mechanisms of the brain are strengthened and the typically

---

37. William M. Compton, Yonette F. Thomas, Kevin P. Conway, & James D. Colliver, *Developments in the Epidemiology of Drug Use and Drug Use Disorders*, 162 AM. J. PSYCHIATRY 1494, 1498 (2005) (stating drug use disorders are "genetically and phenotypically complex" and arise from "multiple genes exerting small effects," and inter alia, "gene-by-environment" interactions).

38. *E.g.*, Nestler, *supra* note 3, at 278.

39. *E.g.*, Barry J. Everitt & Trevor W. Robbins, *Neural Systems of Reinforcement for Drug Addiction: From Actions to Habits to Compulsion*, 8 NATURE NEUROSCI. 1481 (2005); Steven E. Hyman, *The Neurobiology of Addiction: Implications for Voluntary Control of Behavior* 7 AM. J. BIOETHICS 8 (2007); *Addiction: A Disease of Learning and* Memory, 162 AM. J. PSYCHIATRY. 1414 (2005); Steven E. Hyman, R. C. Malenka, and E. J. Nestler, *Neural Mechanisms of Addiction: The Role of Reward-related Learning and Memory*, 21 ANN. REV. NEUROSCIENCE 565 (2006); Peter W. Kalivas and Nora D.Volkow, *The Neural Basis of Addiction: A Pathology of Motivation and Choice*, 162 AM. J. PSYCHIATRY 1403 (2005); *see generally*, Trevor Robbins, Rudolf Cardinal, Patricia DiCiano et al. *Neuroscience of Drugs and Addiction* DRUGS AND THE FUTURE: BRAIN SCIENCE, ADDICTION AND SOCIETY, *supra* note 9, at 11, 19–26.

longer-term "stop" mechanisms are weakened.[40] This mechanistic causal account is consistent with addictive behavior and plausibly relates to two excusing conditions—impaired capacity for rationality and compulsion—and may help us understand why, whether, and to what degree individual drug users should be excused for their drug-related actions.

It is of course possible that in many cases these addiction-predisposing biological variables might be affected by environmental causes and that genetics or neural mechanisms of reward might play only a trivial role. It would make no difference to the analysis of responsibility, however, that the causes of the predisposition were environmental rather than biological. Both the brain and the mind can be changed by both biological and psychological variables, and environmental causes may be every bit as powerful as biological causes. From the purely causal perspective, once again, a cause is just a cause.[41] For the purpose of analysis, however, let us make the simplifying assumption that genetic and neural causes over which the agent has no rational control always play a nontrivial role in causing the anatomical, physiological, and psychological changes associated with prolonged substance use and consequent addiction.

VIII. RESPONSIBILITY AND ADDICTION

An agent will not be held responsible for anatomical, physiological, or psychological states associated with addiction, but the addict potentially may be held responsible for addiction-associated actions such as possession, use, or other crimes motivated by the desire to obtain and use drugs. Thus, the addict must be evaluated as an acting agent, a person who acts for reasons, and not simply as a biophysical mechanism. This would be true even if craving and compulsive seeking and using drugs were the inevitable, mechanistic outcome of a single-gene defect. The question, then, is how to assess the responsibility of an agent acting intentionally and unlawfully, but apparently compulsively in response to cravings.

The criminal actions of addicts are in fact actions, not mechanisms, even if they may also be properly characterized as signs of disease or brain pathology, and discovery of biological or psychosocial causes does not per se negate agency and create an excusing condition. All actions have biological and

---

40. *See generally* Samuel M. McClure et al., *Separate Neural Systems Value Immediate and Delayed Monetary Rewards*, 306 SCIENCE 503, 505–06 (2004) (finding that different areas of the brain are activated by short-term and long-term rewards; these findings are consistent with the view that our "passions" particularly affect short-term reward choices).

41. *See* JANET RADCLIFFE RICHARDS, HUMAN NATURE AFTER DARWIN: A PHILOSOPHICAL INTRODUCTION (2000) (providing a complete analysis of the indistinguishability of biological and social causation as threats to personhood and ordinary responsibility).

nonbiological causes. The agent is not an addict unless the person seeks and uses the drug. And when he seeks and uses, he acts. He is not legally unconscious, even according to the most extravagantly narrow definition of action, and he surely acts intentionally. Genetically predisposed neural pathology may be a prime source of a craving, and compulsive action to satisfy the craving may produce harmful consequences, but activity to satisfy the craving for drugs is nonetheless action. The core definition of addiction entails this.

The question, therefore, is whether addicts should be excused for their addiction-related actions. This part begins with the prior question of whether addicts can be held responsible for becoming addicted and further held responsible for the foreseeable consequences of addiction. No matter what answer we may obtain after considering whether an addict is responsible when his actions are motivated in part or wholly by his addiction, if the addict is responsible for being in that state, it is possible that analysis of responsibility need go no further. Thus, before turning to the responsibility of those people who are already addicted, this chapter begins with responsibility for becoming addicted. The chapter then turns to the responsibility of addicts without regard to how they became addicted. To determine whether addicts should be excused, it is first necessary to consider those features of addiction-related behavior—craving and compulsion—that are most relevant to an assessment of the criminal law's excusing conditions of lack of rationality and legal compulsion. The chapter continues by addressing the two primary theoretical candidates for why actions motivated by cravings and compulsions might be excused—the internal compulsion and irrationality theories. Finally, it turns to society's responsibility for addiction-related behaviors and whether such responsibility negates or lessens individual responsibility.

A. Responsibility for Becoming Addicted

Let us start with preaddiction use. Before they reach the age of reason, some children and many early and middle adolescents have substantial experience with alcohol, nicotine, and other drugs, and a small number of them become problem users. Moreover, early experimentation with substances such as nicotine is highly predictive of later behavior that risks health. Still, the simplifying assumption will be made that virtually all people do not have their first substantial experience with potentially addicting substances until they are mid-adolescents, an age at which adolescents are in general cognitively indistinguishable from adults.[42]

---

42. *See* Stephen J. Morse, *Immaturity and Irresponsibility*, 88 J. CRIM. L. & CRIMINOLOGY 15, 52–56 (1997) (reviewing evidence that the formal reasoning powers of middle and late adolescents are indistinguishable from those of adults, but recognizing that there may be behavioral differences involving impulsiveness and susceptibility to peer pressure).

By the age of reason, any competent person knows generally about the dangers of addicting substances. Most people who use potentially addicting substances do not become addicts, but between 15 and 17 percent do.[43] Whether one considers this a high or low risk is a normative question. On the other hand, they may overestimate the benefits of drug use and underestimate the risks of becoming addicted, especially how bad it will feel to be addicted.[44] Experience with and empathy for those already addicted is simply no substitute for the real thing. Consequently, perhaps addicts are not fully responsible for their addictions because they operate with insufficient information.

This claim appears plausible and not unlike one objection to advanced directives for health care. For example, if one has never faced death or has never faced it while fully competent, how does the person know what he would really want under the circumstances? Although plausible, the claim that non-addicted drug users have insufficient information about the dangers of drug use seems too strong. There is sufficiently good information as a result of both observation and indirect sources about the perils of addiction to warrant the conclusion that those who take drugs understand the risks sufficiently to be held responsible if addiction ensues. After all, as long as people have general normative competence, including the ability to gather relevant information, perfect information is hardly required for responsibility.

One can deny that any drug use is rational because all drug use is immoral and choosing immorality is always irrational. Claiming generically that immorality is irrational is philosophically controversial, of course, and in this specific context it suggests highly moralistic, virtue ethics. Why, precisely, is limited experimentation or more general recreational use immoral?[45] Because it feels good? Does all such use degrade the moral personality? Perhaps so. But, after all, limited initial experience genuinely hooks almost no one—even if the experimental or recreational user is a member of a genetically or socially at-risk population and especially if the diagnostic brain changes almost always require repeated use.[46]

---

43. Deroche-Gamonet et al., *supra* note 33, at 1014. The authors refer to this as a "small proportion" of those using, but it is hardly an insignificant risk of an injurious disorder and the number is surely higher in identifiable at-risk populations.

44. *See* Jon ELSTER, STRONG FEELINGS: EMOTION, ADDICTION AND HUMAN BEHAVIOR 185 (1999).

45. *See* Douglas N. Husak, DRUGS AND RIGHTS 65–68 (1992); Sheridan Hough, *The Moral Mirror of Pleasure, in* DRUGS, MORALITY, AND THE LAW 153 (Steven Luper-Foy & Curtis Brown, eds., 1994); cf. Rem B. Edwards, *Why We Should Not Use Some Drugs for Pleasure, in ibid.* at 183(there is nothing morally suspicious about pleasure, but some drugs are a great danger).

46. Peter W. Kalivas & Nora D. Volkow, supra note 39 at 1405–6 (finding repeated use of addictive drugs induces structural changes in neural circuitry).

The usual response to claims that experimentation or recreational use is not necessarily irrational is that the process of addiction is insidious. No single instance of use seems to cross a threshold; the process is instead stealthily additive, a slippery slope. At some point, however, the addict is hooked without realizing it. Because no initial user can predict whether and when he specifically will become addicted, it is always irrational to start or to continue, even if one is not yet hooked. There is truth to this response, but the insidiousness of the addiction process is well-known generally and proto-addicts are usually aware that they are developing a problem before the problem becomes a diagnosable addiction. They may, of course, be "in denial" or using other defense mechanisms, such as rationalization, to avoid insight into their own conditions, but the use of defense mechanisms, an imperfect shield at best, is not an excusing condition that morality and law will recognize when serious harms occur. Again, one need not act on perfect information to be responsible. It is difficult to resist the conclusions that most and perhaps all users prior to addiction have some awareness of the risk of potential addiction and that pre-addictive use is conduct for which the user is responsible. Consequently, it is also difficult to resist concluding that most addicts are responsible for becoming addicted.

Most addictions probably occur as a result of conscious and not-so-conscious indifference to the risk of becoming addicted, but plausibly it may be rational in some cases to choose intentionally to become an addict and to enter the addictive "life." This claim should be distinguished from the controversial arguments made by Gary Becker and others that addiction is itself rational.[47] My argument is that it can be rational to choose to become irrational, assuming, arguendo, that at least some addicts are irrational about their lives when they are addicted.

Imagine a young person who has lived an extraordinarily deprived life and who therefore has little human capital and few prospects. It is possible that the person could acquire the life skills and education needed to beat the odds, but rational calculation would suggest that the odds are overwhelmingly against success. In such circumstances, one can easily imagine that a life of intermittent "highs" or oblivion, for example, would be preferable to a clean, straight life, despite the threat of poverty, disease, and prison. Such a life would be limited but manageable, employing substances to help ignore or alleviate the misery of existence. Choosing such a life would be quite rational.[48]

Even if consciously risking or intentionally choosing to become an addict is not rational behavior, responsibility for conduct does not require acting for good,

---

47. *See, e.g.*, Gary S. Becker, *A Theory of Rational Addiction, in* ACCOUNTING FOR TASTES 50 (1996); Jim Leitzel, REGULATING VICE: MISGUIDED PROHIBITIONS AND REALISTIC CONTROLS, 29, 35–71 (2008)(evaluating the rationality of addiction).

48. Although addicts may be largely responsible for becoming addicts and also responsible for much of their drug-related activity while addicted, our society should try to help change the odds for those in my nonhypothetical example.

rational reasons. It is sufficient that the agent retain the general capacity for rationality. Until addiction occurs and perhaps thereafter there is little reason to believe that otherwise responsible agents do not retain this general capacity.

Finally, few people are compelled to become addicted. Peer pressure to experiment may be common in adolescence and early adulthood, but it seldom takes a form that would justify a compulsion excuse. Initial use is almost always intentional and in most cases rational, because virtually no one is immediately hooked or harmed (and most people who use frequently are not addicts or generally endangered). The user tries the substance to please friends, for the thrill of experimenting or being on the edge, for the pleasure or arousal the substance produces, and for a host of other reasons that do not suggest excusing irrationality. Moreover, almost no one is literally forced to become an addict by the involuntary administration of substances.[49]

In conclusion, most people who become addicts may fairly be held responsible to a substantial degree for becoming addicted. To the extent that addicts seek to use their addiction as a mitigating or excusing circumstance when they are charged with crimes related to the addiction, they become vulnerable to the claim that they have caused the condition of their own excuse and, therefore, should not be excused. This is a form of strict liability, however, and becoming an addict is distinguishable from committing crimes once one is addicted. Very few would in fact foresee committing specific crimes, although they may be aware that the addicted life poses risks of illness, poverty, and criminality. The only crimes one may specifically foresee would be crimes of buying, possession, and use in the case of people addicted to illicit substances. For those addicted to arguably the most dangerous drug, ethanol, there may be no specific awareness of the risk of future criminality, except, perhaps, driving under the influence. Indeed, in some cases, such as adherence to a properly prescribed regime of addictive analgesics, becoming addicted may be entirely lawful. In short, even if addicts are mostly responsible for becoming addicted and may be aware of the general risks addiction may pose, this responsibility is different from the responsibility necessary to be culpable for specific crimes. The better reason to hold most addicts criminally responsible most of the time, however they became addicted, is that most of the time they retain a sufficient capacity for rationality to be held responsible.[50]

B. The Meaning of Craving and Compulsion

This chapter previously explored the phenomenology of addiction and has implicitly accepted a commonsense understanding of craving and compulsion. Now let us consider whether more precise clinical and scientific definitions of craving and compulsion can be provided.

---

49. Infants born to addicted mothers might be an exception, but this exceptional case does not undermine the general argument.

50. *See supra* Part VIII.C.2.

The American Psychiatric Association's *Diagnostic and Statistical Manual of Mental Disorders, 4th Edition Text Revision* (DSM-IV-TR)[51] does not use the term "addiction" and does not make craving and compulsive seeking or using necessary criteria of a substance disorder. Nonetheless, this chapter will consider what this manual and other authoritative sources teach about these crucial features of addiction.

DSM-IV-TR defines the generic "essential feature" of the class of substance dependence disorders as, "a cluster of cognitive, behavioral, and physiological symptoms indicating that the individual continues use of the substance despite significant substance-related problems. There is a pattern of repeated self-administration that can result in tolerance, withdrawal, and compulsive drug-taking behavior."[52] DSM-IV-TR does state, however, that "[a]lthough not specifically listed as a criterion item, 'craving' (a strong subjective drive to use the substance) is likely to be experienced by most (if not all) individuals with Substance Dependence."[53]

The *International Classification of Disorders* (ICD-10)[54] describes the dependence syndrome generically as follows:

A cluster of physiological, behavioural, and cognitive phenomena in which the use of a substance or class of substances takes on a much higher priority for a given individual than other behaviours that once had greater value. A central descriptive characteristic of the dependence syndrome is the desire (often strong, sometimes overpowering) to take psychoactive drugs . . ., alcohol or tobacco.[55]

Two specific but not necessary ICD-10 criteria for dependence are a "strong desire or sense of compulsion to take the substance" and "difficulties in controlling substance-taking behaviour."[56]

With respect, these definitions of craving and related states are conclusory, vague, and unoperationalized. This problem is not remedied by consulting other analogous criteria or definitions. For example, DSM-IV-TR defines the "essential feature" of an Impulse-Control Disorder as, "the failure to resist an impulse,

---

51. AM. PSYCHIATRIC ASS'N, *supra* note 2.

52. *Id.* at 192. "Compulsion" is assessed inferentially because the addict continues to seek and use despite adverse life consequences. "Compulsion" is not a specific criterion of the disorder, however.

53. *Id.*

54. WORLD HEALTH ORGANIZATION, THE ICD-10 CLASSIFICATION OF MENTAL AND BEHAVIOURAL DISORDERS (1992).

55. *Id.* at 75.

56. *Id.* According to ICD-10, it is thus possible to be diagnosed as dependent in the absence of any analogue to "compulsive" behavior.

drive, or temptation to perform an act that is harmful to the person or to others."[57] In its generic introduction to impulse-control disorders, the manual continues: "For most of the disorders in this section, the individual feels an increasing sense of tension or arousal before committing the act and then experiences pleasure, gratification, or relief at the time of committing the act."[58] Again, this definition may be related in a loose way to what one might mean by craving or compulsion, but it is surely over-inclusive as a precise definition of these terms.

Finally, DSM-IV-TR's formal use of the diagnostic term, "compulsion," which is defined as part of Obsessive-Compulsive Disorder, an anxiety disorder, bears little relation to compulsive drug seeking and using. Compulsions are defined generically as

> repetitive behaviors (e.g., hand washing, ordering, checking) or mental acts (e.g., praying, counting, repeating words silently) the goal of which is to prevent or reduce anxiety or distress, not to provide pleasure or gratification. In most cases, the person feels driven to perform the compulsion to reduce the distress that accompanies an obsession or to prevent some dreaded event or situation. . . . By definition, compulsions are either clearly excessive or are not connected in a realistic way with what they are designed to neutralize or prevent.[59]

Addictive drug seeking and using is excessive, but it is surely realistically designed to prevent anxiety and distress among addicts for whom this is the primary motivation to take drugs. In either case, the compulsions of the person with Obsessive-Compulsive Disorder are distinguishable from the compulsions experienced by an addict.

Neither "compulsion," "compulsive," nor "craving" is among the terms included in DSM-IV-TR's "Glossary of Technical Terms."[60] On the other hand, the most recent edition of the American Psychiatric Glossary does define "compulsive" as follows: "Refers to intensity or repetitiveness of behavior rather than to compulsive behavior strictly defined. Thus, 'compulsive drinking' and 'compulsive gambling' refer to cravings that may be intense and often repeated, but they are not viewed as compulsions."[61] Craving is not defined, but this definition

---

57. AM. PSYCHIATRIC ASS'N, *supra* note 2, at 663. This feature refers to "impulse control disorders not elsewhere classified," but DSM-IV-TR makes clear that other disorders, such as substance-related disorders, "may have features that involve problems of impulse control." *Id.*

58. *Id.*

59. *Id.* at 457; *see also id.* at 462 (listing the specific criteria).

60. *Id.* at 764–65.

61. AM. PSYCHIATRIC GLOSSARY 45 (Narriman C. Shahrokh & Robert J. E. Hales eds., 8th ed. 2003) (emphasis added).

of "compulsive" does seem akin to the generic definition of addiction under consideration.

However it is defined, the crucial criterial term, "compulsive," is frustratingly vague and dependent primarily on assessment of subjective states. For example, DSM-IV-TR's criterion for Impulse-Control Disorder—the failure to resist a drive, impulse, or temptation to engage in harmful activity—does not disclose whether the person is unable or unwilling to resist or how hard it is to resist, nor does it indicate how harmful the act must be.[62] Further, the definition of Impulse-Control Disorder does not reveal how much inner tension and how much release-seeking behavior is necessary to qualify for the diagnosis of an impulse-control problem. ICD-10's criterion of an "often strong, sometimes overpowering" drive again does not specify how strong is strong enough and what is meant by overpowering. In the case of either of these criteria, if simply taking the drug repetitively (or, seemingly, taking it even once if it leads to a predictably harmful outcome) is sufficient, then the definition is essentially circular.

Such vague definitions will depend ultimately on a subjective assessment of the strength of desires and a normative assessment of when the seeking and using itself is sufficiently harmful to the agent to appear like a symptom, rather than like a bad or even harmless habit or a hobby.[63] And how bad it will be for the agent will in turn depend a great deal on environmental variables that are entirely independent of brain states, such as the cost, availability, and legality of the substance.[64]

The definitional problems apparently can be remedied in various ways. First, compulsion (or addiction) could be defined operationally in terms of scores on various scales. There are many virtues to such an approach and it should be applauded. Even if various scales are reliable, however, validity problems will remain because there is no diagnostic gold standard. Moreover, there is no consensual agreement on the scales. Second, compulsion can be defined in terms of objective behavior without regard to subjective experience—or in economic or rational choice terms, definitions that have theoretical, measurement, and esthetic advantages.[65] Indeed, there is clear evidence that classical and

---

62. Attempts to measure the strength of compulsions have been conceptually confused or methodologically suspect. See Stephen J. Morse, From 'Sikora' to 'Hendricks': Menial Disorder and Criminal Responsibility, in THE EVOLUTION OF MENTAL HEALTH LAW 129, 160–63 (Lynda E. Frost & Richard J. Bonnie eds., 2001).

63. See H.L.A. HART, PUNISHMENT AND RESPONSIBILITY 33 (1968) (describing the difficulty assessing the vague term, "self-control," because we must depend on the agent's own statements and broad generalizations about human nature).

64. See ELSTER, supra note 44 at 166–69; Leitzel, supra note 47, at 64–66; Alan Schwartz, Views of Addiction and the Duty to Warn, 75 VA. L. REV. 509, 517–23 (1989) (rejecting the "strong substance caused view" of addiction).

65. See generally GEORGE AINSLIE, BREAKDOWN OF WILL (2001) [hereinafter BREAKDOWN OF WILL]; GEORGE AINSLIE, PICOECONOMICS: THE STRATEGIC INTERACTION OF SUCCESSIVE MOTIVATIONAL

operant conditioning best explain some addictive phenomena, and some researchers believe that any definition including subjective experiences such as craving will be circular. Nevertheless, a purely objective definition will fail to consider the addict's subjectivity, which most investigators and informed observers believe is crucial to adequate understanding.[66] If craving is crucial to the definition, including it does not threaten circularity because craving can exist in the absence of seeking and using behavior. Finally, addiction could be defined in terms of tolerance and withdrawal because these physiologically related states might be relatively objectively measured. Indeed, these criteria are included in both DSM-IV-TR and ICD-10, but they are neither necessary nor sufficient. Compulsive drug seeking and using can exist without them, and they can exist without accompanying compulsive activity and consequent harms.

In sum, present authoritative sources tell us, mostly conclusorily, that agents are driven, that they feel strong or overpowering desires, that they have intense cravings, and, least helpfully, that they are compelled. We are left where we began, with a descriptive phenomenological account of the addict's subjective mental states and behavior and commonsense understanding of those mental states and behavior.

Although the present understanding of craving and compulsion is often vague and inferential, the terms do have commonsense content and they are clearly both continuum concepts. Not all agents who experience craving and compulsion experience these states with the same intensity. If craving and compulsion may be predicates of an excuse for addiction-related action, it seems to follow that the intensity of these states would be crucial to responsibility assessment. But we do not have scientifically validated measures for the intensity of craving and compulsion, and even the discovery of clear biological (or other) causes for these states may not help in this regard. Craving and compulsion are intentional mental states. They take objects; people crave a specific thing or feel compelled to do a specific thing. A crucial feature about such states is that agents have privileged first-person access to them. Unless mental states are identical to and reducible to physical states—a highly controversial position in the philosophy of mind[67]—identification of biological causes will not indicate the subjective intensity of craving and compulsion. The upshot is that analysis of the

STATES WITHIN THE PERSON 96–273 (1992). But see Gideon Yaffe, *Recent Work on Addiction and Responsible Agency*, 30 PHIL. & PUB. AFF. 178 (2001) (criticizing the usefulness of rational choice and related models of addiction for thinking about individual responsibility).

66. *See* ELSTER, *supra* note 44 at 62–65.

67. *See generally* PAUL M. CHURCHLAND, MATTER AND CONSCIOUSNESS 7–49 (rev. ed. 1988) (reviewing various approaches to understanding the mind-body problem). It is not known how the brain produces the mind. Until the mind-body problem is "solved," which will revolutionize our understanding of biology, such questions will remain. PAUL R. MCHUGH & PHILIP R. SLAVNEY, THE PERSPECTIVES OF PSYCHIATRY 11–12 (2d ed. 1998).

responsibility of addicts for addiction-related behavior, however the addiction is caused, must at present rely on concepts about the mental states of intentional agents that can be best evaluated using common sense.

C. Addiction and Individual Responsibility[68]

Once addicted, should addicts be responsible for use and further drug-related activity? By definition, addicts—or anyway most of them—experience subjective craving and compulsion to seek and use drugs. In some cases, withdrawal also might be feared, but most addicts know that the physical symptoms are manageable, and for some of the "hardest" drugs, addicts experience no physical withdrawal or any withdrawal syndrome at all.[69] If compulsion and lack of the capacity for rationality are the law's primary excusing conditions,[70] do craving and compulsion to use addictive substances or to engage in other addiction-related crimes provide a compulsion or rationality excuse?

1. The Internal Coercion Theory[71] Although the biological models and the discovery of biological causes imply that the addict's symptomatic behaviors are solely mechanisms, this is simply not true. Compulsive states are marked by allegedly overwhelming desires or cravings, but whether the cravings are produced by faulty biology, including genetic predispositions or neural defects, faulty psychology, faulty environment, or some combination of the three, a desire is just a desire and its satisfaction by seeking and using is human action. The addict desires, broadly, either the pleasure of intoxication, the avoidance of the pain of withdrawal or inner tension or both. The addict believes that using

---

68. Much of the analysis in this part necessarily involves philosophical, abstract concepts. The issue of responsibility is conceptual, moral, social, and political; it is not scientific, although scientifically discovered data and theories can provide important inputs to moral, social, and legal thinking. See generally Comm. on Addictions, supra note 23; Yaffe, supra note 65 (reviewing and analyzing empirical and philosophical concepts).

69. Withdrawal from cocaine, for example, produces dysphoric mood rather than the uncomfortable physical symptoms that accompany opiate withdrawal. Margaret Haney, Neurobiology of Stimulants, in THE AMERICAN PSYCHIATRIC PUBLISHING TEXTBOOK OF SUBSTANCE ABUSE TREATMENT 31, 36–37 (Marc Glanter & Herbert D. Kleber eds., 3d ed. 2004). Some "hard" drugs, such as PCP, have no withdrawal syndrome or inner tension, or both. Shelly F. Greenfield & Grace Hennessy, Assessment of the Patient, in id. at 101, 112.

70. There is no uncontroversially correct descriptive model of the law's responsibility doctrines and practices. Some model must implicitly or explicitly be used to assess responsibility, however. I have argued that the model being used is the best overall description of our law and is normatively desirable. See infra Part IV; see also Morse, supra note 18; Morse, supra note 27. The general model may not convince everyone concerning all details, but it is clearly a standard type of view and not idiosyncratic.

71. See generally Stephen J. Morse, Uncontrollable Urges and Irrational People, 88 VA. L. REV. 1025, 1054–63 (2002) (explaining the meaning of internal compulsions generally).

the substance will satisfy the desire and consequently forms the intention to seek and to use the substance.

To attempt to demonstrate that people suffering from compulsive states are similar to mechanisms, the following type of analogy is often used. Imagine that a person is hanging by the fingernails from a cliff over a very deep chasm. The hapless cliffhanger is strong enough to hold on for a while, but not strong enough to save his life by pulling himself up. As time passes and gravity and muscle physiology do their work, he inevitably weakens and it becomes harder and harder to hang on. Finally it becomes impossible and the cliffhanger falls to his death. We are asked to believe that the operation of compulsive desires or cravings is like the combined effect of gravity and muscle physiology. At first the hapless addict can perhaps resist, but inevitably he weakens and satisfies the desire for drugs.

Brief reflection demonstrates that the analogy is flawed as an explanation of why compulsive states are "just like" mechanisms. Unlike action to satisfy a desire, the fall is a genuine mechanism. Holding on indefinitely is physically impossible and the ultimate failure of strength is not intentional. Imagine the following counterexample: A vicious gunslinger trails the addict closely and threatens to kill him instantly if he seeks or uses drugs. Assuming that the addict wants to live as much as the cliffhanger does, no addict would yield to the desire.[72] Conversely, even if the same gunslinger threatened to shoot the cliffhanger immediately if he started to fall, he will fall every time. Of course, our liberal society does not force or even permit addicts to employ such a self-management technique.Moreover, ascriptions of responsibility would appear unfair if such powerful self-management techniques were necessary. Nonetheless, the counterexample, like Leroy Powell's case,[73] indicates that the addict's behavior is not a mechanism.

An addict is not a cliffhanger, of course, so let us consider some closer analogies, such as a powerful, persistent itch, or an increasingly full bladder, or the motor and verbal tics of those suffering from Tourette's Disorder.[74] It can be

---

72. Addicts need sufficiently good reason not to yield. One might object that they only need sufficiently good inducement, rather than good reason, but in this case the inducement is in fact a good reason. Another possibility is that the variable motivating abstinence is not a good reason, but simply one that is so salient that it creates motivational force. This is undoubtedly possible, but in most cases of genuine addiction, what induces abstinence will almost certainly be a good reason, rather than simply a salient rationale. Geoffrey Sayre-McCord, Professor of Philosophy, University of North Carolina, provided helpful insight on these points.

73. *See* Powell v. Texas, 392 U.S. 514, 517–18 (1968) (suggesting that Powell was able to stop drinking the day of his trial for public drunkenness because he knew that he had to be in court).

74. The itch example was given by George Ainslie, Chief of Psychiatry at the Coatesville, Pennsylvania Veterans Administration Hospital. Dr. Ainslie is a leading theorist and

damnably hard not to scratch an itch, even if it is contraindicated. An increasingly full bladder can cause dreadful discomfort and an overwhelming feeling of the need to void. The premonitory buildup of tension that precedes and is relieved by tic behavior among those suffering from Tourette's is usually intense and far more bothersome than the tics themselves. In all cases, the "pressure" to satisfy the desire, to end the discomfort, can be immense. But even in such cases the agent will be to some degree reward sensitive or reason responsive. The gun at the head will work again. If people with itches, full bladders, or pre-tic tension satisfy the desire to rid themselves of the itch, discomfort, or tension, surely their behavior will be action and not mechanism.[75]

Still, although the addict's behavior is not mechanism, perhaps not seeking and using is as hard as not scratching an itch, voiding one's bladder, or engaging in tic behavior. Is it fair to expect the addict to self-regulate successfully in ordinary circumstances that do not permit brute techniques, such as threatening oneself with instant death, just in case one lapses? Is yielding to the desire an appropriate basis for blame and punishment, especially in extreme cases? Perhaps, after all, drug-related activity is sufficiently like mechanistic movement to qualify for an excuse, but this requires an argument rather than an analogy. Too often we are seduced by medical metaphors that strongly suggest mechanism. Nevertheless, the disease model and ordinary language—the addict allegedly "can't help using," or is "impelled to use," or, more bluntly, is "compelled to use"—suggest that addiction primarily produces a control or volitional problem.

Volition is a vexing foundational problem for philosophy, psychology, and law.[76] Even if "black box" models of control problems seem to explain the phenomena deemed addiction, the law's concept of the person as a conscious, intentional agent implies that such models cannot provide the law with adequate guidance to decide if an excuse is warranted either in general or in individual cases. Any model must translate into terms of human agency.

Consider some alternatives. If one adopts Professor Michael Moore's influential, widely noticed contention that volition is a functional mental state of

---

researcher on addictions. *See generally* AINSLIE, *supra* note 51. The bladder example was first suggested by an anonymous participant at a conference. Jon Elster also uses it. On Tourette's Disorder, *see* Charles W. Popper, G. Davis Gammon, Scott A. West & Charles E. Bailey, *Disorders Usually First Diagnosed in Infancy, Childhood, or Adolescence, in* TEXTBOOK OF CLINICAL PSYCHIATRY, 833, 906–11 (Robert E. Hales & Stuart C. Yudofsky eds., 4th ed. 2003).

75. If a full bladder finally simply "overflows" because the pressure prevents the agent from controlling the sphincter muscles, voiding is purely a mechanism. Moreover, in some cases Tourette's may be so extreme that tic-ing is more like a reflex than action and responsibility would be blocked for the tic-ing because the agent did not act at all.

76. *See* Bernard J. Bams, *Why Volition is a Foundation Problem for Psychology*, 2 CONSCIOUSNESS & COGNITION 281 (1993); Morse, *Culpability and Control*, *supra* note 25, at 1595–97.

executory intention,[77] the problem of volition disappears because virtually no addict has a volitional problem. Their wills translate their desires for the drug into the necessary action quite effectively. Indeed, on this account of the will, almost no intentional conduct will raise a problem of volition.[78] Moore's account is persuasive to many, but like all accounts of the philosophical foundations of action, it is controversial. Some competitors that consider volition a species of desire,[79] a view that Moore and others reject, may raise volitional problems in the case of addicts.[80] Unless these alternatives can be reduced to ordinary language concepts that apply to human agency, however, it will be impossible for legislatures and courts to resolve disputes about the metaphysics of mind and action rationally.[81]

An "internal coercion" model is one possible explanation of a control or volitional excuse based on "disorders of desire."[82] The model employs a moralized, commonsense approach that is analogous to the criminal law excuse of duress and that requires no implausible, unverifiable empirical assumptions about how the mind works.[83] Consequently, the criteria for duress will be considered before turning to whether the model can be applied to addictions.

Duress obtains if the defendant is threatened with the use of deadly force or grievous bodily harm against himself or another unless the defendant commits

---

77. MICHAEL S. MOORE, ACT AND CRIME: THE PHILOSOPHY OF ACTION AND ITS IMPLICATIONS FOR CRIMINAL LAW 113–65 (1993).

78. Id.

79. E.g., Galen Strawson, FREEDOM AND BELIEF 66–67 (1986) (citing Kant).

80. 67. See, e.g., William Charlton, WEAKNESS OF THE WILL: A PHILOSOPHICAL INTRODUCTION (1988) (discussing competing accounts of weakness of the will); R. Jay Wallace, Addiction as Defect of the Will: Some Philosophical Reflections, 18 L. & PHIL. 621 (1999) (see especially Section 2).

81. A classic, well-known example of a theory of volition that can be understood in ordinary language terms and that has therefore received much attention in the legal as well as philosophical literature is Harry Frankfurt's hierarchical theory. HARRY G. FRANKFURT, THE IMPORTANCE OF WHAT WE CARE ABOUT: PHILOSOPHICAL ESSAYS 11, 24 (1988). For reasons considered elsewhere, however, this seemingly attractive model does not succeed. See Morse, Culpability and Control, supra note 29, at 1626–28.

82. The next subsection suggests that irrationality provides a better explanation of why we might excuse or mitigate the responsibility of an agent suffering from a disorder of desire such as addiction.

83. The analysis in this subsection has been enormously influenced by Alan Wertheimer's treatment of similar issues. See ALAN WERTHEIMER, COERCION (1987). It is assumed that duress can sometimes be an excusing condition. See Joshua Dressler, Exegesis of the Law of Duress: Justifying the Excuse and Searching for its Proper Limits, 62 S. CAL. L. REV. 1331 (1989). Some believe, however, that duress is always a justification. See WALLACE, supra note 7, at 144–47; Peter Westen & Joseph Mangiafico, The Criminal Defense of Duress: A Justification, Not An Excuse—And Why It Matters, 6 BUFF. CRIM. L. REV. 833 (2003). The differences are discussed in the text infra.

an equally or more serious crime, and a person of reasonable firmness would have been "unable to resist" the threat.[84] In other words, an agent faced with a particularly "hard choice"—commit a crime or be killed or grievously injured—is legally excused if the choice is too hard to expect the agent to buck up and obey the law. The defense, however, is not based on empirical assumptions about the subjective capacity of an individual agent to resist threats; it is moralized and objective.[85] For example, the defense is not available to a defendant allegedly "unable" to resist if the threats were less than death or grievous bodily harm or if a person of reasonable firmness would have been able to resist.

The moralized criterion of the person of reasonable firmness necessary to support the excuse of duress appears to risk unfairness. Suppose a person would find it extraordinarily difficult to resist threats that a person of reasonable firmness could resist. Under such conditions, criminal penalties would be retributively unjust because a person does not deserve punishment for conduct that is so difficult for that agent to avoid. Moreover, specific deterrence is bootless in such cases. A purely consequential view might justify punishment to buck up the marginal people, but only at the cost of injustice to those who find it supremely difficult to resist. Because fault is a necessary condition for blame and punishment in our system, denying the defense would be unjust. Those who take this position should argue for a purely subjective view of the duress excuse, which would require difficult empirical assessment of the defendant's capacity to resist. This standard would be a nightmare to adjudicate, but worth the effort if it were necessary to avoid injustice.

There is a good argument, however, that the moralized, objective standard that uses the person of reasonable firmness as the criterion is not unfair. If a person is threatened with death, for example, the defense of duress should be potentially available unless the balance of evils is so remarkably negative that every person would be expected to resist. In all other cases, the question would at least "go to the jury." Thus, there will be few cases involving sufficiently serious threats in which the person incapable of resisting would lose the potential defense. The person who genuinely finds resisting extremely difficult even when the threats are relatively mild— say, kill or be touched—will almost certainly be a person with irrational fears that will qualify for some type of irrationality defense. Duress might not obtain, but exculpation will be available on other grounds.

The formulation, "unable to resist," has the unmistakable implication of mechanism. Unless *force majeure* or genuine mechanism is at work, we virtually

---

84. MODEL PENAL CODE § 2.09 (1962).

85. Using the term "objective" is not meant to suggest that the "person of reasonable firmness" criterion has a reality independent of our practices that can be discovered by reason or empirical investigation. It is only meant to be a thoroughly normative standard that expresses what we all expect of each other in our legal and moral culture.

never know whether the agent is in some sense genuinely unable or is simply unwilling to resist, and if the latter, how hard it is for the agent to resist. In the present state of knowledge, research evidence concerning the characteristics that help people maintain control when faced with temptation or experiencing impulses is no more than a general guide.[86] No metric and no instrumentation can accurately resolve questions about the strength of craving and the ability to resist. This was in large part the reason that both the American Psychiatric Association and the American Bar Association recommended the abolition of the control or volitional test for legal insanity in the wake of the ferment concerning the defense of legal insanity following the *Hinckley*[87] verdict.[88] Moreover, courts faced with deciding whether to adopt a volitional test after Hinckley refused to do so for the same reason.[89] If strength of craving or of resistance are to be the touchstones, legal decision makers will have to act with little scientific guidance and lots of common sense.[90]

---

86. ROY F. BAUMEISTER, TODD F. HEATHERTON & DIANNE M. TICE, LOSING CONTROL: HOW AND WHY PEOPLE FAIL AT SELF-REGULATION 242–56 (1994) (considering self-regulation techniques and distinguishing underregulation, in which the agent often actively participates, and misregulation, in which the agent seldom actively participates). *See generally* BREAKDOWN OF WILL, *supra* note 65 (applying hyperbolic discounting theories to problems of willpower and loss of control); ALBERT BANDURA, SELF-EFFICACY: THE EXERCISE OF CONTROL (1997) (providing an overview of human agency and presentation of "self-efficacy" theory); HOWARD RACHLIN, THE SCIENCE OF SELF-CONTROL (2000) (providing a review of research and theoretical account of self-control based on "teleological behaviorism").

87. United States v. Hinckley, 525 F. Supp. 1342 (D.C. 1981).

88. *See* AM. BAR ASS'N CRIMINAL JUSTICE STANDARDS COMM., A.B.A CRIMINAL JUSTICE MENTAL HEALTH STANDARDS 330, 339112 (1989); AM. PSYCHIATRIC ASS'N, INSANITY DEFENSE: POSITION STATEMENT (1982).

89. *E.g.*, United States v. Lyons, 731 F.2d 243 (5th Cir. 1984) (en banc). The Court also held that narcotics addiction alone, without other physiological or psychological involvement, was not a mental disease or defect for the purpose of raising the insanity defense. *Id.* Presumably, the court meant physiological or psychological effects that were not per se part of the criteria for addiction. Congress later abolished the volitional wing of the insanity defense in federal criminal trials and retained only a cognitive test for legal insanity. Insanity Defense Reform Act of 1984, 18 U.S.C. §17 (2000).

90. For example, one writer explains, "The strength of the craving may be gauged by how willing the person is to sacrifice other sources of reward or well-being in life to continue engaging in the addictive behavior." Dennis M. Donovan, *Assessment of Addictive Behaviors: Implications of an Emerging Biopsychosocial Model, in* ASSESSMENT OF ADDICTIVE BEHAVIORS 3, 6 (Dennis M. Donovan & G. Alan Marlatt eds., 1988) [hereinafter Donovan, *Assessment of Addictive Behaviors*]. Although written by an estimable researcher, it is no more than an operationalized, commonsense measure. There are more recent scales to measure craving, but there is controversy about their validity. Ned L. Cooney, Ronald M. Kadden & Howard R. Steinberg, *Assessment of Alcohol Problems, in* ASSESSMENT OF ADDICTIVE BEHAVIORS, SECOND EDITION 71, 91–92 (Dennis M. Donovan & G. Alan Marlatt eds.2005). Moreover, there is difficulty achieving a valid cross-cultural definition of

The analogy often used to demonstrate that craving is like duress is that the intense cravings or desires of "compulsive" states are like an "internal" gun to the head. The sufferer's fear of physical or psychological withdrawal symptoms and of other dysphoric states[91] is allegedly so great that it is analogous to the "do-it-or-else" fear of death or grievous bodily injury that is necessary for a duress defense. Yielding to a compulsive desire, a craving, is therefore like yielding to a threat of death or grievous bodily harm.[92] The argument is that we cannot expect a person of reasonable firmness not to yield in the face of such an internally generated hard choice, much as we cannot expect such a person not to yield in the face of an external threat of death or grievous bodily harm.

The analogy is attractive, but theoretically and practically problematic. First, the analogy suggests no problem with the defender's will, which operates effectively to execute the intention to block or to remove the dysphoria.[93] Further, it is entirely rational, at least in the short term, to wish to terminate ghastly dysphoria, even if there are competing reasons not to, such as criminal sanctions or moral degradation. And it is simply not the case that addicts always act to satisfy their cravings because they fear dysphoria. Many just yield because it is unpleasant to abstain, not because they substantially fear dysphoria. In addition, the phenomenology of the sufferer's response to craving, unlike the phenomenology of the victim threatened by death, often is not, and perhaps never is, clear or the product of unitary, simple causes. Suppose, for example, that the primary motive is the pleasure or satisfaction of yielding or that such pleasure is an important, additional motive. The possibility of pleasure seems more like an offer than a threat, and offers expand rather than contract freedom. The strong desire for pleasure is not a hard-choice excusing condition in law or morals.

Assuming that fear of dysphoria is a sufficient motive and that the analogy to the fear of death or grievous bodily harm is initially plausible, two problems remain: assessing the strength of the fear and deciding what degree of fear of dysphoria is sufficient to excuse what types of conduct. Based on ordinary experience and common sense, the criminal law uses threats of death or grievous bodily harms as objective indicators of the type of stimulus that would in ordinary people create sufficient hard choice to justify an excuse. Of course, people subjected to such threats will differ markedly in their subjective fear responses and in their desires to live or to remain uninjured, but ordinary, average people

---

craving. Arthur W. Blume,, Osvaldo F. Morera & Berenice Garcia de la Cruz, *Assessment of Addictive Behaviors in Ethnic-Minority Cultures, in id.* at 49, 51–52.

91. *See* AM. PSYCHIATRIC ASS'N, *supra* note 2, at 663 (stating that most "impulse-control disorders" include an increase of tension and arousal before committing the harmful act).

92. In most cases of "impulse-control disorders," there is an experience of pleasure, satisfaction, or relief after committing the impulsive act. *Id.*

93. FINGARETTE & HASSE, *supra* note 30, at 61.

will have very substantial fear and find the choice to resist very difficult.[94] We have all experienced dysphoric states, and many have experienced intense dysphoria, but dysphoria as a source of present and potential pain is more purely subjective than death or grievous bodily injury. Consequently, assessing the average or ordinary intensity of craving or inner tension, including seemingly strong states, is simply more difficult than assessing the fear of death or grievous bodily injury. Focusing on more objective markers of compulsive states, such as physical withdrawal symptoms, will surely help, but fear of such symptoms is unlikely to support an excuse.

Fear of the physical symptoms of withdrawal from most drugs is not likely to be as intense as the fear of death or grievous bodily harm because in most cases withdrawal is not terribly painful—withdrawal from heroin is often likened to a bad flu—and can be medically managed to reduce the discomfort.[95] Withdrawal from alcohol dependence can be extremely severe, but it, too, can be medically managed, and because alcohol is freely and inexpensively available for adults, those who fear withdrawal and do not want treatment seldom need to commit crimes or other wrongs to obtain alcohol to avoid withdrawal.

Dysphoric mental or emotional states are surely undesirable, but does their threat, especially if medical management is available, produce a sufficiently hard choice to warrant an excuse? The answer to this question is not obvious, but perhaps at the extreme they do. People suffering from severe depressive disorders, for example, report subjective pain that is apparently as great and enduring as the reported pain from many forms of grievous bodily harm, and sometimes depressed people kill themselves to avoid the psychological pain. For another example, some people addicted to alcohol who are being treated with a drug that makes them dreadfully sick if they ingest any alcohol, including trace amounts, will "drink through" the miserable sickness.[96] These examples and common

---

94. The subjective experience of fear is not strictly required for standard duress cases. It is sufficient if the choice is extremely difficult for the person of ordinary firmness, even if a particular defendant is cool in the face of threat. Nonetheless, what makes the choice hard is the unpleasantness of the alternative—death or grievous bodily harm—and thus most ordinary people will fear the threat.

The analysis of duress presented could apply to moral dilemmas that the criminal law does not address. Imagine a person who possesses a monetarily worthless locket that contains an equally financially worthless but emotionally priceless memento, say, a strand of a sainted parent's hair. One could easily imagine that a threat to destroy the locket might morally excuse quite serious property crime and perhaps crimes against the person, although the criminal law would recognize no excuse in this case.

95. *See* John Kaplan, The Hardest Drug: Heroin and Public Policy 35–36 (1983).

96. Arnold M. Ludwig, Understanding the Alcoholic's Mind: The Nature of Craving and How to Control It 58–59 (1988). Such cases are surely rare, however, and most alcoholics who wish to drink either discontinue their aversive therapy or find ways to disable its effect. Interestingly, some East Asian populations have a genetically caused variation

sense suggest that fear of or aversiveness to psychologically dysphoric states may be very strong, indeed.[97] But is it as strong as the fear of death?

Even assuming that the feared dysphoria of unconsummated cravings can be substantial, it will likely seldom be as severe as the fear of death or grievous bodily harm. If this is right and assuming, too, that we could reliably assess the fear of dysphoria, few addicts would succeed with a hard-choice excuse. On the other hand, if the drug-related activities were solely possession for personal use and use itself, then perhaps the justification of necessity should obtain.[98] Even if the harm of such activity is less than the harm of dysphoria, however, the law would hold most addicts responsible for becoming addicted and thus for placing themselves in the situation that created the need for the defense. The law disallows the justification in such cases.[99] Finally, even if addicts were not responsible for becoming addicted, all legislatures would today resist permitting a justification for possession and use on policy grounds and would surely reject an excuse for other, possibly related crimes, such as theft or robbery, to pay for drugs. The disease model is powerful, but the moral failure model is resilient.

In sum, the internal coercion or duress approach uses understandable terms and has a moral basis derived from a defense that the criminal law and ordinary morality already accept. Nevertheless, currently insurmountable practical problems beset attempting to assess the appropriateness of an excuse in individual cases. What is more, thinking about excuse in terms of control difficulties inevitably will invite misleading metaphorical thinking about mechanism and expert testimony that is little more than moral judgment wrapped in the white coat of allegedly scientific or clinical understanding. The law should not adopt an internal coercion excuse.

2. The Irrationality Theory Irrationality is the most straightforward, persuasive explanation of why some addicts should perhaps be excused. Moreover, irrationality will excuse any addict who may apparently qualify under the internal coercion theory. If the craving sufficiently interferes with the addict's ability to grasp and be guided by reason, then a classic irrationality problem arises and there is no need to resort to compulsion as the ground for excuse. Finally, it is simply more practicable to assess rationality than to assess the strength of compulsive desires.

---

in the enzymes that metabolize alcohol that create effects of ingestion similar to the effects of the aversive therapy medication. Alcohol addiction is consequently infrequent in such populations. Nestler, *supra* note 3, at 277.

97. *See* Donovan, *Assessment of Addictive Behaviors, supra* note 90.

98. *E.g.*, Model Penal Code § 3.02 (1962).

99. *See, e.g.*, N.Y. PENAL LAW § 35.05 (McKinney 2003) (allowing the defense as an emergency measure to avoid an imminent harm if the situation occurred "through no fault of the actor").

How does it feel to crave intensely? The subjective experience of addicts is diverse, but a modal tale about severe addiction may be useful. Despite different historical pathways to addiction, descriptions of the subjective experience are broadly of a piece,[100] although different descriptors and metaphors are and could be used. The story is not meant to include all the features of the addictive process; rather, it is an approximation of the subjective experience preceding use that may bear on responsibility.

Between episodes of use of the substance, the addict commonly experiences a buildup of tension, irritation, anxiety, boredom, depression, or other dysphoric states. As time passes since the last use, these dysphoric states typically become stronger, more persistent, more intense, and more demanding. In some cases, the buildup is described as sheer desire, sheer wanting. As the wanting remains unsatisfied, increased dysphoric states or, in some cases, excitement, accompany the wanting. For illicit drug addicts, anxiety or fear about obtaining the substance often adds to the dysphoria.

At some point, the addict metaphorically, and in some cases literally, can think of nothing but the desire to use the substance. One informant described the desire like "a buzzing in my ears that prevents me from focusing." It is like an extreme version of being dehydrated or starved: the addict can ordinarily think of nothing except getting and using the stuff. It is like the moment just before orgasm during an episode of exceptional excitement, but usually without the pleasurable feeling of sexual excitement. There is only one tune or story in the addict's head and nothing else drives it out.[101] When the addict cannot get the tune out of his head, it is very difficult to concentrate the mind on the good reasons not to use, especially because, in almost all instances, there is no police officer at the elbow or other available "self-management technique" sufficiently powerful to motivate the addict to think clearly about drug-related activity. Fundamental components of rationality—the capacities to think clearly and self-consciously to evaluate one's conduct—are compromised. The agent may not recognize the various options at all or may not be able coherently to weigh and assess those that are recognized. For moral and legal purposes, however, the precise mechanisms by which addiction can compromise rationality are less

---

100. See, e.g., Donovan, Assessment of Addictive Behaviors, supra note 90, at 5–11 (describing "commonalities across addictive behaviors").

101. See, e.g., Michael B. Ross, It's Time for Me to Die: An Inside Look at Death Row, 26 J. PSYCHIATRY & L. 475, 482–83 (1998) (providing a first-person account given by a death row inmate with persistent, allegedly overwhelming urges to degrade, rape, and kill, who describes the urges as a song one cannot get out of one's head). This example does not involve addictions, of course, but certain disorders of sexual desire, the paraphilias, produce impulse control problems similar to those associated with substance-related problems and impulse control disorders generally. AM. PSYCHIATRIC ASS'N, supra note 2, at 663. Moreover, many think that certain types of sexual behavior are usefully characterized as an addiction.

important than the clear evidence that it can do so.[102] On the other hand, the addict's characteristic ambivalence about addiction suggests that addicts recognize that they have good reason to stop, at least during lucid or inter-use intervals.[103]

The degree to which the general capacity for rationality is compromised can vary widely among addicts. The modal tale is told as an extreme case and is anyway only an approximation. Still, addiction can compromise rationality and therefore can potentially excuse drug-related activity, especially for those most severely affected. Thus, the question remains whether the law should consider addiction as a potential excuse. This is an important question for social and legal policy because drugs are a factor in much criminal conduct. Possession and use offenses are rampant, and in most big cities, well over half of all people arrested for felonies test positive for addictive substances.[104] Many of these are surely addicts. Society may believe that it is fair to blame and punish them, but is it?

Whether or not addicts were responsible for becoming addicted, they will not lack mens rea for their substance-related criminal activity.[105] Virtually all potential addicts are consciously aware of the risk that if addicted they will persistently and intentionally seek and use substances. Nevertheless, the previous conscious

---

102. *See* ELSTER, *supra* note 44, at 169–79 (reviewing the potential mechanisms through which cravings resulting from drug addiction can affect rational choice); Peter W. Kalivas, *Choose to Study Choice in Addiction*, 161 AM. J. PSYCHIATRY 193 (2004) (stating that at some point in a developing addiction disorder, decision-making ability becomes compromised); Louk J.M.J. Vanderschmen & Barry J. Everitt, *Drug Seeking Becomes Compulsive After Prolonged Cocaine Self-Administration*, 305 SCIENCE 1017, 1017 (2004) ("Addicts display drug-dominated, inflexible behavior and are unable to shift their thoughts and behavior away from drugs and drug-related activities," which increases with prolonged use); A. David Redish, Steve Jensen & Adam Johnson, *A unified framework for addiction: Vulnerabilities in the decision process*, 31 BEHAV. & BRAIN SCI. 415 (2008) (identifying the key vulnerabilites in the decision making process that can lead to maladaptive choices).

103. This point is courtesy of George Ainslie, Chief of Psychiatry at the Coatesville, Pennsylvania Veterans Administration Hospital.

104. PAIGE M. HARRISON & ALLEN J. BECK, BUREAU OF JUSTICE STATISTICS, PRISONERS IN 2002, 10, 11 (2003) (finding that 20.4% of sentenced state inmates in 2001 incarcerated for drug offenses; 55% of sentenced federal inmates incarcerated for drug offenses); ZHANG, *supra* note 2; *see also* DORIS JAMES WILSON, BUREAU OF JUSTICE STATISTICS, DRUG USE, TESTING, AND TREATMENT IN JAILS 1 (2000) (finding that in 1998, 70% of jail inmates had used drugs regularly or had committed a drug offense).

105. The major exception will be cases in which the addict offends while in a state of unconsciousness or blackout induced by substance use. Most jurisdictions would permit only limited use of such evidence to negate mens rea and some would not permit it at all. The Supreme Court has declared constitutional the total exclusion of intoxication evidence, even when it is undeniably relevant and probative of culpability. Montana v. Egelhoff, 518 U.S. 37 (1996).

awareness of this risk is distinguishable from forming the intention pre-addiction to seek and use after becoming addicted. For most addicts, however, there will be no mens rea problem when they seek and use. They are not automatons and they do form the intent to buy, possess, and use. In most cases of serious criminal wrongdoing, the potential addict may be unaware of the risk of committing such offenses unless the addict has a history of such wrongdoing. Even if this is true, however, there still will be no mens rea problem. An addict who burgles, robs, or kills surely forms the intent to do so. In the narrow legal sense, most addicts have the true purpose to engage in their drug-related conduct.If they deserve mitigation and excuse, it is because they are not fully rational, not because they lack the mental state required by the definition of the offense.

As a result of addiction, some addicts are sufficiently irrational to warrant mitigation or excuse at the time they commit their substance-related crimes. Should they be held responsible nonetheless? Two theories suggest in general that virtually all should be. The first is that by experimenting with drugs, the addict knowingly took the risk that he would become irrational, including the possibility that the irrationality would operate specifically in contexts involving substance-related behavior. This theory comes dangerously close to strict liability in many instances, however, because most people who experiment with drugs probably are not consciously aware that they might become involved in criminal behavior beyond buying and possessing and using drugs. And even the latter is not a feature for licit addictive drugs such as ethanol.

The second and more convincing theory is that almost all addicts have lucid, rational intervals between episodes of use during which they could act on the good reasons to seek help quitting or otherwise to take steps to avoid engaging in harmful drug-related behavior. This has been termed a case of potential dia-chronic self-control because the person knows that at a later time he will be in a state of nonresponsible irrationality.[106] Again, the ambivalence about addiction that characterizes addicts implies that they are capable of and do recognize these good reasons during their lucid intervals. Even if some addicts are unable to think rationally when they are in a state of intense craving, they are capable of rationality in refractory periods and have a duty to take steps to avoid future offending.

Both theories for holding addicts responsible are potentially subject to the same objection, however. Addiction can become an entire lifestyle and the consequences of prolonged use of substances can so debilitate some addicts physically and psychosocially that this group has exceptional difficulty at all times exercising substantial rationality concerning their status and behavior. Although potential addicts may be aware of the risk of irrationality, they may not be fully

---

106. JEANNETTE KENNETT, AGENCY AND RESPONSIBILITY: A COMMON-SENSE MORAL PSYCHOLOGY 134–35 (2001).

aware of the risk of extreme irrationality that can arise in some cases. In such instances, perhaps, one cannot find responsibility for extreme irrationality by referring back to pre-addiction, knowing conduct, or by considering quiescent intervals. In cases of extreme debilitation, the intervals between episodes of use may not be fully rational.

The foregoing objection does not seem decisive, however. In those few cases in which prolonged drug use produces a permanent, major mental disorder that compromises rationality at the time of criminal conduct, the addict will have available a traditional insanity defense based on "settled insanity" resulting from the use of intoxicants.[107] But except in such rare cases, most addicts' rational intervals are probably sufficiently rational to hold them largely or fully responsible for diminishing their own rationality at the time of use or of other drug-related crimes. In addition, as a result of both street wisdom and personal history, experienced addicts typically know during these intervals both what treatment alternatives are available and the type of criminal behavior beyond seeking and using in which they are likely to engage. Indeed, much of the further criminal activity probably takes place during the rational intervals and involves harm to others, which carries greater criminal penalties, giving the addict even stronger self—and other—regarding reasons not to offend than in the case of personal possession and use.

Finally, suppose one concludes that some addicts deserve mitigation or excuse for at least some criminal conduct. The previous subsection on the internal coercion theory suggests that irrationality would excuse any addict that the internal coercion theory might fairly excuse. The argument, in brief, is this: A person driven crazy by fear is crazy. Or, in the alternative, people so fearful of mild dysphoric states that they appear incapable of bucking up when reasonable people would are irrationally fearful. Any plausible story about allegedly compulsive cravings motivating the criminal conduct, especially in cases of serious crime, also will be a story in which the addict is less than fully rational or not rational at all. In such cases, irrationality would be the appropriate excusing claim; there would be no need to resort to problematic internal coercion.

The conclusion is that most addicts are responsible for seeking and using and almost none should be excused for further criminal activity, and especially not for serious wrongdoing. There are simply too many periods of rationality and there is simply too much awareness of alternative possibilities to permit excuse in more than a small number of cases.[108]

---

107. It is assumed that almost all jurisdictions would permit this defense for cases in which the settled insanity resulted from illicit drugs. See WAYNE R. LAFAVE, CRIMINAL LAW 481–82 (4th ed. 2003).

108. Part IX.A *infra* considers the case for mitigation in more detail. This part also suggests that current criminal law overcriminalizes much drug-related activity. Even if addicts might be responsible for that activity, it does not follow that it is sensible to criminalize it.

C. "Social Responsibility"

Socioeconomic arrangements, culture, life stories, legal regulation, and other "external" causal variables can seem much to blame for addiction and its consequences. Even if most addicts are personally responsible for becoming addicted and for their behavior while addicted, whether one becomes an addict and how one lives as an addict are not solely due to the intentional conduct of an agent who becomes an addict.

Consider the following examples. It is entirely understandable that people living in communities of deprivation, with few life chances, may find a life of addiction preferable to the misery of an impoverished straight life. Some subcultures particularly encourage and celebrate the use of potentially addictive substances, increasing the risk of addiction among members of that subculture. For those who have lived lives of desperation or who suffer from psychological miseries for any reason, substance use can be a welcome escape. Finally, legal regulation can affect the probability of addiction, the lifestyles of addicts, and the further behavioral consequences of addiction. It is more difficult to bum a dime bag than to bum a smoke or to cadge a free drink, even from friends, and the addict can never be sure that a dealer is not an undercover narc, an informant, or cutting the dope. Lawful availability and price affect all the following: rates of consumption; the development of informal customs and conventions for controlled use; the health, safety, and legal dangers of seeking and using drugs; and the probability that other criminal behavior beyond possession and use will occur as a result of addiction. Explanations such as these, especially when considered in the context of a sympathy-arousing life history, can tug at our hearts and influence our responsibility attributions. As Gary Watson concluded in his discussion of the case of a murderer who had suffered a dreadful childhood, in many cases our reaction will be, "No wonder."[109]

How should we respond to powerful social explanations? Social variables account undeniably for a great deal of the variance in addictions and related behavior, and many of these variables are potentially modifiable by sound social policy. For example, millions of lives will be affected by resolution of the current debates concerning decriminalization of illicit drugs,[110] by differential penalties for essentially similar substances such as crack and powdered cocaine, by the

---

109. Gary Watson, *Responsibility and the Limits of Evil: Variations on a Strawsonian Theme, in* RESPONSIBILITY, CHARACTER, AND THE EMOTIONS: NEW ESSAYS IN MORAL PSYCHOLOGY 256, 275 (Ferdinand Schoeman ed., 1987). Watson's description is of the life of Robert Alton Harris, a notorious multiple murderer who seemed to have no empathy for other people. Indeed, his cellblock mates on death row detested him. Yet if one reads his life history, it is difficult not to have at least a modicum of sympathy for Harris and to think that a dreadful outcome was entirely understandable for reasons in no way Harris' fault *Id.*

110. *See infra* Part IX.

propriety of needle exchanges, and by whether nicotine should be regulated by the Food and Drug Administration. A just society should try to minimize the inevitable ill effects of its policies. Nonetheless, crimes and moral wrongs are ultimately committed by individual agents, and social causal variables, or any other kind of causal variable, cannot excuse addicts who are individually responsible without threatening all individual responsibility.[111]

All behavior is caused by innumerable variables over which we have no control. Some causal stories surely arouse more sympathy than others, but sympathy and an unfortunate life history are not excusing conditions per se. One may wish to consider such variables for disposition on consequential grounds or as an expression of mercy, but they do not excuse unless they produce sufficient irrationality or a sufficiently hard choice. Focusing on individual responsibility should not blind us to the remediable causes of wrongdoing and should not diminish justifiable sympathy for wrongdoers, but neither should explanations and sympathy undermine our view that most wrongdoers are responsible agents.

IX. PROPOSALS: DIMINISHED RESPONSIBILITY, DRUG TREATMENT & SENSIBLE CRIMINAL JUSTICE

Three potential legal reforms might produce more proportionate blame and punishment for addiction-related offenses and might reduce addiction-associated costs overall. First, the criminal law should adopt a generic partial excuse to crime that might well apply to cases of addiction-related crime. Second, forced treatment of addicts using the leverage of the criminal law would be fair and likely to be effective. Last, sensible criminalization policy in response to addiction and addiction-related crime would have profound effects.

A. Diminished Responsibility

Some addicts might not be responsible for seeking and use or for further drug-related or drug-affected activity because they are not rational or not fully rational, or perhaps, because they faced a sufficiently hard choice. This would certainly be true if morality and the law held a less demanding set of criteria for responsibility than now obtains. How could the law respond to such claims?

According to almost any definition, rationality and hard choice are continuum concepts.[112] Consequently, responsibility must be a matter of infinite variation.

---

111. *See* Stephen J. Morse, *Deprivation and Desert, in* FROM CRIMINAL JUSTICE TO SOCIAL JUSTICE 114 (William C. Heffernan & John Kleinig eds., 2000) (considering and rejecting the various theories proposed to excuse criminal behavior solely on the basis of an unfortunate life history).

112. For ease of exposition, only rationality will be discussed. The argument applies equally well, however, to an internal coercion theory of excuse.

But even if rationality is easier to assess than irresistibility, it is beyond human ability to measure it precisely enough to ascribe infinite degrees of responsibility. As a result, the law adopts bright-line tests, such as legal insanity, and does not include a generic partial responsibility doctrine.[113] Nevertheless, the law should consider a limited, generic partial excuse of "partial responsibility."[114] Although there are practical objections that might fairly be raised, the moral claim for a partial excuse is sufficiently weighty to justify bearing the potential practical costs.

As the extant, mitigating doctrines of homicide imply, such as reducing murder to manslaughter in cases of "heat of passion" induced by legally adequate provocation, some legally responsible defendants suffer from impaired rationality that warrants mitigation and triers of fact can fairly make the relatively gross culpability judgment required. The underlying theory of excuse that supports these doctrines—impaired capacity for rationality—and the doctrines themselves are perfectly generalizable to all crimes. There is no reason that juries could not reasonably make the same judgments about mitigation for other crimes that they routinely make to determine if murder should be reduced to manslaughter.

Justice would be better served if the criminal law adopted a generic partial excuse, reflected in another possible verdict, "Guilty but Partially Responsible" (GPR). Many crimes are committed when the defendant's rationality may be substantially impaired by a wide variety of factors, including the cognitive and affective changes that addiction may produce. Fairness may demand mitigation in such cases, but except within homicide or at sentencing, the criminal law has no means to do justice, and the existing means suffer from various deficiencies. A verdict such as GPR would provide a remedy. Because GPR would be a partial affirmative defense, the Constitution would permit the state to place the burden of persuasion on either the prosecution or the defense.[115]

---

113. The major exceptions are the mitigating doctrines of homicide that reduce murder to manslaughter and sentencing practices generally.

114. *See* Stephen J. Morse, *Diminished Rationality, Diminished Responsibility*, 1 OHIO ST. J. CRIM. L. 289 (2003) (providing a full defense of a proposal for a generic partial excuse to crime and considering the practical objections).

115. *See* Patterson v. New York, 423 U.S. 197 (1977). It is important to distinguish GPR from "Guilty But Mentally Ill" (GBMI), a verdict adopted by a substantial minority of the states. GBMI reflects a jury finding that the defendant was mentally ill at the time of the crime, but that the defendant was nonetheless fully responsible for her conduct. A GBMI defendant receives no necessary reduction in sentence—indeed, in some jurisdictions capital punishment may be imposed—nor does it guarantee treatment for the defendant that otherwise would not have been available. Thus, *unlike* GPR, it is not a mitigating (or excusing) "defense." Indeed, it is not a defense at all. In my opinion, GBMI is a useless, confusing alternative that impermissibly allows juries to avoid finding a defendant not

Any formula that expressed the central mitigating notion would work as long as it addressed the underlying, normative excusing condition, used common-sense terms, and was not tied to any limiting model of why a defendant suffered from the requisite disturbance. As studies of the insanity defense have shown, the words of the test are not crucial.[116] Juries just need some formulation roughly to guide their normative judgment.

Sentencing partially responsible defendants is a critical issue. Although such defendants may be less culpable, in many cases the defendant's impaired rationality may present a continuing, substantial danger. Ex-addicts often relapse and return to addictive lifestyles that may involve related, dangerous criminal conduct, especially if they return to the setting in which the addictive activity previously occurred. Unless a purely retributivist theory governs punishment—in which case, punishment must be strictly proportional only to desert—a sensible, legislatively mandated sentencing scheme must try to balance culpability and public safety interests. The legislature should set a fixed reduction in sentence for GPR. But however the reduction is characterized, applying it would be no different in principle from the penalty reduction from murder to manslaughter or from the sentence reduction for mitigation that a judge might order. Moreover, if the reduction were legislatively mandated, and assuming the continued importance of plea bargaining, its application would be more consistent than if it were left to pure judicial discretion. Again, any reasonable scheme would do.

This proposal would lump together defendants of disparately impaired rationality, and consequently, different responsibility. This may seem to be a denial of equal justice, but it results inevitably from the epistemological difficulties confronting more fine-grained assessments. To permit many degrees of partial excuse and corresponding degrees of punishment reduction would require juries and judges to make judgments with a precision beyond the capacity of both our moral theories and our ability to understand the necessary facts. Confusion and arbitrary decisions, rather than more justice, would follow from attempts at greater exactitude. If GPR were adopted, defendants in general would have the potential to obtain just mitigation that is not currently available for most. The failure to provide perfect justice in this imperfect world is not a decisive, or even a weighty objection in this instance.

---

guilty by reason of insanity in cases in which legal insanity appears justified. GBMI is like "Guilty But Hepatitis."

116. RITA J. SIMON & DAVID E. AARONSON, THE INSANITY DEFENSE: A CRITICAL ASSESSMENT OF LAW AND POLICY IN THE POST-HINCKLEY ERA 125–27 (1988) (demonstrating on the basis of vignette methodology that the insanity defense test used made little difference in injury verdicts); HENRY J. STEADMAN ET AL., BEFORE AND AFTER HINCKLEY: EVALUATING INSANITY DEFENSE REFORM 8, 45–62 (1993) (demonstrating using California data that the test for legal insanity made little difference in operation of the insanity defense and jury verdicts).

In sum, GPR might be the fairest way to respond to the diminished rationality claims that some addicts and others present as a partial excuse to crime. If adopted, the law might have more flexibility in responding than under the current all-or-none approach, whereby few addicts could claim complete nonresponsibility. Nothing in this scheme would prevent the law from also offering voluntary treatment, and, perhaps, from imposing treatment on addicted and partially excused criminals.

B. Drug Treatment

Successful treatment of addictive states would immensely reduce the personal and social costs of addiction. But, alas, highly effective and safe treatments are not yet generally available for most substances. The new biology, including increased understanding of genetics and neural mechanisms, has not yet led to major discoveries of successful biological interventions.[117] Given the complex genetic basis for addiction, a simple gene therapy does not seem to be an imminently foreseeable possibility. Other drugs, such as methadone or naltrexone, may help some addicts kick some addictions, but no one claims that these drugs cure the underlying pathophysiology or anatomical pathology. Better understanding of the biological mechanisms of addiction has not produced magic bullets. Even abstinence for long periods of time, with or without treatment, does not guarantee that compulsive seeking and use will not recur. If the brain disease model is right, prolonged use changes brain structure and function, but prolonged abstinence following addiction does not make the brain normal again,

---

117. *See, e.g.,* TEXTBOOK OF SUBSTANCE ABUSE TREATMENT, *supra* note 69, at Part III, *Treatment for Specific Drugs of Abuse.* This authoritative text has chapters on the treatment of all specific drugs of abuse. Successful biological treatments are rare and virtually never are sufficient by themselves. But *see* COMM. TO IDENTIFY STRATEGIES TO RAISE THE PROFILE OF SUBSTANCE ABUSE AND ALCOHOLISM RESEARCH, INSTITUTE OF MEDICINE, DISPELLING THE MYTHS ABOUT ADDICTION: STRATEGIES TO INCREASE UNDERSTANDING AND STRENGTHEN RESEARCH 73–87 (1997) (stating a more optimistic view based on recent research, but still admitting limited effectiveness and substantial knowledge gaps). Others are considerably more optimistic about the possibility of using naltrexone in a long-acting depot form to treat opioid addiction., Letter from Charles P. O'Brien, M.D., Ph.D., Department of Psychiatry, University of Pennsylvania to Stephen J. Morse (Sept. 17, 2003) (on file with the author); *see also* James W. Cornish, David Metzger, George Woody, David Wilson, A. Thomas McLellan, Barry Vandergris & Charles P. O'Brien, *Naltrexone Pharmacotherapy for Opioid Dependent Federal Probationers,* 14 J. SUBSTANCE ABUSE TREATMENT 529 (1997) (reporting a successful naltrexone treatment program in a small and nonrandom sample of federal probationers); *see generally* Charles P. O'Brien, *Anticraving Medications for Relapse Prevention a Possible New Class of Psychoactive Medications* 162 AM. J. PSYCHIATRY 1423 (2005) (reviewing anticraving treatments); Frank J. Vocci, Jane Acri & Ahmed Elkashef, *Medication Development for Addictive Disorders: The State of the Science* 162 AM. J. PSYCHIATRY 1432 (2005) (reviewing the development of pharmacotherapies for several substance abuse disorders).

or at least, not normal enough. Although the brain is famously resilient, the brain disease model implies that prolonged drug use is an apparently exceptional insult that changes the brain permanently for the worse.

Despite the basic biological advances, the most successful general treatment strategies to date have been behavioral and social, including the quasi- (and not-so-quasi-) religious regimens associated with Alcoholics Anonymous and the like.[118] Indeed, self-efficacy is the crucial variable in preventing relapse.[119] Those committed to the primarily biological model or to the currently popular "biopsychosocial" model do not deny the importance of behavioral variables and of social context and cues. Keeping the addict away from the setting in which use typically occurs is powerfully prophylactic, for example. Nonetheless, these methods, too, have limited efficacy.

We should be modest about treatment efficacy, but treatment can be helpful, and, presumably, increasingly effective biological and psychosocial treatment methods for addictions will become available. Should such treatments be offered voluntarily to addicts within the control of the criminal justice system (and to addicts not under such control) and may it be imposed on addicts who will not consent to treatment?

Assuming that resources to treat addicts are available without diminishing resources for other, more worthy goals, social justice plausibly requires that society try to help people who suffer from conditions that debilitate their own lives and are costly to the lives of others, especially if such people are imprisoned and thus entirely under the state's control.[120] Moreover, substances play such a large role in criminal behavior that it simply makes good sense to try to reduce the costs of drug- and addiction-related crime through treatment.

The more difficult question is whether the state may impose treatment, either forcibly or by coercive practices[121]. The Supreme Court has held that prisoners have a liberty interest in avoiding unwanted psychotropic drug treatment, but

---

118. *See, e.g.,* TEXTBOOK OF SUBSTANCE ABUSE TREATMENT, *supra* note 69, at 151–321 (detailing treatments for specific drugs); David Ball, *Genetic Approaches to Alcohol Dependence,* 185 BRIT. J. PSYCHIATRY 449, 450 (2004) ("Psychiatric genetics has yet to deliver on its early promise and it has not yielded any major advance in the management of people who are alcohol-dependent").

119. C. Robert Cloninger, *Genetics of Substance Abuse, in* TEXTBOOK OF SUBSTANCE ABUSE TREATMENT, *supra* note 69, at 73, 78–79.

120 This point is weakly stated as only a "plausible claim," even though it is my belief, because what social justice demands is notoriously controversial. Many might deny the premise about resources or claim that prisoners have the least strong claim in our society to limited social resources. For such people, only consequential arguments might be persuasive.

121 Richard J. Bonnie, Donna T. Chen, & Charles P. O'Brien, The Impact of Modern Neuroscience on the Treatment of Parolees: Ethical Considerations in Using Pharmacology to Prevent Addiction Relapse Cerebrum, Nov. 25, 2008, http://dana.org/news/cerebrum/

that the state may override that interest and treat prisoners involuntarily if treatment is medically warranted and necessary to insure the safety of the inmate or others in the institution.[122] Probably few addicts in prison would qualify for involuntary treatment based on substance disorder alone,[123] but could the state offer better conditions in prison or shorter prison terms to induce addicted prisoners to enter drug treatment programs? Could prisoners give informed consent to such treatment? Would such conditions violate ethical or constitutional prohibitions because they were too coercive and would coercive programs be effective even if they were ethically and legally acceptable? Many believe that such conditions are implicitly and unacceptably coercive and that informed consent is impossible in such circumstances. Therefore, unless the state has a sufficiently strong interest to override the prisoner's liberty interest in avoiding unwanted treatment, such treatment cannot be employed.

Coercion is a notoriously fraught concept. The most common account distinguishes between offers, which are thought to increase freedom and are thus not coercive, and threats, which decrease freedom and are potentially coercive.[124] The problem is to distinguish the two, which is difficult to do except against a political and moral baseline that will itself be contestable. For example, assume that a person is lying injured and helpless by the side of the road. A physician arrives, identifies himself as a doctor, and asks if he can be of assistance. The injured person asks the doctor to help. The doctor responds that he will do so for a fee. If physicians have a duty in that society to help in such circumstances without a fee, then the response is a threat; if physicians have no such duty, then the response is an offer. Many cases cannot be so neatly distinguished, however, and whether physicians should have to offer services without a fee in such case is a controversial moral and political question. Assuming that the baseline can be justified and the case can be identified as a threat, another difficult question is how serious the threat must be to be deemed unacceptably coercive. For example, assume that everyone has a right not to be touched without consent. Suppose a malefactor says that he will touch you without your permission unless you kill an innocent bystander. The case is clearly one of threat, but the situation would be insufficiently coercive to satisfy the criteria for duress that might excuse a threatened agent who does wrong in response. The criterion of "sufficient threat," although standard, is contestable and underdeterminative. Nonetheless, it can help clarify the coerciveness of drug treatment programs.

---

detail.aspx?id=13932 (discussing the ethical issues involved in voluntary, leveraged, and "no choice" treatment).

122 Washington v. Harper, 494 U.S. 210 (1990).

123. Many addicts, of course, suffer from co-morbidities, and it is possible that such treatment might be permissible based on nonaddiction disorders.

124. Wertheimer offers a particularly complete account of the various legal and philosophical approaches in addition to his own theory. See WERTHEIMER, supra note 83.

In *McKune v. Lile*, the Supreme Court was asked to determine whether the conditions accompanying a prison treatment program for sex offenders were coercive and unconstitutional.[125] The treatment program was voluntary, but it required all participants to confess without immunity to any prior uncharged sex offenses that they may have committed. Although no participant had ever been subsequently charged for an uncharged but confessed offense, it was a theoretical possibility. If a sex offender refused to participate in the program, he was subject to much harsher prison conditions than those who did participate. The Supreme Court held that the program did not violate the prisoner's Fifth Amendment rights and was not coercive.[126] Although the Court rejected a threat/ offer mode of analysis, the holding was based on the argument that the state had a right to impose the harsher conditions in the absence of a treatment program, so the situation was not coercive. Thus, it appears that the best explanation for the Court's holding is that the program was an offer, not a threat.

By analogy to *McKune*, it seems that the state can to some undetermined extent use the leverage of the criminal justice system to induce an otherwise unwilling prisoner to enter a treatment program. Indeed, the acceptance of much current mental health treatment is motivated by various forms of leverage used by the state's agents.[127] And there is no clear evidence that arguably or undeniably coercive treatment is ineffective.[128] Given the costs that addicts impose on our society, there will be strong pressure to find various inducements morally and constitutionally acceptable, especially if the treatments available are efficacious at reasonable cost in reducing drug-related criminal behavior.

C. Sensible Criminalization Policy

According to the dominant legal model of the person, the criminal law operates by providing rules and consequences for violating the rules that give potential miscreants good reasons not to offend. The model assumes that the creatures to whom these reasons are addressed are generally capable of using them as premises in practical reasoning that should in most cases lead to the conclusion that the agent should not violate the law. Of course, society is delighted if other forms of social control, such as internalized conscience and informal sanctions, also tend to limit criminal conduct.

---

125. McKune v. Lile, 536 U.S. 24 (2002).

126. *Id.*

127. John Monahan et al., *Use of Leverage to Improve Adherence to Psychiatric Treatment in the Community*, 56 PSYCH. SERV. 37, 37 (2005).

128. *See* John Monahan et al., *Mandated Community Treatment Beyond Outpatient Commitment*, 52 PSYCH. SERV. 1198,1199–1204 (2001) (citing evidence for efficacy of mandated outpatient treatment but querying whether legally mandated treatment is necessary to achieve this result).

The question for the law is whether and to what degree we should criminalize drug-related offenses committed by addicts and nonaddicts. No sensible person thinks that the criminal law is sufficient to reduce the level of criminalized harms to acceptable levels in a world of morally imperfect beings who inhabit a nonpolice state. Noncriminal justice approaches to addiction can be extremely useful, even if criminalization also can help. There is no reason to believe that our thinking about addiction must be polar, that it is only brain disease or only intentional conduct, that it is best treated only medically or psychologically or only by criminalization. Addiction-related conduct can be both a sign of brain disease and intentional action, both a proper subject for treatment and for moral judgment.

No one suggests that we should criminalize and punish the status of being an addict. Indeed, doing so would be unconstitutional.[129] Moreover, failure to criminalize recreational substance use is no guarantee of an effective social response. Two of the most addictive drugs, ethanol (alcohol) and nicotine, which cause untold personal and social harm, are entirely lawful, freely available, and relatively inexpensive. The medical model's preferred mode of response to seeking and using these lawful substances is largely unfettered by nasty criminalization, but the problems these substances cause remain grave. When people manage to quit—as many do—it is more a response to reason and self-efficacy generally than a result of medical or psychological intervention in the addicts' brains or minds.

Few people who adopt a unitary medical model suggest that production, possession, sale, and use of currently illicit drugs should be entirely decriminalized and deregulated. Criminal justice apparently plays a necessary role concerning these drug activities.[130] Seeking and using drugs are distinguishable from production, sale, and other criminal activities related to drug use. Even if one desired on "medical grounds" to decriminalize possession for personal use and such use itself, few would argue further that we should decriminalize or deregulate production, possession for sale, sale itself, or other property and personal crimes that might be part of the drug life or necessary to support addiction. Unless the authorities have some legal tool, such as the threat of criminal sanctions or enhanced punishment, to coerce users to accept treatment, many, perhaps most, will not do so willingly. Most addicts already know the other good reasons they ought to enter treatment, but many engage in denial and other defense

---

129. *See* Robinson v. California, 370 U.S. 660 (1962) (holding that criminal punishment solely for the status of being addicted is cruel and unusual and thus constitutionally impermissible under the Eighth and Fourteenth Amendments).

130. Powell v. Texas, 392 U.S. 514, 528–31(1968). For a contemporary view, see Leitzel, *supra* note 47, at 77–81 (arguing that a "robustness" approach to regulating drugs would permit substantial regulation, including the use of criminal law, but that rational consumers should have relatively free access to substances).

mechanisms that may prevent them from keeping such reasons present to their minds. Finally, given the limited success of available treatment programs, the criminal justice response may ultimately be more effective at reducing drug use than providing treatment, and indeed, may protect liberty more than a paternalistic treatment approach.[131] Indeed, some sophisticated observers believe that general decriminalization would produce catastrophic increases in addiction.[132] The important questions, of course, are what the proper role of moral evaluation and criminal justice should be and whether this role is inconsistent with sensible medical responses, such as treatment. Common sense suggests that all such approaches are not necessarily inconsistent and can be simultaneously and usefully employed.

One reform that might do much to reduce both drug-related harms and criminal justice costs would be limited decriminalization of small amounts of substances possessed solely for personal use and simple use itself, coupled with enhanced enforcement of common, further drug-related harms.[133] Consider by analogy our response to drunk driving. Adult possession and use of alcohol is not criminal, but the carnage produced by intoxicated drivers is well-understood. Prohibition would surely reduce the carnage, but, as we learned during our experiment with this approach, it produces vast harms of its own. A potentially sensible approach would more strictly enforce laws against drunk driving, which is probably the most foreseeably dangerous alcohol-related behavior. Similarly, limited decriminalization of currently illicit substances would probably not have catastrophic social effects and would almost certainly avoid the many appalling costs that our complete war on illicit substances now produces. Using produces harms primarily to oneself and might be better approached medically than legally. This regime certainly would facilitate voluntary seeking of treatment by addicts and others with drug problems.

A second promising reform would be diversion from the criminal justice system of minor drug-related offenders coupled with treatment in cases in

---

131. *Id*. Writing for the plurality, Justice Marshall wrote that there might be deterrent and civil liberties virtues to using the criminal justice system to respond to the behavioral consequences of alcoholism *Id*. We have learned a great deal about the causes and consequences of alcoholism since this 1968 opinion, but the reasoning is still applicable.

132. See James Q. Wilson, *What to Do About Crime*, 98 COMMENT. 25 (1994).

133. Proposing any form of decriminalization of currently illicit substances raises enormously complicated and extremely controversial issues. For the purposes of this chapter, however, the full argument cannot be produced. I can only gesture superficially and conclusorily at the recommended approach. For a balanced, data-driven analysis of the costs and benefits of decriminalization, *see* LEITZEL, supra note 47, at 102–28, 134–37; ROBERT J. MACCOUN & PETER REUTER, DRUG WAR HERESIES: LEARNING FROM OTHER VICES, TIMES, & PLACES (2001). *See also* Douglas Husak, OVERCRIMINALIZATION (2007) & LEGALIZE THIS: THE CASE FOR DECRIMINALIZING DRUGS (2002); FRANKLIN E. ZIMRING & GORDON HAWKINS, THE SEARCH FOR RATIONAL DRUG CONTROL (1992).

which treatment seems likely to be successful.[134] The drug courts that have been established in many states are one attempt to provide such diversion and treatment.[135] This approach is controversial for many of the reasons that involuntary treatment generally raises questions, but avoiding the necessity of costly imprisonment and inducing treatment for minor offenders engaged in drug-related criminal activities are potentially cost-effective, especially if more effective and safe treatment modalities become available.

Limited decriminalization has much to recommend it as a solution to drug-related problems. Nevertheless, in the current climate of opinion concerning controlled substances, it seems very unlikely that Congress, whose power over drug regulation is near absolute,[136] will move toward any form of decriminalization.

X. CONCLUSION

Despite the exciting, undoubted advances in the biological understanding of addiction, and despite the plausibility of considering addictions diseases, the disease model does not and cannot fully explain addiction or inform social and legal policy concerning addiction. Addiction inevitably involves human action and is therefore subject to moral evaluation. Although addiction might cause a condition warranting mitigation or excuse, primarily by compromising rationality, there is good reason to believe that most addicts are responsible for seeking-and-using behavior and for other immoral or criminal activity related to addiction. For those who may not be fully responsible, however, modification of the existing doctrines of mitigation and excuse would be necessary to respond fairly to the claims of diminished responsibility addicts might present. Finally, although the criminal justice system might play a useful role in responding to addiction-related action, noncriminal, nonjudgmental interventions also should play a substantial role. The criminal justice system response should be limited and reformed to enhance the potential efficacy of treatment approaches.

---

134. Douglas Longshore, Angela Hawken, Darren Urada, & M. Douglas Anglin, SAPCA Cost Analysis Report (First and Second Years), available at http://www.uclaisap. org/prop36/documents/ SACPA_COSTANALYSIS.pdf at 21–23 (2006) (studying the costs and benefits of a legislatively-mandated diversion program that offered probation and treatment to nonviolent drug offenders found that incarceration costs were substantially reduced, that there were greater cost savings for some eligible offenders than for others, and that the program could be improved). *See also, Bonnie, Chen & O'Brien, supra* note 121.

135. *See generally* DRUG COURTS: IN THEORY AND IN PRACTICE (James L. Nolan, Jr. ed., 2002).

136. *See* Gonzales v. Raich, 125 S. Cf. 2195 (2005) (holding that Congress's Commerce Clause authority includes the power to prohibit local cultivation and use of marijuana for medical purposes that is in compliance with state law).

PART FOUR

IMPLICATIONS FOR CRIMINAL JUSTICE AND SOCIETY

9. GENOMICS, BEHAVIOR, AND TESTIMONY AT CRIMINAL TRIALS

WILLIAM BERNET AND ANAS ALKHATIB

The remarkable advances in the scientific study of human inheritance have created opportunities that are both fascinating and frightening. Since 1940, this cascade of genetic and genomic research has discovered the chemical in the nucleus that conveys genetic information (deoxyribonucleic acid [DNA]) (1944); the three-dimensional structure of DNA (1953); the correct count for human chromosomes (46) (1956); the genetic code by which messenger ribonucleic acid (mRNA) is the template for amino acids (1966); specific genes that cause specific diseases, for example, Huntington's disease (1983); "DNA fingerprinting" and its forensic applications (1989); and the sequence of our genes through the Human Genome Project (2003).

While genetic and genomic research typically originated among basic scientists—such as biochemists, cellular biologists, and, more recently, molecular biologists—there were immediate applications in almost every aspect of life, from agriculture to the cloning of animals to every branch of medicine to the identification of criminals. Psychiatrists and psychologists have been eager to use genetic paradigms in studying and understanding human behavior. As early as the eighteenth century, physicians thought that criminal and violent behaviors were caused partly by one's family background ("nature"), partly by unfortunate life experiences ("nurture"), and partly by malicious intentions, or free will. Mental health professionals in the twenty-first century have been able to apply modern methods to the study of behavioral genomics, and discoveries in this area will quickly find their way into court.

This chapter describes how testimony regarding behavioral genomics is currently used in legal settings and how it may be used in the future. The focus of this chapter is on three ways in which a specific individual's genetic makeup may be relevant to his or her behavior: First, the person's genotype may exactly designate a psychiatric or medical diagnosis that clearly explains the person's abnormal behavior. An example is Huntington's disease, an autosomal dominant neurodegenerative disorder that causes psychosis, dementia, and sometimes violence. In this circumstance, the genotype determines the diagnosis, and there is a distinct causal relationship between the genotype and the behavior. Second, the person's genotype may support a psychiatric diagnosis that has been made on clinical grounds. For example, a person who is homozygous for the short allele of the *SLC6A4* gene is more likely to become depressed and suicidal after stressful situations than a person who is homozygous for the long allele of that gene. If a person has this genotype and stressful life experiences, it would support the contention that the person had a predisposition to a major depressive disorder and suicidality at the time of the alleged offense. In this circumstance, the genotype does not *make* the diagnosis of severe depression, but it *supports* the diagnosis that was made on clinical grounds. Third, the person's genotype may help to explain his or her violent or criminal behavior. For example, a man who has the low-activity allele of the *MAOA* gene and who experienced serious child maltreatment is more likely to manifest violent and antisocial behavior as an adult than is a man who has the high-activity allele of this gene. In this circumstance, the genotype does not make a specific diagnosis or support a specific diagnosis, but it does help to explain that a particular person may have a predisposition to maladaptive behaviors.

There are several aspects of forensic genetics and behavioral genomics that this chapter does not address at all. It is obvious, for instance, that courts already fully and happily accept the science of forensic genetics and genotyping to establish whether a rape occurred and who did it, to clarify who was and was not present at a crime scene, and to prove paternity. This chapter does not discuss these topics at all.

Likewise, this chapter does not review the many missteps that occurred during the last century and a half with regard to behavioral genetics. By way of praeteritio, this chapter does not discuss the following: the theory of Lombroso, inspired by the evolutionary theories of Darwin, that some criminals were throwbacks to a primitive or subhuman type of person with distinct physical stigmata and characteristics reminiscent of apes and lower primates[1]; the trial of Charles Guiteau and the debate over the hereditary origin of moral insanity[2]; the notorious opinion by Justice Oliver Wendell Holmes in 1927 that an allegedly retarded woman, Carrie Buck, should be subjected to forcible sterilization because "three generations of imbeciles are enough"[3]; the use of genetics to justify the ethnic cleansing practiced by the Nazi regime in the 1930s and 1940s[4]; Sheldon's theory that a mesomorphic

1. CESARE LOMBROSO, L'UOMO DELINQUENTE (Fratelli Bocca, 1876); Marvin E. Wolfgang, *Pioneers in Criminology: Cesare Lombroso* (1835–1909), 52 J CRIM LAW CRIMINOL POLICE SCIENCE 361 (1961).

2. H. H. ALEXANDER, THE LIFE OF GUITEAU AND THE OFFICIAL HISTORY OF THE MOST EXCITING CASE ON RECORD: BEING THE TRIAL OF GUITEAU FOR ASSASSINATING PRES. GARFIELD (N. G. Hamilton, 1882); CHARLES E. ROSENBERG, THE TRIAL OF THE ASSASSIN GUITEAU: PSYCHIATRY AND LAW IN THE GUILDED AGE (1968).

3. Buck v. Bell, 274 U.S. 200 (1927).

4. ROBERT PROCTOR, RACIAL HYGIENE: MEDICINE UNDER THE NAZIS (Harvard University Press, 1988); UNITED STATES HOLOCAUST MEMORIAL MUSEUM, DEADLY MEDICINE: CREATING THE MASTER RACE (United States Holocaust Memorial Museum, 2004).

body type was predictive of criminal behavior[5]; the idea that men with an XYY genotype were predisposed to violence[6]; the proposal that a defendant should be tested for a very rare particular point mutation of the *MAOA* gene as part of his defense in a murder trial[7]; or the practice of testing the cerebrospinal fluid (CSF) of defendants for a metabolite of serotonin (5-hydroxyindoleacetic acid or 5-HIAA) because a low level of CSF 5-HIAA was associated with violence and suicide[8].

GENOTYPE DESIGNATES THE DIAGNOSIS

In some circumstances, the introduction of genetic information at a trial is easy to understand and readily fulfills *Daubert* and *Frye* criteria for reliability and acceptance in the professional community. That is the case when the genetic information is used to show that a specific individual has a specific genetic disorder. This section describes two genetic disorders—Down syndrome and Huntington's disease—that may arise in a legal context. There are highly specific and reliable methods for genotyping individuals who may have these conditions. Of course, simply having a diagnosis is usually not sufficient all by itself to justify a legal conclusion. In addition, it is necessary to show that the defendant's mental functioning or behavior was impaired to a significant degree. The nature and required extent of impairment depends on the legal issue being addressed— which might be competency to stand trial, the insanity defense, diminished capacity, or mitigation.

Most genetic disorders that directly cause cognitive and behavioral symptoms— such as mental retardation and violence—are identified in childhood. For example, Down syndrome occurs when a mutation of maternal or paternal origin causes a chromosomal abnormality—that is, the child has three copies of chromosome 21 instead of two.[9] Down syndrome occurs in about one out of eight hundred

---

5. WILLIAM H. SHELDON, EMIL M. HARTL, & EUGENE MCDERMOTT, VARIETIES OF DELINQUENT YOUTH: AN INTRODUCTION TO CONSTITUTIONAL PSYCHIATRY (1949).

6. H. A. Witkin, S. A. Mednick, F. Schulsinger, E. Bakkestrom, K. O. Christiansen, D. R. Goodenough et al., *Criminality in XYY and XXY men*, 193 SCIENCE 547 (1976); M. J. Gotz, E. C. Johnstone, & S. G. Ratcliffe, *Criminality and Antisocial Behaviour in Unselected Men with Sex Chromosome Abnormalities*, 29 PSYCHOL. MED. 953 (1999).

7. Mobley v. State, 455 S.E.2d 61 (Ga. Sup. Ct. 1995).

8. State v. Payne, 2002 WL 31624813 (Tenn. Crim. App. 2002); State v. Godsey, 2001 WL 1543474 (Tenn. Crim. App. 2001); State v. Sanders, 2000 WL 1006574 (Ohio App. 2 Dist. 2000); Paul Rossby, *The Biology of Violence: Serotonin, Alcoholism, Hypoglycemia*, 17 CRIM. JUST. 20 (2007).

9. G. Howells, *Down's Syndrome and the General Practitioner*, 39 J. R. COLL. GEN. PRACT. 470 (1989); Bryan H. King et al. *Mental Retardation, in* COMPREHENSIVE TEXTBOOK OF PSYCHIATRY 3076–106 (Benjamin. J. Sadock & Virginia A. Sadock eds., 8th ed., Williams & Wilkins, 2005).

live births. Individuals with Down syndrome may be severely retarded and may commit a criminal offense out of ignorance or naïveté. These individuals may also become irritable and frustrated and commit a violent act. Persons with Down syndrome have a serious mental defect that affects their ability to appreciate the wrongfulness of their behavior, and they may lack the mental capacity to participate in legal procedures because of their mental retardation. For example, they may not be competent to stand trial or testify as witnesses at a trial, as illustrated by the following example.

The case of *Commonwealth v. Louis Santos*[10] involved a man with Down syndrome, Charles Bartick, who witnessed a robbery. Mr. Bartick's testimony regarding the robbery was important because the perpetrators of the robbery committed a murder several minutes later. Mr. Bartick was described as moderately retarded because of Down syndrome. Mr. Bartick made a stationhouse identification of Louis Santos as one of the robbers, which was accepted by the trial court. On appeal, however, the Supreme Judicial Court of Massachusetts said that the identification procedure was unconstitutionally suggestive and that the witness, Mr. Bartick, was overly suggestible. Also, the trial court denied the defense counsel's motion that Mr. Bartick be examined for competency. On appeal, the Supreme Judicial Court said that the trial court should have ordered a competency evaluation. Because of these errors and for other reasons, the Supreme Judicial Court reversed the conviction of Mr. Santos and remanded the case for a new trial.

In this case, the fact that Charles Bartick had Down syndrome was important, but not determinative. What was determinative was that this witness had specific impairments such as cognitive limitations and high suggestibility. This is almost always the case when psychiatric testimony is introduced at criminal trials. Thus, establishing the correct diagnosis may be important, but the most important proof relates to the person's functional ability. Having a particular diagnosis in itself does not mean that a person is not competent or is insane, but it does explain why a person has specific impairments.

Some individuals are born with a genetic disorder, but the diagnosis is not made until adulthood. It may be that the person's genetic condition is first manifested by some form of aberrant behavior, which leads to his arrest. In this set of circumstances, it is possible for the mental health professional who conducts the pretrial forensic evaluation to be the first person to accurately diagnose the person's medical and psychiatric condition. Huntington's disease, which was previously called Huntington's chorea, is the classic example of an adult-onset genetic disorder that causes psychiatric and behavioral symptoms. The diagnosis of Huntington's disease—based on the defendant's genotype—may have a bearing on the outcome of a criminal case.

---

10. Commonwealth v. Santos, 402 Mass. 775 (Sup. Jud. Ct. Mass. 1988).

George Huntington's original paper[11] in 1872 described "hereditary chorea" in this manner: "There are three marked peculiarities in this disease: 1. Its hereditary nature. 2. A tendency to insanity and suicide. 3. Its manifesting itself as a grave disease only in adult life."[12] The psychiatric and behavioral symptoms of Huntington's disease may not appear until the person is in his forties or fifties. According to Huntington, "As the disease progresses the mind becomes more or less impaired, in many amounting to insanity, while in others mind and body both gradually fail until death relieves them of their sufferings."[13] Huntington was only 21 years old when the paper was published, which was based on the case files of his father and grandfather who practiced medicine in East Hampton, Long Island.

In 1983, Gusella et al.[14] studied two large families—one in the United States and one in Venezuela—that included individuals with Huntington's disease. They were able to determine that the genetic locus for Huntington's disease was on chromosome 4. In 1993, the Huntington's Disease Collaborative Research Group[15] found that the genetic etiology of Huntington's disease was a type of mutation called a repeat expansion—that is, the genetic abnormality is that a specific sequence of three nucleotides (cytosine, adenine, and guanine, or CAG) repeats multiple times at a particular locus on chromosome 4. Since the nucleotide sequence CAG encodes for the amino acid glutamine, the body produces proteins with very long stretches of residues of glutamine, which is a neurotoxin. When a person with Huntington's disease has a child, the child tends to have a longer series of repeats than the parent, which means that the child's onset of symptoms is earlier than was the onset in the parent. For instance, if the parent first manifested symptoms in his forties, the child might manifest symptoms in his thirties. In fact, the parent may die from some other cause before he or she ever manifests symptoms of Huntington's disease. For this and other reasons, it is fairly common for a person to have no awareness of his family history of Huntington's disease and then to develop this illness.

The case of *Commonwealth v. Bobby Gene Parker* illustrates how testimony regarding a specific genetic condition in a specific person may be very helpful in determining the outcome of a criminal proceeding. In early 2001, when he was

---

11. George Huntington, *On Chorea*, 26 THE MEDICAL AND SURGICAL REPORTER: A WEEKLY JOURNAL 317 (1872).

12. *Id.* at 320.

13. *Id.*

14. J. F. Gusella, N. S. Wexler, P. M. Conneally, S. L. Naylor, M. A. Anderson, R. E. Tanzi et al., *A Polymorphic DNA Marker Genetically Linked to Huntington's Disease,* 306 NATURE 234 (1983).

15. Huntington's Disease Collaborative Research Group, *A Novel Gene Containing a Trinucleotide Repeat That Is Expanded and Unstable on Huntington's Disease Chromosomes. The Huntington's Disease Collaborative Research Group,* 72 CELL 971 (1993).

61 years old, Mr. Parker was found to have Huntington's disease. He had uncontrollable movements in his face, legs, and feet, and cognitive impairment in concentration and memory. Mr. Parker manifested a variety of psychiatric and behavioral symptoms: physical violence toward both people and property; threatening state police with a gun; delusions regarding his wife; and squandering the family's assets. In January 2003, Mr. Parker allegedly arranged for another person to burn down the family farm in a rural area of Kentucky. He reportedly stated various motives at different times to different people: he wanted to collect the insurance on the house; he thought his wife was having an affair with the sheriff; he thought the fire would bring his wife closer to him. The forensic psychiatrist thought Mr. Parker met the criteria for the insanity defense because he had a severe mental disease that caused him to lack substantial capacity to conform his conduct to the requirements of the law. The defense attorney presented the forensic psychiatric evaluation to the district attorney, and the charges against Mr. Parker were dismissed.

There are many other genetic or chromosomal disorders that may be manifested by psychological or behavioral symptoms. Fragile X syndrome, the most common form of heritable mental retardation, is caused by unstable expansions of CGG trinucleotide repeats located on the long arm of the X chromosome. Individuals with this syndrome may have a variety of physical features (long, narrow face; large ears; prominent jaw); a range of mental retardation from moderate to severe); and behavior problems (such as autistic features, attention problems, and sometimes externalizing behaviors).[16] Prader-Willi syndrome is a genetic disorder characterized by obesity, short stature, and learning disabilities, but also by psychiatric conditions such as temper tantrums, depressive psychosis, bipolar disorder, and obsessional traits[17]. Wilson's disease is a genetic disorder of copper metabolism that affects the liver, kidney, eyes (the Kayser-Fleischer ring, a yellow-brown discoloration of the limbic area of the cornea), and the central nervous system.[18] Many patients with Wilson's disease have prominent

---

16. B. B. de Vries, D. J. Halley, B. A. Oostra, & M. F. Niermeijer, *The Fragile X Syndrome*, 35 J. MED. GENET. 579 (1998); S. Eliez & A. L. Reiss, *Genetics of Childhood Disorders: XI. Fragile X Syndrome*, 39 J. AM. ACAD. CHILD ADOLESC. PSYCHIATRY 264 (2000); D. D. Hatton, S. R. Hooper, D. B. Bailey, M. L. Skinner, K. M. Sullivan, & A. Wheeler, *Problem Behavior in Boys with Fragile X Syndrome*, 108 AM. J. MED. GENET. 105 (2002).

17. A. J. Holland, J. E. Whittington, J. Butler, T. Webb, H. Boer, & D. Clarke, *Behavioural Phenotypes Associated with Specific Genetic Disorders: Evidence from a Population-Based Study of People with Prader-Willi Syndrome*, 33 PSYCHOL. MED. 141 (2003); A. Vogels, Hert M. De, M. J. Descheemaeker, V. Govers, K. Devriendt, E. Legius, et al., *Psychotic Disorders in Prader-Willi Syndrome*, 127 AM. J. MED. GENET. A 238 (2004); S. Soni, J. Whittington, A. J. Holland, T. Webb, E. Maina, H. Boer et al., *The Course and Outcome of Psychiatric Illness in People with Prader-Willi Syndrome: Implications for Management and Treatment*, 51 J. INTELLECT. DISABIL. RES. 32 (2007).

18. M. El-Youssef, *Wilson Disease*, 78 MAYO CLIN. PROC. 1126 (2003).

psychiatric symptoms such as depression, compulsions, and antisocial behavior.[19] Velo-cardio-facial syndrome is a genetic disorder—caused by a deletion on the long arm of chromosome 22—characterized by multiple congenital abnormalities including cleft palate and cardiac malformations. A high proportion of individuals with velo-cardio-facial syndrome have psychiatric disorders, primarily schizophrenia.[20]

After it was shown that a person's genetic makeup was the cause of specific psychiatric and neurologic disorders such as Huntington's disease and Wilson's disease, researchers were enthusiastic about identifying specific genes that cause other psychiatric conditions. However, it soon became clear that the inheritance of most psychiatric disorders—including schizophrenia and bipolar disorder—was not mediated by single genes. Investigators proposed more complex genomic models such as interaction among several genes; interaction among genes and epigenetic and other intracellular factors; and interaction among genes and the environment.

The interaction between genetic and environmental factors has been called G×E interaction. In the future, it will be common for forensic psychiatrists to evaluate defendants in terms of G×E interactions and to testify regarding their findings in criminal trials. As explained in the following sections of this chapter, a G×E interaction may support the diagnosis that has been made on clinical grounds and may help explain the defendant's behavior.

G×E INTERACTION AS SUPPORT FOR DIAGNOSIS

In some criminal trials, there is a dispute over whether the defendant had a specific mental illness or perhaps any mental illness at the time of the alleged offense. For instance, the defense may assert that the defendant had major depressive disorder, severe, with psychotic features, and that was why he killed his baby. The prosecution may claim the defendant did not have a significant mental illness at all but simply pretended to have severe depression and command hallucinations after his arrest in order to avoid responsibility for the baby's death. In this circumstance, the forensic psychiatrist may want to evaluate the defendant for a particular G×E interaction because this finding may support the diagnosis of major depressive disorder. The possibility of a G×E interaction does

19. G. J. Brewer, *Behavioral Abnormalities in Wilson's Disease*, 96 ADV. NEUROL. 262 (2005).

20. K. C. Murphy, *Schizophrenia and Velo-Cardio-Facial Syndrome*, 359 LANCET 426 (2002); K. C. Murphy, *The Behavioural Phenotype in Velo-Cardio-Facial Syndrome*, 48 J. INTELLECT. DISABIL. RES. 524 (2004); R. J. Shprintzen, A. M. Higgins, K. Antshel, W. Fremont, N. Roizen, & W. Kates, *Velo-Cardio-Facial Syndrome*, 17 CURR. OPIN. PEDIATR. 725 (2005).

not prove the diagnosis in the way genotyping proves the diagnosis of Huntington's disease, but it may support the diagnosis of major depressive disorder that has been made through a traditional forensic psychiatric evaluation.

Since the early twentieth century, G×E interactions have been described in nature and in several fields of medicine. Ronald A. Fisher, a famous statistician and one of the fathers of population genetics, developed mathematical models for characterizing the interaction of inheritance and environment.[21] Lancelot Hogben, an early geneticist, described a genetic and environmental interaction in *Drosophila*.[22] The history of the concept of G×E interaction was recently related by Tabery.[23]

Avshalom Caspi and his colleagues were the first to demonstrate a psychiatrically relevant G×E interaction.[24] In one of their studies, the genetic factor was the polymorphism of the serotonin transporter gene, which is referred to as *5-HTT* or *SLC6A4*. The environmental factor was severe psychosocial stressors. Caspi et al. addressed "why stressful experiences lead to depression in some people but not in others."[25] The New Zealand subjects in this study were members of the Dunedin Multidisciplinary Health and Development Study. The authors found that a particular allele of the serotonin transporter gene appeared to protect individuals from the harmful biopsychosocial impact of multiple stressors.

The transporter is the cell membrane structure that recycles synaptic serotonin (5-hydroxytryptamine or 5-HT) for repackaging and subsequent re-release. The *SLC6A4* or serotonin transporter gene is located on chromosome 17. The *SLC6A4* gene can have either a "long allele" or a "short allele." The short allele of the *SLC6A4* gene causes low activity of the transporter system, which means that once in the synapse, serotonin remains there longer and ultimately that less serotonin appears to be available for reuse. For people with the short allele, the serotonin system is not working efficiently. In Caspi et al., 17 percent of the subjects had two copies of the short allele (S/S homozygotes), 31 percent had two copies of the long allele (L/L homozygotes), and 51 percent had one copy of each allele (S/L heterozygotes).

Caspi et al. characterized the subjects as to whether they had had stressful life events after their 21st birthday and prior to their 26th birthday. For example, they asked about stressful life events related to employment, finances, housing,

---

21. Ronald A. Fisher, Statistical Methods for Research Workers (1925).

22. Lancelot Hogben, Nature And Nurture, Being the William Withering Memorial Lectures (George Allen and Unwin, Ltd., 1933).

23. J. Tabery, *Biometric and Developmental Gene-Environment Interactions: Looking Back, Moving Forward*, 19 Dev. Psychopathol 961 (2007).

24. A. Caspi, K. Sugden, T. E. Moffitt, A. Taylor, I. W. Craig, H. Harrington et al., *Influence of Life Stress on Depression: Moderation by a Polymorphism in the 5-HTT Gene*, 301 Science 386 (2003).

25. *Id.* at 386.

health, and relationships. They found the following frequency of stressful life events: no stressful life events, 30 percent of the sample; one event, 25 percent of the sample; two events, 20 percent of the sample; three events, 11 percent of the sample; and four or more events, 15 percent of the sample. Starting at about age 26, the subjects were characterized as to whether they had symptoms of serious depression. They found that 17 percent of study members met criteria for a past-year major depressive episode, and 3 percent of study members reported past-year suicide attempt or recurrent suicidal ideation. The authors showed that individuals with the short allele of the 5-HTT were more susceptible to stress. Specifically, people with one or two copies of the short allele "exhibited more depressive symptoms, diagnosable depression, and suicidality in relation to stressful life events"[26] than did individuals with two long alleles.

For this research to be usable in expert testimony in the U.S. legal system, it must be replicated. Thus far, Caspi et al. has been replicated by several other research teams, which used varying definitions of psychosocial stressors, psychological distress, and genetic risk. They used a variety of study designs. For example, Wilhelm et al.[27] studied 127 males and females in Australia who had been followed prospectively for 25 years, from about age 23 to about age 48. The cohort was assessed every five years, when the authors recorded episodes of major depression and anxiety disorders and also a range of both positive and negative life events. They said, "An interaction between the [serotonin transporter gene polymorphism] and adverse life events was found to significantly predict the onset of major depression for the 5 years before depression onset. Specifically, the influence of adverse life events on the onset of major depression was significantly greater for individuals with the s/s genotype."[28] Of all the studies of the serotonin transporter gene × environment interaction, the Wilhelm et al. research design collected the most accurate and thorough information regarding the life histories of psychiatric disorders and adverse events.

Table 9.1 contains a list of published studies that either replicated or failed to replicate Caspi et al. Research regarding the *SLC6A4* polymorphism, stressful life events, depression, and neuroimaging studies was summarized by Wurtman,[29] Zammit and Owen,[30] and Bernet et al.[31]

---

26. *Id.* at 386.

27. K. Wilhelm, P. B. Mitchell, H. Niven, A. Finch, L. Wedgwood, A. Scimone et al., *Life Events, First Depression Onset and the Serotonin Transporter Gene*, 188 Br. J. Psychiatry 210 (2006).

28. *Id.* at 211.

29. R. J. Wurtman, *Genes, Stress, and Depression*, 54 Metabolism 16 (2005).

30. S. Zammit & M. J. Owen, *Stressful Life Events, 5-HTT Genotype and Risk of Depression*, 188 Br. J. Psychiatry 199 (2006).

31. W. Bernet, C. L. Vnencak-Jones, N. Farahany, & S. A. Montgomery, *Bad Nature, Bad Nurture, and Testimony Regarding* MAOA *and* SLC6A4 *Genotyping at Criminal Trials*, 52 J. Forensic Sci. 1362 (2007).

TABLE 9.1. REPLICATIONS OF CASPI ET AL. (2003)

Study	Sample Composition, Location	Sample Size, Gender, Age
Caspi et al.[1]	Community birth cohort, New Zealand	847 males and females, age 26
Eley et al.[2]	Nonclinical adolescents, United Kingdom	157 males, 220 females, age 12–19
Grabe et al.[3]	Nonclinical adults, Germany	302 males, 674 females, mean age 52
Kaufman et al.[4]	Children in state custody and community controls, United States	57 subjects, 44 controls, males and females, age 5–15
Kendler et al.[5]	Twin registry, United States	549 males and females, mean age 35
Sjöberg et al.[6]	Nonclinical adolescents, Sweden	66 males, 114 females, age 19–22
Wilhelm et al.[7]	Nonclinical adults, Australia	127 males and females, mean age 48
Zalsman et al.[8]	Depressed patients and controls, United States	191 subjects, 125 controls, males and females, mean age 38

NONREPLICATIONS OF CASPI ET AL. (2003)

Study	Sample Composition, Location	Sample Size, Gender, Age
Gillespie et al.[9]	Twin registry, Australia	1091 males and females, mean age 39
Surtees et al.[10]	Nonclinical adults, United Kingdom	4175 males and females, age 41–80

[1] A. Caspi, K. Sugden, T. E. Moffitt, A. Taylor, I. W. Craig, H. Harrington, et al., *Influence of Life Stress on Depression: Moderation by a Polymorphism in the 5-HTT Gene*, 301 SCIENCE 386 (2003).

[2] T. C. Eley, K. Sugden, A. Corsico, A. M. Gregory, P. Sham, P. McGuffin, et al., *Gene-Environment Interaction Analysis of Serotonin System Markers with Adolescent Depression*, 9 MOL. PSYCHIATRY 908 (2004).

[3] H. J. Grabe, M. Lange, B. Wolff, H. Volzke, M. Lucht, H. J. Freyberger, et al., *Mental and Physical Distress is Modulated by a Polymorphism in the 5-HT Transporter Gene Interacting with Social Stressors and Chronic Disease Burden*, 10 MOL. PSYCHIATRY 220 (2005).

[4] J. Kaufman, B. Z. Yang, H. Douglas-Palumberi, S. Houshyar, D. Lipschitz, J. H. Krystal, et al., *Social Supports and Serotonin Transporter Gene Moderate Depression in Maltreated Children*, 101 PROC. NATL. ACAD. SCI. U.S.A. 17316 (2004).

[5] K. S. Kendler, J. W. Kuhn, J. Vittum, C. A. Prescott, & B. Riley, *The Interaction of Stressful Life Events and a Serotonin Transporter Polymorphism in the Prediction of Episodes of Major Depression: A Replication*, 62 ARCH. GEN. PSYCHIATRY 529 (2005).

(continued)

[6] R. L. Sjöberg, K. W. Nilsson, N. Nordquist, J. Ohrvik, J. Leppert, L. Lindstrom, et al., *Development of Depression: Sex and the Interaction Between Environment and a Promoter Polymorphism of the Serotonin Transporter Gene*, 9 INT. J. NEUROPSYCHOPHARMACOL. 443 (2006).

[7] K. Wilhelm, P. B. Mitchell, H. Niven, A. Finch, L. Wedgwood, A. Scimone, et al., *Life Events, First Depression Onset and the Serotonin Transporter Gene*, 188 BR. J. PSYCHIATRY 210 (2006)

[8] G. Zalsman, Y. Huang, M. A. Oquendo, A. K. Burke, X. Hu, D. A. Brent, S. P. Ellis, D. Goldman, J. J. Mann, *Association of a Triallelic Serotonin Transporter Gene Promoter Region (5-HTTLPR) Polymorphism with Stress Life Events and Severity of Depression*, 163 AM. J. PSYCHIATRY 1588 (2006),

[9] N. A. Gillespie, J. B. Whitfield, B. Williams, A. C. Heath, & N. G. Martin, *The Relationship Between Stressful Life Events, The Serotonin Transporter (5-HTTLPR) Genotype and Major Depression*, 35 PSYCHOL. MED. 101 (2005).

[10] P. G. Surtees, N. W. Wainwright, S. A. Willis-Owen, R. Luben, N. E. Day, & J. Flint, *Social Adversity, The Serotonin Transporter (5-HTTLPR) Polymorphism and Major Depressive Disorder*, 59 BIOL. PSYCHIATRY 224 (2006).

The following case, *State of Tennessee v. Jason Clinard*, illustrates how an investigation of possible G×E interactions might be appropriate to introduce at a criminal trial. The G×E data does not prove that a person has a particular diagnosis, but it may support the diagnosis that has been made through a traditional forensic psychiatric evaluation.

Jason was a 14-year-old, ninth-grade student who experienced an unusual number and intensity of psychosocial stressors. He became seriously depressed and suicidal. One morning in March 2005, Jason woke up and thought about committing suicide that day. Jason obtained a handgun from his father's gun cabinet and loaded it. When it was time to go to school, Jason approached the school bus and fatally shot the bus driver. Immediately after his arrest, Jason was admitted to a state psychiatric hospital for a forensic evaluation. The mental health professionals who evaluated Jason on the same day as the offense said his diagnosis was major depressive disorder, severe, with psychotic features.

As part of a comprehensive, pretrial, forensic psychiatric evaluation, Jason had genetic testing. He was homozygous, S/S, for the *SLC6A4* gene. A juvenile, Jason was transferred to criminal court. At the trial, a forensic psychiatrist testified for the defense and explained the significance of the *SLC6A4* genotyping (i.e., that Jason had a genetic vulnerability to become depressed and suicidal under severe stress). The expert testified that the following factors were all present in Jason's case: he had experienced a large number of severe psychosocial stressors; he had the genetic vulnerability to become depressed under these conditions; and he, in fact, became severely depressed and was given that diagnosis when evaluated on the day of the offense.

The genetic testing supported the testimony that Jason had a serious mental disorder at the time of the alleged offense. The defense attorney's argument was that the jury should consider this information when deciding whether Jason committed first-degree murder (requiring premeditation, i.e., the exercise of reflection and judgment) or second-degree murder. The prosecution did not object to the presentation of mental disorder evidence. However, the testimony did not appear to benefit Jason; the jury found him guilty of first-degree murder.

In this use of forensic genotyping, the defendant's genetic makeup did not prove the diagnosis, but his being homozygotic for the short allele of the *SLC6A4* gene was consistent with and supported the diagnosis of major depressive disorder. Basically, the diagnosis of major depressive disorder was made on clinical grounds—that is, based on a detailed history, the clinical interview, and psychological testing. Testimony regarding the GxE interaction (the S/S genotype of the *SLC6A4* gene and the multiple psychosocial stressors) was intended to explain why Jason had severe depression and to counter the implication that Jason was malingering.

Studying GxE interactions with behavioral and psychiatric implications is trendy, and we have simply crossed the threshold into a world of research that will flourish in coming years. We predict there will be many GxE interactions that will be highly correlated with major depressive disorder, bipolar disorder, schizophrenia, posttraumatic stress disorder, obsessive-compulsive disorder, panic disorder, substance abuse, and violent sexual predation. These interactions will usually not prove that a person has a particular diagnosis, but they will support and explain the diagnosis that has been made through traditional evaluation methods. Also, if the defendant is suspected of malingering, an investigation of the person's genetic makeup and relevant life experience may be used to support the claim that he or she actually has a serious mental disorder.

GxE INTERACTION AS AN EXPLANATION OF BEHAVIOR

This chapter is moving from very specific applications of genetic data to rather general applications of this type of information. We started with cases in which a specific genotype essentially proves that a person has a specific mental disorder; the example was Huntington's disease. We moved on to situations in which a specific GxE interaction may support a particular diagnosis—that is, the interaction of the S/S genotype of the *SLC6A4* gene and multiple life stressors predisposing a person to depression and suicidality. We now proceed to situations in which a specific GxE interaction merely helps to explain why a person had a particular behavior. The concept is that these genetic and environmental factors may interact and, later in life, predispose a person to have antisocial, violent behavior.

Avshalom Caspi and his colleagues also studied this type of G×E interaction. In Caspi et al.[32], the genetic factor was the monoamine oxidase A gene (*MAOA*), and the environmental factor was severe childhood abuse. The researchers "studied a large sample of male children from birth to adulthood to determine why some children who are maltreated grow up to develop antisocial behavior, whereas others do not."[33] These subjects were also members of the Dunedin Multidisciplinary Health and Development Study.

In selecting the *MAOA* gene, the Caspi team knew that both humans and mice that lacked the gene altogether (*MAOA* "knock-outs") became violent and aggressive, respectively. The *MAOA* gene is located on the X chromosome (Xp11.23-11.4). This gene encodes the MAOA enzyme, which metabolizes neurotransmitters such as serotonin, norepinephrine, and dopamine. There are two alleles of the *MAOA* gene: one results in high activity of the MAOA enzyme; the other results in low activity of the MAOA enzyme. Since this gene is on the X chromosome, a male has only one allele, either the high-activity *MAOA* or the low-activity *MAOA* allele. A male with the low-activity *MAOA* allele will not metabolize serotonin, norepinephrine, and dopamine in an efficient manner. In the Caspi et al. study, about 37 percent of the males had low activity of the MAOA enzyme.

When they characterized the subjects regarding childhood maltreatment, Caspi et al. found that 8 percent of the children had suffered "severe" maltreatment between ages 3 and 11; 28 percent of the children suffered "probable" maltreatment; and 64 percent experienced no maltreatment. Regarding the G×E interaction, these researchers found that when male subjects had a low activity of the MAOA enzyme *and also* were maltreated as children, there was a much greater likelihood that the person would manifest violent antisocial behavior in the future. As they stated, "For adult violent conviction, maltreated males with the low-*MAOA* activity genotype were more likely than nonmaltreated males with this genotype to be convicted of a violent crime by a significant odds ratio of 9.8".[34] The authors suggested that the high activity *MAOA* allele protects the child against the harmful biopsychosocial impact of maltreatment.

Caspi et al. has been replicated by several other teams, which used varying definitions of child maltreatment, violent behavior, and genetic risk. Table 9.2 contains a list of published studies that either replicated or failed to replicate Caspi et al.

For purposes of testimony in criminal trials, it is useful to compare subjects who had low MAOA activity and severe maltreatment with subjects who had high MAOA activity and no maltreatment. If presented to mitigate sentencing,

---

32. A. Caspi, J. McClay, T. E. Moffitt, J. Mill, J. Martin, I. W. Craig et al., *Role of Genotype in the Cycle of Violence in Maltreated Children*, 297 SCIENCE 851 (2002).

33. *Id* at 851.

34. *Id.*at 853.

TABLE 9.2. REPLICATIONS OF CASPI ET AL. (2002)

Study	Sample Composition, Location	Sample Size, Gender, Age
Caspi et al.[1]	Community birth cohort, New Zealand	442 males, age 26
Foley et al.[2]	Community twins, United States	514 males, age 8–17
Huang et al.[3]	Psychiatric outpatients and normal controls, United States	342 males, average age 38
Jaffee et al.[4]	Community twins, United Kingdom; genetic risk inferred by zygosity of twins.	1116 pairs of same-sex twins, age 5
Kim-Cohen et al.[5]	Community twins, United Kingdom	975 males, age 7
Nilsson et al.[6]	Community adolescents, Sweden	81 males, age 16–19

NONREPLICATIONS OF CASPI ET AL. (2002)

Haberstick et al.[7]	Community young adults, United States	774 males, age 22
Young et al.[8]	Psychiatric inpatients, United States	247 males, age 12–18

[1] A. Caspi, J. McClay, T. E. Moffitt, J. Mill, J. Martin, I. W. Craig et al., *Role of Genotype in the Cycle of Violence in Maltreated Children*, 297 Science 851 (2002).

[2] D. L. Foley, L. J. Eaves, B. Wormley, J. L. Silberg, H. H. Maes, J. Kuhn, et al., *Childhood Adversity, Monoamine Oxidase a Genotype, and Risk for Conduct Disorder*, 61 Arch.Gen. Psychiatry 738 (2004).

[3] Y. Y. Huang, S. P. Cate, C. Battistuzzi, M. A. Oquendo, D. Brent, & J. J. Mann, *An Association between a Functional Polymorphism in the Monoamine Oxidase a Gene Promoter, Impulsive Traits and Early Abuse Experiences*, 29 Neuropsychopharmacology 1498 (2004).

[4] S. R. Jaffee, A. Caspi, T. E. Moffitt, K. A. Dodge, M. Rutter, A. Taylor, et al., *Nature X Nurture: Genetic Vulnerabilities Interact with Physical Maltreatment to Promote Conduct Problems*, 17 Dev. Psychopathol. 67 (2005).

[5] J. Kim-Cohen, A. Caspi, A. Taylor, B. Williams, R. Newcombe, I. W. Craig, et al., *MAOA, Maltreatment, and Gene-Environment Interaction Predicting Children's Mental Health: New Evidence and a Meta-Analysis*, 11 Mol. Psychiatry 903 (2006).

[6] K. W. Nilsson, R. L. Sjöberg, M. Damberg, J. Leppert, J. Ohrvik, P. O. Alm, et al., *Role of Monoamine Oxidase A Genotype and Psychosocial Factors in Male Adolescent Criminal Activity*, 59 Biol. Psychiatry 121 (2006).

[7] B. C. Haberstick, J. M. Lessem, C. J. Hopfer, A. Smolen, M. A. Ehringer, D. Timberlake, et al., *Monoamine Oxidase A (MAOA) and Antisocial Behaviors in the Presence of Childhood and Adolescent Maltreatment*, 135 Am. J. Med. Genet. B Neuropsychiatr. Genet. 59 (2005).

[8] S. E. Young, A. Smolen, J. K. Hewitt, B. C. Haberstick, M. C. Stallings, R. P. Corley, et al., *Interaction between MAO-A Genotype and Maltreatment in the Risk for Conduct Disorder: Failure to Confirm in Adolescent Patients*, 163 Am. J. Psychiatry 1019 (2006).

the defense attorney would argue that the defendant did not choose to have low MAOA activity and did not choose to experience child maltreatment. These events were outside of his control, but taken together these factors created a vulnerability toward violent behavior. In analyzing the data of Caspi et al., one can calculate that the relative risk for being convicted of a violent offense was 4.6 for individuals who had low MAOA activity and severe maltreatment compared to subjects who had high MAOA activity and no maltreatment.

The case of *Tennessee v. Thompson* illustrates how testimony regarding this GxE interaction might help explain the defendant's behavior and influence sentencing. Adrian Thompson was a 22-year-old man who was charged with aggravated assault and reckless endangerment in 2006. Mr. Thompson was a passenger in an automobile and, in a moment of rage, grabbed the steering wheel of the car and turned it into a telephone pole. Both Mr. Thompson and his girlfriend were injured.

As a child, Mr. Thompson was a victim of child maltreatment and also witnessed severe domestic violence. As an adult, Mr. Thompson had episodes of violence consistent with the psychiatric diagnosis of intermittent explosive disorder. As part of a comprehensive, pretrial, forensic psychological evaluation, Mr. Thompson had genetic testing. Mr. Thompson had the low-activity allele of the *MAOA* gene and also was heterozygous, S/L, for the *SLC6A4* gene. Mr. Thompson pleaded guilty at trial, and the forensic psychologist testified at the sentencing hearing. The psychologist explained the significance of the *MAOA* genotyping. He thought that the genetic (low-activity allele of the *MAOA* gene) and environmental (history of severe child abuse) interaction might help to explain Mr. Thompson's history of violent behavior. With this combination of genetic vulnerability and early life experience, Mr. Thompson's chances of being a violent adult were four to five times what they would have been otherwise. The forensic psychologist also outlined an appropriate treatment regimen for Mr. Thompson, which included both psychopharmacological and psychotherapeutic approaches. Mr. Thompson was sentenced to a prison term of one year—at the low end of the possible range of sentences—and was ordered to comply with a treatment program after release from prison.

In this use of forensic genotyping, the GxE interaction that was identified did not prove that Mr. Thompson had any particular diagnosis. However, having the low-activity allele of the *MAOA* gene and the history of severe child abuse helped to explain his pattern of violent behavior. Simply explaining a person's bad behavior does not typically reduce responsibility for that behavior, but in some circumstances it may have an influence on the sentence that is imposed.

APPLICATIONS OF FORENSIC GENOTYPING IN CRIMINAL TRIALS

The relevance of this testimony regarding behavioral genomics to criminal trials depends on the exact nature of the genetic findings and their role in the person's case—that is, whether the genotyping is intended to establish a specific diagnosis, to support a diagnosis made on clinical grounds, or simply to explain a person's criminal acts. Also, the significance of this testimony depends on what legal issue is being addressed—that is, whether it relates to competency to stand trial or engage in some other aspect of the legal procedures, sanity, capacity to achieve the mental state required for particular offenses, or mitigation. Information regarding the defendant's genotype might be relevant in several ways, summarized as follows.

A. Insanity Defense

Most jurisdictions in the United States have some version of the insanity defense, although there are various definitions of what constitutes insanity. A typical definition is that "at the time of the commission of the acts constituting the offense, the defendant, as a result of a severe mental disease or defect, was unable to appreciate the nature or wrongfulness of such defendant's acts" (Tennessee Code § 39-11-501).

In some cases, genetic testing may help to establish that the defendant has one of the prerequisites for an insanity defense (i.e., "a severe mental disease or defect"). For example, Huntington's disease is considered a severe mental disease or mental illness within the psychiatric community. Down syndrome typically causes a severe mental defect or mental retardation. Although a medical definition of mental disease or defect may not satisfy the legal definition of mental disease or defect, it will substantially assist the defendant's claim. The exact genetic basis for these conditions has been known for decades, and testimony regarding these and similar diagnoses would easily fulfill the *Frye* and *Daubert* criteria.

The diagnosis of a genetic condition does not, however, prove the second prerequisite for an insanity defense (i.e., the defendant's inability "to appreciate the nature or wrongfulness of such defendant's acts"). To determine if the defendant had the capacity to appreciate the wrongfulness of his actions at the time of the alleged offense, a forensic evaluator must collect information regarding the person's functional abilities by relying upon interviews and psychological testing of the defendant; interviews of collateral sources, such as family members, who observed the defendant around the time of the alleged offense; and the investigation by law enforcement personnel regarding the circumstances of the crime and the defendant's behavior and statements when he was arrested. Testimony regarding this information assists the trier of fact in evaluating the defendant's insanity defense claim.

B. Diminished Capacity

Most crimes are defined by a particular *mens rea* ("guilty mind") and *actus reus* ("guilty act"). For example, the actus reus for first-degree murder is the killing of another person. In Tennessee, the mens rea for first-degree murder is that the killing of another person was done in a premeditated and intentional manner. Furthermore, "premeditation" is defined as "an act done after the exercise of reflection and judgment," and it is required that "the mental state of the accused at the time the accused allegedly decided to kill . . . was sufficiently free from excitement and passion as to be capable of premeditation" (Tennessee Code § 39-13-202). "Diminished capacity" refers to a defendant's inability, as a result of subjective impairment, to achieve the mental state required for a particular crime. For example, a person who is very intoxicated on cocaine or a person who is extremely depressed might not be able to exercise reflection and judgment and might lack the capacity to commit first-degree murder.

Some states allow for the introduction of testimony by mental health professionals regarding diminished capacity, and it is easy to see how information regarding the defendant's genotype might be relevant. As in the discussion regarding the insanity defense, the diagnosis of Huntington's disease or Down syndrome help to explain why a defendant's mental abilities were severely impaired at the time of the alleged offense. The diagnosis by itself would not prove diminished capacity, but it would be part of the testimony to show why the person lacked the capacity to form a particular mental state.

Suppose, for example, that a defendant who is accused of first-degree murder had a history of severe child abuse and a genotype that included the low-activity allele of the *MAOA* gene. Because of his genetic makeup and life experiences, the defendant is at a high risk of committing violent acts. Suppose the circumstances of the alleged offense were such that the defendant may have been in a state of excitement or passion. Suppose also that the defendant was using cocaine and marijuana at the time of the alleged offense. One can see how all of this information—including the *MAOA* genotyping—could be considered by the trier of fact to decide that the defendant did not have the mental capacity to commit first-degree murder.

C. Mitigation

In the guilt phase of the trial, the jury or the judge decides whether the defendant committed the crime. If the defendant is found guilty, additional evidence is presented in the penalty phase of the trial, and the jury or the judge decides what the defendant's sentence will be. During the penalty phase, the defense attorney can present a very broad range of information to influence the jury and judge to be lenient toward the defendant. If the defendant is found guilty of a capital crime such as first-degree murder, the jury may forego the death penalty and sentence the person to life in prison, either with or without the possibility of parole. If the defendant is found guilty of a felony and the range of imprisonment is 15 to 25 years, the judge may rely on mitigation testimony to impose a sentence at the lower end of that range.

Is genetic testimony relevant during the penalty phase of a trial? Many topics may be relevant during the penalty phase of a trial including the defendant's

youth; the defendant's old age; his having acted under duress or under the dom-
ination of another person; the defendant's mental or physical condition, which
significantly reduced his culpability; and his having had a mental or physical
condition that reduced his ability to appreciate the wrongfulness of his conduct
or to conform his conduct to the requirements of the law. Often, the defense
presents testimony about the defendant's difficult childhood, such as experiencing chronic illness, child maltreatment, or poverty.

It may be relevant to present testimony that a person's genetic makeup—
along with other factors such as physical or sexual child abuse—predisposed a
person to commit a violent, antisocial act. The defense attorney would argue that
the defendant did not ask to have a particular genetic makeup. He did not ask to
be physically or sexually abused as a child. But these factors—without his desire,
knowledge, or awareness—made it more likely that he would commit a violent
act later in life.

D. Dangerousness

The prosecution also has an opportunity at the penalty phase of a trial to present
additional evidence. In some circumstances, the prosecution may argue that
behavioral genomic testimony is not mitigating but is an aggravating factor that
should increase the length of a sentence. For instance, the prosecution may say
that because of his genetic makeup and his childhood experiences, the defendant has violent tendencies and should have a longer sentence in order to protect
society for a longer time.

Whether testimony regarding behavioral genomics favors the defense or the
prosecution depends on the circumstances. In a case of aggravated robbery, for
instance, it may be logical for the prosecution to argue that a person's genotype
and bad life experiences mean that he should be imprisoned longer in order to
protect society. In a case of capital murder, on the other hand, the defendant
is never going to live outside of prison and threaten society. In that situation,
it may be logical for the defense to argue that the person's genotype and bad
life experiences mean he should have a life sentence rather than the death
penalty.

E. Malingering

In some trials in which psychiatric or psychological testimony is offered, there is
a dispute about whether the defendant is malingering mental illness. If the prosecution can show that the defendant was malingering, then the jury is less likely
to find the person insane or eligible for a reduced sentence. The defense may be
able to use behavioral genomic testimony to bolster the argument that the
defendant has an actual mental disorder. For example, suppose a male defendant has the low activity allele of the MAOA gene and a history of severe child
abuse. The research indicates that this individual is more likely than a typical
person to engage in violent, antisocial acts. This combination of genetic and

environmental vulnerabilities may support the diagnosis of intermittent explosive disorder. Or, suppose a defendant has the short allele of the *SLC6A4* gene and a history of multiple, severe psychosocial stressors. The research indicates that this individual is more likely than a typical person to become seriously depressed and suicidal and to have poor coping skills when stressed. This combination of genetic and environmental vulnerabilities supports the diagnosis of major depressive disorder.

In the future, it is likely that researchers in behavioral genomics will show that groups of genes or various G×E interactions greatly increase the risk that a particular person will have a serious psychiatric condition (i.e., schizophrenia, bipolar disorder, obsessive-compulsive disorder, autism, etc.). It is likely that this kind of information will be one aspect of what the forensic psychiatrist or psychologist considers is assessing whether a defendant is malingering. It would raise suspicions of malingering if a person had no genetic risks and no environmental risks for schizophrenia but sometimes manifested symptoms that seemed consistent with schizophrenia. Of course, genetic testing would only be one part of a comprehensive evaluation and would not be determinative all by itself. It is possible for a person to have the genetic risk factors for schizophrenia but to not have the illness. Also, it is possible for a person with actual schizophrenia to also be malingering.

F. Competency

Mental competency is a very important issue in many aspects of the criminal justice system. In an important decision of the Supreme Court, *Dusky v. United States*, the Court endorsed the position taken by the solicitor general that the test for competency to stand trial "must be whether [the defendant] has sufficient present ability to consult with his lawyer with a reasonable degree of rational understanding—and whether he has a rational as well as factual understanding of the proceedings against him."[35] In another important case, *Miranda v. Arizona*, the Supreme Court established the principle that a person who has been arrested has a right to remain silent and a right to an attorney. The Supreme Court also said that an individual may waive these rights, "provided the waiver is made voluntarily, knowingly and intelligently."[36]

Mental health professionals are frequently asked to assess whether a defendant was competent in the past when he waived Miranda rights and made a statement to investigators. They are asked to evaluate whether a defendant is currently competent to stand trial or competent to waive his right to have an attorney represent him at the trial. After conviction, there may be an issue of

---

35. *Dusky v. United States*, 362 U.S. 402 (1960).
36. *Miranda v. Arizona*, 384 U.S. 436 (1966).

whether an inmate is competent to waive his appeals or even competent to be executed.

In conducting a competency evaluation, the mental health professional would ordinarily assume the person is competent unless there is some reason to think otherwise. To conclude that an individual is not competent, the evaluator would have to identify some mental disorder that is causing the impairment in mental functioning. As in the previous discussion—regarding insanity, diminished capacity, and malingering—genetic testing may help to establish that a person has a mental illness that would cause enough impairment to compromise the individual's competency. Of course, making the diagnosis of mental illness or mental defect does not in itself mean the person is not competent, and thatconclusion would require additional assessment of the person's actual functioning.

G. Juvenile Court

Since most juvenile courts are organized around the principle of rehabilitation, juvenile court judges are usually very interested in having a full understanding of the youngster's biological, psychological, and social background. Juvenile court judges—in order to arrive at an appropriate disposition of each case—take into consideration lengthy social histories, the results of psychological testing, and psychiatric evaluations. There is a search for why this particular boy or girl got into so much trouble in the past, and then an effort to devise an intervention or corrective action to reduce the likelihood of more trouble in the future.

Preliminary research regarding GxE interactions has started to explain why some children manifest oppositional defiant disorder and conduct disorder, while others do not.[37] Of course, juvenile court judges are not interested merely in research and theories: they want solutions, interventions, and rehabilitation that actually works. As both genetic and environmental risk factors and their interactions become better understood, it is certain that practitioners will develop more specific and more effective treatments. For example, it will be determined

---

37. A. Caspi, J. McClay, T. E. Moffitt, J. Mill, J. Martin, I. W. Craig et al., *Role of Genotype in the Cycle of Violence in Maltreated Children*, 297 SCIENCE 851 (2002); D. L. Foley, L. J. Eaves, B. Wormley, J. L. Silberg, H. H. Maes, J. Kuhn et al., *Childhood Adversity, Monoamine Oxidase A Genotype, and Risk for Conduct Disorder*, 61 ARCH. GEN. PSYCHIATRY 738 (2004); S. R. Jaffee, A. Caspi, T. E. Moffitt, K. A. Dodge, M. Rutter, A. Taylor et al., *Nature x Nurture: Genetic Vulnerabilities Interact with Physical Maltreatment to Promote Conduct Problems*, 17 DEV. PSYCHOPATHOL. 67 (2005); K. W. Nilsson, R. L. Sjoberg, M. Damberg, J. Leppert, J. Ohrvik, P. O. Alm et al., *Role of Monoamine Oxidase A Genotype and Psychosocial Factors in Male Adolescent Criminal Activity*, 59 BIOL. PSYCHIATRY 121 (2006); J. Kim-Cohen, A. Caspi, A. Taylor, B. Williams, R. Newcombe, I. W. Craig et al., *MAOA, Maltreatment, and Gene-Environment Interaction Predicting Children's Mental Health: New Evidence and a Meta-analysis*, 11 MOL. PSYCHIATRY 903 (2006).

that some forms of adolescent violence are treatable with medication, while other forms of violence require lengthy residential treatment. In the future, an assessment of a youngster's risk factors based on G×E interactions will be a common feature of biopsychosocial evaluations conducted for juvenile courts.

H. Sex Offenders

This section pertains to a future application of behavioral genomics that someday may be much more important than the topics previously discussed in this chapter. Sexual offending is an enormous problem for our society. It is roughly estimated that 40 percent of girls and 15 percent of boys experience at least one incident of sexual abuse (including both contact and noncontact abuse) at some time during their childhood and adolescence. About thirty thousand individuals are convicted of a sexual offense each year.

Mental health professionals frequently conduct evaluations of sexual offenders for the purpose of identifying any psychopathology that may be driving the sexual offending, assessing the person's capacity for treatment and rehabilitation, and assessing the person's risk for future dangerousness as a sexual offender. Thousands of these evaluations—sometimes called psychosexual evaluations—are conducted every year. The most common circumstance for a psychosexual evaluation is after a person has been found guilty of a sexual offense and prior to sentencing, so the evaluation is intended to help the court decide on the sentence or other disposition of the case. In some states, a psychosexual evaluation is performed when a convicted, imprisoned sexual offender is about to be released. In this case, the purpose of the evaluation is to determine if the inmate is a sexually violent predator and appropriate for civil commitment. It is also possible that an individual who has no involvement with the criminal justice system might have a psychosexual offender evaluation. For example, if a psychiatric inpatient revealed abnormal sexual urges, the attending psychiatrist might conduct a psychosexual evaluation in order to guide the inpatient treatment and disposition of the patient.

Sexual offenders are a heterogeneous lot. At one extreme, some are compulsive, violent, and sadistic—and very likely to offend again at the earliest opportunity. At the other extreme, some sexual offenders have simply manifested transitory bad judgment and are very unlikely to re-offend. In the future, an analysis of G×E interactions may help distinguish the malignant from the benign sexual offenders. We are not suggesting that an assessment based on behavioral genomics would be used in isolation as the basis of a conclusion or recommendation. However, we are predicting that current components of a psychosexual evaluation—the clinical interview, actuarial methods, deception detection through polygraphy, and measuring sexual arousal by penile plethysmography and visual reaction time—will be supplemented with genomic studies such as G×E interactions.

CAUSATION AND LEVELS OF PROOF

Most of the applications of behavioral genomics that have been discussed in this chapter pertain to the person's past or current behavior or mental state. For example, the issues of insanity and mitigation relate to the defendant's past behavior, while competency pertains to the person's current mental status. However, if genetic testing were incorporated into a comprehensive psycho-sexual evaluation, it would involve using behavioral genomics to predict a person's future behavior or mental state. We believe the legal standard for introducing evidence based on behavioral genomics should be relatively low when its purpose is to explain past and present behavior but should be higher when it relates to predicting future behavior.

A. Level of Proof for Mitigation

Suppose the defendant—having been found guilty of first-degree murder—wants to present some aspect of GxE interaction to support has case for mitigation. Generally, courts allow defendants to present a rather wide range of information for the purpose of mitigation. It seems reasonable that the defendant should be able to introduce testimony regarding GxE interactions and their relationship to past criminal behavior if the expert witness can show it is more likely than not that there is such a relationship.

B. Level of Proof for Commitment

On the other hand, suppose an inmate was found guilty of a sexual offense twenty years ago and has served his time. As the date for his release approaches, the government proposes to conduct genetic testing to see if the inmate is likely to be a dangerous sexual offender in the future. There is no such genetic test at the present time, but it is plausible that scientists will determine a biological basis for sexual violence and that such information may be the basis for civil commitment in the future. It seems reasonable that the government should be able to introduce testimony regarding GxE interactions and their relation ship to possible future criminal behavior if the expert witness can show in a clear and convincing manner that there is such a relationship. In other words, the level of proof for civil commitment is higher than is the level of proof for mitigation.

C. Causation vs. Correlation

This chapter discusses a wide range of testimony regarding behavioral genomics. In some of the examples cited (such as Down syndrome and Huntington's disease), there is an obvious relationship between the genetic abnormality and the behavioral outcome that is universally accepted by the scientific community. Both scientists and legal scholars would agree that having three copies of chromosome 21 is a sufficient cause for the clinical phenotype known as Down syndrome.

Trisomy 21 is not a necessary cause of this condition because other chromosomal abnormalities also cause Down syndrome.

The relationship between the G×E interactions (*SLC6A4* and psychosocial stressors; *MAOA* and childhood maltreatment) and behavior discussed in this chapter is not so obvious. There certainly is a correlation between the G×E interactions and the behavior, but one cannot say definitely that there is a causal relationship. Based on the replicated research, we conclude that the interaction of the *SLC6A4* gene and psychosocial stressors is a probabilistic cause of depression and suicidality, which means the G×E interaction increases the chance that depression and suicidality will occur. Likewise, we conclude that the interaction of the *MAOA* gene and childhood maltreatment is a probabilistic cause of violence. More likely than not, there is a causal relationship, so a forensic psychiatrist or psychologist should be able to testify about this topic with regard to past criminal behavior (e.g., regarding mitigation in criminal court or disposition in juvenile court).

In the future, it may be possible to apply the criteria proposed by Sir Austin Bradford Hill[38] to this topic. Van Reekum[39] suggested that some of Hill's criteria for causation are particularly suited to neuropsychiatry: demonstration of an association between the causative agent and the outcome, consistency of the findings, a biologic rationale, and the appropriate temporal sequence. For example, "consistency of the findings" may be established for some G×E interactions by appropriate replication studies. There is, of course, a biologic rationale, for interactions that involve *SLC6A4* and *MAOA*. It is known, for instance, that a genetic absence of *MAOA* activity causes aggressive behavior in animals and violence in humans.

The goal of future research is to establish linkages along the following lines: individuals with a combination of allelic polymorphisms have specific changes in brain functioning, manifested by functional magnetic resonance imaging (fMRI); there is a physiological relationship between these changes, such as modification in the activity of a particular neurotransmitter; these changes in the brain cause specific alterations in emotional and/or cognitive functioning; the functional alterations cause a consistent pattern of behavior; and the pattern of emotional, cognitive, and behavioral changes may constitute a diagnosis. When these linkages are established, it may become appropriate for forensic psychiatrists and psychologists to incorporate behavioral genomics as one part of comprehensive evaluations of a person's risk of future dangerousness.

---

38. Austin Bradford Hill, *The Environment and Disease: Association or Causation?*, 58 PROC. R. SOC. MED. 293 (1965).

39. Reekum R. van, D. L. Streiner, & D. K. Conn, *Applying Bradford Hill's Criteria for Causation to Neuropsychiatry: Challenges and Opportunities*, 13 J. NEUROPSYCHIATRY CLIN. NEUROSCI. 318 (2001).

ARRANGING FOR GENOTYPING

Usually, it would not be practical or useful for a defense or prosecuting attorney to request genotyping of a defendant just to gauge the results. Genotyping is not a test that can be interpreted or presented all by itself. If genotyping is conducted on a criminal defendant, it should be part of a comprehensive psychiatric or psychological forensic evaluation. A pretrial forensic evaluation typically consists of many parts including a review of medical records, a review of the investigation of the crime, interviews with the defendant, psychological testing, neuropsychological testing, interviews with family members and other collaterals, and sometimes other investigations such as brain scans, electroencephalograms, and consultation with other medical specialists. As a small part of this elaborate evaluation, genotyping for *MAOA*, *SLC6A4*, and perhaps other genes might included.

The forensic evaluator would need to establish a relationship with a laboratory that conducts genotyping. For example, the authors have used the Molecular Biology Laboratory of Vanderbilt University School of Medicine for genotyping the *MAOA* gene, the *SLC6A4* gene, and the gene for Huntington's disease. As genetic testing becomes more common for many medical and psychiatric conditions, these tests may begin to be conducted by commercial laboratories.

If genotyping is being considered as part of a comprehensive psychiatric or psychological pretrial forensic evaluation, the evaluator should discuss the pros and cons with the defendant's attorney. Whether to conduct genotyping depends on the circumstances of the individual case and the legal questions that are being posed. The same type of decision making applies to other aspects of the forensic evaluation, such as whether to arrange for brain scans and neuropsychological testing.

In order to conduct genotyping, the laboratory will require a sample of venous blood or cells scraped from the cheek inside the mouth. The blood sample should be preserved in an anticoagulant, ethylenediaminetetraacetic acid (EDTA), or lavender-top tube. In either case, the sample should be collected under forensic conditions—that is, the chain of custody of the sample should be documented from the time of its collection to its arrival at the laboratory.

CONCLUSIONS

Because of the Human Genome Project and the introduction of technologies that make it much more efficient to map the entire genome of a specific person, we are observing the first rumblings of an avalanche of new information regarding medical and behavioral genomics. Much of the current research is tentative, and usually one cannot draw hard and fast relationships between a person's genetic makeup, the person's life experiences, and his or her ultimate psychiatric condition and behavioral quirks and abnormalities. Science is cumulative, and we predict that future research will be much more precise and will sometimes establish a direct causal interaction among these three factors. Of course, we do not want to be buried by this avalanche of behavioral genomic data. We suggest watching the process from a safe distance and being ready to make use of suitable behavioral genomic information in court in an honest and scientific manner.

10. BEHAVIORAL GENETICS EVIDENCE IN CRIMINAL CASES: 1994–2007

DEBORAH W. DENNO

I. INTRODUCTION

In 1994, convicted murderer Stephen Mobley became a cause célèbre when he appealed his death sentence before the Georgia Supreme Court.[1] According to Mobley's counsel, the trial court should have enabled Mobley to be tested for genetic deficiencies. The counsel's interest in genetics testing was straightforward: Mobley's family history revealed generations of relatives with serious behavioral disorders. Indications that Mobley shared a genetic propensity for misconduct could help explain some of his troubling tendencies and why he should not be executed.[2] In a highly publicized

---

1. Mobley v. State, 455 S.E.2d 61 (Ga. 1995).

2. *See generally* Deborah W. Denno, *Legal Implications of Genetics and Crime Research*, *in* GENETICS OF CRIMINAL AND ANTISOCIAL BEHAVIOUR 248, 248–64 (Gregory Bock & Jamie Goode eds., 1996) (presented at the 1995 Ciba Foundation Symposium 194) (discussing the *Mobley* case in light of historical and contemporary arguments concerning the use of genetics evidence in criminal law cases). The news media focused on detailing the behavioral disorders across generations of the Mobley family. *See, e.g.*, Carolyn Abraham, *DNA at 50: The First of a 3 Part Series, The Bad Seed*, GLOBE & MAIL (Toronto), Mar. 1, 2003, at F1 ("[Mobley's lawyer] knew that arguing a genetic defect would never earn an acquittal. No credible expert would testify that genes made Mr. Mobley kill. But if there was any evidence that bad behaviour ran in the Mobley family, it might hold up at the sentencing as a mitigating factor."); Steve Connor, *Do Your Genes Make You a Criminal?*, INDEP. ON SUN. (London), Feb. 12, 1995, at 19 ("'There is no legal defence to his crime,' says . . . Mobley's attorney. 'There is only the mitigating factor of his family history. His actions may not have been a product of totally free will.' Murder, rape, robbery, suicide, 'you name it,' the Mobley family has had it, he says."); *Convicted Killer Seeks Brain Test*, TIMES (London), Feb. 14, 1995, at 6 ("Violence, aggression and anti-social behaviour dominate the family tree of Stephen Mobley. . . . Lawyers acting for Mobley asked a court to allow him to undergo neurological tests to determine whether he was suffering from an imbalance of brain chemicals that may have contributed to his behaviour."); Michelle Henery, *Killer Blamed His Family History*, TIMES (London), Oct. 2, 2002, at 5 (According to Mobley's counsel, Mobley's criminality derived from "four generations of Mobley men," either successful or violent, "including a murderer, a rapist, an armed robber, spouse abusers, several substance abusers and Mobley's father, a self-made millionaire."); Kathryn Holmquist, *Nature, Nurture, the "Criminal Gene"—What Makes Men Violent?*, IRISH TIMES, May 9, 1996, at 12 ("After [Mobley] was sentenced to death, his lawyers won an appeal. They argued that he was not acting on the basis of 'free will' but due to a genetic

decision,[3] the Georgia Supreme Court rejected that reasoning and affirmed the trial court's holding, explaining that the genetics theory involved in Mobley's case "will not have reached a scientific stage of verifiable certainty in the near future and . . . Mobley could not show that such a stage will ever be reached."[4]

One year later, Mobley's family history evidence again became an issue. This time, new counsel representing Mobley filed a petition for writ of habeas corpus claiming Mobley's trial counsel were inadequate for a range of reasons: failing to research sufficiently Mobley's background for mitigating evidence, neglecting to acquire funds so that a psychologist could provide expert testimony during Mobley's sentencing phase, wrongly declining an offer of financial assistance from Mobley's father to support Mobley's genetics testing, and incompetently raising an "unorthodox mitigating defense that attempted to show a possible genetic basis for Mobley's conduct."[5] The habeas court vacated Mobley's death sentence on grounds that Mobley's trial counsel were ineffective;[6] on appeal,

---

predilection. Virtually his entire family, they said, were violent."); Minette Marrin, *Freedom Is a Better Bet than the Gene Genie*, SUN. TIMES (U.K.), Oct. 6, 2002, at 3G ("Generations of Mobleys, starting with [Stephen's] great-grandfather, had been antisocial and violent, and his lawyers tried to argue that he was hard-wired to be bad.").

3. Various news accounts illustrated the degree of attention the *Mobley* case received. *See, e.g.*, Mike Pezzella, *Violence DNA Researchers Mum on Meeting, Hoping to Avoid Protests*, BIOTECH. NEWSWATCH, Apr. 15, 1996, at 14 ("The [*Mobley*] case became a minor landmark when Mobley's . . . attorney . . . attempted to get Georgia to pay for a DNA analysis of Mobley in order to obtain evidence based on four generations of violence and aggressive business behavior in his family."); Babs Brockway, *Mobley's Death Sentence Is Upheld*, TIMES (Gainesville, Ga.), Mar. 18, 1995, at 1 ("The [*Mobley*] case gained international attention when [Mobley's lawyer] Summer contended his defense was hurt by Hall Superior Court Judge Andy Fuller's refusal to approve $1,000 for the tests . . . [which] could have shown that Mobley had a genetic predisposition toward violence."); *Not by Our Genes Alone*, NEW SCI., Feb. 25, 1995, at 3 ("Mobley's case became headline news in Britain last week, thanks to a scientific meeting on the links between genes and crime, held in London . . . "); Kam Patel, Adrian Raine & Steven Rose, *Perspective: An Inside Job Or A Set-Up?*, TIMES HIGHER EDUC. SUPPLEMENT, Feb. 10, 1995, at 16 ("[W]hat appears to be pretty much an open and shut case—even Mobeley [sic] has never denied his guilt—has been catapulted on to the battlefield of a fierce worldwide debate."); *see also* Sarah Boseley, *Second Front: Genes In The Dock*, GUARDIAN (London), Mar. 13, 1995, at T2 ("Even if [the Georgia Supreme Court turns down Mobley's appeal], lawyers believe it is now no longer a case of *whether* genetic evidence will be allowed in court but *when*."); Connor, *supra* note 2 ("[Mobley's] last chance of reprieve rests with a plea from his lawyer that the murder was not the evil result of free will but the tragic consequence of a genetic predisposition."); Edward Felsenthal, *Legal Beat: Man's Genes Made Him Kill, His Lawyers Claim*, WALL ST. J., Nov. 15, 1994, at B1 ("The [*Mobley*] case seeks to break new legal ground by bringing into court a growing body of research linking genes and aggressive behavior.").

4. *Mobley*, 455 S.E.2d at 66.

5. Turpin v. Mobley, 502 S.E.2d 458, 463 (Ga. 1998).

6. *Id.* at 461.

however, the Georgia Supreme Court reversed and reinstated the sentence, concluding counsel had been adequate.[7] Likewise, the Georgia Supreme Court denied reconsideration of the potential for testing Mobley for genetic deficiencies, but for a somewhat different reason than it had expressed three years earlier.[8] In the court's view, Mobley had in fact been "able to present the genetics theory" through a relative's testimony about the family's generations of behavioral problems;[9] however, even if the court had allowed genetics testing, "there had been no showing that a geneticist would have offered additional significant evidence."[10] In 2005, after more appeals, Mobley was executed.[11]

Mobley's request for genetics testing spawned an international debate on the political and scientific acceptance of behavioral genetics evidence in criminal law.[12] Near the time of Mobley's 1994 appeal, for example, the Ciba Foundation[13] sponsored a symposium in London on the Genetics of Criminal

---

7. *Id.* at 467.

8. *Id.* at 463–66.

9. *Id.* at 466; *see also infra* notes 54–58 and accompanying text (discussing the testimony of Joyce Ann Mobley Childers).

10. *Turpin*, 502 S.E.2d at 466.

11. Mark Davis, *Final Appeals Fail; Killer Mobley Dies*, ATLANTA J. CONST., Mar. 2, 2005, at B3; Mark Davis, *Mobley Dies for 1991 Murder; Supreme Court Denies Last Appeals Half-Hour Before Execution*, ATLANTA J. CONST., Mar. 2, 2005, at 1JJ.

12. *See, e.g.*, Mariya Moosajee, *Violence—A Noxious Cocktail of Genes and the Environment*, 96 J. ROY. SOC'Y MED. 211, 213 (2003) ("[S]ince genetic make-up is predetermined, some might seek to make genes an excuse for misbehavior. . . . The case of Stephen Mobley . . . is a case in point."); Sarah Boseley, *Genes' Link To Crime May Be Cited in Court*, GUARDIAN (London), Feb. 14, 1995, at 4 (describing the difficulties and misconceptions regarding genetic predisposition to criminal behavior related by participants in the Ciba conference on the Genetics of Criminal and Antisocial Behaviour); Connor, *supra* note 2 ("[A]t a closed meeting of scientists at the Ciba Foundation in London, Mobley's family tree will again come under intense scrutiny, this time by researchers studying the link between genes and violence."); Roger Highfield, *Scientists Can Test Foetus For Violent Gene*, DAILY TELEGRAPH (U.K.), Feb. 14, 1995, at 4 ("Discovery of a genetic link to aggression may soon have an impact on America's legal system.") (referring to *Mobley*); Kenan Malik, *Refutation: No Such Thing as a Born Killer*, INDEPENDENT (London), Feb. 14, 1995, at 15 (describing the *Mobley* appeal and the Ciba conference as being "[t]wo recent events [that] have revived the debate about whether criminal behaviour is genetically determined"); Colin Wilson, *Are Some People Born Criminal?*, DAILY MAIL (U.K.), Aug. 2, 2002, at 12 (considering "whether there is such a thing as a 'criminal gene'" to be "one of the great debates of modern times"); *see also* Denno, *supra* note 2, at 251–53 (citing articles discussing the controversy surrounding the *Mobley* case).

13. The Ciba Foundation is a scientific organization now called the Novartis Foundation. Information on Novartis Foundation Symposia can be found at http://www.novartisfound.org.uk/symp.htm (last visited Aug. 12, 2007). For purposes of clarity, this Chapter continues to refer to the Ciba Foundation in the context of discussions about the Ciba conference.

and Antisocial Behaviour.[14] Because the symposium examined the legal implications of behavioral genetics and crime research[15] and contributed to the publicity surrounding the *Mobley* case,[16] the issues discussed at Ciba are significant to this Chapter.[17] Furthermore, the Ciba symposium was relevant to the legal field as a whole because the symposium's themes squarely addressed a topic that had seemed dormant for years: the interdisciplinary links between behavioral genetics and crime.[18] Such interdisciplinary contributions were just as relevant in 2007, a year when behavioral genetics evidence showed a relative upswing in application to criminal cases.[19] Also that year, the United States Supreme Court responded to the attempted introduction of behavioral genetics evidence in *Schriro v. Landrigan*,[20] another death penalty case.

---

14. The three-day Ciba Foundation symposium was held on February 14–16, 1995. *Contents, in* GENETICS OF CRIMINAL AND ANTISOCIAL BEHAVIOUR, *supra* note 2, at v. The papers presented at the symposium were published in *Genetics of Criminal and Antisocial Behaviour. Id.* For the purposes of the symposium, I wrote a chapter about the *Mobley* case. *See* Denno, *supra* note 2, at 248.

15. *See* Denno, *supra* note 2, at 248.

16. For further descriptions of the debates surrounding the issue of genetics and crime outside the context of the *Mobley* case but in the wake of the Ciba conference on the Genetics of Criminal and Antisocial Behaviour, see Clive Cookson, *Controversial Search for the Criminal Gene: A Conference the Americans Would not Allow*, FIN. TIMES (U.K.), Feb. 14, 1995, at 8 ("Ten of the 13 speakers [at the Ciba conference] are from the US, where criminal genetics is a particularly controversial issue."); Patel et al., *supra* note 3, at 16 (exploring opposing viewpoints on the connections between genes and crime and the implications of such on the legal system); Richard W. Stevenson, *Researchers See Gene Link to Violence but Are Wary*, N.Y. TIMES, Feb. 19, 1995, at 29 ("Researchers [at the Ciba symposium] said . . . there was tentative but growing evidence of a genetic basis for some criminal and aggressive behavior. But clearly mindful of the controversy on this issue, most . . . emphasized that the 'nature versus nurture' debate was not an either-or proposition in this case"); and Tom Wilkie, *Genes Link to Violence and Crime Condemned*, INDEPENDENT (London), Feb. 15, 1995, HOME, at 2 (noting that the controversy surrounding the issues discussed at the Ciba symposium had "now reached the European Parliament").

17. *See infra* Part III.

18. For example, the 25 symposium attendees represented a range of different academic areas, including genetics, psychology, philosophy, and law. *See Participants, in* GENETICS OF CRIMINAL AND ANTISOCIAL BEHAVIOUR, *supra* note 2, at vii. For insightful analyses of the breadth of such interdisciplinary interactions, see Owen D. Jones, *Behavioral Genetics and Crime, In Context, in* THE IMPACT OF BEHAVIORAL SCIENCES ON CRIMINAL LAW 125 (Nita A. Farahany ed., 2009) and Brent Garland & Mark S. Frankel, *Considering Convergence: A Policy Dialogue About Behavioral Genetics, Neuroscience, and Law, in* THE IMPACT OF BEHAVIORAL SCIENCES ON CRIMINAL LAW, *supra*, at 147.

19. *See infra* app. B. Appendix B, which consists of 48 cases arranged chronologically beginning with the most recent case, shows that most of the criminal cases using behavioral genetics evidence between 1994 and June 1, 2007, were published in 2006.

20. 127 S. Ct. 1933 (2007).

These developments stir the genetics and crime debate by prompting a key question: how have courts and litigators treated behavioral genetics evidence in criminal cases during the 13 years between Mobley's 1994 appeal and the Supreme Court's decision in *Landrigan*? Much of the controversy concerning *Mobley* was based on the presumption that behavioral genetics evidence would skyrocket in use and abuse. The following pages seek to determine if such forecasts have been realized.[21]

From 1994 to June 1, 2007, at least 48 criminal cases relied on behavioral genetics evidence in a wide range of ways, but mostly as some sort of mitigating evidence in a death penalty case.[22] While the number 48 is sizable, it does not constitute a surge.[23] Nor have the legal strategies using the evidence been especially controversial. Contrary to predictions voiced around *Mobley*'s appeal, then, the fears and frenzy that *Mobley* generated are not warranted.

At the same time, attorneys should be wary about how courts view behavioral genetics evidence. As in *Landrigan*,[24] a substantial number of courts have either ignored or downplayed such information, or they have considered it negatively. For example, some courts have regarded a defendant's family history of behavioral disorder to be indicative of that defendant's potential for future dangerousness[25] or to be a misguided attempt to sidestep responsibility for violence.[26] These kinds of judicial reactions suggest that at least some of the legal strategies

---

21. This Chapter is less concerned with conceptual debates on whether behavioral genetics evidence should have a role in the criminal justice system than with what role it has actually assumed and why. Superb commentaries exist on whether behavioral genetics evidence should have any evidentiary contribution in the criminal justice system. *See* Nita A. Farahany & James E. Coleman, Jr., *Genetics, Neuroscience, and Criminal Responsibility, in* THE IMPACT OF BEHAVIORAL SCIENCES ON CRIMINAL LAW, *supra* note 18, at 183; Stephen J. Morse, *Addiction, Science, and Criminal Responsibility, in* THE IMPACT OF BEHAVIORAL SCIENCES ON CRIMINAL LAW, *supra* note 18, at 241. For research results on the interaction between genetic and environmental factors in violent criminal behavior and an overview of genetic testimony in murder trials, see William Bernet et al., *Bad Nature, Bad Nurture, and Testimony Regarding MAOA and SLC6A4 Genotyping at Murder Trials*, 52 J. FORENSIC SCI. 1362 (2007).

22. *See infra* Part IV & app. B.

23. This author's prior article on the use of behavioral genetics evidence in criminal cases from 1994 to 2004 had concluded "that little has occurred in the area of genetics and crime warranting the concern that *Mobley* generated." Deborah W. Denno, *Revisiting the Legal Link Between Genetics and Crime*, 69 LAW & CONTEMP. PROBS. 209, 212 (Winter/Spring 2006). That conclusion does not account for the relative growth in the use of such evidence in the past two-to-three years.

24. 127 S. Ct. 1933 (2007).

25. *See infra* Part IV.B.3.

26. *See, e.g.,* People v. Mertz, 842 N.E.2d 618, 663 (Ill. 2005), *cert. denied,* Mertz v. Illinois, 127 S. Ct. 47 (2006) ("We believe the effort to blame defendant's drinking problems upon an alleged genetic or family predisposition was little more than a thinly veiled effort to divert responsibility from defendant for his failure to address his problems and take responsibility for them.").

using behavioral genetics evidence are without question a double-edged sword for defendants.[27]

The criminal justice system must be alert to the potential vulnerabilities of behavioral genetics evidence,[28] and attorneys must weigh whether the information could be more prejudicial than probative for defendants.[29] At the same time, a balance is needed between concern and overreaction. Unsupported fears, for example, could also curtail some capital defendants' constitutionally legitimate attempts to submit mitigating factors during their death penalty cases, in particular, behavioral genetics evidence that could validate the existence of more traditionally accepted mitigating conditions, such as mental illness. Judges and juries may be less likely to think that a defendant is malingering by presenting evidence of states such as schizophrenia or alcoholism if such disorders commonly occurred across generations of the defendant's family. Again, in these cases and evidentiary circumstances, context is critical.[30]

---

27. *See infra* Part IV.

28. For comprehensive and sophisticated accounts of the frailties and dangers of behavioral genetics research, see D. H. Kaye, *Behavioral Genetics Research and Criminal DNA Databases: Laws and Policies, in* THE IMPACT OF BEHAVIORAL SCIENCES ON CRIMINAL LAW, *supra* note 18, at 355; Erica Beecher-Monas & Edgar Garcia-Rill, *Genetic Predictions of Future Dangerousness: Is There a Blueprint for Violence?, in* THE IMPACT OF BEHAVIORAL SCIENCES ON CRIMINAL LAW, *supra* note 18, at 389; and Karen Rothenberg & Alice Wang, *The Scarlet Gene: Behavioral Genetics, Criminal Law, and Racial and Ethnic Stigma, in* THE IMPACT OF BEHAVIORAL SCIENCES ON CRIMINAL LAW, *supra* note 18, at 439.

29. *See* Diane E. Hoffman & Karen H. Rothenberg, *When Should Judges Admit or Compel Genetic Tests?*, 310 SCIENCE 241, 241 (2005). The authors' survey of all trial court judges in Maryland included two hypothetical questions concerning the admissibility of behavioral genetics evidence in criminal cases. *Id.* One question in particular was relevant to this Chapter's topic: "whether they [the judges] would admit a positive genetic test for schizophrenia to establish that the defendant did not have the necessary criminal intent (*mens rea*) to commit the crime." *Id.* According to the survey's results, the judges "were almost equally divided," *id.*, with "[s]everal" judges characterizing the matter "as a 'gray area' where the ultimate question would be whether the information would be more prejudicial than probative," *id.* at 242. The second question concerned a less defined condition: "whether, in a sentencing proceeding, they [the judges] would compel a test for a condition that predisposes an individual to bouts of rage (proclivity to 'future dangerousness')." *Id.* at 241. In response to this question, "[a] large majority of judges" explained that they would not compel such a test because "the test was an 'inexact' instrument that could brand someone for life and would be especially stigmatizing in the context of mental health." *Id.* at 242. "A few judges" contended, though, "that because the defendant had been convicted, his privacy interest was already diminished" and such "information might assist them in predicting future dangerousness, especially when the defendant has no prior criminal record." *Id.*

30. *See id.* (recommending that "judges scrutinize the admitting or compelling [of behavioral genetics evidence] in the context in which its use is proposed").

Discussions of an interdisciplinary subject of this sort require clear terminology, especially because of the close ties between biological and social factors and the frequent muddling of the terms "biological" and "genetic." Therefore, this introduction briefly sets forth definitions of major terms according to how they are used in much of the research literature and in this Chapter.[31] In general, *social variables*, such as socioeconomic status, consist of environmental influences on a person's behavior.[32] *Biological variables*, on the other hand, constitute "physiological, biochemical, neurological, and genetic" effects on how an individual may act.[33] *Genetic factors* are a subset of biological variables, distinguishable because they are inherited; in contrast, *social factors* are not inherited.[34] All these categories—social, biological, and genetic—are related in interesting ways. For example, being male is a genetic attribute that strongly predicts crime.[35] Yet most men never commit an officially recorded crime, particularly a violent crime.[36] Likewise, other biological factors and a wide range of social factors mediate the relationship between sex and criminal behavior, so much so that social variables greatly dominate a researcher's ability to determine who among a small group of people will engage in criminality.[37]

A common stereotype is that an individual's "genotype" or "genetic constitution"[38] is static, as though there is a "crime gene" that "hardwires" certain people to violate the law.[39] But this perspective, however entrenched in the public's mind, has no scientific support. Rather, an overwhelming amount of evidence shows that "environments influence gene expression."[40] In other

---

31. For an excellent discussion of the basics of behavioral genetics and assessments of how it relates to human behavior, see Laura A. Baker, Serena Bezdjian & Adrian Raine, *Behavioral Genetics: The Science of Antisocial Behavior, in* THE IMPACT OF BEHAVIORAL SCIENCES ON CRIMINAL LAW, *supra* note 18, at 3, and Jonathan Kaplan, *Misinformation, Misrepresentation, and Misuse of Human Behavioral Genetics Research, in* THE IMPACT OF BEHAVIORAL SCIENCES ON CRIMINAL LAW, *supra* note 18, at 45.

32. Jasmine A. Tehrani & Sarnoff A. Mednick, *Crime Causation: Biological Theories, in* 1 ENCYCLOPEDIA OF CRIME & JUSTICE 292, 292 (Joshua Dressler et al. eds., 2d ed. 2002).

33. *Id.*

34. *Id.*

35. *See* Deborah W. Denno, *Gender, Crime, and the Criminal Law Defenses*, 85 J. CRIM. L. & CRIMINOLOGY 80, 80–180 (1994) (examining a broad range of statistics on sex differences in crime).

36. *See id.*

37. *See* DEBORAH W. DENNO, BIOLOGY AND VIOLENCE: FROM BIRTH TO ADULTHOOD 7–28 (1990) (detailing a large longitudinal study of various biological and sociological predictors of sex differences in crime).

38. GREGORY CAREY, HUMAN GENETICS FOR THE SOCIAL SCIENCES 68 (2003).

39. Denno, *supra* note 2, at 254; *see also* Holmquist, *supra* note 2 (referring to a "criminal gene" in the title of a news article about the *Mobley* case); Marrin, *supra* note 2 ("[Mobley's] lawyers tried to argue that [Mobley] was hard-wired to be bad.").

40. CAREY, *supra* note 38, at 452.

words, an individual's genetic structure may act developmentally and probabilistically in the context of social variables by potentially predisposing an individual to certain behavioral tendencies, such as shyness.[41] In turn, "genotype influences societal response," which explains, for example, why men are far more likely than women to wear a tuxedo rather than a dress at formal events.[42] These kinds of interlinkages between genotype and the environment become helpful in assessing how behavioral genetics evidence may be viewed in a criminal law case such as *Mobley*.

Part II of this Chapter briefly reviews the facts and legal arguments in *Mobley*. Part III addresses the primary issues that concerned the court in *Mobley*, noting that many of the reasons for the controversy over the potential use of behavioral genetics evidence in 1994 remain the same today. Part IV discusses the 48 behavioral genetics and crime cases occurring between 1994 and 2007, during the time *Mobley* and *Landrigan* spurred the topical dispute. These cases share several important characteristics: they overwhelmingly constitute murder convictions in which defendants attempted to use genetics evidence as a mitigating factor in a death penalty case (as Mobley and Landrigan did), and the evidence is introduced mostly to verify a condition (such as a type of mental illness) that is commonly acceptable for mitigation. Part V concludes that, contrary to some commentators' warnings during the *Mobley* appeal, the last 13 years have not revealed a legally irresponsible application of behavioral genetics factors in criminal cases. Rather, courts continue to regard behavioral genetics variables skeptically, and society still embraces the same political and moral concerns over the role of such information. At the same time, courts have failed to provide sound and conceptually consistent reasons either for denying defendants' offers of behavioral genetics evidence or for viewing such evidence in the worst light for defendants.

Unwarranted constraints or stereotypical perspectives on the admissibility of behavioral genetics factors in death penalty cases can undercut some defendants' efforts to fight their executions through the use of traditional mitigating evidence. As a result, the criminal justice system may be undermining the very principles and progressive thinking the cap on behavioral genetics information was originally intended to achieve.

---

41. Denno, *supra* note 2, at 254; *see also* Terrie E. Moffitt, *Genetic and Environmental Influences on Antisocial Behaviors: Evidence from Behavioral-Genetic Research, in* 55 ADVANCES IN GENETICS 41, 41–104 (Jeffrey C. Hall ed., 2005) (analyzing the interaction between genes and the environment with respect to antisocial behavior).

42. CAREY, *supra* note 38, at 452. For an excellent discussion and analysis of these issues, see Owen D. Jones & Timothy H. Goldsmith, *Law and Behavioral Biology*, 105 COLUM. L. REV. 405 (2005).

II. THE STEPHEN MOBLEY CASE

The facts and legal arguments raised in *Mobley* provide a broad context for analyzing the applicability of behavioral genetics evidence for purposes of mitigation. On February 17, 1991, Stephen Mobley entered a Domino's Pizza store in Oakwood, Hall County, Georgia, to steal money. In the course of the robbery, he shot John Collins, the store's manager, in the back of the head as Collins begged for his life. Mobley was caught a month later and immediately confessed to the crime.[43]

The two court-appointed attorneys assigned to Mobley, Daniel Summer and Charles Taylor,[44] faced a daunting dilemma. There was little about Mobley that aroused legal sympathy or provided "'traditional mitigation evidence.'"[45] Mobley's father was a multimillionaire.[46] White and young (age 25 at the time of his crime), Mobley had recently left a home of economic privilege[47] having experienced "a childhood standard of living [that] had ranged from middle class to affluent."[48] Mobley's parents and sister, as well as Mobley himself, stated that he had never been neglected or abused, sexually or physically.[49] Rather, Mobley showed an early and continuous history of personal and behavioral disorders that became ever more troubling with age. As a young child, Mobley cheated, lied, and stole. Such conduct worsened in adolescence, resulting in prison sentences for forgery and culminating in numerous armed robberies during Mobley's mid-twenties. Following this years-long crime spree, Mobley robbed and murdered Collins. While awaiting trial for Collins's death, Mobley's aggression was out of control: he fought continually with other inmates, sodomized his cellmate, tattooed the word "Domino" on his own back, and

---

43. Mobley v. State, 426 S.E.2d 150, 151 (Ga. 1993); Mobley v. State, 455 S.E.2d 61, 65 (Ga. 1995); Turpin v. Mobley, 502 S.E.2d 458, 461 (Ga. 1998); Denno, *supra* note 2, at 251.

44. *Turpin*, 502 S.E.2d at 463; *see infra* note 51 and accompanying text.

45. *Turpin*, 502 S.E.2d at 463.

46. Denno, *supra* note 2, at 251.

47. *Id.*; *Turpin*, 502 S.E.2d at 463–64.

48. *Turpin*, 502 S.E.2d at 464.

49. *Id.* at 463. Journalist Tom Junod depicted Mobley's comfortable childhood in blunter terms:

Deprivation? Want? Hey, they may explain your typical murderer, your average every-day ghetto shooter, but they sure . . . don't explain *Tony Mobley*. Nothing does. Sure, his father's hard and his mother harder; sure, they divorced when Tony was at a deli-cate age; sure, he resents . . . his older sister. But please, Dr. Freud, you have to believe him: There is nothing any of them did—father, mother, sister, grandpa, grandma, maiden aunt—to deserve *him*. He didn't get beat, he didn't get [sexually abused]; no, beating and [sexual abuse], they were what *he* did, and that's how it has always been.

Tom Junod, *Pull the Trigger*, Gentlemen's Q., July 1994, at 92, 92–94.

verbally taunted and threatened prison guards. As a youth and as an adult, seemingly no amount of counseling or punishment could contain Mobley's outbursts.[50]

Mobley did have one advantage at the time of his trial—his attorneys, Summer and Taylor,[51] proved to be creative and concerned advocates determined to put forward the best case that someone like Mobley could possibly have. According to Summer's account of his trial tactics, he and Mobley "realized that they had no legal defense to the armed robbery and murder charges because of Mobley's numerous confessions, and they also recognized that they had no traditional 'mitigating' evidence that they could offer the jury to convince them to spare [Mobley's] life."[52] In light of these circumstances, Summer attempted to collect a wide range of other information in order to provide some kind of explanation for Mobley's history and disposition.[53] In the course of analyzing Mobley's family, for example, Summer interviewed Joyce Ann Mobley Childers, the first cousin of Mobley's father.[54] At Mobley's sentencing hearing, Ms. Childers testified that four generations of Mobleys—including Mobley's uncles, aunts, and a grandfather—consistently engaged in acts of violence, aggression, and behavioral disorder.[55] Such behavior ranged from serious crimes (murder and rape) to extreme spousal abuse, alcoholism, explosive temperaments, and antisocial conduct.[56] At the same time, a substantial number of Mobleys were highly successful at business.[57] This split created a family reputation of peculiar renown: the Mobleys were either behaviorally disturbed or business achievers, and, in a number of cases, they were both.[58]

What instigated Stephen Mobley's violence? No one knew, but Summer attempted to find out. He and Taylor requested experts and financial support of

---

50. *Turpin*, 502 S.E.2d at 463–64; Denno, *supra* note 2, at 251–52; Daniel A. Summer, *The Use of Human Genome Research in Criminal Defense and Mitigation of Punishment*, in Genetics and Criminality: The Potential Misuse of Scientific Information in Court 182, 189 (Jeffrey R. Botkin et al. eds., 1999).

51. *Turpin*, 502 S.E.2d at 463.

52. Summer, *supra* note 50, at 189; *see also Turpin*, 502 S.E.2d at 463–66 (recognizing the lack of available mitigating evidence in Mobley's background).

53. *Turpin*, 502 S.E.2d at 463–66.

54. *Id.* at 465; Denno, *supra* note 2, at 251. At the time of her trial testimony, Joyce Ann went by the name of Joyce Ann Mobley Childers. Denno, *supra* note 2, at 251. The *Turpin* court, however, refers to her using two different last names: Joyce Ann Elders, *see Turpin*, 502 S.E.2d at 465, and Joyce Ann Childers, *see id.* at 467 (basically the name she used at trial). The court does not explain the discrepancy in names.

55. *Turpin*, 502 S.E.2d at 465.

56. *Id.*; Denno, *supra* note 2, at 251 & fig.1.

57. Denno, *supra* note 2, at 251 & fig.1.

58. *Id.*

$1000 so that scientific tests could be conducted to determine if Mobley showed any kind of genetic or neurochemical imbalance.[59]

In an effort to bolster the demonstrated need for funding, Summer introduced into evidence a then-recent article by Han Brunner and others, published in the prestigious journal *Science*.[60] The article (and other publications following it)[61] reported the results of genetics testing of a Dutch kindred of four generations.[62] The kindred included 14 males affected by a syndrome characterized by border-line mental retardation and serious behavioral dysfunction. Brunner and his coauthors had sufficient documentation on eight of these males to note more specific and consistent disorders among them, including impulsivity, verbal and physical aggression, and violence.[63] A number of the kindred's males also had committed serious crimes. One man had raped his sister and, after he was insti-tutionalized, stabbed the institution's warden in the chest. Another man habitu-ally forced his sisters to undress at knife point, while another tried to kill his boss. Yet two more were arsonists, and several regularly groped or grasped female family members.[64] Tests on these males showed a defect on the X chro-mosome, known as monoamine oxidase A (MAOA) deficiency, which was passed from mother to son and linked to regulating aggression.[65]

According to Summer, it seemed reasonable to investigate whether Mobley was also afflicted by the MAOA deficiency or by a comparable kind of disability. Indeed, a coauthor of the *Science* article[66] had volunteered to perform genetics testing on Mobley to determine whether Mobley shared the same or a similar kind of genetic mutation.[67] Other researchers offered to assess whether Mobley demonstrated abnormal levels of additional kinds of chemicals that can be linked

---

59. *Id.* at 252; Summer, *supra* note 50, at 189.

60. H.G. Brunner et al., *Abnormal Behavior Associated with a Point Mutation in the Structural Gene for Monoamine Oxidase A*, 262 Science 578 (1993) [hereinafter Brunner et al., *Abnormal Behavior*]; *see also* Paul S. Appelbaum, *Behavioral Genetics and the Punishment of Crime*, 56 Psych. Services 25, 25 (2005) (discussing the Brunner et al. study).

61. For a general overview of the research, see Han G. Brunner, *MAOA Deficiency and Abnormal Behaviour: Perspectives on an Association*, in Genetics of Criminal and Antisocial Behaviour, *supra* note 2, at 155, 155–67 [hereinafter Brunner, *MAOA Deficiency*]. For details on the studies, see Brunner et al., *Abnormal Behavior*, *supra* note 60; H.G. Brunner et al., *X-Linked Borderline Mental Retardation with Prominent Behavioral Disturbance: Phenotype, Genetic Localization, and Evidence for Disturbed Monoamine Metabolism*, 52 Am. J. Hum. Genetics 1032 (1993) [herinafter Brunner et al., *X-Linked*].

62. Brunner, *MAOA Deficiency*, *supra* note 61, at 156.

63. *Id.*

64. Brunner et al., *X-Linked*, *supra* note 61, at 1035.

65. Brunner et al., *Abnormal Behavior*, *supra* note 60, at 578–79.

66. *See id.* at 578.

67. Denno, *supra* note 2, at 252. The coauthor who volunteered to test Mobley was Xandra Breakefield. *Id.*

to aggression, such as serotonin, noradrenaline, and adrenaline.[68] As the Supreme Court of Georgia explained,

> [Summer's] strategy in the penalty phase centered around the following theme: Mobley has a personality disorder that has affected his behavior since he was a child, this behavior may be the result of a genetic problem that he cannot control, the jury should show him mercy because people with personality disorders tend to "mellow out" as they age, and Mobley has accepted responsibility for his crimes by cooperating with the police and offering to plead guilty.[69]

Of course this plan failed in Mobley's case.[70] Yet the implications of the court's holding raise many issues that were underscored by the Ciba symposium[71] and that remain relevant today.

III. ISSUES RAISED BY *MOBLEY*

A. *Mobley* Themes at Ciba

Several themes that emerged at the Ciba symposium were fueled specifically by *Mobley*. First, the symposium's mere occurrence highlights the unusual interdisciplinary concern with the possible link between behavioral genetics and crime.[72] The second theme was the narrowness with which the press and public viewed the *Mobley* case, focusing mainly on the tie between the case and the Brunner article in *Science*. This emphasis was unfortunate but not surprising, partly because Mobley's counsel had introduced Brunner's study into evidence in support of a request for funds for genetic and neurochemical testing of Mobley.[73] Yet medical analyses of Mobley were intended to be far broader than simply an investigation of MAOA deficiency, in part because Mobley did not appear to fit the common characteristics of an individual suffering from MAOA deficiency syndrome. At the Ciba symposium[74] and in the *Mobley* case itself,[75] commentators emphasized that Mobley's tested IQ was average, a sharp contrast

---

68. *Id.*

69. Turpin v. Mobley, 502 S.E.2d 458, 466 (Ga. 1998).

70. *See supra* notes 8–11 and accompanying text.

71. *See supra* notes 12–18 and accompanying text.

72. Typically, symposia at the Ciba Foundation do not involve topics that would interest nonscientists. *See* The Novartis Foundation, http://www.novartisfound.org.uk (last visited Aug. 12, 2007); *see also supra* note 16 and accompanying text.

73. *See supra* notes 59–60 and accompanying text. The MAOA deficiency issue has come about in other cases. *See* Appelbaum, *supra* note 60, at 25–27.

74. Denno, *supra* note 2, at 252.

75. Turpin v. Mobley, 502 S.E.2d 458, 463 (Ga. 1998) ("[P]sychological reports showed that Mobley had an average IQ. . . . Although some psychological reports early in Mobley's childhood suggested that he might have a learning disability or organic brain disorder, later reports found no evidence of either.").

to the borderline IQ shown by the males in Brunner's study.[76] Likewise, Mobley's disorder, if it had any genetic basis whatsoever, seemed to be transmitted through males, not through females.[77] Therefore, the proposed Mobley evaluations were geared toward uncovering a wide range of neurochemical imbalances, the origins of which could be biological or even environmental.

The Ciba symposium prompted interest in a third theme—the future legal use of behavioral genetics evidence. A symposium chapter, Legal Implications of Genetics and Crime Research,[78] estimated that after *Mobley*, attorneys would increasingly attempt to introduce behavioral genetics evidence in criminal cases.[79] This estimate was not based on the perceived quality or moral acceptability of the evidence, but simply on a belief that defense counsel would progressively investigate scientific discoveries in their various efforts to provide mitigation for death row clients.[80]

B. *Mobley* Themes since Ciba

Historically, behavioral genetics evidence has been no stranger to law.[81] Now, however, the themes of the Ciba symposium take on new significance as research grows. Behavioral genetics studies are gaining in sophistication,[82] and criminal defense attorneys are becoming more interdisciplinary.[83]

Despite the enhanced acceptance of behavioral genetics research, however, behavioral genetics evidence[84] continues to be plagued by the same problems

---

76. Brunner et al., *Abnormal Behavior*, *supra* note 60, at 578.

77. Denno, *supra* note 2, at 251 & fig.1.

78. *Id.* at 248.

79. *Id.* at 252.

80. *Id.* at 252–55.

81. It is beyond the scope of this Chapter to analyze either the research or the publications examining the link between genetics and crime in legal cases. For a few overviews of this literature, see CAREY, *supra* note 38; Denno, *supra* note 2; Jones & Goldsmith, *supra* note 42; Moffitt, *supra* note 41; and Matthew Jones, *Overcoming the Myth of Free Will in Criminal Law: The True Impact of the Genetic Revolution*, 52 DUKE L.J. 1031, 1039–40 (2003) (describing XYY syndrome–related studies in the context of the early history of genetic defenses in criminal trials).

82. For recent research reviews, see CAREY, *supra* note 38, at 431–57; Tehrani & Mednick, *supra* note 32, at 292–302; Moffitt, *supra* note 41, at 41–104; and Terrie E. Moffitt, *The New Look of Behavioral Genetics in Developmental Psychopathology: Gene-Environment Interplay in Antisocial Behaviors*, 131 PSYCHOL. BULL. 533 (2005).

83. *See* Summer, *supra* note 50, at 182–90.

84. Of course, there are vastly different types of genetics evidence, ranging from family history to modern medical testing. It is artificial to aggregate all the research under one heading. This type of lumping also confuses debates about when and where the evidence should be appropriately applied. The umbrella heading of "genetics evidence" is used in this Chapter, however, to make general points, while recognizing that the points made could differ in their accuracy depending on the type and quality of evidence being discussed.

and concerns that were raised 12 years ago at the Ciba symposium. Such concerns include the following: (1) the historical association of genetics evidence with abuses by the Nazis during the Holocaust; (2) the meaning accorded the evidence in terms of the potential chilling of society's notions of free will; (3) the possible stigmatizing effect of such evidence, exemplified by past efforts to screen and genetically follow targeted children or to corral through preventive detention those individuals deemed genetically predisposed to violence; (4) the absolution of societal responsibility for the social and economic factors that lead to crime if legal actors find a "genetics" defense acceptable; and (5) suggestions that juries may be more readily swayed in court by genetic or biological studies because such research seems more objective and precise than do social or behavioral factors.[85] All five issues, which remain unresolved, influence how the criminal justice system perceives behavioral genetics research.

At the same time, however, modern research continues to emphasize the importance of environmental effects on behavior,[86] thereby debunking the common myth that an individual's genetic structure is static.[87] Indeed, during the past 13 years, criminological investigations have increasingly incorporated genetic, biological, and social factors as vehicles for understanding crime. When these studies employ many different kinds of variables, their results show that genetics and biology continually accentuate the significance of social factors on behavior—so much so that the three interactive categories ("genetic," "biological," and "social") are often difficult to separate and decipher.[88] In light of these kinds of discoveries, the next part examines cases that have used behavioral genetics evidence since the time *Mobley* was decided.

IV. BEHAVIORAL GENETICS EVIDENCE CASES: 1994–2007

The various arguments about the role of behavioral genetics in criminal law are still largely theoretical. Behavioral genetics evidence has not gained widespread acceptance in current case law despite *Mobley* and the decisions since that have resembled it. Those criminal cases that have used behavioral genetics evidence, however, reflect the interdisciplinary efforts of attorneys to help explain defendants' behaviors. At least 48 criminal cases have referred to behavioral

---

85. Denno, *supra* note 2, at 254; *see also infra* note 219 (describing the reactions to a 1995 University of Maryland conference on *The Meaning and Significance of Research on Genetics and Criminal Behavior*, in which the public and some conference participants voiced many of these same five concerns).

86. *See* DENNO, *supra* note 37.

87. Denno, *supra* note 2, at 254.

88. For examinations of the relationship among these variables, see CAREY, *supra* note 38; DENNO, *supra* note 37; Jones & Goldsmith, *supra* note 42; and Moffitt, *supra* note 41.

genetics evidence over the past 13 years, that is, since 1994, when Mobley first appealed his death sentence, to June 1, 2007, shortly after the Supreme Court decided *Landrigan*.[89]

A. An Overview of the Behavioral Genetics Evidence Cases

The charts in Appendix A[90] and the cases summarized in Appendix B[91] give an aggregate overview of the genetics issues involving the 48 defendants. As Chart 1 shows, most of the cases are appellate court decisions in which the defendant either received the death penalty (37 cases) or life in prison (three cases).[92] This

---

89. These cases, which are summarized in Charts 1–3 of Appendix A and in Appendix B, were compiled using legal research databases only. Other cases may exist in which genetic predisposition evidence was at issue or potentially could have been at issue; however, such cases were either not published or were not made known publicly in a way that made them readily verifiable. (A general Internet search turned up references to cases in which behavioral genetics evidence was relevant; in most instances, however, efforts to locate such cases on Westlaw or LexisNexis were unsuccessful.) The 48 cases discussed in this Chapter also do not include *Mobley*, 455 S.E.2d 61 (Ga. 1995), which already has been examined in some detail, or other decisions in which behavioral genetics evidence may have been an issue in a context not relevant to this Chapter. For example, in *People v. Rodriguez*, 764 N.Y.S.2d 305 (N.Y. Sup. Ct. 2003), the New York Supreme Court held a defendant may be compelled to provide a blood sample for DNA testing so the defendant's DNA could be compared to DNA evidence from a crime scene. *Id.* at 311–15. The court ruled that the defendant's DNA could be used only for that criminal proceeding, however, and could not be placed into a DNA database for comparison with DNA evidence from other unsolved crimes. Results of DNA testing must be kept confidential—defendant has an "'exclusive property right' to control dissemination of his genetic makeup." *Id.* at 311. In essence, the opinion concerns privacy rights and DNA samples, as well as ways in which genetic material has been abused in the past. *Id.* at 307–15.

90 *See infra* app. A, charts 1–3.

91 *See infra* app. B.

92. *See infra* app. A, chart 1; app. B. In 37 of the 48 examined cases, the defendant received the death penalty. *See* Johnson v. Quarterman, 483 F.3d 278 (5th Cir. 2007); Marquard v. Sec'y for Dep't of Corrections, 429 F.3d 1278 (11th Cir. 2005), *cert. denied*, Marquard v. McDonough, 126 S. Ct. 2356 (2006); Dennis *ex rel.* Butko v. Budge, 378 F.3d 880 (9th Cir. 2004); Landrigan v. Stewart, 272 F.3d 1221 (9th Cir. 2001), *aff'd in part and rev'd in part en banc*, Landrigan v. Schriro, 441 F.3d 638 (9th Cir. 2006), *rev'd*, Schriro v. Landrigan, 127 S. Ct. 1933 (2007). West v. Bell, 242 F.3d 338 (6th Cir. 2001); Mickey v. Ayers, No. C-93-0243 RMW, 2006 WL 3358410 (N.D. Cal. Nov. 17, 2006); Hamilton v. Ayers, 458 F. Supp. 2d 1075 (E.D. Cal. 2006); Jones v. Schriro, 450 F. Supp. 2d 1023 (D. Ariz. 2006); Hendricks v. Calderon, 864 F. Supp. 929 (N.D. Cal. 1994), *aff'd*, 70 F.3d 1032 (9th Cir. 1995); Loving v. United States, 64 M.J. 132 (C.A.A.F. 2006); Fudge v. State, 120 S.W.3d 600 (Ark. 2003); People v. Lancaster, 158 P.3d 157 (Cal. 2007); People v. Smith, 150 P.3d 1224 (Cal. 2007); Rogers v. State, 783 So. 2d 980 (Fla. 2001); Head v. Thomason, 578 S.E.2d 426 (Ga. 2003); People v. Mertz, 842 N.E.2d 618 (Ill. 2005), *cert. denied*, Mertz v. Illinois, 127 S. Ct. 47 (2006); People v. Armstrong, 700 N.E.2d 960 (Ill. 1998); People v. Franklin, 656 N.E.2d 750 (Ill. 1995); Stevens v. State, 770 N.E.2d 739

breakdown in disposition is critical because it indicates that behavioral genetics evidence is submitted primarily as a mitigating factor in death penalty cases rather than as a defense relating to the defendant's level of culpability at the trial court level. The criteria for evaluating and admitting mitigating evidence are far broader and more flexible than those used for defenses.[93] For example, the trial

---

(Ind. 2002); Benefiel v. State, 716 N.E.2d 906 (Ind. 1999); *State v. Frank*, 957 So. 2d 724 (La. 2007); *State v. Manning*, 885 So. 2d 1044 (La. 2004); Billiot v. State, 655 So. 2d 1 (Miss. 1995); State v. Ferguson, 20 S.W.3d 485 (Mo. 2000); State v. Timmendequas, 737 A.2d 55 (N.J. 1999); State v. Hartman, 476 S.E.2d 328 (N.C. 1996); State v. Ketterer, 855 N.E.2d 48 (Ohio 2006), *cert. denied*, Ketterer v. Ohio, 127 S. Ct. 2266 (2007); State v. Scott, 800 N.E.2d 1133 (Ohio 2004); State v. Hughbanks, 792 N.E.2d 1081 (Ohio 2003); State v. Spivey, 692 N.E.2d 151 (Ohio 1998); State v. Wilson, No. Civ. A. 92CA005396, 1994 WL 558568 (Ohio Ct. App. Oct. 12, 1994); Von Dohlen v. State, 602 S.E.2d 738 (S.C. 2004); Morris v. State, No. W2005-00426-CCA-R3-PD, 2006 WL 2872870 (Tenn. Crim. App. Oct. 10, 2006); Keen v. State, No. W2004-02159-CCA-R3-PD, 2006 WL 1540258 (Tenn. Crim. App. June 5, 2006), *cert. denied*, Keen v. Tennessee, 127 S. Ct. 2250 (2007); Cauthern v. State, 145 S.W.3d 571 (Tenn. Crim. App. 2004); Alley v. State, 958 S.W.2d 138 (Tenn. Crim. App. 1997); Hall v. State, 160 S.W.3d 24 (Tex. Crim. App. 2004) (en banc). In three cases, the defendant was sentenced to life imprisonment. *See* Davis v. State, No. M2003-00744-CCA-R3-PC, 2004 WL 253396 (Tenn. Crim. App. Feb. 11, 2004); State v. Maraschiello, 88 S.W.3d 586 (Tenn. Crim. App. 2000); State v. Arausa, No. 2002-439113 (Dist. Ct. Lubbock County July 5, 2002), *aff'd*, Arausa v. State, No. 07-02-0396-CR, 2003 WL 21803322 (Tex. Ct. App. Aug. 6, 2003). Three of the cases were remanded. State v. Madey, No. 81166, 2002-Ohio-5976, 2002 WL 31429827 (Ohio App. 8 Dist. Oct. 31, 2002) (vacating and remanding sentencing decision of trial court); State v. Sexton, 904 A.2d 1092 (Vt. 2006) (affirming in part, reversing in part, and remanding); State v. Idellfonso-Diaz, No. M2006-00203-CCA-R9-CD, 2006 WL 3093207 (Tenn. Crim. App. Nov. 1, 2006) (remanding decision of trial court). In one case, the defendant was acquitted. State v. DeAngelo, No. CR 97010866S, 2000 WL 973014 (Conn. Super. June 20, 2000). In one case, the defendant was sentenced to 35 years of imprisonment. People v. Hammerli, 662 N.E.2d 452 (Ill. App. Ct. 1996). In one case, the defendant was sentenced to 28 years of imprisonment. Miller v. State, No. 01-06-00034-CR, 2007 WL 1559822 (Tex. App. Hous. 1 Dist. May 31, 2007). In one case, defendant's application for transfer from a state mental hospital was denied. People v. Allaway, No. G030307, 2003 WL 22147632 (Cal. App. 4 Dist. Sept. 18, 2003). Finally, in one case, the defendant's driving privileges remained suspended. Sanchez v. Ryan, 734 N.E.2d 920 (Ill. App. Ct. 2000).

93. Mitigation evidence can be introduced during the penalty phase of a death penalty case to support attorneys' explanations for why a defendant should not be executed. LINDA E. CARTER & ELLEN KREITZBERG, UNDERSTANDING CAPITAL PUNISHMENT LAW 137 (2004). The evidence, which is typically introduced through the use of expert testimony, focuses on a potentially wide range of individualized circumstances—for example, that the defendant had no prior criminal record, came from an abusive home, is remorseful, will not be dangerous in the future, is young, has a mental disorder, or suffers from any one of various life circumstances. *Id.* at 137–38. Although the Supreme Court permits substantial flexibility in the kind of evidence that can be admitted for mitigation purposes, the Court

judge in Landrigan's sentencing hearing concluded that one of the two non-statutory mitigating circumstances operating on Landrigan's behalf was that "Landrigan's family loved him,"[94] feelings that would hardly be viable for Landrigan as a defense against a murder conviction.

Chart 2 in Appendix A indicates that most of the behavioral genetics evidence is applied to validate the existence of a serious condition, typically a mental illness or addiction, which the defendant could introduce as mitigating evidence in a death penalty case or at trial, irrespective of the genetics issue.[95] For example, the majority of cases involve a mental disorder of some sort, such as depression (five cases), "mental illness" in general (seven cases), or other problems reflecting a range of impairments. Notably, 12 cases concern a defendant's arguing a genetic predisposition to addiction, either to alcohol (seven cases) or drugs and alcohol combined (five cases).[96]

---

also allows states considerable discretion in how that evidence can be structured. *Id.* A substantial case law and literature on this topic are discussed in detail elsewhere. *See generally id.* at 137–56 (providing a general overview of the key cases and literature on mitigation evidence in death penalty cases).

94. Schriro v. Landrigan, 127 S. Ct. 1933, 1938 (2007) (citations omitted).

95. The total number of cases will be more than the number of examined cases (48), because in some cases the evidence was applied to validate more than one condition.

96. *See infra* app. A, chart 2; app. B. Behavioral genetics evidence has been used to validate the existence of a wide range of serious conditions. *See Johnson,* 483 F.3d at 288 n.* (substance abuse); *Marquard,* 429 F.3d at 1288 (personality disorders); *Dennis ex rel. Butko,* 378 F.3d at 895 (Berzon, J., concurring) (mental illness); *Landrigan,* 272 F.3d at 1228–29 (predisposition towards violence); *West,* 242 F.3d at 344 (mental illness); *Mickey,* 2006 WL 3358410, at *19 (predisposition to alcohol and drug dependency); *Hamilton,* 458 F. Supp. 2d at 1091 (extreme mental and emotional impairment, serious psychiatric disorders); *Jones,* 450 F. Supp. 2d at 1031 (substance abuse, affective disorder, mental health difficulties); *Hendricks,* 864 F. Supp. at 935 (mental illness); *Loving,* 64 M.J. at 151 (alcoholism); *Fudge,* 120 S.W.3d at 602–03 (violence towards women); *Lancaster,* 158 P.3d at 165 (antisocial personality); *Smith,* 150 P.3d at 1234 (psychopathy, antisocial characteristics); *Allaway,* 2003 WL 22147632, at *3 (mental illness, psychotic behavior); *DeAngelo,* 2000 WL 973104, at *6 (bipolar disorder); *Rogers,* 783 So. 2d at 996 (porphyria); *Thomason,* 578 S.E.2d at 429, 435 (alcohol and drug abuse/addiction); *Mertz,* 842 N.E.2d at 662 (alcohol dependence, alcoholism, mood disorder); *Armstrong,* 700 N.E.2d at 970 (alcoholism); *Franklin,* 656 N.E.2d at 761 (mental illness, predisposition towards violence); *Sanchez,* 734 N.E.2d at 922 (alcohol tolerance); *Hammerli,* 662 N.E.2d at 456 (severe mood disorder); *Stevens,* 770 N.E.2d at 750 (dissociative disorder); *Benefiel,* 716 N.E.2d at 913 (schizotypal personality disorder); *Frank,* 957 So. 2d at 734 (PTSD); *Manning,* 885 So. 2d at 1097 (alcoholism); *Billiot,* 655 So. 2d at 8 (schizophrenia); *Ferguson,* 20 S.W.3d at 509 (depression); *Timmendequas,* 737 A.2d at 71 (pedophilia); *Hartman,* 476 S.E.2d at 342 (alcoholism); *Ketterer,* 855 N.E.2d at 83 (mental illness, depression, bipolar disorder); *Scott,* 800 N.E.2d at 1148 (chemical dependencies); *Hughbanks,* 792 N.E.2d at 1101 (schizophrenia); *Madey,* 2002 WL 31429827, at *1 (alcoholism); *Spivey,* 692 N.E.2d at 165 (extra Y chromosome); *Wilson,* 1994 WL 558568, at *43 (alcoholism); *Von Dohlen,*

Chart 3 in Appendix A provides information on the nature of the evidence the defendant seeks to admit. Most of the information is based on some kind of expert evaluation or family history (30 and 25 cases, respectively), rather than on a medical study of the defendant.[97] This revelation is important to the extent that

---

602 S.E.2d at 741–42 (depression, mental disorders); *Idellfonso-Diaz*, 2006 WL 3093207, at *2 (depression); *Morris*, 2006 WL 2872870, at *22 (bipolar disorder); *Keen*, 2006 WL 1540258, at *24 (mental illness); *Cauthern*, 145 S.W.3d at 588 (impulsive behavior); *Davis*, 2004 WL 253396, at *4 (depression, mental illness); *Maraschiello*, 88 S.W.3d at 598 (delusional disorder); *Alley*, 958 S.W.2d at 140–43 (physical abnormalities, neurosis, multiple personality disorder); *Miller*, 2007 WL 1559822, at *2 (acute intermittent porphyria); *Hall*, 160 S.W.3d at 32–33 (Fetal Alcohol Syndrome, Fragile X Syndrome, Klinefelter's Syndrome, extra Y chromosome); *Arausa*, 2003 WL 21803322, at *4 (propensity of abused to become abusers); *Sexton*, 904 A.2d at 1105 n.13 (schizophrenia).

97. *See infra* app. A, chart 3; app. B. Chart 3 illustrates the frequency with which defendants sought to admit different forms of genetics evidence. The total number will be more than the number of examined cases (48), because in some cases the defense attempted to introduce more than one form. Defendants sought to admit expert testimony regarding a direct evaluation of the defendant in 30 instances. *See Johnson*, 483 F.3d at 288 n.* (expert was a mitigation specialist rather than a psychologist or medical doctor); *Marquard*, 429 F.3d at 1288; *West*, 242 F.3d at 344 (Moore, J., dissenting); *Mickey*, 2006 WL 3358410, at *19; *Hamilton*, 458 F. Supp. 2d at 1091; *Jones*, 450 F. Supp. 2d at 1027; *Lancaster*, 158 P.3d at 165; *Smith*, 150 P.3d at 1234; *Allaway*, 2003 WL 22147632, at *3; *DeAngelo*, 2000 WL 973104, at *6; *Rogers*, 783 So. 2d at 997; *Thomason*, 578 S.E.2d at 429 n.1; *Mertz*, 842 N.E.2d at 641; *Hammerli*, 662 N.E.2d at 456; *Stevens*, 770 N.E.2d at 750; *Frank*, 957 So. 2d 734; *Manning*, 885 So. 2d at 1096-97; *Billiot*, 655 So. 2d at 8; *Timmendequas*, 737 A.2d at 71; *Ketterer*, 855 N.E.2d at 78; *Scott*, 800 N.E. 2d at 1148; *Hughbanks*, 792 N.E.2d at 1101; *Madey*, 2002 WL 31429827, at *4 n.4; *Spivey*, 692 N.E.2d at 165; *Idellfonso-Diaz*, 2006 WL 3093207, at *2; *Morris*, 2006 WL 2872870, at *15; *Keen*, 2006 WL 1540258, at *23; *Alley*, 958 S.W.2d at 140–43; *Hall*, 160 S.W.3d at 32–33; *Sexton*, 904 A.2d at 1106. Defendants also attempted to introduce evidence regarding their family histories in 25 instances. *Johnson*, 483 F.3d at 288 n.*; *Mickey*, 2006 WL 3358410, at *19; *Hamilton*, 458 F. Supp. 2d at 1091; *Hendricks*, 864 F. Supp. at 934-5; *Loving*, 64 M.J. at 151; *Rogers*, 783 So. 2d at 997; *Thomason*, 578 S.E.2d at 429 n.1; *Mertz*, 842 N.E.2d at 641; *Armstrong*, 700 N.E.2d at 970; *Franklin*, 656 N.E.2d at 761; *Sanchez*, 734 N.E.2d at 922–23; *Benefiel*, 716 N.E.2d at 913; *Frank*, 957 So. 2d at 734; *Hartman*, 476 S.E.2d at 339–42; *Ketterer*, 855 N.E.2d at 78; *Scott*, 800 N.E.2d at 1148–49; *Madey*, 2002 WL 31429827, at *4; *Wilson*, 1994 WL 558568, at *43; *Morris*, 2006 WL 2872870, at *15; *Keen*, 2006 WL 1540258, at *23; *Cauthern*, 145 S.W.3d at 588; *Davis*, 2004 WL 253396, at *4; *Maraschiello*, 88 S.W.3d at 599; *Miller*, 2007 WL 1559822, at *2; *Sexton*, 904 A.2d at 1118. Defendants attempted to introduce evidence regarding their behavioral histories three times. *See Landrigan*, 272 F.3d at 1228-29; *Ferguson*, 20 S.W.3d at 509; *West*, 242 F.3d at 344. Defendants also attempted to introduce their medical records in five instances. *See Benefiel*, 716 N.E.2d at 913; *Von Dohlen*, 602 S.E.2d at 741–42; *Miller*, 2007 WL 1559822, at *2; *West*, 242 F.3d at 344; *Sexton*, 904 A.2d at 1106. Three defendants attempted to introduce medical studies as evidence. *See Arausa*, 2003 WL 21803322, at *4; *Keen*, 2006 WL 1540258, at *23; *Mickey*, 2006 WL 3358410, at *19. One defendant attempted to introduce

both the judiciary and the public appear more concerned about the direct medical testing of a defendant than, for example, descriptive accounts of the defendant's family history. Regardless, both direct testing and family history strongly reflect environmental influences.[98]

Seventeen cases[99] make only brief, passing references to behavioral genetics evidence. Typically in these cases, courts merely listed the behavioral genetics evidence among the mitigating factors offered by the defense during the sentencing or penalty phases of a death penalty trial. In the remaining 33 cases, behavioral genetics evidence is an issue of varying significance. Even when the behavioral genetics evidence is not pivotal, however, subtleties in the opinions of all 48 cases may provide some insight concerning courts' future stances toward behavioral genetic and environmental factors as mitigation.

B. Tactical Strategies for Using Behavioral Genetics Evidence

Tactical strategies for using behavioral genetics evidence varied among the 48 cases. In general, however, most cases employed behavioral genetics evidence in three primary ways: (1) to support a claim of ineffective assistance of counsel, (2) to provide proof and diagnosis of a defendant's genetic condition, and/or (3) to indicate some likelihood of the defendant's future dangerousness.

Any association between the type of strategy and the court's acceptance of the behavioral genetics evidence is difficult to garner, given the range of other factors influencing these cases and the varying legal standards that were raised. As Appendix B indicates, for example, attorneys introduced behavioral genetics evidence to bolster claims spanning from defendant's incompetency to stand

---

medical testing as evidence. *Idellfonso-Diaz*, 2006 WL 3093207, at *1. One case did not describe the nature of the evidence sought to be introduced. *See Fudge*, 120 S.W.3d at 600. Finally, one case examined did not involve the introduction of genetics evidence, genetics being mentioned only in passing. *See Dennis ex rel. Butko*, 378 F.3d at 895 (Berzon, J., concurring).

98. For further discussion of the tendency of individuals to overplay the powerful effect of biology on behavior, see Deborah W. Denno, *Commentary, in* UNDERSTANDING CRIME: A MULTIDISCIPLINARY APPROACH 175, 175–80 (Susan Guarino-Ghezzi & A. Javier Treviño eds., 2005).

99. *See infra* app. B. Those 17 cases are *Johnson*, 483 F.3d at 288 n.*; *Marquard*, 429 F.3d at 1288; *West*, 242 F.3d at 344; *Loving*, 64 M.J. at 151; *Lancaster*, 158 P.3d at 165; *DeAngelo*, 2000 WL 973104, at *6; *Rogers*, 783 So. 2d at 997; *Stevens*, 770 N.E.2d at 754; *Frank*, 957 So. 2d at 734; *Manning*, 885 So. 2d at 1096–97; *Ferguson*, 20 S.W.3d at 509; *Timmendequas*, 737 A.2d at 71; *Scott*, 800 N.E.2d at 1148; *Wilson*, 1994 WL 558568, at *43; *Davis*, 2004 WL 253396, at *4; *Maraschiello*, 88 S.W.3d at 598; and *Miller*, 2007 WL 1559822, at * 2. Although these cases reference behavioral genetics evidence only in passing, some of the cases are relevant nonetheless to discussions that appear elsewhere in this Chapter's analysis.

trial to insanity to traditional forms of mitigation.[100] Other factors, such as what kind of expert was testifying when about which kinds of evidence and whether the alleged conditions were medically evaluated or derived from family histories, further compound efforts to designate any kind of cohesive approach to how courts viewed such information. Of course, courts and evidentiary standards also vary by state and over time.

In addition, the application of these three strategies was not rigid or discrete. While behavioral genetics evidence was used disproportionately in claims of ineffective assistance of counsel—the only strategy for which a clear breakdown of cases was possible because defendants must raise a distinct legal claim— many of the 48 cases employed more than one strategy.[101] In general, then, defense attorneys raised behavioral genetics evidence in numerous and varied ways.

1. Ineffective Assistance of Counsel Twenty cases involved petitions and appeals by defendants based on claims of ineffective assistance of counsel.[102] In some of these cases, the court held that including behavioral genetics evidence was a valid defensive strategy. In *Head v. Thomason*,[103] for example, the defendant successfully argued his ineffective assistance of counsel claim on the basis that his counsel did not raise important mitigation evidence that included a social worker's opinion that the defendant's family "had a strong genetic disposition to

---

100. *See infra* app. B.

101. For example, both *Landrigan*, 272 F.3d at 1221, and *Franklin*, 656 N.E.2d at 750, are mentioned in the discussions of all three categories.

102. *See* Johnson v. Quarterman, 483 F.3d 278 (5th Cir. 2007); Marquard v. Sec'y for Dep't of Corrections, 429 F.3d 1278 (11th Cir. 2005), *cert. denied*, Marquard v. McDonough, 126 S. Ct. 2356 (2006); Landrigan v. Stewart, 272 F.3d 1221 (9th Cir. 2001), *aff'd in part and rev'd in part en banc*, Landrigan v. Schriro, 441 F.3d 638 (9th Cir. 2006), *rev'd*, Schriro v. Landrigan, 127 S. Ct. 1933 (2007); Mickey v. Ayers, No. C-93-0243 RMW, 2006 WL 3358410 (N.D. Cal. Nov. 17, 2006); Hamilton v. Ayers, 458 F. Supp. 2d 1075 (E.D. Cal. 2006); Jones v. Schriro, 450 F. Supp. 2d 1023 (D. Ariz. 2006); Hendricks v. Calderon, 864 F. Supp. 929 (N.D. Cal. 1994), *aff'd*, 70 F.3d 1032 (9th Cir. 1995); Loving v. United States, 64 M.J. 132 (C.A.A.F. 2006); Head v. Thomason, 578 S.E.2d 426 (Ga. 2003); People v. Franklin, 656 N.E.2d 750 (Ill. 1995); Stevens v. State, 770 N.E.2d 739 (Ind. 2002); Benefiel v. State, 716 N.E.2d 906 (Ind. 1999); State v. Ferguson, 20 S.W.3d 485 (Mo. 2000); State v. Ketterer, 855 N.E.2d 48 (Ohio 2006), *cert. denied*, Ketterer v. Ohio, 127 S. Ct. 2266 (2007); Von Dohlen v. State, 602 S.E.2d 738 (S.C. 2004); Morris v. State, No. W2005-00426-CCA-R3-PD, 2006 WL 2872870 (Tenn. Crim. App. Oct. 10, 2006); Keen v. State, No. W2004-02159-CCA-R3-PD, 2006 WL 1540258 (Tenn. Crim. App. June 5, 2006), *cert. denied*, Keen v. Tennessee, 127 S. Ct. 2250 (2007); Cauthern v. State, 145 S.W.3d 571 (Tenn. Crim. App. 2004); Alley v. State, 958 S.W.2d 138 (Tenn. Crim. App. 1997); Miller v. State, No. 01-06-00034-CR, 2007 WL 1559822 (Tex. App. Hous. 1 Dist. May 31, 2007).

103. 578 S.E.2d 426 (Ga. 2003).

alcohol and drug abuse."[104] In other kinds of cases, defendants succeeded in an ineffective assistance of counsel claim even if it had an outcome a defendant may not have originally intended. For instance, in *Stevens v. State*,[105] defendant's counsel had presented the defendant as a "passive victim of abuse," based in part on testimony from a psychologist who stated that the defendant's genetic predisposition was partly to blame for his behavior.[106] The court held that this defense strategy was sound but affirmed the lower court's denial of postconviction relief because the strategy conflicted with defendant's alternative claims of ineffective assistance of counsel.[107] *Stevens* is one of a number of cases in which genetics evidence ultimately backfired on a defendant's efforts toward mitigation when a court accepted its validity.

Other ineffective assistance of counsel claims were based on the failure to present behavioral genetics evidence adequately. The court in *Von Dohlen v. State*[108] remanded the defendant's case due to his counsel's failure to sufficiently prepare a defense expert witness for sentencing-phase testimony regarding the extent of the defendant's mental illness.[109] The remand was based in part on subsequent testimony from the expert witness that if he had been given certain medical and psychiatric records that were available before the trial, he would have diagnosed the defendant with a far more serious mental illness.[110] These records indicated, in part, the defendant's genetic predisposition for mental disorders.[111] In turn, in *Mickey v. Ayers*,[112] the court accepted arguments that the defendant's counsel was inadequate, not only because defendant's counsel downplayed the mental health experts,[113] but also because the available information would have enabled a forensic psychologist to testify at the penalty phase about the "strong correlation between [defendant's] genetic history of addictive disorders and predisposition to developing addictions."[114]

---

104. *Id.* at 429; *see also Loving*, 64 M.J. at 151–52 (remanding so that an evidentiary hearing could determine whether defendant's counsel unreasonably dropped a full investigation of mitigating evidence concerning defendant's abusive family history, including information indicating a "parental and family history of alcoholism and substance addiction").

105. 770 N.E.2d at 739.

106. *Id.* at 754.

107. *Id.* at 755. *Stevens*, 770 N.E.2d at 739, may be seen as implicit approval of a behavioral genetics defense because the court did not consider a defense theory partially based on genetics evidence to constitute ineffective assistance of counsel. Yet the theory was obviously considered unsuccessful, nonetheless.

108. 602 S.E.2d 738 (S.C. 2004).

109. *Id.* at 746.

110. *Id.* at 741.

111. *Id.* at 741–42.

112. No. C-93-0243 RMW, 2006 WL 3358410 (N.D. Cal. Nov. 17, 2006).

113. *Id.* at *15.

114. *Id.* at *19.

Cases like *Ayers* and *Von Dohlen* appear to be in the minority, however. In other situations, courts placed less importance on behavioral genetics evidence. In particular, these courts rejected defendants' petitions or appeals claiming their counsels' ineffectiveness in failing to offer mitigating genetics evidence during the penalty phase. In *State v. Ferguson*,[115] for example, the defendant argued that his counsel should have investigated and presented information concerning the defendant's genetic predisposition to a major depressive disorder.[116] The court concluded that because sufficient mitigation evidence had been introduced, the loss of this additional predisposition evidence did not constitute ineffective assistance of counsel.[117] In *Benefiel v. State*,[118] the genetics evidence involved the defendant's predisposition to a personality disorder.[119] Testimony regarding this predisposition had been offered during the guilt phase, and the court was satisfied that the jury had been able to consider it in the sentencing phase, even though it was not reintroduced; its absence from that phase had therefore not affected the jury's sentencing recommendation.[120] In *People v. Franklin*,[121] the court held that, even if the defendant's counsel had investigated and offered such mitigating evidence as the defendant's "family's history of mental illness and violence," it would have made no difference to the jury's recommended sentence.[122] Similarly, in *Landrigan v. Stewart*,[123] the Ninth Circuit's initial decision in the case determined that evidence of the defendant's alleged

---

115. 20 S.W.3d 485 (Mo. 2000).

116. *Id.* at 509.

117. *Id.*; *see also* Jones v. Schriro, 450 F. Supp. 2d 1023, 1024 (D. Ariz. 2006) (holding in part that trial counsel's failure to seek neuropsychological testing did not prejudice defendant, and thus could not amount to ineffective assistance of counsel); Keen v. State, No. W2004-02159-CCA-R3-PD, 2006 WL 1540258, at *46 (Tenn. Crim. App. June 5, 2006), *cert. denied*, Keen v. Tennessee, 127 S. Ct. 2250 (2007) (concluding that generational evidence of mental illness and substance abuse did not outweigh the aggravating circumtances in the case); State v. Ketterer, 855 N.E.2d 48, 80-81 (Ohio 2006), *cert. denied*, Ketterer v. Ohio, 127 S. Ct. 2266 (2007) (determining that despite defendant's evidence of "severe mental problems" which were supported by a genetic connection, aggravating circumstances in the case outweighed mitigating factors).

118. 716 N.E.2d 906 (Ind. 1999).

119. *Id.* at 913.

120. *Id.*

121. 656 N.E.2d 750 (Ill. 1995).

122. *Id.* at 761; *see also* Johnson v. Quarterman, 483 F.3d 278, 279-80 (5th Cir. 2007) (disregarding a mitigation specialist's mention of the defendant's genetic predisposition to substance abuse and focusing instead on the limited potential impact the defendant's history of child abuse would have had on a jury).

123. 272 F.3d 1221 (9th Cir. 2001), *aff'd in part and rev'd in part en banc*, Landrigan v. Schriro, 441 F.3d 638 (9th Cir. 2006), *rev'd*, Schriro v. Landrigan, 127 S. Ct. 1933 (2007).

genetic predisposition to violence would have been unlikely to affect the outcome of the defendant's case.[124]

Landrigan's procedural aspects, which are described in detail elsewhere,[125] are particularly interesting for two reasons: The appellate court opinion cites *Mobley* as precedent,[126] and the case reached the Supreme Court.[127] While the Court only briefly analyzed the evidence, even the Court's limited perspective is nonetheless telling in the context of this Chapter's other behavioral genetics evidence cases.

Timothy Landrigan was convicted of murder and sentenced to death in 1993,[128] one year before Mobley.[129] After the Arizona Supreme Court affirmed Landrigan's conviction and sentence[130] and the district court rejected Landrigan's petition for habeas corpus relief, Landrigan appealed to the Ninth Circuit Court of Appeals.[131] Landrigan's numerous postconviction appeals and petitions were based in part on a claim of ineffective assistance of counsel, arguing that trial counsel did not investigate and introduce mitigating evidence during the trial and sentencing phases.[132] The three-judge appellate panel denied Landrigan's ineffective assistance of counsel claim and affirmed the district court's decision.[133] Citing *Mobley v. Head*[134] and *Turpin v. Mobley*,[135] the panel emphasized that the "rather exotic . . . genetic violence theory" proposing that "Landrigan's biological background made him what he is" would not have affected the outcome of his trial, even if the theory had been introduced.[136] As the panel explained, "although Landrigan's new evidence can be called mitigating in some slight sense, it would also have shown the court that it could anticipate that he would continue to be violent."[137] Given Landrigan's reluctance to express remorse or

---

124. *Id.* at 1228.

125. *Schriro*, 127 S. Ct. at 1937–39; Denno, *supra* note 23, at 226–29.

126. Landrigan, 272 F.3d at 1228 n.4 (citing Turpin v. Mobley, 502 S.E.2d 458, 458 (Ga. 1998)).

127. *Schriro*, 127 S. Ct. at 1933.

128. State v. Landrigan, 859 P.2d 111, 112 (Ariz. 1993).

129. *Turpin*, 502 S.E.2d at 460.

130. *Landrigan*, 859 P.2d at 118.

131. *Landrigan*, 272 F.3d at 1223.

132. *Id.* at 1228.

133. *Id.* at 1229.

134. 267 F.3d 1312 (11th Cir. 2001).

135. 502 S.E.2d 458 (Ga. 1998).

136. *Landrigan*, 272 F.3d at 1228 n.4. Landrigan refuted the panel's reliance on the *Mobley* cases in a subsequent supplemental brief. Supplemental Brief of Petitioner-Appellant at 2, Landrigan v. Stewart, 397 F.3d 1235 (9th Cir. 2005) (No. 00-99011). Citing a wide range of research for support, the brief emphasized that Landrigan's genetic predisposition does not render violent behavior a certainty but simply indicates a higher risk for antisocial tendencies. *Id.* at 1.

137. *Landrigan*, 272 F.3d at 1229.

provide the reasons for his crimes, "assuring the court that genetics made him the way he is could not have been very helpful."[138]

After further petitions,[139] in 2005, the Ninth Circuit Court of Appeals ordered that Landrigan's case be reheard en banc.[140] On rehearing, the Court of Appeals affirmed in part, reversed in part, and remanded the case in an opinion that indicated a considerable amount of openness and receptivity concerning Landrigan's efforts to introduce mitigating genetic and family history evidence.[141]

Such receptivity was short lived, however. In 2007, on grant of certiorari, the Supreme Court reversed and remanded, forcefully supporting a number of the concerns about Landrigan's dangerousness that were articulated by the Ninth

---

138. *Id.*

139. Schriro v. Landrigan, 127 S. Ct. 1933, 1937–39 (2007); Denno, *supra* note 23, at 226–29.

140. Landrigan v. Stewart, 397 F.3d 1235, 1235 (9th Cir. 2005).

141. Landrigan v. Schriro, 441 F.3d 638, 650 (9th Cir. 2006). In considering Landrigan's claim of ineffective assistance of counsel in the penalty phase of his capital sentencing proceeding, the en banc court found that Landrigan had "tried and failed, through no fault of his own, to develop the facts supporting his ineffective assistance claim at the state-court level." *Id.* at 643. The court noted that Landrigan's counsel did not develop potential mitigating evidence, including "information regarding his . . . family history of violence." *Id.* Also seemingly disregarded was a neuropsychological evaluation revealing that factors including "Landrigan's genetic makeup" led to "disordered behavior." *Id.* at 645. Although the en banc court conceded that Landrigan's attorney had "prepared to present two mitigation witnesses . . . and Landrigan was unwilling to have these two particular people testify," the court also noted that "there is no indication that Landrigan would have precluded the introduction of mitigating evidence by other means." *Id.* at 646. Indeed, the issue of Landrigan's willingness to permit other mitigating evidence was never explored, "doubtless because defense counsel had no other evidence to present." *Id.* Moreover, the notion that Landrigan prevented his counsel from presenting mitigating evidence is "overly broad," the result of taking "out of context" the sentencing judge's questioning of Landrigan. *Id.* at 647. Finally, the en banc court noted, an attorney must seek mitigating evidence regardless of a client's desires, and the trial court was required to determine whether Landrigan "[had the] capacity to appreciate his position and make a rational choice with respect to continuing or abandoning further litigation." *Id.* Neither Landrigan's counsel nor the lower court satisfied these obligations. The en banc court thus held Landrigan's claim of ineffective assistance to be "colorable," with "proper basis for an evidentiary hearing" and remanded the case to the district court. *Id.* at 650. The court did, however, "adopt the panel's holdings with respect to the additional sentencing issues raised in Landrigan's certificate of appealability." *Id.* The dissent, meanwhile, argued against remand due to Landrigan's failure to demonstrate prejudice. In partial support for this position, the dissent contended that "[t]he mitigating value of any proven genetic predisposition for violence would not have outweighed its aggravating tendency to suggest Landrigan was undeterrable and, even from prison, would present a future danger to society." *Id.* at 651.

Circuit's initial decision.[142] Addressing Landrigan's alleged genetic predisposition to violence, for example, the Court found it "difficult to improve upon the initial Court of Appeals panel's conclusion" that Landrigan "'not only failed to show remorse or offer mitigating evidence, but he flaunted his menacing behavior'"; therefore, "'assuring the court that genetics made him the way he is could not have been very helpful.'"[143] Describing Landrigan's mitigation evidence as "weak," and noting that "the postconviction court was well acquainted with Landrigan's exceedingly violent past and had seen first hand his belligerent behavior," the Court concluded that the District Court did not abuse its discretion "in declining to grant Landrigan an evidentiary hearing."[144]

The final outcome of *Landrigan* could have implications for other kinds of behavioral genetics evidence cases, irrespective of the types of factors they may try to introduce.[145] Like *Mobley*, *Landrigan* touches on many of the key and varied issues pertaining to behavioral genetics evidence. At the same time, the Court has in no way dismissed the potential applicability of behavioral genetics evidence in cases where the Court may perceive the evidence as more acceptable and the defendant more remorseful. While the Court does not provide a test or standard suggesting how it may weigh such information in the future, the Court does suggest that there are particular aspects of Landrigan's history and demeanor that may have prompted the Court's final determination in a way that other defendants may avoid.

It is also helpful to put *Landrigan* in context with other behavioral genetics and crime cases. In *Hendricks v. Calderon*,[146] for example, the court remanded because defense counsel had not offered mitigating evidence of the defendant's predisposition to mental illness during the penalty phase.[147] In doing so, the

---

142. Schriro v. Landrigan, 127 S. Ct. 1933, 1936 (2007). The Supreme Court also disagreed with the en banc court's opinion regarding Landrigan's refusal to permit the introduction of mitigating evidence, finding that Landrigan "plainly . . . informed his counsel not to present any mitigating evidence." *Id.* at 1935. Given that much of the testimony of the proffered witnesses would have "overlap[ped] with the evidence Landrigan now wants to present," the Supreme Court held it to be clearly established that "Landrigan would have undermined the presentation of any mitigating evidence that his attorney might have uncovered." *Id.* at 1941. With regard to the question of whether "Landrigan's decision not to present mitigating evidence was 'informed and knowing,'" the Supreme Court noted first that "[w]e have never imposed [such a] requirement upon a defendant's decision not to introduce evidence," and then proceeded to outline several additional reasons that the claim was without merit. *Id.* at 1942 (citations omitted).

143. *Id.* at 1944 (citations omitted).

144. *Id.*

145. *See infra* Part V.

146. 70 F.3d 1032 (9th Cir. 1995).

147. 70 F.3d at 1045. The court rejected the defendant's claim that his counsel was ineffective for failing to present this same evidence during the guilt phase. *Id.*

court suggested that mitigating evidence regarding the defendant's "difficult life" (including his genetic predisposition to mental illness) might have affected the case's outcome regarding sentencing.[148] This argument was at odds with the reasoning in *Benefiel*, *Landrigan*, and *Franklin*, in which behavioral genetics evidence had been offered and admitted.[149]

Conversely, behavioral genetics evidence suggesting a predisposition to impulsive behavior was proffered by the defendant's counsel but omitted by the trial court in *Cauthern v. State*.[150] In rejecting the defendant's claim that he was prejudiced by the omission of this mitigating evidence, the court noted that the defendant's stepsiblings experienced similarly abusive upbringings but did not appear to suffer from violent inclinations.[151] *Alley v. State*[152] was comparatively dismissive of behavioral genetics evidence.[153] But the court readily accepted the testimony of medical experts who saw no need to investigate the possibility of genetic problems during their evaluation of the defendant despite their statements that he suffered from various physical problems that could potentially "point to a syndrome with genetic origin."[154] The experts' decision was particularly notable given their acknowledgment that certain genetic conditions can potentially influence people's behavior.[155]

---

148. *Id.*

149. The reasoning in *Hendricks* markedly contrasts with the arguments presented in *State v. Hartman*, 476 S.E.2d 328 (N.C. 1996). Hartman argued the trial court's restructuring of his requested jury instruction regarding his family history of alcoholism prevented the jury from considering relevant mitigating evidence—specifically, Hartman's genetic predisposition to alcohol abuse. *Id.* at 342. The trial court instead submitted the following instruction: "'Consider whether the defendant is an alcoholic.'" *Id.* Stated this way, Hartman posited, the jury "'was more likely'" to view Hartman's alcoholism "'simply as weakness or unmitigated choice.'" *Id.* The court rejected this argument, holding that a "catchall mitigating circumstance" instruction that had been submitted was sufficient to address any such concerns. *Id.*

150. 145 S.W.3d 571, 613 (Tenn. Crim. App. 2004). Cauthern appealed the denial of his petition for post-conviction relief based in part on a claim of ineffective assistance of counsel at his earlier sentencing hearings: his psychiatric expert witness at the postconviction hearing testified that mitigation evidence could have been presented of Cauthern's family history suggesting a genetic predisposition to impulsive behavior. *Id.* at 588. The Tennessee Court of Criminal Appeals affirmed the denial of postconviction relief, holding any shortcomings by counsel would have made no difference to the outcome. *Id.* at 578.

151. *Id.* at 609.

152. 958 S.W.2d 138 (Tenn. Crim. App. 1997).

153. *Id.* at 149–50.

154. *Id.* at 143. A mental health program specialist explained that these problems appeared to be unrelated to Alley's defense of multiple personality disorder and thus did not merit further investigation. *Id.*

155. *Id.* A psychologist who had examined Alley testified that "genetic defects would possibly affect behavior," but noted that "at the time of the evaluation . . . the team deemed as unnecessary any investigation of genetic problems." *Id.*

2. Proof and Diagnosis of Genetic Conditions A second use of behavioral genetics evidence is to prove or support a diagnosis of a genetic condition. The cases in which behavioral genetics evidence was employed for this purpose demonstrate the challenges of applying legal principles to complex scientific information. According to the concurring opinion in *Dennis* ex rel. *Butko v. Budge*,[156] for example, courts have difficulty distinguishing mental illness from "the myriad . . . memories, experiences and genetic predispositions that go to make up each individual's unique personality."[157] Likewise, "judges and lawyers attempt to capture these philosophical dilemmas in words that can have very different meanings to different people, and that often may not respect the concepts that mental health professionals would use to capture cognitive and volitional capacity."[158]

These challenges have been well documented over the years.[159] For one, courts are reluctant to embrace behavioral genetics evidence, which may be due in part to the seemingly arbitrary standards for determining what constitutes mitigation and the vague criteria for diagnosis of genetic conditions. Even among the sizable number of cases analyzed in this Chapter for example, there is great variety in the types of mitigating factors proposed.[160]

In most cases in which the defendant's counsel offers behavioral genetics evidence, the information consists almost wholly of the defendant's family history.[161] It stands to reason, of course, that a defendant's family members could suffer from the same genetic condition(s) as the defendant. Yet proof limited to family history seems to invite responses such as that of the Tennessee Court of

---

156. 378 F.3d 880 (9th Cir. 2004).

157. *Id.* at 895.

158. *Id.*

159. See Denno, *supra* note 2, for an overview of some of these challenges.

160. *See infra* app. A, chart 2; app. B. These types of mitigating factors include predispositions to alcoholism, depression, impulsive behavior, violence, and aggression. *See infra* app. A, chart 2; *supra* note 84 (discussing the different types of genetics evidence). The conditions range from the specific (such as XXY syndrome, porphyria, and bipolar disorder) to the general (for example, mental disorders, personality disorders, mood disorders, and "genetic defects"). *See infra* app. A, chart 2; *supra* note 96 (listing the ways behavioral genetics evidence validates the existence of serious conditions).

161. *See, e.g.*, Landrigan v. Stewart, 272 F.3d 1221 (9th Cir. 2001), *aff'd in part and rev'd in part en banc*, Landrigan v. Schriro, 441 F.3d 638 (9th Cir. 2006), *rev'd*, Schriro v. Landrigan, 127 S. Ct. 1933 (2007). Hendricks v. Calderon, 864 F. Supp. 929 (N.D. Cal. 1994), *aff'd*, 70 F.3d 1032 (9th Cir. 1995); People v. Franklin, 656 N.E.2d 750 (Ill. 1995); Sanchez v. Ryan, 734 N.E.2d 920 (Ill. App. Ct. 2000); State v. Hartman, 476 S.E.2d 328 (N.C. 1996); State v. Hughbanks, 792 N.E.2d 1081 (Ohio 2003); Cauthern v. State, 145 S.W.3d 571 (Tenn. Crim. App. 2004); Davis v. State, No. M2003-00744-CCA-R3-PC, 2004 WL 253396 (Tenn. Crim. App. Feb. 11, 2004); State v. Maraschiello, 88 S.W.3d 586 (Tenn. Crim. App. 2000); Morris v. State, No. W2005-00426-CCA-R3-PD, 2006 WL 2872870 (Tenn. Crim. App. Oct. 10, 2006).

Criminal Appeals, which emphasized in *Cauthern* that the defendant's stepsiblings did not suffer from the alleged predisposition.[162] Even in cases such as *State v. Hughbanks*,[163] in which the court acknowledged the negative effects of a family history of mental illness on a defendant, such mitigating evidence does not appear likely to affect the outcome of the case.[164]

In some circumstances, proving a genetic predisposition through family history may even backfire. In rejecting the defendant's ineffective assistance claim in *Landrigan*, the initial Ninth Circuit decision set forth a proposition eventually echoed by the Supreme Court: "It is highly doubtful that the sentencing court would have been moved by information that [the defendant] was a remorseless, violent killer because he was genetically programmed to be violent, as shown by the fact that he comes from a family of violent people, who are killers also."[165] Citing *Franklin*,[166] the Ninth Circuit further warned, "although [defendant's] new evidence can be called mitigating in some slight sense, it would also have shown the court that it could anticipate that he would continue to be violent."[167] Of course, this argument takes on a double-edged-sword rationale that wrongly

162. *Cauthern*, 145 S.W.3d at 609.

163. 792 N.E.2d at 1101–03.

164. *Id.* at 1104. In *Hughbanks* and at least two other cases, *State v. Spivey*, 692 N.E.2d 151 (Ohio 1998), and *State v. Wilson*, No. Civ.A. 92CA005396, 1994 WL 558568 (Ohio Ct. App. Oct. 12, 1994), the courts did not expressly reject mitigating evidence regarding genetics, but held that the aggravating circumstances of the crime outweighed any mitigating factors. The appellate court in *Hughbanks* appeared to include "genetic tendency" among the defendant's relevant background factors. 792 N.E.2d at 1101. It acknowledged that many of Hughbanks's family members suffered from mental illness and noted the likely negative effect on his "growth and development." *Id.* at 1103. Yet the court found that the aggravating circumstances of the crime outweighed such mitigating factors. *Id.* at 1104. Family history was not specifically offered as proof of a genetics defense in *Spivey* and *Wilson*. *Spivey* involved a diagnosis of XYY syndrome. 692 N.E.2d at 165. A defense expert testified that although the syndrome itself does not cause aggression, the defendant's family environment exacerbated his condition and resulted in his criminal behavior. *Id. Wilson* merely listed the defendant's genetic predisposition to alcoholism among the mitigating factors presented during the penalty phase and offered no further information concerning its origins. 1994 WL 558568, at *13 n.5.

165. *Landrigan*, 272 F.3d at 1228–29.

166. People v. Franklin, 656 N.E.2d 750 (Ill. 1995).

167. *Landrigan*, 272 F.3d at 1229. The *Franklin* court further concluded the following: The proffered evidence regarding defendant's psychological problems and his family's violent and psychological history was not inherently mitigating. Although this evidence could have evoked compassion in the jurors, it could have also demonstrated defendant's potential for future dangerousness and the basis for defendant's past criminal acts. The evidence of defendant's mental illness may also have shown that defendant was less deterrable or that society needed to be protected from him. 656 N.E.2d at 761 (citations omitted).

presumes a genetic attribute is static.[168] Despite the questionable accuracy of this presumption, such approaches appear to be highly persuasive to courts and the public alike.

Nor does genetics evidence appear to flag the attention of the trial court when proof other than family history is offered. In *Arausa v. State*,[169] the defendant had requested appointment of a psychiatrist in part to help him assess the mitigation value of a research study that indicated a genetic predisposition among victims of abuse to become abusers.[170] The appellate court skirted the genetics issue, finding no error in the trial court's rejecting the defendant's request: the defendant's original request for a court-appointed medical health expert had been based on a need to analyze the defendant's competency, not the research study.[171] In *State v. Maraschiello*,[172] the defendant claimed his genetic predisposition for a delusional disorder (as demonstrated by his family history) was exacerbated by Gulf War syndrome.[173] This appellate court also followed the lead of the trial court in avoiding the matter of genetics. The testimony pertaining to Gulf War syndrome had been excluded on unrelated grounds, and the defendant's alleged predisposition did not come up again at trial (or on appeal).[174] Only in *Hendricks v. Calderon*[175] did an appellate court consider it a mistake not to offer as mitigation evidence pretrial hearing testimony on the defendant's genetic predisposition to mental illness and its aggravation by an abusive childhood.[176]

3. Future Dangerousness Evidence regarding genetic predispositions brings with it the third use of genetics evidence in criminal law: the debate over the prediction of future dangerousness,[177] as discussed in *Franklin*[178] and *Landrigan*.[179] In many of the cases this Chapter analyzes, genetics evidence takes the form of

---

168. See *infra* Part V for further discussion of this issue in the context of additional conceptual problems with the genetics evidence cases.

169. No. 07-02-0396-CR, 2003 WL 21803322, at *1 (Tex. App. Aug. 6, 2003), *aff'g* State v. Arausa, No. 2002-439113 (Dist. Ct. Lubbock County July 5, 2002).

170. *Id.* at *2.

171. *Id.* at *4. More generally, the court did not consider the request for a psychiatrist to be relevant to the defense. *Id.*

172. 88 S.W.3d 586 (Tenn. Crim. App. 2000).

173. *Id.* at 599. On appeal, Maraschiello claimed in part that the trial court had wrongfully excluded testimony that he suffered from the syndrome. *Id.* at 590.

174. *Id.* at 599–611.

175. 864 F. Supp. 929 (N.D. Cal. 1994), *aff'd*, 70 F.3d 1032 (9th Cir. 1995).

176. *Id.* at 934–35.

177. Future dangerousness and other issues raised by genetics evidence are discussed in *People v. Rodriguez*, 764 N.Y.S.2d 305 (N.Y. Sup. Ct. 2003), which concerns defendants' privacy rights in the context of the recent trend to collect DNA samples. See *supra* note 89 for a more detailed account of *Rodriguez*.

178. People v. Franklin, 656 N.E.2d 750, 761 (Ill. 1995).

179. Landrigan v. Stewart, 272 F.3d 1221, 1228–29 (9th Cir. 2001), *aff'd in part and rev'd in part en banc*, Landrigan v. Schriro, 441 F.3d 638 (9th Cir. 2006), *rev'd*, Schriro v. Landrigan, 127 S. Ct. 1933 (2007).

an individual's predisposition toward some condition or behavior.[180] This approach does not, of course, guarantee that the afflicted individual will develop that condition or engage in that behavior; it indicates merely that the likelihood of occurrence may be heightened. For example, in *State v. Spivey*,[181] the doctor who diagnosed the appellant with XYY syndrome testified that this abnormality put the defendant "at risk for committing criminal acts, but that the syndrome itself did not cause him to be aggressive and to commit violent acts."[182] Instead, the defendant's family environment was faulted for triggering his preexisting tendencies toward violence.[183]

The issue of future dangerousness was explored in further detail in *State v. DeAngelo*,[184] in which several psychiatrists evaluated the mental condition of an individual who had been acquitted of criminal charges because he was unable to recognize or control the wrongfulness of his behavior.[185] The evaluating experts disagreed on their diagnoses and treatment recommendations for the individual, as well as on their assessment of the risk he posed to the public if released.[186] The court ultimately determined that the individual should be committed to a maximum security psychiatric unit because he was a danger to society.[187] As the court stated, "[p]sychiatric predictions of future dangerousness, while of some value, must not be unduly relied upon. The court's main concern must be the protection of society, and not necessarily therapeutic goals."[188]

DeAngelo and comparable kinds of cases[189] illustrate the strain between the legal and mental health fields when they consider genetic information. Such tension is accentuated because genetics evidence is typically introduced into trials through

---

180. *See infra* app. A, chart 2; app. B.

181. 692 N.E.2d 151 (Ohio 1998).

182. *Id.* at 165.

183. *Id.*

184. No. CR 97010866S, 2000 WL 973104, at *2 (Conn. Super. Ct. June 20, 2000).

185. *Id.* at *1.

186. *Id.* at *3–6. One psychiatrist testified that DeAngelo "need[ed] supervision; especially if he has a genetic predisposition to bipolar disorder." *Id.* at *6. He concluded that "if [DeAngelo] suffer[ed] another manic episode, he could be dangerous to himself and dangerous to others." *Id.*

187. *Id.* at *11.

188. *Id.*

189. *See, e.g., People v. Allaway*, No. G030307, 2003 WL 22147632 (Cal. App. 4 Dist. Sept. 18, 2003). In *Allaway*, behavioral genetics evidence worked against the defendant for purposes of evaluating future dangerousness. Allaway's application for transfer from a state mental hospital to an outpatient treatment facility was denied in part based on the testimony of an independent evaluator who stated that Allaway had a "genetic predisposition" to mental illness and psychotic behavior. *Id.* at *3. The court seemed to accept the genetics link, albeit in a way that ensured a negative result for the defendant.

testimony from mental health professionals.[190] Establishing consistent criteria for assessing the expertise of these witnesses is therefore likely to be a critical step toward the general acceptance of behavioral genetics evidence. In *DeAngelo*,[191] for example, the court questioned the credentials and objectivity of at least one testifying psychiatrist.[192] In turn, the court in *People v. Hammerli*[193] likewise seemed dubious of the defense's expert witness testimony.[194] The court emphasized that although the defendant's treating psychiatrist had diagnosed the defendant with depression (yet had noted improvement), all four defense experts "found defendant to be legally insane at the time of the murder and were able with hindsight to fit defendant's actions into their various diagnoses."[195] As the court explained, each of the experts detected "in defendant's behavior facts to support [that expert's] own opinion."[196] In *Billiot v. State*,[197] the court exhibited a more overt lack of deference toward the treating mental health expert, who diagnosed the defendant with a genetic predisposition. Instead, the court relied on the combined testimony of the majority of expert witnesses in determining that the defendant was competent to be executed.[198] Acknowledging that the lone, treating mental health expert who testified otherwise "had done more recent and more extensive research on the issue of [defendant's] sanity," the court nonetheless refused to give that witness's testimony greater weight than that of the other witnesses.[199] In *People v. Armstrong*,[200] the court concluded that a social worker lacked the expertise to testify concerning the defendant's genetic predisposition to alcoholism.[201] Perhaps *Armstrong* could be interpreted as indicating that the genetic predisposition evidence might have received greater consideration if the testifying witness had had the necessary expertise.

Even among qualified experts, however, conflicting diagnoses are another factor likely to hinder general acceptance of behavioral genetics evidence. The drawbacks of such incongruity are indicated in cases such as *Hall v. State*.[202] In *Hall*, psychologists for the defense testified that the defendant suffered from various genetic afflictions; in contrast, the state's psychologist offered directly opposing testimony, asserting that the defendant did not exhibit the symptoms

---

190. *See infra* app. A, chart 3; app. B.
191. No. CR 97010866S, 2000 WL 973014 (Conn. Super. June 20, 2000).
192. *Id.* at *11.
193. 662 N.E.2d 452 (Ill. App. Ct. 1996).
194. *Id.* at 458.
195. *Id.*
196. *Id.*
197. 655 So. 2d 1 (Miss. 1995).
198. *Id.* at 17.
199. *Id.* at 13.
200. 700 N.E.2d 960 (Ill. 1998).
201. *Id.* at 970.
202. 160 S.W.3d 24 (Tex. Crim. App. 2004) (en banc).

of any such disorders.[203] Not surprisingly, courts are quick to point out such disparities. The *DeAngelo*[204] court, for example, noted the psychiatrists' inability to agree on a diagnosis of the defendant,[205] an outcome that encouraged the court to have him committed.[206]

Overall, this analysis of the last 13 years of behavioral genetics evidence cases shows how courts generally have continued to constrain the admissibility or use of genetic factors, even as mitigation in the penalty phase of a death penalty trial. Thus, there is little overt indication that behavioral genetics evidence has reinforced concerns expressed in the context of *Mobley*, most particularly worries that actors in the criminal justice system would increasingly and irresponsibly rely on such evidence in their decision making. So far, evidentiary rules and procedures continue to keep the evidence in a relatively safe place substantively. Therefore, a concern may be that defendants do not have available the full range of mitigating factors to which they are constitutionally entitled in death penalty cases.

Indeed, concerns over behavioral genetics evidence in criminal cases can also prove to be a red herring of sorts, deflecting attention from the realization that courts can genetically stereotype defendants irrespective of any attempt made by those defendants to submit genetics arguments. In *State v. Madey*,[207] for example, the defendant, who pled guilty to misdemeanor assault after two police officers tried to take her into protective custody for public intoxication,[208] challenged the court's probation requirements, one of which mandated that she

---

203. *Id.* at 30. Hall submitted affidavits from two psychologists stating that he was mentally retarded. *Id.* at 32. One affidavit described Hall's appearance as typical of fetal alcohol syndrome and stated that he also exhibited characteristics resembling other genetic disorders (e.g., XXY), which had existed at birth. *Id.* at 33. The State submitted a rebuttal affidavit from a neuropsychologist who had testified during the guilt phase of the trial. *Id.* at 35. This witness explicitly stated that Hall did not exhibit symptoms of such genetic disorders. *Id.* The habeas trial court concluded that Hall was not mentally retarded, and therefore denied relief. The Texas Court of Criminal Appeals determined that the trial court was in the best position to evaluate conflicting evidence regarding the defendant's mental state, and thus affirmed the trial court's decision. *Id.* at 40.

204. No. CR 97010866S, 2000 WL 973104 (Conn. Super. Ct. June 20, 2000).

205. *Id.* at *11.

206. *Id.* In addition, there is no assurance that the expert's testimony is going to satisfy the tough legal standards for mental state even if that testimony is considered credible. *See, e.g.,* State v. Idellfonso-Diaz, No. M2006-00203-CCA-R9-CD, 2006 WL 3093207 (Tenn. Crim. App. Nov. 1, 2006) (remanding decision of trial court) (rendering testimony inadmissible because the impairment at issue was not sufficiently detrimental to negate the defendant's mental capacity to commit the crimes).

207. State v. Madey, No. 81166, 2002-Ohio-5976, 2002 WL 31429827 (Ohio App. 8 Dist. Oct. 31, 2002) (vacating and remanding sentencing decision of trial court).

208. *Id.* at *1.

write an essay on "alcoholism and American Indians."[209] The requirements were also made in the context of the court's numerous and unsubstantiated comments about Madey's ethnic proclivity for alcoholism. These comments included asking Madey's mother whether "she knew 'anything about genetic predisposition to alcoholism?'" or "if she had 'ever been on an Indian reservation?' and if she had ever seen 'the Scotch or Irish drinking?'"[210] The court even asked the mother whether she "had a concern that her daughter would become 'a flaming alcoholic' because, with such an ethnic background, 'there [was] nothing she can do about it.'"[211] In turn, the court continually speculated about the degree of the defendant's future dangerousness, even characterizing the defendant's potential state of being a murder victim as a danger to others: *"[I]f you start drinking like this, you're a danger.* You will go out and get yourself attacked, or murdered, or something, and put yourself in these hopeless conditions, which is a bad example, and every time somebody is killed or raped in society, that diminishes the public safety overall."[212]

In vacating the defendant's sentence and remanding, the appellate court noted that not only were the trial court's comments completely unrelated "to an interest in doing justice," but that the defendant did not "[attempt] to use her family background to excuse her behavior."[213] The genetic stereotyping was in the court's eyes only, a potential cause for concern in any case, no matter the defense or evidentiary circumstances.

V. CONCLUDING COMMENTS

In 1994, *Mobley v. State*[214] garnered substantial notice because of defense counsel's strenuous efforts to test for genetics evidence for mitigation in Stephen Mobley's death penalty case.[215] According to some commentators at the time, if such testing had been allowed, it could encourage political and moral abuses of such highly controversial information.[216] Yet the survey here of the 48 cases that have used behavioral genetics evidence in the 13 years following *Mobley* shows

---

209. *Id.* at *2.
210. *Id.* at *1.
211. *Id.*
212. *Id.* at *2.
213. *Id.* at *4.
214. 455 S.E.2d 61 (Ga. 1995).
215. *See supra* note 12 and accompanying text.
216. *See* Denno, *supra* note 2, at 254 (outlining the political and moral concerns over genetics evidence); *see also supra* note 12 (discussing potential abuses in the context of the *Mobley* case); *infra* note 219 (discussing potential abuses in the context of the 1995 University of Maryland conference on *The Meaning and Significance of Research on Genetics and Criminal Behavior*).

no apparent basis for these worries.[217] When attorneys do attempt to introduce such evidence during the penalty phase of a death penalty trial, most courts still question its applicability, an approach that is also seemingly followed by the Supreme Court's position in *Landrigan*.[218]

In essence, since *Mobley*, little has changed legally in the area of behavioral genetics and crime. The topic remains controversial for many of the same reasons it did 13 years ago.[219] Likewise, the press and public still seem confused about the meaning and role of mitigating evidence in death penalty cases.[220]

---

217. *See supra* Part IV; *infra* app. B.

218. 127 S. Ct. 1933 (2007).

219. Few conferences on the topic of genetics and crime have occurred since the Ciba symposium. For example, shortly after the Ciba symposium took place, the University of Maryland held a conference on *The Meaning and Significance of Research on Genetics and Criminal Behavior*. David Wasserman, a legal scholar and organizer of the conference, noted at the time, "There are a hell of a lot of people attending this conference who think the dangers of genetic research are as great in the long term as the dangers of atomic energy." Pezzella, *supra* note 3; *see also* Wade Roush, *Conflict Marks Crime Conference*, 269 SCIENCE 1808, 1808 (1995) ("The [Maryland] conference . . . has been protested, canceled, rescheduled, and otherwise dogged by controversy ever since it was first planned . . ."). Previously, the conference had been cancelled because of the controversial nature of the topic. Abraham, *supra* note 2 ("In 1992, just a year before Mr. Summer seized on the Dutch family study, the U.S. National Institutes of Health cancelled a conference on crime and genetics at the University of Maryland after black groups protested that such research was racially motivated."); Cookson, *supra* note 16, at 8 ("Public pressure forced the US National Institutes of Health to cancel a conference on [genetics and behavior] in 1992 after opponents of the research detected racial overtones in some of the proposed contributions."); Pezzella, *supra* note 3 ("Even participants [of the Maryland conference] found the meeting somewhat distasteful. Paul R. Billings, a professor at Stanford University . . . said he feared the current concentration on genetics could bring back the kind of eugenics movement that was espoused by the Nazis."); Richard W. Stevenson, *Researchers See Gene Link To Violence But Are Wary*, N.Y. TIMES, Feb. 19, 1995, at 29 ("[The Maryland] conference was called off after critics said that it was too accepting of the idea that inherited personality traits were the primary causes of crime and violence and that it would promote the notion that criminals could be identified by genetic markers."); Tom Wilkie, *Scientist Denounces Criminal Gene Theory*, INDEPENDENT (London), Feb. 13, 1995, HOME, at 2 ("'[The Maryland conference] was seen as overtly racist.'").

220. This confusion was particularly apparent at the time of the Stephen Mobley case. Some news media referred to the genetics evidence as a culpability defense, not as a basis for mitigation. *See* Moosajee, *supra* note 12, at 213; Robert Davis, *'We Live in an Age of Exotic Defenses'*, USA TODAY, Nov. 22, 1994, at 1A ("Stephen Mobley blames his genes for making him kill. . . . [E]xperts say these defenses are typical of the bizarre and unusual rationales that increasingly are being heard in courtrooms across the USA as defendants try to find something—anything—to blame."); Felsenthal, *supra* note 3 ("In a novel and highly controversial defense, [Mobley's lawyers] are arguing that Mr. Mobley's genes may have predisposed him to commit crimes."); Holmquist, *supra* note 2; Marrin, *supra* note 2. *But see* Abraham, *supra* note 2 ("[P]eople are concerned [the argument] nullifies the idea

A key question remains, however. What is the overall framework courts use to rationalize their skepticism regarding behavioral genetics evidence? Not all courts have viewed genetics evidence negatively. In *Von Dohlen v. State*,[221] for example, the court considered such information (in conjunction with other evidence) sufficiently compelling to remand the defendant's case for resentencing: the defendant's counsel had not provided a testifying expert with records that indicated, among other things, the defendant's genetic predisposition for mental disorder.[222] *Von Dohlen* is one of a number of exceptions,[223] however, among a larger group of cases that have considered behavioral genetics evidence either insignificant or possibly indicative of a defendant's continuing violent tendencies.

As in *Mobley*, courts have provided various reasons for excluding a defendant's offer of behavioral genetics information, including the following: (1) counsel had already submitted sufficient mitigation evidence and additional data on the defendant's genetic proclivities would probably not have affected the outcome of the defendant's case;[224] (2) genetics evidence has questionable credibility when compared to other evidence introduced at trial,[225] particularly when testimony from different experts conflicts;[226] (3) the theory of a link between genetics and violence is "unorthodox"[227] or "exotic";[228] (4) genetics evidence can cut against a defendant's case because it suggests the defendant will continue to be violent;[229]

---

of free will and responsibility. But I'm not using it as a defence, per se, but as a mitigating factor—you know, 'If you're thinking about putting this guy to death, think about this.'") (quoting Daniel Summer); Connor, *supra* note 2 ("'There is no legal defence to his crime,' says . . . Mobley's attorney. There is only the mitigating factor of his family history.'"). On occasion, the media also assumed Mobley founded his appeal on having a genetic disorder, although the appeal was based on the denial of his motion for funding to test for any genetic disorder. *See* Boseley, *supra* note 3; Malik, *supra* note 12.

221. 602 S.E.2d 738 (S.C. 2004).

222. *Id.* at 741–46.

223. See also *supra* notes 175–76 and accompanying text discussing Hendricks v. Calderon, 864 F. Supp. 929 (N.D. Cal. 1994), *aff'd*, 70 F.3d 1032 (9th Cir. 1995). For other exceptions, see Mickey v. Ayers, No. C-93-0243 RMW, 2006 WL 3358410 (N.D. Cal. Nov. 17, 2006); Loving v. United States, 64 M.J. 132 (C.A.A.F. 2006); and Head v. Thomason, 578 S.E.2d 426 (Ga. 2003).

224. *See, e.g.,* Landrigan v. Stewart, 272 F.3d 1221 (9th Cir. 2001), *aff'd in part and rev'd in part en banc*, Landrigan v. Schriro, 441 F.3d 638 (9th Cir. 2006), *rev'd*, Schriro v. Landrigan, 127 S. Ct. 1933 (2007). Mobley v. State, 455 S.E.2d 61 (Ga. 1995); People v. Franklin, 656 N.E.2d 750 (Ill. 1995); State v. Ferguson, 20 S.W.3d 485 (Mo. 2000).

225. People v. Hammerli, 662 N.E.2d 452 (Ill. App. Ct. 1996); Cauthern v. State, 145 S.W.3d 571 (Tenn. Crim. App. 2004).

226. Hall v. State, 160 S.W.3d 24, 26 (Tex. Crim. App. 2004) (en banc).

227. Turpin v. Mobley, 502 S.E.2d 458, 463 (Ga. 1998).

228. *Landrigan*, 272 F.3d at 1228 n.4.

229. *Id.* at 1229.

and (5) genetics evidence does not comport with some courts' theories of criminal responsibility, which may emphasize, for example, the protection of society over "therapeutic goals."[230]

There is little or negligible foundation for any of these five rationales, however. First, there is only a fragile basis for questioning the credibility or impact of behavioral genetics evidence when such evidence is so rarely admitted into court. Indeed, part of the controversy over the admissibility of behavioral genetics research has usually involved the opposite claim—that because of its aura of scientific sophistication and precision, genetics information would weigh too heavily on a jury and have a disproportionate effect on a case's disposition. The extent of this influence would be particularly significant if the evidence were compared to other, more traditionally accepted, mitigating information.[231] For example, there are compelling arguments that some behavioral genetics evidence could be relevant and useful if applied in a limited way, such as buttressing other proffered mitigating conditions,[232] as in cases when the defendant's veracity concerning the existence of a condition is questioned.[233]

Likewise, courts' rendering of genetic factors as "unorthodox" or "exotic" is ironic, given that courts themselves perpetuate this supposed status of unusualness. Regardless, a factor need not be conventional in order for it to be considered mitigating. The claim of "exoticism" is also dubious on its face. Genetics evidence has a long history in legal cases,[234] even if that past was controversial or has seemingly been forgotten by modern courts, such as those deciding *Mobley v. State*[235] and *Landrigan v. Stewart.*[236] In turn, this Chapter's survey has uncovered a sizable number of such cases over the past 13 years.

The double-edged-sword aspect of behavioral genetics evidence stressed by some courts[237] has also long been acknowledged. But this dilemma characterizes many other mitigating factors, for example, those available to juvenile offenders. In *Roper v. Simmons,*[238] the Supreme Court held that the Eighth and Fourteenth

---

230. State v. DeAngelo, No. CR 970010866S, 2000 WL 973104, at *11 (Conn. Super. Ct. June 20, 2000).

231. Denno, *supra* note 2, at 253–54; *see also supra* note 85 and accompanying text (discussing the five stated problems concerning the use of genetics evidence in criminal cases).

232. *See supra* note 96 (listing the ways that genetics evidence validates the existence of a serious condition); *infra* app. B.

233. *See infra* app. B (listing Alley v. State, 958 S.W.2d 138, 142 (Tenn. Crim. App. 1997) and Billiot v. State, 655 So. 2d 1, 8 (Miss. 1995)).

234. *See supra* note 81 and accompanying text.

235. 455 S.E.2d 61 (Ga. 1995).

236. 272 F.3d 1221 (9th Cir. 2001), *aff'd in part and rev'd in part en banc,* Landrigan v. Schriro, 441 F.3d 638 (9th Cir. 2006), *rev'd,* Schriro v. Landrigan, 127 S. Ct. 1933 (2007).

237. *See* Denno, *supra* note 2, at 254.

238. 543 U.S. 551 (2005).

Amendments prohibited the execution of persons aged younger than 18 at the time their crimes were committed.[239] The Court reasoned that relative to adults, juveniles are more immature and irresponsible, vulnerable to negative pressures from their peers and environment, and fragile and unstable in their identities.[240] Although these disparities explained why juveniles may be less culpable, they also heightened the likelihood that juveniles would engage in impulsive thinking and criminality.[241] In other words, the very factors that argued against juveniles' eligibility for the death penalty also made them more prone to misconduct. Youth can be a double-edged sword, although the Court has taken steps to contain that possibility.

Similarly, courts that exclude behavioral genetics evidence because it does not mesh with their theory of criminal responsibility seemingly confuse the requirements for mitigating evidence with other criminal law doctrines. This problem also arose when the media covered the *Mobley* case. Basically, some journalists and commentators treated mitigation in a death penalty case synonymously with criminal defenses pertaining to a defendant's culpability.[242] The admissibility criteria for mitigation, however, are far more encompassing than criminal defenses because the criteria serve substantially different goals.[243]

Part of the general difficulty with these cases also involves courts' apparent ignorance of the interactions among social, biological, and genetic variables. As this Chapter has noted, however, biological, genetic, and social variables are highly interactive and difficult to separate without creating artificial categories.[244]

Overall, this Chapter has taken a relatively narrow view of the use of behavioral genetics evidence, thereby excluding or limiting a number of topics of interest: (1) the question of whether such evidence should be applied outside the context of mitigation in death penalty cases; (2) the doctrinal differences in how the evidence has been implemented within the mitigation context (for example, the differences between the evidentiary requirements necessary for proving a claim of ineffective assistance of counsel as opposed to future dangerousness); (3) a comparison of courts' treatment of behavioral genetic factors with other kinds of social and behavioral research (even though much of the criticism of behavioral genetics evidence could pertain to social science evidence in general); (4) a comparison of the different types of genetics factors used in cases; and (5) an analysis of the broader philosophical debates and exchanges concerning

---

239. *Id.* at 578 ("The Eighth and Fourteenth Amendments forbid imposition of the death penalty on offenders who were under the age of 18 when their crimes were committed.").

240. *Id.* at 569–70.

241. *Id.*

242. *See supra* note 220 and accompanying text.

243. *See supra* note 93 and accompanying text.

244. *See supra* note 88 and accompanying text.

the role of behavioral genetic factors in the criminal justice system and theoretical models of criminal responsibility. All these issues are significant, but they exceed this Chapter's scope.

At the same time, the topic of behavioral genetics and crime will not go away. Although courts do not appear to be exploiting genetics information in the way commentators on *Mobley* feared, the criminal justice system still lacks a sound conceptual framework for handling behavioral genetics research no matter what it decides to do with it. The warnings of the past are important to heed. As surveyed attorneys agreed over a decade ago in the context of *Mobley*, "the question is not if this kind of genetic testing is admissible as mitigating evidence in criminal trials, but when."[245]

---

245. Mark Curriden, *His Lawyer Says It's in the Killer's Genes*, NAT'L L.J., Nov. 7, 1994, at A12.

11. BEHAVIORAL GENETICS RESEARCH AND CRIMINAL DNA DATABASES: LAWS AND POLICIES[*]

D.H. KAYE

DNA identification databases have made it possible to apprehend the perpetrators of crimes ranging from auto theft and petty burglary to serial rapes and murders. Yet the laws establishing these databases have been the subject of persistent litigation and repeated criticism. One recurrent refrain plays on the fear of research into genes and behavior. The public has been told that

> There are no limits on who uses [the tissue sample]. Even if [a law enforcement agency] decides they're only going to use it for identification purposes, there's no restriction on their turning it over to somebody else who will use it to look for a crime gene. . . .[1]

Other advocacy groups and individuals have trumpeted the prospect of research seeking a "crime gene"[2] or have pointed to the sordid history of biological theories of racial inferiority[3] as grounds for resisting or reversing DNA database initiatives.[4]

---

[*] Copyright©2009 by David Kaye.

1. Interview by Ira Flatow, NPR *Talk of the Nation*, with Nadine Strossen (May 25, 2001), *available at* http:// www.sciencefriday.com/pages/2001/May/hour1_052501.html; see also Speeding DNA Evidence Processing: Hearing on H.R. 2810, H.R. 3087, and H.R. 3375 before the Subcomm. on Crime of the H. Comm. on the Judiciary, 106th Cong., 2000 WL 342540 (2000) (testimony of Barry Steinhardt, Associate Director, American Civil Liberties Union, Washington, D.C.) [hereinafter Hearing] (describing DNA samples as harboring our "most intimate secrets," possibly including "genetic markers for aggression, substance addiction, criminal tendencies and sexual orientation").

2. Benjamin Keehn, *Strands of Justice: Do DNA Databanks Infringe on Defendants' Rights?*, PBS Newshour Online Forum, July 17, 1998, http:// www.pbs.org/newshour/ forum/july98/dna_databanks03.html ("The hunt is already on for the 'crime gene'. . . [and] the process of searching for it may well be the path to totalitarianism"); *cf.* Jean E. McEwen, *Storing Genes to Solve Crimes: Legal, Ethical, and Public Policy Considerations, in* STORED TISSUE SAMPLES: ETHICAL, LEGAL, AND PUBLIC POLICY IMPLICATIONS 311, 323 (B.F. Weir ed., 1998) ("Banked samples from convicted offenders . . . could someday come to be seen as an especially valuable resource for behavioral geneticists—such as those interested in studying the possibility of a genetic predisposition to violence, pedophilia, or alcoholism") (footnote omitted).

3. Nachama L. Wilker et al., *DNA Data Banking and the Public Interest, in* DNA ON TRIAL: GENETIC INFORMATION AND CRIMINAL JUSTICE 141, 147 (Paul R. Billings ed., 1992) (opposing research "designed to identify genes associated with criminal behavior" because it lacks scientific merit and "could be used as a new biological justification to bolster racist and ethnic prejudice").

4. Michael Avery, Landry v. Attorney General: *DNA Databanks Hold a Mortgage on Privacy Rights*, 44 BOSTON B. J. 18, 18 (2000) ("Researchers are currently attempting to

How valid are these objections to the DNA database laws now on the books? It seems clear that talk of a "crime gene" is scientifically naive and that the databases themselves would be of little or no value in behavioral genetics research. The DNA information in these databases is limited to a small number of DNA base-pair variations that have been selected because they are useful for identification. These particular DNA variations are unlikely to reveal anything significant about an individual's genes, let alone the "polygenes" that might affect behavior.[5] However, the DNA samples that are on file could be reanalyzed at more informative sites, and statistical studies of possible correlations between the new data and behavioral traits might be of some scientific interest. As such, fears about the law enforcement databases contributing to genetic research into crime cannot be so easily dismissed.

Accordingly, this chapter surveys state and federal database legislation. It shows that several previous studies have overlooked or understated the restrictions on medical or behavioral genetics research with convicted offender samples. Many of the pertinent statutes, although not drafted with precision, preclude such research. Nevertheless, even clear statutory provisions are subject to amendment through the legislative process. Inasmuch as the Constitution, as currently interpreted, offers rather weak protection for informational privacy, the policy question of allowing such behavioral genetics research with the samples in the law enforcement repositories must be confronted.

As to this question, this chapter identifies and assesses some of the bioethical and social arguments against allowing such research. These include concerns about the possible misuse of or misunderstandings about the fruits of the research and the lack of consent on the part of the "donors" of DNA samples. This issue also raises the related policy issue of whether the DNA samples should be retained at all—as well as the question addressed in Part II of the research value of DNA databases and repositories. In these regards, I conclude that an absolute prohibition on behavioral genetics research is not necessary. Instead, I propose that if the samples are to be retained (as they currently are), then an independent body with appropriate expertise should evaluate proposals for research projects on a case-by-case basis.

develop genetic profiles that would identify or predict homosexuality, aggression, criminality, mental illness, alcoholism, obesity and other conditions [and conducting] more than 200 clinical studies on the genetic basis of criminal behavior, [creating obvious] unfairness and potential for harm to individuals and families inherent in such social stereotyping").

5. D. H. Kaye, *Please, Let's Bury the Junk: The CODIS Loci and the Revelation of Private Information*, 102 Nw. Univ. L. Rev. Colloquy 70 (2007).

THE LEGAL "IS": PERMISSIBILITY OF RESEARCH ACCESS
TO OFFENDER DATABASES

As noted at the outset, a commonly expressed concern about DNA databases for law enforcement is that the laws authorizing or funding the databases allow, if not invite, genetic information collected to catch rapists, murderers, and other criminals to be used for genetic research into criminal conduct as well as mental illness and other diseases. The following alarms are typical:

(1) "In about fifteen of the fifty states, the statutes expressly permit that the databanks. . . can be used for research purposes in . . . medical research, humanitarian needs, and what have you."[6]

(2) "Twenty-four states allow DNA samples that have been collected only for law enforcement identification to be used for a variety of other non–law enforcement purposes."[7]

(3) "[T]wenty states allow law enforcement to use DNA samples to improve forensic techniques, 'which could mean searching . . . DNA samples for genetic predictors of recidivism, pedophilia or aggression.'"[8]

(4) "[M]any state statutes allow access to the samples for undefined law enforcement purposes and humanitarian identification purposes, or authorize the use of samples for assisting medical research."[9]

---

6. Peter Neufeld, Remarks at the Conference on DNA and the Criminal Justice System (Nov. 19–21, 2000), http://www.ksg.harvard.edu/dna/transcribe_ table_page.htm.

7. Barry Steinhardt, *Privacy and Forensic DNA Data Banks*, in DNA AND THE CRIMINAL JUSTICE SYSTEM 173, 176 (David Lazer ed., 2004); *cf.* Jonathan Kimmelman, *The Promise and Perils of Criminal DNA Databanking*, 18 NATURE BIOTECH. 695, 696 (2000) ("On the negative side, ... 23 states (directly or indirectly) authorize release of samples or records for research uses that would assist law enforcement. . . . Retaining samples sustains the possibility that they will find ethically problematic uses in the future; authorizing research on samples, even if they are stripped of individual identifiers (as mandated by most laws) nearly delivers them to this unseemly fate").

8. Jill C. Schaefer, *Comment, Profiling at the Cellular Level: The Future of the New York State DNA Databanks*, 14 ALB. L. J. SCI. & TECH. 559, 576 (2004) (citation omitted); *see also* Troy Duster, *Selective Arrests, an Ever-expanding DNA Forensic Database, and the Specter of an Early-Twenty-First-Century Equivalent of Phrenology*, in DNA AND THE CRIMINAL JUSTICE SYSTEM, 315, 328 (David Lazer ed., 2004) ("Twenty states authorize the use of data banks for research on forensic techniques [that] could easily mean assaying genes or loci that contain predictive information").

9. Mark Rothstein & Sandra Carnahan, *Legal and Policy Issues in Expanding the Scope of Law Enforcement DNA Data Banks*, 67 BROOK. L. REV. 127, 156 (2001) (citations omitted); *see also* Mark A. Rothstein & Meghan K. Talbott, *The Expanding Use of DNA in Law Enforcement: What Role for Privacy?*, 34 J. L. MED. & ETHICS 153, 159 (2006) (describing DNA databases).

Even the FBI has endorsed this view, conceding that in most states "there appear to be no protections against the dissemination of DNA samples."[10] At the other pole, it has been said that "the fear that DNA information or samples in law enforcement databases will be turned over to medical researchers is largely unfounded" because no statutes allow DNA samples taken by compulsion from convicted offenders to be used for medical research.[11]

The explanation for these antipodal views lies, at least in part, in the expansive readings some commentators have given to certain phrases, or to the absence of direct mention of research uses for samples, in the statutes establishing offender databases. The disagreement, therefore, is one of statutory construction, and it can be illustrated and clarified by examining four statutes.

A. Federal Law

For years, the federal government did not take DNA from any convicted offenders. Instead, the FBI merely maintained the national database (NDIS), as part of the "Combined DNA Index System" (CODIS), composed of records derived from samples collected by participating states. When police were unable to find a match in the state or local databases, they could turn to CODIS to see if the source of the crime-scene sample might be an offender from another state. The DNA Analysis Backlog Elimination Act of 2000,[12] however, authorized the collection and analysis of samples from individuals convicted of violating a set of federal criminal laws and the inclusion of the identifying DNA genotype records in NDIS.[13] As of October 2008, NDIS contained DNA identification profiles from well over six million state, federal, and military offenders.[14]

---

10. Randall S. Murch & Bruce Budowle, *Are Developments in Forensic Applications of DNA Technology Consistent with Privacy Protections?*, in GENETIC SECRETS: PROTECTING PRIVACY AND CONFIDENTIALITY IN THE GENETIC ERA 212, 226 (Mark A. Rothstein ed., 1997).

11. Davina Dana Bressler, *Note, Criminal DNA Databank Statutes and Medical Research*, 43 JURIMETRICS J. 51, 54, 63–66 (2002); *cf.* Jonathan Kimmelman, *Risking Ethical Insolvency: A Survey of Trends in Criminal DNA Databanking*, 28 J. L. MED. & ETHICS 209, 212 (2000) ("[S]everal statutes brush perilously close to involuntary uses of banked DNA samples for research purposes.... Five states appear to authorize release of DNA samples for the support of 'identification research and protocol development'").

12. 42 U.S.C. § 14135 (2000).

13. Under 42 U.S.C. § 14135a(a)(1), the Director of the Bureau of Prisons must "collect a DNA sample from each individual in the custody of the Bureau of Prisons who is, or has been, convicted of a qualifying Federal offense. . . ." Section 14135a(b) states that "[t]he Director of the Bureau of Prisons or the probation office responsible (as applicable) shall furnish each DNA sample collected under subsection (a) of this section to the Director of the Federal Bureau of Investigation, who shall carry out a DNA analysis on each such DNA sample and include the results in CODIS." Section 14135b contains analogous provisions for the DNA from individuals convicted for crimes in the District of Columbia, and 10 U.S.C. § 1565 establishes a similar regime for the military.

14. On September 2, 2005, an FBI website reported that NDIS contained 2,599,959 convicted-offender samples. Federal Bureau of Investigation, NDIS Statistics,

Under federal law, for a state to participate in CODIS—as every state does—it must operate "pursuant to rules that allow disclosure of stored DNA samples and DNA analyses only" for the purposes enumerated in 42 U.S.C. § 14132(b):

(A) to criminal justice agencies for law enforcement identification purposes;
(B) in judicial proceedings, if otherwise admissible pursuant to applicable statutes or rules;
(C) for criminal defense purposes, to a defendant, who shall have access to samples and analyses performed in connection with the case in which such defendant is charged; or
(D) if personally identifiable information is removed, for a population statistics database, for identification research and protocol development purposes, or for quality control purposes.[15]

These limitations apply equally to the samples and records of federal offenders.[16]

The upshot of these restrictions is clear. Behavioral genetics researchers wanting to use the samples in CODIS (and in the state and local databases feeding CODIS) are excluded. Their research would not qualify under subsection (A) as undertaken "for law enforcement identification purposes" because the CODIS legislation was adopted to support and expand a well-defined system of identification—namely, an operational, computerized database of records of identifying DNA genotypes that would let investigators search for DNA matches between crime scene samples and convicted offender samples. In the abstract, checking people for genes that might bear some statistical association to antisocial behavior might be said to be a "law enforcement identification purpose," but this ignores the fact that the statute refers to a system of using trace DNA to link individuals to completed crimes—not to "identify" people who might be predisposed to some behaviors. Prediction of possible behavior is not comparable to the retrospective, definitive system of "identification" authorized and funded by Congress.

This contextual reading of subsection (A) is confirmed by subsection (D), which defines the allowable scope of "research" with the samples. Subsection (D) allows only research designed to improve the paradigmatic use of DNA to match trace evidence to possible perpetrators. It permits research on anonymized—and only on anonymized—samples for only three purposes: "for

http://www.fbi.gov/hq/lab/codis/clickmap.htm. By July 2, 2007, the number had climbed to 4,457,313. Id. On December 3, 2008, the reported number was over 6,384,379 offender profiles. Id.

15. 42 U.S.C. § 14132(b) (2000).

16. Id. § 14135e(b). "A person who knowingly—(1) discloses a sample or result described in subsection (a) of this section in any manner to any person not authorized to receive it; or (2) obtains, without authorization, a sample or result described in subsection (a) of this section, shall be fined not more than $100,000." Id. § 14135e(c).

a population statistics database, for identification research and protocol development purposes, or for quality control. . . ."

Population statistics databases are collections of data from various populations on the DNA alleles and genotypes used in forensic identification. They are used to estimate allele frequencies that are then combined according to population genetics theory to ascertain the frequencies of the DNA genotypes used in criminal identification.[17] "Identification research and protocol development" refers to work that could enhance the efficacy of matching individuals to traces of DNA found at crime scenes. Developing or testing additional polymorphisms to assist in individualization or to investigate new methods for typing loci would fall into this category. Likewise, "quality control" research fits squarely into the approved identification paradigm, being nothing more than work intended to keep analytical or clerical errors to a minimum.

B. Massachusetts Law

The Massachusetts statute merits attention because it frequently is held up as an example of a law that is shockingly devoid of constitutionally required safeguards against medical or behavioral research with DNA samples. The public has been told, for example, that "[t]he Massachusetts law set no limits on the purposes for which the samples could be used" and that "samples could be used for research, a practice prohibited by the Nuremberg Code."[18] A similar argument was made to the Supreme Judicial Court of Massachusetts by outstanding law professors and students at several universities.[19] The argument is untenable.

The Massachusetts statute distinguishes between "DNA records" and "DNA samples."[20] A sample is "biological evidence of any nature that is utilized to

---

17. *See, e.g.,* Ian W. Evett & Bruce S. Weir, Interpreting DNA Evidence: Statistical Genetics for Forensic Scientists (1998); National Research Council Committee on DNA Forensic Science, The Evaluation of Forensic DNA Evidence 89–90 (1996); David H. Kaye, *DNA Evidence: Probability, Population Genetics, and the Courts,* 7 HARV. J. L. & TECH. 101 (1993); Neil J. Risch & B. Devlin, *On the Probability of Matching DNA Fingerprints,* 255 SCIENCE 717 (1992); B. S. Weir, *Independence of VNTR Alleles Defined as Fixed Bins,* 130 GENETICS 873 (1992); B. Devlin et al., *No Excess of Homozygosity at Loci Used for DNA Fingerprinting,* 249 SCIENCE 1416 (1990).

18. Paul R. Billings, *Op-Ed, DNA Data Banks Would Taint Justice,* BOSTON GLOBE, Jan. 14, 1999, at A19.

19. D. H. Kaye, *Bioethics, Bench, and Bar: Selected Arguments in* Landry v. Attorney General, 40 JURIMETRICS J. 193 (2000) (analyzing the arguments in amicus curiae briefs filed by Lori Andrews, Harold Krent, and Michelle Hibbert, then at the Chicago-Kent School of Law, and by the Owen M. Kupperschmid Holocaust Human Rights Project of Boston College Law School and the Criminal Justice Clinic of Boston College Law School).

20. The discussion of the Massachusetts statute that follows is adapted from Kaye, *supra* note 19.

conduct DNA analysis."[21] A record is "DNA information that is derived from a DNA sample and DNA analysis. . . ."[22] The statute specifies the permissible uses for the records,[23] and it penalizes all unauthorized uses.[24] In particular, the statute gives the director of the state police laboratory discretion to

> make DNA records available . . . for the limited purpose of (1) advancing DNA analysis methods and supporting statistical interpretation of DNA analysis, including development of population databases; provided, however, that personal identifying information shall be removed from DNA records . . . and (4) advancing other humanitarian purposes.[25]

However, the law contains no corresponding list of the authorized uses for samples and imposes no penalty for their misuse.[26] Should this lack of parallelism be interpreted to mean that state employees are free to use and disseminate the samples for any purpose, including medical research? Or does it mean exactly the opposite—that the legislature assumed the samples would not be used for any purpose except to produce the records and therefore deemed it unnecessary to develop a list of allowable uses for the samples?

The Supreme Judicial Court adopted the latter interpretation. It construed the authorization to disclose the records for certain purposes, combined with the omission of any such authorization for disclosure of the sample, as a prohibition on any release of the samples.[27] The court concluded,

> the Act confines the use of the samples to a DNA analysis which generates only "numerical identification information." In most cases, only the resulting "DNA record," which contains the numerical identification information derived from the samples by the analysis, may be distributed. In addition, the Act limits the purposes for which the DNA records may be distributed, and does not permit dissemination of the DNA samples themselves. . . . The plaintiffs

---

21. Mass. Gen. Laws Ann. ch. 22E § 1 (LexisNexis 2003).

22. Id.

23. Id. § 10.

24. See id. §§ 12–13 (making it a crime punishable by a fine of not more than $1000 or imprisonment of up to six months for an official to disclose a record or a part of it to "any person or agency not authorized to receive such record" and making it a similar crime to obtain a record or part of it "without proper authorization").

25. Id. §10(d).

26. The director merely is instructed to "promulgate regulations governing the . . . storage and disposal of DNA samples." Id. § 6.

27. Landry v. Att'y Gen., 709 N.E.2d 1085, 1096 (Mass. 1999) ("[T]he Act limits the purposes for which the DNA records may be distributed, and does not permit dissemination of the DNA samples themselves"). In addition, the court noted that under the regulations promulgated by the state crime laboratory, even the STR profiles could not be released for "humanitarian purposes." Id. at 1089 n.5.

assert that [a section] of the Act, which compels disclosure of the records to comply with Federal statutory or grant obligations, and allows disclosure of records for various scientific or humanitarian purposes, may somehow lead to leakage of complete genetic profiles. Their speculation that data may be used wrongfully is contrary to the language of the Act. . . .[28]

This result seems clearly correct. It is the samples, not the essentially random numbers contained in the databases, that pose a serious privacy question and that make DNA database systems more threatening than, say, fingerprint databases. The critics of DNA databases have made precisely this point in legislative hearings[29] and briefs.[30] It would be perverse to maintain that a law adopted in this setting makes the sensitive samples freely available while imposing strict confidentiality constraints on the purely identifying data that reveal no personally sensitive information. Yet this view of the statute persists, at least among advocacy groups.[31]

C. Nevada Law

Another statute that has been portrayed as authorizing "a variety of non-law enforcement uses" for samples "collected only for law enforcement identification"[32] is Nevada's DNA database law. But the Nevada law, like the Massachusetts statute, is silent on this score. It merely provides for the collection

---

28. *Id.* at 1096 (citations omitted). In a footnote, the court remarked,

When promulgating final regulations for the Act, the director may want to provide more detail as to tests that may be performed on the DNA samples that are being collected and stored. While the Act only authorizes use of those portions of DNA samples that are relevant for identification purposes, the indefinite storage of the entire DNA sample, see 515 Code Mass. Regs. § 1.05(4), creates some concern that the samples could be misused at some point in the future to search for and disclose private genetic information.

Id. at 1096 n.20.

29. E.g., Hearing, *supra* note 1 (testimony of Barry Steinhardt).

30. E.g., Brief of Electronic Privacy Information Center as Amici Curiae Supporting Appellant at 7–9, United States v. Kincade, 379 F.3d 813 (9th Cir. 2004) (*en banc*) (No. 02-50380), *available at* http:// www.epic.org/privacy/genetic/kincade_amicus.pdf.

31. Notwithstanding the structure of the statute and the state's highest court's interpretation of it, the Director of the ACLU's Program on Technology and Liberty continues to cite the Massachusetts statute as a prime example of a database law that permits unbounded circulation of "both the forensic DNA profiled and the raw biological sample that contains DNA." Steinhardt, *supra* note 7, at 176; *see also id.* at 185 ("[T]he law the Massachusetts legislature passed allows virtually unlimited use of DNA").

32. *Id.* at 176; *see also* Kimmelman, *supra* note 11, at 212 (suggesting only eight states, not including Nevada, "prohibit any meaningful use of banked tissues for genetic research").

of "a biological specimen"[33] from certain categories of offenders[34] and for the analysis of "genetic markers"[35] by a "forensic laboratory."[36] However, whereas the Massachusetts law imposes explicit limitations on the use of the bio-identification records, the Nevada statute makes no mention of any allowed uses. Should this omission be taken to mean that anything goes for records and samples alike?

In a brief discussion of this point, the Nevada Supreme Court rejected such an expansive construction of the law. In *Gaines v. State*,[37] the defendant entered a negotiated plea to the unlawful use of coins in a gaming machine, burglary, and forgery arising from a failed attempt to cash three fake $100 Visa travelers' checks at a Las Vegas casino, and to another burglary charge stemming from a check forgery at a Las Vegas bank. The district court sentenced Gaines and ordered him to undergo "DNA genetic marker testing"; Gaines appealed.[38] In a shotgun attack on the constitutionality of the DNA database statute, Gaines maintained that the law was unconstitutional due to "overbreadth."[39] In particular,

> Gaines argues that NRS 176.0913 [the Nevada DNA database statute] is overbroad because there are no restrictions on the amount of blood drawn, the testing of the blood, the time period for keeping the test results, and no requirement that the State dispose of the remaining portions of blood not used in the DNA testing. Essentially, Gaines is concerned that the State will use the DNA test results for a discriminatory or invasive purpose, such as determining a convict's predisposition to physical or mental disease.[40]

---

33. Nev. Rev. Stat. § 176.0913(1)(b) (2003).

34. *Id.* § 176.0913(4).

35. *Id.* § 176.0913(1)(b).

36. Id. § 176.0913(2). Although the law does not define the term "genetic markers," it is plain from the manner in which the term is used (not to mention the background of the law) that these encompass only those "genetic markers" that are useful for forensic identification. See id. §§176.0918(1), 176.0918(6)(a) (creating procedures under which "[a] person convicted of a crime and under sentence of death" may obtain "a genetic marker analysis of evidence" if "[a] reasonable possibility exists that the petitioner would not have been prosecuted or convicted if exculpatory results had been obtained through a genetic marker analysis of the evidence" and other conditions relating to a traditional forensic identification analysis are satisfied).

37. 998 P.2d 166, 168 (Nev. 2000).

38. *Id.* at 169.

39. The "constitutional attacks on NRS 176.0913 [include] claims that the statute is overbroad and that it violates his right to be free from unreasonable search and seizure, right to equal protection, right to due process, and right to be free from cruel and unusual punishment." *Id.* at 171.

40. *Id.* at 175.

The court deemed these concerns speculative and conjectural[41] and dismissed them as inconsistent with "[t]he plain language of [the statute, which] limits the purpose of testing to identification."[42]

Taken together, *Landry* and *Gaines* indicate a tendency to construe the scope of allowable uses for the law enforcement DNA records and samples narrowly, if only to blunt the force of constitutional attacks on the database laws. They also stand for the proposition that the meaning of statutory terms should not be divorced from historical context and statutory purpose. If other states follow the same approach, then the number of statutes that allow non–law enforcement research with offender DNA samples approaches zero.

D. Alabama Law

Alabama's statute is noteworthy because it has been depicted as authorizing every imaginable type of biomedical research with offender DNA samples.[43] Again, the truth is much less alarming. In its declaration of the statute's purpose, the legislature found that forensic DNA matching had become "generally accepted in the relevant scientific community"[44] and declared that

---

41. The court wrote

Gaines' contentions concerning abuse of the genetic marker data are merely speculation and conjecture, as he has provided this court with no evidence regarding such abuse. Finally, we note that the Supreme Court of the United States has rejected an analogous argument: "While this procedure [collection of blood and urine for mandatory drug testing] permits the Government to learn certain private medical facts that an employee might prefer not to disclose, there is no indication that the Government does not treat this information as confidential, or that it uses the information for any other purpose."

Id. at 175 (quoting Skinner v. Ry. Labor Executives' Ass'n, 489 U.S. 602, 626 n.7 (1989)).

42. The only "plain language" the court identified was subsection 1(b) of NRS 176.0913 that "mandat[es] the samples be used for 'determin[ing] the genetic markers of the blood.'" *Id.*

43. *See* Gaia Bernstein, *Accommodating Technological Innovation: Identity, Genetic Testing and the Internet*, 57 VAND. L. REV. 965, 1009 (2004) (stating that the Alabama statute "expressly provides for use of the samples for research related to genetic disease"); Eric T. Juengst, *I-DNA-fication, Personal Privacy, and Social Justice*, 75 CHI.-KENT L. REV. 61, 68–69 (1999) (suggesting that the sole limitation on research with these samples is that they be anonymized, which is not "technically possible"); Jean E. McEwen, *DNA Data Banks, in* GENETIC SECRETS, *supra* note 10, at 231, 238 ("[The Alabama] data banking law specifically authorizes the use of samples collected for its data bank for 'educational research or medical research or development'—an authorization that would presumably encompass behavioral research into, for example, genetic predispositions to violence."); Schaefer, *supra* note 8, at 576.

44. *Id.* § 36-18-20(e).

the Alabama Department of Forensic Sciences should be authorized and empowered to analyze, type and record any and all genetic markers contained in or derived from DNA and to create a statewide DNA database system for collection, storage and maintenance of genetic identification information as the same may pertain to the identification of criminal suspects.[45]

The legislature's purpose in "creat[ing] and establish[ing] a statewide DNA database" was to implement "the most reasonable and certain method or means to rapidly identify repeat or habitually dangerous criminals."[46] But the legislature recognized that the database might also "serve an array of humanitarian purposes, including . . . the identification of human remains from natural or mass disasters or the identification of missing, deceased or unidentified persons."[47] Moreover, "through the development of a population statistical database which does not include therein individual personal identification information an important research mechanism is obtained for the causation, detection and prevention of disease."[48]

These legislative findings have a common and circumscribing theme—using molecular biology to establish the origin of two or more DNA samples. The last declaration, though, expresses the hope that the frequencies of the alleles used in this type of forensic work would be valuable in medical research as well. While this belief does not seem to be true for the CODIS STR loci that dominate law enforcement work today, it was more plausible for some of the loci used in earlier years.[49] In any event, the DNA database system authorized in Alabama adheres to the trace-evidence paradigm of matching DNA samples, not to the dubious theory that "identification" includes prediction of what someone might someday do.[50]

---

45. *Id.* § 36-18-20(h).

46. Ala. Code § 36-18-20(g) (LexisNexis 2001).

47. *Id.* § 36-18-20(i).

48. *Id.* § 36-18-20(j). The statute defines a "DNA population statistical database" as "[t]hat system established by the Director of the Alabama Department of Forensic Sciences for collecting, storing, and maintaining genetic information relating to DNA population frequencies." *Id.* § 36-18-21(h).

49. *See, e.g.,* M. A. Pani et al., *Vitamin D Receptor Allele Combinations Influence Genetic Susceptibility to Type 1 Diabetes in Germans,* 49 DIABETES 504 (2000); Matthias Wjst, *Variants in the Vitamin D Receptor Gene and Asthma,* 6 BIOMED. CENT. GENETICS 2 (2005).

50. The statute lists these sole purposes for the database:

(a) Assisting federal, state, county, municipal, or local criminal justice and law enforcement officers or agencies in the putative identification, detection, or exclusion of persons who are the subjects of investigations or prosecutions of sex related crimes, other violent crimes or other crimes in which biological evidence is received or recovered.

(b) Supporting identification research and protocol development of DNA forensic methods.

(c) Creating and maintaining DNA quality control standards.

366 THE IMPACT OF BEHAVIORAL SCIENCES ON CRIMINAL LAW

In particular, the Alabama law includes no express provision for using samples in medical research, and such use would exceed the scope of disclosure allowed for the operational "records."[51] Only the "DNA population statistical database which shall not include therein individually identifiable information"[52] can be utilized to "provide data relative to the causation, detection and prevention of disease or disability" or "to assist in other humanitarian endeavors including, but not limited to, educational research or medical research or development."[53] One can debate the merits of giving away, for any bona fide scientific or educational purpose, a database listing all observed forensic DNA types, and the notion that they have much medical value is farfetched. However, it should be remembered that defendants in criminal cases often demanded the release of the population databases and sometimes argued that evidence of a DNA match was not admissible unless the databases from which the estimates of genotype probabilities were drawn were made available to the scientific community. Publicly accessible research databases are generally desirable, and researchers who refuse to make their data available to their colleagues often are viewed with suspicion.

In sum, it is literally true but potentially quite misleading to say "the authorized uses of DNA databases extend beyond criminal identification purposes into the realm of humanitarian and statistical research purposes" or to refer to "the use of their DNA database for genetic research" without clarifying the nature of the database and the genetic research.[54] The "databases" are electronic data on

---

    (d) Assisting in the recovery or identification of human remains from natural or mass disasters.
    (e) Assisting in other humanitarian purposes including the identification of missing, deceased or unidentified persons.

Ala. Code § 36-18-24 (LexisNexis 2001).

    51. Alabama Code § 36-18-27 specifies

DNA records collected and maintained for the purpose of the identification of criminal suspects or offenders shall be disclosed only:

    (a) To criminal justice agencies for law enforcement identification purposes.
    (b) In judicial proceedings, if otherwise admissible.
    (c) For criminal defense purposes, to a defendant, who shall have access to samples and analyses performed in connection with the case in which such defendant is charged.

Id. § 36-18-27.

    52. Id. § 36-18-31(a).
    53. Id. § 36-18-31(b).
    54. Seth Axelrad, American Society of Law, Medicine, and Ethics, Survey of State DNA Database Statutes (Jan. 12, 2005), http://www.aslme.org/dna_ 04/grid/guide.pdf. This publication of the American Society of Law, Medicine, and Ethics wisely cautions that

Statutes provide an informative yet limited picture of each state's DNA database system. Administrative rules and regulations, as well as the policies and procedures of individual forensic laboratories, play a large role in defining the real-world operation

identification loci that constitute an infinitesimal fraction of the genome and that are no more stigmatizing than a passport number. They are not "future diar[ies],"[55] "a chapter in the book of life,"[56] "a glimpse into a person's most intimate self,"[57] or any of the other exaggerated characterizations of the human genome that have reinforced a false sense of genetic determinism or essentialism.

Even the full set of human chromosomes does not match these metaphors, although it assuredly contains personal and sensitive information. As a result, laws like Alabama's distinguish between the identifying records and the physical samples. Even in Alabama, whose law is most favorable to genetics research outside of the trace-evidence paradigm, only the anonymized forensic records—and not the underlying samples—can be released. Behavioral genetics researchers who come knocking on the doors of state or federal administrators for the DNA of convicted offenders will find them locked, and the key cannot be located within the disclosure and usage provisions of the current database laws.

However, the case law is thin, and it may be a mistake to think that courts will continue to reject extravagant and noncontextual constructions of the database laws. Moreover, inasmuch as statutes are subject to change,[58] it is important to ask what the legal regime should be.

---

of these databases. Furthermore, statutes are subject to various interpretations, and the impact of any DNA database statute depends in large part on the interpretations and actions of law enforcement agencies and courts.

Id. In addition, it correctly notes that

Because the terms used in the statutes are often vague or undefined, one cannot predict with certainty the scope of the databases' authorized uses; examples include "law enforcement purposes" and "other humanitarian purposes." The construction of each statute may provide clues as to whether these terms will be interpreted broadly or narrowly.

Id.

55. *See* George J. Annas, *Privacy Rules for DNA Databanks: Protecting Coded 'Future Diaries,'* 270 J. AM. MED. ASS'N 2346, 2348 (1993).

56. *See* Nicholas Wade, *Life Is Pared to Basics; Complex Issues Arise*, N.Y. TIMES, Dec. 14, 1999, at F3 ("[A] medical ethicist . . . noted when biologists sequenced the first human chromosome last month, they called it 'the first chapter in the book of life, as if life is chromosomes'").

57. LORI ANDREWS, FUTURE PERFECT: CONFRONTING DECISIONS ABOUT GENETICS 31 (2001).

58. In considering the likelihood of changes at the state level, it should be remembered that states that wish to participate in CODIS, as all do, would still need to comply with the DNA Identification Act of 1994. 42 U.S.C. §§ 14131–34 (2000). In addition, it could be argued that an expansive interpretation of existing laws or a revision to allow identified DNA samples to be used to search for genes that might influence behavior would violate constitutional protections of liberty or privacy or the right to be free from unreasonable searches and seizures. Under existing doctrine, however, such claims are unlikely to succeed. *See generally* Edward J. Imwinkelried, *Can We Rely on the Alleged Constitutional Right to Informational Privacy to Secure Genetic Privacy in the Courtroom?,*

THE SOCIAL "OUGHT": SHOULD THE CRIMINAL DATABANKS BE AVAILABLE FOR BEHAVIORAL RESEARCH?

The millions of DNA samples collected for investigating crime involving biological trace evidence could prove useful in research into genes and behavior. Although the notion of "crime genes" is simplistic, offender DNA repositories might be of some value in confirming reports of loci influencing behaviors such as novelty-seeking or impulsiveness or even in identifying previously unsuspected quantitative trait loci (QTL) in polygenetic systems influencing behavior. Although it is hard to know the range of practical applications of such knowledge, a clearer picture of what leads to extreme behaviors conceivably could be of benefit both inside and outside of the criminal justice system. If this assessment is accurate and the research cannot be summarily dismissed as worthless, then it becomes important to consider the dangers that research with these samples might pose and the human rights upon which the research might infringe.[59]

A. Popular Misunderstanding of Research Results

One danger of behavioral genetics research (and other areas of genetics research) is public misunderstanding. The first report of an association may receive considerable publicity even though later efforts at replication fail. Even if an association is real, it may be spurious (the result of a third variable) or not especially predictive of any behaviors. In short, "while behavioral genetic studies do not provide any justification for simplistic talk about 'a gene for starting to smoke' or 'a gene for divorce,' people sometimes talk like that anyway."[60]

Now, public misunderstanding is not always a major evil. The Big Bang theory is routinely misunderstood, but the universe goes on. Normally, the antidote to public misunderstanding of research is public discourse and a free flow of scientific information. On issues ranging from transcendental meditation to homeopathy to fluoridated water, scholars, publicists, and journalists promulgate pernicious or unvalidated theories, thinly or thickly garbed in the dress of science. The research can be, and often is, initially misleading, but we tolerate it,

---

31 SETON HALL L. REV. 926 (2001); D. H. Kaye, *The Constitutionality of DNA Sampling on Arrest*, 10 CORNELL J. L. & PUB. POL'Y 455 (2001).

59. As I have argued elsewhere, "biometric research" designed to validate or improve the use of DNA analysis as a means of post hoc identification in the criminal justice system should be permissible without the consent of the individuals whose DNA has been obtained involuntarily but lawfully. *See* Kaye, *supra* note 19, at 215–16. Research that is unrelated to the use for which the samples were collected is more problematic.

60. CATHERINE BAKER, BEHAVIORAL GENETICS: AN INTRODUCTION TO HOW GENES AND ENVIRONMENTS INTERACT THROUGH DEVELOPMENT TO SHAPE DIFFERENCES IN MOOD, PERSONALITY, AND INTELLIGENCE 18 (2004).

trusting the "marketplace of ideas" to separate fact from fiction, science from pseudoscience.

However, this does not mean that government resources must support the research. If the public cannot be trusted to get it right, and if there are immediate and significant harms from getting it wrong, then discouraging the research itself could be defended. The unfortunate fact is that there are harms that might flow from false beliefs in genetic behavioral determinism. These fall into three categories: discrimination based on an individual's actual genotypes, discrimination based on an individual's membership in a genetically related group, and misguided public policy choices.

1. **Discrimination against Individuals with Known Genotypes** The bearers of "bad" alleles may be unjustly stigmatized. For example, when the effects of particular mutations are exaggerated, the individuals who are known to have them could be misjudged and disadvantaged in having access to education, employment, or health insurance. Moreover, they could be shunned and treated as pariahs in personal relationships.

There are several responses to this possible stigmatization, short of policies to discourage the acquisition of knowledge.[61] A barrage of laws to foster "genetic privacy" or to prevent "genetic discrimination" in the workplace and in health insurance already have been enacted.[62] In addition, as knowledge of human genetics matures, a more realistic appraisal of the limitations of behavioral predictions may come to permeate the public consciousness. Even so, laws against any kind of discrimination can only reduce, not eliminate, the objectionable conduct, and at the interpersonal level, genetic features can join with cultural ones

---

61. In this context, "discourage" may be too strong a term. The issue is whether to facilitate research by making a public resource (a DNA repository) available.

62. *See, e.g.*, Genetic Information Nondiscrimination Act of 2008, P. L. 110-233, May 21, 2008, 122 Stat. 881; Lawrence O. Gostin & James G. Hodge, Jr., *Genetic Privacy and the Law: An End to Genetics Exceptionalism*, 40 JURIMETRICS J. 21, 46–47 (1999). Indeed, "in one year in the late'90s, more bills were introduced into the nation's state legislatures about the regulation of genetic information than any other single topic." *Life Sciences, Technology, and the Law Symposium Transcript*, 10 MICH. TELECOMM. & TECH. L. REV. 175, 180 (2003) (address by Philip Reilly). Of course, the practical value of the laws is open to question, but so is the extent of genetic discrimination. *See* 1 National Bioethics Advisory Commission, *Research Involving Human Biological Materials: Ethical Issues and Policy Guidance* 5 (1999), *available at* http://www.georgetown.edu/research/nrcbl/nbac/hbm. pdf ("[T]o date there is little empirical evidence documenting extensive employment or insurance discrimination based on genetic status"); PHILIP R. REILLY, GENETIC DISCRIMINATION, IN GENETIC TESTING AND THE USE OF INFORMATION 106, 106–7 (Clarisa Long ed., 1999). *But see* Karen H. Rothenberg & Sharon F. Terry, *Before It's Too Late—Addressing Fear of Genetic Information*, 297 SCIENCE 196, 197 (2002) (explaining how there could be "widespread cases of genetic discrimination" even though they have not been observed).

in defining social hierarchies that privilege some groups at the expense of others.

2. Attitudes toward Racial and Ethnic Groups A second mode of stigmatization might arise if people were led to believe that undesirable alleles are more prevalent in some racial, ethnic, or socioeconomic groups. Because linking behavioral traits and capacities with race-related genes has a particularly ugly history, research that could rekindle such racial stereotyping deserves special scrutiny. "For a variety of complex factors, the population of those arrested and convicted is disproportionately male, minority, and poor."[63] Hence,

> The possibility exists that a researcher conducting genome scans on samples collected for a criminal database might find an allele that occurs more than randomly and claim (or be misreported in the media as claiming) to have found a "gene for" criminal behavior. What the researcher might actually have found is an allele that is more common among, say, poor whites from the Bayou who couldn't afford good lawyers, Mexicans caught up by immigration violations, or African Americans who faced racist juries. Such a claim could lead to discriminatory actions against others of the same demographic group who share the allele.[64]

There seem to be two somewhat poorly knitted threads to this argument. The first concerns the statistical problem of confounding variables—of thinking that one variable causes a result when a third variable (correlated with the first) is the true cause. The threat of confounding is a pervasive issue in observational studies. Suppose that there is an allele S that is more common in African Americans than in Caucasians.[65] Because African Americans comprise a greater proportion of the convicted offender database than of the general population,[66] the relative

---

63. Baker, *supra* note 60, at 89.
64. *Id.* The AAAS Report provides another variation on this theme:
Another consequence of genetic research that relies on arrest or conviction as synonyms for the criminal phenotype is that it will disproportionately focus on those who have committed "blue collar" crimes (assaults, property theft, petty drug offenses, etc.) compared to subjects who have committed "white collar" crimes (tax evasion, information theft, large-scale drug dealing, etc.). This is because those committing the latter type of crime are caught less often. Such research would inevitably reinforce the stereotype that the working class is more deviant than the professional class.
Id. at 89–90.
65. For example, S could be the sickle cell allele, which "has an allele frequency of 0.10–0.20 in Africans, compared with less than 0.001 in U.S. Whites. . . ." Daniel C. Rowe, *Under the Skin: On the Impartial Treatment of Genetic and Environmental Hypotheses of Racial Differences*, 60 AM. PSYCHOL. 60, 61 (2005).
66. In 2002, there were 586,700 blacks out of 1,291,326 (45 percent) sentenced state and federal prisoners. PAIGE M. HARRISON & ALLEN J. BECK, BUREAU OF JUSTICE STATISTICS, PRISONERS IN 2002 9, Tbl. 13 (2003). The 2000 census calculated a total population of

frequency of S will be larger in the convicted offender database than in the overall population—even though it does not change the probability that an individual will engage in criminal conduct. This kind of confounding, however, is easily detected in this situation. To avoid mistaking S for an allele that influences behavior, one can compare the DNA samples from convicted African Americans with samples collected from African American controls in the general population.[67] Since the presence or absence of S is uncorrelated with the existence of a criminal conviction of an African American, a significant difference is unlikely. In short, confounding due to racial or ethnic differences may not be an intractable problem.

But even research reports—and media reports about the research—that avoid confusing correlation with causation are not free from the risk of prompting discrimination on the basis of a group's genotype. Suppose, for the sake of argument, that certain alleles do affect behavior in a manner that makes it more likely that someone will be convicted of a crime and that these alleles are much more prevalent in African Americans (or some other group) than in Caucasians. The discovery of both these hypothetical facts could promote the belief that African Americans (or the other group) are "racially inferior" and prone to crime. In this situation, there is a genetic difference between two groups, and it is used stereotypically to disparage an entire group.[68]

But it may be unrealistic to posit the discovery of alleles that are both (a) strongly related to crime and (b) substantially more prevalent in one race than another. Each relevant allele in such a complex system of behavior is likely to be a small factor, and "[t]he polygenic nature of antisocial behaviour also means that even if a susceptibility allele is found at a high frequency in a particular ethnic group, it is likely that a different susceptibility allele will be found at a

---

281.4 million, of which 34.7 million people, or 12 percent, reported only Black, while "an additional 1.8 million people reported Black and at least one other race"). JESSE McKINNON, U.S. CENSUS BUREAU, THE BLACK POPULATION: 2002 (2001).

67. This type of statistical control is the norm in association studies in genetic epidemiology. *See* Stephen P. Daiger, *Was the Human Genome Project Worth the Effort?*, 308 SCIENCE 362, 362–63 (2005) ("[C]ase-control association studies look for differences in the frequencies of common genetic variants *between ethnically matched* cases and controls to find variants that are strongly associated with the disease") (emphasis added). However, it can be "very difficult to design a sampling strategy to avoid the effects of population stratification, especially if the specific locus has allele frequencies that vary among populations." Cathy L. Barr & Kenneth K. Kidd, *Population Frequencies of the A1 Allele at the Dopamine D2 Receptor Locus*, 34 BIOLOGICAL PSYCHIATRY 204, 205 (1993).

68. This is rather different than the concern expressed in the AAAS report over "discriminatory actions against others of the same demographic group who share the allele." Baker, *supra* note 60, at 89. The group-discrimination problem arises when members of the demographic group who do not share the allele are treated as if they do by virtue of their membership in the group.

similarly high frequency in another ethnic group."[69] Furthermore, even if a few alleles that fulfilled both conditions (a) and (b) were to be discovered, and if no alleles with a counterbalancing racial or ethnic distribution were known, the social consequences would still be unclear. Women are biologically and genetically different from men in many ways—including some clear differences in the functioning and maturation of parts of the brain—but this knowledge does not seem likely to lead to a new wave of discrimination against women or to retard efforts to achieve gender equality.[70] The vector sum of the social forces that encourage racism and sexism and those that moderate these attitudes may not be significantly affected by finding that a few alleles are more common in some groups than others—at least not when the alleles are found in all racial groups and when they do not ineluctably determine anyone's behavior.

3. Misguided Public Policies A third harm that has been attributed to behavioral genetics research relates to the impact of knowledge on governmental action. Thus, it has been said that

> [L]ike the old eugenic studies and the new MAOA studies, genetic studies tend to misdirect attention from the overwhelming social causes of the behaviors they purport to explain by encouraging a determinism that suggests that efforts at social reform are ultimately futile. Where this misdirection reinforces existing social policy inequities, it is likely to have an even more pronounced effect.[71]

Not only is it said that social progress might be forestalled, but the identification of genes that affect behavior could be seen as "legitimizing draconian 'medical' responses to the targeted behavior, like eugenic sterilization."[72] In fact, one eminent historian of biology predicts that "to proceed under [the] assumption" that human behavioral genetics research could generate useful knowledge "will certainly lead to a legal and ethical quagmire equivalent to that encountered by the eugenics

---

69. Katherine I. Morley & Wayne D. Hall, *Is There a Genetic Susceptibility to Engage in Criminal Acts?*, in TRENDS AND ISSUES IN CRIMINAL JUSTICE, No. 263, Oct. 2003, at 5. Of course, if such discoveries come, they will not emerge simultaneously.

70. *See, e.g.,* Natalie Angier & Kenneth Chang, *Gray Matter and the Sexes: Still a Gray Area Scientifically*, N.Y. TIMES, Jan. 24, 2005, at A1. Indeed, understanding these differences could lead to strategies better calculated to enhance the development of, say, mathematical ability in women. *See* Amanda Ripley, *Who Says a Woman Can't Be Einstein?*, TIME, Mar. 7, 2005, at 50.

71. Juengst, *supra* note 43, at 70.

72. *Id.*

movement of 1910–1940 and its push towards massive sterilization, and eventually, euthanasia, of the so-called unfit."[73]

To the extent that these are warnings that the dissemination of new research results will promote repressive laws or thwart enlightened policies of reform, they pose a fundamental question about democratic self-government. Is it right for the state to withhold resources that might advance knowledge not because the information causes direct and immediate harm to individuals, but because it might lead the electorate or its representatives to follow misconceived or misguided policies? The proposition that government should not advance knowledge because the electorate or the elected representatives might misuse that knowledge in the political process is surely problematic.

Even assuming that the government can be justified in failing to support the acquisition of information it believes would promote the "wrong" laws, the question arises of how high the probability of this democratically endorsed "harm" must be for the knowledge to be officially discouraged. In this instance, the theory apparently is that if researchers refer to specific alleles as weakly associated with criminal conduct, then the public and the politicians will abandon or forego efforts to rehabilitate offenders or to reduce crime by improving the economic and social conditions that breed crime.

These possibilities cannot be excluded. Yet it seems equally possible that the people who believe that rehabilitation is impossible will adhere to this pessimism regardless of news about genetics, while those who are inclined to hope for reformation and redemption will continue to regard individual behavior as a malleable function of both genetic endowment and life history. It is far from obvious that criminals as a group will come to be more stigmatized than they already are by the identification of individual genes having indirect and small influences on criminality. Similarly, the further diminution of social welfare programs is all too possible, but the role of genetic findings due to access to offender databases in this political process is likely to be marginal at best. As for the more dire predictions of a resurrection of eugenics laws, contemporary legal and public attitudes toward compulsory sterilization are quite different than they were in the days of *Buck v. Bell*,[74] and it is hard to conceive of discoveries about

---

73. Garland Allen, *DNA and Human-Behavior Genetics: Implications for the Criminal Justice System, in* DNA AND THE CRIMINAL JUSTICE SYSTEM: THE TECHNOLOGY OF JUSTICE 287, 294–95 (David Lazer ed., 2004).

74. 274 U.S. 200, 206 (1927) (upholding a state law allowing compulsory sterilization of certain individuals on the ground that "experience has shown that heredity plays an important part in the transmission of insanity, imbecility, &c").

QTLs that would lead legislatures to enact[75]—and courts to sustain[76]—laws resembling the one upheld in *Buck*.[77]

In many ways the objections to research into crime and genetics track the arguments made against research into intelligence and race. For example, when Arthur Jensen, a psychologist at the University of California at Berkeley, published a paper in 1969 asserting that it was "not an unreasonable hypothesis that genetic factors are strongly implicated in the average Negro-white intelligence difference,"[78] and suggesting that efforts to enhance educational opportunities

---

75. *See* DANIEL J. KEVLES & LEROY HOOD, REFLECTIONS, IN THE CODE OF CODES: SCIENTIFIC AND SOCIAL ISSUES IN THE HUMAN GENOME PROJECT 300, 318 (Daniel J. Kevles & Leroy Hood eds., 1992):

> Eugenics profits from authoritarianism—indeed, almost requires it. The institutions of political democracy may not have been robust enough to resist altogether the violations of civil liberties characteristic of the early eugenics movement, but they did contest them effectively in many places. The British government refused to pass eugenic sterilization laws. So did many American states, and where eugenic laws were enacted, they were often unenforced. It is far-fetched to expect a Nazi-like eugenic program to develop in the contemporary United States so long as political democracy and the Bill of Rights continue in force. If a Nazi-like eugenic program becomes a threatening reality, the country will have a good deal more to be worried about politically than just eugenics.

76. *See* Skinner v. Oklahoma, 316 U.S. 535, 536 (1942) (striking down a sterilization law for certain criminals on Equal Protection grounds and describing "the right to have offspring" as "basic"); *id.* at 546 (Jackson, J., concurring) ("There are limits to the extent to which a legislatively represented majority may conduct biological experiments at the expense of the dignity and personality and natural powers of a minority—even those who have been guilty of what the majority define as crimes."); JANET L. DOLGIN & LOIS L. SHEPERD, BIOETHICS AND THE LAW 359 (2005) ("The *Skinner* Court did not overrule *Buck v. Bell*. However, the Court's categorization of procreation as a fundamental right and its later application of the most stringent review to statutes that interfered with that right left little room for future courts to invoke Justice Holmes' 1927 decision in *Buck v. Bell* as precedent for the state's right to compulsorily sterilize members of social groups deemed marginal by the state").

77. Indeed, well-designed studies of behavior can help reveal the effect of environmental variables, suggesting possible interventions rather than the abandonment of hope. Thus, it has been suggested that "genetic research is more likely to refine social policies by better specification of environmental risk factors than to divert funds from environmental crime prevention strategies." Morley & Hall, *supra* note 69, at 5.

78. Arthur Jensen, *How Much Can We Boost IQ and Scholastic Achievement?*, 39 HARV. EDUC. REV. 1, 82 (1969).

could not remove the racial divide in occupational achievement, the immediate result was "a national furor":[79]

> Many of Jensen's academic colleagues attacked his thesis on methodological grounds, but others criticized the nature of the inquiry itself. . . . The Society for the Psychological Study of Social Issues, an organization of social and behavioral scientists, expressed concern that hereditarian statements could be seriously misinterpreted, and used to justify repressive social policies. Elizabeth Alfert, a colleague of Jensen at Berkeley, wrote that many persons read and quoted Jensen's work but failed to notice the many qualifiers it contained. Bernard Diamond, professor of law and psychiatry at Berkeley, found that race-IQ studies risked "social denigration" of the groups singled out and urged that researchers be required to obtain the consent of parents who might not wish their children to participate in studies aimed at discovering ethnic differences.[80]

These themes—the public will be mislead, social progress will be retarded, and groups will be stigmatized by the research[81]—are precisely those that are sounded once again.[82] And they should be, for they are important and valid concerns. Yet they sound suspiciously like calls for content-based suppression of inquiry. Is it better to avoid "inopportune" knowledge altogether or to subject it to scientific scrutiny and public debate?[83] American society has taken the latter approach in response to the theories and studies of Jensen and others.[84] It is the bumpier

---

79. Richard Delgado et al., *Can Science Be Inopportune? Constitutional Validity of Governmental Restrictions on Race-IQ Research*, 31 UCLA L. Rev. 128, 137 (1983).

80. *Id.* at 140.

81. One geneticist editorialized "It perhaps is impossible to exaggerate the importance of the Jensen disgrace, for which we must all now share responsibility. It has permeated both science and the universities, and hoodwinked large segments of government and society. Like Vietnam and Watergate, it is a contemporary symptom of serious affliction." Jerry Hirsch, *Jensenism: The Bankruptcy of "Science" without Scholarship*, 25 Educ. Theory 3, 3–4 (1975).

82. Indeed, sometimes the old social science and IQ data are simply repackaged as if they were modern "genetic research." *See* Andrews, *supra* note 57, at 94 (describing the *The Bell Curve* as a contemporary case of "genetic research . . . being used to 'demonstrate' the genetic inferiority of people of color").

83. *Cf.* Delgado et al., *supra* note 78, at 153–225 (discussing First Amendment limitations on government responses to research that might show, or purport to show, racial inferiority).

84. Officially, there may be no constraints on research, but it can be severely inhibited by unofficial funding policies and sanctions for research on certain topics. *See, e.g.,* Lila Guterman, *Scientists Censor What They Study to Avoid Controversy and 'Lunatic-Proof' Their Lives, Researchers Find*, Chron. Higher Educ., Feb. 11, 2005, *available at* http:// chronicle. com/daily/2005/02/2005021104n.htm.

road, but the historical record does not demonstrate that these publications have had a lasting, or even a measurable, impact on public policy. The same appears to be true of reports of a link between XYY trisomy and criminality.[85] Although the social response to the early reports often is cited as a modern example of genetic discrimination,[86] the scientific criticism of the reports (or, rather, the more sensational interpretations of them) was extensive,[87] no repressive legislation emerged, no American courts accepted the condition as a defense to criminal conduct,[88] and no instances of actual discrimination have been documented.[89]

---

85. See Patricia A. Jacobs et al., *Aggressive Behaviour, Mental Sub-normality and the XYY Male*, 208 NATURE 1351, 1352 (1965) ("[T]he finding that 3.5 percent of the population [of institutionalized men] were XYY males must represent a marked increase in frequency by comparison with the frequency of such males at birth"); Herman A. Witkin et al., *Criminality in XYY and XXY Men*, 193 SCIENCE 547, 553–54 (1976) (reporting that XYY males showed evidence of a higher rate of criminality although they displayed no disproportionate tendency toward violence).

86. E.g., Paul A. Lombardo, *Genetic Confidentiality: What's the Big Secret?*, 3 U. CHI. L. SCH. ROUNDTABLE 589, 596 (1996) (claiming that "[t]he more recent history of genetic discrimination is exemplified by the XYY controversy screening programs to deter criminality were proposed" but pointing to no instances of discriminatory acts against men with this karyotype).

87. See, e.g., Digamber S. Borgaonkar & Saleem A. Shah, *The XYY Chromosome Male—or Syndrome?*, in PROGRESS IN MEDICAL GENETICS 135, 202 (Arthur G. Steinburgh & Alexander G. Bearn eds., 1974) ("Because of the relatively small numbers, the absence of matched controls and of blind assessment procedures, and the inconsistent findings, there are relatively few psychologic, psychiatric, and behavioral characteristics which clearly and consistently distinguish the XYY males from comparable controls . . . [and] the few which do appear tend to refute the notion that XYY males are predisposed toward aggressive and violent behavior"); Greogy Carey, *Genetics and Violence*, in 2 NATIONAL RESEARCH COUNCIL, UNDERSTANDING AND PREVENTING VIOLENCE: BIOBEHAVIORAL INFLUENCES 21, 26 (Albert J. Reiss, Jr., et al. eds., 1994) ("[P]rospective [studies] dispel the myth of the XYY as a 'hyperaggressive, supermasculine sociopath' and, in its place, portray a group of individuals within the normal range but with an array of relatively nonspecific behavioral differences in attention and cognition, motoric skills, and personality"); NUFFIELD COUNCIL ON BIOETHICS, GENETICS AND HUMAN BEHAVIOUR: THE ETHICAL CONTEXT 160 (2002), *available at* http:// www.nuffieldbioethics.org/fileLibrary/pdf/nuffieldgeneticsrep.pdf ("[A 1976 study concluded] XYY males were more likely to be imprisoned, but that this was due to their low intelligence and low socioeconomic status[,] which placed them at higher risk of being caught").

88. See Deborah W. Denno, *Comment, Human Biology and Criminal Responsibility: Free Will or Free Ride?*, 137 U. PA. L. REV. 615, 620–21 (1988).

89. There are suggestions that some individuals have aborted XYY fetuses, but the basis for these statements is not apparent. E.g., Virginia Morell, *Evidence Found for a Possible 'Aggression Gene,'* 260 SCIENCE 1722, 1723 (1993) ("[J]onathan Beckwith cautioned, i]t would be a disaster if people suddenly decided to begin screening babies for monoamine oxidase deficiencies—as some did for the XYY defect."). It also has been claimed that "genetic test results" for the XYY karyotype conducted on "6,000 young men . . . were routinely passed to courts to use however they chose." Andrews, *supra* note 57, at 94.

"Learning from history is indispensable," but "[g]enetics today is not the same as eugenics and racial hygiene in the 1930s,"[90] and superficially respectable arguments for eugenics or sterilization laws are no longer at hand.[91]

This is not to say that the worst could never happen. Human beings have a remarkable capacity for self-deception and credulity. If eternal vigilance is the price of liberty, it also is the price of avoiding the mistakes of the past.[92] In the end, how much harm actually would flow from discoveries about genes, environment, and crime as a result of discoveries aided by the criminal offender DNA repositories is an open question.

B. The "Right to Informed Consent"

Harms to individuals are not the only line of argumentation against permitting behavioral genetics research with law enforcement DNA repositories. A second line of argumentation involves an asserted "right to informed consent," which builds on the assumption that individuals should choose how their samples are used. Invocations of some version of this right pepper the literature on the research uses of the databases and databanks. But it is not enough to assert, in the broadest possible terms, that "[t]he right to consent or refuse to take part in research is an important right for individuals and for society."[93] A demonstration

---

The basis for this claim is a story in the now defunct news magazine, *Emerge*. Harriet A. Washington, *Human Guinea Pigs*, EMERGE, Oct. 1994, at 24. However, the *Emerge* article merely states that "[a]ccording to the *Washington Daily News* [another defunct publication], the children's confidentiality was not protected and the blood tests results were passed to the courts to use as they saw fit." *Id.* Years ago, the principal investigator of the NIMH study noted that the stories published in the *Washington Daily News* amounted to "inaccurate publicity" with "erroneous accusations." Digamber S. Borgaonkar, *Cytogenetic Screening of Community-Dwelling Males, in* GENETIC ISSUES IN PUBLIC HEALTH AND MEDICINE 215, 218 (Bernice H. Cohen et al. eds., 1978). The consent form promised that "the results will be used only by our medical researchers for scientific study and will not be disclosed to any other person or agency." *Id.* at 230. The researchers realized that it would not then have been possible to maintain this confidentiality in the face of a court subpoena, but they reported that, fortunately, no court ever requested the information, and the "results have been disclosed only to parents" of the juveniles. *Id.* at 227. In sum, the claim that XYY findings were routinely passed to courts appears to be another urban myth.

90. Manfred D. Laubichler, *Frankenstein in the Land of Dichter and Denker*, 286 SCIENCE 1859, 1860 (1999).

91. *See* Kevles & Hood, *supra* note 75, at 318 ("Awareness of the barbarities and cruelties of state-sponsored eugenics in the past has tended to set most geneticists and the public at large against such programs. Geneticists today know better than their early-twentieth-century predecessors that ideas concerning what is 'good for the gene pool' are highly problematic").

92. *Cf.* GEORGE SANTAYANA, LIFE OF REASON: REASON IN COMMON SENSE 284 (1905) ("Those who cannot remember the past are condemned to repeat it").

93. KRISTINA STALEY, GENEWATCH UK, THE POLICE NATIONAL DNA DATABASE: BALANCING CRIME DETECTION, HUMAN RIGHTS AND PRIVACY 8 (2005), *available at* http://www.genewatch. org/HumanGen/Publications/Reports/NationalDNADatabase.pdf; *see also id.* at 46

that a particular use of the tissue samples violates an "important right" requires explicating the boundaries of this right, and that task cannot be accomplished without a theory of the reasons for insisting on informed consent in medical research.

In this regard, there is no plausible moral right "to informed consent" as a prerequisite for any and all scientific research into human behavior, physiology, or anatomy. Rather, consent serves to waive other individual rights that stand between the subject and the research. These include the rights to be free from intentional bodily harm, from offensive touching or intrusion, from unnecessary confinement and physical restraint, and from serious and reasonable emotional distress. Thus, physicians are not at liberty to perform experimental (or even clinically accepted) surgery on their patients even when the surgery is the only hope for the patient.[94] Social psychologists cannot freely conduct experiments that might produce psychological harm or stress (although they may deceive subjects about some aspects of the study when this deception is essential and the risk of harm from the deception is de minimis).[95]

A counterargument to the thesis that research that infringes no independent, protected interests is morally permissible without prior consent builds on the Kantian perspective that a research subject is an autonomous agent who must not be used as a means to the researcher's ends, no matter how beneficent those ends may be. But this pronouncement is too glib. It knows no bounds and does not accord with historical and contemporary practices. Consider the following case: traffic engineers want to study the effect of altering the timing of stoplights at the entrance ramps to certain freeways. Would this study infringe the freeway

---

("Seeking informed consent protects the freedoms, rights and dignity of the people who take part. . . . Consent should have to be obtained from the individuals on the database before genetic research is allowed to go ahead").

94. *See, e.g.,* Chambers v. Nottebaum, 96 So. 2d 716, 718 (Fla. Dist. Ct. App. 1957) ("The rule is well established which prevents a doctor from operating on a patient without his express or implied consent"); Schloendorff v. Soc'y of New York Hosp., 105 N.E. 92, 93 (N.Y. 1914) ("Every human being of adult years and sound mind has a right to determine what shall be done with his own body; and a surgeon who performs an operation without his patient's consent commits an assault, for which he is liable in damages"). On the ethical constraints on human experimentation, *see, e.g.,* INSTITUTE OF MEDICINE, NATIONAL RESEARCH COUNCIL, RESPONSIBLE RESEARCH: A SYSTEMS APPROACH TO PROTECTING RESEARCH PARTICIPANTS (2002), *available at* http:// www.iom.edu/Object.File/Master/4/157/0.pdf.

95. E.g., PANEL ON INSTITUTIONAL REVIEW BOARDS, SURVEYS, AND SOCIAL SCIENCE RESEARCH, NATIONAL RESEARCH COUNCIL, PROTECTING PARTICIPANTS AND FACILITATING SOCIAL AND BEHAVIORAL SCIENCES RESEARCH 25 (Constance F. Citro et al. eds., 2003), *available at* http:// www.nap.edu/books/0309088526/html/. Historians and other scholars have chafed at the rigid application of human subjects protections to their work. *See, e.g.,* Jeffrey Brainard, *The Wrong Rules for Social Science?*, CHRON. HIGHER EDUC., Mar. 9, 2001, at A21.

drivers' dignitary interest unless they first gave their informed consent to be observed?

A dedicated adherent to the no-research-without-consent rule might concede the validity of the counterexample but seek to rescue the broad rule by admitting the narrowest of exceptions. This reformulated thesis would hold that informed consent is required for all research except in those cases in which the research consists of observations of public behavior visible to any bystander.

Even with this amendment, however, the modified principle is too broad. Consider a data set consisting of records of blood or breath alcohol concentrations taken from drivers suspected of driving while intoxicated. Most of these data, let us assume, have not been obtained with the voluntary consent of the drivers (especially if they were, in fact, intoxicated at the time), but rather under threat of having one's driving license suspended as provided for in the jurisdiction's "implied consent law." Would it be unethical for the sheriff's office to make these records available to a researcher to analyze the distribution of alcohol levels in the sample?

Such counterexamples[96] suggest that no absolute requirement of obtaining consent can pertain to all "research" seeking information on human subjects.[97] Rather, the proposed research must entail some invasion of the subject's interests that would create a duty on the part of the researcher to the subject. That duty, moreover, does not arise simply because the words "medical" or "controversial" are placed in front of "research"[98] or because the Nuremburg Code

---

96. *See also* 45 C.F.R. § 46.116(c) (2004) (allowing federally funded or conducted researchers evaluating public benefit or service programs to dispense with informed consent); Kaye, *supra* note 19.

97. *Cf.* 45 C.F.R. § 46.101(I) (2004) (permitting waiver for unspecified reasons of the consent requirement in federally funded or federally conducted research on human subjects); 45 C.F.R. § 46.116(d) (2004) (permitting waiver of the consent requirement in cases of "minimal risk").

98. For examples of this phrasing, see Staley, *supra* note 92, at 37 ("Using the [United Kingdom's national DNA database] for research would violate the right of research participants to opt out of potentially controversial studies"); Kimmelman, *supra* note 7, at 696 ("Although many potential benefits of such research can be envisioned (for example, determining suitable treatment regimens for particular prisoners), transferring databanked DNA for research protocols would violate the right of research subjects to opt out of participating in potentially controversial medical research . . .").

Dr. Kimmelman also noted that research use of convicted-offender samples "would also run counter to the guidelines on handling genetic materials proposed by several commentators. . . ." Kimmelman, *supra* note 7, at 696. However, even if the tissue-banking guidelines of other commentators are generally desirable, it is not obvious how they should be applied to law enforcement databases and databanks. Unlike many tissue repositories of samples created in the context of a trust relationship between medical providers and patients, the law enforcement repositories are not part of a consent-based regime. *See* Kaye, *supra* note 19.

is invoked.[99] Inasmuch as the theory that "research can risk harming the individuals who are being studied"[100] supports the general rule that people should not be forced to participate in research unless they have given their informed consent, one must then ask whether the research threatens to cause personal harms before one can conclude that the general rule should apply.[101]

Research with tissue samples certainly could fall into this category. Concrete harms, already noted, might flow from the revelation to potential employers or insurers of certain genotypes. In addition, an individual has an autonomy interest in not knowing that he has particular alleles. For example, individuals should not be forced to undergo genetic testing to discover whether they carry the allele for Huntington's disease. Some individuals with a family history that puts them at risk may prefer a life with ambiguity to one in which they know that they are destined for an early death. This personal choice as to how to live one's life should be respected.[102]

---

99. For an instance of this polemic, see *supra* Part I.B (citing statements of Paul Billings, Lori Andrews, and others). The applicability of the Nuremburg Code to research on archival tissue samples is discussed in Kaye, *supra* note 19.

100. Ellen Wright Clayton et al., *Informed Consent for Genetic Research on Stored Tissue Samples*, 274 JAMA 1786, 1786 (1995) (explaining the position of several participants who advocated demanding more rigorous standards for consent in a 1994 workshop "to develop recommendations for securing appropriate informed consent when collecting tissue samples for possible use in genetic research and for defining indications for additional consent if samples in hand are to be used for genetic studies").

101. The "rule" I am speaking of is one of morality, not law. It might be argued that behavioral genetics research with DNA samples, particularly those from prisoners, would violate the "Common Rule" that applies to federally funded or federally conducted research. *See* 45 C.F.R. pt. 46 (2004). For present purposes, let us assume that these administrative regulations, as they are interpreted by the Department of Health and Human Services' Office for Human Research Protections, would not allow the research with the law enforcement samples to be funded or conducted. *But see* Henry T. Greely, *Breaking the Stalemate: A Prospective Regulatory Framework for Unforeseen Research Uses of Human Tissue Samples and Health Information*, 34 WAKE FOREST L. REV. 737 (1999) (discussing the generous interpretation of the Common Rule recommended by the National Bioethics Advisory Commission); Daniel S. Strouse, *Informed Consent to Research on Banked Human Tissue*, 45 JURIMETRICS J. 135, 150–52 (2005) (discussing ambiguities in the Common Rule and mechanisms for dispensing with informed consent). Although these regulations are intended to reflect the ethical norms of the research community, when one is asking what is morally justified, it is not enough that government regulations come out one way or the other. The rules are at most indicative of a descriptive morality, of the practices considered ethical in the research community. They are not a final answer in a critical morality, which asks whether these practices are justified.

102. Of course, it could be argued that if precautions are taken to render the possibility of data leakage (both to the research subject and to third parties) extremely remote, then the hypothetical possibility of these harms is not enough to trigger a duty to obtain consent.

Beyond the potentially harmful or autonomy-threatening consequences of possible "data leakage" lies a distinct and, as yet, ill-defined and inchoate concept of "genetic privacy"—a widely shared feeling that one's genome should not be on display to any and all interested parties, that this information is part of one's private sphere, and that this realm is wrongly invaded even if no one learns of the invasion. It is one thing to photograph a neighbor as she is walking in the corridor on the way to her high-rise apartment. It is another to photograph her naked body in her bedroom from the building across the way. Regardless of the woman's awareness of his conduct, the "peeping Tom" might have a duty not to look.

This analogy, however, is inapposite. The source of the duty not to peep does not arise because of the sensitivity of the "information." It is part of a comprehensive set of protections to assure people that, for a time, they can be alone and unobserved. Exactly where the protective line should be drawn is open to debate—perhaps the burden should be on the apartment-dweller to draw the blinds—but if there is a justification for according similarly stringent privacy protections to DNA samples, it rests on some other personal interest that has yet to be articulated. At this point, therefore, the rubric of "genetic privacy" seems inadequate as a specification of a personal interest that would give rise to a duty to seek consent.

Even assuming that individuals have a right to preclude others from studying their DNA because they might be harmed by data leakage, the resulting requirement to obtain informed consent before examining the samples could still be avoided—by anonymizing the samples. If the researchers have no realistic chance of discovering which sample goes with which offender, then there is no real possibility of harmful data leakage.[103]

Federal regulations for the protection of research subjects have never imposed a blanket requirement of obtaining informed consent in this situation.

103. With some research designs, it will be possible to infer the identities of the participants in the study. *See* National Commission on the Future of DNA Evidence, Proceedings, Privacy Considerations and Database Sample Retention Discussion (July 26, 1999) (statement of Philip Reilly), http://www.ojp.usdoj.gov/nij/topics/forensics/events/dnamtgtrans6/trans-h.html:

[Y]ou cannot tell me that the statutes include currently an absolute guarantee of a pure anonymous and anonymity function in the research. . . . [B]ecause they will be a very limited sample of people, and a very limited sample of questions, . . . it will be possible to reconstruct . . . in a small cohort who were the subjects of the research. . . . Let's imagine that in the State of Massachusetts, I want to do research on 400 convicted pedophiles, and I want to ask whether an allele has a certain frequency that has a relative risk much higher in that group than the general population; and I find out that that is, in fact, true. . . . [I]t would be possible . . . to find out who was [in] the set of convicted pedophiles during those years.

Even with anonymized samples, however, a further objection to the research might be raised. An individual might worry that the results of the study will stigmatize a group of which he is a member. Native Americans, for instance, may wish to block a genetic study for alcoholism on a reservation for fear that it will reinforce the image of the "drunken Indian." Genetic research on "Jewish diseases" like Tay-Sachs raises a similar concern in Jewish communities. Do these concerns create a duty for the researcher to obtain consent from the "donors"? The donors are not the community, although they are a part of it. If the duty runs to the community, who speaks for that group, and why are their views about whether the risk of harm is justified privileged over those of everyone else?

As these questions reveal, the group-harm argument fits awkwardly into the doctrine of informed consent. The harms that are supposed to trigger a duty on the part of the researcher extend to all members of the group who might be harmed, not just to the individuals whose DNA samples are on file. Their interest lies in not being misjudged by other people who do not appreciate the limitations or implications of the research. The view that researchers owe a duty to acquire the consent of everyone who might be affected by new knowledge is a recipe for frustrating all research about human beings.

A more plausible view is that if this possible change in status is the only harm to individuals—particularly to individuals who are not contributing to the research by any voluntary action—then no obligation to obtain their permission arises. No man, to be trite, is an island. We are all members of intersecting, overlapping, and interacting groups. All research on humans can affect one or more of these groups.

This connectedness is not a reason to ignore the possibility of harm in deciding whether the research is, on balance, justified. In appropriate cases, "community consultation" may be valuable in designing or implementing the research as well as in deciding whether the possible benefits justify the research itself. But the possibility of group harm does not give the group veto power over

---

However, knowing that an individual's DNA was included in a study does not imply that the individual has the allele for which the "relative risk [of pedophilia is] much higher." As in the general population, most of the study population will not have that allele. The knowledge about the individual Dr. Reilly described is no different than the knowledge that an individual is a member of a group that has an elevated risk factor. This fact is not a breach of anonymity, but it might be the basis for an argument that group harm warrants requiring informed consent. This line of argument is considered below.

Another puzzling argument is that because DNA is unique to individuals (and monozygotic twins), "samples cannot ever be truly anonymized." Andrews, *supra* note 57, at 24; *cf.* Juengst, *supra* note 43, at 68–69 (suggesting that anonymization of DNA samples is not "technically possible"). These ethicists do not explain how the researchers will obtain access to the data in NDIS (or elsewhere) that would permit the names of individuals to be linked to the DNA samples. If personal identification is not feasible, then the "technical" possibility is of no practical concern.

the research. In other words, it does not create a right to informed consent that resides in the group as a whole. Instead, it simply constitutes a harm-based argument based on false beliefs in genetic determinism. Depending on the circumstances, this argument may be compelling or it may be flimsy, but it is not sufficient warrant for the claim that it is the group that has the right to decide whether the research can proceed.

Consider, for example, a geographically defined community. Researchers doing contract research for the local police enter the area and go to barber shops in different neighborhoods to gather hair off the floor for drug testing. This testing reveals that some locales are drug-infested, while others are not. Did the researchers have an obligation to obtain the informed consent of the residents of each neighborhood before collecting the convenient samples of hair?

The situation differs from the usual medical research context, in which the system seeks to foster trust between researchers and patients or subjects and in which legitimate acquisition of biological samples in the first instance depends on informed consent. It is closer to the convicted offender biobanks that house samples legitimately acquired without consent. As to these tissue repositories, the justification for demanding informed consent from the involuntary "donors" must be that the potential harms to these individuals are sufficiently palpable to require the "donors" to make the decision as to whether this research should proceed with their samples. The immediacy, probability, and severity of the harms, like the possible harms to individuals or racial or ethnic groups with known genotypes, are far from clear.[104]

C. Sample Retention and Research

Recognizing that repositories of individually labeled DNA samples create at least a theoretical possibility that personally sensitive information will be extracted, many commentators have questioned the need to retain the samples in the first place.[105] The National Commission on the Future of DNA Evidence debated this issue without success. Unable to reach a consensus, it recommended that another commission address the issue within five years.[106] In arguing before the

---

104. With regard to research with offender samples, the group potentially stigmatized is not an extended family or a racial or ethnic minority that is evident in advance, but rather the group of potential or convicted criminals. This class already is about as stigmatized as any group could be. Admittedly, finding that some alleles occur more frequently among convicted criminals than among the rest of the population might reinforce perceptions of "natural born killers." Yet, regardless of whether killers are born or made (or both), their social and legal status is not likely to change dramatically as a result of these kinds of studies.

105. E.g., Rothstein & Carnahan, *supra* note 9, at 156; Steinhardt, *supra* note 7, at 190.

106. *See* NATIONAL COMMISSION ON THE FUTURE OF DNA EVIDENCE, PROCEEDINGS, COMMISSION DISCUSSION ON CONTINUED TRACKING OF FORENSIC DNA ISSUES: AS TECHNOLOGY EXPANDS, HOW SHOULD LEGAL, PRIVACY, FUNDING AND RESEARCH ISSUES BE ADDRESSED IN THE

commission, the FBI adduced four reasons for sample retention. First, it indicated that "[o]nly one state requires the destruction of samples after analysis."[107] That a parochial practice[108] (or even a universal one) exists, however, is not a reason to perpetuate it.

Second, the FBI pointed to the "tremendous difficulty in regenerating or retyping databases after the samples have been destroyed."[109] Throwing the samples away could lock the system into the 13 STR loci now in place, which might be unfortunate if a superior typing technology were to emerge. Nonetheless, it would seem that the STR loci are satisfactory and could continue to be used in parallel with a new system.[110]

Third, the FBI maintained that "destruction of samples would affect the quality assurance of the DNA database."[111] In particular, the Bureau noted that "mistakes can happen" and that "going back to the original sample and retyping that sample and confirming the accuracy of the identity of the individual prior to the name being released to law enforcement would identify mistakes" and spare individuals from the trauma of false accusations.[112]

FUTURE? (Apr. 10, 2000) (statement of Michael Smith), http://www.ojp.usdoj.gov/nij/topics/forensics/events/dnamtgtrans9/trans-n.html ("[At a previous meeting] what we said was something like in no more than five years a body should be assembled which is not the creature of the labs or the law enforcement interests to revisit the question whether or not it's necessary or desirable to retain samples").

107. NATIONAL COMMISSION ON THE FUTURE OF DNA EVIDENCE, PROCEEDINGS, Sept. 26, 1999, http:// www.ojp.usdoj.gov/nij/topics/forensics/events/dnamtgtrans7/trans-c.html (statement of Tom Callaghan).

108. At least four countries—Belgium, Germany, the Netherlands, and Norway—"destroy reference samples so as to remove any possibility or perception that government be able to perform any other inappropriate or illegal testing on the sample." Christopher H. Asplen, *International Perspectives on Forensic DNA Testing*, paper presented at the International Society for the Reform of Criminal Law Conference, Aug. 24–28, 2003, at 4–5.

109. NATIONAL COMMISSION ON THE FUTURE OF DNA EVIDENCE, *supra* note 108 (statement of Tom Callaghan).

110. However, Dr. Callaghan, Program Manager of the Federal Convicted Offender Database, pointed to one subtlety in this regard:

One of the difficulties in current DNA analysis is resolving mixtures. When mixtures cannot be resolved, the entire mixture profile would be searched against the database, generating a lot of hits that would have to be further investigated. There may be markers in the future that are discovered that are far more discriminating and therefore mixtures would be much easily, much easier to resolve and to profile, not associated or only associated with one individual could be put in the DNA database and searched.

Id.

111. *Id.*

112. *Id.*

Finally, the FBI suggested that there was no real problem that warranted the destruction of potentially useful samples. "DNA databasing," it noted, "has occurred for ten years, and there has been no record of misuse of any sample in a DNA analysis database."[113] Of course, this fact is not an affirmative reason to retain the samples.

Neither these arguments nor the additional value of the samples to behavioral genetics research provide compelling reasons to retain samples indefinitely. If a strong case for indefinite retention cannot be made, then eliminating the stockpile of samples might be a politically appealing strategy because it would assure the public that misuse of samples cannot occur.[114] Such a change in current policy would, of course, foreclose the use of the samples for behavioral or medical research, but this might be a small price to pay for enhanced public trust.

D. Independent Review of Research Proposals and Protocols

Even if the existing sample retention policy is continued, and even if arguments for a categorical ban on behavioral genetics research with law enforcement databanks or for requiring consent from all criminal "donors" are rejected, it does not follow that researchers should have unchecked discretion to proceed with studies of human behavior. Some research may be ill conceived or may not be likely to achieve adequate anonymization of samples (where that is necessary). Therefore, procedures should be implemented to ensure that the merits of the particular research justify the risks it creates.

The usual procedural mechanism for avoiding excesses on the part of individual researchers in federally funded or directed research is an institutional review board (IRB) that is charged with verifying that the research is not unduly

---

113. *Id.*

114. *See, e.g.,* D. H. Kaye & Michael E. Smith, *DNA Identification Databases: Legality, Legitimacy, and the Case for Population-wide Coverage,* 2003 Wis. L. Rev. 413, 438 (proposing a population-wide identification database in which "[l]aw enforcement agencies would not need—and should not be permitted—to handle, much less retain, the samples"); Rothstein & Talbott, *supra* note 9, at 159 ("Destruction of samples immediately after analysis would go a long way in assuring the public that their DNA will not be used for purposes unrelated to legitimate law enforcement. After the DNA sample is destroyed, the remaining information would consist merely of thirteen sets of numbers with no diagnostic, prognostic, or research significance"); Rothstein & Carnahan, *supra* note 9, at 163 ("[t]he retention of samples, however, even under conditions of stringent security, raises concerns among the public that the samples could be re-analyzed for purposes other than identification. Therefore, samples should be destroyed immediately after analysis").

harmful.[115] IRBs are no panacea,[116] but they are better than nothing.[117] If tissue samples in law enforcement databanks are to be made available for biomedical or behavioral (rather than for biometric) research, then the proposed research should be reviewed by an independent board with expertise in this type of research. This review could help ensure that the specific research has sufficient merit to justify the risks of stigmatization or discrimination. IRB approval already is required for researchers seeking federal grants for projects that would make use of law enforcement biobanks. It would be reasonable to add this same layer of review to private or state projects that fall outside this regulatory framework.

CONCLUSION

Behavioral geneticists are not yet massing at the gates of law enforcement DNA databanks preparing to breach these citadels in the search for "crime genes." Nevertheless, concerns that DNA samples collected from convicted offenders for the construction of DNA identification databases also might be used in behavioral genetics research are legitimate. For better or worse, not all such research can be dismissed as devoid of scientific merit, making it necessary to decide whether the samples should be available for studies of alleles that might be linked to behavioral traits such as impulsiveness, novelty-seeking, or aggressiveness.

Existing legislation in the United States seems to preclude these uses of the samples, but one could argue that this limitation is squandering a useful resource for genetic research. Conversely, it can be argued that this research should be discouraged and that the samples should not be used for any purpose other than biometric identification. These competing arguments produce no clear winners. On one hand, the risks of psychosocial harms, informational privacy, and the protection of human subjects may not justify banning all behavioral genetics research with the samples. On the other hand, the research need for these

---

115. On the nature and role of IRBs, see 1 NAT'L BIOETHICS ADVISORY COMM'N, ETHICAL AND POLICY ISSUES IN RESEARCH INVOLVING HUMAN PARTICIPANTS: REPORT.

116. *See, e.g.,* James F. Childress, *The National Bioethics Advisory Commission: Bridging the Gap in Human Subjects Research Protection,* 1 J. HEALTH CARE L. & POL'Y 105, 113–14 (1998); Jay Katz, *Human Experimentation and Human Rights,* 38 ST. LOUIS U. L. J. 7, 9 (1993); ANNE WOOD ET AL., THE CRISIS IN HUMAN PARTICIPANTS RESEARCH: IDENTIFYING THE PROBLEMS AND PROPOSING SOLUTIONS (2002), http://bioethics.gov/background/emanuelpaper.html.

117. For reviews of recent books on IRBs, see Kenneth A. DeVille, *Book Review Essay,* 28 J. LEGAL MED. 579 (2007); see also INSTITUTE OF MEDICINE, *supra* note 94; Carl H. Coleman, *Rationalizing Risk Assessment in Human Subject Research,* 46 ARIZ. L. REV. 1 (2004); Sharona Hoffman, *Continued Concern: Human Subject Protection, the Institutional Review Board, and Continuing Review,* 68 TENN. L. REV. 725 (2001); Lars Noah, *Deputizing Institutional Review Boards to Police (Audit?) Biomedical Research,* 25 J. LEGAL MED. 267 (2004).

samples may not be pressing. But even if the existing categorical rule against using the samples is thought to be unwarranted, the doors to the law enforcement biobanks should not be thrown wide open. Some studies will be better designed to uncover interesting discoveries and to respect the privacy interests of the "donors" of the samples than others. With ordinary biomedical research involving human subjects, the peer review process for grant requests by academic investigators offers some assurance that the study design is appropriate, and review by IRBs offers further protection for the interests of "donors." Comparable review should be required before releasing law enforcement samples for behavioral genetics or other biomedical research.

12. GENETIC PREDICTIONS OF FUTURE DANGEROUSNESS: IS THERE A BLUEPRINT FOR VIOLENCE?

ERICA BEECHER-MONAS AND

EDGAR GARCIA-RILL

INTRODUCTION

The brave new world of genomics, spurred on by the Human Genome Project, presents tantalizing possibilities for developments in criminal law as well as advances in medicine and understanding disease. DNA identification testing has become commonplace in the courts, transforming the criminal justice system, demonstrating innocence, and identifying perpetrators. Already it is clear that DNA testing will be used as a way of predicting which medical treatments will be effective. With predictive medicine becoming a reality, surely predicting human behavior cannot be far behind.

 . The link between crime and genetics is hardly a new idea. At least since the late nineteenth century, courts and prisons have attempted to discriminate between the innately criminal and those who acted merely by force of circumstance, meaning that their crimes would not pose a future danger to society.[1] In order to distinguish the dangerous criminals from the merely circumstantial ones, predictions of future dangerousness became vital to the criminal justice system. This legacy has persisted despite the enactment of civil rights legislation, doing away with the more overtly racist laws deriving from eugenics. As a result, predictions of future dangerousness now dominate death penalty sentencing determinations and sexually violent predator commitments.[2]

---

1. Cesare Lombroso, an influential criminologist, claimed that criminals were atavistic throwbacks to the apes, characterized by physical "stigmata," as well as by a high threshold for pain, an inability to blush, and a propensity for tattoos. CESARE LOMBROSO, CRIME: ITS CAUSES AND REMEDIES 365 (Henry P. Horton trans., 1918). *See also* STEPHEN J. GOULD, THE MISMEASURE OF MAN 153–72 (1996) (discussing Lombroso's influence on criminal law and the fallacy of his claims to predict innate criminality). According to Lombroso, while dangerous criminals should be removed from society, little would be gained by incarcerating those who were the victims of circumstance, including those men who kill their adulterous wives in the heat of passion. LOMBROSO, *supra*, at 138.

2. Lest one think that racism and bigotry have disappeared from predictions of future dangerousness, it is worth noting that "whites are more likely to view African-American defendants as dangerous and violent than they view white defendants." Donna Coker,

Surprisingly, although the stakes are high in these predictions, they receive little judicial or legislative scrutiny. Although courts and legislatures are well aware of the unscientific nature of these predictions, they nonetheless continue to demand them.[3] Responding to the continued legislative and judicial demand, researchers attempted to improve the accuracy of future dangerousness predictions by developing actuarial instruments to assess the risk of repeated violence in offenders and psychiatric patients by examining a number of factors, scored on a scale with points varying according to the particular instrument.[4] Each instrument evaluates different risk factors, and also scores them differently, but there is a general consensus that such instruments are superior to clinical judgment alone.[5] None of these methods is particularly predictive.[6] Whether future dangerousness predictions can meet standards of scientific validity and what, if anything, can be done to improve them, are highly debatable issues.[7] The question posed by behavioral genetics is whether molecular biology can improve this dismal record.

Foreword: Addressing the Real World of Racial Injustice in the Criminal Justice System, 93 J. CRIM. L. & CRIMINOLOGY 827, 876 (2003).

3. *See* Alexander Scherr, *Daubert & Danger: The "Fit" of Expert Predictions in Civil Commitments*, 55 HASTINGS L. J. 1, 2–3 (2003) (commenting that courts are extraordinarily receptive to expert future dangerousness testimony, even though they are well aware of its scientific unreliability).

4. Actuarial risk assessment "uses an equation, a formula, a graph, or an actuarial table to arrive at a probability, or expected value, of some outcome." William M. Grove & Paul E. Meehl, *Comparative Efficiency of Informal (Subjective, Impressionistic) and Formal (Mechanical, Algorithmic) Prediction Procedures: The Clinical-Statistical Controversy*, 2 PSYCHOL. PUB. POL'Y & L. 293, 294 (1996).

5. For a more in-depth examination and appraisal of each of these instruments, *see generally* Erica Beecher-Monas & Edgar Garcia-Rill, *Chaos at the Edge of Danger: Predicting Violent Behavior in a Post-Daubert World*, 24 CARDOZO L. REV. 1845 (2003).

6. *See, e.g.*, Neil M. Malamuth et al., *Risk Assessment: Discussion of the Section, in* 989 ANNALS OF THE NEW YORK ACADEMY OF SCIENCES, SEXUALLY COERCIVE BEHAVIOR: UNDERSTANDING AND MANAGEMENT 236, 237 (Robert A. Prentky et al. eds., 2003) [hereinafter SEXUALLY COERCIVE BEHAVIOR] (explaining that at best, current actuarial instruments are only moderately predictive, having Reciever Operating Characteristic curve statistics of about 0.70, or correlations of 0.30). Even with the best assessment instrument, the VRAG, only 55 percent of the individuals scoring as high risk actually recidivated compared with 19 percent recidivism in the low-scoring group. *See* John Monahan, *Violence Risk Assessment: Scientific Validity and Evidentiary Admissibility*, 57 WASH. & LEE L. REV. 901, 906–8 (2000).

7. *See, e.g.*, Caroline M. Mee & Harold V. Hall, *Risky Business: Assessing Danger in Hawai'i*, 24 U. HAW. L. REV. 63, 63 (2001) (noting that "dangerousness prediction has heretofore been rudimentary and inaccurate, relying on clinical judgment rather than on objective measures"). Even where actuarial risk assessment is used, the results, while better than clinical predictions, are only moderately predictive. *See, e.g.*, Malamuth et al., *supra* note 6.

Genetic information, including behavioral genetics, has exploded under the influence of the Human Genome Project. Virtually everyone agrees that genes influence behavior.[8] Scandinavian twin and adoption studies are widely touted as favoring a genetic role in crime.[9] "Everyone knows" that the cycle of violence is repeated across generations.[10] Recently, alleles of specific genes, such as those transcribing for monoamine oxidase A (MAOA), have been identified and linked with propensities to violence.[11] Shouldn't adding genetic information to the mix produce more accurate predictions of future dangerousness?

This question must be answered with a qualified yes and no. First, there is unfortunate history in this regard, and while we might wish to put the bad old days behind us, the shocking absence of scientific scrutiny for eugenics assertions has managed to persist in the astonishing failure of courts and legislatures

---

8. *See, e.g.*, Richard P. Ebstein et al., *Behavioral Genetics, Genomics, and Personality, in* BEHAVIORAL GENETICS IN THE POSTGENOMIC ERA 365, 380 (Robert Plomin et al. eds., 2003) (noting that "the importance of genetic factors in determining human temperament has been recognized for two decades"); Patrick Bateson, *The Corpse of a Wearisome Debate,* 297 SCI. 2212 (2002) (reviewing STEPHEN PINKER, THE BLANK SLATE: THE MODERN DENIAL OF HUMAN NATURE (2002) and noting that "the center of th[e] academic debate is not whether genes influence behavior but rather how they do so").

9. *See, e.g.*, DEBRA NIEHOFF, THE BIOLOGY OF VIOLENCE: HOW UNDERSTANDING THE BRAIN, BEHAVIOR, AND ENVIRONMENT CAN BREAK THE VICIOUS CIRCLE OF AGGRESSION 238 (1999) (noting that "twin and adoption data favor a role for genetic influences" in crime but cautioning that "when concordance rates for violent crime were extracted from the Scandinavian data, none of the studies made a very convincing case for an appreciable genetic influence on violence"); MATT RIDLEY, THE AGILE GENE 19–20 (2004) (noting that twin studies demonstrate that "personality is about as heritable as body weight").

10. *See, e.g.*, NAT'L INST. OF JUST., THE CYCLE OF VIOLENCE REVISITED (1996), *available at* http://www.ncjrs.org/pdffiles/cyclepre.pdf (studying 1575 subjects over a 26-year period, and concluding that abused and neglected children were twice as likely to be arrested as juveniles as children without such a history, and more likely to be arrested for a violent offense).

11. MAOA regulates neurotransmitters such as serotonin, dopamine, and epiniephrine and has been associated with psychopathy, childhood hyperactivity, childhood aggression, impulsivity, and substance abuse. *See* Grant T. Harris et al., *The Construct of Psychopathy,* 28 CRIME & JUST. 197, 224 (acknowledging that "findings on all of these laboratory-based theories of psychopathy often seem somewhat ephemeral"). *See also* Avshalom Caspi et al., *Role of Genotype in the Cycle of Violence in Maltreated Children,* 297 SCI. 851–53 (2002) (studying 442 men in New Zealand for differences in MAOA activity alleles and correlating these differences with maltreatment in childhood and subsequent violent behavior). The results demonstrated that the high-activity form of the gene did not manifest in violent propensities even if the men had been mistreated as boys, while those with the low-active form of the gene, who had been mistreated, committed four times as many rapes, assaults, and robberies as the average). *Id.*

to examine the scientific validity of expert future dangerousness predictions.[12] Throwing away the key when someone has already committed a grisly crime is an all-too-human response to the specter of tragedy and nasty headlines. But it is precisely to counter such responses that we have the rule of law, and inquiry into the relevance and reliability of proffered evidence is a foundational aspect of this process.

Second, while information from the biology of violence, including genomics, could vastly improve the way predictions are made, it is urgent that the information be tested, scrutinized, and properly limited, such that the promise of science is not once again perverted into the cynicism of political expediency. This leads to the third point: while genes may constrain, influence, or impact behavior, they do so only in concert with each other and the environment, both internal and external to the organism carrying the genes.

Initially, future dangerousness predictions were based on mostly wrong and mostly unchallenged notions of heredity[13] and acted upon mostly in such "preventive" measures as mass sterilizations,[14] indeterminate sentencing, and ethnically biased immigration laws.[15] Because the idea was that genes were deterministic,

---

12. *See, e.g.*, Erica Beecher-Monas, *The Epistemology of Prediction: Future Dangerousness Testimony and Intellectual Due Process*, 60 Wash. & Lee L. Rev. 353, 359 & passim (2003) (discussing the courts' failure to examine the scientific validity of future dangerousness testimony).

13. They were also based on fallacious notions about genetic differences among ethnic groups. *See, e.g.*, John Tooby & Leda Cosmides, *On the Universality of Human Nature and the Uniqueness of the Individual: The Role of Genetics and Adaptation*, 58 J. PERSONALITY 1, 34–35 (1990) (explaining that modern molecular genetics have shown that there is no basis for believing that "each ethnic group has a set of genes shared by members of the group, but not shared by others"). Rather, the genetic difference between individuals of the same ethnic group is much larger than the genetic difference between groups. *Id.* at 35 (noting that "within-group variance is 12 times greater than the between-group variance"). From an evolutionary standpoint, this is consistent with the pathogen theory of sexual recombination, where because people "catch diseases from their neighbors, . . . it is important to be genetically different from them; such selection . . . promot[es] local within-group diversity and reduc[es] intergroup diversity." *Id.* (observing that "[a]lthough there is a sea of genetic diversity (measured at the protein level), it is a well-mixed sea").

14. *See, e.g.*, Charles C. Mann, *Behavioral Genetics in Transition*, 264 SCI. 1686 (1994) (noting that "[b]y 1930, 24 states had enacted laws to sterilize the 'feeble-minded,'" who were believed to be responsible for a degenerate society and the crime that was rampant within it).

15. *See id.*, at 1684 (noting that Calvin Coolidge signed the Immigration Restriction Act in 1924, restricting immigration from "supposedly inferior Latin and Slavic genes"); *see also* Michael Willrich, *The Two Percent Solution: Eugenic Jurisprudence and the Socialization of American Law, 1900–1930*, 16 LAW & HIST. REV. 63, 84 (1998) (remarking on the "link between heredity, feeblemindedness and criminality" as the focus of prison and mental institution reformers in the early part of the twentieth century).

these hereditarian notions of crime control were coupled with the idea of diminished responsibility.[16] Thus, at the same time that legislatures were enacting these preventive crime control measures, Clarence Darrow managed to save his clients Nathan Leopold and Richard Loeb from the death penalty by arguing that they were the "product of heredity."[17] These twin themes linking genetics to crime prevention and exoneration have resurfaced with the massive attention given to the Human Genome Project. Behavioral genetics has been heralded as the future of criminal justice.[18]

The question now facing social policymakers is whether and how to use these scientific advances in a manner that avoids the pitfalls of eugenics.

---

16. *See, e.g.,* Albert W. Alschuler, *The Changing Purposes of Criminal Punishment: A Retrospective on the Past Century and Some Thoughts About the Next,* 70 U. Chi. L. Rev. 1, 3–5 (2003) (discussing the influence of Darwinism on criminal theory).

17. Clarence Darrow, The Crime of Compulsion, Address of Case Summation Before John R. Caverly, Chief Justice of the Criminal Court of Cook County (Aug. 22, 1924), *in* ATTORNEY FOR THE DAMNED: CLARENCE DARROW IN THE COURTROOM 65–66 (Arthur Weinberg ed., University of Chicago Press, 1989) (1957).

18. *See, e.g.,* Lori B. Andrews, *Predicting and Punishing Antisocial Acts: How the Criminal Justice System Might Use Behavioral Genetics,* in Behavioral Genetics: The Clash of Culture and Biology 116, 1354–35 (1999) (suggesting that, in the future, the state might "take into consideration not just genes for criminal behavior, but genes thought to be associated with precursors to criminal behavior"); David Wasserman, *Is There Value in Identifying Individual Genetic Predispositions to Violence?,* 32 J. L. & Med. Ethics 24, 24 (2004) (forecasting the expanded use of behavioral genetics in crime control); Lindsay A. Elkins, Note, *Five-Foot Two With Eyes of Blue: Physical Profiling and the Prospect of a Genetics-Based Criminal Justice System,* 17 Notre Dame J. L. Ethics & Pub. Pol'y 269, 271 (2003) (arguing that "DNA analysis could serve as an antidote to racial profiling" and exploring the "broader implications of using genetic research"); Rhonda J. Yen, *Tourette's Syndrome: A Case Example for Mandatory Genetic Regulation of Behavioral Disorders,* 27 L. & Psychol. Rev. 29, 29 (asserting that "the vision of *Gattaca* [a 1997 movie depicting a society driven by genetic engineering] is closer than many of us realize"); Keynote Address, 51 Am. L. Rev. 431, 443 (2002) (forecasting changes when behavioral genetics enters into the criminal justice system in terms of defenses and predisposition to commit crime); Nicole H. Rafter, *Seeing and Believing: Images of Heredity in Biological Theories of Crime,* 67 Brook. L. Rev.71, 96 (2001) (forecasting that "pop criminologists may soon come up with recommendations for genetic engineering"); Jasmine A. Tehrani & Sarnoff A. Mednick, *Genetic Factors and Criminal Behavior,* 64 DEC Fed. Prob. 24 (2000) (concluding that "crime prevention efforts may be most effective when all risks, social and genetic, are evaluated"); Nikolas Rose, *The Biology of Culpability, Pathological Identification and Crime Control in a Biological Culture,* 4 THEORETICAL CRIMINOLOGY 5 (2000); Bettyann Kevles & Daniel J. Kevles, *Scapegoat Biology: As Violence Continues to Ravage Our Society, Researchers are Raising Hopes that Science Alone Can Save Us From Our Worst Natures—Again,* Discover, Oct. 1, 1997 at 58, 59–60 (noting that crime joins "many aspects of human life for which it can be claimed that biology is destiny").

Although involuntary sterilization statutes were largely repealed by 1974,[19] determinate sentencing guidelines have imposed some uniformity on punishment,[20] and immigration laws no longer retain language of ethnic bias, the criminal justice system's reliance on future dangerousness predictions has increased dramatically, and without scientific scrutiny. Although future dangerousness predictions are required in a wide range of proceedings, including civil commitments, juvenile adjudications, bail hearings, competency hearings, insanity determinations, and sentencing, "dangerousness prediction has heretofore been rudimentary and inaccurate, relying on clinical judgment rather than on objective measures."[21]

On the other hand, apart from Clarence Darrow's clients, defendants who have attempted to use the idea of innate propensities to negate individual responsibility have met with great resistance. Unless the accused independently meets the criteria for legal insanity, criminal defenses built on behavioral genetics have been overwhelmingly defeated.[22] Putting aside for a moment the question of

---

19. The Virginia statute that was upheld in *Buck v. Bell*, 274 U.S. 200 (1927) was repealed in 1974. 1974 Va. Acts ch. 296. However, a voluntary sterilization statute mandating castration as a condition of parole for repeat sex offenders was enacted in California in 1996. CAL. PENAL CODE § 645 (West 2005). Florida, Georgia, and Montana have similar statutes. *See* FLA. STAT. ANN. § 794.0235 (West 1997); GA. CODE ANN. § 49-9-44.2 (West 1997); MONT. CODE ANN. § 45-5-512 (1997).

20. *See* United States v. Booker, No. 04-1142 (8th Cir. July 29, 2005) (ruling that sentencing guidelines must be merely discretionary). However, the post-*Booker* consequences for determinate sentencing are anybody's guess.

21. Mee & Hall, *supra* note 7, at 63. Indeed, predictions of future dangerousness (on which are based the death penalty, sex offender registration, and postsentence commitment, to name just a few) have become pervasive in the criminal justice system. For example, Deborah Denno ascribes the "dramatic surge in sexual psychopath legislation" to the "medicalization of deviance." Deborah Denno, *Life Before the Modern Sex Offender Statutes*, 92 Nw. U. L. REV. 1317, 1320 (1998). It is not a far leap from "medicalization" to assuming a genetic basis for sexually deviant behavior. *See* Lori B. Andrews, *Predicting and Punishing Antisocial Acts, in* BEHAVIORAL GENETICS: THE CLASH OF CULTURE AND BIOLOGY 116, 134 (Ronald A. Carson & Mark A. Rothstein eds., 1999) (noting that because racial prejudice affects surveillance, arrests, and sentencing, "it is often taken for granted that [blacks'] higher representation in arrests and in prison means they are more violence prone" without acknowledging the skewed sampling). For example, Professor Andrews points out that "[p]regnant white women are slightly more likely to abuse drugs than pregnant black women, but pregnant black women are 9.58 times as likely to be reported for substance abuse during pregnancy." *Id.*

22. As soon as studies linking XYY chromosomal abnormalities with criminal propensities became available, defense attorneys argued that their clients should be exonerated. In the United States, the four cases that attempted such a genetic defense were unsuccessful. *See* State v. Roberts, 544 P.2d 754 (Wash. Ct. App. 1976) (affirming trial court's denial of genetic testing because of the uncertain causal connection between XYY and criminal conduct); People v. Yukl, 372 N.Y.S.2d 313 (N.Y. Sup. Ct. 1975)

whether the courts were correct about the poor science behind these assertions denying culpability due to genetic predispositions, it appears odd, as a practical matter, that the same courts rely on predictions of dangerousness that are even less scientific.

Following this introduction, Part II of this chapter discusses and critiques the courts' use of future dangerousness predictions in sentencing and postsentence commitment proceedings for capital murderers and sex offenders and in community notification requirements for sex offenders. Part III addresses the growth of knowledge about the biology of violence and sexual violence and questions whether such information could be incorporated into actuarial instruments that might more reliably form the basis for sentencing and postsentencing determinations. Part IV examines the problems of predicting violence based on genetic information. Part V concludes that the courts' insistence on future dangerousness predictions is ill conceived for both legal and scientific reasons. Nevertheless, in the face of their unwillingness to abandon such predictions, they must at a minimum insist on the most accurate information available, and that information includes the role of genes in the biology of violence.

FUTURE DANGEROUSNESS IN THE COURTS

Predictions of future dangerousness are widely admissible without any judicial inquiry into their scientific validity.[23] This is astonishing in a system that embraces as a fundamental tenet that only facts having rational probative value should be admissible in the search for truth.[24] Yet judges continue to admit

---

(refusing to order genetic testing or to permit defendant's father to pay for genetic testing because the evidence of a genetic link to violence was not reliably established); People v. Tanner, 91 Cal. Rptr. 656 (Cal. Ct. App. 1970) (finding that neither the link to aggressive behavior nor a chromosomal contribution to legal insanity were established); Millard v. State, 261 A.2d 227 (Md. Ct. Spec. App. 1970) (upholding trial court's refusal to submit the genetic issue to the jury because the expert failed to demonstrate a link between the XYY condition and the legal definition of insanity). An attempt to obtain expert testimony to mitigate the sentence of a capital murder defendant on the basis of MAOA gene abnormality has also been unsuccessful. See Turpin v. Mobley, 502 S.E.2d 458 (Ga. 1998) (finding no ineffective assistance of counsel in failing to accept defendant's father's offer to pay for genetic testing for MAOA deficiency analysis after the trial court refused to pay for it).

23. See Scherr, *supra* note 3.

24. The doctrines of relevance and probativity are expressed as follows under the federal rules of evidence:

"Relevant evidence" means evidence having any tendency to make the existence of any fact that is of consequence to the determination of the action more probable or less probable than it would be without the evidence.

predictions that no one seriously argues can meet these standards. If the test by which an evidentiary practice should be judged is whether it increases the likelihood that the truth, defined as correspondence to the real world, will be attained, then expert future dangerousness testimony fails to make the grade.[25]

Basic rule of law precepts appear to be tossed out with the bathwater when it comes to gruesome murders and violent sex offenses. Not only are people deemed to be at risk for sexually violent recidivism singled out for involuntary postsentence commitment, community registration, or lifetime parole, but even the determination of guilt for sexual offenses is based on evidence of past crimes, which is impermissible "character evidence" for other felony defendants.[26]

FED. R. EVID. 402. And:

Although relevant, evidence may be excluded if its probative value is substantially outweighed by the danger of unfair prejudice, confusion of the issues, or misleading the jury, or by considerations of undue delay, waste of time, or needless presentation of cumulative evidence.

FED. R. EVID. 403.

25. Beecher-Monas & Garcia-Rill, *supra* note 5, at 1856–60 (explaining that clinical future dangerousness testimony cannot meet the *Daubert* standards because it is entirely subjective, ungrounded in empirical data, and therefore unfalsifiable; because it has been overwhelmingly castigated by the profession, and thus fails peer review, publication, and general acceptance; and because it has no standards for its methodology and cannot meet the requirements for an acceptable error rate). We are not, as Professor Scherr contends, seeking a "bare relevance" standard. *See* Scherr, *supra* note 3, at 3 (arguing that because future dangerousness testimony fills a perceived need of the courts it is justified under *Daubert*'s "fit" requirement). Rather, we contend that with respect to expert testimony, relevance under *Daubert* and rule-of-law principles consists of two prongs: reliability (scientific validity) and a logical tendency to prove or disprove an issue in the case. Beecher-Monas & Garcia-Rill, *supra* note 5. Sometimes the concept of "fit" is called "materiality," but it is considered to be one of the generative principles of the law of evidence. *See* Robert P. Burns, *Notes on the Future of Evidence Law*, 74 TEMP. L. REV. 69, 70 (2001) (noting that the generative principle of materiality, now subsumed under the relevance requirement, permits into evidence only that evidence that is of consequence to the "legitimate determination of the action"). Contrary to the Court's contention in *Barefoot v. Estelle*, the adversary process cannot be trusted "to sort out the reliable from the unreliable evidence and opinion about future dangerousness." 463 U.S. 880, 901 (1983). Rather, as the Supreme Court explained in *Daubert*, the requirement that expert testimony be helpful to the jury, "supported by appropriate validation–i.e., 'good grounds,' based upon what is known," is a condition of relevance. 509 U.S. 579, 590–91 (1993). And relevance is not "merely" a matter of evidentiary rules; it is a constitutional minimum, "a requirement of due process and a fundamental fairness requirement of the rule of law." Erica Beecher-Monas, *The Epistemology of Prediction: Future Dangerousness Testimony and Intellectual Due Process*, 60 WASH. & LEE L. REV 353, 361 (2003).

26. *See* FED. R. EVID. 413 (stating that evidence of similar crimes in sexual assault cases is admissible) *and* FED. R. EVID. 414 (permitting evidence of similar crimes in molestation cases to be admissible) (enacted by Congress as part of the Violent Crime Control and Law

The justification for this disparate treatment is that sex crimes are different from other crimes of violence and that sex offenders are more incorrigible and less likely to be deterred by the threat of incarceration.[27] In sentencing sex offenders and capital murderers, as well as in the postsentencing disposition of sex offenders, predictions of future dangerousness are rampant, although generations of scientists have explained that such predictions cannot meet the standards of science. As argued elsewhere,[28] this is a far cry from the truth-generating methodologies supposedly fundamental to due process and runs counter to what is happening in civil trials, where experts must demonstrate the reliability of their testimony.[29]

Predicting future dangerousness has become important as the criminal justice system has changed its focus from punishment to violent recidivism.[30]

Enforcement Act of 1994; effective July 9, 1995) *with* FED. R. EVID. 404(b) (federal evidentiary rule stating that "[e]vidence of other crimes, wrongs, or acts is not admissible to prove the character of a person in order to show action in conformity therewith").

27. There is, however, little evidence for this, and Congress cited none in passing the Violent Crime Control and Law Enforcement Act of 1994. For example, in *Seling v. Young*, the Supreme Court held, in a postsentence sexual offender commitment, that even where there were serious concerns over confinement conditions, release from commitment was unavailable. 531 U.S. 250 (2001). The Court rejected ex post facto and double jeopardy claims, although it left open the possibility that there might be due process claims available. *Id.* at 263. Eric Janus argues that the constitutionality of sexual predator commitments is premised on only the most dangerous being committed, a premise that is "dubious because of the limitations in our ability to predict dangerousness." Eric S. Janus, *Closing Pandora's Box: Sexual Predators and the Politics of Sexual Violence*, 34 SETON HALL L. REV. 1233, 1237 (2004). Professor Janus considers the other bases for finding these commitments constitutional—that somehow this small group of offenders is "different" from normal people because they are mentally disordered, and that confinement would be only for the period of treatment—equally flawed. *Id.* at 1236.

28. Beecher-Monas & Garcia-Rill, *supra* note 5.

29. *See, e.g.,* Julie G. Shoop, *Judges are Gaining Confidence in Assessing Expert Evidence, Study Finds*, 38 TRIAL 92, 92 (2002) (discussing a report by the Rand Institute for Civil Justice, which found that *Daubert* has had a significant impact on admissibility of expert testimony in civil trials, such that judges are closely scrutinizing relevance and reliability, resulting in a dramatic increase in the percentage of excluded expert testimony in products liability trials and a surge in summary judgments against the plaintiffs). This increased scrutiny of scientific evidence has not affected criminal trials nearly so dramatically. *See, e.g.,* Paul C. Gianelli, *Scientific Evidence in Civil and Criminal Cases*, 33 ARIZ. ST. L.J. 103, 119 (2001) (discussing the myriad instances in which criminal judges fail to take *Daubert* seriously); Erica Beecher-Monas, *Blinded by Science: How Judges Avoid the Science in Scientific Evidence*, 71 TEMP. L. REV. 55, 78–82 (1998).

30. *See* Christopher Slobogin, *A Jurisprudence of Dangerousness*, 98 NW. U. L. REV. 1, 62 (2003) (stating that "[p]reventive detention is a pervasive, routine occurrence in our society."); *cf.* Stephen J. Morse, *Preventive Confinement of Dangerous Offenders*, 32 J.L. MED. & ETHICS 56, 56 (2004) (contending that "pure preventive detention is more common than we usually

Although "most offenders have only one recorded violent offense"[31] and only a small proportion of criminal offenses are violent, the focus of criminal justice has shifted from punishment to deterrence through incarceration, civil commitment, or death.[32] For specific sexual offenders, not only are sentences vastly increased for second and third offenses, but sexually violent predator statutes provide for indefinite postsentence civil commitment.[33] These, as well as sexual offender registration laws; three-strikes laws, which authorize life sentences for repeat offenders; and the lowering of the age at which juveniles may be tried as adults, are all based on the notion of preventing future crimes.[34]

In capital sentencing, for example, Texas requires the jury to decide "whether there is a probability that the defendant would commit criminal acts of violence that would constitute a continuing threat to society."[35] Similarly, the Virginia sentencing guidelines use a sex offender risk assessment instrument to recommend that judges consider increased sentences; for nearly half of all sex offenders,

---

assume, but that this practice violates fundamental assumptions concerning liberty under the American constitutional regime").

31. David P. Farrington, *Predictors, Causes, and Correlates of Male Violence*, 24 CRIME & JUST. 421, 434 (1998) (citing studies).

32. Paul H. Robinson, *Punishing Dangerousness: Cloaking Preventive Detention as Criminal Justice*, 114 HARV. L. REV. 1429, 1450 & n.77 (2001) (noting the shift to preventing future violations and observing that most felony offenders are not convicted of a subsequent offense).

33. *See, e.g.,* Va. Code Ann. §§37.1-70.1 (2005). The Virginia Statute defines a sexual predator as

> Any person who (i) has been convicted of a sexually violent offense or is unrestorably incompetent to stand trial . . . and (ii) because of a mental abnormality or personality disorder, finds it difficult to control his predatory behavior, which makes him likely to engage in sexually violent acts.

34. *See id.* at 1432 (arguing that this approach perverts the justice system). In addition to three-strikes laws, a number of states have enacted two-strikes laws, with enhanced sentences for violent sexual offenders. *See* Roxane Lieb et al., *Sexual Predators and Social Policy*, 23 CRIME & JUST. 43, 70 (1998) (observing a "trend toward sentences that incapacitate offenders" and noting increased sentences for sex offenders). Experts estimate that two-thirds of offenders affected by the three-strikes law in California are nonviolent offenders. FRANKLIN E. ZIMRING & GORDON HAWKINS, CRIME IS NOT THE PROBLEM: LETHAL VIOLENCE IN AMERICA 182, 182 (1997).

35. TX. CODE CRIM. PROC. ANN. § (Vernon 1996). Virginia also explicitly requires a finding of future dangerousness in capital sentencing proceedings. VA. CODE ANN. § 19.2-264.2-4 (West 2003). Even when jurors are not explicitly required to consider future dangerousness, studies of capital jurors have shown that "discussion of the defendant's dangerousness occupies a large portion of the time jurors spend deliberating on whether a death sentence is appropriate, regardless of how or whether this information is included at any point during the sentencing phase." Aletha M. Claussen-Schulz et al., *Dangerousness, Risk Assessment, and Capital Sentencing*, 10 PSYCHOL. PUB. POL'Y & L. 471, 480 (2004).

this results in an upward guidelines modification.[36] For the top scorers, it can result in trebled sentences.[37]

Sexually violent predator statutes similarly rely on predictions of dangerousness to commit people who have already served their prison sentences to indefinite terms of confinement.[38] Legislatures in 16 states and the District of Columbia have enacted sexually violent predator laws that civilly commit sexual offenders who have already served their criminal sentences to further indefinite incarceration.[39] A common definition of a sexual predator is someone who has committed

---

36. The Virginia guidelines present the judge with "a midpoint recommendation" for each defendant and a range of sentencing options, in which the high end is increased for the riskiest group of offenders. Richard P. Kern & Meredith Farrar-Owens, *Sentencing Guidelines with Integrated Offender Risk Assessment*, 16 FED. SENT. R. 165, 2004 WL 2189126, at *5. The factors used for this instrument are age at the time of conviction (paradoxically, one gets a worse sentence for being young); prior history of sex offense arrests; criminal record; relationship with the victim; victim's age; whether there was penetration (or attempted penetration); whether the defendant had received treatment; and education level. *Id.* There was apparently no testing of this instrument outside the Virginia Sentencing Commission, and it was neither peer-reviewed nor published in scientific journals before being implemented. *Id.* Although two cases have challenged the use of the sex offender instrument, neither was successful. *See* Brooks v. Commonwealth, No. 2540-02-3, 2004 WL 136090 (Va. Ct. App. Jan. 28, 2004) (upholding constitutionality of guidelines system because they were discretionary with the judge); Lutrell v. Virginia, No. 2092-02-4 (Va. Ct. App. Feb. 17, 2004) (rejecting appeal based on unreliability of instrument because Virginia exempts from appeal judicial use of sentencing guidelines).

37. See Kern & Farrar-Owens, *supra* note 36 at *6 (noting that 48 percent of rapists and 41 percent of felony sex assault offenders received an upward modification, although only 3 percent of rapists and 2 percent of sexual assault offenders received the highest increase, which tripled their possible sentence).

38. Most state sexually violent predator statutes require a finding of future dangerousness, plus current mental illness. *See, e.g.*, WASH. REV. CODE § 71.09.010 (1990) (civil commitment proceedings require a determination of future danger and mental illness). The Supreme Court upheld the constitutionality of such indefinite postsentence commitments in *Kansas v. Hendricks. See* 521 U.S. 346, 346–47 (1997) (holding that civil commitment of sexual predators does not constitute punishment and that states may confine individuals whose mental abnormality makes them likely to commit future offenses).

39. These states include Arizona, ARIZ. REV. STAT. ANN. §§ 36-3701–3717 (2003) (effective July 1, 1996); California, CAL. WELF. & INST. CODE §§ 6600–09.3 (West 1998 & Supp. 2004); Florida, FLA. STAT. ANN. §§ 394.910–.931 (West 2002 & Supp. 2004) (effective Jan. 1, 1999); Illinois, 725 ILL. COMP. STAT. 207/1–99 (2002 & Supp. 2004) (effective Jan. 1, 1998); Iowa, IOWA CODE ANN. §§ 229A.1–.16 (West Supp. 2004) (effective May 6, 1998); Kansas, KAN. STAT. ANN. §59-29a02 (West 2005); Massachusetts, MASS. GEN. L. ANN. CH. 123A (West Supp. 1998); Minnesota, MINN. STAT. ANN § 253B.02 (West 2002); Missouri, MO. STAT. ANN. §632.480 (LWest Supp. 1999); New Jersey, N.J. STAT. ANN. § 30:4-27.24 (West Supp.1999); Oregon, OR. REV. STAT. § 426.005 (1998); South Carolina, S.C. CODE ANN. §§ 44-48-10 (West Supp. 1998); Texas, TEX. STAT. ANN. §841.002 (West 2005);

a crime of sexual violence, and has a mental or personality disorder that makes future acts of sexual violence likely.[40] Although definitions of sexual predator may vary by statute, they all require findings that future acts of sexual violence are likely.[41] Clinical predictions alone, or in combination with actuarial risk assessment instruments, have been widely accepted as being adequately reliable for the severe deprivations of liberty authorized by the violent sexual predator statutes.[42]

Community notification statutes, the first of which was Megan's Law, are also based on predicting the dangerousness of sex offenders.[43] Selective community notification is now commonplace for released sex offenders. In New Jersey, and most other states, offenders are scaled on a risk assessment instrument and entitled to a hearing on their dangerousness.[44] If the offenders are deemed to be a danger to the community, they must register, leading to dire consequences for their ability to obtain housing, employment, and other resources.

Virginia; Washington, WASH. REV. CODE WASH. ANN. § 71.09 (West 2005); Wisconsin, WISC. STAT. ANN. §980.01 (West 1998).

40. *See, e.g.*, KAN. STAT. ANN. § 59-29a01 (West 2004). Some states, like Minnesota require that the victim be a stranger, which virtually guarantees that the most prevalent, and arguably the most devastating, form of sexual offense—that which occurs within the family—remains unaddressed. *See, e.g.*, Eric S. Janus, *Minnesota's Sex Offender Commitment Program: Would an Empirically-Based Prevention Policy be More Effective?*, 29 WM. MITCHELL L. REV. 1083, 1087 (2003) (arguing that Minnesota's sex offender policy is misconceived because "the overwhelming majority of sexual crimes . . . [are] committed by acquaintances and intimates of the victims").

41. *See* John M. Fabian, Kansas v. Hendricks, Crane *and Beyond: "Mental Abnormality," and "Sexual Dangerousness": Volitional vs. Emotional Abnormality and the Debate Between Community Safety and Civil Liberties*, 29 WM. MITCHELL L. REV. 1367, 1369 (2003) (noting that the term "predator" is "usually applied to offenders who offend against strangers, have multiple victims, have prior sexual offenses, are sexually deviant and suffer from paraphilias such as pedophilia, commit violent offenses, and may have exhibited other antisocial and criminal behaviors").

42. *See, e.g., In re* Commitment of R.S., 773 A.2d 72 (N.J. Super. Ct. App. Div. 2001) (upholding use of actuarial instruments to assess future dangerousness); Johnson v. Missouri, 2001 WL 527494 (Mo. Ct. App. May 18, 2001) (finding that expert testimony was necessary to determine that a defendant incarcerated since his teens had a mental abnormality that made him likely to commit sexual violence); *In re* Blodgett, 510 N.W.2d. 910, 917 n.15 (Minn. 1994) (giving broad deference to expert predictions of future dangerousness); State v. Post, 541 N.W.2d 115, 132 (Wis. 1995) (rejecting challenge based on impossibility of prediction).

43. The New Jersey legislature in 1994 adopted a series of measures under the name Megan's Law, including extending prison terms, involuntary civil commitment, lifetime parole supervision, and mandatory DNA sampling for identification. N.J. STAT. ANN. 2C §§ 7-1 to 7-11 (West 1994). The registration provisions require sex offender registration with law enforcement and community notification. *Id.*

44. *In re* Registrant G.B., 685 A.2d 1252, 1260–61 (N.J. 1996).

While future dangerousness is often explicitly a factor in determining the sentence for violent murders and sex offenses, some courts are predicting future criminality even for nonviolent offenders. In Virginia, for example, two kinds of risk assessment instruments are being used for sentencing determinations.[45] In addition to the violent offender instrument, the nonviolent offender risk assessment instrument was developed in response to overcrowding of Virginia's prisons and is used to determine who should receive a jail sentence and who could be placed on probation.[46]

A. Gatekeeping Dilemmas

In a trio of evidentiary cases,[47] the Supreme Court demanded that judges examine the empirical foundations of expert assertions made in their courts to ensure that the data on which they rest is sound. This trio commands that judges admit into evidence only expert testimony that passes scientific muster. At a very minimum, these cases explain that expert testimony should be admissible only if it can meet the standards and methods of science.[48] No such trustworthiness inquiry, however, is made in one critical area: expert testimony about the defendant's future dangerousness.[49]

---

45. *See* Kern & Farrar-Owens, *supra* note 36, at *8 (discussing Virginia's risk assessment instruments and remarking that they believe that "Virginia is the only structured sentencing guidelines system in the nation that has formally integrated offender risk assessment tools grounded in criminological research").

46. *See* Emily Bazelon, *Sentencing by the Numbers*, N.Y. TIMES MAGAZINE, Jan. 2, 2005, at 18–19 (discussing the Virginia sentencing program). These tables are based on factors such as adult and juvenile criminal records, gender, age, employment, and marital status. *Id.* Judges use a 71-point scale of risk assessment employing these factors to aid in sentencing. *Id.* A score of 35 or less means the defendant is eligible for house arrest or probation. *Id.* If a defendant receives a score of 35 or more, the recommendation is jail time. *Id.* The Virginia sentencing commission's chair claims that in testing the scale on prisoners who had been released five years previously, the table was accurate in three out of four cases. *Id.*

47. *See* Daubert v. Merrell Dow Pharmaceuticals, Inc., 509 U.S. 579 (1993); Gen. Elec. Co. v. Joiner, 522 U.S. 136, 140 (1997) (reiterating the trial judge's mandate to review testimony for scientific validity and "fit"); Kumho Tire Co., Ltd. v. Carmichael, 526 U.S. 137 (1999) (extending the scope of the *Daubert* inquiry to technical as well as scientific evidence).

48. Notably, one-third of the prisoners exonerated by the Actual Innocence Project had been convicted on the basis of "tainted or fraudulent science." JIM DWYER ET AL., ACTUAL INNOCENCE: FIVE DAYS TO EXECUTION AND OTHER DISPATCHES FROM THE WRONGLY CONVICTED 246 (2000).

49. *Cf.* Morse, *supra* note 30, at 59 (explaining that "[t]he incentive structure predisposes the gatekeepers in cases involving danger to over-predict").

In capital sentencing, this is a result due, in large part, to the Supreme Court's decision in *Barefoot v. Estelle*, finding such expert testimony constitutional.[50] In sexual offender commitment proceedings, the Supreme Court's decision in *Kansas v. Hendricks* similarly constitutionalized indefinite sexual offender commitments based on future dangerousness testimony.[51] Although civil commitment has been a staple of handling the mentally ill who pose a danger to self or others in society, this decision vastly expanded criteria for civil commitments. No longer were strict mental illness criteria, together with a showing of current facts demonstrating danger to self or others, required. Rather, confinement could be based on remote past behavior if it was coupled with some "mental abnormality" or "personality disorder" deemed to make recidivism likely.[52] Although "death is different," and postsentence civil commitment is draconian, juries are permitted to hear—and judges to rely on—expert testimony that even the most optimistic could characterize only as not "always wrong."[53] Neither due process concerns for the truth-generating capacity of the methodologies of the justice system,[54] nor the precept that, in order to reach a justifiable decision,

---

50. 463 U.S. 880 (1983) (permitting experts to testify about future dangerousness as a constitutional matter, despite challenges to the validity of such testimony, absent a showing that predictions were always wrong). Notably, none of the opinions in the *Daubert* trilogy referred to *Barefoot*. *Kumho*, however, did castigate astrology as unscientific. 526 U.S. at 151.

51. 521 U.S. 346 (1997).

52. *Id.* at 357. Although the ostensible reason for these sexual offender civil commitments was treatment, the preamble to the Kansas statute noted that sex offenders were usually treatable. *See* 1994 KAN. SESS. LAWS, ch. 140 (asserting in its preamble that "sexually violent predators generally have antisocial personality features which are unamenable to existing mental illness treatment modalities").

53. *Barefoot*, 463 U.S. at 901 (refusing to exclude future dangerousness testimony because the defense could not show that "psychiatrists are always wrong with respect to future dangerousness, only most of the time.").

54. In other words, "a process reasonably designed to ascertain the truth." JOHN RAWLS, A THEORY OF JUSTICE 239 (1971). *See also* WILLIAM L. TWINING, RETHINKING EVIDENCE 107 (1990) (discussing the rationalist tradition in evidence scholarship and its main epistemological assumption that the purpose of adjudication is to discover an objectively knowable truth, while at the same time acknowledging that "the notion of 'fact' in adjudication is more problematic than the orthodox view suggests . . ." and thus that it is "misleading to suggest that legal enquiries into questions of fact are value-free"). Even law and economics adheres to the notion of legal process as a search for truth. *See, e.g.*, Richard A. Posner, *An Economic Approach to Legal Procedure and Judicial Administration*, 2 J. LEGAL STUD. 399, 401 (1978) (remarking that judicial error is "a source of social costs and the reduction of error is a goal of the procedural system"). That is why, Posner explains, a procedural rule such as the constitutional exclusionary rule "is exceptional, and is recognized—and often bitterly criticized—as such." *Id.*

reasoning must be based on trustworthy information,[55] appears to have penetrated the thicket of judicial future dangerousness jurisprudence.[56] And in *Kansas v. Crane*,[57] the Court revisited the Kansas statute, once more failing to address the problematic nature of expert future dangerousness testimony.[58] None of these cases has required the trustworthiness demonstration that rule of law principles, the *Daubert* trio, and the Federal Rules of Evidence appear to require of expert testimony. Death, incarceration, and preventive detention based on predictions that the courts acknowledge as scientifically flimsy seem somewhat cynical to say the least.

B. Gatekeeping under *Daubert*

Explicitly addressing the Federal Rules of Evidence, *Daubert* requires judges to examine the empirical basis of statements made by experts in federal courts.[59] *Daubert* held that scientific validity and "fit" of expert testimony to the facts in the case are questions of reliability and relevance.[60] Four "general observations" guide the inquiry into scientific validity: (1) testability; (2) peer review and publication; (3) the existence of methodological standards, including the error rate of

---

55. Twining, *supra* note 54, at 107. The belief that decisions based on correct information come closer to the truth is the basis of normative epistemology, including "norms governing how individuals should acquire and weigh evidence as well as, ultimately, form beliefs." Ronald J. Allen & Brian Leiter, *Naturalized Epistemology and the Law of Evidence*, 87 VA. L. REV. 1491, 1498 (2001) (contending that the rules of evidence "structure the epistemic process by which jurors arrive at beliefs about disputed matters of fact at trials").

56. Beecher-Monas, *supra* note 5.

57. 534 U.S. 407 (2002).

58. *Id.* at 411–12. In *Kansas v. Hendricks*, the Court had relied on Hendricks' testimony that the only way he could control his impulses to molest children was "to die." 521 U.S. 346, 355 (1997). Thus, Crane contended that the state had to show an absence of control. The Supreme Court disagreed, holding only a showing of "serious difficulty in controlling dangerous behavior," rather than a complete absence of control, was necessary to meet constitutional standards. *Crane*, 534 U.S. at 408.

59. *See* Paul C. Gianelli, Daubert: *Interpreting the Federal Rules of Evidence*, 15 CARDOZO L. REV. 1999 (1994) (observing that "*Daubert* required a higher standard for money damages than *Barefoot* required for the death penalty."). Although the argument has been made that *Daubert* is not technically inconsistent with *Barefoot* because *Daubert* involved interpretation of the Federal Rules of Evidence, while *Barefoot* involved interpretation of the Due Process clause of the Constitution, nearly everyone acknowledges the tension between the two decisions. *See, e.g.*, Craig J. Albert, *Challenging Deterrence: New Insights on Capital Punishment Derived from Panel Data*, 60 U. PITT. L. REV. 321 (1999) (asserting that "it goes too far to say simply that *Daubert* impliedly overruled *Barefoot*," but acknowledging that "they cannot co-exist as a matter of common sense").

60. *Daubert*, 509 U.S. at 590–91.

the methodology; and (4) general acceptance.[61] The overall goal of these flexible guidelines is to evaluate expert testimony by the standards scientists themselves use to critique each other's work.[62] In two subsequent cases, *General Electric Co. v. Joiner*[63] and *Kumho Tire Co. Ltd. v. Carmichael*,[64] the Court reiterated the *Daubert* standards, expounded on its notion of "fit," and explained that not only do judges have to evaluate the scientific validity of testimony based on the traditional "hard" sciences but that they must also evaluate the validity of expert testimony based on what are often referred to as the "soft" sciences, such as psychology.[65] Congress subsequently amended the Federal Rules of Evidence to codify these cases.[66]

These changes have profoundly affected not only the federal courts, but state courts as well.[67] Even jurisdictions that eschew the *Daubert* standard in favor of the general acceptance standard of *Frye*, are beginning to insist that expert testimony meet standards of scientific validity.[68] Thus, even in courts in which the *Daubert* standard is not followed, there is an increased awareness that whatever evidence is considered should be based on a sound empirical foundation. Such awareness supports the argument that *Daubert*'s general principles of judicial screening for scientific validity should apply to all expert testimony.[69]

Future dangerousness testimony based on clinical judgment alone has been overwhelmingly castigated by the profession (and so fails peer review, publication, and the general acceptance prongs of *Daubert*).[70] Clinical predictions of future dangerousness are not based on scientific study, nor do they even purport to be based on the scientific method. Because such predictions are frequently wrong, they cannot meet the error rate inquiry.[71] Even actuarial predictions, though somewhat more accurate than clinical predictions, still are tenuous.[72]

---

61. *Id.* at 593–94.

62. *See Daubert*, 509 U.S. at 580, 593 (characterizing the inquiry as a "flexible one").

63. 522 U.S. 136 (1997).

64. 526 U.S. 137 (1999).

65. *See id.* at 137 (addressing issue of expert's engineering testimony).

66. FED. R. EVID. 702.

67. For an article describing some of these changes, *see generally* Clark Hedger, Note, *Daubert and the States: A Critical Analysis of Emerging Trends*, 49 ST. LOUIS U. L.J. 177 (2004) (describing state court reactions to *Daubert* and FED. R. EVID. 702 [2000 amendments]).

68. *See, e.g.*, Blum v. Merrell Dow Pharms., Inc., 705 A.2d 1314, 1323 (Pa. Super. Ct. 1997)(reviewing expert testimony under *Frye* standard and addressing scientific validity).

69. Beecher-Monas & Garcia-Rill, *supra* note 5.

70. *Id.*

71. Although they made bald assertions that they were invariably accurate, the experts in *Barefoot* offered no substantiation for their claims. Barefoot v. Estelle 463 U.S. 880, 896–97 (1983).

72. Beecher-Monas & Garcia-Rill, *supra* note 5, at 1845 n.3.

Nonetheless, even though they cannot meet criteria for valid science, expert predictions are widely used as a basis for deprivations of life and liberty.[73] The admission of such testimony appears to be a result of the extraordinary public pressure on courts and legislatures to control crime.

C. Barefoot v. Estelle

At issue in *Barefoot* was the constitutionality of permitting psychiatrists to testify about the defendant's future behavior, given that such predictions were shown to be wrong two out of three times.[74] At the sentencing proceeding in *Barefoot*, two psychiatrists testified that the defendant "would probably commit further acts of violence and represent a continuing threat to society,"[75] based on a hypothetical question about the crime and the defendant's conduct.[76] The Court acknowledged the American Psychiatric Association's opposition to future dangerousness testimony because of its extreme unreliability[77] but upheld its admissibility because it felt that disallowing such testimony would be like "disinvent[ing] the wheel."[78] Reliability, then as now, was the touchstone for admissibility

---

73. *See* Scherr, *supra* note 3, at 2 (acknowledging that although "we should expect the rules of evidence . . . to require the exclusion of predictive expertise . . . no appellate court has ever ordered exclusion"). Professor Scherr contends that this is because it is expedient for the courts to rely on expert opinions and that they therefore meet the "fit" requirements of *Daubert*. *Id.* at 2–3. While courts overwhelmingly admit expert future dangerousness testimony (and probably do so because they find it expedient), they rarely articulate any principled basis for doing so. We disagree with Professor Scherr that unscientific predictions can meet *Daubert* requirements, either for reliability or fit. Rather, we argue that the courts should not circumvent their gatekeeping duties in this way.

74. *See* 463 U.S. 880, at 899–902 (1983). Before the Court was an amicus brief by the American Psychiatric Association explaining that no one, including psychiatrists, can predict with any degree of reliability that an individual will commit other crimes in the future. *Id.* at 899. Some scholars argue that clinical predictions have improved since *Barefoot*, but even these scholars only contend a slightly better-than-chance record for clinical predictions. *See* Monahan, *supra* note 6.

75. *Barefoot*, 463 U.S. at 884.

76. The prosecutor's hypothetical asked the psychiatrists to assume a number of facts about the defendant; his conviction for five nonviolent criminal offenses; arrests for sexual offenses against children; a bad reputation in the eight communities the defendant had lived in over ten years; unemployment during the two months preceding the crime; drug use; boasting of plans to commit crimes to acquaintances; shooting a police officer without provocation from a distance of six inches; and acting as though there were nothing unusual after the crime. Brief for the American Psychiatric Association as Amicus Curiae Supporting Petitioner at 5, Barefoot v. Estelle, 463 U.S. 880 (1983) (No. 82-6080).

77. *Barefoot*, 463 U.S. at 904.

78. *Id.* at 896.

of evidence at sentencing.[79] Nonetheless, the Court found that because the Association did not claim that psychiatrists were *always* wrong with respect to future dangerousness predictions—only that they were wrong more often than not—it would not exclude such testimony.

The Supreme Court decided that the state could sentence the defendant to death based on scientifically questionable testimony because the state's evidentiary rules permitted such testimony.[80] The Supreme Court distinguished its decision in *Barefoot* from scientific evidence cases in which testimony about future dangerousness had been disallowed by explaining that *Barefoot* sought a constitutional rule barring an entire category of expert testimony.[81] The Court was "not persuaded that such testimony is almost entirely unreliable" and so found that the adversary system would be competent to take account of its shortcomings.[82]

Although the Court found "no constitutional barrier to applying the ordinary rules of evidence governing the use of expert testimony,"[83] as noted previously, the ordinary rules of evidence have changed, and these changes have illuminated the extreme unreliability and irrelevance of expert testimony that has no empirical foundation masquerading as science. We argued that *Barefoot* was wrongly decided, both as a matter of evidentiary due process and because it was empirically wrong about the ability of the adversary system to sort out the reliable from the unreliable expert testimony.[84] It has further been argued that *Barefoot* is egregiously wrong-headed by current standards for reliability[85] and that *Barefoot*'s effect on capital sentencing proceedings has been pernicious and pervasive,

---

79. *See* Flores v. Johnson, 210 F.3d 456, 464 n.10 (5th Cir. 2000) (Garza, J., concurring) (noting that "the cardinal concern of the rules of admissibility for expert testimony— reliability—is also the paramount concern in addressing the constitutionality of capital sentencing procedures").

80. *Barefoot*, 463 U.S. at 898 (noting that "the rules of evidence generally extant at the federal and state levels anticipate that relevant, unprivileged evidence should be admitted and its weight left to the fact finder, who would have the benefit of cross-examination and contrary evidence by the opposing party"). Post-*Daubert*, the rules of evidence require judges to act as gatekeepers to ensure that only scientifically valid expert testimony be admitted.

81. *Id.* at 899.

82. *Id.*

83. *Id.* at 904.

84. *See* Beecher-Monas & Garcia-Rill, *supra* note 5; Daniel A. Krauss & Bruce D. Sales, *The Effects of Clinical and Scientific Expert Testimony on Juror Decision Making in Capital Sentencing*, 7 PSYCHOL. PUB. POL'Y & L. 267, 273–77 (2001) (discussing research that suggests jurors are incapable of differentiating more scientifically valid expert testimony from less accurate testimony).

85. No one persuasively argues that the testimony at issue in *Barefoot* could meet *Daubert* standards. *See, e.g.,* 1 DAVID L. FAIGMAN ET AL., MODERN SCIENTIFIC EVIDENCE: THE LAW AND SCIENCE OF EXPERT TESTIMONY 298–99 (1997).

undermining fundamental fairness in a way wholly contrary to the rule of law. Perhaps it is true, as Justices Blackmun and Powell contended, that the death penalty cannot be administered in a way that meets constitutional requirements.[86] If so, it appears that sexual offender statutes are similarly impervious to rule-of-law precepts.

D. Hendricks and Crane

In *Kansas v. Hendricks*,[87] the Supreme Court examined the constitutionality of the Kansas Sexually Violent Predator Act (Kansas Act),[88] which provided for the indefinite civil commitment of people who were likely to engage in future "predatory acts of sexual violence" due to a "mental abnormality or personality disorder."[89] Because it requires a finding of likely future violence, the statute appears to provide for an expert future dangerousness prediction. In *Hendricks*, both the state's expert and the defendant's expert testified about future dangerousness.

The defendant, Leroy Hendricks, had been "convicted of taking 'indecent liberties' with two thirteen-year old boys."[90] He served a ten-year sentence for his crime. Shortly before he was due to be released to a halfway house, the state sought civil commitment under the Kansas Act.[91] During his commitment jury trial, Hendricks testified that he had five prior convictions for sexually molesting children and had been treated at and discharged from a state psychiatric institution, after which he had continued to abuse children, including his own stepchildren.[92] He testified that when he was under stress he could not "control the urge," and that the only way he could keep from sexually molesting children in the future was "to die."[93]

---

86. *See* Callins v. Collins, 510 U.S. 1141, 1145–46 (1994) (Blackmun, J., dissenting) (observing that "the inevitability of factual, legal, and moral error gives us a system that we know must wrongly kill some defendants, a system that fails to deliver the fair, consistent, and reliable sentences of death required by the Constitution."); Jeffrey L. Kirchmeier, *Aggravating and Mitigating Factors: The Paradox of Today's Arbitrary and Mandatory Capital Punishment Scheme*, 6 WM. & MARY BILL RTS. J. 345, 347 (1998) (noting that "Justice Powell came to a similar conclusion after his retirement"). Notably, two states, Illinois and Maryland, have reached similar conclusions and have placed a moratorium on death penalty prosecutions because of due process concerns. *See* Dirk Johnson, *Illinois, Citing Verdict Errors, Bars Executions*, N.Y. TIMES, Feb. 1, 2000, at A1.

87. 521 U.S. 346 (1997).

88. KAN. STAT. ANN. § 59-29a01 et seq. (1994).

89. *Id.* at §§ 59-29a01, -29a01, -29a07.

90 *Hendricks*, 521 U.S. at 353.

91. *Id.* at 354.

92. *Id.*

93. *Id.* at 355.

The state's experts were a clinical social worker and a psychologist, both of whom opined that Hendricks was a pedophile.[94] The psychologist testified that, unless confined, Hendricks was likely to commit sexual offenses in the future.[95] Hendricks' expert, a psychiatrist, testified that "it was not possible to predict with any degree of accuracy the future dangerousness of a sex offender."[96] The jury nonetheless was persuaded beyond a reasonable doubt by the state's evidence that Hendricks was likely to commit a future crime, the judge determined that pedophilia qualifies as a mental abnormality under the statute, and Hendricks was committed.

The issues on appeal included due process, double jeopardy, and ex post facto clause claims. The Kansas Supreme Court accepted Hendricks's due process claim, holding that substantive due process requires a showing, by clear and convincing evidence, that the person to be committed is both mentally ill and poses a danger to self or others.[97] The Supreme Court disagreed, holding that the Kansas Act's definition of mental abnormality satisfied due process requirements.

Although the Court acknowledged that involuntary commitment statutes must adhere to "proper procedures and evidentiary standards," it did not discuss those evidentiary standards. The Court made no mention of *Barefoot*, *Daubert*, the need for reliability, or any scientific basis for the expert testimony on dangerousness. The Court did cite to a 1984 case for the proposition that "there is nothing inherently unattainable about a prediction of future criminal conduct."[98] It did not, however, elaborate. Although it acknowledged the need for a showing of "more than a mere predisposition to violence," the Court determined that the Kansas Act's twin requirements of evidence of past sexual offenses and present mental abnormality making recidivism likely were sufficient.[99] Nowhere did the court grapple with the scientific basis for a prediction of future dangerousness.

In *Kansas v. Crane*,[100] the Supreme Court revisited the Kansas Act to determine the application of *Hendricks* to the indefinite civil commitment of a convicted flasher.[101] Michael Crane was convicted and served time for lewd and

---

94. *Id.* at 355 n.2.

95. *Id.*

96. *Kansas v. Hendricks*, 521 U.S. 346, 355 n.2 (1997).

97. *Id.* at 356.

98. *Id.* at 358 (citing Schall v. Martin, 467 U.S. 253, 278 (1984)).

99. *Id.* The Court acknowledged that dangerousness alone was not enough for indefinite involuntary commitment but held that a showing that the offender continues to have inadequate control over his behavior due to a present mental abnormality would suffice. *Id.* at 358, 364.

100. 534 U.S. 407 (2002).

101. Crane was convicted of lewd and lascivious behavior for exposing himself to a tanning salon attendant. *In re* Crane, 7 P.3d 285, 286 (Kan. 2000). The prior conduct required for commitment under the Kansas Act consisted of an aggravated sexual battery

lascivious behavior, after which the state sought civil commitment under the Kansas Act. Crane argued that the state had not proved that he completely lacked control over his behavior and that *Hendricks* required such a showing.

The Supreme Court held that the state need not prove a complete lack of control under the Kansas Act.[102] Nonetheless, the Supreme Court held that the Constitution does require some "proof of serious difficulty in controlling behavior."[103] On this basis, the Court vacated and remanded for such a determination. Once more, however, the Court avoided any discussion of the reliability of predictions of dangerousness or what such predictions could mean in the context of an exhibitionist.

DATA ON VIOLENCE AND SEXUAL VIOLENCE

This public pressure for strengthened crime control measures is fueled by stories of sexual murders, especially those of children, as well as of gang homicides and rape, which occupy the national and international media and feed the fears of an increasingly violent society.[104] Certainly, the U.S. prison population is growing at an alarming rate.[105] Violence in America is world famous, is perceived

---

conviction that was overturned on appeal. *Id.* The event giving rise to the sexual battery charges actually occurred 30 minutes after Crane left the tanning salon. *Id.* He entered a video store, grabbed a clerk, exposed himself, and threatened to rape her before suddenly stopping and running out of the store. *Id.* Crane pled guilty to aggravated sexual battery, which met the requirement for prior sexual offense history. *Id.*

102. *Crane*, 534 U.S. at 411.

103. *Id.* at 413.

104. There is some question about whether this perception that violence is increasing in society is accurate. Some commentators have asserted that violence is actually decreasing over time as society industrializes and remark that violence in tribal societies is still prevalent. Martin Daly & Margo Wilson, Homicide 291 (Sarah Blaffer Hrdy & Richard W. Wrangham eds., Aldine De Gruyter 1988) (1944). For example, homicide is estimated to have accounted for 35 percent of the adult male mortality and 29 percent of the adult female mortality among tribal peoples in New Guinea and the Amazon. *Id.* Daly and Wilson further note that "[e]ven the gentle Kung San foragers of the Kalahari desert had a homicide rate approximately equivalent to that of the most violent urban American ghettos." *Id.* Moreover, most crimes labeled "violent" are really batteries involving no physical injuries; when physical injuries are present, they usually do not require medical treatment, and even if they do, they do not require hospitalization. Bureau of Just. Stat., Criminal Victimization in the United States 18–19, 22–23, 75–76, 95 (2000), *available at* http://www.ojp.usdoj.gov/bjs/pub/pdf/cvus00.pdf.

105. *See* Joseph E. Kennedy, *Monstrous Offenders and the Search for Solidarity Through Modern Punishment*, 51 Hastings L. J. 829, 831 (2000) (stating that, "The number of people in prison in the United States has increased by almost 500% since 1972 while the population itself has increased by only 28%"). In 1997 the prison population had grown

to be increasing over time, and is considered a threat to civil society.[106] Violent recidivism is perceived to be a horrifying reality, although the base rate of violent recidivism is actually quite low.[107] In response, there has been an increased emphasis on preventive detention and death, magnifying the role of future dangerousness predictions. Predictions about behavior, however, are empirically problematic.

A. Actuarial Predictions

Concerned about the inaccuracy of clinical predictions, researchers began to study ways to improve the accuracy of future dangerousness predictions.[108] Their goal was to develop an empirically based actuarial instrument that would reflect a state of the art understanding of the factors correlated with violence and their interrelationships.[109] These risk factors were then combined to create a scoring instrument that takes into account the interrelationship of various risk factors and of the population base rates, and then assigns weights to the individual risk factors. The instrument then yields an overall "score" that ranks levels of risk.[110]

---

to 1.2 million from 200,000 in 1972. *Id.* at 831 n.6. When probation and parole are included, 3 percent of the population was under some form of correctional supervision in 1998. *Id.* at 832–33 (citing the high number of Americans under correctional supervision and espousing a Durkheimian view that excessive punishment is the attempt of a fragmenting society to bind itself together).

106. *See* Franklin E. Zimring, *Will Success Spoil James Q. Wilson?*, 85 J. Crim. L. & Criminology 828, 830 (1995) (reviewing Crime (James Q. Wilson & Joan Petersilia eds., (1995)) (noting that "U.S. rates of property crime other than robbery are near the rates of other Western nations, while U.S. lethal violence rates are four to eight times the rates of other highly developed nations").

107. *See* R. Karl Hanson et al., *Sex Offender Recidivism: What We Know and What We Need to Know, in* Sexually Coercive Behavior, *supra* note 6, at 154, 163 (finding that, "Overall, the observed rates [of sexual recidivism] are between 10 percent and 15 percent after 5 years and approximately 20% after 10 years."). The base rate of sexual recidivism rates for rapists was reported at 18.9 percent, and 12.7 percent for child molesters. R. Karl Hanson & Monique T. Bussière, *Predicting Relapse: A Meta-Analysis of Sexual Offender Recidivism Studies*, 66 J. Consulting & Clinical Psychol. 348, 351 (1998).

108. Christopher Webster et al., The Violence Prediction Scheme: Assessing Dangerousness in High Risk Men xi, xii (1994) (describing the genesis and goals of the violence risk assessment guide).

109. *See id.; see also* Vernon L. Quinsey et al., Violent Offenders: Appraising and Managing Risk 190 (1998).

110. *See* Monahan, *supra* note 6, at 905–10 (evaluating risk assessment instruments). The concept of risk encompasses not only the presence of danger but also its probability of occurrence. *See* Eric S. Janus & Robert A. Prentky, *Forensic Use of Actuarial Risk Assessment with Sex Offenders: Accuracy, Admissibility and Accountability*, 40 Am. Crim L. Rev. 1443, 1448–49 (2003) (addressing the concept of risk in predictions).

Currently, it is well accepted that actuarial instruments offer the most accurate way of making future dangerousness predictions.[111] The predominant instrument used in assessing violence (including sexual violence) is the Violence Risk Assessment Guide (VRAG).[112] The predominant instruments for sexual offender risk assessment are the Sexual Offender Risk Assessment Guide (SORAG)[113] and the Rapid Risk Assessment for Sexual Offense Recidivism (RRASOR).[114] Of these, the VRAG is "the best currently available method to predict future violence."[115] Its close cousin, the SORAG, is not quite as predictively accurate.[116]

In each of these instruments, violent behavior (violent sexual behavior in the SORAG and RRASOR) is statistically correlated[117] with specific factors either in

---

111. A number of studies of these instruments have shown that actuarial measures are more accurate predictors than are clinical judgment. *See, e.g.,* Mark D. Cunningham & Thomas J. Reidy, *Don't Confuse Me With the Facts: Common Errors in Violence Risk Assessment at Capital Sentencing,* 26 CRIM. JUST. & BEHAV. 20, 28 (1999) (stating that repeated studies of actuarial methods have demonstrated them to be superior to clinical judgment standing alone); Mairead Dolan & Michael Doyle, *Violence Risk Prediction: Clinical and Actuarial Measures and the Role of the Psychopathy Checklist,* 177 BRIT. J. PSYCHOL. 303, 305–09 (2000) (citing results of studies on clinical risk assessment tools and their predictive validity); Robert A. Prentky, *A 15-Year Retrospective on Sexual Coercion: Advances and Projections, in* SEXUALLY COERCIVE BEHAVIOR, *supra* note 6, at 13, 21 (noting that "the predictive efficacy of actuarial methods of risk assessment are superior to clinically derived assessments of risk"). One reason for this may be that "much of the information commonly assessed in these [clinical] interviews, such as low victim empathy, denial, and lack of motivation for treatment, were unrelated to sexual offense recidivism." Hanson et al., *supra* note 107, at 158.

112. QUINSEY ET AL., *supra* note 109, at 141.

113. *Id.* at 155–59 (proposing SORAG as an enhancement to VRAG).

114. RRASOR is based on four factors: prior sexual offenses, age at release (younger is worse), gender of the victim (male is worse), and relationship to the victim (related is better). Mee & Hall, *supra* note 7, at 102. In their discussion, Mee and Hall included the Minnesota Sex Offender Screening Test–Revised (MnSOST-R) as a sex offender instrument. *Id.* at 107. However, Barbaree's study found that it "failed to meet conventional levels of statistical significance in the prediction of serious and sexual recidivism," and so it has been omitted here. *See* Howard E. Barbaree et al., *Evaluating the Predictive Accuracy of Six Risk Assessment Instruments for Adult Sex Offenders,* 28 CRIM. JUST. & BEHAV. 490, 512 (2001).

115. Mee & Hall, *supra* note 7, at 102.

116. Mee & Hall, *supra* note 7, at 102 n.227 (citing interview with the developer of both the VRAG and the SORAG).

117. As Stephen Gould explains, "[c]orrelation assesses the tendency of one measure to vary in concert with another." GOULD, *supra* note 1, at 269. Correlation, with regard to linear relationships, is measured by using Pearson's product moment correlation coefficient, which ranges from +1 for perfect positive correlation, to 0 for no correlation, to -1 for perfect negative correlation. *Id.* at 270.

the person's past behavior (a pattern of past violence, for example), circumstances (such as poverty), attitudes toward others (failure to marry or form equivalent relationships); medical and psychiatric history (age when problems began and any injuries to the brain); and substance abuse (alcohol or drugs).[118] The sexual violence instruments tend to include phallometric studies.[119] They also include factors such as whether the victim was a stranger and whether the victim was male.[120] These factors are then used in combination to probabilistically assess a level of risk for the future. The variables considered for the instruments were drawn from empirical studies showing a statistical association[121] with violent (or sexually violent) behavior.

---

118. *See* R. Karl Hanson & Monique T. Bussiere, *A Meta-Analysis of Sexual Offender Recidivism Studies*, 66 J. CONSULTING & CLIN. PSYCHOL. 348, 353–56 (1998) (discussing and comparing risk factors). These factors are not "causes" of violence. They are factors that are associated with violence. *See* Stephan F. Lanes, *Error and Uncertainty in Causal Inference, in* CAUSAL INFERENCE 173, 182–85 (Kenneth J. Rothman ed., 1988) (stating that "[t]he uncertainty in causal inference is attributable to the fact that we cannot establish that an association is valid"). An unidentifiable error may exist and it may cause the observation. *Id.* The most that can be expected of strength of association and the level of statistical significance is that they affect subjective beliefs. *See id.* at 186.

119. "Phallometry is a diagnostic method to assess sexual arousal by measuring blood flow (tumescence) to the penis during the presentation of potentially erotic stimuli in the laboratory." CTR FOR SEX OFFENDER MGMT., UNDERSTANDING JUVENILE SEXUAL OFFENDING BEHAVIOR: EMERGING RESEARCH, TREATMENT APPROACHES, AND MANAGEMENT PRACTICES (1999), http://www.csom.org/pubs/juvbrf10.html. The report also notes that this is a controversial practice and explains the pitfalls involved, especially with juvenile offenders. *Id.*

120. *See* Hanson et al., *supra* note 107, at 157 (discussing risk factors as predictors of sexual offense recidivism).

121. "Association" means that there is a statistically significant correlation of a particular factor with violent behavior. Statistical significance is set by convention at a level of significance, or p-value of.05, which corresponds to a confidence level of 95 percent. The object of statistical significance tests is to keep the scientist from asserting a positive effect when the effect may actually be due to chance. *See* David Ozonhoff & Leslie I. Boden, *Truth & Consequences: Health Agency Responses to Environmental Health Problems*, 12 SCI., TECH. & HUM. VALUES 70, 73–74 (1987) (stating that statistical significance testing tries to avoid accepting results as significant when they may have been arrived at only by chance). If the p-value is.01, then the evidence is said to be highly statistically significant. Stephen E. Fienberg et al., *Understanding and Evaluating Statistical Evidence in Litigation*, 36 JURIMETRICS J. 1, 22 (1995). Fienberg further clarifies that "By rejecting a hypothesis only when the test is statistically significant, we have placed an upper bound, 5% on the chance of rejecting a true hypothesis." *Id.* Another way of explaining this is that it describes the probability that the procedure produced the observed effect by chance. *See id.* If the test is not statistically significant, it may either be because the results were due to chance or because the test lacked the power to discern a difference between the null hypothesis and the proposed effect. *See id.* Power increases with the size of the study and with the degree of difference from the null hypothesis (the more extreme the alternatives, the better the power). *See id.*

Even such instruments, however, with their structured reasoning requirements, do not obviate all the problems of human judgment.[122] Although structured analysis offers many advantages in light of the difficulty people have in synthesizing differently weighted likelihoods of varying significance such as risk factors for violent behavior,[123] the actuarial instrument is only as effective as the risk factors used in it and the weight that is given them, making accurate prediction elusive in all but the highest of the risk categories.[124] For example, the risk factor descriptions may be vague, decreasing their reliability,[125] and sometimes the factors are not independent, as with anger and the inability to sustain relationships.[126]

Moreover, all future dangerousness predictions rely heavily on prior criminal record as an important factor, which is both under- and overinclusive. It is underinclusive because it misses the highest percentage of violence, that between intimates. Also, many people with violently aggressive behaviors and a high likelihood of repeating violent behavior, such as chronic spouse abusers and stalkers, do not have criminal records. Using one's criminal record as an important factor is also overinclusive, because it does not allow for the changes that occur with aging, or for other dynamic factors.[127]

---

122. It is important to bear in mind that risk is a social construct. Although it uses probabilistic analysis and quantification, it is not an exact science. *See* The Royal Society, Risk: Analysis, Perception and Management 7 (1992) (explaining that some subjectivity is always a part of risk assessment). Indeed, all science is value laden, and risk assessment is not different in that regard. *See generally* Erica Beecher-Monas, *The Heuristics of Intellectual Due Process: A Primer for Triers of Science,* 75 N.Y.U. L. Rev. 1563 (2000) (acknowledging the subjectivity inherent in all scientific methodologies and proposing a five-step framework to follow for sound analysis of scientific evidence).

123. J. Richard Eiser & Joop van der Pligt, Attitudes and Decisions 100 (1988) (observing that human decision "accuracy declines considerably when the number of features or the number of alternatives increases" and the "reliability with which choice rules are used tends to decrease as the decision-maker's information load increases").

124. *See* Morse, *supra* note 30, at 59 (noting that "[i]t is a truism of behavioral science that statistical, 'cookbook' prediction based on empirically validated risk factors is more accurate than clinical prediction, but despite advances in the database that have improved the cookbook, highly accurate prediction by any method eludes us in all but the most obvious cases").

125. *See* David Carson, *A Risk-Management Approach to Legal Decision-Making about 'Dangerous' People, in* Law and Uncertainty: Risks and Legal Processes 255, 258 (Robert Baldwin ed., 1997) (noting the problem of reliability). For example, even trained clinicians may differ on what exactly is meant by "glibness" (a factor on the PCL-R) or "lack of insight" (a factor on the VRAG and HCR-20).

126. *Id.*

127. For example, three-strikes rules premised on the notion that repeated bad behavior escalates in violence, overlook the natural decrease in aggression after adolescence. *See* David P. Farrington, *Predictors, Causes and Correlates of Male Youth Violence,* 24 Crime & Just.

Although testimony based on actuarial instruments is more accurate than clinical predictions,[128] and thus is preferable to clinical testimony, these predictions are still tenuous bases for making important decisions about sentencing, such as death and indefinite confinement. At best, these actuarial instruments correlate only moderately with violent and violent sexual recidivism.[129] Thus, if they are to meet standards for scientific validity, the expert must carefully

---

421, 425 (1998) ("the highest prevalence of homicide is between the ages seventeen and twenty-two"). Thus, while offending rates drop after the twenties, three-strikes rules are often triggered "just when the natural forces of aging would rein in the offenders." Robinson, *supra* note 32, at 1451. Moreover, with treatment, most adolescent brains can be retrained. The abnormal stress responses in violent offenders can be normalized with medication. NIEHOFF, *supra* note 9, at 265 (advocating the "selective and thoughtful use of medications that normalize stress responses, delay impulsive reactions, block the craving for drugs, or suppress nonlethal paraphilias"). Furthermore, the time period that the risk assessment is to cover, the circumstances under which it will be implemented (confinement or release), and the individual's motivation to refrain from violence (including motivation to comply with treatment), are all dynamic factors that should be taken into consideration in assessing risk, but which currently are not. *See, e.g.,* Eric S. Janus & Robert A. Prentky, *Forensic Use of Actuarial Risk Assessment with Sexual Offenders: Accuracy, Admissibility, and Accountability,* 40 AM. CRIM. L. REV. 1443, 1479 (2003) (acknowledging that the absence of dynamic factors "may seriously undermine the assessment power of ARA [actuarial risk assessment] tools" but contending nonetheless that they are superior to clinical judgment).

128. There is some evidence that a multidisciplinary team may be able to rival the accuracy of actuarial instruments. *See* Julian Fuller & Justin Cowan, *Risk Assessment in a Multidisciplinary Forensic Setting: Clinical Judgement Revisited,* 10 J. FORENSIC PSYCHIATRY. 276, 286 (1999) (acknowledging that a multidisciplinary team may provide increased accuracy, approaching that of actuarial instruments). However, such teams are unlikely to be employed in capital sentencing or sexual predator determinations. *See, e.g.,* Beecher-Monas, *supra* note [Wash, & Lee] at 362 (describing clinical future dangerousness testimony at capital sentencing hearings).

129. *See* Barbaree et al., *supra* note 114, at 492–93 (noting VRAG correlations of .44 with violent recidivism and RRASOR correlations of .27 with sexual recidivism); Janus & Prentky, *supra* note 110, at 1471 (noting the efficacy of VRAG, SORAG, and RRASOR and explaining that the "correlation between the SORAG and violent recidivism was .38"). As Janus and Prentky observed, "all . . . [actuarial] instruments have shortcomings, and these shortcomings detract from the reliability of the instruments." *Id.* Another measure of accuracy is a statistical analysis known as the Relative Operating Characteristic (ROC). Mark Binderman, *Understanding VRAG: The Violence Risk Assessment Guide,* 10(1–2) FORENSIC EXAMINER, 28, 29 (2001). A test that is no better than chance would have an ROC of .50; the VRAG's ROC was .76, which means that "if an offender were drawn randomly from each of the recidivist and nonrecidivist groups, there was a probability of .76 that the recidivist had the higher score on the VRAG." QUINSEY ET AL., *supra* note 109, at 148. This is a statistically significant result, comparable to ROC scores for predictions in meteorology and medical imaging. Binderman, *supra,* at 29.

explain the limits of such testimony.[130] In order to be helpful, the expert needs to educate the jury in a scientifically sound manner, which includes explicitly stating the statistical basis for the opinion.[131] Violence risk assessment is not a yes-or-no dichotomy; instead, actuarial assessments are probabilistic risk estimates that should be acknowledged as uncertain.[132] At most, these instruments offer a partial answer, and courts should demand more.[133]

B. The Biology of Violence and Sexual Violence

What is missing from any of the actuarial instruments is causal theory, recognition of the biology of violence, and explicit discussion of the interrelatedness of genes, organisms, and their environment. Thus, the instruments do little to advance our understanding about violent behavior and do not give us any insight into prevention, other than removal from society. However, there has been an explosion of knowledge about how biological, including genetic, factors, combined with environmental factors, such as stress and substance abuse,[134] can

---

130. *Cf.* John Monahan & Henry J. Steadman, *Violent Storms and Violent People: How Meteorology Can Inform Risk Communication in Mental Health Law*, 51 AM. PSYCHOLOGIST, 931, 935–36 (1996) (explaining that predictions of the risk of future violence should be modeled explicitly on weather predictions, with all their qualifiers and uncertainties).

131. *See* Cunningham & Reidy *supra* note III at 34–35 (advocating that experts limit their testimony to predominantly statistical analyses, in order to avoid going beyond the limits of their scientific expertise).

132. Beecher-Monas & Garcia-Rill, *supra* note 5, at 1868. It is important that juries be informed that even the most accurate of the actuarial instruments made predictions of dangerousness for people who did not, in fact, later commit acts of violence. *Id.* at 1898–99. For example, of people who were placed in the "high risk" category under the VRAG, only 55 percent actually committed violent acts upon release. *Id.* at 1878. That means 45 percent did not. Had the "high risk" prediction been the basis for a death sentence, nearly half the people sentenced to death would not, in fact, go on to commit any more acts of violence.

133. *Cf.* David L. Faigman, *The Law's Scientific Revolution: Reflections and Ruminations on the Law's Use of Experts in Year Seven of the Revolution*, 57 WASH. & LEE L. REV. 661, 667, 678 (opining that "[a] lot of previously admitted evidence, especially evidence offered by prosecutors, appears excludable for want of a research base" and that "[p]sychologists should hesitate before seeking to bring their findings to policymakers, fearful that when tested the research might be thought not-yet-done").

134. Alcohol consumption, which can effectively shut down the activity of small brain cells responsible for cortical function, figures into two out of every three violent crimes. J. Roizen, *Issues of Epidemiology of Alcohol and Violence*, in ALCOHOL AND INTERPERSONAL VIOLENCE: FOSTERING MULTIDISCIPLINARY PERSPECTIVES 20 (Susan E. Martin ed., 1993). We use the cerebral cortex to assess and plan responses, rather than "knee-jerking." If the cortex loses some of its inhibitory power, such as by deactivation of cortical circuits under the influence of alcohol, then some of that regulation will be lost, and "primordial," instinctive behaviors will be released. The frontal lobes of the brain, of which the cerebral cortex is a part, are our most highly evolved brain structures. They are in charge of critical

increase the chances that a particular individual will become violent. Indeed, many of the risk factors measured by actuarial assessments of violence risk may be tied to an underlying biological function. But no testable theoretical basis is advanced for why the risk factors correlate with violence. Thus, a major problem with each of the risk instruments is their failure to correlate the risk factors with the biology of violence and to articulate a hypothesis for the mechanisms of violence.[135] Until there is an understanding of how violence occurs, there will be little ability to control or predict it.

1. The Evolutionary Perspective Current research on the biology of violence suggests that violence is "normal" aggression gone awry.[136] In this view, aggression is thought to be part of the normal repertoire of behaviors that has arisen to balance the need of the individual to look out for himself and still maintain good standing within the group.[137] That it is part of our normal repertoire of responses to certain situations does not mean that violent behavior is desirable.[138] It does mean that, in order to understand and control violence, we need to probe the situations that elicit violent responses and the complex biological mediators of these responses.[139]

From the perspective of evolutionary biology, the situations eliciting aggression and violence commonly involve competition for reproductive resources.[140]

---

judgment and learning. Frank N. Dempster, *The Rise and Fall of the Inhibitory Mechanism: Toward a Unified Theory of Cognitive Development and Aging*, 12 DEV. REV. 45, 48–51 (1992).

135. *See* Harris et al., *supra* note 11, at 197 (attempting to correlate the Psychotherapy Checklist–Revised (PCL-R) with neuroscience and conceding that much research still needs to be done).

136. Richard J. Davidson et al., *Dysfunction in the Neural Circuitry of Emotion Regulation: A Possible Prelude to Violence*, 289 SCI. 591, 591 (2000).

137. NIEHOFF, *supra* note 9, at 76.

138. Daly & Wilson, *supra* note 104, at 57 (noting that although violence may be abhorrent, it cannot be pathological, because pathology connotes a breakdown in biological systems and "people and other animals possess complex psychophysiological machinery that is clearly designed *for* the production and regulation of violence").

139. *See id.* at 60–61 (giving the example of bird mate-guarding for paternity assurance as a testable hypothesis arising from "explanations of why particular proximal objectives and motivators have evolved to play their particular roles in the causal control of behavior, and why they are calibrated as they are"). The mate-guarding behavior of birds, for example, varies in relation to observable clues about female fertility, as well as the proximity, abundance, and attractiveness of male rivals. *Id.*

140. *See id.* at 294–95 (young men with dismal prospects are the most likely to be victims and perpetrators of homicide, competing for control over the reproductive capacities of women); JARED DIAMOND, COLLAPSE: HOW SOCIETIES CHOOSE TO FAIL OR SUCCEED 319–28 (2005) (arguing that societal collapse, including the Rwandan genocide, is frequently the result of a confluence of factors resulting in Malthusian population pressures exploding into violence when large numbers of young men cannot command

In humans, demographically speaking, most violence is perpetrated by young males against other unrelated young males, under circumstances in which risk-taking improves their chances of reproductive success.[141] Even spousal murders and infanticide can be viewed as aggressive responses to threats to reproductive success.[142] Most spousal homicides result from male attempts to exert control over women's reproductive capacities and women's efforts at independence from coercion.[143] Whether rape is a reproductive strategy is more contentious, with some scholars claiming it as a "natural" genetically based reproductive strategy[144] and others claiming that rape is not a reproductive but an aggressive and dominance strategy, a weapon, not an appetite.[145] No one has yet advanced an evolutionary strategy as the basis for pedophilia.

---

the assets to attract women and begin their own families). For example, in mice bred for aggression, the aggression trait did not begin to manifest until the animals reached sexual maturity, and it began to wane with age and repeated interactions with less aggressive mice. *See* Robert B. Cairns, *Aggression from a Developmental Perspective: Genes, Environments and Interactions, in* GENETICS OF CRIMINAL AND ANTISOCIAL BEHAVIOUR 45, 47–48 (Gregory R. Bock & Jamie A. Goode eds., 1996). Aggressive behavior, including violent behavior, may be a flexible response to social conditions that reflect dynamic interactions realigning the nervous system with the outside social world. *Id.* at 48.

141. *See* WILSON & DALY, *supra* note 104, at 294 (noting that the predominant form of homicide is between "unrelated men, especially young men whose dismal prospects make dangerous escalation of social competition attractive").

142. For example, in gorillas, a victorious challenging male will kill all the suckling offspring in the vanquished male's harem, thus causing the female to stop lactating and go into estrus. *See* MATT RIDLEY, THE AGILE GENE: HOW NATURE TURNS ON NURTURE 19–20 (2004) (noting that "[i]nfanticide is common among gorillas, as it is among many primates").

143. *See* Margo Wilson et al., *Lethal and Nonlethal Violence Against Wives*, 17 CAN. J. CRIMINOLOGY 331, 343–44 (1995) (observing escalation of violence toward wives as a correlate of other controlling behaviors); WILSON & DALY, *supra* note 104, at 295 (remarking that "male sexual proprietariness is the principal source of conflict in the great majority of spousal homicides").

144. RANDY THORNHILL & CRAIG T. PALMER, A NATURAL HISTORY OF RAPE: BIOLOGICAL BASES OF SEXUAL COERCION 59 (2000) (claiming that rape may be an adaptation favored by natural selection because it increases male reproductive success by increasing a male's mating partners). *But see* Elizabeth A. Lloyd, *Violence Against Science, in* EVOLUTION, GENDER AND RAPE 235, 235–57 (Cheryl B. Travis ed., 2003) (discrediting Thornhill and Palmer's "reduced view of rape as sex" and identifying weaknesses in their evolutionary theory of why men rape.

145. *See* NIEHOFF, *supra* note 9, at 164 (claiming that rape is motivated by aggression and noting that testosterone blocking drugs chill sexual behavior but not antisocial aggression); Grant T. Harris et al., *Appraisal and Management of Risk in Sexual Aggressors: Implications for Criminal Justice Policy*, 4 PSYCHOL. PUB. POL'Y & L. 73, 85 (1998) (observing that "although rapists are more dangerous [than child molesters] (i.e., more likely to

2. Behavioral Traits Of course, individuals vary in their responses to given situations, and this must be due at least in part to genetic variations among individuals.[146] Differences in personality account for a large percentage of behavioral differences.[147] But while behavioral diversity within populations undoubtedly has some genetic aspects, behavioral differences also may be due in part to differences in the environment in which each individual matured and resides. All behavior is a complex intermingling of nature and nurture.[148]

a. Stress Responses. Stress responses also demonstrate this complex interaction. Although most violence is perpetrated by young men against other young men, violent tendencies can develop prenatally,[149] in early infancy,[150] or can emerge after the onset of puberty.[151] Environmental factors often play a role.[152] Disruption of the early environment can cause increased nervous system sensitivity to stress in animals.[153] Variations in maternal care also influence the development of hormonal stress response.[154] All mammals, including humans,

---

exhibit violent recidivism) overall, much of that violence does not appear to be sexually motivated").

146. *See* V. Elving Anderson, *Genes, Behavior, and Responsibility: Research Perspectives, in* THE GENETIC FRONTIER: ETHICS, LAW AND POLICY 105, 105–06 (Mark S. Frankel & Albert H. Teich eds., 1994) (explaining that although few behaviors are completely without genetic and environmental influences, "genes do not *determine* one's destiny in a predictable manner," and the effects are not unidirectional: genes can influence behavior, but behavior can also affect genetic expression).

147. *Cf.* Tooby & Cosmides, *supra* note 13, at 18 (noting the challenge individual variation poses to theories of evolutionary psychology).

148. *See* Niehoff, *supra* note 9 at 51–53 (discussing the complex interrelationship of biology and the environment).

149. *See, e.g.,* Constance Holden, *The Violence of the Lambs,* 289 SCI. 580 (2000) (noting that "[r]esearchers are increasingly coming to view violence as the end result of multiple risk factors that may include a biological vulnerability—either genetic or created in the prenatal environment—that can be brought out or reinforced in the social environment.").

150. Frans B. M. De Waal, *Primates: A Natural Heritage of Conflict Resolution,* 289 SCI. 586, 588 (2000) (discussing the violence between two infant monkeys after displaying aggression and biting each other).

151. E.g., NIEHOFF, *supra* note 9, at 159.

152. *See, e.g.,* Darlene Francis et al., *Nongenomic Transmission Across Generations of Maternal Behavior and Stress Responses in the Rat,* 286 SCI. 1158 (1999) (finding that "individual differences in the expression of genes in brain regions that regulate stress reactivity can be transmitted from one generation to the next through behavior . . . [through] differences in maternal care during the first week of life").

153. Niehoff at 274.

154. Francis, *supra* note 152, at 1155.

socialize their young. It may be that "neuropsychological impairments disrupt normal development and increase vulnerability" to poor social environments.[155]

Curiously, although crowding has often been considered a factor in aggressive behavior, this does not appear to be the case in primates.[156] Even in rodents, social isolation can produce aggression that intensifies as the isolation time increases, particularly when such isolation takes place at puberty.[157] Physiological responses to environmental stimuli can also predispose individuals to engage in violent behavior. For example, while some violent criminals have lowered central nervous system (CNS)[158] and autonomic nervous system (ANS) arousal,[159] others have heightened arousal.[160] Depression, violent aggression, and antisocial

---

155. James C. Howell & J. David Hawkins, *Prevention of Youth Violence*, 24 CRIME & JUST. 263, 268 (1998) (citing Terrie E. Moffitt, *Adolescence-Limited and Life-Course-Persistent Antisocial Behavior: A Developmental Taxonomy*, 100 PSYCHOL. REV. 674–701 (1993)). *Cf.* Morse, *supra* note 30, at 56 (remarking that "all societies that survive surely place limits on risk and will act to prevent danger from those for whom socialization has apparently failed").

156. *See* FRANS B. M. DE WAAL, TREE OF ORIGIN: WHAT PRIMATE BEHAVIOR CAN TELL US ABOUT HUMAN SOCIAL EVOLUTION 48 (2001) (observing that "the connection between crowding and aggression, initially demonstrated in rodents, fails to hold in monkeys and apes").

157. D. Brunner & R. Hen, *Insights into the Neurobiology of Impulsive Behavior from Serotonin Receptor Knockout Mice*, 836 ANNALS N.Y. ACAD. SCI. 81 (1997); *see also* Niehoff, *supra* note 9 at 269 (discussing studies finding that aggression in isolated rats becomes expressed most strongly after puberty).

158. The normal human CNS displays immediate, short-term, instinctive reflexive activity as a first line of defense to real or perceived threats.

159. Measures of antisocial behavior in 15-year-old males have been correlated with reduced autonomic nervous system activation. *See* Adrian Raine et al., *Autonomic Nervous System Factors Underlying Disinhibited, Antisocial, and Violent Behavior: Biosocial Perspectives and Treatment Implications*, 794 ANNALS N.Y. ACAD. SCI. 46, 48 (1996) (reviewing nine-year prospective study of crime development and noting that it is the "first study providing evidence for underarousal in an antisocial population in all three psychophysiological response systems"). Further studies showed that measures of underarousal of the CNS and ANS taken at 15 years of age were related to criminality status assessed at 24 years of age. Adrian Raine et al., *Relationships Between Central and Autonomic Measures of Arousal at Age 15 Years and Criminality at Age 24 Years*, 47 ARCHIVES GEN. PSYCHIATRY 1003, 1003 (1990).

160. NIEHOFF, *supra* note 9, at 181. Lowered levels of arousal were accompanied by decreased activation of the reticular activating system (RAS), which is the part of the brain that controls sleep/wake cycles and arousal, and lowered hypothalamic-modulated stress responses. *See id.* Generally speaking, the hypothalamus, along with the RAS, helps regulate the body's physiological response to stress, often referred to as "fight or flight." ROBERT M. SAPOLSKY, STRESS, THE AGING BRAIN, AND THE MECHANISMS OF NEURON DEATH 3–9 (1999). For a more detailed discussion of the stress response, *see* Edgar Garcia-Rill & Erica Beecher-Monas, *Gatekeeping Stress: The Science and Admissibility of Post-Traumatic Stress Disorder*, 24 U. ARK. LITTLE ROCK L. REV. 9, 12–14 (2001). In order to initiate "fight or flight"

personality disorder have all been linked to problems with the stress response.[161] Although each of these disorders has a different pattern of expression, all are associated with abnormal endocrine feedback, norepinephrine and serotonin functions, and altered glucocorticoid levels.[162] Studies of recidivistic violent offenders, adults with antisocial personality disorder, and antisocial adolescents have all documented statistically significant reductions in levels of cortisol, which is the main circulating stress hormone.[163] This suggests that inappropriately violent behavior may sometimes involve a stress response disorder, one in which the response to a threat is too weak rather than too strong. People who appear to lack a conscience may actually lack the biological machinery necessary to warn them that they are heading for disaster.[164]

Tooby and Cosmides postulate that early environmental cues may calibrate behavior irrevocably.[165] These early cues may indicate the kind of social environment the child has been born into. For example, "[v]iolent treatment in childhood increases the likelihood that a person has been born into a social environment where violence is an important avenue of social instrumentality."[166] Thus, exposing a child to violence may permanently lower the threshold for activation of the "fight or flight" response and may account for the disproportionate aggression in adults who were abused as children.[167] Undoubtedly, some of these effects may have a genetic component. As noted below, however, genes

---

responses, there must be an initial arm, an arousal response, and the part to the brain that fulfills that function is the RAS. The RAS projects into many regions, simultaneously alerting the cortex to the event and priming the motor system to be able to fight or flee. Another projection is to the hypothalamus, where the arousal response triggers the stress response.

161. NIEHOFF, *supra* note 9, at 183.

162. *Id.*

163. NIEHOFF, *supra* note 9, at 181. For additional information on the studies cited by Niehoff, *see also* Bo Bergman & Bo Brismar, *Hormone Levels and Personality Traits in Abusive and Suicidal Male Alcoholics*, 18 ALCOHOLISM: CLINICAL & EXPERIMENTAL RES. 311, 311–15 (1994); Keith McBurnett et al., *Anxiety, Inhibition, and Conduct Disorder in Children: II. Relation to Salivary Cortisol*, 30 J. AM. ACAD. CHILD & ADOLESCENT PSYCHIATRY 192 (1991); Matti Virkkunen et al., *CSF Biochemistries, Glucose Metabolism, and Diurnal Activity Rhythms in Alcoholic, Violent Offenders, Fire Setters, and Healthy Volunteers*, 51 ARCHIVES GEN. PSYCHIATRY 20 (1994); Matti Virkkunen, *Urinary Free Cortisol Secretion in Habitually Violent Offenders*, 72 ACTA PSYCHIATRICA SCANDANAVICA 40, 40 (1985).

164. *See* NIEHOFF, *supra* note 9, at 181 (stating that "no warning bell of anxiety or disgust sounds when . . . [antisocial individuals are] about to commit an atrocity.").

165. Tooby & Cosmides, *supra* note 13, at 54.

166. *Id.*

167. *Id.*

do not determine behavior. They may increase the likelihood (probability or risk) that a behavior will occur, but they do not cause it directly.[168]

b. Sex Hormones. Hormones, which are regulated by the hypothalamus and the ANS, can play a role as well. Testosterone affects levels of aggression even in the womb, at least in mice, whose intrauterine positioning between sibling males and females affects levels in postbirth aggression.[169] Testosterone in boys surges at age 10, rising to a plateau by age 14, when aggressive behavior starts accelerating.[170] Males start to kill each other at an appreciable rate only after they reach adolescence.[171] This is also the age at which hormone levels are fluctuating widely. However, delinquent behavior, adjustment problems, and rebelliousness are actually more likely to be associated with lower testosterone levels.[172] Apparently, testosterone functions as a sensitizer, permitting males to match the social environment with an appropriate response.[173]

3. Impaired Brains Structural dysfunction may also contribute to violent behavior. Damage, decreased uptake of glucose, reduced blood flow or metabolism to the frontal lobes, and reduced function have all been observed in the frontal cortex of violent individuals and murderers.[174] Studies using positron emission tomography (PET) and single photon emission computed tomography (SPECT), which are imaging devices designed to measure brain function by showing changes in the metabolism of glucose, have demonstrated that murderers have decreased glucose utilization in the frontal lobes compared to age- and gender-matched subjects.[175]

---

168. Robert Plomin & Michael Rutter, *Child Development, Molecular Genetics, and What to Do with Genes Once They Are Found*, 69 CHILD DEVELOPMENT 1223, 1224 (1998).

169. Frederick S. vom Saal, *Models of Early Hormonal Effects on Intrasex Aggression in Mice, in* HORMONES AND AGGRESSIVE BEHAVIOR 197, 198 (Bruce B. Svare ed., 1983).

170. NIEHOFF, *supra* note 9, at 159.

171. *See* DALY & WILSON, *supra* note 104, at 22 (noting that "14 is about the age at which people begin to kill one another at an appreciable rate").

172. NIEHOFF, *supra* note 9, at 160.

173. Renee J. Primus & Carol K. Kellogg, *Gonadal Hormones During Puberty Organize Environment-Related Social Interaction in the Male Rat*, 24 HORMONES & BEHAV. 311, 320 (1990) (finding in a study done with rats that "[t]he presence of testosterone . . . appears to be critical for the expression of environment-related changes" in social interaction).

174. Adrian Raine et al., *Brain Abnormalities in Murderers Indicated by Positron Emission Tomography*, 42 BIOLOGICAL PSYCHIATRY 495, 495–504 (1997); Adrian Raine et al., *Selective Reductions in Prefrontal Glucose Metabolism in Murderers*, 36 BIOLOGICAL PSYCHIATRY 365, 365–73 (1994). The subjects in these studies did not differ in handedness, schizophrenia, ethnicity, etc. *Id.* at 365.

175. Adrian Raine et al., *Reduced Prefrontal and Increased Subcortical Brain Functioning Assessed Using Positron Emission Tomography in Predatory and Affective Murderers*, 16 BEHAV. SCI. & L. 319, 319–30 (1998). This study was extended to a population of impulsive murderers compared to a group of predatory violent offenders, and the results suggest

How do we perceive the world around us? We process information first through evolutionarily conserved, instinctive systems.[176] That is, we inherited a spinal cord and brainstem that is very similar to those in lower species. These parts of the brain have virtually identical functions in lower species and include basic processes like sleep-wake cycle control and respiration and locomotion, along with primordial drives such as those related to feeding, drinking, procreation, and emotions. These systems were conserved in evolution because of their survival value, their success in "fight or flight" responses.

On the other hand, more advanced species evolved a series of newer brain structures, in particular, the cerebral cortex.[177] Humans have much greater amounts of cerebral cortex than do primates and apes, which allows us to reach unheard of, in evolutionary terms, heights. On an everyday basis, these newly evolved parts of the brain, such as the cerebral cortex, receive their information from the older, primordial, emotional systems. However, they do this in the context of a complex environment and, importantly, within the process of enculturation.

In general, the role of the cortex is to control, through inhibition, those old parts of the brain.[178] Therefore, if the cortex loses some of its inhibitory power, "primordial" behaviors are released. This can occur when the cortex, for example, suffers from decreased blood flow, or metabolism, known as "hypofrontality." Instinctive behaviors then can be released including exaggerated "fight or flight" responses to misperceived threats (i.e. violent or exaggerated behavior in an attempt to attack or flee). Hypofrontality is evident in such disorders as schizophrenia, posttraumatic stress disorder, and depression.[179] Damage, decreased

---

that impulsive murderers have decreased glucose metabolism in the frontal lobes while predatory murderers do not. *Id.* at 319; *see also* Nora D. Volkow & Laurence Tancredi, *Neural Substrates of Violent Behaviour: A Preliminary Study with Positron Emission Tomography*, 151 BRIT. J. PSYCHOL. 668, 668–72 (1987) (showing a pattern of decreased activity in the frontal cortex of a group of murderers as compared to controls and hypothesizing that temporocortical dysfunction may implicate emotional reasoning).

176. ANTONIO R. DAMASIO, DESCARTES' ERROR: EMOTION, REASON, AND THE HUMAN BRAIN, 111 (1994).

177. Dempster, *supra* note 134.

178. Joaquin M. Fuster, *Frontal Lobe and Cognitive Development*, 31 J. NEUROCYTOLOGY 373–85 (2002).

179. *See, e.g.*, Edgar Garcia-Rill, *Disorders of the Reticular Activating System*, 49 MED. HYPOTHESES 379, 379–82 (1997) (reviewing study that showed hypofrontality in schizophrenic patients). Hypofrontality may also lead to the release of "fixed action patterns," which are more complex than instincts. "Fixed action patterns" are automatic brain modules that make complex movements. Rodolfo R. Llinas, *I of the Votex, From Neurons to Self* 133, MIT Press (2001). These patterns can result in repetition of sequences of movements (e.g., stabbing repeatedly) and may be part of uncontrolled action patterns rather than rage. Hypofrontality has been shown to occur during dreaming, Pierre Maquet

uptake of glucose, reduced blood flow, and reduced function have all been observed in the frontal cortex of violent individuals and murderers.[180]

Additional studies have found abnormal temporal lobe metabolism[181] and lesions of the frontal lobes to be associated with an increased risk of aggressive and violent behavior.[182] Reduced volumes of the frontal and temporal cortex have been observed in violent and antisocial personality disorder patients.[183] Interestingly, adolescents on average show a mild form of this condition. The brain, especially the frontal lobes, is still maturing, so the full-blown inhibition exercised by this region in adulthood is not yet in play during adolescence.[184] Magnetic resonance imaging (MRI) testing in adolescents shows mild decreases in frontal lobe function compared to adults, which, coupled with increased levels of sex hormones, can lead to hyper-responsiveness to stimuli.[185] These results

---

et al., *Functional Neuroanatomy of Human Rapid-Eye-Movement Sleep and Dreaming*, 383 NATURE 163, 163 (1996). This may explain why we accept our dreams so readily, why we do not question that we are flying or embroiled in an unrealistic situation. Overreactions to innocuous stimuli are likely in these disorders, particularly the anxiety disorders. Events or conditions could easily lead to exaggerated responses such as panic attacks or incapacitation like fear of leaving the house. Cornering such individuals or placing them under undue stress, could elicit exaggerated reactions, striking out due to overperceived threats.

180. Raine et al., *supra* note 174. *See also* Hugo D. Critchley et al., *Prefrontal and Medial Temporal Correlates of Repetitive Violence to Self and Others*, 47 BIOLOGICAL PSYCHIATRY 928, 931 (2000); J. Graffman et al., *Frontal Lobe Injuries, Violence, and Aggression: A Report of the Vietnam Head Injury Study*, 46 AM. ACAD. NEUROLOGY 1231, 1231 (1996).

181. *See* David Seidenwurm et al., *Abnormal Temporal Lobe Metabolism in Violent Subjects: Correlation of Imaging and Neuropsychiatric Findings*, 18 AM. J. NEURORADIOLOGY 625, 625 (1997) (discussing study finding abnormalities in the glucose metabolism in the temporal lobe correlated with violent behavior in humans); Henrik Soderstrom et al., *Reduced Regional Cerebral Blood Flow in Non-Psychotic Violent Offenders*, 98 PSYCHIATRY RES. NEUROIMAGING 29, 40 (2000). The temporal lobe contains limbic structures like the hippocampus and amygdala, which are associated with emotional states.

182. Graffman et al., *supra* note 180.

183. Critchley et al., *supra* note 180; Raine et al., *Reduced Prefrontal Gray Matter Volume and Reduced Autonomic Activity in Antisocial Personality Disorder*, 57 ARCHIVES GEN. PSYCHIATRY 119, 119 (2000).

184. Jay N. Giedd et al., *Brain Development during Childhood and Adolescence: A Longitudinal MRI Study*, 2 NATURE NEUROSCI. 861, 861–62 (1999); Elizabeth R. Sowell et al., *In Vivo Evidence for Post-Adolescent Brain Maturation in Frontal and Striatal Regions*, 2 NATURE NEUROSCI. 859, 859–61 (1999).

185. Younger individuals (8–20 years of age) show less efficient activation of the frontal lobes than do older adults. L. Tamm, V. Menon, & A. Reiss, *Maturation of Brain Function Associated with Response Inhibition*, 41 J. AMERICAN ACAD. CHILD & ADOLESCENT PSYCH. 1213–38 (2002). Normal adolescents also appear to have a sensory gating deficit, which is an overresponsiveness to repetitive or inconsequential stimuli. Lisa Rasco et al., *Effect of Age on Sensory Gating of the Sleep State-Dependent P1/P50 Midlatency Auditory Evoked*

suggest that reduction of function in the frontal lobes may be responsible for impaired critical judgment and poor impulse control. [186]

On the other hand, lack of empathy, rather than impaired impulse control, may result from damage to the amygdala.[187] Studies on amygdalar function suggest that damage to this part of the brain might lead to disengagement and lack of empathy.[188] While electrically stimulating the amygdala can elicit the physiological and behavioral signs of emotional states,[189] lesions to the amygdala induce an unusually placid and emotionally unengaged individual, a condition known as the Kluver-Bucy syndrome.[190] Those affected are unable to recognize the context of danger although they are capable of emitting the right gestures. Such lack of empathy may be at the root of multiple, premeditated, and serial, rather than impulsive, killing.[191]

4. Sexual Violence Far less is known about sexual paraphilias[192]—the offenses other than rape that the sexually violent predator statutes encompass. These statutory offenses typically involve molesting children. There has been surprisingly little biological research done on sex offenders.[193] Demographically, nearly half the sex offenses against children are perpetrated by other children, usually

---

Potential, 3 Sleep Res. Online 97, 97–105 (2000), http://www.sro.org/bin/article. dll?Paper&1930&0&0. This can lead to increased distractibility, which can also create unnecessary responsiveness to inconsequential stimuli. *Id.* Given a stressful environment or other condition that increases arousal, such as hormones, the chances of exaggerated responsiveness—too much "fight" or too much "flight"—are increased.

186. R. J. R. Blair, *Neurocognitive Models of Aggression, The Antisocial Personality Disorder, and Psychopathy*, 71 J. Neurology, Neurosurgery, & Psychiatry 727, 728 (2001).

187. The amygdala is an almond shaped structure deep inside the front end of the temporal lobe and part of the limbic system, the "emotional" part of the brain. Niefhoff, *supra* note 9, at 94.

188. *Id.* at 96–7 (stating that the removal of the amygdalar can turn an animal into an emotionally unavailable being).

189. *Id.* at 92.

190. Antonio R. Damasio, Descartes' Error: Emotion, Reason, and the Human Brain 134–39 (1994).

191. *See* Beecher-Monas & Garcia-Rill, *supra* note 5, at 1866.

192. *See* Martin P. Kafka, *The Monoamine Hypothesis for Pathophysiology of Paraphilic Disorders: An Update*, in Sexually Coercive Behavior, *supra* note 6, at 86–87 (explaining that "paraphilias found predominantly in males, are repetitive, compelling, socially deviant behaviors that are associated with personal distress, harm to others, or other expressions of significant psychosocial impairment"). This definition excludes adult rapists. *Id.* at 87.

193. *See, e.g.*, Grant T. Harris & Marnie E. Rice, *Actuarial Assessment of Risk Among Sex Offenders*, in Sexually Coercive Behavior, *supra* note 6, at 199 (noting that the actuarial instruments for sexual recidivism were "based on a surprisingly small amount of empirical work").

the victim's family members,[194] and 90 percent of the rapes of children younger than 12 are committed by someone the victim knows.[195]

Most sexual predator statutes apply, however, only when the victim was a stranger. The primary impetus for passage of the sex offender statutes was the sexual murder of children by strangers, yet statistics show that these represent fewer than 1 percent of all murders.[196] In contrast to other murders, most of the child victims of sexual murders are female, although a greater risk of recidivism occurs when the victim is male.[197] The base rate of sexual re-offending appears to be low, well below that of general or even violent recidivism.[198]

Very little is known about pedophilia in adult males. They seem to be an older crowd, with nearly 25 percent of child victimizers being forty or older,[199] although

194. CTR. FOR SEX OFFENDER MGMT., AN OVERVIEW OF SEX OFFENDER MANAGEMENT 1, 2 (2002), *available at* http://www.csom.org/pubs/csom_bro.pdf. There are several reasons to exclude this population. It is overwhelmingly characterized by psychiatric disorders (80 percent) and learning disabilities (30–60 percent). CTR. FOR SEX OFFENDER MGMT., MYTHS AND FACTS ABOUT SEX OFFENDERS (2000), http://www.csom.org/pubs/mythsfacts. html. Moreover, there is no evidence to show that sexually abusive youth become sex offenders as adults. AN OVERVIEW OF SEX OFFENDER MANAGEMENT, *supra*, at 2. Unfortunately, this has not stopped the increasing treatment of juveniles as adults in the criminal justice system, where juvenile court waivers have become increasingly common, the age at which juveniles may be tried as adults has been lowered, and minimum age restrictions for trying juveniles as adults in certain serious crimes have been abandoned. *See id.* at 4–6 (noting the increasing level of accountability in the criminal justice system).

195. LAWRENCE A. GREENFIELD, BUREAU OF JUST. STAT., AN ANALYSIS OF DATA ON RAPE AND SEXUAL ASSAULT: SEX OFFENSES AND OFFENDERS, i., iii (1997), *available at* http://www.ojp. usdoj.gov/bjs/pub/pdf/soo.pdf (last visited Mar. 26, 2005).

196. *Id.* at *vi; *see also* Roxanne Lieb et al., *Sexual Predators and Social Policy*, 23 CRIME & JUST. 43, 52–53 (1998) (noting that about 1.5 percent of murders involve rape or sexual assault).

197. LAWRENCE A. GREENFIELD, BUREAU OF JUST. STAT., CHILD VICTIMIZERS: VIOLENT OFFENDERS AND THEIR VICTIMS, iv (1996), *available at* http://www.ojp.usdoj.gov/bjs/pub/ pdf/cvvoatv.pdf (reporting "3 in 4 child victims of violence were female").

198. The exact numbers appear to be somewhat in dispute. The Bureau of Justice Statistics reports that sexual offender recidivism is set at about 5 percent, and child molesters' recidivism appears at about 3 percent. BUREAU OF JUST. STAT., CRIMINAL OFFENDER STATISTICS (2005), http://www.ojp.usdoj.gov/bjs/crimoff.htm. However, the Center for Sex Offender Management reports that recidivism is set at a 13 percent reconviction rate for child molesters and 19 percent for rapists. MYTHS AND FACTS ABOUT SEX OFFENDERS, *supra* note 194. In either event, the "recidivism rates for sex offenders are lower than for the general criminal population." *Id.*; *cf.* Hanson et al., *supra* note 107, at 353 (finding that although recidivism rates for rapists and child molesters are about equal for sexual offenses, rapists are more likely to commit another violent act).

199. *See* U.S. Dep't of Just., Bureau of Just. Statistics, *Sexual Assault of Young Children as Reported to Law Enforcement: Victim, Incident, and Offender Characteristics*, www.ojp. usdoj.gov/bjs/abstract/saycrle.htm (last visited Mar. 25, 2005).

most recidivists are younger.[200] While exposure to physical violence in childhood predisposes adults to violence, it is unclear whether exposure to sexual abuse in childhood has the same effect on sexual offending.[201] Approximately 30 percent of all adult sex offenders were sexually abused as children.[202]

Some potentially important anomalies have been observed in pedophiles. Right temporal lobe hypometabolism has been identified in adult pedophiles,[203] as have lower baseline cortisol levels[204] and monoaminergic dysfunction.[205] Although pedophilia is not well studied, some researchers believe that neurological deficits, chromosome aberration, or early childhood abuse or sexual experience may imprint desire onto inappropriate outlets.[206] The best available evidence suggests some disruption in the development of the neurosystem.[207] There may well be a genetic component.

Therefore, violent behavior appears to be both universal and individual, both normal aggression gone awry and pathological breakdowns in biological systems, both nature and nurture. Multiple hormones and neurotransmitters, and a multitude of genes, contribute to aggression, as do the social environment, context, and timing. Personality and genetics are undoubtedly involved, as are social circumstances, like status, future prospects, and relative wealth. Violence is

---

200. Hanson et al., *supra* note 107, at 353.

201. *See, e.g.*, John Monahan et al., Rethinking Risk Assessment: The MacArthur Study of Mental Disorder and Violence 54–55 (2001) (noting that "[a]lthough prior physical abuse as a child . . . [is] associated with post-discharge violence, prior sexual abuse was not."); Ctr. for Sex Offender Mgmt., Understanding Juvenile Sexual Offending Behavior: Emerging Research, Treatment Approaches and Management Practices (1999), *available at* http://www.csom.org/pubs/juvbrf10.html (reporting that 20 to 50 percent of sexually abusive youth had a history of physical abuse, while 40 to 80 percent had a history of sexual abuse).

202. Myths and Facts about Sex Offenders, *supra* note 194.

203. Mario F. Mendez et al., *Pedophilia and Temporal Lobe Disturbances*, 12 J. Neuropsychiatry & Clinical Neurosci. 71–76 (2000) (suggesting that "[a] predisposition to pedophilia may be unmasked by hypersexuality from brain disease").

204. *See* Michael Maes et al., *Lower Baseline Plasma Cortisol and Prolactin Together with Increased Body Temperature and Higher mCPP-Induced Cortisol Responses in Men with Pedophilia*, 24 Neuropsychopharmacology 37, 37–44 (2001) (studying hormonal and serotonergic alterations in pedophiles).

205. *See* Kafka, *supra* note 192, at 91 (reviewing data on the role of monoamine neuromodulators in paraphiliacs and concluding that "a specific role for these neuromodulators in the paraphilic condition remains neither proven nor rejected").

206. *See* F. S. Berlin & E. Kraut, *Pedophilia Diagnostic Concepts, Treatment and Ethical Considerations*, 7 Am. J. Forensic Psychol. 13 (1986); F. S. Berlin et al., *A 5-Year Follow-Up Survey of Criminal Recidivism*, 12 Am. J. Forensic Psychol. 5 (1991).

207. Berlin et al., *supra* note 206, at 208 (observing that "the best available evidence suggests that most sexual deviance and paraphilia is caused by very early biomedical events leading to neurodevelopmental disruption").

complex behavior. Why wouldn't identifying the genetic contributions aid the accuracy of future dangerousness predictions?

BEHAVIORAL GENETICS AND FUTURE DANGEROUSNESS

A. Assumptions about Human Nature

The explosion of scientific information related to the determination of the human genome has created an unfortunate misunderstanding by many, lay and scientist alike, of the role that genes play in behavior.[208] The assumptions go something like this: Genes made us the way we are; therefore, we are driven by a set of rigid, genetically determined predilections toward some behaviors. The force of this genetic dictatorship makes us less responsible for our actions, mainly because genetic "determinism" is absolute and irreversible. Such views are used to influence increasingly restrictive laws presumably aimed at curbing the worst in us. How did we arrive at such a state? Is this really true?

A prime example of how such views came to be integrated into our assumptions, our "belief system," is the publication of *The Selfish Gene*, by Richard Dawkins in 1976.[209] This book became very influential soon after being published and has been reissued in a number of more recent editions. Dawkins argues that "we, and all other animals, are machines created by our genes."[210] This theory prompted the writer to argue that a predominant quality in a "successful gene," defined as one that is passed on from generation to generation, is ruthless selfishness, and that it will usually give rise to selfishness in individual behavior. Dawkins essentially used the theory of natural selection proposed by Darwin as one potential mechanism behind evolution and applied it to gene selection. Presumably genetic selection was simply too dry a subject. It needed some pizzazz, and "voilà": the dog-eat-dog process of natural selection was an ideal concept to muster interest. The gene became "selfish" because it tends to perpetuate itself; it became "ruthless" because it was in "competition" with its alleles. This series of unsupported conclusions was used to further argue that, since genes can influence behavior (unsupported conclusion), we tend toward selfish behavior (unsupported conclusion). As usual, two wrongs do not make a right.

---

208. *See, e.g.*, Anderson, *supra* note 146, at 105, 126 (explaining that because of the complex pathways between genes, environment and behavior, "[g]enes do not directly *cause* behavior, since their effect is expressed indirectly through physiological systems" and warning that even if genetic correlates to violence are identified, "many individuals with abnormal genotypes will be completely normal")

209. RICHARD DAWKINS, THE SELFISH GENE (Oxford University Press, 1989) (1976).

210. *Id.* at 2.

Such unfortunate categorical language has led to great misunderstanding. To the author's credit (and in response to the uproar), he tempered this extreme notion by arguing that, rather than being deterministic, genes "determine" our behavior only in a statistical sense[211] (adding another unsupported conclusion). Many readers, and some who never read the book, stopped at the inflammatory basic theory that the "gene is the basic unit of selfishness"[212] (unsupported conclusion) and have applied the concept to complex behaviors (unsupported conclusion).[213] The author, seemingly ineffectively considering how easily this misunderstanding has been perpetuated, further argued that the effect of the gene depends on the environment, including other genes: that "[s]ometimes a gene has one effect in the presence of a particular other gene, and a completely different effect in the presence of another set companion genes."[214] While this provides a glimpse into the precarious conditions mandating gene expression, this position still gives genes far too much power—power they do not have. There is no evidence to suggest that genes dictate behavior "in a statistical sense" or otherwise.

B. Nature vs. Nurture, Again

One of the basic questions regarding the development of the nervous system is how much influence genetic programming, or nature, has compared to environmental, or nurture, factors.[215] Nowadays, there is a false belief that there is a gene for this behavior and a gene for that behavior, that some genes make us violent, some genes make us depressed, and other genes make us gregarious. On the other hand, the attitude only a few years ago was that it was the environment that made us who and what we are.[216] This approach made our parents responsible for our neuroses; behaviors such as failed relationships and divorce were considered learned behaviors. Even the environment we lived in caused depression.

Now, the reigning mode of explanation of development, of individual differences and even of behavior, is genetic.[217] Hopefully, it will become evident that the major factor influencing the development of the brain is neither nature nor

---

211. *Id.* at 37–40.

212. *Id.* at 36.

213. Deterministic theories of mind, such as those espoused by Dawkins, make "great inferential leaps from genes to culture and ignore[e] a good deal of what we know about the brain." MERLIN W. DONALD, A MIND SO RARE: THE EVOLUTION OF HUMAN CONSCIOUSNESS 4 (2001).

214. *Id.* at 37.

215. *See generally,* DAVID S. MOORE, THE DEPENDENT GENE 72 (2001).

216. RICHARD LEWONTIN, THE TRIPLE HELIX: GENE, ORGANISM, AND ENVIRONMENT 16 (1998).

217. *Id.*

nurture, not one or the other, but both. In fact, the effect of environment or nurture is what makes individuals of a species different. That is, the differences between rats, tigers, chimps, and humans can be explained by differences in their genetic makeup, but to explain the differences between two individual chimps or two individual humans, more is needed than their genetic differences.[218] Some believe that the organism is determined neither by its genes nor by its environment, or by the interactions between them, but that "developmental noise" introduces a random process that leads to great variation in individual differences.[219]

First, put genes in perspective. Inside the nucleus of a cell is deoxyribonucleic acid, or DNA, which is like two strings of pearls twisted around each other in a double helix. There are four different types of pearls in each string, with the particular sequence of a number of pearls being a gene, a code for the manufacture of a protein.[220] That is, DNA contains many, many genes, each of which codes for one or more proteins. DNA can be thought of as a blueprint for a building. Genes or pieces of DNA, when activated, make different kinds of proteins.[221] Those proteins are incorporated into a cell, for example, a nerve cell. Each cell exists because many genes provided the building material of brick protein, mortar protein, wood protein, metal protein, and so forth that went into building the structure called a "cell."[222] The DNA contains a blueprint that determines more or less what a cell should look like when all the construction is done. DNA is not two-dimensional like a blueprint; it is a linear chain of coding, a specific sequence of pearls. On the other hand, the organism to be created will be three-dimensional. Therefore, the cell, or building, actually created may only resemble that blueprint in principle.

One reason for this is that a particular gene does not always code for a particular protein. Although scientists previously believed that a single gene coded for a single protein, it is now known that, while many genes appear to produce only one primary protein, other genes produce alternative forms of these proteins.[223] These proteins may start or end at different sites along the coded region and may have more than one site for alternative splicing of proteins. A single stretch of DNA may thus encode a variety of proteins.

Sometimes a cell may express these different proteins; in other cases, the pattern is subject to "developmental regulation." That is, one gene can encode many

---

218. *Id.* at 17.
219. *Id.* at 38.
220. *See generally* DAVID S. MOORE, THE DEPENDENT GENE, 67–81 (2001).
221. J. Z. YOUNG, AN INTRODUCTION TO THE STUDY OF MAN 60 (1971).
222. Id. at 53.
223. BASIC NEUROCHEMISTRY: MOLECULAR, CELLULAR AND MEDICAL ASPECTS 421 (George J. Siegel et al. eds., 6th ed., 1999).

different proteins, often with divergent functions.[224] Environmental factors may also play a role in cellular structure. For example, the construction of a building can be influenced by many factors during construction, such as the experience of the builder, the dedication of the workers, the terrain, weather, and economic conditions—basically, a very complex set of "environmental" circumstances. Our brand-new research building looks fantastic, but eighty of its windows leak because workers forgot to seal around them. Assuming a detached attitude, this can be termed "noise" in the environment.

The environment in turn can alter genetic expression. For example, water fleas, those fast little bugs that skip along on the surface of water, when raised in a lab aquarium containing the scent of fish (their main predator), will express a "helmet" that makes them harder to swallow. When no scent of fish is present in the water, water fleas with identical DNA will not express a "helmet."[225] That is, the environment can elicit markedly different traits from the same DNA. This and other examples of developmental "plasticity" show that a given genotype can develop in different ways depending on the environment.

A gene in rats that makes them fearful and jumpy can be altered by how regularly the mother licks and grooms the pups.[226] Maternal care, therefore, can change the expression of the gene, and the rat grows up to be calm and curious. In a species closer to home, geneticists investigated the claim that a gene called 5-HTT is associated with depression and suicide.[227] They found that people who carry this gene are more likely to suffer from depression than are people with the "healthy" variant, unless they also experience very stressful events. That is, these genes are not connected to depression or aggression in the absence of exposure to environmental risk. Again, differing environments can produce different traits from the same or different genotype. It may be that what genes give us is the "plasticity" to respond to the environment, rather than "hardwiring" our behavior. What is "innate," our human nature, is actually our flexibility to respond to a complex environment.

C. Genes Make Proteins, Not Behavior

A complex nervous system is necessary in order to generate behavior. Genes do not make behavior, they make proteins. A collection of proteins makes a nerve cell, but it takes more than nerve cells alone to generate behavior. That is, brain cells, once constructed, must be connected together accurately into working circuits called "systems," such as our motor systems or visual systems. Within each

---

224. Id.

225. Niles Lehman, et al., *A Hierarchical Molecular Phylogeny within the Genus Daphnia*, 4 MOLECULAR PHYLOGENETICS & EVOLUTION 395–407 (1995).

226. Eric W. Fish, et al., *Epigenetic Programming of Stress Responses through Variations in Maternal Care*, 1036 ANN. N.Y. ACAD. SCI. 167–80 (2004).

227. Avsalom Caspi, et al., *Influence of Life Stress on Depression: Moderation by a Polymorphism in the 5-HTT Gene*, 301 SCI. 386 (2003).

of these systems, every cell needs to find its specific synaptic targets, other nerve cells with which they will synapse and communicate to create the working system. If that search is thwarted, the cell may never find a target and may die. This is the process of "programmed cell death."[228]

A pervasive and well-supported theory of brain development, "programmed cell death" describes the development of some systems in the brain as follows: The developing brain system makes about twice as many cells as it will end up with in the adult.[229] Every distinct group of cells within that system must link up with its appropriate synaptic target or targets in order to create a circuit or circuits within that system. The target for a specific group of cells expresses a specific growth factor, like a perfume that attracts only certain suitors, and the cells begin to send out processes, arm-like appendages called axons, chasing the chemical gradient of growth factor, growing toward the target. Those axons that reach the target first will feast on the growth factor secreted by the target, thereby consolidating their synaptic link, feeding on the growth factor, and keeping the cell of origin alive. The axons of cells that arrived too late will not find a site at which to synapse and be nurtured and will consequently die.

"Programmed cell death" is very much like developmental natural selection, survival of the fastest. The process of establishing appropriate connections in many brain regions is, therefore, essentially stochastic, and, as such, extremely vulnerable to environmental conditions. For example, if the environment of the fetus is disturbed during the time when the main links are being made, namely the first and second trimesters, abnormal connectivity may result. If the neurochemical environment is changed dramatically, with too few cells (as in oxygen compromise that leads to mental retardation because too few cortical cells survive) or too many (as in overexpression of growth factors that allows too many cells to survive, as may be the case in some schizophrenics),[230] then cells survive. Between these extremes there must be a great number of milder effects on cell survival, none genetically determined, that may give rise to individual differences. Even if all goes well and one group of cells connects appropriately with another, all such a process creates is a very basic nervous system. Such a nervous system is still incapable of "behavior."

Lots of different cells and several different systems interconnected in sufficiently complex ways will lead to behavior, but only simple behavior, as long as there is no "environmental" influence. For example, imagine that we can grow a complex nervous system but in the absence of an environment, or in a "neutral" environment.[231]

---

228. Robert R. Buss & Ronald W. Oppenheim, *Role of Programmed Cell Death in Normal Neuronal Development and Function*, 79 ANATOMICAL SCI. INT'L. 191, 191 (2004).

229. *See generally*, DAVID S. MOORE, THE DEPENDENT GENE 72, 82–103 (2001).

230. E. Garcia-Rill et al., *Mesopontine Neurons in Schizophrenia*, 66 NEUROSCI. 321, 321 (1995).

231. This is strictly an intellectual exercise, as there can be no organism without an environment, just as there can be no environment without an organism. LEWONTIN, *supra* note 216, at 48.

Such a nervous system, no matter how complex, will carry out only simple behaviors. It may eat, breathe, walk—basically carry out survival and presumably "innate" functions. Without an appropriate environment, that nervous system will not be shaped appropriately, and will not function "normally." It will not learn, remember, plan, or behave in socially acceptable, or unacceptable, ways. One example of the pervasive effects of environment is the classic sensory deprivation study of Melzack, in which puppies were brought up in the dark, without social interaction, in a white noise environment and wearing collars to prevent grooming or contact with extremities.[232] These dogs grew up to sniff an open flame without realizing their noses would burn and without reacting in pain. However, when the study was repeated, the results could not be replicated. One night, returning to the lab, Melzack found the reason. A cleaning person felt sorry for the dogs and released them from their collars and cages in the evening. Only brief exposure to the environment "normalized" complex behaviors.

Not until all the brain systems are in place, coupled with exposure to an appropriate environment, do we start "behaving" normally or abnormally. Early in development, we learn to move, plan, and interact with others. The combination of a good genetic program and the exposure to a proper environment creates a well-functioning nervous system.

But even then, these behaviors are not written in stone. We modify our brain connections throughout our lifetime, usually in response to our surroundings. Some of these modifications are carried out by proteins, proteins that are coded by genes. For example, consolidation of memories is believed to be caused by the triggering of genes for the manufacture of proteins that fortify a set of synapses so that, given activation of this circuit, the memory may be recalled.[233] What this means is that genes remain an active part of our everyday functions, of our behavior. But what triggers the genetic expression? Nerve activity as a result of interaction with the environment. That is, such genes are at the beck and call of our now fully functioning nervous system; they are not dictating what the nervous system does but are tools that our nerve cells use to mold the ever-changing brain.

Moreover, we are capable of changing our behavior as long as we live. The end result of what each of us becomes is influenced by multiple environmental factors at many points during our lifetime, from conception (microenvironment) to birth and adulthood (macroenvironment). One way to look at it is that human beings are born with genetically determined musical instruments, but how well

---

232. Ronald Melzack & T. H. Scott, *The Effects of Early Experience on the Response to Pain*, 50 J. COMP. PHYSIOL. PSYCHOL. 155, 155–60 (1957). Note that such procedures are unlikely to meet approval from regulatory committees today.

233. Subimal Datta, *Avoidance Task Training Potentiates Phasic Pontine-Wave Density in the Rat: A Mechanism for Sleep-Dependent Plasticity*, 20 J. NEUROSCI. 8607, 8607–13 (2000).

and what kinds of music we will play is determined by so many environmental factors that it would be impossible to predict how well the instruments will play the music, the kind of music they will play, or the kind of behavior they will display in the future. By practicing on our musical instruments, we can improve performance; our consistent use of the instrument makes minor changes in its structure by using genes to make more proteins, proteins that "tune up" the system.

Thus, the sequence of events is that genes make proteins, which make cells, which make connections, which make systems, which make brains—only then does behavior result. In other words, the brain needs to have networks before its potential for behavior can be realized. At every point in this building and tuning process, the environment plays a hand, for better or for worse. All traits, from biological traits such as hair color and height to complex psychological traits such as intelligence, are caused by dependent interactions of genes and the environment. Human beings live in a complex world of interdependent conditions.

The overemphasis on molecular biology and genetic research has created the impression that it is the wave of the future, the answer to our illnesses, medical and even social. The fact is that there are limits to the methodology and no reason to believe that safer or more economic ways of dealing with disease will emerge in many, many areas. Some believe that the most fruitful research should be done on diseases whose emergence and course can *not* be significantly modified by personal habits or the environment.[234] Such disorders as Type 1 diabetes and Alzheimer's disease appear to be induced by genetic mechanisms that may not be voluntarily or environmentally modified. However, Type 2 diabetes can be avoided by exercise and weight loss, alcohol consumption can be reduced by higher taxes and better oversight of sales, and nicotine addiction can be modified by smoking bans, social pressure, and taxes. Environmental approaches are not as "sexy" as gene-based high-tech methods, but they do work.

There are also reasons for caution regarding the evidence suggested by genetic studies. Studies associating genes with specific diseases are typically wrong.[235] For example, a 1992 study found that people with two copies of a dopamine D3 receptor have a risk for schizophrenia roughly two to four times higher than do those without it.[236] A flood of follow-up studies found that no statistically significant link existed where researchers had initially found one.[237] Two recent studies

---

234. Kathleen R. Merikangas & Neil Risch, *Genomic Priorities and Public Health*, 302 Sci. 599 (2003).

235. Jack Lucentini, *Gene Association Studies Typically Wrong: Reproducible Gene-Disease Associates Are Few and Far Between* 18 The Scientist 20, 20 (2004).

236. M. A. Crocq et al., *Association Between Schizophrenia and Homozygosity at the Dopamine D3 Receptor Gene*, 29 J. Med. Genetics 858, 859 (1992).

237. Erik G. Jonsson et al., *Meta-analysis of the Dopamine D3 Receptor Gene (DRD3) Ser9Gly Variant and Schizophrenia*, 14 Psychiatric Genetics 9, 9–11 (2004).

found that when a finding is first published linking a given gene with a complex disease, there is only roughly a one-third chance that other studies will confirm the finding.[238] Another recent report suggested that the first report is usually spurious; if it is true, the association is exaggerated. Worse yet, there may be no way to predict which new gene-association studies will be verified with multiple replications.[239]

D. Brave New Mind

Neo-Darwinian hardliners, scholars who share the uncompromising belief in the irrelevance of the conscious mind and the illusory nature of free will, argue that human nature, including the intellect itself, is fixed in genetic concrete.[240] According to these hardliners, we do not just have emotions, we have them for specific reasons; we do not just see, we parse the world in a particular fashion; we have built-in cognitive tools such as "cheater detectors," which recognize people who do not give a good return on investment. Under this view, these are all hardwired capacities, complex and completely unconscious and automatic.[241]

Merlin Donald argues that, on the contrary, the capacity for consciousness is our distinguishing trait, a trait that defines human nature. The emergence of languages, symbols, many social institutions, and religions has all been driven by a felt need to extend the reach of human consciousness. The conscious mind assembles memories and skills, supervising the processes that make culture possible. Our capacity for consciousness is what makes us human and provides the biological basis for the generation of culture, including symbolic thought

---

238. Kirk E. Lohmuller et al., *Meta-analysis of Genetic Association Studies Supports a Contribution of Common Variants to Susceptibility to Common Disease*, 33 NATURE GENETICS 177, 177 (2003); John P. A. Ioannidis et al., *Replication Validity of Genetic Association Studies*, 29 NATURE GENETICS 306, 306–08 (2001).

239. *See* Thomas A. Trikalinos et al., *Establishment of Genetic Associations for Complex Diseases is Independent of Early Study Findings*, 12 EUR. J. HUM. GENETICS 762, 768 (2004) (stating "evidence collection and comprehensive synthesis may be useful in probing genetic associations of complex diseases, but cautious interpretation is probably always warranted").

240. *See* MERLIN DONALD, A MIND SO RARE: THE EVOLUTION OF HUMAN CONSCIOUSNESS 1–4 (2001) (referring to authors Daniel Dennett, Richard Dawkins, and Steven Pinker as "neo-Darwinian Hardliners"). Donald coined the term "Brave New Mind" to describe the implications of a number of recent books on the nature of consciousness. *See id.* at 1. *See also* DANIEL C. DENNETT, DARWIN'S DANGEROUS IDEA: EVOLUTION AND THE MEANINGS OF LIFE (1995); DAWKINS, *supra* note 209; STEVEN PINKER, THE BLANK SLATE: THE MODERN DENIAL OF HUMAN NATURE (2002).

241. *See* DONALD, *supra* note 240, at 2 (stating that "[a]ccording to . . . [Hardliners'] scheme of things, all that prating religious nonsense about moral self-discipline, denying the flesh, turning the other check, gaining control over one's base desires, not coveting thy neighbor's wife, and so on is bound to fail because it contradicts our biology").

and language.[242] Donald goes on to argue that, while many brains collectively and over time generated our culture, culture in turn is shaping our brains.[243] According to Donald, "The nature and range of human conscious experience are no longer a biological given."[244] Rather, they depend on "a somewhat unpredictable interaction of brain and culture, whereby the processes of mind can be endlessly rewritten and rearranged by cultural forces."[245]

CONCLUSION

Despite an ocean of literature explaining the flaws of expert behavioral predictions, legislatures continue to demand future dangerousness predictions in the statutes they write. Courts, long aware that these predictions are tenuous at best, ignore their gatekeeping duties and admit future dangerousness predictions into evidence. Experts, whose training and professional literature excoriate such testimony, continue to make future dangerousness predictions. Although the eugenics experiment in social control is long discredited, a skeptic might be forgiven for observing that it too was characterized by a flagrant disregard for the standards and methods of science, though many of its most prominent advocates, like those experts testifying to future dangerousness, were nominally scientists.

As William K. Clifford wrote in his famous essay "The Ethics of Belief," "The danger to society is not merely that it should believe wrong things, though that is great enough; but that it should become credulous, and lose the habit of testing things and inquiring into them; for then it must sink back into savagery."[246] The development of a rational set of laws requires that they be founded on sound evidence. Implementation of laws through judicial decisions similarly requires sound evidence. The intellectual culture of today is one in which science, instead of literature or philosophy, takes center stage in the debate over "human nature" and the nature of the universe.[247] However, that does not mean that scientists are

242. *Id.* at 8, 11.

243. *Id.* at 11.

244. *Id.* at 321.

245. *Id.* at 321–22 ("The human conscious process is a specialized adaptation for navigating the turbulent waters of culture as well as the primary channel through which cultural influence can be transmitted back to us").

246. Timothy J. Madigan, *Introduction* to W. K. CLIFFORD, THE ETHICS OF BELIEF AND OTHER ESSAYS 76 (1999).

247. The face-off between these two cultures has been supplanted by a "third culture." John Brockman was convincing in showing that it is scientists, not literary intellectuals, who have the most to say on the important questions facing humankind. JOHN BROCKMAN, THE THIRD CULTURE 17 (1995).

always "right," that they have a lock on the "truth." Nor does it make them immune from scientific critique.

As preeminent twentieth-century philosopher Karl Popper proposed, there is no such thing as absolute truth; what science provides is a better and better approximation of the truth.[248] Popper explained that we should strive not to attempt to prove our theories correct but to try to prove them wrong, because only by passing repeated tests, and being constantly refined in the process, may the theory approach being closer to the truth.[249] This is his famous principle of "falsifiability." As you would suspect, few scientists treat their pet theories so disdainfully. Nonetheless, it was Popper's philosophy that formed the foundation for the *Daubert* decision, requiring judges to examine the validity of scientific testimony before admitting it in evidence.[250]

Legislatures and judges are under enormous public pressure to "solve" the problem of violent (and sexually violent) crime. Admitting the dubious testimony of experts willing to testify that an individual poses a future danger to society is an easy but disingenuous answer. Unfortunately, another easy answer to the problem of crime control, finding a "genetic" basis for killing or locking a violent individual away and throwing away the key, is similarly unsupported by the evidence. Genetic determinism is simply unfounded when it comes to complex behavior. Rather, to reduce the level of violence in our society and help prevent those who either impulsively or intentionally have committed acts of violence from doing so again, we need to develop more constructive methods of expression.[251]

---

248. KARL R. POPPER, REALISM AND THE AIM OF SCIENCE 25 (W. W. Bartley, III ed., 1983).
249. *Id.*
250. Erica Beecher-Monas & Edgar Garcia-Rill, *The Law and the Brain: Judging Scientific Evidence of Intent*, 1 J. APP. PRAC. & PROCESS 243, 247 (1999).
251. Whether one justifies the enforcement of social norms through a utilitarian calculus or by retributivist principles, or by some hybrid combination of the two, science ought to inform the debates both about what violence is preventable and about what controls are likely to be effective. As Owen Jones noted, "law is a lever for moving human behavior." Owen D. Jones, *Law and Biology: Toward an Integrated Model of Human Behavior*, 8 J. CONTEMP. LEGAL ISSUES 167, 167 (1997). We ought to be fairly sure we are moving it in the right direction. There is a great need for research into early childhood intervention and for methods that are effective in rehabilitating offenders, methods that will certainly need to be individually tailored depending on the individual's major negative environmental influences. Such methods will certainly be criticized as expensive and time-consuming, which they will be. The cost of treatment and intensive supervision in the community is estimated at about $5000–$15,000 per individual per year; the cost of incarceration is significantly higher, at $22,000 per year, excluding treatment costs. See MYTHS AND FACTS ABOUT SEX OFFENDERS, *supra* note, at 194. What we are doing now is expensive in money and human capital, too. The question then becomes, how long are we willing to stand current conditions?

Law's moral authority is based on the accuracy of its assumptions and predictions. Admitting scientifically baseless expert testimony on future dangerousness into evidence is not only cynical: it undermines law's moral authority. The very least we can do in a system that aspires to do justice is to be sure that the scientific testimony admitted in our courts has been tested, scrutinized, and properly limited. If what we seek is justice, and if justice depends on the willingness to seek the truth, then the current charade undermines the rule of law. A far better solution is to require that experts testifying about human behavior acknowledge the complexity of the environmental (nurture) and biological (nature) interactions, and ultimately recognize that human beings can and do change their behavior.

13. THE SCARLET GENE: BEHAVIORAL GENETICS, CRIMINAL LAW, AND RACIAL AND ETHNIC STIGMA

KAREN ROTHENBERG AND ALICE WANG

INTRODUCTION

Imagine that a scientist from the state university asks you and your family to participate in a study on a particular gene variant associated with alcoholism. The project focuses on your ethnic group, the Tracy Islanders, who have a higher incidence of alcoholism, as well as a higher incidence of the gene variant, than the general population. You will not be informed whether you have the gene variant, but your participation in the study might help scientists develop drugs to help individuals control their addiction to alcohol. You have a family history of alcoholism, and you are concerned that your 21-year-old son may be susceptible to the condition as well. Do you agree to participate in the study?

Now imagine that, with your participation, the study concludes that Tracy Islanders with the particular gene variant have a 10 percent chance of becoming alcoholics, whereas Tracy Islanders without the gene variant have only a 5 percent chance. Although the scientists are careful to note that the gene variant exists in the general population and is not "the cause" of alcoholism, the sound-bite reported by the media is that Tracy Islanders are hardwired to become alcoholics.

That same day, your son gets drunk at a bar and pushes an off-duty police officer through a window, killing him. Your son is charged with murder, and his lawyer wants to use his genetic predisposition toward alcoholism as a defense. Some members of your family and community are concerned that this approach will only further stigmatize Tracy Islanders as alcoholics. How do you advise your son and his lawyer?

These scenarios were presented to a panel of scientists, legal experts, journalists, and community leaders in a PBS television program entitled *Genes on Trial: Genetics, Behavior, and the Law*.[1] This chapter uses the television program as a framework for exploring the implications of behavioral genetics research for

---

1. GENES ON TRIAL: GENETICS, BEHAVIOR, AND THE LAW (Films for the Humanities & Sciences, 2004) (*transcript available at* http://www.pbs.org/fredfriendly/ourgenes/transcripts/GENES_ TRANSCRIPT.pdf).

the individual, family, community, and society. In particular, it focuses on the unique potential for behavioral genetics research, when placed in the context of criminal law, to stigmatize racial and ethnic minority groups through the blame-shifting mechanisms of genetic reductionism and genetic determinism. Like the scarlet "A" in Nathaniel Hawthorne's famous novel,[2] DNA associated with criminal or antisocial behavior might become a "scarlet gene" that marks the individual, his family, and his racial or ethnic community as "flawed, compromised, and somehow less than fully human."[3]

This chapter proceeds in six parts. The remainder of Part I summarizes the *Genes on Trial* program and introduces the issues raised by it. Part II explains why behavioral genetics research tends to focus on discrete and insular populations that overlap with socially constructed racial or ethnic groups. Part III locates behavioral genetics research on a spectrum spanning from single-gene disorders to complex behavioral traits, positing that the behavioral end of the spectrum carries the most potential for stigma. Part IV explores how the blame-shifting mechanisms of genetic reductionism and genetic determinism affect the individual, family, community, and society when genetics research focuses on criminal or antisocial behavior. Part V analyzes how racial and ethnic stigma arise from behavioral genetics research and perpetuate inequality. Part VI concludes by considering the ethical dilemmas that geneticists face when choosing who and what to study.

* * *

The *Genes on Trial* program was part of a series of Fred Friendly Seminars entitled *Our Genes/Our Choices*.[4] Fifteen panelists were sequestered together for several days and assigned to play roles in the hypothetical scenarios described above. Professor Charles Ogletree of Harvard Law School moderated the discussion by posing questions and introducing factual complications into the scenarios. The purpose of this role-playing format was to create a "human drama" that

---

2. NATHANIEL HAWTHORNE, THE SCARLET LETTER (William Charvat et al. eds., Ohio State University Press, 1962) (1850).

3. John F. Dovidio et al., *Stigma: Introduction and Overview, in* THE SOCIAL PSYCHOLOGY OF STIGMA 1, 3 (Todd F. Heatherton et al. eds., 2000).

4. OUR GENES/OUR CHOICES, http://www.pbs.org/inthebalance/archives/ourgenes/index.html (last visited Oct. 1, 2005). The other two programs in the series were WHO GETS TO KNOW? GENETICS AND PRIVACY (Films for the Humanities & Sciences, 2004) (*transcript available at* http://www.pbs.org/fredfriendly/ourgenes/transcripts/WHOKNOWS_TRANSCRIPT.pdf) and MAKING BETTER BABIES: GENETICS AND REPRODUCTION (Films for the Humanities & Sciences, 2004) (*transcript available at* http://www.pbs.org/fredfriendly/ourgenes/transcripts/BABIES_TRANSCRIPT.pdf).

would help both the panelists and the audience "to consider the issues in all their complexity."[5]

The program began with a discussion of the implications of participating in behavioral genetics research. Stanley Crouch, a columnist for the *New York Daily News*, and Karen Rothenberg played the roles of the Tracy Islander parents who were asked to participate in a study on a gene variant associated with alcoholism. While they were concerned about their son's growing symptoms of alcoholism, they were also wary of the study's potential impact on their family. Supreme Court Justice Stephen Breyer played the role of the uncle who encouraged the family to participate in the research for its contribution to scientific knowledge, while Professor Patricia King of Georgetown University Law Center played the role of another family member who feared that the research would stigmatize all Tracy Islanders as alcoholics. Dean Hamer, a geneticist at the National Cancer Institute, and David Goldman, a geneticist at the National Institute on Alcohol Abuse and Alcoholism, played the roles of university scientists, while Francis Collins, Director of the National Human Genome Research Institute, played the role of the university president.

When the conversation turned to the potential impact of the research on the Tracy Islander community, Reverend Colin Gracy of Northeastern University, playing the role of a religious leader in the Tracy Islander community, questioned the study's focus on Tracy Islanders, as did Evan Balaban, a neuroscientist at the College of Staten Island at the City University of New York, and Nadine Strossen, President of the American Civil Liberties Union, who expressed concern about the status of Tracy Islanders as a historically oppressed immigrant group. Barry Mehler, a professor of history at Ferris State University, questioned whether discovering a gene variant correlated with alcoholism would have any positive impact on social problems associated with alcoholism, such as homelessness.

The program then considered the media's role in interpreting and disseminating the results of the research. Playing the role of a journalist covering the study, Gwen Ifill, the managing editor of *Washington Week*, defended the media's role in exploring the impact of the study on the Tracy Islander community, while Alan McGowan, President of the Gene Media Forum, criticized unscrupulous journalists for reporting that "the gene for alcoholism" had been discovered. Meanwhile, Charles Ogletree switched into the role of "Brad Blueblood," the host of a syndicated show called *I'm Always Right*, who treated the study as evidence that Tracy Islanders were inherently inferior.

On the same day the study was released, the fictional Tracy Islander parents learned that their son Joseph had killed an off-duty police officer while drunk at

---

5. About Fred Friendly Seminars, http://www.pbs.org/inthebalance/archives/ourgenes/about.html (last visited Oct. 1, 2005).

a bar and was being charged with murder. Playing the role of Joseph's defense attorney, Johnnie Cochran explored the possibility of a "DNA defense," suggesting that Joseph was not responsible for murder because his genetic predisposition toward alcoholism had "taken away his free will." Meanwhile, playing the role of the prosecutor, attorney Victoria Toensing argued that Joseph should not be released on bail because, by his own admission, he had a genetic proclivity to drink and to become violent.

The program concluded with a new proposal to study the genetic influences on impulse control and aggression. While several panelists expressed skepticism about the value of such research, others emphasized the potential for behavioral genetics research to remedy social problems and to alleviate human suffering. Using the program as a springboard, this chapter explores how genetics research on criminal or antisocial behavior has the unique potential to stigmatize racial and ethnic minority groups in a manner that both reflects and reinforces social inequality.

BEHAVIORAL GENETICS RESEARCH AND "DISCRETE AND INSULAR MINORITIES"[6]

> From a geneticist's perspective, the Tracy Islanders are very interesting because they had a very small set of original founders, so there is less heterogeneity than we would expect to find in their DNA—which, simply put ... means we have a better chance of finding an answer than if we look at a very outbred group with a lot of different genetic contributions coming from a lot of places.
> —Francis Collins, Director, National Human Genome Research Institute[7]

One of the issues raised in the *Genes on Trial* program was why the genetics research on alcoholism "targeted" an ethnic minority group like the Tracy Islanders—an issue that becomes even more acute in the context of criminal law. Several factors explain why the intersection of behavioral genetics research and criminal law disproportionately affects racial and ethnic minority groups. First, genetics research tends to focus on discrete and insular populations that share a common ancestry and that often overlap with socially constructed racial or ethnic minority groups. Second, the study of genetic differences between racial or ethnic groups appeals to the persistent impulse in our society to explain racial and ethnic differences in biological terms. Finally, because racial and ethnic minority groups are disproportionately represented in the criminal

---

6. United States v. Carolene Prods. Co., 304 U.S. 144, 152 n.4 (1938). *See also infra* note 24 and accompanying text.

7. GENES ON TRIAL, *supra* note 1 (playing the role of the university president).

justice system, efforts to analyze the DNA of criminals will inevitably be skewed toward these groups.

A. Race, Ethnicity, and Genetics

While race and ethnicity are difficult and contentious terms to define, this chapter treats them both as social constructs with overlapping meanings.[8] Whereas race refers to groups identified by physical traits and geographic origin, ethnicity refers to groups sharing a common kinship, nationality, religion, language, or culture.[9] Because these categories are socially constructed, their definitions depend on the social context. What is considered "black" in the United States, for example, might be considered "white" in Brazil.[10] The U.S. Census Bureau recognizes five racial groups ("American Indian or Alaska Native," "Asian," "Black or African American," "Native Hawaiian or Other Pacific Islander," and "White") and one ethnic group ("Hispanic or Latino").[11] Although race and ethnicity are distinct concepts, this chapter analyzes them together for the purpose of exploring the impact of behavioral genetics on populations that have socially constructed group identities.

While recent forensics research suggests that race and ethnicity can be identified by DNA analysis,[12] it is commonly accepted among geneticists that race and ethnicity are not biologically determined categories and that greater genetic variation exists within racial groups than between them.[13] Nevertheless, race and

---

8. *See* Stephen Cornell & Douglas Hartmann, Ethnicity and Race: Making Identities in a Changing World 25–34 (1998).

9. *See id.* at 15–25. The federal hate crimes statute offers the following definitions: "the term 'racial group' means a set of individuals whose identity as such is distinctive in terms of physical characteristics or biological descent," 18 U.S.C. § 1093(6) (2000), and "the term 'ethnic group' means a set of individuals whose identity as such is distinctive in terms of common cultural traditions or heritage," *id.* § 1093(2).

10. Michael J. Bamshad & Steve E. Olson, *Does Race Exist?*, 289 Sci. Am. 78, 80 (2003).

· 11. *See* U.S. Census Bureau, Racial and Ethnic Classifications Used in 2000 Census and Beyond (Apr. 12, 2000), http://www.census.gov/population/www/socdemo/race/racefactcb.html; Revisions to the Standards for the Classification of Federal Data on Race and Ethnicity, 62 Fed. Reg. 58,782 (Oct. 30, 1997). The Office of Management and Budget, which sets the standards used in the U.S. Census, defines "Hispanic or Latino" as "a person of Cuban, Mexican, Puerto Rican, South or Central American, or other Spanish culture or origin, regardless of race." *Id.* at 58,789.

12. *See, e.g.*, B. Devlin & Neil Risch, *Ethnic Differentiation at VTNR Loci, with Specific Reference to Forensic Applications*, 51 Am. J. Hum. Genetics 534 (1992); Alex L. Lowe et al., *Inferring Ethnic Origin by Means of an S.T.R. Profile*, 119 Forensic Sci. Int'l 17 (2001). For a discussion of this research, *see* Troy Duster, *Selective Arrests, an Ever-Expanding DNA Forensic Database, and the Specter of an Early-Twenty-First-Century Equivalent of Phrenology, in* DNA and the Criminal Justice System 313, 322–27 (David Lazer ed., 2004).

13. *See, e.g.*, Joseph L. Graves, The Emperor's New Clothes: Biological Theories of Race at the Millennium 1–7, 193–97 (2001); Guido Barbujani et al., *An Apportionment of Human*

ethnicity can serve as rough proxies for ancestry and may therefore be salient to genetics research.[14] For example, a particular racial or ethnic group may exhibit a higher incidence of a particular gene variant than other groups, as illustrated by the example of "the alcoholism gene" and the fictional Tracy Islanders in the *Genes on Trial* program. Real-life examples of this phenomenon include the sickle-cell anemia gene in African Americans and the Tay-Sachs gene in Ashkenazi Jews.[15] This phenomenon does not indicate, however, that race and ethnicity are genetically defined; rather, it reflects evolutionary forces such as genetic drift, the founder effect, and the bottleneck effect that affect the genetic composition of small, reproductively isolated populations.[16]

Genetic drift is the fluctuation of gene frequencies within a small population caused by random mutations.[17] One form of genetic drift, known as the founder effect, occurs when a population originates from a small set of ancestors and maintains a random mutation through inbreeding because of voluntary or forced isolation.[18] This mechanism helps explain, for example, the high incidence of the Tay-Sachs gene among Ashkenazi Jews[19] and the virtual absence of the B blood type among Native Americans.[20] Another form of genetic drift, known as the bottleneck effect, occurs when a catastrophic event, such as famine, war, or an epidemic, wipes out a large portion of the population, thereby changing the composition of the gene pool that will serve as the source of repopulation.[21] In both the founder effect and the bottleneck effect, it is the inbreeding within a small

---

DNA Diversity, 94 PROC. OF THE NAT'L ACAD. OF SCI. 4516 (1997); Eliot Marshall, *Cultural Anthropology: DNA Studies Challenge the Meaning of Race*, 282 SCIENCE 654 (1998).

14. *See* Erik Lillquist & Charles A. Sullivan, *The Law and Genetics of Racial Profiling in Medicine*, 39 HARV. C.R.-C.L. L. REV. 391, 408–09 (2004); *cf.* Deborah Hellman, *Two Types of Discrimination: The Familiar and the Forgotten*, 86 CAL. L. REV. 315 (1998) (distinguishing between proxy and nonproxy discrimination).

15. *See* Lillquist & Sullivan, *supra* note 14, at 410.

16. *See id.* at 395, 418–26; *see also* Jacqueline Stevens, *Racial Meanings and Scientific Methods: Changing Policies for NIH-Sponsored Publications Reporting Human Variation*, 28 J. HEALTH POL. POL'Y & L. 1033, 1046–48 (2003).

17. *See* FRIEDRICH VOGEL & ARNO G. MOTULSKY, HUMAN GENETICS: PROBLEMS AND APPROACHES 504–05 (2d ed., 1986); *see also* STEVE OLSON, MAPPING HUMAN HISTORY: DISCOVERING THE PAST THROUGH OUR GENES 164–65 (2002) ("Genetic drift is more obvious in such small interbreeding populations because an individual who has many children can flood a population with distinctive genetic variants").

18. *See* Karen H. Rothenberg & Amy B. Rutkin, *Toward a Framework of Mutualism: The Jewish Community in Genetics Research*, 1 COMMUNITY GENETICS 148, 150 (1998). For a technical explanation of how rare recessive diseases can become prevalent in small populations due to the founder effect, *see* VOGEL & MOTULSKY, *supra* note 17, at 508.

19. Lillquist & Sullivan, *supra* note 14, at 425.

20. *See* ANTHONY J.F. GRIFFITHS et al., AN INTRODUCTION TO GENETIC ANALYSIS 807 (6th ed., 1996).

21. *See* Rothenberg & Rutkin, *supra* note 18, at 150.

population that is responsible for the unusually high incidence of the mutation, not the genetic distinctiveness of the population itself.[22]

In seeking to estimate the genetic influence on a particular trait, behavioral geneticists tend to study populations with a relatively homogeneous gene pool in order to isolate the effects of a particular gene variant on that behavioral trait.[23] Accordingly, they often focus on small, reproductively isolated populations that share a common ancestral background. Such populations tend to overlap with socially constructed racial or ethnic minority groups—what are known in constitutional law as "discrete and insular minorities."[24] This overlap is significant because the very features of discreteness and insularity that make a population useful for genetics research are also the features that make them vulnerable to societal and governmental discrimination.

In genetics, populations affected by the founder and bottleneck effects are "discrete" in that they can be identified by a common ancestral and geographical origin, and they are "insular" in that they historically have been reproductively isolated from the mainstream population. In constitutional law, racial and ethnic minority groups are "discrete" in that they generally can be identified by a distinct and often immutable trait, and they are "insular" because they historically have been segregated from mainstream society and excluded from the political process.[25] Of course, the genetic, social, and legal categories do not overlap entirely. Latinos, for example, are discrete and insular minorities in the constitutional sense but not in the genetic sense because their gene pool is relatively diverse. Likewise, while the Amish are discrete and insular minorities in the genetic sense because their culture forbids intermarriage, they are not considered racial or ethnic minorities in the constitutional sense because they cannot be identified by a distinct physical trait and historically have not been subject to the widespread discrimination and forced segregation that African Americans, Jews, Latinos, Asians, and Native Americans have experienced. Nonetheless, many of the discrete and insular populations studied in behavioral genetics happen to be racial or ethnic minority groups that have been subject to discrimination and segregation. Because such treatment has included eugenics in the form of forced sterilization, anti-miscegenation laws, and exclusionary immigration policies,

---

22. *See* Stevens, *supra* note 16, at 1046.

23. *See* Lon R. Cardon, *Practical Barriers to Identifying Complex Trait Loci, in* BEHAVIORAL GENETICS IN THE POSTGENOMIC ERA 55, 61 (Robert Plomin et al. eds., 2003).

24. United States v. Carolene Prods. Co., 304 U.S. 144, 152 n.4 (1938).

25. *See generally* JOHN HART ELY, DEMOCRACY AND DISTRUST: A THEORY OF JUDICIAL REVIEW 145–70 (1980). In defining "suspect classifications" that warrant strict judicial scrutiny under the Equal Protection Clause of the Fourteenth Amendment, the Supreme Court has identified three criteria for discrete and insular minorities: those who exhibit "obvious, immutable, or distinguishing characteristics that define them as a discrete group"; those who historically have been subject to discrimination; and those who are a "minority or politically powerless." Lyng v. Castillo, 477 U.S. 635, 638 (1986).

genetics research that focuses on these groups comes with specific historical baggage that contributes to racial and ethnic stigma.[26]

B. The Allure of Genetic Difference

Besides the methodological advantage of studying discrete and insular minority groups to isolate the effect of a particular gene variant, there is the allure of explaining racial and ethnic differences in terms of genetics.[27] In their book *The DNA Mystique*, Dorothy Nelkin and Susan Lindee document how the rhetorical and imagistic power of the gene has permeated American culture, especially in explaining and justifying social inequalities.[28] It is no surprise, then, that the focus on racial and ethnic minority groups in behavioral genetics research is readily accepted and appropriated by a popular culture that embraces the idea of genetic differences between socially constructed groups.

This phenomenon is reflected in the growing body of research on the genetic bases for differences in disease susceptibility and drug reactions among racial and ethnic groups.[29] One of the most well-known examples is research on the BRCA mutations associated with breast cancer in Ashkenazi Jewish women.[30] Other examples include research on a genetic link to prostate cancer in African American men, genetic mutations linked to asthma in individuals of Middle Eastern descent, and a gene variant associated with scleroderma in Native Americans.[31] Based on genetics research on variations in drug reactions among

---

26. *See* ALLEN BUCHANAN ET AL., FROM CHANCE TO CHOICE: GENETICS AND JUSTICE 27–46 (2000); Rothenberg & Rutkin, *supra* note 18, at 150. For cases discussing these policies, *see* Loving v. Virginia, 388 U.S. 1 (1967) (anti-miscegenation); Buck v. Bell, 274 U.S. 200 (1927) (forced sterilization); and The Chinese Exclusion Case, 130 U.S. 581 (1889) (immigration).

27. *See* BUCHANAN ET AL., *supra* note 26, at 23; Stevens, *supra* note 16, at 1072.

28. DOROTHY NELKIN & M. SUSAN LINDEE, THE DNA MYSTIQUE: THE GENE AS A CULTURAL ICON (1995).

29. Lillquist & Sullivan, *supra* note 14, at 393; Stevens, *supra* note 16, at 1034.

30. *See generally* Karen H. Rothenberg, *Breast Cancer, The Genetic "Quick Fix," and the Jewish Community*, 7 HEALTH MATRIX 98 (1997); Stevens, *supra* note 16, at 1042. For a technical explanation of the BRCA mutations, *see* JACK J. PASTERNAK, AN INTRODUCTION TO HUMAN MOLECULAR GENETICS: MECHANISMS OF INHERITED DISEASES 490–92 (2d ed., 2005).

31. Stevens, *supra* note 16, at 1056–57. One of the most controversial examples is the "slavery hypothesis," which seeks to explain the higher incidence of hypertension among African Americans by positing that when their ancestors were brought as slaves from Africa to America, those with genetic predispositions toward salt retention were more likely to survive the arduous voyage and thus form the original gene pool of African Americans. *See id.* at 1071–73; Stephen J. Dubner, *Toward a Unified Theory of Black America*, N.Y. TIMES MAG., Mar. 20, 2005, at 54 (describing the work of Harvard economist Roland Fryer); Jay S. Kaufman, *The Anatomy of a Medical Myth*, SOCIAL SCIENCE RESEARCH COUNCIL, http://raceandgenomics.ssrc.org/Kaufman (last visited Oct. 1, 2005).

different racial and ethnic groups,[32] pharmaceutical companies are now marketing drugs for specific racial and ethnic groups, such as BiDil, a hypertension drug targeted at African Americans.[33] On a broader scale, the newly launched International HapMap Project seeks to "find genes that affect health, disease, and individual responses to medications and environmental factors" by studying four population groups from Nigeria, Japan, China, and the United States.[34]

Such research is driven in part by government policies that seek to include racial and ethnic minority groups in medical research. As mandated by federal statute,[35] for example, the National Institutes of Health (NIH) requires all federally funded clinical research to include racial and ethnic minorities as subjects unless such inclusion is "inappropriate," and to review any evidence of "significant" racial or ethnic differences in the intervention effect.[36] Similarly, the Food and Drug Administration advocates the collection of race and ethnicity data in all clinical trials.[37] As a form of affirmative action in medical research, these guidelines engender tension analogous to that surrounding racial and ethnic affirmative action in higher education and employment. While colorblindness in those contexts may only perpetuate "the effects of centuries of law-sanctioned inequality,"[38] singling out racial and ethnic minorities for special treatment threatens to stigmatize them as "undeserving."[39] Similarly, when placed in the context of genetics research, the focus on racial and ethnic minorities may be a mixed blessing: while it may draw attention and resources to problems afflicting the minority community, it may also stigmatize the community as genetically inferior and reify the socially constructed notion of race.[40] This tension exists, for example, in the Jewish community regarding research on the BRCA gene variants associated with breast cancer. While some members of the community welcome such research for its potential to advance both the community's health and society's scientific knowledge, others view the research as targeting Jews for genetic screening in the historical shadow of Nazi eugenics.[41]

---

32. See Stevens, *supra* note 16, at 1058–59.

33. Sally L. Satel, *I Am a Racially Profiling Doctor*, N.Y. Times Mag., May 5, 2002, at 58.

34. International HapMap Project, About the HapMap (2002), http://www.hapmap. org/thehap map.html.en.

35. NIH Revitalization Act of 1993, 42 U.S.C. § 289a-2 (2000).

36. National Institutes of Health, NIH Policy and Guidelines on the Inclusion of Women and Minorities as Subjects in Clinical Research (Oct. 2001), http://grants.nih. gov/grants/funding/women_min/ guidelines_amended_10_2001.htm.

37. See Draft Guidance for Industry on the Collection of Race and Ethnicity in Clinical Trials for FDA Regulated Products, 68 Fed. Reg. 4788 (Jan. 30, 2003).

38. Gratz v. Bollinger, 539 U.S. 244, 298–304 (2003) (Ginsburg, J., dissenting).

39. Grutter v. Bollinger, 539 U.S. 306, 373 (2003) (Thomas, J., dissenting).

40. See Lillquist & Sullivan, *supra* note 14, at 399–400.

41. See Rothenberg & Rutkin, *supra* note 18, at 149–50; Marc D. Schwartz, Karen Rothenberg, Linda Joseph, Judith Benkendorf, & Caryn Lerman, *Consent to the Use of*

A related concern in the African American community is that genetics research on racial differences in health traits will legitimize genetics research on racial differences in behavioral traits.[42] Indeed, the allure of genetic difference is not limited to medical research. Traits that recently have been attributed to heredity in the mass media include aggression, intelligence, homosexuality, impulsiveness, exhibitionism, family loyalty, addiction, religiosity, deviance, learning disability, and happiness.[43] As illustrated by the controversial bestseller *The Bell Curve*,[44] perhaps one of the most pervasive and perverse ideas in American society is that blacks are genetically less intelligent than whites and Asians.[45] This impulse to seek genetic explanations for racial and ethnic differences may explain why behavioral genetics research that focuses on racial and ethnic minority groups is so readily sensationalized in the popular press.

C. Racial and Ethnic Bias and the Criminal Justice System

When placed in the context of criminal law, behavioral genetics research is even more likely to focus on racial and ethnic minority groups. Although "stereotypes about race and crime may make it more likely that researchers will look for a gene for aggression or criminality in a minority population,"[46] the more likely scenario is that genetics research on criminal behavior will focus on blacks and Latinos simply because they are disproportionately represented in the criminal population. From 1990 to 2004, blacks were five times more likely than whites to be incarcerated,[47] and in 2000, blacks and Latinos comprised 63 percent of incarcerated adults, even though together they represented only 25 percent of the total population.[48]

Attributing these trends to the War on Drugs, racial profiling, discriminatory sentencing, and general racial bias in the criminal justice system, sociologist Troy Duster warns that because African Americans are disproportionately represented

---

Stored DNA for Genetics Research: A Survey of Attitudes in the Jewish Population, 98 AM. J. MED. GENETICS 336 (2001).

42. *See* Lillquist & Sullivan, *supra* note 14, at 392, 399–40.

43. *See* Dorothy Nelkin, *Behavioral Genetics and Dismantling the Welfare State*, in BEHAVIORAL GENETICS: THE CLASH OF CULTURE AND BIOLOGY 156, 156 (Ronald A. Carson & Mark A. Rothstein eds., 1999) [hereinafter BEHAVIORAL GENETICS].

44. RICHARD J. HERRNSTEIN & CHARLES MURRAY, THE BELL CURVE: INTELLIGENCE AND CLASS STRUCTURE IN AMERICAN LIFE (1994).

45. *See* GRAVES, *supra* note 13, at 157–72; NELKIN & LINDEE, *supra* note 28, at 112–17.

46. Lori B. Andrews, *Predicting and Punishing Antisocial Acts: How the Criminal Justice System Might Use Behavioral Genetics*, in BEHAVIORAL GENETICS, *supra* note 43, at 116, 133.

47. Bureau of Justice Statistics, U.S. Department of Justice, Blacks Were Two Times More Likely Than Hispanics and Five Times More Likely Than Whites To Be in Jail (Apr. 24, 2005), http://www.ojp.usdoj.gov/bjs/glance/jailrair.htm.

48. Human Rights Watch, Race and Incarceration in the United States (Feb. 27, 2002), http://www.hrw.org/backgrounder/usa/race.

in the criminal justice system, behavioral genetics research relying on the DNA samples of convicted criminals will inevitably be skewed toward that population.[49] All fifty states, along with the U.S. Army and the FBI, now contribute to the Combined DNA Index System (CODIS), a national database containing the DNA profiles of nearly 2.5 million convicted offenders.[50] Although currently used only for identification and forensic purposes, these DNA profiles could potentially be used for behavioral genetics research, resulting in a study implicitly focusing on African Americans and Latinos.[51] The results of that study, in turn, could stigmatize all African Americans and Latinos as prone to criminal behavior, thereby reinforcing existing stereotypes and promoting discrimination in other contexts.

FROM DISEASE TO BEHAVIOR: THE SPECTRUM OF GENETICS RESEARCH

[G]enetics is an incredibly powerful science when... [we] know what we're studying. When we have a condition that is medically defined, like heart disease, we have a clearly defined population of things that we're trying to study and learn about. When we move to something like alcoholism, that may be a whole lot more nebulous, [but] at least there is clinical agreement on patterns of behavior that constitute a problem. Now, we have moved into a brand new arena. We are using terms—"impulsiveness," "aggression"— that are very difficult to define in the operational ways that scientists need to define things.
—Evan Balaban, Professor, College of Staten Island, City University of New York[52]

The *Genes on Trial* program concluded with a hypothetical proposal to study the genetic bases of impulsiveness and aggression. As reflected in the skepticism expressed by several of the panelists, the strength and impact of genetics research vary along the spectrum of traits that are studied. As one moves toward the behavioral end of the spectrum, the genetic influence on a trait becomes more uncertain and difficult to isolate, while the stigma associated with such influence becomes more significant. Because criminality is a stigmatic trait, any research on genetic influences on criminal behavior threatens to stigmatize the population being studied.

---

49. *See* Duster, *supra* note 12, at 316–22, 328–29; Troy Duster, *Genetics, Race, and Crime: Recurring Seduction to a False Precision, in* DNA ON TRIAL: GENETIC INFORMATION AND CRIMINAL JUSTICE 129, 132–33 (Paul R. Billings ed., 1992); Troy Duster, *Race and Reification in Science,* 307 SCIENCE 1050, 1051 (2005); *see also* Andrews, *supra* note 46, at 134.

50. Federal Bureau of Investigation, National DNA Index System (July 2005), http://www.fbi.gov/hq/lab/codis/national.htm.

51. *See* Chapter 11, David Kaye, *Behavioral Genetics Research and DNA Databases, in* THE IMPACT OF BEHAVIORAL SCIENCES ON CRIMINAL LAW (Nita A. Farahany, ed., 2009).

52. GENES ON TRIAL, *supra* note 1.

A. The Spectrum of Genetics Research

Genetics research exists on a spectrum that varies in the complexity and precision of the traits being studied. At one end of the spectrum is the study of single-gene disorders, such as sickle-cell anemia and Huntington's disease, which are caused by a single gene variant. Even at this end of the spectrum, however, where the relationship between genotype and phenotype is the closest, geneticists cannot always predict with certainty when the condition will develop or how severe it will be.[53]

Next on the spectrum is the study of complex medical diseases, such as cancer, caused by the interaction of multiple genetic and environmental factors. Although a single gene variant, such as the BRCA mutations associated with breast cancer, may increase the probability of developing the disease, it remains difficult to isolate the effect of the mutation from that of other genetic and environmental factors.[54] Thus, even if an individual has the gene variant associated with cancer, one cannot predict whether that individual will actually develop cancer, much less when she will develop it and how severe it will be.[55]

Further on the spectrum is the study of complex behavioral conditions or diseases, such as alcoholism, drug addiction, and depression. The genetic influence on these conditions is even more difficult to isolate because their symptoms often involve an element of individual choice. Moreover, such conditions are more elusive research subjects because they are more difficult to define and to diagnose than medical diseases like hypertension and breast cancer. Nevertheless, as Evan Balaban pointed out during the *Genes on Trial* program, these conditions at least have clinical definitions upon which scientists can agree.

Finally, at the other end of the spectrum is the study of behavioral traits, such as aggression, intelligence, and impulsiveness. Like behavioral conditions or diseases, these traits are influenced not only by genetic and environmental factors, but also by individual choices, thus making their heritability difficult to identify. And because of their social and political implications, the definitions of these traits are often as hotly contested as their heritability.[56] Thus, behavioral traits

---

53. Mark A. Rothstein, *Behavioral Genetic Determinism: Its Effects on Culture and Law, in* BEHAVIORAL GENETICS, *supra* note 43, at 89, 92; Francis S. Collins et al., *Heredity and Humanity*, NEW REPUBLIC, June 25, 2001, at 27–28.

54. *See* Rothstein, *supra* note 53, at 92–93.

55. Rothenberg & Rutkin, *supra* note 18, at 151.

56. *See* Rothstein, *supra* note 53, at 93. The line between behavioral conditions or diseases and behavioral traits is blurry and tentative; it may well be that if research were to definitively link aggression to a particular gene, it would be considered a disease. However, it is useful for the purpose of this chapter to distinguish between conditions or diseases that have clinical definitions on which scientists commonly agree and traits that lack operational definitions and criteria for diagnosis.

are the most indeterminate and controversial subjects of genetics research. At the same time, they may be the most relevant to criminal law. Although genetic disorders like Huntington's disease and XYY trisomy have formed the bases of criminal defenses in the past,[57] criminal law is now particularly interested in behavioral conditions that contribute to violence, such as alcoholism and mental illness, and antisocial behavioral traits, such as aggression.[58]

B. The Stigma of Behavior

The behavioral end of the spectrum of genetics research is not only the most scientifically problematic, but also the most potentially stigmatic. As explained above, behavioral traits are not as precisely defined as diseases and thus are subject to manipulation and misunderstanding. Moreover, because behavioral traits involve a strong element of individual choice, they are more closely associated with fault, even if they are deemed genetic. Ironically, the weaker the causal link between the gene and the condition, the more stigmatizing the gene may be, since those who carry the gene are grouped with those who are at "fault" for their condition. For example, as long as some cases of alcoholism can be attributed entirely to individual choice, then alcoholics who are genetically predisposed toward the condition bear the burden of demonstrating that they, unlike their counterparts, did not "choose" to become alcoholics—a burden that individuals with sickle-cell anemia, for example, never have to bear.

Furthermore, traits that potentially threaten society, such as aggression, are more stigmatic than traits that potentially threaten individual health, such as Tay-Sachs disease.[59] Whereas the latter is a basis for making individual decisions about marriage and childbearing,[60] the former is a basis for making social

---

57. See TED PETERS, PLAYING GOD? GENETIC DETERMINISM AND HUMAN FREEDOM 69–72 (2d ed., 2003); Andrews, supra note 46, at 124–26. For examples of defenses based on Huntington's disease, see United States v. Click, 807 F.2d 847 (9th Cir. 1987); Caldwell v. State, 354 S.E.2d 124 (Ga. 1987); Scammahorn v. State, 506 N.E.2d 1097 (Ind. 1987); and People v. Ponke, No. 180310, 1997 WL 33354421 (Mich. Ct. App. Jan. 24, 1997). For examples of defenses based on XYY trisomy, see People v. Tanner, 91 Cal. Rptr. 656 (Cal. Ct. App. 1970); Millard v. State, 261 A.2d 227 (Md. Ct. Spec. App. 1970); People v. Yukl, 372 N.Y.S.2d 313 (N.Y. Sup. Ct. 1975); and State v. Roberts, 544 P.2d 754 (Wash. Ct. App. 1976).

58. See, e.g., PETERS, supra note 57, at 77 (discussing the connection between crime and alcohol).

59. Cf. id. at 72 ("If we carry a defective gene for breast cancer, then we certainly can feel empathy for someone else who carries the gene for cystic fibrosis. But if that other person carries a gene predisposing him or her to harm us, then this adds an additional element of considerable consequence"). But see id. at 66–67 (noting that individuals with Huntington's disease are stigmatized as violent).

60. See, e.g., Rothenberg & Rutkin, supra note 18, at 151.

policies about surveillance and preventive detention.[61] Similarly, stigma associated with criminal or antisocial behavior is more far-reaching and disabling than stigma associated with disease because one's behavior is relevant to a wider range of social contexts. While there already is extensive literature on the potential for genetic discrimination in insurance and employment, genetics information has many other potential applications, such as in educational placement, tort liability, loan approval, and child custody.[62] A genetic predisposition toward impulsiveness, for example, might not only increase one's car insurance rates but also count against one's creditworthiness in a mortgage application. More immediately, many of the bases for termination of parental rights, such as cruelty, alcoholism, mental illness, sexual promiscuity, and criminal activity, are traits being studied in behavioral genetics research.[63] Because a genetic predisposition toward criminal or antisocial behavior is relevant to nearly every aspect of life, the stigma associated with that predisposition is especially threatening.

THE FAULTY GENE: REDUCTIONISM, DETERMINISM, AND BLAME SHIFTING

Let's say you do this study and you find out that our family or groups of families have these predispositions [toward alcoholism]. I'm worried he's going to drink more because now he's going to have an excuse. And he's going to say, "See, I'm not a bad guy. You did it, Mom and Dad, both of you did it to [me]."

—Karen Rothenberg, Dean, University of Maryland School of Law[64]

What the study tells me is that your problems are not the result of job discrimination; it's not the result of any kind of ethnic bias; it's not the result of poverty or anything else. The problem is inside of you. It's not the environment. It's you.

—Charles Ogletree, Professor, Harvard Law School[65]

[T]he flip side of the defense of this particular individual is an indictment, so to speak, of not only him but the entire community.

—Nadine Strossen, President, American Civil Liberties Union[66]

---

61. *See* Andrews, *supra* note 46, at 132–38.

62. *See id.* at 131, 138; Rothstein, *supra* note 53, at 107.

63. *See* Andrews, *supra* note 46, at 138. For a discussion of statutes and case law governing the termination of parental rights based on behavioral traits, *see* Sherry S. Zimmerman, Annotation, *Parents' Mental Illness or Mental Deficiency as Ground for Termination of Parental Rights*, 113 A.L.R. 5th 349 (2003).

64. GENES ON TRIAL, *supra* note 1 (playing the role of the mother).

65. *Id.* (playing the role of "Brad Blueblood").

66. *Id.*

As illustrated by the *Genes on Trial* program, behavioral genetics research, like other genetics research, is vulnerable to the fallacies of genetic reductionism and genetic determinism. By overstating the genetic influence on human behavior, these fallacies shift blame among the individual, family, community, and society. Like the individual's decision to participate in behavioral genetics research, the individual's decision to use such research to support a criminal defense can operate as a double-edged sword: while it may mitigate his culpability by shifting blame away from his "free will," it may also stigmatize him, his family, and his racial or ethnic community as being prone to criminal behavior.

A. Genetic Reductionism, Genetic Determinism, and Blame Shifting

Genetic reductionism is the impulse to treat genetics, or even a single gene, as the sole cause of a particular trait, discounting the interaction of other genes, the environment, and "free will."[67] The idea of "the alcoholism gene" is an example of genetic reductionism, as it treats alcoholism as a single-gene disorder unaffected by other genes, the environment, or individual choice. Genetic determinism is the impulse to treat DNA as destiny, discounting the possibility of deviating from one's genetic predisposition.[68] The idea that an individual is "hardwired" to become an alcoholic is an example of genetic determinism, as it suggests that a predisposition toward alcoholism cannot be changed by individual choice or social intervention.[69] Together, genetic reductionism and genetic determinism describe different aspects of the same fallacy: the overemphasis on the influence of genes on human behavior.[70] Whereas genetic reductionism is a backward-looking framework for understanding the cause of a trait, genetic determinism is a forward-looking framework for predicting the future. Both are appealing in part because they "extend the certainty and predictability of science to troubling and controversial terrains."[71] They also reflect the emphasis in

---

67. Rothenberg, *supra* note 30, at 102–3 ("Genetic reductionism results when all traits, health problems, and behaviors become attributable to genes and no attention is paid to other potential factors").

68. *See id.* ("Genetic determinism results when an individual believes her future is defined and predicted by genetic makeup and cannot be changed").

69. *See* NELKIN & LINDEE, *supra* note 28, at 195–96 ("Traits that are genetic appear as immutable, deeply resistant to change initiated through individual action or external intervention. . . . The ideology of genetic essentialism encourages submission to nature and to constraints on the possibilities for social change").

70. *See* Rothenberg, *supra* note 30, at 102–3 ("Genetic myopia is a condition that results from viewing everything from the perspective of genetics"). Dorothy Nelkin and Susan Lindee call this condition "genetic essentialism," which "reduces the self to a molecular entity, equating human beings, in all their social, historical, and moral complexity, with their genes." NELKIN & LINDEE, *supra* note 28, at 2.

71. Nelkin, *supra* note 43, at 158.

current American political culture on individual responsibility, as opposed to societal or governmental intervention.[72]

Because the concept of fault is closely linked to the concept of causation,[73] and because genetic reductionism and genetic determinism treat the gene as the ultimate and determinative cause of a particular behavior, they shift blame for the behavior away from both individual "free will" and the environment created by the family, community, and society.[74] In the context of criminal law, as illustrated by the *Genes on Trial* program, the defendant can invoke a reductive and determinist view of behavioral genetics to shift blame away from his "free will" and thus demonstrate either that he lacked the mens rea to commit the offense or that he does not deserve the full extent of punishment because he is not fully culpable for the crime.[75]

B. Effects of Blame Shifting on the Individual, Family, Community, and Society

When viewed through a determinist lens, behavioral genetics research can create a self-fulfilling prophecy. For example, when an individual learns that she is genetically predisposed to alcoholism, she may react in one of two ways: If she believes her genetic background is only a predisposition and not predestination, she may be more vigilant about not drinking in order to avoid triggering her heightened appetite for alcohol. But if she takes the determinist view and believes that she cannot control her drinking and thus cannot be blamed for becoming addicted to alcohol, she may actually drink more than she would otherwise.[76] By shifting blame to her genes and away from her individual autonomy, she fulfills the prophecy of genetic determinism.

In some cases, behavioral genetics research may provide "moral relief for stigmatized conditions" by framing the behavioral trait as a "natural" result of human biology rather than a conscious choice of moral depravity.[77] Many gay rights activists, for example, welcome research on the so-called gay gene because

---

72. *See* NELKIN & LINDEE, *supra* note 28, at 128–29.

73. In tort law, for example, a person who causes an injury is deemed to be at fault and thus responsible for compensating the victim of the injury. For a philosophical discussion of the relationship between causal responsibility and moral blameworthiness, *see* MARION SMILEY, MORAL RESPONSIBILITY AND THE BOUNDARIES OF COMMUNITY (1992).

74. *See* Andrews, *supra* note 46, at 119.

75. *See id.* at 120–21; *see* Chapter 7, Nita A. Farahany & James E. Coleman Jr., *Genetics, Neuroscience, and Criminal Responsibility, in* THE IMPACT OF BEHAVIORAL SCIENCES ON CRIMINAL LAW (Nita A. Farahany, ed., 2009).

76. *See* Allison Morse, *Searching for the Holy Grail: The Human Genome Project and Its Implications*, 13 J. L. & HEALTH 219, 241–42 (1999) ("[Research demonstrates that] a person who believes she is an alcoholic, when informed a particular drink contains alcohol, will consume more of the drink than the average person, even if there is no alcohol in the drink").

77. Nelkin, *supra* note 43, at 158.

it responds to charges that homosexuality is "unnatural" and shifts blame away from individual choices.[78] Indeed, such research was pioneered by gay men, including geneticist Dean Hamer and neuroscientist Simon LeVay.[79] Some members of the gay community expect genetics research on homosexuality to advance gay rights, as courts have denied gays and lesbians heightened constitutional protection from discrimination precisely because they view homosexuality as "behavioral" and not "immutable" like race and sex.[80] Others point out, however, that attributing homosexuality to a genetic mutation may suggest that gays and lesbians are "abnormal" and that homosexuality can be "cured" like other "disorders."[81] Even more troubling, discovery of a "gay gene" could lead to genetic screening, genetic engineering, and selective abortion of gay fetuses.[82]

Similar dynamics exist with respect to the family. In some instances, behavioral genetics research may shift blame away from the environment that parents create for their children. In the 1950s and 1960s, for example, schizophrenia was blamed on poor parenting, particularly the uncaring mother.[83] The National Alliance for the Mentally Ill thus supported research on the genetic link to schizophrenia "because it relieved the parents of the mentally ill from blame."[84] At the same time, however, parents of the mentally ill fear that they may be blamed for passing on "defective" genes and thus be restricted in their reproductive freedom.[85]

When behavioral genetics research associates a gene with both a deviant behavior and a racial or ethnic community, genetic reductionism and genetic

---

78. See PETERS, supra note 57, at 97–98; Rothstein, supra note 53, at 96.

79. See, e.g., DEAN HAMER & PETER COPELAND, THE SCIENCE OF DESIRE: THE SEARCH FOR THE GAY GENE AND THE BIOLOGY OF BEHAVIOR (1994); Dean H. Hamer et al., A Linkage Between DNA Markers on the X Chromosome and Male Sexual Orientation, 261 SCIENCE 321 (1993); Simon A. LeVay, A Difference in Hypothalamic Structure Between Heterosexual and Homosexual Men, 253 SCIENCE 1034 (1991). For a discussion of this research, see NELKIN & LINDEE, supra note 28, at 119–20, and PETERS, supra note 57, at 98–102.

80. High Tech Gays v. Def. Indus. Sec. Clearance Office, 895 F.2d 563, 573–74 (9th Cir. 1990); Woodward v. United States, 871 F.2d 1068, 1076 (Fed. Cir. 1989).

81. See NELKIN & LINDEE, supra note 28, at 122 (quoting a National Enquirer headline: "Simple injection will let gay men turn straight, doctors report"); PETERS, supra note 57, at 106–7; Rothstein, supra note 53, at 96.

82. See NELKIN & LINDEE, supra note 28, at 122 (quoting Harvard Law School Professor Janet Halley's prediction that genetic explanations for homosexuality will encourage "the development of anti-gay eugenics"); PETERS, supra note 57, at 107. The prospect of aborting a gay fetus was the subject of Jonathan Tolins's 1993 Broadway play The Twilight of the Golds.

83. David C. Rowe & Kristen C. Jacobsen, In the Mainstream: Research in Behavioral Genetics, in BEHAVIORAL GENETICS, supra note 43, at 12, 14–15.

84. Nelkin, supra note 43, at 167; see also NELKIN & LINDEE, supra note 28, at 147; Allan J. Tobin, Amazing Grace: Sources of Phenotypic Variation in Genetic Boosterism, in BEHAVIORAL GENETICS, supra note 43, at 1–2.

85. See NELKIN & LINDEE, supra note 28, at 147; Nelkin, supra note 43, at 167.

determinism may shift blame to the community itself in the form of racial or ethnic stigma. Because behavioral genetics research draws statistical conclusions about a sample population and not about specific individuals, it is likely that an individual who possesses a trait will not know whether he possesses the gene variant associated with the trait. The only thing he will know is that he is a member of the racial or ethnic group associated with the gene. Because the only known "cause" of the trait is membership in the racial or ethnic group, it is the group itself that bears the brunt of the blame.

By attributing a trait entirely to genetic factors, a reductive and determinist view of behavioral genetics research can also shift blame away from environmental factors created by society. To avoid legal liability and social disapproval for causing medical and behavioral maladies, industries are now funding genetics research to shift blame away from their products. For example, the Ernest Gallo Clinic and Research Center established by Gallo Winery at the University of California San Francisco conducts research on the genetic link to alcoholism. If such a link is established, "some of the social pressure against alcoholic beverages and their purveyors might be deflected onto 'faulty' genes."[86] Tobacco companies fund similar research on lung cancer,[87] and genetic predisposition to a disease is a common defense in toxic tort litigation.[88] By locating the cause of the trait in the individual's genome, genetic reductionism shifts blame away from the industry. By framing the trait as predestined and immutable, genetic determinism alleviates pressure for the industry to change the toxic environment that it creates.

Similarly, research that seeks to explain racial or ethnic inequality in terms of genetics both shifts blame away from societal and governmental discrimination and alleviates pressure for society and the state to change the discriminatory environments that they create. Genetic reductionism justifies racial and ethnic inequality as the "natural" result of innate differences. Genetic determinism rejects societal and governmental efforts to eliminate inequality as futile, since such inequality is genetically predestined.[89] The Bell Curve, for example, argued that social welfare programs and affirmative action are futile because blacks are

---

86. Rothstein, supra note 53, at 96; see also Nelkin, supra note 43, at 160.

87. See Nelkin, supra note 43, at 167 (citing Jon Cohen, Tobacco Money Lights Up a Debate, 272 SCIENCE 488 (1996)).

88. See id.; cf. Karen Rothenberg et al., Genetic Information and the Workplace: Legislative Approaches and Policy Challenges, 275 SCIENCE 1755, 1756 (1997) ("Some state laws provide for genetic testing by employers in order to determine an employee's susceptibility to toxic chemicals or substances in the workplace, even though cleaning up the environment would enhance the working conditions for all employees and would alleviate the need for genetic testing of individual employees").

89. See Rothstein, supra note 53, at 95 ("[G]enetic determinism is the scientific justification for social inequality, social Darwinism, and the status quo"); see also Nelkin, supra note 43, at 164.

genetically less intelligent than whites and Asians.[90] As Dorothy Nelkin concludes,

> [B]y locating the source of social problems within the individual, theories of genetic causation also serve political agendas, for they reduce the responsibility of the state. Moreover, genetic explanations of behavior translate into moral guidelines about normal, or natural behavior. At the same time, they provide the equivalent of moral absolution, exonerating individuals by attributing antisocial acts to an independent biological force beyond the influence of volition—the DNA.[91]

C. Blame Shifting as a Double-Edged Sword in Criminal Law

Although blame shifting may seem attractive to a criminal defendant, invoking genetic reductionism and genetic determinism to support a criminal defense can be a double-edged sword. As illustrated by the scenario presented in the *Genes on Trial* program, an individual's decision to introduce evidence of a genetic predisposition toward criminal behavior can backfire on himself, his family, and his community. If the defendant claims that he cannot control his genetic tendency toward violence, then the government may turn that against him and argue that he should not be released on bail or given the possibility of parole, as he poses a permanent danger to society. And if this particular defendant has the "gene for aggression," the argument goes, then members of his family and racial or ethnic group likely have the gene too. Nelkin warns, "If it is accepted that genetic endowment determines the propensity to commit bad acts, then hereditary traits, which often reduce to ethnic group membership, may one day be considered evidence of the commission of the crime."[92]

This possibility is not as remote as one would hope. In a recent case, an Ohio trial court sentenced a Native American defendant, who had been convicted of assaulting two police officers while she was drunk, to quit her job as a waitress in a bar, to refrain from consuming alcohol for two years, to undergo alcoholism counseling, and to "write a paper regarding your [sic]—for educational purposes— on alcoholism and the American Indians."[93] During trial, the court asked the defendant's mother whether she knew "anything about genetic predisposition to alcoholism," whether she had "ever been on an Indian reservation," and whether "she had ever seen 'the Scotch or Irish drinking.'"[94] The trial court also asked the

---

90. PETERS, *supra* note 57, at 82–83 (describing *The Bell Curve*'s hypotheses).

91. Nelkin, *supra* note 43, at 158.

92. Rochelle Cooper Dreyfuss & Dorothy Nelkin, *The Jurisprudence of Genetics*, 45 VAND. L. REV. 313, 331 (1992).

93. State v. Madey, No. 81166, 2002 WL 31429827, at *2 (Ohio Ct. App. Oct. 31, 2002) (emphasis removed) (quoting the trial court).

94. *Id.* at *1 (quoting the trial court).

defendant's mother whether she was concerned "that her daughter would become 'a flaming alcoholic' because, with such an ethnic background, 'there [was] nothing she can do about it.'"[95]

Similarly, employing genetic reductionism and genetic determinism in a criminal defense may stigmatize those who carry the "faulty" gene in other contexts. When research in the 1960s suggested a link between XYY trisomy and violence, for example, not only did criminal defendants blame their violence on their extra Y chromosome,[96] but thousands of law-abiding XYY males were stigmatized as "congenital criminals," and hospitals began screening newborns for XYY, potentially for selective abortion.[97] Likewise, when Huntington's disease was raised as part of an insanity defense by a woman who had shot her children,[98] the Huntington's Disease Society of America worried that the defense would stigmatize all Huntington's sufferers as violent and lead to discrimination in other areas, such as employment.[99] As theologian Ted Peters puts it, "One possible scenario from such a precedent is that genetic determinism might end up declaring those committing crimes innocent and stigmatizing those not committing crimes as potentially guilty."[100]

THE DISCREDITING GENE: RACIAL AND ETHNIC STIGMA

Tracy Islanders are going to be known as the alcoholics of the country. And so whenever I go someplace and they say, "Oh, you're a Tracy Islander," they will say, "Oh, we don't want to hire you." Or they will say, "Oh, you come from that group, that genetically deformed, defective group. You carry the gene for alcoholism."
—Patricia King, Professor, Georgetown University Law Center[101]

When viewed through the lenses of reductionism and determinism, behavioral genetics research has a unique potential to stigmatize racial and ethnic minority groups. Because of the "discrete and insular" character of these groups, and because of the salience of race and ethnicity in our society, racial and ethnic stigmas are more powerful and pervasive than other types of stigma.

---

95. *Id.* (alteration in original) (quoting the trial court).

96. *See, e.g.,* cases cited *supra* note 57.

97. *See* PETERS, *supra* note 57, at 69–72. *See generally* DAVID SUZUKI & PETER KNUDTSON, GENETHICS: THE CLASH BETWEEN THE NEW GENETICS AND HUMAN VALUES 141–59 (1989).

98. Caldwell v. State, 354 S.E. 2d 124 (Ga. 1987).

99. PETERS, *supra* note 57, at 66–67; Andrews, *supra* note 46, at 119–20, 125.

100. PETERS, *supra* note 57, at 67.

101. GENES ON TRIAL, *supra* note 1 (playing the role of a Tracy Islander).

A. Deconstructing Stigma

The term "stigma" historically refers to a physical mark branded on a criminal or slave to identify the person as dangerous or subhuman.[102] Like the "A" that marks the adulteress in *The Scarlet Letter*, a stigma serves as a badge of opprobrium, signaling to society that the individual should be "discredited, scorned, and avoided."[103] Racial and ethnic stigmas are "dishonorable meanings socially inscribed on arbitrary bodily marks," such as skin color, that identify an individual as a member of a racial or ethnic group.[104] A racially stigmatized person is "reduced in our minds from a whole and usual person to a tainted, discounted one," undeserving of full participation in mainstream society.[105]

Not coincidentally, these definitions of racial and ethnic stigma overlap with the constitutional criteria for "discrete and insular minorities" who, because of their stigmatized social status, require special judicial solicitude.[106] The notion of stigma provides a conceptual link among the criteria: it is because the discrete marks of race and ethnicity signal inferiority that racial and ethnic minority groups historically have been subject to discrimination and excluded from mainstream society. In addition, just as the discreteness and insularity of racial and ethnic minority groups are what make them "interesting" subjects of genetics research,[107] they are also what make racial and ethnic stigmas more pernicious than other types of stigma.

---

102. *See* ERVING GOFFMAN, STIGMA: NOTES ON THE MANAGEMENT OF SPOILED IDENTITY 1 (1963); R. A. Lenhardt, *Understanding the Mark: Race, Stigma, and Equality in Context*, 79 N.Y.U. L. REV. 803, 814–15 (2004); *see also* OXFORD ENGLISH DICTIONARY 689 (2d ed., 1989).

103. Lenhardt, *supra* note 102, at 814 (quoting Steven L. Neuberg et al., *Why People Stigmatize: Toward a Biocultural Framework*, in THE SOCIAL PSYCHOLOGY OF STIGMA, *supra* note 3, at 31, 31).

104. *Id.* at 809 (quoting GLENN C. LOURY, THE ANATOMY OF RACIAL INEQUALITY 59 (2002)).

105. *Id.* at 818 (quoting GOFFMAN, *supra* note 102, at 3).

106. *See supra* Part II.A. *See generally* Deborah Hellman, *The Expressive Dimension of Equal Protection*, 85 MINN. L. REV. 1 (2000). Glenn Loury defines "race" as "a cluster of inheritable bodily markings carried by a largely endogamous group of individuals, markings that can be observed by others with ease, that can be changed or misrepresented only with great difficulty, and that have come to be invested in a particular society at a given historical moment with social meaning. This definition has three aspects: ease of identification, relative immutability, and social signification." LOURY, *supra* note 104, at 20–21. This definition also overlaps with the Supreme Court's definition of "discrete and insular minorities" as those who exhibit "obvious, immutable, or distinguishing characteristics that define them as a discrete group"; those who historically have been subject to discrimination; and those who are a "minority or politically powerless." Lyng v. Castillo, 477 U.S. 635, 638 (1986).

107. GENES ON TRIAL, *supra* note 1 (Francis Collins).

In the context of behavioral genetics, the "faulty" gene associated with criminal or antisocial behavior is the mark that identifies the individual as dangerous and subhuman. The potential for racial or ethnic stigma arises when behavioral genetics research associates the faulty gene with a racial or ethnic minority group.[108] Because the faulty gene cannot be readily perceived and thus serves as a poor signaling device,[109] the physical marks of race or ethnicity, such as skin color, take its place, serving as outward reflections of the faulty gene. Thus, while the faulty gene stigmatizes those who carry it, the link between the faulty gene and the racial or ethnic minority group stigmatizes all members of the group, regardless of whether they carry the faulty gene.

B. Racial and Ethnic Stigma in Context

The racial or ethnic stigma that arises from the "faulty" gene is even more powerful when the behavior associated with the gene maps onto preexisting stereotypes about the racial or ethnic group. Because racial and ethnic stigmas are social constructs, their existence and salience depend on the social context in which the behavioral genetics research is conducted.[110] For example, studying the genetic influence on alcoholism in the Irish or the Native American community has greater potential for stigma than studying alcoholism in the Jewish community. Likewise, studying the heritability of aggression in the African American community has greater potential for stigma than studying aggression in the Amish community.[111]

As mentioned above, racial and ethnic stigmas are especially threatening because of the discreteness and insularity of the racial or ethnic minority group. First, because the physical marks of racial and ethnic identity are distinct, observable, and generally immutable, racial and ethnic stigmas are more difficult to avoid by "converting," "passing," or "covering."[112] In other words, because the groups are discrete and insular, it is more difficult for members of the group to assimilate into the mainstream in order to avoid the shadow of stigma. Second, a history of discrimination, especially genetic discrimination, lends additional resonance to racial and ethnic stigma because it echoes a message that is deeply ingrained in the social psyche. Third, racial and ethnic stigmas reinforce

---

108. *Cf.* PETERS, *supra* note 57, at 73 ("If we identify crime with genes and then genes with race, then we may inadvertently provide a biological support for prejudice and discrimination").

109. *Cf.* GOFFMAN, *supra* note 102, at 43–51 (explaining how stigma symbols convey negative social information and thus must be readily perceived by others).

110. *See* Lenhardt, *supra* note 102, at 821.

111. *Cf. id.* at 359 (describing the "black beast" stereotype as "a violent brute with an unusually powerful sexual appetite for white women who was completely devoid of humanity").

112. Kenji Yoshino, *Covering*, 111 YALE L. J. 769 (2002); *see also* GOFFMAN, *supra* note 102 at 73–91, 102–04.

insularity: while stigma encourages the mainstream population to avoid contact with the stigmatized group, it is only through increased social contact between groups that racial and ethnic stereotypes can be dispelled. Finally, the political powerlessness of many racial and ethnic minorities makes the racial and ethnic stigma associated with behavioral genetics research more likely to be translated into social policy. In the *Genes on Trial* program, Francis Collins pointed out that men are "predisposed to get in trouble with the law at about a tenfold increased risk than [women]."[113] But the fact that the Y chromosome is strongly correlated with crime is not touted as a rationale to change social policy, perhaps in part because most policymakers are men.

C. The Harms of Racial and Ethnic Stigma

The harms of racial and ethnic stigma come in various forms. At the individual level, they include heightened anxiety about racial or ethnic bias, self-hate, and stereotype threat. When an individual is stigmatized because of her race or ethnicity, she may feel "insecure and uncertain in interactions with others," constantly fearing prejudice and discrimination.[114] As a result, she may distrust others and view all her social interactions through the lens of race or ethnicity. At the same time, she may internalize the racial or ethnic stigma that she faces every day.[115] In *Brown v. Board of Education*, for example, the Supreme Court recognized this form of self-stigma when it observed that segregating schoolchildren by race "generates a feeling of inferiority as to their status in the community that may affect their hearts and minds in a way unlikely to ever be undone."[116] Finally, racial or ethnic stigma may create "stereotype threat," a type of performance anxiety that stems from the desire not to confirm negative stereotypes about the racial or ethnic group.[117]

These psychological harms are not necessarily unique to race and ethnicity, but they are more acute when membership in the stigmatized group is important to the individual's personal identity. For example, if being black is an important aspect of one's personal identity but being tall is not, then the message that blacks are genetically predisposed to violence carries more stigmatic harm than the message that tall people are genetically predisposed to violence.

---

113. *See* GENES ON TRIAL, supra note 1.

114. Lenhardt, *supra* note 102, at 839–41; *see also* GOFFMAN, *supra* note 102, at 13–14.

115. Lenhardt, *supra* note 102, at 841–42; *see also* GOFFMAN, *supra* note 102, at 7.

116. 347 U.S. 483, 494 (1954).

117. Lenhardt, *supra* note 102, at 843–44 (citing Claude M. Steele & Joshua Aronson, *Stereotype Threat and the Intellectual Test Performance of African-Americans*, 69 J. PERSONALITY & SOC. PSYCHOL. 797 (1995)). For a review of the recent literature on stereotype threat, *see* S. Christian Wheeler & Richard E. Petty, *The Effects of Stereotype Activation on Behavior: A Review of Possible Mechanisms*, 127 PSYCHOL. BULL. 797 (2001).

At the group level, the harms of racial and ethnic stigma include discrimination, racial or ethnic profiling, and racial or ethnic stereotyping.[118] Although these harms are also felt at the individual level, they are attacks on the racial or ethnic community as a whole and represent the experiences of many members of the group.[119] The harm may be a tangible deprivation of property or liberty, such as being denied a job or being stopped by the police, or it may be an intangible deprivation of dignity, such as being called a racial epithet or being asked whether one knows how to speak English. Like the harms that affect the individual psyche, these harms draw their impact in part from the group's historical and collective experiences. Therefore, the stigmatic harm of behavioral genetics research depends on both the context in which it is conducted and the group on which it focuses.

CONCLUSION

There is a certain risk here that [the study] could foment prejudice. And the risk arises not just out of the study, but out of the way the study is presented. . . . And the bigger the mess it is, and the [more] it's about how the study was done, and the more confusing it gets, there's only one thing I remember. And that is that Tracy Islanders drink a lot. . . . I'm committed to research, so I might do it anyway. But nonetheless, there's a point here.
—Justice Stephen Breyer, United States Supreme Court[120]

In the *Genes on Trial* program, the hypothetical research on "the alcoholism gene" in Tracy Islanders had no immediate clinical application.[121] It did, however, have an immediate stigmatic impact on the Tracy Islander community. In concluding the program, Charles Ogletree asked, "Should any of this scientific inquiry be off limits?"[122]

For many scientists, this question is blasphemous, as they view all scientific knowledge as inherently valuable, no matter what its social and political consequences. Others point to the promise of improving the human condition through scientific inquiry: "If we want to see a better day for medical treatments, for public health, for improving our lot, for reducing suffering, it is this engine of

---

118. *See* Lenhardt, *supra* note 102, at 836–39.

119. *See id.* at 836.

120. GENES ON TRIAL, *supra* note 1 (playing the role of the uncle).

121. *Id.* (Francis Collins).

122. *Id.* This same question was asked in 1992 when David Wasserman at the University of Maryland planned a conference on "Genetic Factors in Crime: Findings, Uses, and Implications." In response to public protest and outcry from the African American community, the National Institutes of Health revoked its funding, and the conference was canceled. *See* PETERS, *supra* note 57, at 72–73.

research that will get us there."[123] But even if behavioral genetics research could theoretically lead to a "cure" for antisocial behavior, this benefit is unlikely, whereas the harm of racial and ethnic stigma is all too likely, as our history has shown.[124] Moreover, although "curing" alcoholism is almost certainly beneficial to the individual's health and to society's productivity, there would be less consensus about other traits, such as homosexuality and impulsiveness. Is the scientific ability to change these behaviors beneficial to the individual or to society? Or is it a frightening move toward eugenics? In a world of limited resources, should we fund research that has remote benefits but obvious harms?

It is unlikely that the tide of behavioral genetics research can be, or even should be, stopped. But in answering these questions, and in deciding who and what to study, we must consider the implications of behavioral genetics research for the individual, the family, the community, and society. We should question not only the purpose of the study but also whether a strong scientific justification supports focusing on a racial or ethnic minority group. We should consider who is being studied, what is being studied, and who is doing the study. It is through heightened sensitivity to the context of behavioral genetics research that we can try to avoid the stigma of a "scarlet gene."

---

123. GENES ON TRIAL, *supra* note 1 (Francis Collins).
124. *See* Stevens, *supra* note 16, at 1070; *cf.* Rothenberg, *supra* note 30, at 106–7.

APPENDICES TO CHAPTER 10: BEHAVIORAL GENETICS EVIDENCE IN CRIMINAL CASES: 1994–2007

DEBORAH W. DENNO

APPENDIX A: CHARTS 1–3

CHART 1
SEVERITY OF SENTENCING BY NUMBER OF CASES

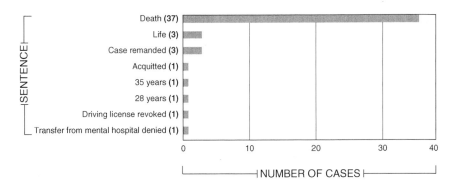

CHART 2
REASONS FOR INTRODUCING GENETICS EVIDENCE
BY NUMBER OF CASES

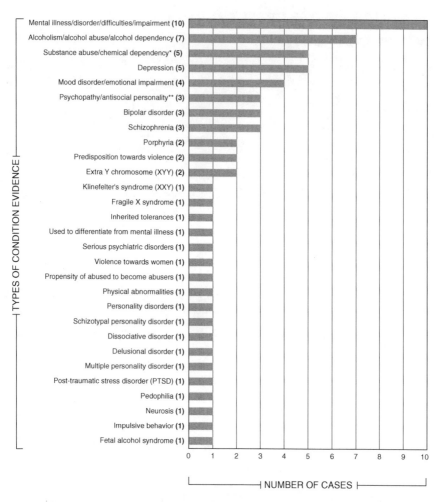

* Cases in this category appear to refer to alcohol and drugs combined; in addition to abuse and dependency, they may also refer to addictions.
** Cases in this category may refer more specifically to antisocial characteristics and psychotic behavior.

CHART 3
NATURE OF EVIDENCE SOUGHT TO BE ADMITTED
BY NUMBER OF CASES

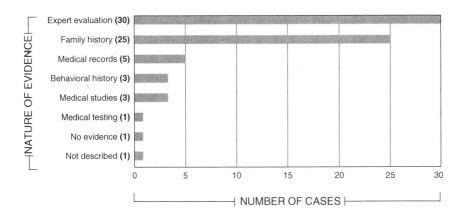

APPENDIX B: CASES REFERENCING GENETICS EVIDENCE, 1994 TO JUNE 1, 2007

Case	Summary	Comments
Miller v. State, No. 01-06-00034-CR, 2007 WL 1559822 (Tex. App. Hous. 1 Dist. May 31, 2007).	Miller was convicted of aggravated robbery. 2007 WL 1559822, at *1. His appeal was based in part on a claim of ineffective assistance of trial counsel. The appellate court affirmed. *Id.* At the punishment phase, Miller's mother testified that various family members, including Miller, had been diagnosed with a genetic condition that "can cause rapidly changing behavior," including paranoia and anxiety. *Id.* at *2.	Miller's mother testified that Miller and other family members had been diagnosed with the genetic condition, "acute intermittent porphyria." *Id.* at *2. The appellate court did not refer to this condition in affirming the lower court's decision. Genetics evidence, then, was mentioned only in passing.
People v. Lancaster, 158 P.3d 157 (Cal. 2007).	Lancaster was convicted of murder, among other offenses, and sentenced to death. 158 P.3d at 162. During the penalty phase, a psychologist testified for the defense that Lancaster has an antisocial personality that might have a genetic component. *Id.* at 165.	Genetics evidence was mentioned primarily in passing by a testifying psychologist.
State v. Frank, 957 So. 2d 724 (La. 2007).	Frank was convicted of murder and was sentenced to death. 957 So. 2d at 727. On appeal, the state supreme court affirmed in part and remanded in part. *Id.* On remand, a psychiatrist testifying for the state noted that "there is a possibility that susceptibility to PTSD may be partly genetic and that someone who has inherited a predisposition to the disorder may be vulnerable to mental illness if he or she is traumatized under the stress of environmental influences."	Frank argued that she should be given a new sentencing phase, presumably to bring up past sexual abuse. In the context of stating that her claims of sexual abuse were dubious, an expert "conceded" that vulnerability to

Case	Summary	Comments
	Id. at 734. The district court held that Frank refused the assistance of a mental health expert and concluded that she was not entitled to a new sentencing phase of her trial. On appeal, the state supreme court affirmed, holding in part that Frank did not demonstrate prejudice because she did not have expert assistance funded by the state.	PTSD may be partially genetic and therefore, when combined with environmental stressors, may heighten the likelihood of acquiring a mental illness. *Id.* at 734. However, Frank was denied a new sentencing phase since she had already refused the assistance of a mental health expert, so the issue went no further. Genetics evidence, then, was mentioned only in passing.
Johnson v. Quarterman, 483 F.3d 278 (5th Cir. 2007).	Johnson was convicted of capital murder and sentenced to death. 483 F.3d at 279. The district court dismissed his subsequent petition for writ of habeas corpus and denied his application for certificate of appealability. The court held that the state court did not unreasonably deny relief on Johnson's claim that his counsel rendered ineffective assistance, in part by failing to conduct a complete and thorough mitigation investigation. *Id.* In support of this claim, Johnson submitted an affidavit of a mitigation specialist who stated that she had discovered evidence concerning numerous potentially mitigating factors, including a genetic predisposition to substance abuse. *Id.* at 278. Johnson then requested a certificate of appealability, to appeal the district court's denial of relief. This request, too, was denied.	The mitigation specialist seemed to refer to Johnson's family history of substance abuse and his genetic predisposition to substance abuse as two separate but related items. *Id.* at 288 n.*. Also, the appellate court acknowledged the district court's comments that childhood abuse evidence was not compelling enough to create a "reasonable

Case	Summary	Comments
	Because the district court was found not to have erred in its procedural ruling, the appellate court rendered it unnecessary to address the ineffective assistance claim. *Id.* at 279. The court did note, however, the district court's holding that "even if considered, the mitigation specialist's affidavit would provide no grounds for relief because, in the context of Johnson's extensive history of extreme and brutal violence, it is highly unlikely that evidence of Johnson's childhood abuse and privations in foster homes was so compelling that there is a reasonable probability that at least one juror could have reasonably determined that death was not an appropriate sentence." *Id.* at 288 n.*.	probability that at least one juror" would have voted against a death sentence; however, the court made no mention of the alleged genetic predisposition in this context. *Id.* at 288. In general, genetics evidence was mentioned in passing.
People v. Smith, 150 P.3d 1224 (Cal. 2007).	Smith was charged with two counts of first degree murder, among other offenses, and entered a plea of not guilty by reason of insanity. 150 P.3d at 1231. One of several doctors appointed to evaluate Smith testified during the sanity phase that Smith had a genetic predisposition for psychopathy and other untreatable antisocial characteristics. *Id.* at 1234. The jury returned a verdict that Smith was sane at the time of the offenses. He was subsequently convicted and sentenced to death. The state superior court denied Smith's automatic application to modify the death verdict and sentenced him accordingly. On automatic appeal to the state supreme court, Smith's conviction for receiving stolen property was reversed but the judgment was otherwise affirmed. *Id.* at 1257.	Genetics evidence appeared—if relevant at all—to work against the defendant. An expert who evaluated Smith during the sanity phase of his trial "opined that defendant had a genetic predisposition for psychopathy and antisocial characteristics, and that such disorders were essentially untreatable," *id.* at 1234, but "found no psychiatric evidence that defendant was legally insane at the time of the offenses." *Id.* At 1235.

Case	Summary	Comments
Mickey v. Ayers, No. C-93-0243 RMW, 2006 WL 3358410 (N.D. Cal. Nov. 17, 2006).	Mickey was convicted of murder and sentenced to death. 2006 WL 3358410, at *1. The state supreme court affirmed, and Mickey's application for a writ of certiorari from the U.S. Supreme Court was denied. Following several unsuccessful petitions, Mickey petitioned the district court for habeas corpus relief. His petition was denied on the guilt phase claims, but was granted on the penalty phase claim of ineffective assistance of counsel. *Id.* The court stated that the performance of Mickey's counsel was deficient in part because they failed to "effectively utilize the expertise of their mental health experts" in the "preparation and presentation of [Mickey's] mitigation case. . . ." *Id.* at *15. Based on available information regarding Mickey's background, a forensic psychologist would have testified at the penalty phase regarding the "strong correlation between a genetic history of addictive disorders and predisposition to developing addictions," and stated that "Mickey's genetic loading, combined with his family environment and underlying mental illness, caused him to be predisposed to alcohol and drug dependency." *Id.* at *19.	As the court noted, "[t]he defense could have presented a mitigation case that Mickey was a psychiatrically disturbed individual who was exposed to abuse and surrounded by family members who had psychiatric problems themselves." *Id.* at *20. In essence, the difference between what the defense could have done and did do was "substantial." *Id.*
State v. Idellfonso-Diaz, No. M2006-00203-CCA-R9-CD, 2006 WL 3093207 (Tenn. Crim. App. Nov. 1, 2006) (remanding decision of trial court).	Idellfonso-Diaz was charged with murder. 2006 WL 3093207, at *1. On interlocutory appeal, the state contended that the trial court erroneously permitted expert testimony regarding Idellfonso-Diaz's diminished mental capacity at the time of the crimes. *Id.* The expert witness had arranged genetic testing for Idellfonso-Diaz and testified that he "had a genetic vulnerability to becoming depressed and dysfunctional, especially in stressful, crisis-type situations." *Id.* at *2. The witness also stated that "considered separately, [Idellfonso-Diaz's] genetic	The appellate court considered expert testimony that genetic vulnerability was one factor that may have contributed to defendant's behavior; however, the court determined that such impairment, along with the defendant's other disorders, was

Case	Summary	Comments
	vulnerability . . . would not have been particularly serious," but would have "'impaired him, to some extent'" when combined with other factors such as intoxication, PTSD, and depression. *Id.* The state argued that because the witness's testimony did not indicate that Idellfonso-Diaz "completely lacked the mental capacity to commit the crimes, his testimony is inadmissible. . . ." *Id.* at *4. The appellate court agreed and remanded the case.	not sufficiently detrimental to negate the defendant's mental capacity to commit the crimes. The expert's testimony was rendered inadmissible .
Hamilton v. Ayers, 458 F. Supp. 2d 1075 (E.D. Cal. 2006).	Hamilton was convicted of murder and sentenced to death. 458 F. Supp. 2d at 1086. His conviction and sentence were affirmed, and his petition for habeas corpus was denied. Hamilton then petitioned for federal writ of habeas corpus. Hamilton argued that he was incompetent to stand trial and that his attorneys did not investigate his mental state. *Id.* at 1085–86. An expert witness opined that "Hamilton's family history of genetic disorders," among other factors, "burdened him with extreme mental and emotional impairments . . . that compromised his ability to fully appreciate the nature and consequences of his acts or to conform his conduct to the requirements of the law." *Id.* at 1091. The witness also stated "that both sides of Hamilton's family have histories of genetically transmitted disorders which expressed themselves early in Hamilton's life," while another expert stressed "that Hamilton was raised in an environment of intergenerational alcoholism, child abuse and domestic violence. . . ." *Id.* at 1127. The court noted, however, the lack of medical records to support Hamilton's claim of incompetence. *Id.* at 1091. The court also emphasized that Hamilton's behavior did not appear to be irrational, and he had "not shown that he	Despite substantial testimony by mental health professionals concerning Hamilton's genetically transmitted disorders and family background of violence and abuse, the court spotlighted other factors relatively more heavily— specifically, Hamilton's lack of medical records, behavioral irrationality, or indications that he could not understand the proceedings.

Case	Summary	Comments
	was unable to understand the nature of the proceedings against him or to assist counsel." *Id.* at 1092. The court concluded that "the evidence presented . . . does not raise a 'bona fide doubt' as to Hamilton's competence to stand trial" and that "defense counsel was not ineffective for failing to raise the issue of Hamilton's competence." *Id.*	
State v. Ketterer, 855 N.E.2d 48 (Ohio 2006), *cert. denied, Ketterer v. Ohio,* 127 S. Ct. 2266 (2007).	Ketterer pleaded guilty to murder and was sentenced to death. 855 N.E.2d at 56. His appeal was based in part on a claim of ineffective assistance of counsel, due to his attorneys' failure to effectively present mitigating evidence. *Id.* at 66. At the penalty phase, a clinical psychologist testified that Ketterer "does have a 'severe mental disease or defect,'" which has a "genetic component . . . in that Ketterer's family is 'filled with people with depression, bipolar disorder, and suicides.'" *Id.* at 78. The state supreme court described "evidence of Ketterer's severe mental problems as a significant mitigating factor," *id.* at 80, but "conclude[d] that the aggravating circumstances outweigh the collective mitigating factors," *id.* at 81, and affirmed the trial court's ruling, *id.* at 58.	The concurrence also emphasized the genetic links to defendant's mental illness, noting that "many of Ketterer's family members suffer from depression and bipolar disorder," including a brother treated for "major depressive disorder" as well as bipolar disorder, a second brother who was institutionalized at a state mental hospital, a cousin treated for depression, and another cousin and uncle who both committed suicide. *Id.* at 83.
Morris v. State, No. W2005-00426-CCA-R3-PD, 2006 WL 2872870 (Tenn. Crim. App. Oct. 10, 2006).	Morris was convicted of murder and rape and sentenced to death. 2006 WL 2872870, at *1. The state supreme court affirmed, and the trial court denied Morris's petition for postconviction relief. Morris appealed, based in part on a claim of ineffective assistance of counsel. *Id.* Specifically, Morris argued that his counsel was deficient "in failing to uncover information that would have led to a diagnosis	While acknowledging expert testimony concerning the genetic, familial, and environmental components of addiction, the court noted that some of the missing

Case	Summary	Comments
	of Bipolar Disorder II. . . ." *Id.* at *45. A neuropsychiatrist concluded that Morris suffered from "genetically transmitted" bipolar disorder. *Id.* at *22. This neuropsychiatrist stated that affidavits from Morris's family "were crucial with regard to establishing a genetic/family history of mental disorders." *Id.* at *47. An expert in medical addiction testified that "'[i]n terms of addiction medicine . . . [w]e go through the family history because we know that addiction is strongly genetic.'" *Id.* at *18. A mitigation specialist working for Morris testified that because certain mental illnesses are genetic, a "thorough familial investigation" was merited; however, she described "her function in the present case" as "'not very proactive.'" *Id.* at *15. The appellate court affirmed the postconviction court's judgment, however, holding in part that Morris "was not denied effective assistance of counsel at trial or on appeal." *Id.* at *35.	information about the defendant viewed by the defense as potential mitigating evidence would have actually been "harmful" because "it revealed and supported [defendant's] long-time drug use and also indicated that [defendant] relied upon the sale of illegal drugs as a source of income." *Id.* at *61.
Loving v. United States, 64 M.J. 132 (C.A.A.F. 2006).	Loving was sentenced to death. His conviction was affirmed by the appellate court and the Supreme Court. Loving subsequently filed a habeas petition. 64 M.J. at 134–35. In partial support for his claim that his trial counsel did not effectively investigate and present mitigation evidence, Loving presented information related to his "parental and family history of alcoholism and substance addiction," which could have "established [Loving's] genetic proclivity for alcoholism." *Id.* at 151. Noting that Loving "has presented a potentially meritorious claim of ineffective assistance of counsel arising from his trial defense counsel's failure to . . . [expand] the mitigation investigation into the defendant's traumatic life history," *id.* at 151–52, the appellate court held it did "not	In remanding for an evidentiary hearing, the court noted that defendant's "traumatic family background and upbringing" warranted examination of extenuating or mitigating factors. *Id.* at 152. In general, however, genetics evidence was mentioned in passing.

Case	Summary	Comments
	have the factual predicate to determine if [its] prior decision addressing the issue of ineffective assistance of counsel was correct . . . ." *Id.* 134. The appellate court thus remanded for an "evidentiary hearing to address the issue of whether [Loving's] trial defense counsel 'chose to abandon their investigation at an unreasonable juncture, making a fully informed decision with respect to sentencing strategy impossible' thereby prejudicing [Loving] in the capital sentencing phase of the court-martial." *Id.*	
Jones v. Schriro, 450 F. Supp. 2d 1023 (D. Ariz. 2006).	Jones was convicted of first-degree murder and sentenced to death. 450 F. Supp. 2d at 1025. The state supreme court affirmed the convictions and sentences on direct appeal. Jones then filed a petition for writ of habeas corpus, claiming "ineffective assistance of trial counsel based on counsel's failure to investigate and present mitigating evidence." *Id.* Testifying on behalf of Jones at the sentencing hearing, a mental health expert stated that Jones's substance abuse was the result of "genetic predisposition and self-medication." *Id.* at 1031. Another mental health expert identified mitigating factors that included a "genetic loading for substance abuse and affective disorders." *Id.* at 1027. The trial court found, however, that the mitigating circumstances did not outweigh the aggravating circumstances or merit leniency. *Id.* at 1029. The district court denied habeas relief, holding in part that trial counsel's failure to seek neuropsychological testing did not prejudice petitioner and thus could not amount to ineffective assistance of counsel. *Id.* at 1046.	Despite testimony from three expert witnesses concerning defendant's history of abuse and genetic predisposition, the district court was concerned about the lateness with which some of defendant's claims were revealed. As the district court explained, "the sentencing judge would likely have viewed with skepticism [defendant's] more-recent allegations of sexual and physical abuse, given their late disclosure, their inconsistency with other information in the record, and [defendant's] 'obvious motive to fabricate.'" *Id.* at 1047 (citation omitted).

Case	Summary	Comments
State v. Sexton, 904 A.2d 1092 (Vt. 2006) (affirming in part, reversing in part, and remanding).	Sexton was charged with second-degree murder. 904 A.2d at 1095. A court-appointed psychiatrist concluded that Sexton was insane at the time of his offense, with his psychosis possibly occurring as a result of illegal drugs (e.g., LSD) that "exacerbated or activated a preexisting latent illness." *Id.* at 1106. This rare reaction, the psychiatrist noted, is more likely to occur among individuals with a genetic predisposition. *Id.* at 1105 n.13. Another psychiatrist cited research indicating greater susceptibility to a psychotic response to LSD use among individuals with a genetic predisposition to schizophrenia, and stated that Sexton's "'mental health history clearly puts him in this category.'" *Id.* The district court held that Sexton "was entitled to rely on the defense of diminished capacity due to voluntary intoxication" and, in a second decision, "conclude[ed] that [Sexton] was also entitled to argue that he was legally insane at the time of the killing." *Id.* at 1096. On appeal by the state, the state supreme court affirmed in part, reversed in part, and remanded, holding in part that Sexton could not assert an insanity defense "based on the voluntary consumption of illegal drugs that activate a latent mental disease or defect. . . ." *Id.* at 1111.	As the state supreme court explained, even if the defendant possessed "a latent mental illness, it does not alter the fact that . . . defendant would not have been in a psychotic state at the time of the offense had he not chosen to use illegal consciousness-altering drugs." *Id.* at 1106. In essence, the defendant's evidence "demonstrates that his recent, voluntary use of illegal drugs was an essential causal element of the mental illness and psychotic episode that followed." *Id.*
Keen v. State, No. W2004-02159-CCA-R3-PD, 2006 WL 1540258 (Tenn. Crim. App. June 5, 2006), *cert. denied, Keen v. Tennessee*, 127 S. Ct. 2250 (2007).	Keen was convicted of first-degree felony murder and sentenced to death. 2006 WL 1540258, at *1. On direct appeal, his conviction was affirmed, but the state supreme court reversed and remanded. On remand, the jury again imposed the penalty of death and the state supreme court affirmed. Keen's petition for postconviction relief was denied, and Keen appealed, claiming in part ineffective assistance of counsel. *Id.* The attorney who represented Keen in his earlier trials testified that she did not offer any evidence regarding a genetic predisposition	The psychologist's expert testimony emphasized a link between defendant's family history and his criminal behavior, which involved the rape and murder of a young child, noting for example that "[t]he family's sexual dysfunction transcends

Case	Summary	Comments
	to mental illness. *Id.* at *9. A psychologist for the defense testified that within Keen's family, "'there is a significant genetic heritability or genetic predisposition to mental illness.'" *Id.* at *24. He stated that Keen's siblings' backgrounds were also important, since "the children share genetic parenting or partial genetic parenting," as well as "the same climate of abuse and neglect." *Id.* He also noted "the importance of multi-generational family history in capital sentencing evaluations," as "one may be genetically predisposed to many characteristics, such as personality disorders, psychological disorders and substance abuse." *Id.* at *23. Based on the psychologist's overview of Keen's family history, he concluded that "in the context of a capital murder, one may say that [Keen's] behavior is at the end of a generational pyramid that involves genetic influences . . . from generation to generation" and noted that this mitigation evidence was available during Keen's earlier trials. *Id.* However, the appellate court affirmed the judgment of the postconviction court, concluding that "[t]here is no reason to lack confidence as to the outcome in this case because the aggravating circumstances submitted to the jury outweighed the mitigating circumstances." *Id.* at *46.	generations and impacts both genders," and more specifically, the "'generational sexual deviation and abuse directed toward children.'" *Id.* at *23. Likewise, in defendant's family, "there is an increased incidence of persons who abandon their children, of persons who sexually molest children, and persons who have significant alcohol and drug histories . . . ." *Id.* at *24. While Keen voluntary chose to commit the crime, "he did not have the same choice as everyone else due to his background and history" as well as "risk factors" that propelled his behavior. *Id.*
People v. Mertz, 842 N.E.2d 618 (Ill. 2005), *cert. denied, Mertz v. Illinois,* 127 S. Ct. 47 (2006).	Mertz was convicted of first-degree murder, among other crimes, and sentenced to death. 842 N.E.2d at 622. On appeal to the state supreme court, he argued in part that imposition of the death penalty was excessive in light of his inherited alcoholism (as well as other factors, such as military service). *Id.* An expert witness specializing in substance abuse evaluations testified that Mertz	The court specifically addressed Mertz's claim of "'inherited' alcoholism," calling it "highly questionable" and doubting its credibility, as well as the extent of the evidence of drinking

Case	Summary	Comments
	"satisfied the criteria for alcohol dependence" and that this dependence was "genetically influenced." *Id.* at 641. Additionally, a psychologist testified for the defense "that defendant had a genetic predisposition to alcohol dependence and mood disorder." *Id.* at 644. In evaluating Mertz's excessive sentence argument, the court made strong comments about the testimony on Mertz's alcoholism: "[D]efendant's claim of 'inherited' alcoholism is highly questionable in terms of credibility and, in our opinion, did little to help defendant at sentencing. Apparently, defendant believed he would be less blameworthy in the eyes of the jurors for his failure to seek help with his drinking problems, and his failure to earnestly try to overcome them, if he attributed the problems to genetics and family models. We believe defendant was mistaken in this respect. Moreover, the case defendant made for 'inheriting' alcoholism is not convincing." *Id.* at 662.	among his family members. *Id.* at 662. The court also made clear its skepticism about Mertz's links between his alcoholism and his behavior. "We believe the effort to blame defendant's drinking problems upon an alleged genetic or family predisposition was little more than a thinly veiled effort to divert responsibility from defendant for his failure to address his problems and take responsibility for them. To the extent that credible evidence *was* adduced on this subject, and that evidence might be considered mitigating, we find the weight of that evidence was insignificant." *Id.* at 663.
Marquard v. Sec'y for Dep't of Corrections, 429 F.3d 1278 (11th Cir. 2005), *cert. denied, Marquard v. McDonough,*	Marquard was convicted of first-degree murder and armed robbery and sentenced to death. 429 F.3d at 1282. The district court denied his petition for habeas corpus relief. On appeal, Marquard claimed ineffective assistance of counsel during the penalty phase of his trial. *Id.* at 1294. During the penalty phase, a psychologist testified that individual personality traits stem in part from	The role of genetics evidence as related to Marquard is more implied than directly stated. The expert witness testified that Marquard presented "'personality problems,'" and then

Case	Summary	Comments
126 S. Ct. 2356 (2006).	"genetic predisposition." Individuals who develop "maladaptive personality traits" are considered to have a "personality disorder," which varies in type depending on the individual. *Id.* at 1288. The psychologist stated that Marquard "had traits typical of many different personality disorders." *Id.* The court of appeals affirmed, holding in part that the state court's decision that counsel did not meet the standard for ineffective assistance because it did not present some of the mitigation evidence was not "'contrary to' clearly established federal law." *Id.* at 1306.	explained that individual personality traits are "traceable to genetic predisposition and also the individual's environment and upbringing and values in the home." *Id.* at 1288. Genetics evidence, then, was mentioned only in passing.
State v. Manning, 885 So. 2d 1044 (La. 2004).	Defendant was convicted of first-degree murder and sentenced to death. 885 So. 2d at 1057. At the sentencing phase, a forensic psychiatrist offered mitigation expert testimony, stating that during a psychiatric evaluation, defendant "minimized his alcohol problems, which may have stemmed from a genetic predisposition." *Id.* at 1096–97. Defendant appealed to the Louisiana Supreme Court on claims unrelated to the genetics evidence. His conviction was affirmed. *Id.*	Genetic predisposition was mentioned only in passing.
Von Dohlen v. State, 602 S.E.2d 738 (S.C. 2004).	Defendant was convicted of murder and armed robbery and sentenced to death. 602 S.E.2d at 740. His convictions and sentence were affirmed on direct appeal, and he applied for postconviction relief, arguing that during the sentencing phase, a psychiatrist for the defense had understated defendant's mental illness. *Id.* at 741. At the postconviction relief hearing, the psychiatrist testified that had he seen certain medical and psychiatric records (which had been available before the trial), he would have diagnosed the defendant with a more serious	Genetic predisposition was not a pivotal issue but may have formed some of the basis for remand.

Case	Summary	Comments
	mental illness. This diagnosis would have been based in part on records indicating a possible genetic basis for the defendant's chronic depression, as well as on an overall genetic predisposition for mental disorders. *Id.* at 741–42. The hearing judge denied relief, but on appeal the South Carolina Supreme Court reversed and remanded for a new sentencing hearing, holding that defense counsel's lack of preparation prevented a defense expert witness from accurately depicting defendant's mental condition at the time of the crime. *Id.* at 746.	
Dennis ex rel. *Butko v. Budge*, 378 F.3d 880 (9th Cir. 2004).	Defendant pled guilty to first-degree murder and was sentenced to death. 378 F.3d 882. The Nevada Supreme Court affirmed. Defendant filed a petition for writ of habeas corpus, which was dismissed by the state district court. Defendant appealed to the Nevada Supreme Court, but then requested that his appeal be withdrawn. His counsel refused defendant's request, questioning defendant's competence. *Id.* at 883. The Nevada Supreme Court remanded the case to state district court for a competency hearing. Defendant was found competent, and his counsel was directed to withdraw the appeal. *Id.* at 886. Instead, defendant's counsel removed herself from the case and filed a "next-friend" petition for habeas corpus in the federal district court. The petition was dismissed for lack of standing because the defendant was deemed competent. *Id.* at 887–88. Defendant's former counsel appealed. *Id.* at 888. The court of appeals affirmed the dismissal of the petition and denied the request for a stay of execution. *Id.* at 895.	The case itself did not involve genetics evidence, but the concurring opinion mentions genetic predispositions in the context of differentiating such predispositions from mental illness (asking how mental illness can be distinguished from genetic predisposition).

Case	Summary	Comments
	The concurring opinion commented on the difficulty of distinguishing a mental illness from "the myriad . . . memories, experiences and genetic predispositions that go to make up each individual's unique personality . . . ." *Id.* The concurrence also noted that "[w]e as judges and lawyers attempt to capture these philosophical dilemmas in words that can have very different meanings to different people, and that often may not respect the concepts that mental health professionals would use to capture cognitive and volitional capacity." *Id.*	
Hall v. State, 160 S.W.3d 24 (Tex. Crim. App. 2004) (en banc).	Defendant was convicted of capital murder and sentenced to death. 160 S.W.3d at 26. On appeal, the Texas Court of Criminal Appeals affirmed his conviction and sentence. Defendant then appealed to the U.S. Supreme Court and filed a state application for writ of habeas corpus. The Supreme Court vacated the Texas Court of Criminal Appeals's decision and remanded the case for reconsideration in light of *Atkins v. Virginia,* 536 U.S. 304 (2002). *Hall,* 160 S.W. 3d at 27. In defendant's habeas action, the trial court determined that the matter of defendant's mental retardation was an issue of fact that had not been resolved, and it ordered a hearing by way of affidavits. *Id.* at 26–27. The defendant submitted affidavits from two psychologists stating that he was mentally retarded. *Id.* at 32. One affidavit described defendant's appearance as typical of fetal alcohol syndrome and stated that the defendant also exhibited characteristics resembling other genetic disorders (e.g., XXY), which had existed at birth. *Id.* at 33. The State submitted a rebuttal affidavit from a neuropsychologist who had testified during	The Texas Court of Criminal Appeals noted that testimony was presented both by and against the defendant regarding the similarity, or lack thereof, of defendant's mental condition to several genetic disorders. *Id.* at 39–40. The court weighed this testimony collectively with other evidence in finding against the defendant.

Case	Summary	Comments
	the guilt phase of the trial. *Id.* at 35. This witness explicitly stated that the defendant did not exhibit symptoms of such genetic disorders. *Id.* The habeas trial court concluded that the defendant was not mentally retarded, and therefore denied relief. The Texas Court of Criminal Appeals determined that the trial court was in the best position to evaluate conflicting evidence regarding the defendant's mental state, and thus affirmed the trial court's decision. *Id.* at 40.	
Cauthern v. State, 145 S.W.3d 571 (Tenn. Crim. App. 2004).	Defendant was convicted of felony murder and sentenced to death. 145 S.W.3d at 578. On direct appeal, the Tennessee Supreme Court remanded for resentencing, and defendant was again sentenced to death. The sentence was affirmed on appeal, and defendant's subsequent petition for postconviction relief was denied. *Id.* at 579. Defendant appealed the denial of his petition based in apart on a claim of ineffective assistance of counsel at both preceding sentencing hearings: his psychiatric expert witness at the postconviction hearing testified that mitigation evidence could have been presented of defendant's family history suggesting a genetic predisposition to impulsive behavior. *Id.* at 588. The Tennessee Court of Criminal Appeals affirmed the denial of postconviction relief, holding any shortcomings by counsel would have made no difference to the outcome. *Id.* at 578.	In rejecting defendant's claim that he was prejudiced by the failure to present mitigating evidence about his background at the capital resentencing trial, the court noted that defendant's stepsiblings experienced abusive upbringings but did not appear to suffer from violent inclinations. *Id.* at 609.
Davis v. State, No. M2003-00744-CCA-R3-PC, 2004 WL 253396	The only contested issue at the guilt phase of defendant's trial for murder, reckless endangerment, and carrying a weapon on school property, was his mental state at the time of the crimes. 2004 WL 253396, at *4. A psychiatrist testified for the defense that	Defendant's appeal was unrelated to his alleged genetic predisposition. Genetic predisposition was

Case	Summary	Comments
(Tenn. Crim. App. Feb. 11, 2004).	defendant had a genetic predisposition for mental illness because numerous family members had been hospitalized for mental illness. *Id.* Defendant was convicted of first-degree murder and sentenced to life imprisonment. *Id.* at *1. His petition for postconviction relief was dismissed and its dismissal affirmed on appeal to the Tennessee Court of Criminal Appeals. *Id.* at *11.	mentioned only in passing.
State v. Scott, 800 N.E.2d 1133 (Ohio 2004).	Scott was convicted of murder, among other offenses, and sentenced to death. 800 N.E.2d at 1139–40. On appeal, the state supreme court affirmed the lower court's judgment, holding in part that the aggravating circumstances outweighed the mitigating factors. *Id.* at 1151. Included in Scott's mitigation evidence was testimony from a social worker/mitigation specialist, stating in part that Scott was genetically predisposed for chemical dependencies. *Id.* at 1148.	Genetic predisposition was mentioned only in passing.
Fudge v. State, 120 S.W.3d 600 (Ark. 2003).	Defendant was convicted of capital murder and sentenced to death. 120 S.W.3d at 601. The Supreme Court of Arkansas affirmed. Defendant appealed a denial of his petition for postconviction relief to the Arkansas Supreme Court, which concluded that the trial court's order denying defendant's petition had not met statutory requirements for written findings regarding defendant's allegation of ineffective assistance of counsel. *Id.* at 604. The attorneys had failed, among other things, to investigate and present mitigating evidence during the penalty phase, including defendant's propensity for violence towards women, which "either resulted from a genetic condition or is behavior that was learned from his male role models." *Id.* at 602–03. The Arkansas Supreme Court	The alleged genetic condition was listed as a potentially mitigating factor that required consideration by the trial court.

Case	Summary	Comments
	reversed the trial court's decision and remanded the case for specific findings and conclusions of law. *Id.* at 603.	
People v. Allaway, No. G030307, 2003 WL 22147632 (Cal. App. 4 Dist. Sept. 18, 2003).	Allaway was charged with murder, among other offenses, and found not guilty by reason of insanity. 2003 WL 22147632, at *1. His application to be transferred from a state mental hospital to an outpatient treatment facility was denied, and he appealed, claiming that the trial court's decision was not supported by substantial evidence. *Id.* An independent evaluator testified that Allaway is genetically predisposed to mental illness and psychotic behavior, and the court noted that Allaway "seemed to admit as much in his testimony." *Id.* at *3. The appellate court affirmed the trial court's judgment, finding no abuse of discretion. *Id.* at *6.	Here, genetics evidence worked against Allaway for purposes of evaluating future dangerousness. His application for transfer was denied in part based on the testimony of an independent evaluator who stated that Allaway had a "genetic predisposition" to mental illness and psychotic behavior. *Id.* at *3. The court seemed to accept the genetics link, albeit in a way that worked against Allaway's application.
State v. Hughbanks, 792 N.E.2d 1081 (Ohio 2003).	Hughbanks was convicted of murder and sentenced to death. 792 N.E.2d at 1089. The appellate court appeared to include "genetic tendency" among the defendant's relevant background factors: defendant's father was diagnosed with schizophrenia and there can be "sometimes a familial augmentation" because "schizophrenia 'runs in families.'" *Id.* at 1101. The court acknowledged that "many" of defendant's family members suffered from mental illness and noted the likely negative effect on defendant's "growth and development." *Id.* at 1103. Yet the court found	The alleged genetic condition was listed as a potentially mitigating factor. *Id.* at 1103.

Case	Summary	Comments
	that the aggravating circumstances of the crime outweighed such mitigating factors. _Id._ at 1104.	
Head v. Thomason, 578 S.E.2d 426 (Ga. 2003).	Thomason was convicted of murder, among other crimes, and sentenced to death. 578 S.E.2d at 428. Conviction and sentence were affirmed, and Thomason filed for writ of habeas corpus, which was denied on all grounds except one: that Thomason received ineffective assistance of counsel during the sentencing phase, in part due to his counsel's failure to offer available mitigation evidence. _Id._ This evidence included the opinion of a social worker who stated "that Thomason's family had a strong genetic disposition to alcohol and drug abuse." _Id._ at 429 n.1. The habeas court ordered a new sentencing trial, and the warden appealed. Thomason cross-appealed the habeas court's rejection of his other claims. _Id._ at 428. On appeal, the state supreme court affirmed the grant of a new sentencing trial, holding in part that defense counsel was ineffective due to failure to offer available mitigating evidence. _Id._ at 430.	The court stressed "the importance of mitigating evidence in death penalty cases, [explaining] that an attorney has not acted reasonably when he fails to call mental health experts he knows have mitigating evidence and explains his failure to present lay mitigating evidence by asserting that he had no experts to call." _Id._ at 430.
State v. Madey, No. 81166, 2002-Ohio-5976, 2002 WL 31429827 (Ohio App. 8 Dist. Oct. 31, 2002) (vacating and remanding sentencing decision of trial court).	Madey was convicted of misdemeanor assault and appealed. 2002 WL 31429827, at *1. The appellate court found that the trial court abused its discretion in imposing probation conditions related to Madey's drinking, and therefore vacated the sentence and remanded the case. _Id._ The trial court asked Madey's mother whether "she knew 'anything about genetic predisposition to alcoholism?'" and whether she "had a concern that her daughter would become 'a flaming alcoholic' because, with such an ethnic background, 'there [was] nothing she can do about it.'" _Id._ The trial court also required Madey to "both immediately cease her only employment and	The trial court's comments are uniquely disturbing in many ways, particularly in terms of how the court stereotypes the relationship between ethnic or national background and alcoholism. For example, the court asked defendant's mother "if she had 'ever been on

Case	Summary	Comments
	also submit an essay 'on alcoholism and the American Indians,'" *id.* at *4, which it justified "in part because the issue of a 'genetic predisposition toward alcoholism' had been raised in the defense expert's report and Madey therefore was being 'hypocritical' in challenging the terms imposed." *Id.* at *4 n.4. The appellate court found that the trial court's conditions "bear no relation to an interest in doing justice as well as in rehabilitation." *Id.* at *4. In vacating defendant's sentence and remanding, the appellate court also noted that defendant did not "[attempt] to use her family background to excuse her behavior." *Id.*	an Indian reservation?' and if she had ever seen 'the Scotch or Irish drinking?'" *Id.* at *1. In turn, the court continuously projected defendant's danger without any evidence, even characterizing her potential state of being a murder victim as a danger to others: "[I]f you start drinking like this, you're a danger. You will go out and get yourself attacked, or murdered, or something, and put yourself in these hopeless conditions, which is a bad example, and every time somebody is killed or raped in society, that diminishes the public safety overall." *Id.* at *2.
State v. Arausa, No. 2002-439113 (Dist. Ct. Lubbock County July 5, 2002), *aff'd*, Arausa v. State,	Defendant was convicted of first-degree, aggravated sexual assault and sentenced to life imprisonment. 2003 WL 21803322, at *1. Defendant claimed on appeal that although a psychologist appointed by the trial court had found him legally sane and competent to stand trial, the trial court had erred in refusing his request for an appointment with a psychiatrist, instead, to assist him in the	The court responded specifically to the defendant's claim of genetics evidence, but not on a substantive level.

Case	Summary	Comments
No. 07-02-0396-CR, 2003 WL 21803322 (Tex. Ct. App Aug. 6, 2003).	development of mitigation evidence. *Id.* at *2. Defendant argued in part that a psychiatrist had been required to discuss a study indicating a genetic predisposition among victims of abuse to become abusers themselves. *Id.* at *4. The court of appeals responded that the appellant had not based his original request for a psychiatrist on the need to discuss the gene study. On a more general level, the court saw no relevance of the request for the psychiatrist to the defense. It affirmed, concluding defendant was not entitled to a new trial.	
Stevens v. State, 770 N.E.2d 739 (Ind. 2002).	Defendant was convicted of murder and sentenced to death. 770 N.E.2d at 745. His conviction was affirmed on direct appeal to the Supreme Court of Indiana. Defendant's petition for postconviction relief was denied and its denial affirmed by the Indiana Supreme Court. The petition was based in large part on various claims of ineffective assistance of counsel. *Id.* at 746. The supreme court rejected these claims, emphasizing that defense counsel's strategy had been sound. *Id.* at 752. Defendant's proposed alternative strategy, the court pointed out, would have conflicted with the defense's theory that he was a "passive victim of abuse." *Id.* at 754. This theory was supported by the testimony of a psychologist for the defense that the defendant's genetic predisposition was partly to blame for his behavior.	Genetic predisposition was mentioned only in passing, in the context of pointing out why the alternative defense strategy now proposed by the defendant would not have worked (indicating the alternative strategy would have conflicted with the existing defense theory).
Landrigan v. Stewart, 272 F.3d 1221, (9th Cir. 2001), *aff'd in part and rev'd in part en banc, Landrigan v.*	Defendant was convicted of murder and sentenced to death. His conviction was affirmed on direct appeal by the Arizona Supreme Court. 272 F.3d at 1223. His petition for postconviction relief was denied, as was his petition for habeas corpus. On appeal of these, defendant claimed ineffective assistance of counsel based on counsel's	Citing *Mobley v. Head*, 267 F.3d 1312 (11th Cir. 2001), and *Turpin v. Mobley*, 502 S.E.2d 458 (Ga. 1998), the Ninth Circuit characterized the "genetic violence"

Case	Summary	Comments
Schriro, 441 F.3d 638 (9th Cir. 2006), rev'd, *Schriro v. Landrigan*, 127 S. Ct. 1933 (2007).	failure to present mitigating evidence during the sentencing phase of his trial. *Id.* at 1224. The Ninth Circuit noted that defense counsel had attempted to present evidence regarding defendant's drug and alcohol addictions during the guilt phase, but that defendant thwarted all such efforts. *Id.* at 1225. Further, any inadequacies in defense counsel's investigation prior to the sentencing phase resulted from defendant's lack of cooperation. *Id.* at 1230–31. The court was thus skeptical of defendant's insistence "that he would have allowed the presentation of genetic predisposition evidence." *Id.* at 1231. The court concluded that "it is not reasonably probable that the outcome would have been affected," had evidence of the alleged genetic predisposition to violence been introduced. *Id.* The Ninth Circuit Court of Appeals, on rehearing *en banc*, remanded for an evidentiary review, stating that "a defendant can be prejudiced by an attorney's failure to investigate and present mitigating evidence that could influence the judge's appraisal of moral culpability." 441 F. 3d at 649-50. On May 14, 2007, the U.S. Supreme Court reversed the Ninth Circuit, stating that "Landrigan's mitigation evidence was weak, and the postconviction court was well acquainted with Landrigan's exceedingly violent past and had seen first hand his belligerent behavior." 127 S.Ct. at 1944. Further, "the mitigating evidence [Landrigan] seeks to introduce would not have changed the result." *Id.*	theory as "rather exotic at the time, and still is." *Landrigan*, 272 F.3d at 1228. The theory "suggests that [defendant's] biological background made him what he is." *Id.* Likewise, the court stated, "It is highly doubtful that the sentencing court would have been moved by information that [defendant] was a remorseless, violent killer because he was genetically programmed to be violent, as shown by the fact that he comes from a family of violent people, who are killers also." *Id.* at 1228–29. The court also cited *People v. Franklin*, 656 N.E.2d 750 (Ill. 1995), in commenting that although [defendant's] new evidence can be called mitigating in some slight sense, it would also have shown the court that it could anticipate that he would continue to be violent." *Landrigan*, 272 F.3d at 1229.

Case	Summary	Comments
Rogers v. State, 783 So. 2d 980 (Fla. 2001).	Defendant was convicted of first-degree murder and was sentenced to death. 783 So. 2d at 985. On direct appeal, the Florida Supreme Court affirmed, holding in part that the trial court had given proper weight to such mitigating evidence as penalty-phase testimony from a defense mental health expert witness that the defendant suffered from a rare genetic mental disease called porphyria. *Id.* at 997.	Genetics evidence was mentioned only in passing.
West v. Bell, 242 F.3d 338 (6th Cir. 2001).	West was sentenced to death for rape and murder. 242 F.3d at 339. His attorneys at his state postconviction proceedings filed a motion for appointment of counsel and stay of execution to determine whether West "knowingly, voluntarily, and competently waived his right to seek federal habeas." *Id.* The district court entered a stay of execution and scheduled a competency hearing; however, the appellate court vacated the stay of execution, holding in part that West's former counsel was not able to sue for federal habeas relief as West's "next friend." *Id.* at 341–43. The dissent argued in favor of affirming the district court's stay of execution, finding that West's defense counsel could assert rights for West as a next friend in part because there was "reasonable cause to believe that West is incompetent to make a decision to forego filing a federal habeas corpus petition." *Id.* at 344. This reasonable cause stemmed in part from defense counsel's provision of an affidavit from a psychiatrist who indicated that West may be genetically predisposed to mental illness. *Id.*	Genetics evidence was mentioned only in passing.
State v. Maraschiello, 88 S.W.3d 586 (Tenn. Crim. App. 2000).	Defendant was convicted of charges including first-degree murder and arson and sentenced to life in prison. 88 S.W.3d at 590. On appeal, defendant claimed in part that the trial court had wrongfully excluded testimony that he suffered from "Gulf War Syndrome." *Id.*	Genetic predisposition was mentioned in the context of recounting testimony from the trial. *Id.* at 599.

Case	Summary	Comments
	At defendant's trial, a psychiatrist had testified for the defense that due to mental illness in defendant's family, defendant was probably afflicted with a genetic predisposition for a delusional disorder, which was exacerbated by his stressful experiences in the military during the Persian Gulf War. *Id.* at 599. The Tennessee Court of Criminal Appeals affirmed the trial court's decision to exclude subsequent testimony regarding "Gulf War Syndrome." *Id.* at 609.	The alleged predisposition was given only passing mention.
Sanchez v. Ryan, 734 N.E.2d 920 (Ill. App. Ct. 2000).	The Secretary of State denied defendant's petition to have his driving privileges reinstated. 734 N.E.2d at 921. Defendant's appeal was based in part on the rejection of expert testimony regarding defendant's alleged "inherited alcohol tolerance." *Id.* at 925. Defendant had claimed that he inherited a high tolerance for alcohol from his uncle and grandfather. *Id.* at 922. A state circuit court affirmed, as did the Illinois Appellate Court, *id.*, the latter ruling that this testimony had been properly rejected, *id.* at 924.	In upholding the trial court's and hearing officer's rejection of the expert testimony, the court noted that "[t]he record shows that the hearing officer accepted the possibility that a person's tolerance to alcohol could be inherited. The hearing officer simply refused to believe that the [defendant] here had an inherited high tolerance." *Id.* at 925.
State v. DeAngelo, No. CR 97010866S, 2000 WL 973104 (Conn. Super. June 20, 2000).	Defendant was acquitted of robbery, larceny, and attempted assault charges after the court found him unable to control or recognize the wrongfulness of his behavior due to a combined ingestion of alcohol and legally prescribed drugs. 2000 WL 973104, at *1. The court ordered an examination to determine defendant's mental condition. At a subsequent hearing to investigate whether defendant posed a risk of future violent or criminal behavior, *id.* at *2, psychiatrists agreed that defendant suffered from	An alleged genetic predisposition to bipolar disorder played a role in one psychiatrist's recommendation that the defendant required supervision. *Id.* at *6. Genetics evidence was mentioned in passing.

Case	Summary	Comments
	obsessive-compulsive disorder (OCD), but varied in their treatment recommendations and assessment of future risk, *id.* at *3. One psychiatrist testified that defendant "need[ed] supervision; especially if he has a genetic predisposition to bipolar disorder." *Id.* at *6. He concluded that "if the [defendant] suffer[ed] another manic episode, he could be dangerous to himself and dangerous to others." *Id.* The court determined that, overall, the evaluation team had found that defendant's release would put the public in danger and ordered that he be committed to a maximum security psychiatric unit for a maximum of ten years, since he "presently constitutes a danger to himself and others." *Id.*	
State v. Ferguson, 20 S.W.3d 485 (Mo. 2000).	Defendant was convicted of first-degree murder and sentenced to death. 20 S.W.3d at 485. Following appeal and retrial, the defendant was again convicted and sentenced to death. Defendant's postconviction motion was denied. Defendant's appeal was based in part on a claim of ineffective assistance of counsel, *id.* at 505, because his counsel had failed to investigate and present evidence in the penalty phase including proof of defendant's genetic predisposition to a major depressive disorder, *id.* at 509. The Missouri Supreme Court affirmed, concluding that even without the submission of this evidence, there was "ample [other] evidence in support of mitigation, and counsel's failure to present additional evidence that would have been cumulative does not amount to ineffective assistance of counsel." *Id.*	Genetic predisposition was mentioned only in passing.

Case	Summary	Comments
Benefiel v. State, 716 N.E.2d 906 (Ind. 1999).	Defendant was convicted of rape and murder and sentenced to death. 716 N.E.2d at 910. The Indiana Supreme Court affirmed the sentences and conviction on direct appeal. Defendant's petition for postconviction relief based largely on a claim of ineffective assistance of counsel was denied. Id. at 911–12. On appeal, defendant argued in part that his counsel had failed to present mitigating evidence during the penalty phase. Id. at 912. These mitigating factors included a genetic predisposition to "'schizotypal personality disorder.'" Id. at 913. Expert witnesses had testified to this disorder during the guilt phase; therefore, the court reasoned that "[b]ecause the guilt phase evidence was incorporated into the penalty phase, this evidence was available for the jury to consider when it determined its recommended punishment." Id. Finding no reasonable probability that the failure to reintroduce the testimony had affected the death sentence imposed by the jury, the Indiana Supreme Court determined that defendant suffered no prejudice, and affirmed. Id. at 919.	The appeal focused on the phase at which the mitigating evidence, including a genetic predisposition to a personality disorder, was offered. The court concluded that offering this evidence during the guilt phase was sufficient to ensure that the jury could consider it in determining an appropriate sentence.
State v. Timmendequas, 737 A.2d 55 (N.J. 1999).	Defendant was charged with murder, two counts of felony murder, first-degree kidnapping, and four counts of first-degree assault. 737 A.2d at 64. He was convicted and sentenced to death on the murder charge and received two life imprisonment sentences on the other charges. Id. at 65–66. At the sentencing hearing a psychologist called by the defense testified that defendant's "[l]ow IQ and genetic defects may [have] . . . play[ed] a role." Id. at 71. The New Jersey Supreme Court affirmed defendant's conviction and sentence. Id. at 172.	The appeal was not based on alleged genetic predisposition. Id. at 55. Genetics evidence was mentioned only in passing.

Case	Summary	Comments
State v. Spivey, 692 N.E.2d 151 (Ohio 1998).	Defendant was convicted of charges including aggravated murder and was sentenced to death. 692 N.E.2d at 155. Evidence presented by defendant during the penalty phase included testimony from a developmental pediatrics specialist who had earlier diagnosed the defendant with XYY syndrome, a chromosome abnormality resulting in an increased risk of mental disease and behavioral problems. *Id.* at 165. The specialist testified "that [defendant's] chromosome abnormality placed him at risk for committing criminal acts, but that the syndrome itself did not cause him to be aggressive or to commit violent acts." *Id.* Although the Ohio Supreme Court affirmed defendant's conviction and sentence, the court noted that the defendant's "various psychological problems" merited some mitigation. *Id.* at 170.	The specialist elaborated that "family environment plays a vital role in whether a person with XYY syndrome is likely to engage in criminal behavior." *Id.* at 165. Thus, "in this regard . . . [defendant] 'did not have a fair shake either from mother nature or from the environment.'" *Id.* The witness further explained that "'[t]he combination of the two factors, his genetics, the family, and failure of the environment to fulfill his needs leads to his criminal behavior and violent behavior.'" *Id.*
People v. Armstrong, 700 N.E.2d 960 (Ill. 1998).	Defendant was convicted of charges including felony murder and was sentenced to death. 700 N.E.2d at 963. At the sentencing hearing, the trial court had restricted the testimony of a social worker who spoke to the defendant's genetic predisposition to alcoholism because the witness lacked the expertise required to offer an opinion on genetics. *Id.* at 970. The Illinois Supreme Court held that the trial court had properly excluded this and other testimony, *id.* at 970–71, and affirmed the lower court's decision in all respects, *id.* at 963.	The court did not comment on the general admissibility of genetics evidence. This outcome suggests that the evidence might have been admissible if the testifying witness had possessed the necessary expertise.

Case	Summary	Comments
Alley v. State, 958 S.W.2d 138 (Tenn. Crim. App. 1997).	Defendant was convicted of charges including murder and sentenced to death. 958 S.W.2d at 140. The Tennessee Supreme Court affirmed each conviction on direct appeal. *Id.* After he was denied by the trial court, defendant appealed as a matter of right to the Tennessee Court of Criminal Appeals. The Tennessee Court of Criminal Appeals reversed denial of defendant's petition for postconviction relief and remanded the case to the trial court for an evidentiary hearing with a new judge. *Id.* at 147. At the hearing, members of a medical team that had evaluated defendant before trial testified that they had not consulted a geneticist regarding various physical problems that afflicted the defendant. *Id.* at 141. A mental health program specialist explained that these problems appeared to be unrelated to defendant's defense of multiple personality disorder and thus did not merit further investigation. Defendant was classified as a malingerer. A psychiatrist testified that while "a cluster of physical anomalies can point to a syndrome with a genetic origin," the team did not see fit to "consult a geneticist in this case." *Id.* at 143. A psychologist who had examined defendant testified that "genetic defects would possibly affect behavior," but noted that "at the time of the evaluation . . . the team deemed as unnecessary any investigation of genetic problems." *Id.* On appeal, defendant claimed that he had been denied effective assistance of counsel with respect to proving his mental condition. Defendant argued, in part, that "his counsel was ineffective by failing to introduce any significant mitigating evidence during the sentencing phase of the trial." *Id.* at 150.	The appeal implies that defendant's genetic condition may have influenced defendant's behavior. Expert witnesses acknowledged that genetic factors may negatively affect behavior but claimed that this was not true in the present case.

Case	Summary	Comments
State v. Hartman, 476 S.E.2d 328 (N.C. 1996).	Defendant was convicted of charges including first-degree murder and was sentenced to death. 476 S.E.2d at 331. On appeal, defendant argued that the trial court had committed reversible error by refusing his request to submit specific nonstatutory mitigating circumstances (presumably during the sentencing phase), instead combining them to simplify the presentation to the jury. *Id.* at 339–42. Defendant argued in addition that the trial court's instructions had prevented the jury from evaluating relevant mitigating evidence, such as his family history of alcoholism, instead submitting the following instruction: "Consider whether the defendant is an alcoholic." *Id.* Presented this way, this statement did not allow the jury to determine whether the defendant had a "genetic predisposition to alcohol abuse," and the jury "was more than likely" to view the defendant's alcoholism "simply as weakness or unmitigated choice." *Id.* The North Carolina Supreme Court held that the jury was able to consider any mitigating evidence due to a "catchall mitigating circumstance" that had been submitted, *id.*, and affirmed, *id.* at 349.	The North Carolina Supreme Court ruled that even if the trial court erred by not submitting evidence of defendant's "'genetic predisposition to alcohol abuse'" as a mitigating factor, the "error was harmless beyond a reasonable doubt." *Id.* at 342.
People v. Hammerli, 662 N.E.2d 452 (Ill. App. Ct. 1996).	Defendant was charged with first-degree murder, found guilty but mentally ill, and sentenced to 35 years in jail. 662 N.E.2d at 452. At the trial, a forensic psychiatrist testified for the defense that defendant was afflicted with a "genetic predisposition to severe mood disorder." *Id.* at 456. On appeal, defendant claimed the trial court had incorrectly rejected his insanity plea. *Id.* at 458. The appellate court affirmed, noting that the circuit court "did not specifically embrace or reject any of the expert testimony," but "clearly found defendant mentally ill, but able to conform his conduct to the requirements	The Appellate Court appeared dubious of the defense expert witnesses' testimony, noting, for example, that although the defendant's treating psychiatrist had diagnosed him with improving depression, all four experts "found defendant to be legally insane at the

Case	Summary	Comments
	of the law at the time of the crime." *Id.* Because "[t]his determination was not against the manifest weight of the evidence," the court concluded "that defendant failed to sustain his burden of proving he was insane by a preponderance of the evidence." *Id.* at 458–59.	time of the murder and were able with hindsight to fit defendant's actions into their various diagnoses." *Id.* at 458. "Each [expert] found in defendant's behavior facts to support his own opinion." *Id.*
People v. Franklin, 656 N.E.2d 750 (Ill. 1995).	Once defendant's murder conviction and death sentence were affirmed by the Illinois Supreme Court, he sought postconviction relief, alleging, inter alia, ineffective assistance of counsel. 656 N.E.2d at 760–61. The Circuit Court of Cook County's denial of relief was appealed to the Illinois Supreme Court, and defendant's conviction was affirmed. *Id.* at 754. In support of his claim of ineffective assistance, defendant alleged that an investigation by counsel would have revealed mitigation evidence including "his family's history of mental illness and violence." *Id.* at 761. The court found it unlikely that such evidence would have affected defendant's sentence. "The proffered evidence regarding defendant's psychological problems and his family's violent and psychological history was not inherently mitigating. Although this evidence could have evoked compassion in the jurors, it could have also demonstrated defendant's potential for future dangerousness and the basis for defendant's past criminal acts. The evidence of defendant's mental illness may also have shown that defendant was less deterrable or that society needed to be protected from him." *Id.* (citation omitted). The Illinois Supreme Court affirmed. *Id.* at 754.	A genetics defense was alluded to and rejected, although it was never actually identified as such. In support of his claim of ineffective assistance of counsel, defendant also argued that his counsel had failed to request a jury instruction explaining that "the alternative sentence to death is natural life in prison without parole, if the State places the defendant's future dangerousness at issue." *Id.* at 760. However, this court concluded that "the prosecution did not place the defendant's future dangerousness at issue during the second stage of the sentencing hearing,"

Case	Summary	Comments
		thus rendering defendant's claim without merit. *Id.*
Billiot v. State, 655 So. 2d 1 (Miss. 1995).	Defendant was convicted of capital murder and sentenced to death. 655 So. 2d at 2. At a postconviction evidentiary hearing to determine the defendant's competency to be executed, a psychology professor who had interviewed and examined defendant testified that he did not believe that the allegedly schizophrenic defendant was malingering because of defendant's "genetic predisposition for the symptoms" of schizophrenia. *Id.* at 8. The court nevertheless found the defendant competent. On appeal, the Mississippi Supreme Court held the trial court had not erred in refusing to weigh the testimony of this one witness more heavily than the combined testimony of the other expert witnesses, all of whom opined that defendant was competent to be executed. *Id.* at 14. Categorizing defendant's competency to be executed as a "post-conviction relief question" properly deferred to the judgment of the trial and circuit judges, that court refused to conduct de novo review. *Id.* at 12.	The appellate court acknowledged that the witness testifying to defendant's genetic predisposition to schizophrenia "had done more recent and more extensive research on the issue of [defendant's] sanity" than had the other expert witnesses. *Id.* at 13.
State v. Wilson, No. Civ. A. 92CA005396, 1994 WL 558568 (Ohio Ct. App. Oct. 12, 1994).	Defendant was convicted of aggravated murder, kidnapping, and aggravated arson and was sentenced to death. 1994 WL 558568, at *1. On appeal, the Ohio Court of Appeals affirmed, determining, in part, that the aggravating circumstances of the crime outweighed the mitigating factors presented during the penalty phase, such as defendant's genetic predisposition to alcoholism. *Id.* at *43.	Genetic predisposition was mentioned only in passing.

Case	Summary	Comments
Hendricks v. Calderon, 864 F. Supp. 929 (N.D. Cal. 1994), *aff'd*, 70 F.3d 1032 (9th Cir. 1995).	Defendant was convicted of two counts of first-degree murder, including felony murder, and was sentenced to death. 70 F.3d at 1035. His petition for writ of habeas corpus was denied. On appeal, the denial was reversed and remanded. *Hendricks v. Vasquez*, 908 F.2d 490, 491 (9th Cir. 1990). Defendant's amended petition was denied and remanded again for a postconviction hearing on defendant's claim of ineffective assistance of counsel as to the penalty phase of his trial. *Hendricks*, 70 F.3d at 1035 n.1. Defendant claimed his counsel had failed to call two expert witnesses who could have testified about mitigating circumstances. These witnesses stated at the hearing that defendant had a family history of mental illness and that he therefore had a genetic predisposition to serious mental illness. 864 F. Supp. at 934–35. The experts explained that the predisposition was "exacerbated by . . . [a] violent and traumatic upbringing" that included physical, emotional, and sexual abuse. *Id.* at 935. One expert stated that the defendant was "genetically predisposed and vulnerable to serious mental illness." *Id.* Another would have testified at trial that defendant "was insane and that he had diminished capacity at the time of the homicides." *Id.* The Ninth Circuit Court of Appeals agreed with the district court that although it was reasonable for trial counsel not to call the experts to testify about an insanity defense during the guilt phase, withholding this potential mitigating evidence of a genetic predisposition to mental illness and insanity at the sentencing phase was not unreasonable under the circumstances and was prejudicial. 70 F.3d at 1044–45. The Ninth Circuit further suggested that mitigating evidence regarding the defendant's "difficult life" might have affected the outcome of the case. *Id.* at 1045.	"Quoting *Penry* [v. Lynaugh, 492 U.S. 302 (1989)], the *Hendricks* court reiterated that 'the jury must be able to consider and give effect to any mitigating evidence relevant to a defendant's background, character, or the circumstances of the crime.' In Hendricks's case, evidence of a genetic predisposition to mental illness would certainly be classified as 'relevant to a defendant's character.' Thus, the court held that Hendricks's trial counsel's failure to offer, among other things, mitigating evidence of a genetic predisposition to mental illness and insanity at the sentencing phase resulted in prejudice." Cecilee Price-Huish, *Born to Kill? "Aggression Genes" and Their Potential Impact on Sentencing and the Criminal Justice System*, 50 SMU L. REV. 603, 617–18 (1997) (citations omitted).

INDEX

NOTE: Page numbers followed by an *n* or *nn* and a number refer to a note(s) on the designated page. For example, 72*n*90 refers to note 90 on page 72 and 241*nn*2–3 refers to notes 2 and 3 on page 241.

and death penalty, 129, 176, 320, 353. *See also* Roper v. Simmons
and evidence, 275*n*105, 396*n*25, 406
and Fifth Amendment, 285
and intent, 222
and Kansas v. Hendricks, 399*n*38, 401, 403*n*58, 409
and Landrigan case, 127, 202–203, 339, 341
and mens rea, 223*n*245
and mitigation evidence, 332*n*93, 350
United States v. Hinckley, 270
United States v. Moore, 187–188, 211, 216
University of Maryland conference on Research on Genetics and Criminal Behavior, 125, 350*n*219
Urdiales case. *See* People v. Urdiales

V

Vandalism, 15
and serotonin, 33
Variation, causes of, 47
Velo-cardio-facial syndrome, 297
Ventral tegmental area (VTA), 85–86, 112
Ventrofrontal-striatal pathway, 111
Violence, 333*n*96, 409*n*194, 413, 451. *See also* Aggression; Domestic violence
and age, 418
and alcohol use, 26–27, 26*n*128
and brain function, 423, 423*n*181
Brunner study, 67–68, 163
causes of, 412*n*118, 426
and child abuse, 53, 68–69
combined risk factors, 40–41
and dopamine, 35
and drug use, 26
Dunedin study, 68–69, 390*n*11
and environment, 74–76
family history of, 199
genetic predisposition, 199, 203*n*133
heritability of, 57, 64, 66, 68–69
and MAOA, 303, 305, 308–309, 390*n*11
and pathology, 416*n*138
and serotonin, 192*n*46
and women. *See* Battered woman syndrome (BWS); Fudge v. State; Gender differences

and XYY syndrome, 137*n*41, 157
Violence Risk Assessment Guide (VRAG), 411
Volition, xv, 187*n*11, 191, 212, 214, 215*n*202, 343. *See also* Agency; Insanity defense
and addiction, 267–268
and depression, 189
involuntary acts, 215
and substance abuse, 204
Voluntary manslaughter, 188, 189
Von Dohlen v. State, 189, 211, 214, 216, 332*n*92, 334*n*97, 336*n*102, 337, 351
Vygotsky, Lev, 101–102

W

Wasserman, David, 133, 462*n*122
Weapon on school property, charges of carrying, 193
Web sites, 148*n*3
West v. Bell, 331*n*92, 333*n*96, 334*n*97, 335*n*99
Wilson and Daly article, 74–76
Wilson case. *See* State v. Wilson
Wilson's disease, 296–297
Women, 394*n*21. *See also* Gender differences
violence toward, 413. *See also* Battered woman syndrome (BWS); Fudge v. State
Writ of habeas corpus. *See* Habeas corpus, writ of

X

X chromosome, 163, 296, 303. *See also* Fragile X syndrome
XXY syndrome, 343*n*160, 348*n*203
XYY syndrome, 162–163, 376*n*89
and aggression, 136–137, 137*n*41, 157, 201*n*119, 376, 376*nn*85–87, 458
in criminal cases, 333*n*96, 334*n*96, 344*n*164, 346, 394*n*22, 458
and free will, 207*n*154
and insanity defense, 194–195, 196–197

Y

Y chromosome. *See* Chromosomes; XXY syndrome; XYY syndrome